Wiltshire Record Society

(formerly the Records Branch of the Wiltshire Archaeological and Natural History Society)

VOLUME 53

FOR THE YEAR 1997

Impression of 750 copies

Memorial to Henry Danvers (died 1654) in West Lavington church.
The epitaph is transcribed on page 247.

MONUMENTAL INSCRIPTIONS OF WILTSHIRE

AN EDITION, IN FACSIMILE, OF *MONUMENTAL INSCRIPTIONS IN THE COUNTY OF WILTON*, BY SIR THOMAS PHILLIPPS, 1822

EDITED BY

PETER SHERLOCK

TROWBRIDGE

2000

ISBN 0 901333 30 1

THIS VOLUME IS DEDICATED TO THE MEMORY OF
MICHAEL LANSDOWN, 1916 – 1999,
HONORARY TREASURER OF THIS SOCIETY
FOR FORTY-EIGHT YEARS UNTIL HIS DEATH

Michael Lansdown was a great-grandson of the founder of the *Trowbridge Advertiser* (predecessor of the *Wiltshire Times*). Another great-grandfather was William Millington, the Victorian Trowbridge artist. After a degree at Cambridge and war service he joined the newspaper in 1946 and retired as editor in 1981.

His knowledge of Victorian Trowbridge was encyclopaedic, and he wrote many pieces of local history in the newspaper, as well as several pamphlets on aspects of the town's history.

He managed the finances of the Wiltshire Record Society with a success probably unparalleled by any similar body. The enthusiasm and humour with which he reported the intricacies of postage, packing, and covenants, and the quirks of printers and booksellers will remain a vivid memory with all who served on the Society's committee.

Produced for the Society by
Salisbury Printing Company Ltd, Salisbury
Printed in Great Britain

CONTENTS

PREFACE

For permission to reproduce in facsimile the copy of *Monumental Inscriptions* in their possession the Society wishes to express formally its thanks to the Wiltshire Archaeological and Natural History Society, and to that Society's Sandell Librarian, Mrs Lorna Haycock.

Mr Sherlock, the Editor of this volume, wishes to acknowledge also the help given to him by Jane Freeman, Clive Holmes, and Judith Maltby; and the staff of the Bodleian Library, the College of Arms, and the British Library. He is grateful too for the financial support of the Commonwealth Scholarship Scheme of the Association of Commonwealth Universities, and of the Hungerford and Associated Families Society. Mr Sherlock and I are both indebted to Lorna Haycock for her kind co-operation in enabling the facsimile to be made.

JOHN CHANDLER

INTRODUCTION

In 1822 Sir Thomas Phillipps ordered his printer, Adolphus Brightley, to produce six copies of his transcriptions of the monumental inscriptions of Wiltshire at the Middle Hill Press in his home. By 1824 the work was complete, yet it passed almost immediately into obscurity. For the last 175 years, the handful of copies have remained largely unconsulted in Phillipps's collections and in a small number of libraries. Despite its inaccuracies and omissions the volume is of value to genealogists, those with an interest in Wiltshire, and historians of death and commemoration, not least because many of the epitaphs recorded no longer exist. This edition is intended to make Phillipps's work available to a wider audience, with the much-needed addition of an index.

SIR THOMAS PHILLIPPS

Thomas Phillipps entered the world on 2 July 1792 at 32 Cannon Street, Manchester, and was baptised at the city's church on 22 July 1792. He was born out of wedlock, but was raised by his father Thomas Phillipps (1742-1818) as his only son and heir. He had little contact with his mother, Hannah Walton (1770-1851) who in 1812 married Frederick Judd of London. The few surviving letters between mother and son relate to an annuity due to her until her death.

Phillipps grew up at 'Middle Hill', a property purchased by his father in 1794, near the town of Broadway, Worcestershire, where his grandfather had been a farmer. His early education was at the academy at Fladbury run by John Harward, prior to entering Rugby School in 1807. In 1811 he matriculated to University College Oxford, from which he graduated B.A. in 1815 and M.A. in 1820. At the death of his father in November 1818 he inherited the substantial Middle Hill estates. Due to their entailment under the terms of his father's will, he had access to their annual income only and not the capital itself, a source of later frustration.

His father's death allowed Phillipps to marry the woman who had captured his affections but who had incurred the disapproval of the senior Thomas. The wedding took place in February 1819, the bride being Henrietta, daughter of an army General, Sir Thomas Molyneux. The couple made their home at Middle Hill, not far from the Molyneux residence in Cheltenham. They had three daughters, Henrietta (1819), Maria (1821) and Katharine (1823), who prior to marriage would dutifully assist their father by transcribing manuscripts and preparing copy for his printer.

A. N. L. Munby, Phillipps's biographer, argues that the early 1820s were his happiest years. Besides a happy family life, Phillipps enjoyed social success: he was elected a Fellow of the Royal Society in 1820 and created a Baronet the following year, thanks to his father-in-law's connections. Financial difficulties soon followed, however, then in

1832 Phillipps's wife died aged 37. After a long, unsuccessful quest for a bride (with a large income to solve his financial woes), he was married a second time in 1842 to Elizabeth Harriet Anne Mansell, who survived him.

During his early years, Phillipps had begun collecting books and manuscripts, at the age of 16 compiling a precocious catalogue of the 110 volumes in his possession. Once he was settled at Middle Hill, this became his life's occupation, accompanied by a series of antiquarian endeavours. His manuscript collection was considerably enhanced by sojourns in continental Europe during the 1820s, where he was able to purchase voluminous quantities at auctions. By his death, Phillipps's 'vellomania' had led to his possession of the largest personal manuscript library in the world. He was well-known to all major booksellers and auction houses, and on two occasions had been arrested for unpaid debts as he consistently bought beyond his means. Besides collecting, Phillipps also maintained a private press at his residence and printed various manuscripts in his possession alongside his antiquarian researches. Most of these offerings appeared in such small numbers that they retain the status of manuscripts. No complete catalogue of his publications exists.

In 1862 the size of his collection forced Phillipps to remove to the larger Thirlestane House, near Cheltenham, formerly owned by Lord Northwick. Sir Thomas died here on 6 February 1872, aged 79. The Middle Hill estates passed according to their entailment to his eldest daughter Henrietta and her husband James Halliwell-Phillipps, the Shakespearean scholar. His second and favourite daughter, Maria, wife of the Reverend John Walcot, predeceased him in 1858. Due to Phillipps's estrangement from his eldest daughter and son-in-law, he left his personal assets – Thirlestane House and his library – to his youngest child Katherine, wife of the Reverend John Fenwick.

The Fenwicks did not have sufficient means to maintain such an enormous collection of manuscripts and books. The library was gradually dispersed in a series of auctions between 1886 and 1913, beginning with duplicate copies of books. Large purchases were made by foreign governments, ensuring the repatriation of important manuscripts. In 1945 the remainder of the collection, the contents of which could only be guessed at, was sold by the Fenwick family to the Robinson firm of booksellers, who deposited Phillipps's voluminous personal papers in the Bodleian Library.[1]

WILTSHIRE HISTORY AND TOPOGRAPHY

Phillipps's interest in Wiltshire is intertwined with the beginning of his antiquarian and collecting career. He began his research on the county while at University, during visits to Ferne in Donhead St Andrew, the Wiltshire residence of his closest friend Charles Grove, where he calendared the family's deeds and compiled genealogies.[2] The county was one of only many interests, for Phillipps's time in Oxford led to an interest there as

1 On Phillipps's life and work, see Edward Kite, 'Wiltshire Topography [1659-1843] with some Notes on the late Sir Thomas Phillipps, and his Historical Collections for the County', *Wiltshire Notes and Queries*, vol.6, December 1908, pp.145-161; A.N.L. Munby, *Phillipps Studies*, 5 vols., Cambridge, 1951-60, particularly vol.2; idem, *Portrait of an Obsession*, London, 1967.
2 Ibid, p.6.

well, one which saw him employ William Kirtland in the 1810s and 1820s as a scribe in the Bodleian and nearby archives.[3] Wiltshire became the primary region of interest from 1819, however, when he encountered the circle of antiquaries centred on Sir Richard Colt Hoare and his library at Stourhead.

In 1818, Colt Hoare was in the midst of completing his *Ancient Wiltshire* (1812-21), and was desirous of undertaking a modern history to match. In his pamphlet of that year, *Hints on the Topography of Wiltshire*, he urged local folk from the noble to the artisan classes to join with him in producing a multi-volume history of the county by adopting a parish or a hundred. Phillipps wrote offering to take responsibility for the entire northern half of the county, having already arranged to spend the summer of 1818 in the archives of Salisbury. Colt Hoare responded enthusiastically, and thus began a productive partnership which saw Phillipps acquire the status of Sir Richard's second-in-command of the Wiltshire history project over the following few years.[4]

Phillipps produced his first publication in 1819, a miscellaneous set of *Collections for Wiltshire*, privately printed at Salisbury. It set the tone for a series of similar volumes by either Phillipps or Colt Hoare published over the next twenty years, in which primary records from Wiltshire archives were transcribed and made accessible for the convenience of all researchers. For his part, Phillipps produced the *Collections*, the *Monumental Inscriptions*, and the *Institutiones Clericorum in Comitatu Wiltoniae* (Middle Hill, 1821-5), while Colt Hoare offered *Repertorium Wiltonense* (Bath, 1821) and *Monasticon Wiltonense* (Salisbury, 1822). Colt Hoare, meanwhile, also produced finished historical syntheses, most notable the first volume of the *History of Modern Wiltshire*, on Mere Hundred, in 1822, and a study of the Hungerford family, *Hungerfordiana*, in 1823. By this time he was fully convinced of Phillipps's commitment and ability to the history of north Wiltshire, referring to him in the history of Mere as, 'a most active, intelligent, and zealous coadjutor', and in correspondence as, 'Our Hero of the north'.[5]

Phillipps attended an early gathering of Wiltshire historians at Stourhead on 1 January 1821, along with Lord Arundell, Henry Wansey, Robert Benson and others.[6] The group exchanged their printed work as soon as it came off the presses. Colt Hoare was always impatient for Phillipps's latest publications, urging him to organise and print his many notebooks, and to put pressure on his various printers to work faster. This was particularly true of the *Institutiones*, which were printed by J. A. Gilmour of Salisbury as slowly as a page a week over a four year period to Colt Hoare's frustration.[7]

3 Phillipps Correspondence, Bodleian Library, Oxford, Phillipps-Robinson MSS [hereafter PRMS] b.107/27 (William Kirtland to Thomas Phillipps [TP], 23 November 1820).
4 Richard Colt Hoare, *Hints on the Topography of Wiltshire*, 1818, Salisbury; PRMS c.405/138-141 (TP to Richard Colt Hoare [RCH], ca.1818; RCH to TP, 28 June 18[18]).
5 Richard Colt Hoare, *History of Modern Wiltshire: Mere Hundred*, London, 1822, p.vii; PRMS b.112/155 (RCH to TP, n.d.).
6 On the Stourhead gatherings, see Joseph Hunter, 'The Topographical Gatherings at Stourhead, 1825-1833', *Memoirs of the History and Antiquities of Wiltshire*, 1851.
7 See for example PRMS b.106/149 (RCH to TP, 16 November 1820), b.106/155 (RCH to TP, December 1820), b.110/150 (RCH to TP, 21 September 1821), b.112/115 (RCH to TP, 3 April 1822).

The academic partnership was accompanied by a series of friendships. Wansey in particular kept in touch with Phillipps for a few years, encouraging him to visit whenever he was able. He also kept him informed of Colt Hoare's health, mainly his gout and deafness, for the latter made it, 'difficult to converse with him ... [and] makes him fonder of his pen than ever'.[8] All were keen for Phillipps to make his residence in Wiltshire, and kept on the lookout for potential properties, such as Blacklands near Calne, put up for sale through the owner's bankruptcy in 1821. Due to the depths of Sir Thomas's financial problems, these were impossible purchases.[9] As it turned out, Phillipps was not as regular a guest at Stourhead and Salisbury as the other historians would have liked, and he had a tendency to fall out of contact with them; but they met his wife and daughter and became fond of his family.[10]

The collaboration between Sir Richard and Sir Thomas had reached its high point by the end of 1821, coinciding with the happiest times in Phillipps's life, when the two historians agreed to provide funding for a third collaborator to work alongside them. This was the Reverend John Offer, a relatively poor schoolmaster but a meticulous researcher. He was provided with £200 per annum by Colt Hoare and Phillipps, and worked alternately with his patrons in various archives. The resulting frenzy of Wiltshire research was to be shortlived, however, for in 1822 Phillipps decided to travel to Europe for an extended period, and the following year Offer died from a stomach obstruction.[11]

Colt Hoare's concerns about Phillipps's commitment to his *History of Modern Wiltshire* appeared in April 1822 as soon as his 'foreign sojourn' was mentioned. He argued against any such venture, 'for depend upon it, you will *gain* nothing by a foreign sojourn – lose the comforts of an English home – and the great resources which your extensive collection will afford daily'. By June, Colt Hoare was urging Phillipps to take on and complete the history of a single hundred in north Wiltshire, fearing that his 'great Mass of Materials' would be forever neglected if he embarked on his 'continental progress'. Phillipps had made up his mind, however, partly as he wished to avoid his many financial problems, and departed in August 1822 for Switzerland.

In April 1823 Colt Hoare believed that his fear of being deserted was becoming reality, as Phillipps embarked upon his voluminous manuscript purchases, leading him to comment that, 'I hope your vellum-mania does not encrease – & that you will confine it unto Wilts'. Colt Hoare wrote to Phillipps's printer, Adolphus Brightley, to ensure that he was receiving any work from the Middle Hill presses, and the reply came that Phillipps was in Rome. Brightley concluded pessimistically that if Phillipps, 'sets his foot in the Vatican I am afraid it will be a long time before he returns'.[12]

8 PRMS b.111/253 (Henry Wansey to TP, 18 May 1821).

9 PRMS b.111/249-50 (Henry Wansey to TP, 6 February 1821).

10 PRMS b.113/142-3 (Henry Wansey to TP, 22 May 1822).

11 PRMS b.112/121 (RCH to TP, May? 1822), PRMS b.112/149 (RCH to TP, July 1822), PRMS b.112/157-159 (agreement between RCH, TP and John Offer, early 1822), c.412/231 (RCH to TP, Dec 1822 or Jan 1823).

12 PRMS b.112/121 (RCH to TP, May? 1822), PRMS b.112/129 (RCH to TP, 3 June 1822), PRMS b.112/137 (RCH to TP, Jun 1822), PRMS c.412/238 (RCH to TP, April 1823), PRMS c.412/245 (Adolphus Brightley to RCH, November 1823).

Phillipps did not abandon his Wiltshire interests by any means, and returned to England at the end of 1823. Yet, just as Colt Hoare had come to suspect, he never published a volume of north Wiltshire history to match those produced on south Wiltshire, although he still maintained that this was his intention as late as the 1850s. He continued to edit and print privately various manuscripts related to Wiltshire, but it was once again one county among many which occupied his mind and pen.

Of greater concern to other Wiltshire historians was Phillipps's increasing reluctance to make his work available to others, particularly after Colt Hoare's death in 1838. When the Wiltshire Topographical Society was formed in 1839, he refused to participate, writing in 1843 that he was still committed to the history of north Wiltshire, and believed that individual efforts were better than societies, a sentiment typical of his eccentricity, intolerance and prejudice. In 1854 the *Wiltshire Archaeological and Natural History Magazine* commenced publication, its first issue including a catalogue of Wiltshire manuscripts in Phillipps's possession. He again refused to participate in this venture, withholding permission for such documents to be consulted or reprinted and instead inviting submissions to his own publications. Such attitudes often stemmed from personal grudges Phillipps held against other historians. He disliked the elderly John Britton, instrumental in the foundation of both the Wiltshire Topographical Society and the Wiltshire Archaeological and Natural History Society. Canon Jackson, one of the most prolific contributors to the *Wiltshire Archaeological and Natural History Magazine*, also incurred Phillipps's ire in 1862 by publishing his own, fully annotated edition of Aubrey's *Wiltshire Topographical Collections* which Sir Thomas had printed himself in a much criticised version between 1825 and 1838.[13]

Despite Phillipps's many publications in Wiltshire topography and genealogy, it is difficult to regard him as highly as his contemporaries. For, while characters such as Britton and Colt Hoare were not free of jealousy or obsessiveness themselves, they fostered collective, ongoing efforts. Moreover, Sir Thomas's many publications had a restricted circulation due to his tiny print runs, and were hampered by errors and omissions. Sir Frederic Madden, prejudiced by Phillipps's purchases of many manuscripts he had wanted to acquire for the British Library, wrote bitterly on Sir Thomas's death that: 'his greatest pleasure was to abstract a Parish Register! As to his publications, they are all but worthless from their inaccuracies. Learning or scholarship he never possessed in any degree.'[14] Nevertheless, the *Monumental Inscriptions of Wiltshire* is a substantial work published at the zenith of Phillipps's career as a researcher, and is unique in its content.

13 Eric Holzenberg, *The Middle Hill Press: a checklist of the Horblit collection of books, tracts, leaflets, and broadsides printed by Sir Thomas Phillipps at his press at Middle Hill, or elsewhere to his order, now in the library of the Grolier Club*, New York, 1997; Ken Rogers and Douglas Crowley, 'Wiltshire', in *A Guide to English County Histories*, eds. C.R.J. Currie and C.P. Lewis, Stroud, 1994, pp.411-422; Jenny Stratford, *Catalogue of the Jackson Collection of Manuscript Fragments in the Royal Library Windsor Castle: with a Memoir of Canon J.E. Jackson and a List of his Works*, London, 1981, p.65.

14 Bodleian Library, Oxford, Madden Journals, vol.43, p.323, quoted in Munby, *Portrait of an Obsession*, p.261.

COLLECTING MONUMENTAL INSCRIPTIONS

The *Monumental Inscriptions* did not begin as a cohesive project. In 1819 Phillipps began employing an amanuensis, William Hensley, to transcribe manuscripts in London, Salisbury and elsewhere, and, it would seem, to copy down epitaphs from certain churches in Hampshire. Once he had committed himself to the history of north Wiltshire, Phillipps decided to make full collections for each parish. Thus, Hensley was sent in the summers of 1820 and 1821 to note down the monumental inscriptions in churches across Wiltshire, and to obtain what information he could about manorial descents, clergy past and present, charitable donations and curiosities in each place.

William Hensley appears to have been in the employ of the Phillipps family prior to 1819, probably as a gamekeeper or manager on the Middle Hill estate in the service of Sir Thomas's father prior to his death in 1818.[15] He was born at Broadway and baptised at St Eadburgh's church on 6 October 1790, the eldest child of Thomas and Anne Hensley. A note by Phillipps amidst his correspondence with Hensley for 1821 states that, 'This Man was my Amanuensis & afterwards became an Architect & made much money'. He was employed by Phillipps as a scribe throughout his life, as was his son, Christopher French Hensley, from 1855. The Hensley family, whose members may have been tenants of Sir Thomas, was still resident in Broadway in the early twentieth century.[16]

In 1820 and 1821 Hensley worked according to Phillipps's orders, though these were somewhat sporadic and unpredictable, and on more than one occasion he had to beg for more money or return to Middle Hill to await further instruction. He usually stayed at a public house in the main town of a hundred and travelled each day to visit up to four or five different churches. At night he would write up his findings and as he completed two folio sheets would fold, seal and post them to Sir Thomas at Middle Hill or Salisbury, resulting in several letters each week. Some of these were pure epitaphs, but others contained small notes begging money or further orders. He began in May 1820 with Cricklade Hundred, then Malmesbury, before joining Phillipps to work jointly in Salisbury archives in June. In September he took up lodgings at the Castle Inn, Devizes, and by October was at Avebury. The next collecting season ran from May to October 1821 and included the south as well as the north of the county, proceeding from Chippenham to Highworth, Swindon, Burbage, Devizes, Melksham, Bradford, Trowbridge, Westbury and Warminster.[17]

Hensley's letters to his employer provide a unique and entertaining window into the daily grind of antiquarian pursuits in the early nineteenth century. He was required to be a jack of all trades, not only transcribing epitaphs, but also inscriptions on bells, and as need arose executing brass rubbings or drawings of curious monuments.

15 Hensley reports his activities as a gamekeeper at Middle Hill in PRMS b.112/97-98 (William Hensley [WH] to TP, 9 October 1822), c.405/137 (WH to TP, 8 December 1818), c.412/225-6 (WH to TP, 11 January 1823).

16 PRMS b.110/110.

17 Hensley's letters containing the epitaphs are preserved at PRMS c.270 (1821) and c.313 (1820). What appear to be his original notebooks, in pencil, are at PRMS e.236-243. These latter notebooks were used to prepare the printed edition.

In October 1820 he wrote from the Red Lion Inn at Avebury noting that he had made, 'the Sketch of 4 Saxon Arches two Brass figures and some curious fonts'. Likewise, from Chippenham in May 1821 he reported that,'I have taken some Copy's of some handsome Brass figures from Lacock Church of Robt and Elizth Baynard & 17 children'.[18]

Health, and the weather, were prominent concerns as was Hensley's fear of displeasing his infamously short-tempered employer. In June 1820 he wrote from the Good Will Arms at Swindon, concerned that Phillipps was disappointed with his rate of progress:

> I have been ill great part of the time as I have been in Wilts but for this last week past I have been better, and live in hopes of Continuance of it, but it have made my work seem very hard, but I think I shall enjoy my usual state of health again. I do not understand you by giving up my employment whither you mean because of me being ill or whether you think me not capable of collecting your Inscriptions, so far as my education I have done to the best of my knowledge for you . . .

At the end of October 1820 he begged to be allowed home, hoping Phillipps 'will not persist in my Collecting any more this Season, as it is so far advanced. I taken a bad cold in my bones the second day at Marlbro St Mary's and have been unwell ever since . . . I find the Churches very damp.'[19]

The constant travelling could result in loneliness. Hensley complained in 1820 of always staying in lodgings, which also incurred extra costs for Phillipps: 'I shall go on as long as I have a sixpence and then walk home . . . I cannot find any friend in a strange place except I have one in my pocket.' He expressed similar sentiments the following year: 'I shall take it a pleasure to travell any part of England for you, But I hope you will consent to me to come home one day or two to see my friends.'[20] Unexpected difficulties on top of these ordinary hurdles caused Hensley to joke about his sanity in 1819: 'But I have all the misfortunes as can be with my Box, for when I open'd it there was the jar of ink broke and run all over it. I think if I have any more trouble with it I shall stand in need of a strait waistcoat.'[21]

While Phillipps himself may have had strained relations with the likes of John Britton, who during these years was researching the third volume of *The Beauties of Wiltshire*, it was his amanuensis who had to deal with the competition in person. Hensley first became aware of Britton in 1820, writing that, 'A gentleman by name Britton is Collecting for History Chippenham and north Damersham Hund which part of it is in great forwardness for the Press. And is Enquiries are the same as yours.'[22] In 1821 Hensley encountered or nearly missed Britton on several occasions, and began to wonder if his work was futile. At Christian Malford in May 1821 he realised, 'every day I still witness that I am walking the ground that Mr Britton previously have done', and the clergyman, 'told me that it was a pity that I interfered into his Collections'. A postscript added, 'Write to me as I cannot work with any courage, unless I know whether you wish me so to do, as he is writing the same'. A further note showed

18 PRMS b.106/117 (WH to TP, 22 October 1820), b.110/99 (WH to TP, 14 May 1821).
19 PRMS c.313/327 (WH to TP, 10 June 1820), b.106/117 (WH to TP, 22 October 1820).
20 PRMS b.106/115 (WH to TP, 7 September 1820), b.110/99 (WH to TP, 14 May 1821).
21 PRMS c.406/122 (WH to TP, 20 July 1819).
22 PRMS c.313/373-6 (WH to TP, 2 June 1820).

resentment of Britton's method of getting the clergy to do the transcribing, for 'he gives them a Call, and pays them a Morning visit, & receives their Copies good Morn and his Collection has made'. Phillipps's reply commanded Hensley 'to go on even if he met Britton himself'.[23]

Hensley's next letter showed that Britton's spectre still haunted him. He attempted to meet Britton at Nettleton, but missed him, and was then annoyed to discover that the minister at Colerne wanted Hensley to pay a fee for permission to copy down the epitaphs there. He vented his anger in poetry:

'Ev'ry day as my travells advance
I expect for to meet with that deaf one
But as far as my knowledge or strength will admit
I never will yeild to one Britton.'[24]

The gentleman concerned shortly wrote to Phillipps, opening, 'I have often heard of you during my late Tour in Wiltshire . . .'.[25] Not all such encounters were competitive. Hensley was pleased to meet Richard Colt Hoare at Malmesbury Abbey and receive extra help in May 1820, for Sir Richard, 'directed his discource to me respecting the difference of Architecture in the Arches'.[26]

The antiquarian competition was not, in the long run, a stumbling block for either Hensley or Phillipps. A major complaint was the lack of local historical knowledge amongst the clergy, or indeed amongst any of the local gentry:

I have been very unfortunate in meeting with Clergymen, I have not met with but one Rector or V as yet & two Curates, in general the diligent Curates Serve 3 or 4 Churches in one Day, and they now as much about it as I do, on Monday last I was at Great Somerford where I met with the present Rector & he told me that he should be happy to give all the Infirmation he could and which he did, which I askd him if he could tell the Glebe at Little Somerford but he could not, but is answer was, that the best way to have all the Glebes Correct was to get a Coppy of them at the register Office Sarum, where they may all be had, (the Revd S Demainbrey) Yesterday I went to Hankerton where I could get no Inteligence of the Glebe nor register nor else, I was informed that the Rector keeps all at his house at Crudwell which I went & Collected all Inscriptions and then to go to the Rector which I found all under his care and he was at Bath & I made great Inquire in the Village with the upper Class of men but no true Account could I get, for I general Ask these thick headed people twice or thrice and very rare to find one but what deviate in their discourse and know but little at last, as I do not like to write after all men, and I have made my self very ill in fretting about it as I cannot collect as I wish, if I could meet with any Inteligent Clergymen or others it would be a pleasure to me, & greater satisfaction to you.[27]

By the end of 1821, Hensley had finished his work of collecting monumental inscriptions and could move on to other tasks closer to home. Unforeseen difficulties

23 PRMS b.110/97 (WH to TP, 4 May 1821).
24 PRMS b.110/99 (WH to TP, 14 May 1821).
25 PRMS b.108/158 (John Britton to TP, 18 October 1821).
26 PRMS c.313/355 (WH to TP, 21 May 1820).
27 PRMS c.313/323 (WH to TP, 8 June 1820).

with clergy, and a lack of money on Phillipps's part, meant that details such as manorial descents had not been compiled, but the epitaphs were recorded and ready for the Middle Hill Press.

PRINTING AND DISTRIBUTION

From 1818 to 1822 Phillipps used the services of a variety of printers, chiefly in Salisbury or London. He decided to employ his own, and placed an advertisement in *The Times* in December 1821, seeking someone with a knowledge of Latin who had sets of Saxon characters and Latin abbreviations. This solicited the application of Adolphus Brightley, a native of Bungay, Suffolk, who was appointed to the post, taking up residence at Middle Hill in August 1822. He remained in Phillipps's service until December 1825. Although his time at Middle Hill was generally pleasant, his arrival and departure were not. In 1822 no residence was prepared for Brightley, Phillipps having decided that he could live in the dilapidated Tower on the estate which would later feature on the frontispieces of Middle Hill publications. Brightley immediately wrote from the inn where he was staying temporarily to Sir Thomas in Paris, complaining about the appalling living conditions, desiring to return to Suffolk, and stating his disillusionment with the entire project. Once the accommodation problem was solved, however, Brightley came to enjoy his 'pretty little office in the octagon room' at Middle Hill and began to work productively. Phillipps soon discovered that he had to keep his printer occupied and thus began his tendency to print material hastily and unedited. Brightley would depart from Middle Hill three years later primarily because he was owed £216 by Phillipps. He had received only £30 from Phillipps between May 1822 and April 1825 towards bills of £191, much of which were incurred in the production of the *Monumental Inscriptions*.[28]

The printing of the Wiltshire epitaphs was Brightley's first major task. He began in September 1822 with Chippenham Hundred, having purchased one hundred sheets of paper for the purpose the previous month. By November Phillipps was able to tell Colt Hoare that the work was well underway, and Sir Richard replied saying that, 'you do right to print (however incorrectly) the inscriptions, as they will assist you much in visiting the Churches'.[29] In April 1823 Brightley sent the following report to Phillipps, now in Berne:

> I am still going on with the Epitaphs, expect to finish them in June; I have not gone on so fast as I expected with them, principally owing to the incorrectness in which they are taken – I print them nearly as I find them, – I cannot correct them although I know they certainly must be wrong. I began them in the same manner as they were given to me, that is, by beginning a book and going through with it without paying any respect to placing the parishes in the Hundreds to which they belong – I find there is no regard paid to that in the collecting them, for one parish may immediately follow another, which may be situated widely different from each other. I received a letter from Sir Richd

28 PRMS c.410/83-4 (Adolphus Brightley to TP, 21 August 1822), c.416/80-90 (Adolphus Brightley to TP, 1825); Munby, *Portrait of an Obsession*, pp.12-13, 30-33.
29 PRMS b.112/169 (RCH to TP, November 1822), c.410/85 (Adolphus Brightley accounts for TP, August 1822).

> Hoare with your commands for a copy of what I have hitherto done. But it being the northern instead of the southern district, that I have been about, – he wished me instantly to print the latter, and send him portions of it as I get it done, for him to correct upon the spot. I have sent him the Hundreds of Amesbury, Elstub and Everley. He have not had a copy of what I had done previously. "I hope (he says) I shall live till Sir Thos returns, that we may prosecute our researches in the northern district together." He kindly offered to send me his little printed account of the Hundreds and a guide, not having began then in a regular order it will now be of little use, I had only the assistance of a small Map to arrange them from. I chose rather to print them in the order as I find them, than to follow the uncertainty of that. When they are finished I will print an alphabetical Index, they will then be easily found. I have printed six copies perhaps I ought to have printed more but you did not tell me how many you would wish. Should be sorry if I have not printed as many as will be wanted ... The Epitaphs, I doubt you will find sadly incorrect I followed the copy, but wished you could have overlooked them ... I am glad I am not in Broadway, the place and people I cannot bear: the beautiful walks and situation of Middle Hill suits my ideas of retirement and study. I will do anything to stay ...[30]

Colt Hoare's interference in the project did not cease, for, having heard nothing out of Brightley for some months, he wrote to Phillipps asking whether, 'Brightley has finished the Monumental Inscriptions – if so – beg him to send me the *remainder* since his last'. This caused Brightley to write directly to Colt Hoare, apologising for the delay on the grounds that he had been expecting Phillipps to return from Europe every day for the previous two months, when new orders for copying and distribution could be issued.[31]

From this correspondence it appears that the epitaphs for north Wiltshire – some 286 pages – were printed between September 1822 and April 1824. Those for south Wiltshire, comprising 108 pages, were probably done in 1823 as Colt Hoare requested. The dates watermarked on the volume's paper (from Clarke & Horsington or Bitton Mills) range from 1820 to 1823 for north, and 1822 alone for south Wiltshire. As Brightley promised, an (incomplete) index to the parishes covered was added, and a title page printed depicting the Tower at Middle Hill with the words: 'Monumental Inscriptions in the County of Wilton. Edited by Sir T. Phillipps, Bart. Typis Medio – Montanis, in Turre Lativiensi Adolphus Brightley Excudit. 1822.'[32] A secondary title page, with a seemingly erroneous date, reads simply 'Monumental Inscriptions in Co Wilts. – 1821.'

A mere six copies of the volume were printed, and it was fortunate that there were even this many, for Colt Hoare had protested in April 1822 that, 'If you print your MSS Collections, pray say *six* vice *three* or even more – for the additional expense will be only that of paper'.[33] In consequence the volume is one of the great rarities emanating from the Middle Hill, and certainly the rarest of the more substantial publications.

One copy was presented to Colt Hoare at Stourhead, literally as it came off the

30 PRMS c.412/59 (Adolphus Brightley to TP, 8 April 1823).

31 PRMS c.412/250-1 (RCH to TP, September 1823), c.412/245 (Adolphus Brightley to RCH, November 1823).

32 The title page does not accompany Sir Richard Colt Hoare's copy but is found with the other extant copies.

33 PRMS b.112/119 (RCH to TP, April 1822).

presses. This copy is preserved in the Library of the Wiltshire Archaeological and Natural History Society at Devizes, and is the basis of this edition. Another copy was presented on 5 April 1827 by Phillipps himself to the Library of the College of Arms, London, where it remains to this day.[34] At least two copies stayed in Phillipps's library. One of these was disposed at the first of the Sotheby auction sales of duplicate items in the library arranged by the Fenwicks in 1886, selling as lot 2436 for an impressive £14 10*s*.[35] The other remained with the library and passed into the hands of the Robinson booksellers in 1945, from whom Harrison D. Horblit acquired it. Horblit had compiled one of the most comprehensive collection of Phillipps books by his death, including those from the library of the Earl of Lindsey. The entire collection, including the *Monumental Inscriptions*, is now housed at the Grolier Club, New York, to whom it was presented by Horblit's widow.[36] Other copies found their way to the British Library (in 1883) and the Bodleian Library, Oxford; the latter may be the one sold in 1886.[37] The whereabouts of the sixth copy is unknown.

All copies except that in the British Library are interleaved with blank pages. The Bodleian and Grolier copies contain various corrections in Phillipps's handwriting, including pedigrees worked out on the interleaved pages using the content of the epitaphs. The Devizes copy contains similar corrections in Colt Hoare's hand. No copy shows signs of extensive consultation.

CONTENT AND SCHOLARSHIP

Madden criticised all of Phillipps's publications for their shoddy transcribing, editing and printing, and Brightley expressed his concern at the perceived inaccuracies in *Monumental Inscriptions*. Both men had some reason for their views. The volumes of the *History of Modern Wiltshire* include epitaphs from each parish which can be used to check the accuracy of Phillipps's edition, and some discrepancies are immediately noticeable. In the parish of Amesbury, for example, Colt Hoare includes a number of flat stones missing in Phillipps. Yet, conversely, Phillipps includes the heraldry of the larger monuments which Colt Hoare ignores. The two versions do, however, agree on the content of each inscription although the use of abbreviations and layout differs.[38] To Phillipps's credit, his correspondence with Hensley shows his insistence on transcribing all Wiltshire monuments himself, irrespective of the work undertaken simultaneously by Britton or Colt Hoare.

There are undoubtedly mistakes, many of which are the result of Hensley's difficulty in reading old or worn epitaphs in the poor light inside churches. Yet, for north Wiltshire at least, there is now no other source for many of the inscriptions which have long since vanished. The dates cannot be accepted with confidence, but, where survival permits, the original epitaph or parish burial register can be used for verification.

34 Letter of Rouge Dragon Pursuivant, College of Arms, to the editor, 21 September 1999.

35 Munby, *Phillipps Studies*, vol.5, p.56.

36 Holzenberg, *Middle Hill Press*, gives the catalogue number as 'Phill. Coll. 34.52 MH424'.

37 They are shelved at 9915.f.10 and G.A.Wilts.c.5 respectively.

38 See below pp.289-290, and Richard Colt Hoare, *History of Modern Wiltshire: Everley, Ambresbury, Underditch Hundreds*, 1826, pp.74-75.

The chief value of the *Monumental Inscriptions* remains: there is no other publication which can act as a guide to the monuments of Wiltshire extant in 1820-21.

Errors of transcription aside, the volume's chief deficiency is the omission of some major sites of monumental construction. Salisbury Cathedral is not included, though it might be excused on the grounds of its unique status in the county. Phillipps may have known James Harris, who in 1825 would produce a volume recording the epitaphs therein.[39] A number of other churches are missing, mostly in the Swindon area. Notable among these is Lydiard Tregoze, which contains some of the county's most famous tombs in the form of the St John monuments. The reason for this is suggested in a collection of nineteen letters written by J.W. Osborne to Phillipps between 1819 and 1821, now preserved in the Wiltshire and Swindon Record Office. Osborne had been employed by Phillipps as an amanuensis, but appears not to have been paid for his labour. He took down the inscriptions of several churches near Swindon, including Lydiard Tregoze, and it may be that he withheld the transcripts from Phillipps until he could be assured of payment.[40] There are still inexplicable omissions. Transcripts of the monuments of Clyffe Pypard church taken in 1820 exist in Phillipps's notebooks in the Bodleian Library, yet this parish does not appear in the *Monumental Inscriptions*.[41]

The epitaphs included are overwhelmingly from the eighteenth century. This is not due to a poor survival of earlier gravestones, but to the huge upsurge in monumental commemoration which began in the 1660s, culminating in the foundation of public cemeteries in the nineteenth century and crematoria in the twentieth. Hensley did not normally transcribe monuments in churchyards, restricting himself to those inside churches. Exceptions are the churches in Highworth hundred, and the parishes of Chute, Great Bedwyn, Mere, Poulshot, South Marston, Stratton St. Margaret and Wanborough. Tombstones in churchyards have been recorded this century by the Wiltshire Family History Society although no transcriptions have been published.

Phillipps's work with its limited coverage and occasional errors still sits comfortably within the long-established antiquarian tradition of recording and sometimes publishing epitaphs. John Leland noted many monuments, including a number in Wiltshire, as early as the 1530s in his travels across England, and the manuscripts of heralds from Elizabethan times onwards include many notebooks of monumental inscriptions and heraldry. William Camden was the first to publish a collection of epitaphs, in his account of the tombs of Westminster Abbey, printed in 1600.[42]

Of Camden's many contemporaries and seventeenth-century successors, including the likes of William Dugdale, Henry Holland, and Anthony Munday, the most prominent was John Weever. Weever's *Ancient Funerall Monuments* (1631) was a 900-page volume listing epitaphs in the dioceses of Kent, Rochester, London and Norwich. This book is a useful comparison for Phillipps's work, as it has been subjected to similar criticism due to its inaccuracies and omissions. Weever has a major advantage

39 James Harris, *Copies of the Epitaphs in Salisbury Cathedral*, Salisbury, 1825.

40 Wiltshire and Swindon Record Office, WRO 2320/2.

41 PRMS e.236 notebook 3.

42 William Camden, *Reges, reginae, nobilis et alii in Ecclesia S. Petri Westmonasterii Sepulti*, London, 1600. For an account of the tradition of recording monuments, see J.G. Nichols' introduction to Thomas Dingley, *History From Marble*, London, Camden Society vol.94, 1867.

over Phillipps in that the book was circulated in large numbers in the seventeenth century, and in the style of writing which embeds each epitaph within a narrative. Nevertheless it is chiefly prized for its preservation of hundreds of monumental inscriptions which have long since been destroyed, a value which exists equally in Phillipps.

A more pertinent comparison is the set of *Gloucestershire Collections* by the eighteenth-century antiquarian Ralph Bigland. This was clearly a model for Phillipps's vision of his history of north Wiltshire, as Phillipps himself attempted the completion of Bigland's project and left directions in his will for the work of publication to be finished.[43] The *Monumental Inscriptions* contain traces of Bigland's influence in the inclusion of the names of contemporary clergy and manorial lords, or the sporadic listing of donation tablets. Bigland's work as published in the eighteenth and nineteenth centuries benefited from a broader circulation than Phillipps allowed himself, and from the wider scope of coverage for each parish. Yet again, however, its primary value is the transmission of gravestone inscriptions into the more durable medium of print, and it also provides a first port of call for those interested in epitaphs or in Gloucestershire history.

Phillipps's *Monumental Inscriptions* is indeed worthy of fresh consultation if only for its preservation of the material past, and as a source of reference for Wiltshire historians. It is not merely a dry record of names, dates, and places, facts which form the bulk of most epitaphs. A number of the epitaphs are highly colourful, many in English, some in Latin and a few in more than one language. Some are in rather poor taste, like that of Hester, wife of Henry Martyn, who died in 1667, ending: 'If women all would live like thee, Then Men with Wives might happy be' (p.109). A few are of a literary quality, most notably George Herbert's poem 'Sacred Marble safely Keepe', inscribed on the monument of the Earl of Danby who died in 1643.

Several epitaphs record remarkable people and their deaths. One which continues to cause surprise today is that of Hannah Twinnoy, who in 1703: 'was a servant at the White Lion Inn, where was an Exhibition of Wild Beasts, and amongst them a very fierce tyger, which she imprudently took a pleasure in teazing, notwithstanding the repeated remonstrance of its keeper' – and was subsequently torn to pieces (p.118). Then there is Hannah Hyde, died 1787, whose 'voice by nature was so wrought, To shake a D, a fourth above Alt' (p.158). Some inscriptions record events of political significance, such as Gyles Eyre, a Parliamentarian in the English Civil War who was, 'imprisoned for refusing to pay the sum of £400 illegally demanded of him' (p.355). The clergyman John Rolte wrote a fine epitaph for Henry Season of Bromham, died 1775, which called into question the very existence of monuments and inscriptions (p.229).

THIS EDITION

This edition of Phillipps's *Monumental Inscriptions* is a reproduction of the original in facsimile, using Colt Hoare's copy now lodged at Devizes. It follows the original pagination for North Wiltshire, but this is followed in a continuous sequence by South

43 Bigland's work was finally completed and printed by the Bristol and Gloucestershire Archaeological Society as Brian Frith, ed., *Bigland's Gloucestershire Collections*, 4 vols., Stroud, 1989-95.

Wiltshire, beginning at p.289 (Phillipps had begun numbering afresh for South Wiltshire). The few errors in page numbering are corrected, all in North Wiltshire, on pp.87 (81), 100 (96), 166 (164), 167 (163), 168 (162) and 184 (180). Manuscript notes and corrections present on the text pages of Colt Hoare's copy have been retained, but the sometimes heavily annotated interleaved pages have not been reproduced. Readers should be aware that the quality of the original printing leaves much to be desired, and many of its shortcomings are reflected in the facsimile. The need to minimize damage to the original volumes has also affected the quality of reproduction on some pages.

Besides providing wider distribution, an over-riding reason for reprinting the *Monumental Inscriptions* is the need for an index, without which it cannot function as a reference work. All names of persons and places within the text have been indexed, including noble or ecclesiastical titles, but not corporations. Surnames and place names have been grouped under the predominant or official spelling and cross-referenced. The most common first names have been abbreviated, and a list of these with the variant expansions is provided at the beginning of the persons index. (Names on Latin epitaphs have been rendered into English for the purposes of indexing.)

The *Monumental Inscriptions of Wiltshire* was one of Sir Thomas Phillipps's most notable publications. It was conceived and executed during his happiest years of family life, and his most active period as a student of Wiltshire history. The history of its production itself sheds light on the methods and experiences of early nineteenth century antiquaries and topographers. Although in its poor distribution, its errors and omissions, it retains traces of Phillipps's infamous tendency to rush into print, it remains one of his longest works and is worthy of a wider audience. Together with its index, it is now a valuable reference book for local historians, genealogists and biographers.

SUMMARY CONTENTS LIST OF WILTSHIRE PARISHES

CHIPPENHAM.

On Monument, against West End of Chancel.

Near this place lyeth ye Body of the Revd Mr. Robt. Cock, Vicar of this Parish, who, by will, left, for ever the yearly produce of Fifty Pounds, (which was all that he had) for Teaching POOR GIRLS to Read, and Instructing them to the Knowledge and Practice of the Christian Religion, as Professed and Taught in the Church of England. He dy'd October 4th, Anno Dom. 1721, Æt. 57.

Near this Place Lyes Interred the Body of Mr. Gilbert Lake, B. D. who was formerly Student of Christ Church in Oxford, and 15 years Vicar of this place, the Income of which he had the pleasure of Augmenting, by procuring One Hundred Pounds from Mr. Colston, and adding One Hundred Pounds more of his own to Queene Ann Bounty. He also built Part of the Vicaridge House. He was the Son of the Rev. Mr. Wm. Lake, formerly Student of the same Colledge, and Vicar of the same Place. A worthy son of so worthy a Father, who, haveing finished his Allotted time of Trial here, Departed this Life in the 48th year of his Age, and of our Lord 1740.

Against N. Wall.

Near this Stone lies interred the Body of Elizabeth Bayliffe, one of the Daughters of Edward Goddard, late of Hartham, Gent. and late Wife of Wm Bayliffe, now of Mounckton, Gent. who deptd this life Nov. 3, 1652.

Near unto this Stone Lieth the Body of Judeth Snell, Late wife of Richard Snell, of Loxwell, Gent. Eldest dau. of Wm. Bayliffe of Mounton, Esq. whoe depd this Life the 3d of Decem. Ano Dñi 1628.

Near unto this Place lieth interred the Bodies of Mr. Jonathan Clare, the late V. of this Place, and his two Sons, which said V. Depd this life the 26th of Dec. Ano Dñi 168 -.

Stars fall, but in the grossnese of our sight,
A good man dying the world doth lose a light;
While we Lament our Loss such lights put out,
The Heaven Triumph above, the Angels shout.
If virtue it selfe with vertuous men could dy,
Reader, thou mights say, here it doth Ly.

Near unto this Place lyeth interred the Bodie of Anne, the dau. of Sam. Twiford of this Burrough, Gent. who was Baptised the 18th day of Dec. Ao 1672, and Departed this Life the 16 day of June Ao 1674.

Near this place is buried the Body of Elizabeth the daughter of Mr. Saml. Twiford, who was baptised the 8th day of August, Ano Dom. 1681, and departed this life the 29th of Jan. next following.

Near this place lyeth the Body of Anna Maria, Wife of Sam. Twiford, who departed this life, Nov. 19. Anno Dom̃. 1711, Aged 22 years. Near this Place also lyeth the Body of Anna Maria, Dau. of Samuel Twiford, Aged 2 months.

Arms—S. a chev. A.

P. M. S.

Juxta depositum jacet quod mortale fuit Johannes Holland, Hujus Parochiæ, arm. qui ob. 26o Aprilis, Ao salutis 1728, Ætatis 52.

Animam deo Reddidit. Corpus Sepulchro, et Famam (Posteris) Dorothie ux. ej. ob. 3o Aprilis, 1726. Æt...

Roger Holland, filius, hujus Parochiæ, arm. ob. Julii 8. Æt. Sexag. 1762.

Arms—Az. a lion ramp. guard. A. arm G. bt. 6 fleur-de-lis. A. impaling A. a chev. bt. 3 bucks courant S.

On Monument against S. Wall.

Near this place lieth the Body of Ann the wife of Roger Warne, who died June the 24, A.D. 1724, Aged 60 years. Also the Body of Roger Warne, who died Feb. A.D. 1729, Aged 74 years. Also the Body of Philip, son of Roger and Ann Warne, who died Dec. 26, A.D. 1780, Aged 30 years.

In spem beatæ Resurrectionis juxta dormit Gul. Lake, A.M. Eccliæ Hujus Vicari dignissimus Sarum Præbendarius, Æclis. Xti Oxon. olim alumñus omnibus ibidem Semper Charus qui post annos 23. In ministerii munere illibatta, pietate, incorrupta, fide candore, et prudentia singulari: Indefessa et felici diligentia peractos de bonis omnibus, bene beritus plebilis, ob. 9o die Martii, A.D. 1703, Ætatis suæ 57.

On flat stones.

H. S.

Thomas Long, de Rowden, Gent. qui obijt 21° Maij, Anno Dom̃. 1691. Et Margeria uxor ejus, quæ ob. 13° die Decembris, Anno Dom. 1692.

Thomas Long, Esq. died May the 19th, 1730, Aged 73.

Arms—A li. pass. on a chief, 3 cross crosslets. Crest. a li. head issuing out of a marqual coronet.

Here lyeth the Body of Elizth ye wife of Richard Long of this Parish, Gent, who died 22. of October, Anno Dom. 1691.

Ann, the wife of Thos. Long, Esq. died Oct. ye 24, 1724, Aged 72.

Also Mary, Wife of Thomas Long, Esq. who died July the 6, 1773, Aged 72 years.

Arms, a li. ramp. bt. 8 crosslets. impaling. a li. pass. on a chief, 3 crosslets. Crest, a demi li.

Johannes, fil. Jonathæ Rogers, gen: et: Eliz: ux. ej. obijt xx die Decembris 1674.

Maria, ux Jonathæ Rogers, gen. . . . . fil Nath. Long, de Langrish . . . . . Hanton, Ar: ob. 3° Sep. A° Dom. 1711.

Arms—a chev. bt. 3 bucks courant, imp. Long.

Elizth ux: Jonathæ Rogers, gen: et filia Anthony Saunders, S.T.P. obijt nono die Feb. A.D. 1619.

Eorum filia Margareta, obijt 1673.

Hic conditæ jacent Reliquiæ Jonathæ Rogers, gen. qui obiit 30 Aug. Anno { Ætatis 82. Salutis 1715. }

Arms— a chev. bt. 3 bucks courant, impaling pr. chev. 3 elephants heads erased.

Josephus, filius Johannis Holland, arm. obijt die February . . . . 1730 Æ . . .

Elizth filia Jonathæ Rogers, Gen. obijt secundo 10 die Aug. 1677.

Johannes Holland, Ar. obijt 26 Aprilis, Anno Dom. 1723, Æt. 52.

Dorothæ, ux. Johis Holland, Ar. obijt 2° Aprilis, 1726, Æt. 51.

Here lyeth Jane, the daughter of John and Mary Merewether, who was born June the 8, 1729, And died Oct. the 31, 1731.

Also, Eleanor their Daughter, who died Dec, the 6th, A.D. 1739.

Also, William their Son, who died May the 17, A.D. 1741.

Also Edward their son, who dyed February the 13, A.D. 1745.

Also, William their son, who died June 19, 1747.

Here lyeth the Body of Mary, wife of John Merewether, who died July 12, 1756, Aged 50 years.

Hic jacent Ossa
Vire Desideratissimi, Johannis Merewether, M.B.
Œdis Christi apud Oxoniensis olim com.
Qui
Nullius interim seu boni Civis, seu Patris familias
Officii immenior Medicinam miseris Levamen:
Haud minori Liberalitatis
Quam Ingenii Laude
Annos amplius quadraginta
In hoc Municipio feliciter exercuit.
Obiit Maii 24, Anno Domini, 1774, Ætatis suæ. 88.

Richard Pocock, sen. died August the 21, 1777, Aged 68 years.

Also the Body of Sarah, wife of Richard Pocock, who departed this life the 26 day of May 1781, Aged 32 years.

Also, in Memory of Jane, wife of Richard Pocock, Sen. who dep. this life the 21 day of May 1785, Aged 76 years.

Here lyeth the Body of Mary, wife of Richard Lewis, of Corsham, Esq. and Daughter of Giles James, of Sheston-Pinckney, gen. Aged sixty years, who dep. this life ye 27 of Feb. Anno Dom. 1697.

Franciscus Cock, Arm. Roberti fili. Et Pater Ex Agro Norfolciæ | Hic Dormit | Qui hæc Dormiens Verba fecit | Nam Samnians, et vigilana | semper erat Mortis Memor | Cœlo natus | Cœlum spiro | Mundam Calco | Resurrecturus | Doctrinæ fericissimus amator Theologiæ præcipue scientior | Rogis et Ecclesiæ Defensor | Religionis assiduus cultor Peccantes Liberrime arguit | Temperantiam Fidem, Patientiam | Dictis factio Commendavit | Atterenis se abstraxit | Annes ad Superna excitavit | Omnibus ut posset profuit.

Obijt Anno salutis 1704 } Jan. die 11°.
Ætatis autem suæ 81 }

Arms—Quarterly, on a chief a cock.

In Memory of James Hall, who died Dec. A.D. 1750, Aged 35 years.

Roger Warne, Gent. died June 5th 1773, Aged 85.

To the Memory of Mrs. Eliz. Warne, spinster, born in 1686, and died in Jan. 1763.

Sarah ye wife of Henry Singer, gent. died Sept. 9th, 1775.

Henry Singer, gent. died Oct. 18, 1778, Aged 70.

Bazilla Chappall died Feb. 22, A. D. 1752, Aged 61 years.

Here lieth the Body of Wm. Bradbury, who departed this Life, Dec. the 24, A. D. 1763, Aged 43 years.

Also of Clementina his wife, who departed this life, Dec. 27, A. D. 1785, Aged 63 years.

On Monument against North Wall of the Nave.

Near to this Place lyeth the Body of John Ely, gent. Sometime Burgesse of this Towne, who died Nov. 25th 1663.

Tis well I am stone to preserve his name,
Who was (if mortals may be) without blame
In his religious civil Race Tise just.
In his calling no Traytour to his trust.
If this report consuming time shall weare,
And wipe out, search Heaven's Recors, tis there.

Near to this place lyeth also the Body of Mary, relict of John Ely, gent, who died Oct. 9th, 1671.

The Table of my life was Black and White,
Some cloudy dayes I liv'd to see, some bright
But now there is no mixture, All is Cleare,
Tis perfect sunshine, I am with my deare,
Of whom the world was not worthy, nor I,
Happy once more in this Blest Company.

Near this place lyeth the Body of Richard, son of John Ely, Gen. who died the 27 of July, A. D. 1675, Aged 23 years.

Though death would not upon his head
The Almond-tree permit to grow;
Yet shall the virtues of the dead
In dust and ashes bud and blow.

In the next Alley, over against this stone, Lieth the Body of Thomas Batten, of Allington, who departed this life, 26 of Dec. A° Dñi 1628.

To the Memory of John Gould Heath, an Ensign in the Dorset Regt. of Militia, son of John Heath, of this place, gent. He died suddenly at Ivy-Bridge Inn, in the County of Devon, and was interred in the Church-yard of Harford, in which Parish the Inn is situated. Obiit 7th of June, 1810, Ætatis 24.

Arms—Pp Chev. S & O. in chief 2 muttels pierced O, in base a heath cock of the first.

E. end of Nave.

In a Vault underneath are deposited the remains of Esmead Edridge, Esq. of Monkton juxta Chippenham, who died Mar. 13, 1812, Aged 64.

Arms---A li. ramp. in chief, a broad arrow bt. 2 li. hds. erased. Crest, a li. rampant.

In memory of Henry Singer, Esq. who died Oct. 18, 1778, Aged 70 years.

Of Richard Singer, Esq. his son, who died April 27, 1802, Aged 63 years.

And of Harriet, daughter of the above-named Richd Singer, by Maria Parry, his wife, who died Oct 30th, 1790, Aged 7 years.

Their Remains are deposited in the Chancel of this Church.

Also in Memory of Richard Oriel Singer, Esq. late of his Majesty's 32d Regt. only son of the said Rich. Singer, by Maria Parry his wife, who died Oct. 15, 1818, Aged 37 years. His remains are deposited at North Wraxall, in this County.

Arms on a chev. bt. 3 eag. disp. a cross crosslet bt. 2 escalops. Crest, a Phœnix holding in its beak a crosslet fitchey.

On Flat Stones in Nave.

In Memory of Mary, wife of Thos. Sparrow, who died Sept. 22d, A. D. 1763. Aged 41 years.

Also, in Memory of Thos. Sparrow, who died Nov. ye 6th, A. D. 1771, Aged 88 years.

Also, in Memory of Ann, wife of Thomas Sparrow, who died April 15, A. D. 1777, Aged 82 years.

In Memory of George Stucley, who died Feb. ye 23d, 1755, Aged 44 years.

Also, here lyeth the Body of George, son of George and Margaret Stucley, who departed this life the 7th day of Sept. A. D. 1763, Aged 19 years & 6 months.

In Memory of James Barnes, who died Dec. ye 25th, 1744, Aged 57.

In Memory of Abraham Noble, gent. of Maldon, in the county of Essex, who departed this life March 11, 1748, Aged 57 years.

William, son of Wm. and Margaret Lovegrove, died February 22d, 1743, Aged 16 years.

Margt Lovegrove died March 21, 1757, Aged 67 years.

Also Margaret Lovegrove, spinster, died June 10, 1802, Aged 70 years.

William Lovegrove died Feb. ye 18th, 1778, Aged 84 years.

Also Ambrose Lovegrove, died June ye 23d, 1788, Aged 66 years.

Also Mary, Relict of Ambrose Lovegrove, died Sept. ye 9th, 1800, Aged 81 years.

Underneath this stone lies interred the Remains of Ann, wife of Richard Smith of Rowdedown, who died March the 2d, 1770, Aged 63 years.

Also, Richard their son, died March the 8, 1774, Aged 32 years.

Also Richard Smith, who dep. this life, March 6, 1777, Aged 70 years.

John Warne, died Oct. 13, 1759, Aged 38. Elizth Jones, daughter of Roger and Elizabeth Warne, died Oct. 3, 1762, Aged 43. Eliz. wife of Roger Warne, died July 2, 1755, Aged 79. Anna, daughter of John and Eliz. Warne, died April 22, 1787, Aged 27 years. Mary, wife of Archibald Litle, gent. who died Nov. 20, 1799, Aged 42 years. Elizabeth, wife of John Warne, she died July 13, 1802, Aged 74 years.

Frances Hill Verchild, Wife of Lewis Brotherson Verchild (of the Island of St. Christopher, in the West Indies) departed this life 20th Sept. 1810.

In Memory of Wm. Gale, son of Wm. and Eliz. Gale, who died Nov. 24, 1754, Aged 5 months.

Also Mary, their daughter, died May the 27, 1765, Aged 1 year.

Here lieth interred the Body of Eliz. the wife of Wm. Gale, who died ye 13 day of Nov. 1769, aged 40.

Also the Body of the said Wm. Gale, gent. died Jan. 18, 1800, Aged 72.

In Memory of John Wilson, son of Stephen and Mary Wilson, who died Oct. 26, 1764, Aged . .

Here lieth ye Body of John Dunn, who died June the 17, A. D. 1760, aged 84 years.

Also, here lieth the Body of Ann, wife of John Dunn, who died Nov. the 13, A. D. 1760, aged 74 years.

Here lieth the Body of Catherine, wife of Joseph Colborne, who departed this life, June the 16, A. D. 1753, aged 65 years.

Here lieth the Body of Jane, wife of Joseph Colborne, who died Sept. ye 3, 1755, aged 28 years.

Also Jane, daughter of Joseph and Jane Colborne, who died March 3, 17. . aged 3 years.

In Memory of Ann, wife of Thos. Homes, who died July ye 8, 1764, aged 47 years.

Also, in Memory of Thos. Holmes, who died May ye 8, 1788, aged 84 years.

Also, Elizabeth, Wife of Wm. Bowsher, died Jan. 12, 1816, aged 59 years.

Here lieth the Body of John Emmett, who departed this life the 12 of Nov. 1711, aged 52 years.

Here lyeth the Body of Margaret, the Wife of Nicholas Emmett, who departed this life Sep. 13, A. D. 1716, aged 65 years.

Here lyeth the Body of Eliz. wife of Joseph Colborne, who dep. this life 14 day of Feb. A. D. 17. . Aged 21 years.

Also, here lyeth the Body of Joseph Colborne, Burgess of this Borow, who dep. this life, Oct. ye 7, A. D. 1734, Aged 51 years.

On Mon. against E. end of S. aisle.

Near this Place lyeth ye Body of Mary, ye Wife of Thos. Chappell, of this Burrough, Clothier, and daughter of Mr. Thos. Andrews, Minister of God's Word, late of Shaston, in Dorsetshire, who departed her Life ye 15 day of Feb. 1689.

Noe sooner are wee Born to live than dy,
Our first day doth assure us of our Last;
Whilst ev'ry moment wee doe hasten ny
To our Long home, and what we have lived is past.
For man to live here ever cannot bee,
Long to enjoy we must not think, a Chang
Attends us, and thou groneing waitst to see
That day, dear Soule life here at last seemd strange
'Twas sickness now thou Livst when death hath wrought
Its malice, and soe ended Hath all greif,
Happy be those Mishaps which thee have Brought
A gain full los, and in thy Death a life.

Here Lyeth the Bodye of Alice, the Wife of Thomas Longe, gent. late deceased. Shee Depd this Life the 17th day of Nov. Ano Dom. 1741.

Reader, behold, what little staye or trust, is
To bee sett on man whose strength is dust:
Consider well thye brittle stage on earth,
How Everye moment subject unto death.
Amend then whats amisse, thye sins forsake,
Repent in tyme, peace in thy conscience make,
Death spareth none, yet when hee strikes, or how,
For man Before hande, tis too much to know.

Richard Forman, late one of the Burgesses of this Burrough, departed this life the 5th day of March, Anº Dom̃. 1639, whos Bodye here lyeth Buryed.

Erected in Commemoration of Wm. Pew, gent. and Grace his Wife: the said Wm. departed this life, October ye 31. Anº Dom̃. 1648, and Grace departed this life the 25th of August, 1635, whose Bodies Lye here Interred.

MORIENDO VIVIMUS

Upon the Death of Mr. Wm. Pew, and Mrs. Grace, his Wife, buried in the same grave:

Behold my Grave is now my Nuptiall Bed
Whom once on Earth in Earth i now doe wed
Wth chaste embraces Death was not unkind
To part us so that Shee may stronger binde
No Reader, now our blisse is neare complete
For here our Dust—above our souls doe meete.

Here lyeth the Body of Alice Hawkins, daughter of Robert Hawkins, late of Hardenhuish, Clothier, Shee Depd this life on the 31 day of August, A.D. 1657, Ætatis suæ 29.

Nuptiæ replent terram, Virginitas Paradisum.

Here lieth the Body of Thomas Hawkins, gent. late one of the Burgesses of this Borrough, who departed this Life the 4th day of December, Anº Dom̃. 1676.

The Father and two Sones united be
This grave contains what's mortall of ye three,
The Mother also near to those doth ly,
Whose soules no doubt enjoyes felicity.

On an Altar-tomb, at the E. end of S. aisle.

Miger hoc tumulo jacet Hic generosus opaco
Andreas Baynton, qui nominatus Erat
Quem Genuit Miles bene notus ubi que Edouardus
Hujus erat heres nunc Requiescit Humo
Anº Dom̃. 1370 [*or* 1570.]

Arms 1 a bend lozen.
2 . . . . . .
3 a fess. bt. 6 martlets.
4 3 fishes naiant.
5 2 li. passant guard.
6 on a chev. 3 eagles disp.

On a Monument against S. E. corner of Nave.

Near to this place lye interred the bodies of Anthony Martyn, gent, who died on the 19 day of March, 1719, in the 61 year of his age.

His wife, Mary Martyn, expired the 17 of April, 1731, aged 70 years.

Robert Martyn, of the Inner Temple, esq. their only son, died the 12 of August, 1733, in whose Memory this Monument was erected, by Mildred Martyn, his Relict. Also Mildred, wife of the above Robert Martyn, esq. and relict of Roger Holland, esq. departed this life the 28 of January, 1776, in the 77 year of her Age.

Arms, ermine A. eagle displ. G. over an escut. charged with 5 chevronels.

On a brass plate against S. wall of S. aisle.

The Memoriall of Sir Gilbart Pryn, Kt. who married Mary, the eldest daughter of Jayne Davis, daughter to Sir Wymond Carye, Kt. Lord Warden of ye St armeries, Mr. of ye First fruits office, &c. Kt, of ye Bathe, the said Sir Gilbart Pryn having issue by ye said Mary his Wife seven children, 2 sons and 5 daughters, five of which, 2 sons and 3 daughters, are dead, the other daughters, namely, ye eldest of all, Fraunces, is married to Sir Frauncys Seimour, Kt. Youngest sonne of ye Lord Beauchamp Sonne and heire to ye now Erle of Hertford, and ye second daughter, named Seimour, married to Sir George Hastings, Kt. second Brother to Henry, now Erle of Huntingdon,

Eche mans a Plant, and Every tree,
Like man, is subject to Mortalitie:
These Braunches dead and Fallen away, are gone
From us untill the Resurrection;
These Grafted thus, by Wedlocks sacred Dome,
God graunte may flourishe till those other come.

Arms, O. a fess. eng. S. bt. 3 escalops, G. imp. S. a chev. arm. bt. 3 annulets, A.

[Erected 1620.]

S. Wall.

Near this Place lyeth the Body of Thos. Figgins, jun. gent. who departed this life the 9 day of August 1757, Aged 28 years.

Also Jane, wife of Thos. Figgens, sen. gent. died the 20 day of March, 1767, Aged 82 years.

And also the Body of Thos. Figgens, sen. gent. who died the 11 day of 1777, Aged 74 years.

Also Susanna Merewether, Wife of the above Thos. Figgens, jun. gent. and Relict of John Merewether, gent. died 27 August 1807, aged 75 years.

Arms, A. a tree pp.

Sacred to the Memory of Eliz. Norris, Relict of the late Wm. Norris, esq. of Nonsuch House, Wilts. who died May 20, 1805, aged 75.

Also to the Memory of Eliz. Norris, Daughter of the above Elizth Norris, who died March 17, 1805, Aged 56.

Against W. end of S. aisle.

Near this place lyes interred ye Body of John Scott, gent. son of John Scott, Clothier, who departed this life the 4th day of April. Ano Dom̃. 1700, Ætat. . .

Here lyes ye Body of George Scott, Clothier, who departed this life, Aug. ye 24th, Ano Dñi 1628, Ætat. suæ 44.

Near this Place lieth the Body of Alice, the Wife of Henry Gouldney, Clothier, and the daughter of Mr. Richard Scott, who was interred the 4th day of April, 1670, and was baptized the 11th of October 1631.

On Flat Stones in S. aisle.

In Memory of Elizabeth, Wife of George Scott, who died July the 28, 1733, aged 45 years.

Also W . . . er, son of George and Eliz. Scott, died April 20, 17 . . . . . years.

Likewise two of their daughters died infants.

Here Lyeth ye Body of John Wastfield, who dep. this life, Aug. 11. A. D. 1741. Aged 40 years.

Also, here lyeth the Body of Edward Wastfield, who departed this life March 11, A. D. 1742, Aged 33 years.

Wm. Grinfield, Esq. died August ye 17, 1762, Aged 61 years.

Here lyeth ye Body of Martha, the Daughter of William and Mary Gale, who deptd this life the . . . day of June, Ano Dñi 1724.

Sarah Coke died May ye 17th, 1777, Aged 50 years.

Absent or dead, a friend should still be dear:
A sigh the absent claims; the dead, a tear.

Here lieth the Body of Anne ye Wife of Samuel Marten, who exchanged this life for a better September ye 2d, A.D. 1731.

Also Samuel Martyn died June ye 8, 1749.

John Holland, Aged 21 years. A. D. 1740.

The Rev. Christopher Holland, A. M. 22 years Vicar of this Place, died May ye 8th, 1760, Aged 52.

Elizabeth, Wife of the above Christopher Holland, died April 28, A. D. 1776, aged 72 years.

Nicholas Trueman, Esq. died April ye 2d, 1778, Aged 64 years.

Here lieth the Body of John Jennings, gent. who died July ye 3d, 1795, Aged 70 years.

In Memory of Sarah Allen, who died the 5th of Nov. 1769, aged 27 years.

It was not requested to be deposited here with her truly affectionate friend, Frances Batchlor, Wife of Mr. George Batchlor of North Bradley, in this County, and sister to Mr. Jennings, Surgeon, of this Town. She died the 26th of October, 1776, Aged 44 years. Also Mary Jennings, died Sept. 29, 1792, Aged 75 years.

Here lyeth the Body of Robert Martyn, Esq. who Depd this Life August the 12th, A. D. 1783, Aged 44 years.

Mildred Holland died January 28, 1776, Aged 77.

. . . . Alice Hawkins . . . .

[Brass taken out.]

Against the West wall of S. transept.

Near this place lyeth the Body of Elizabeth, the Wife of Jonathan Scott, gent. late of the Ivy, who departed this life the 25th day of April, Anno Domini 1718, Aged 77 years.

Near this place lyeth the Body of Mr. Jonathan Scott, of ye Ivy, who departed this life ye 28th day of Jan. Ano Dom̃. 169$\frac{3}{4}$ Aged 85 years.

Juxta hunc Lapidem jacet sepulta Elinora, uxor Jonathanis Scot, deive hujus Parochiæ, Filia Henrici Bayliffe, nuper de Chippenham, arm̃. quæ obdormivit 4 die Februarii 1664, Anno Ætat. suæ 61.

Quæ modo peccatis mundi vexata dolebatiam Christo et Sanctis consonat illa Deo.

Here Lyeth the Body of John Brookes, who departed this life the 7th of Dec. A. D. 1722, Aged 82 years.

Maria, ux. Johannis Brookes, filia Domini Thomæ Fereby, de Episcopi Cannings, nuper Vicarii dignissimi decimo sertimo die octorris mortua 19° ejusdem mensis, 1666 sepulta.

Cara deo dilecta piis pretiosa marito vicinis lenis pauperibus que fuit.

On a flat stone in S. transept.

Here lieth the Body of Jane, the wife of Jonathan Scott, who died Jan. 2d, 1774, Aged 44 years.

DONATION TABLETS.

Against the S. side of the S. aisle.

In the year 1638, Mrs. Elizabeth Hawkins, of Chippenham, gave by Will to the Bailiff of the Borough of Chippenham. in the county of Wilts, ten Pounds, the Interest to be paid annually to Six poor Freemens' Widows on Candlemas Day, by the Bailiff of the said Borough.

In the year 1735,

Sir Francis Popham, Baronet, by Deed gave to the Bailiff of the Borough of Chippenham for the time being, and other Trustees, certain lands at Foxham, and in Dale Mead in the Parish of Christian Malford, in the County of Wilts; the Rents and Profits to be paid to such poor Freemen or free Burgesses of the said Borough of Chippenham, as the said Trustees should yearly, between the Feast Day of St. Michael the Archangel and the Feast of All Saints, appoint.

These Lands are now Let at £.22 per annum, and the Rent is divided into Forty Shilling Donations, and given to poor Freemen annually.

In the year 1642,

Mr. Henry Smith, formerly a Citizen and Silversmith of London, left an estate at Lonney, near Gloucester, to the Governors of Christ's Hospital, in trust, for the use of 23 Parishes in different parts of the Kingdom, in such proportions as the Donor directed, one of which was Chippenham, in the County of Wilts. The following is a clause in Mr. Henry Smith's Will: Item, The said Henry Smith doth further by those Presents limit and appoint and declare his intent and meaning to be, that the said sums of Money given limited and assigned, or appointed to or for the Relief of the Impotent and aged Poor of the said Parishes respectively, shall be distributed, bestowed, and employed in Apparel, of one colour, with some Badge or other Mark, that the same may be known to be the Gift of the said Henry Smith, or else in Bread, or Flesh, or Fish, upon each Sabbath-day publicly in the Parish Church of each of the said Parishes.

This Estate is Let at £.900 a-year, and the proportionate part of the Rent, received by the Churchwardens of Chippenham, distributed in Great Coats for the Poor annually.

In the year 1664,

Mr. William Woodroffe, of ye Parish of Chippenham, yeoman, gave, by Will, to the Bailiff of ye Borough of Chippenham, and to the Minister of the said Parish for the time being, an Annuity of Five Pounds, to be received by the said Bailiff and Minister on the Feast of All Saints, to be by them paid to a Schoolmaster, for keeping a School, and teaching of Ten poor Boys within the said Borough, such as the said Bailiff and Minister for the time being should think fit.

This Annuity is payable out of the field called the Breach, situate in ye Ivy, in ye Parish of Chippenham. In consequence of Mr. Wm. Woodroffe's Donation, the House given by Mr. Richard Scott, was erected into a Free School, and a Master appointed to the same by the Bailiff of the said Borough, and the Master of the School is appointed by the Bailiff and Burgesses of Chippenham, and ye Boys are nominated alternately by the Bailiff and Minister of the said Parish for the time being.

In the year 1689,

John Wicks, Gentleman, by Will, bearing date the thirteenth day of March, One Thousand Six Hundred and Eighty-seven, devised to the Minister and Churchwardens of the Parish of Chippenham, in the County of Wilts, certain lands, called Pipesmore, containing 6A. 2R. 0P. in Trust, to divide the Rent of the said Lands yearly, on the twenty-ninth Day of March, unless it fell on a Sunday, then the Monday following, amongst the Poor of Chippenham where most needful.

The land is now Lett at £.23 per annum, and the Rent is laid out in the Purchase of Linen Garments, and given to both poor men and women in the said Parish.

In the Year 1719,

The Rev. Robert Cock, Vicar of this Parish, gave by Will to the Ministers of the several Parishes of Chippenham, Melksham, and Box, in the County of Wilts, in Trust, after defraying all his Debts and Funeral Expences, the Residue of his Goods and Chattels, Rights and Credits, to apply the same towards it, and supporting a Charity School for Girls within the said Parish of Chippenham. A Close of Meadow Land was purchased by his Trustees out of the Residuum of his Estate near a House called by the name of the

Folly, on the Bristol road, and bounded partly by the Hardenhuish Estate. See his Monument in the Chancel of this Church.

The Land now lets at the annual Rent of £.9 9s. and Twenty-five Girls are placed at School with the same.

This Charity is now solely under the superintendance of the Minister of Chippenham.

DONATION TABLETS,

Against North Wall of Nave.

June 18, 1615,

Thomas Ray, late of the City of New Sarum, by his Will of this Date, gave the House wherein he dwelt, and all his Tenements in Giggin Street, in the City of New Sarum, to his daughter Martha Ray, during her natural Life, and after her death, bequeathed the same to the Poor Clothiers of the four following Towns, viz. the Rent of the first year to Trowbridge, the second to Chippenham, the third to Westbury, and the fourth to Marlbrough, and so round again for ever, as Sir Thos. White's Money was given. The above Premises are now Let to Thomas Adams of the City of New Sarum, Taylor, for a term of 21 years, from the 29th of Sept. 1795, at the yearly Rent of 15 pounds, and the Charity is under the management of Feoffees, to be chosen in the Towns by the Majority of the poor Clothiers, together with the Churchwardens for the time being, of the Township of Trowbridge, the Bailiff of the Borough of Chippenham for the time being, and for the Towns of Westbury and Marlbrough, the Mayors of the said Towns for the time being.

RALPH GABY, } *Churchwardens*
GEO. BRAMBLE, } *June* 1, 1813.

November the 1. 1681,

Gabriel Goldney, late of Chippenham, in the County of Wilts. Clothier, by his Will of this Date (amongst other things), gave and bequeathed Six Pounds per annum, chargeable on his lands at Tytherton, to purchase six Coats to be given to honest poor labouring men of the Parish of Chippenham, no one Person to receive one of these Coats two successive years following, the disposal of the Coats to be in the Heirs of the said Testator for ever.

These lands are described in the Will by the names of Mill Field, and two other Grounds adjoining to it called Cogswell, and one other Ground, called Hatts, and are now in the occupation of Mr. William Crook, as Tenant to Mrs. Sarah Goldney. *June* 1, 1813.

RALPH GABY, } *Ch.-Wardens.*
GEO. BRAMBLE, }

In the year 1728,

Mr. Robert Gale, Citizen and Vintner of London, left by Will, Twenty Pounds a year to the Poor of the Parish of Chippenham, in the County of Wilts. payable out of certain Estates called Claypool and Brassington, in the Counties of Lincoln and Derby, in these Words following: Twenty Pounds a-year, Part thereof to be distributed yearly on the Feast of St. Thomas the Apostle, at the discretion of the Bailiff and six of the ancientest Burgesses of the said Borough, at the Parish Church of Chippenham, and Twenty Shillings a year yearly for ever for a Preacher to Preach at the Parish Church of Chippenham at the distributing of the said Twenty Pounds a year, and Twenty Shillings a year yearly for ever to the said Bailiff and six of the ancientest Burgesses of the said Borough to drink withal for their pains in distributing of the said Twenty Pounds, as aforesaid.

This Money is received annually of Mr. Wilby, Receiver, Christ's Hospital, London, and distributed to the poor at the Vestry on St. Thomas' Day.

March 31 and April 1, 1802.

By Deed of this Date, made between Sir Andrew Bayntun, Bart., Paul Cobb Methuen, and Richard Long, of the first part, Harry Goldney and Henry Burnett, of the second part, and Paul Methuen, the Rev. John Starkey, Mathew Humphrys, and Gabriel Goldney, of the third part, several Messuages and Lands situate in the Parishes of Chippenham and Laycock, in the several occupation of Mary Tayler, Robert Sadler, Alfred King, Wm. Williams, and John Beames, and were conveyed to the use and behoof of the said Sir Andrew Bayntun, Paul Cobb Methuen, Richard Long, Paul Methuen, John Starkey, Mathew Humphrys, George Norris, and Gabriel Goldney, their Heirs and Assigns for ever, upon Trust to Let and dispose of the Premises to the best advantage, and to employ, or cause to be employed, the Rents, Issues, and Profits thereof for the Maintenance, Upholding, and Reparation of the Parish Church of Chippenham, and for the provision of things necessary for the said Church.

In the year 1661,

Mr. Richard Scott, of Chippenham, gave by Will the present Free School House (whenever a School should be erected, and Maintenance given unto it for the encouragement of the Schoolmaster) for a little more encouragement, and to be disposed of by the Bailiff and Burgesses for ever.

In the year 1764,

Mrs. Mary Bridges, of the Parish of Chippenham, by her Will, left Ten Pounds for the use of the Free School in the Parish of Chippenham, which with interest, amounting to five pounds, was paid in December One Thousand Seven Hundred and Seventy-Four, by the late Mr. Wm. Lovegrove, surviving Executor, into the hands of the then Bailiff of the Borough of Chippenham, in consideration of the Bailiff's engaging for himself and his successors to pay to the master of the said Free School the sum of fifteen shillings yearly for the teaching and instructing two poor Boys, born within the Borough, in Reading, Writing, and Arithmetic. The nomination of these two Boys is with the Bailiff solely.

Nov. the 17, 1769,

Wm. Colborne, late of the City of Bath, Esq. on this day had paid into his hands the sum of One Hundred Pounds, three per cent. consols, in the names of Sir James Tylney Long, and others. And by deed of this date it was declared, That the Dividends thereof should be paid towards the Support and Maintenance of such Freemen of the Borough of Chippenham, and the Widows of Freemen living in Free Houses, and being in the possession of the Freedom of such Houses at such time, in such Parts, Shares, and Proportions, Manner, and Form, either in Money, Clothes, or Provisions, or otherwise, as the said Trustees, and their Successors, or the major part of them, should think proper.

The surviving Trustees are Paul Cobb Methuen, and Gabriel Goldney, Esquires.

RALPH GABY, } *Churchwardens*
GEO. BRAMBLE, } *June* 1, 1813.

At the E. end, in the vaulting of the S. aisle, are Three Shields of Arms.

FIRST SHIELD. { Quarterly,
1. S. 2 bars A. in chief 3 plates.
2. Ppale indented G. & S. over all a chev. O.
3. O on a bend G 3 . . . . . A.
4. Barry of 8. O. & S. impaling A. a Griffin Segrant G.

SECOND SHIELD. {
1. S. 2 bars A. in Chief . . . . A.
2. A. a Griffin, Segrant G.
3. G. 3 Pallets wavy or.
4. G. 3 chev. or.
5. S. 2 Bars A. in chief 3 plates.
6. S. on a fess. G. 3 fusils conj. A.

THIRD SHIELD. { Quarterly, S.
1. 2 Bars A. in chief 3 plates.
2. Ppale, indent. G. & S. over all a chev. or.
3. a Castle A.
4. on 3 bars A. . . . . . S.

Register Commenced 1587.

The Rev. Thomas Weekes, late Vicar 60 years.
The Rev. Edward Ellis present Vicar. (2 Ministers of Westminster.)

In a Window in south aisle is a little painted glass, az. o. G. Likewise in the Chancel Window.

The Church consist of a Chancel, Nave, and South Aisle. At the east end of the Nave is a Saxon Arch, much ornamented, about ten feet in the span.

LANGLEY BURRELL.

On Monuments against North Wall of Chancel.

In Memory of Edward Speke, Esq. who died Jan. 9th, 1732, Aged 40 years.

Also Sarah Speke, his widow, who died Dec. 11th, 1774, Aged 76 years.

Here beneath lieth the Bodie of Mr. Robert Sadlier, who died in the Faith of our Saviour Jesus Christ, the 10th day of January, in the year of our Lord 1643.

Here Lieth the Bodie of Mrs. Rebekah Norborne, lately wife to the . . . . Henry Norborne, Batch. in Divinitie. She died in the Faith of our Saviour Jesus Christ, the 16th of June, in the year of our Lord God 1641.

East Wall.

Lucy-Anne, daughter of the late Richard Watts, of Harnhill, in the county of Gloucester, Esq. died August 16, 1808, aged 23 years.

Her Sister, Mary Jane Jenner, Wife of the Rev. Robert Ashe, died April 4, 1811, Aged 28 Years.

Hunc juxta Locum jacet Depositum,
Viri admondum Reverendi Aylmeri Lynch, B. D.
Hujusæ Ecclesiæ nuperrime Rectoris,
Nepotis Johannis Aylmeri,
Qui
Prænomen illi Dederit
Londinensis quondam Episcopi. Filii antem
Gulielmi Lynch, de Groves, in Parochia de Staple, in agro Cantiensi, Generosi.
Nati 23° Novembris, Anno Domini 1600,
Denati vero 24 Januarii, Anno Dom̄. MDCXCJ.
Resurrectio mortuorum fiducia Christianorum.
Arms, Az. 3 leop. saliant, A. armed G.

On Flat Stones in Chancel.

Here lyeth the Body of Theophilus Lynch, gent. and Anne his late Wife. Theo. was buried the 13th day of March, A. D. 1668, Anne, the 22d day of August, A. D. 1689.

Matilda Ashe died October 8, 1802, Aged 5 years.

Samuel Ashe died November 5, 1802, Aged 18 years.

Margaret-Catherine Ashe died July 1st, 1804, Aged 15 years.

The Rev. Samuel Ashe, late Rector, died the 15th of April, 1807, Aged 54 years.

Here lyeth the Body of Anne, late Wife of William Hulbert, who was buried the 14th day of December, Anno Dom̃. 1670.

Here lyeth the Body of William Hulbert, of this place, who Departed this Life the twenty-third day of December, Anno Dom̃. 1712, Aged 90 years and 5 months.

Subtus dormit beatissime Resurgendi certus,
Thomas Stampe . . . . is infantulus undicimester,
Qui assiduis Omciatibus
Tenui corpusculo longi imparibus Regnum Cœlorum
Hæreditatem talium osi sic seniores,
Tanta innocentia, A. D. iji.
Decimo quarto die Jan. 1699.

H. S. E.

Thomæ Read, per annos quadraginta hujus Parochiæ Rector. Obiit die quinto Augusti, Anno Dom̃. 1743, Ætatis suæ 68.

Juxta hunc Lapidem jacet Henricus, filius Thomæ Read: Obiit die 15° Aprilis, Anno Domini 1740, Ætatis suæ 24.

Arms, a cross charged with a roundel bt. 4 fleur-de-lis, imp. a chev. bt. 3 boars heads.

Here lyeth the Body of Martha, Wife of Adam Tuck, of the Parish of Langley Burrell, Gentleman. And also the Bodys of their three Sons and three Daughters, who all died in their Infancy. The said Martha departed this life the Eleventh day of August 1740, in the 31st year of her Age. Also Martha Tuck died November 8, 1812, Aged 81 years.

Sarah, Wife of the Rev. Robert Ashe, died October 10th, 1772, Aged 53 years.

Also, the Rev. Robert Ashe, Rector of this Church, died January 4, 1774, Aged 55 years.

H. S. E.

Elizabetha, uxor Thomæ Read, hujus Ecc† Rector, Quæ Variolarum labe tabefacta, Obiit 17 Augusti, 1732.

Mater protumulo heu nimis focunda ex undecim enim Nates a dextra sua jacent Quinque quorum pars maxima ecunabulis in Cœlos transibant.

Also Elizabeth Pincke, daughter of the said Thos. and Elizabeth Read, Ob. 23 Nov. 1797, Aged 87 years.

On a White Marble Stone.

Here lyeth the Body of James Ashe (the eldest son of Samuel Ashe of this place, Esq.) who lately married the youngest daughter of Christopher Thomlinson, merchant, of the City of London. He departed this life the 2d day of February, in the 37th year of his age, Anno Dom̃. 1704.

In Cœlo Salutis.

Arms, 2 chev. impaling ppale, 3 greyhounds courant.

On Monuments in S. transept.

In Memory of Mathew Humphrys, of Ivy House, near Chippenham, Esq. who died Sept. 14, 1810, Aged 76 years.

And of Anne Humphrys, his Wife, daughter of the Rev. Robert Ashe, late Rector of this Parish. She died June 15, 1780, Aged 30 years.

Also, of Mathew Humphrys, their eldest Son, who died July 25, 1795, Aged 18 years.

Near this Place lyeth the Body of Mary Rayner, late Wife of Nicholas Rayner, of St. Paul, Covent Garden, in the County of Middlesex, Mercer, and daughter of Samuel Ashe of this Place, Esq. She Departed this Life the 13th of June 1695, Ætatis suæ 25.

Vivit post funera Virtus.

Arms, ermine, on a chief, az. 2 estoils, or. impaling, A. 2 chev. S.

Here lieth the Body of Margaret White, daughter of Henry White, gent. who died in the faith of our Saviour Jesus Christ, the 28th of March, in the year of our Lord God 1640.

Here lyeth the Body of William Duckett, sonne of Lionell Ducket, and Martha his Wife, eldest daughter of Samuel Ashe, Esq. of Langley, who died the second day of August, 1681.

On a Monument against S. side of Nave.

Sacred to the Memory of Susannah Ponting, Wife of N. Ponting, gent. of this Parish, who calmly resigned her life to Him who gave it, on the third day of September, 1795, Aged 41 years.

ROBERT ASHE, Esq. Lord of the Manor.

KEYLWAY CHURCH.

ERECTED CIRC. 1806.

On a Monument against East end of the Church.

In a Vault on the North side of this Church are deposited the Remains of the Rev. Henry Brindley, A. M. Vicar of Holdcombe Burnell, in com̄ Devon. and Rector of Calloes 34 years. He departed this Life 3d April 1819, in the 81st year of his age.

By his zeal and interest this Church was removed and Rebuilt, and the Service, which before was monthly, has since been performed every week. He instituted an annual Lecture on the Sin of Cruelty to the Brute Creation; and he was as pious, generous, and affectionate, as he was humane.

Look down, blest soul, and from thy realms above,
Accept this last sad tribute of my love,
The last—even now my sorrows I resign,
And lose my feelings to rejoice in thine.

MR. LONG, Lord of this Manor.

The Rev. WALTER LONG Rector, Henry Brindley late Rector.

TYTHERTON LUCAS.

Against N. Wall of Chancel.

Hic jacet Corpus Hugonis Barret, generosis, qui obdormivit in Domino vicesimo secundo die Junii, Anno Ætatis suæ octogesimo quinto, Anno Domini millesimo sexentesimo vicesimo septimo.

East end of Chancel.

Here under lieth the Body of Mrs. Alice Jacob, late Wife of Thomas Jacob, of Wootton Basset, gent. who changed this mortall for an Immortall Life the last of February 1653, and left issue,

John Jacob of Norton, gent. Sibilla, the Wife of Nevell Maskeline, of Purton, gent. and Elizabeth, the Wife of Edward Stokes, of this Parish, esq.

On Flat Stones.

In Memory of Mary, the Wife of Richard Uncles, who departed this life May the 15, A. D. 1740, Aged 37 years.

Dear Husband, now life is past,
So long to you my love did last;
Now for me no sorrow take,
But love my Children for my sake.

Also, near this Place lieth the Body of Richard Uncles, of Avon, who departed this life August the 2d, A. D. 1747, aged 55 years.

From grief and trouble I am free,
Of which I had great store;
When Christ doth call, arise I shall,
And Death shall see no more.

Also near this Place lieth the Body of Betty Uncles, who departed this life Oct. 27, A. D. 1750, Aged 21 years.

Here lieth the Body of Dorothy, daughter of Edward and Eliz[th] Crook, who died October 17, 1739, Aged 15 years.

Also John, their son, died July 19, 1773, Aged 52 years.

Here Lieth the Body of Sarah, Wife of John Crook, who died November 24, 1774, Aged 53.

In Memory of Edward Crook, who died July 15, 1743, Aged 64 years.

Elizabeth, wife of Edward Crook, died May 29, 1767, Aged 78 years.

In Memory of Elizabeth, Wife of John Crook, who died August 14, 1779, Aged 29 years.

In Memory of William, son of Simon and Elizabeth Crook, who departed this life July 11, 1778, Aged 3 months.

Against S. side of Nave.

Ann Lloyd Bayliffe, Ob. 20 April 1788, Ætat. 22.
Lucy Bayliffe, Ob. 17th, April 1791, Ætat. 21.

As a tribute of affection, their surviving sister, Mary Susanna Crook, have caused this Tablet to be erected to their memories.

On Flat Stones in Nave.

Here Lieth the Body of William Ponting, who died February 7, A. D. 1767, Aged 52 years.

Here lyeth ye Body of Penelope, the Wife of John Tayler, who departed this Life, August the 20th, A. D. 1727, Aged 68 years.

Against N. Wall of N. aisle.

Near this Place lyeth the Body of Adjohn Stokes, gent. of Tytherton Lucas, jun. who departed this life July 7th An° Dom̃. 1725, Aged 53 years.

And also Sarah his Wife, who departed this life April the 4th, 1734, Aged 53 years.

Underneath this Place lyeth interred the Body of Edward Stokes, Esq. who departed this life, in the Faith of our Lord Jesus Christ, the 31 day of October, in the 56th year of his Age, An° Dom̃. 1667, and left Issue 2 sons, Adjohn in the Parish, Christopher in Hamshire, Liveing in Whitchurch.

In Memory of Edward, son of Thomas and Elizabeth Crook: He died January 24, 1748, Aged 1 year.

Also, of Mary their daughter, died Feb. 2, 1748, Aged 4 years.

Also, of John their son, died December 20, 1767, Aged 15 years.

Also, of Simon, their son, who died May 22, 1779, Aged 28 years.

To the Memory of Thomas Crook, gent. who departed this life Nov. ye 26, 1783, Aged 71 years.

Elizabeth, relict of Thomas Crook, gent. departed this life January 28, 1791, Aged 75 years.

And William their son departed this life, April 19, 1805, Aged 46 years.

Here under lyeth the Body of Thomas Stokes, late of this Parish, gent. who departed this mortal life the 10th of July 1654, about the 37th year of his age.

On Flat Stones.

Under this Stone lyeth the Body of Dorothy, Wife of Thomas Crook. She died the 18th day of March, A. D. 1734, Ætatis suæ 84.

Under this Stone lieth the Body of Mary, daughter of Edward and Alice Crook. She departed this life June the 4th, 173- Aged 21 years.

Robert Crook, died Oct. ye 28, 1777, Aged 52 years.

Catherine, relict of Robert Crook, died May 16, 1809, Aged 78 years.

Also four of their children died Infants. Also William their son died June 3, 1816, Aged 59 years.

No Lord claims the Manor.

BREMHILL.

On Monuments against North Wall of Chancel.

Near this place Lyeth the Body of the Rev. Mr. John Wilson, late Vicar of this Parish, who departed this Life the 30th of October 1724.

Also, the Body of Mrs. Anne Wilson, widow of the late Mr. John Wilson, who died Sept. 24, 1727.

Juxta sitæ sunt Mortales exuviæ Georgii Hungerford, Armigeri: filii natu maximi Georgii Hungerford, de Cadmam, militis, ex Domina Francisca, filia unica Caroli Sancti Mauri, et soror Germana illustrissimi Principis Caroli, Ducis Somersetensis.

Deflendus hic juvenis Nobilissimi sanguinis particeps
A parentibus acceptam haud degener, ad anxit gloriam
Miræ Virtutis,
quæ est vera nobilitas,
Et præclaræ indolis indicia
Ab incumabitis prodidit
Adultus præ Coæraneis ita en...vit
Ut invidiam illi fecisset Doctrina
Nisi amorem conciliarat modestia Sarisburiæ
Latinis, Græcisq. literis apprime instructus
Oxonium migravit
Ubi Philosophiam omnimodam diligenter coluit
Et. Triennii spatio (quod mirere) exhausit
Dein ut nec Patriæ, nec sibi deesset
Municipalium legum peritiam.
Apud Londinensis acquisivit,
Cum a severioribus vacaret studiis
Musicæ etiam jucundam operam dedit,
Clarissimi Purcelli, Fautor Æmulus
Jamq. quæ stantissimis dotib. quæ aut ingenuum
juvenum, Aut bonum decent Civem. ornatus
Ut Patriæ tandem utilior evaderet
Eam aliquantis per reliquit
Interque Batavos commoratus est,
Hospes acceptissimus, simul et sobrius
Qui Angliam pluris habuerunt
In ipso egregium morum exemplar, Admirantes
Rediens brevi in supremum regni senatum,
Plaudentibus bonis co-optatus est
Quorum spem Maximam simul ac superavit
Febre correptus fefillit.
Obiit An° Ætat. 24, Aprilis 23, An° Dñi 1698.

Forma erat eleganti sed virili
In vultu suavitas dignitate temperata,
In sermone ingenium una et subactum judicium,
In vita candor, magnanimitas, constantia, effulsere,
Ob fidem erga amicos sinceram :
Erga parentes obsequium pientissimum :
Erga Pauperes diffusam beneficentiam,
Et quæ omnium instar est,
ob Pietatam erga Deum, non fucatam inclaruit;
Nulli injuriosus, nulli non charus,
Is demum erat, in quo nihil
Prætor diuturniorem viram desiderares.

Arms, ppale indented, G. & az. 3 sickles hand O. bt. 3 garbs O.

M. S.

Optima juvenis hoc amoris et doloris summi Monumentum Parentes posuere.

Arms, S. 2 bars A. in chief, 3 plates, a label G. for diff.

On Monument against S. Wall.

Sacred to the Memory of the Rev. Edward Lambert, of an ancient Family in Wiltshire, many years Rector of the Parishes of Freshford, in the county of Somerset, and of East Horsley, in the county of Surry. He died at Bath the 17th day of March, 1818. His Remains are deposited in the Porch of this Church.

Arms, A. on a bend O. 3 annulets G. bt. 2 lions ramp. az. impaling, quarterly, 1 & 4, az. a crescent, A. in chief the sun in full glory. O. 2. & 3. G. within a bord. engrailed O. a lion ramp. argent.

Near this place lie the Remains of the Rev. Matthew Frampton, L. L. D. late Vicar of this Parish, who died 20th of February, 1782, Aged 63 years.

Sacred to the Memory of the Rev. Nathaniel Hume, late Vicar of this Parish, and many years Precentor of the Cathedral Church of Sarum, he died April 28th, 1804, aged 72 years.

On flat stones in Chancel.

H. S. E.

Walterus Hungerford, clara stirpe ortus,
Nec ipse degener, Utilitatis publicæ
Pro virili assertor, Municipium de Calne, in hoc Agro
Summo Angliæ senatis: Patrii juris peritus,
et fidelis Dispensator
Ad omnia Benevolentiæ, Charitatis, Amicitiæ,
Officia paratus
Ætate provectiore morbis languescens
Animam Cœlo maturam
Expiravit, Natus nono die Julii, 1675,
Denatus tricessimo primo Maii, 1754.

Arms S. 2 bars A. in chief, 3 plates, over all an escutc. S. charged with a chev. or. bt. 3 catherine wheels.

Here lyeth ye Body of John Tounson, Doctor in Divinity, late Rector of this Parish, and Prebendary of the Prebend of Highworth, in the church of Sarum, who departed this life the 24th day of July, 1687, Aged 77 years, 3 months, and 14 days.

Arms, 4 escallops, bt. 5 crosslets fitchey. Crest 3 crosslets fitchey issuing out of an escallop.

Here lyeth the Body of Benjamin D'Aranda, L. L. D. late Vicar of Bremhill, and Prebendary of Sarum, who departed this Life, Dec. 27, 1739, Aged 73 years.

Also, near this Place lyeth the Body of Elizabeth his Wife, who departed this life, April 27, 1742, Aged 35 years.

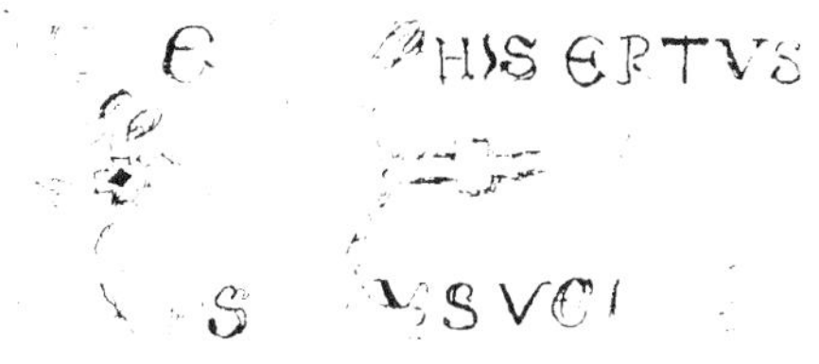

The Rev. Nathaniel Hume died April 28, 1804, Aged 72 years.

Richard James Hume, son of Nathaniel Hume, died June 6, 1783, Aged 9 months and 10 days.

Against S. wall of Nave.

In Memory of William Smith, who died April 3d, 1781, Aged 69 years.

Elizabeth his Wife died Jan. 18, 1781, Aged 69 years.

Sarah, their daughter, died July 28, 1776, Aged 21 years.

Against N. wall of N. aisle.

In Memory of Edward, son of Daniel and Sarah Gale, who died January 13, 1781, Aged 17 years.

Also, Daniel died October 10, 1785, Aged 50 years.

Also, Sarah his Wife, died April 28, 1807, Aged 73 years.

Daniel their son died May 17, 1796, Aged 27 years.

Near this place lyeth the Body of Ann, wife of Joseph Smith, daughter of Daniel and Sarah Gale, who died 16th of May 1789, Aged 28 years. Also, of Mary-Ann their Daughter, who died 29th of Sept. 1789, Aged 14 months.

E

In Memory of Elizabeth, relict of James Gale, and daughter of Richard and Ann Gale, who died Jan. 15, 1802, Aged 54 years.

In Memory of Edward Gale, who died April ye 1st. 1779, Aged 81 years.

Jane his Wife died March the 17th, 1774, Aged 78 years.

Edward their son died May 26, 1775, Aged 48 years.

James their son died Feb. 21, 1779, Aged 50 years.

Against S. wall of S. aisle.

Beneath this Tablet, in a vault, are deposited the mortal Remains of William Smith, Esq. of Chilvester Hill, who departed this life on the 11th day of Feb. 1814, Aged 46 years.

On a shield O. in south window is part of a lion saliant, with do. tail S.

Hatchment in Chancel.

1. S. 2 bars A. in chief 3 plates.
2. Perpale indented G. & . . . . . over all a chev. or.
3. Barry of 6. erm. & G.
4. . . . . . 3 garbs A. band G. a chief O.
5. Erm. a li. ramp. G. within a border engrailed S.
6. G. on a chev O. 3 roses G.
7. O. 3 tortauxes.
8. S. on a fess. A. 3 lozen. conjoined G.
9. O. a li. ramp. double tail S. within a bord. S.
10. O. a saltire engrailed S.
11. A. on a fess. cotised S. 3 crescents or. Crest, a garb or. bt. 2 sickles, A. issuing out of a ducal coronet.

Hatchment.

S. 2 bars A. in chief, 3 plates, impaling perpale, O. on a pile, G. 3 li. pass. guard. of the first bt. 6 fleur-de-lis, S. 2d G. one pair of wings conjoined O.

Lord Lansdown Lord of the Manor.

Dial and Cross.

There rest the Village Dead, and there too I,
When yonder Dial points the hour, must lie.
Look round, the distant prospect is display'd,
Like life's fair landscapes, marked with light and shade.
Stranger, in peace pursue thy onward road,
But ne'er forget thy long and last abode.

As you face this inscription, the dial is on the left, and the landscape on the right.

Hermitage.

From this to the right is a View of the Dial and Cross.

To mark the few and fleeting hours,
I plac'd the Dial midst the flowers;
Which, one by one, came forth and died,
Still with'ring round its ancient side:
Mortal, let the sight impart
Its pensive moral to thy heart.

PEREUNT ET IMPUTANTUR.

Pleasure Seat.

Rest, stranger, in this decorated scene,
That hangs its beds of flowers, its slopes of green;
So from the walks of life the weeds remove,
But fix thy better hopes on scenes above.

From this commands a prospect of Compton-Basset House, and other extensive Views.

LACOCK CHURCH.

On Monuments against North Wall of North Aisle.

Vicino in tumulo conduntur reliquæ Johannis Talbot,
Militis.
Qui Ducis Salopiensis, nobilissima Familiâ natus,
Eidem fuit ornamenta; temperantiâ enim fuæ,
Omnunodâ virtute publicæ,
Consuluit saluti, quam singulari,
Fortitudine ac sumptu, Concilio, ac prudentiâ,
In armis, in comitiis, in senatu, in aulâ,
Plurunum promovit scilicet in omnibus
Tam Monarchiæ, quam ecclesiæ Anglicanæ,
Propugnator fidissimus, non solum insignem,
Et animi constantiam,
Et legitimatæ authoritatis reverentiam,
Sed et egregiam, cum in Deum,
Tum in vicem ejus gerentes,
Tres scilicet principes, periculis undique cinctos
Pietam retinuit, cum gloriæ suæ ineremento
Cum capitis Maximo diserimine, nempe inter hostes,
Plus quam Sicarios, plus quam homicidas,
Plus etiam quam parricidas, Quoram unus quisq.
Sibi fac esse ducebat,
Non solum suum, sed et Patriæ parentem,
Occidere quibus tamen opposuit,
Alacris seissum Animosus unicum,
Quem habuit filium, Paternis hostibus
Formidabilem Quippe in Rebellatores
Armatum,
Cum nefarii gladio, ex improviso conficeratur
Hoc Patriæ vulnus, multo, magis suum
Usque ad senectutem omni laude cumulatam
Pater
Animo sustinuit in victo, qui post privati

Post publici muneris, partes splendide peractis,
Cum gloriæ suæ satis vexisset
Bonus omnibus nimis desideratus obiit,
Natus est vii. die Junii, A. D. 1630,
Obiit 13 Martii, 1713.

H. M. P.

Johannis Talbot, Arm. et Nepos, et Hæres.

Arms, 1. G. a li. ramp. O. within a bord. engrail. O.
2. Az. a li. ramp. O. within a bord. O.
3. Bendy of 11. G. and A.
4. G. 2 patte O. between 2 flanches checkey A. & az.
5. Az. a bend A.
6. perpale indented O. and az. 6 martlets in pale counter changed.

Ser William Sheringtone, Kt. 1566.

Arms, 1. Quarterly, 1 and 4. a cross patee O. bt. 2 flanches checky, az. and S.
2. Az. a bend O.
3. perpale indented, O & S. 6 martlets counter-changed. impaling G. 3 unicorns in pale, A.
4. (the same impaling) Quarterly, 1 & 4 az. a cross O. bt. 20 torteaux, 2 & 3 G. on a bend, az. a garter wavy G. in chief a crosslet fitchy O.

Against S. wall of Chancel.

In Memory of Mary, youngest daughter of the Rev. Thomas Talbot, and Jane his Wife, who departed this life on the 18th day of June, in the 9th year of her age, 1762.

Near this lie the mortal Remains of Catharine Barbara Talbot, third daughter of Thomas Mansel Talbot, Esq, and the Right Hon. Lady Mary Talbot, of Margam, in Glamorganshire. She died on the 10th of March, 1808, Aged 10 years, after a most lingering and painful illness, which she bore with patience, worthy the imitation of those in riper years, and which will ever impress the hearts of her family with the tenderest regret.

Arms, G. a li. ramp. O. within a bordered engrailed of the second, impaling palley of 6 A. and gules, on a chief S. 2 li. passant guard O.

On Flat Stones.

To the Memory of Sarah, fourth daughter of William and Mary Hutchinson, late of Bury, Lancashire, and sister-in-law of the James Paley, vicar of this Parish, who died Sept. 5, 1816, Aged 38 years.

On a Brass.

This Tablet is dedicated to the Memory of Mary Spencer Grossett, the beloved wife of J. R. Grossett, Esq. M. P. She died at Lacock Abbey, on the 31st October, 1820, a few weeks after the birth of a still-born child. Her mortal remains are deposited in a vault in the Cathedral of Bristol. Endowed with meekness of temper, and the genuine feelings of Christian charity, she was a kind friend, an affectionate sister, the best of wives, and the tender mother of seven young children. Conscious of a well-spent life, she saw her end approach with the utmost tranquillity and resignation. After receiving the sacrament, she breathed her last, and her pure spirit returned to its Almighty Creator.

Jesus said, I am the living bread which came down from heaven; if any man eat of this bread he shall live for ever. St. John, c. vi.

On Monuments against E. wall of S. transept.

Heare lyeth the Body of the Lady Vrsula Bagnard, daughter of Sir Robert Stapilton of Wyghall, in the county of York, knight, and wife to Sir Robert Baynard, knight, by whom she had issue Edward her sonne, heare buried, and Mary, her daughter. She lyved to the age of 36 years, and departed to God in most Firme Fayth in Christ, in the yeare of our Lord God 1623. Gods goodnes made her wise, and well Beseeming, discreed and prudent, constant, true, and chaste. Her virtues rare, won her much Esteeming. In Cou . . and Country, still with favour Grace. Fayth could not yelde more pleasing Faythly Blisse. Blest wth two Babes though death brought her to this.

[On wood.]

Arms Quarterly, 1 and 4. O. a li. ramp. S. 2 & 3. G. 3 bars O.
1. Impaling S. fretty O.
2. Bendy of 6. O. & az.
3. O. a li. ramp. az.
4. Checkey, or. & az. on a canton or. a li. ramp. S.
5. G. 3 bars O.
6. S. on a fess. az. 3 fleur-de-lis, or.
7. O. 3 bars, az.
8. G. 2 pat. O. between 2 planches checque O. & az.

To the Memory of James Montague, Esq. third son of Admiral John Montagu, commander of his Majesty's ship MONTAGU, who fell, gloriously fighting for his country, in the action between Earl Howe and the French Fleet, off Ushant, on the 1st of June, 1794, in the 43rd year of his age, and his remains were committed to the deep.

In this Aisle are interred the Bodies of James Montagu, Esq. and Diana his Wife, Edward their eldest son, James their second son, and Elizabeth, daughter of Sir John Eyles, Knight. Anthony, their third son, died at Bengal, in India, and Robert, their fourth son, lies buried in St. Giles's Church, in Middlesex.

Arms, 1 & 4. A. 3 fusils conj. in fess. G. within a bord. S. 2. & 3. O. an eagle disp. S. impaling S. 2 bars A. in chief 3 plates.

To the Memory of Mrs. Mary Wroughton, spinster, Aged 64, and born at Wilcot, in the County of Wilts, in the year 1727. She was buried, by her express desire, in this Church, that her remains might be placed near a Family to whom in her life she had been affectionately attached.

Near this place are deposited the remains of James Montagu, Esq. and Elinor his wife, daughter and heir of William Hedges, Esq. of Aldrington, in this County.

Arms. Quarterly, 1 & 4. 3 fusils conjoined in fess. G. within a bord. S. 2 & 3. O. an eagle displ. S. beaked and taloned G. impaling quarterly 1 & 4. az. 3 swans necks erased A. 2. & 3. O. 3 bulls heads cabossed S.

Near this place are deposited the Remains of John Montagu, Esq. Admiral of the White in the Royal Navy of Great Britain, and born at Lackham, in the County of Wilts, in the year of our Lord 1719. He was, for sixty-three years, with little intermission, employed in the service of his country, and filled some of the most important stations in his profession with honour, reputation, and unshaken integrity. His domestick virtues were equally eminent and conspicuous, and were a dignified example of filial reverence, conjugal attachment, and parental affection.

To the Memory of Colonel Edward Montagu, fourth son of Admiral John Montagu, Aged 64.

He was bred to arms in the service of the East India Company, and passed twenty-eight years in constant and generally very active duty in India. After having rendered the East India Company great and important service in a variety of actions in which he distinguished himself, he received a mortal wound in the lines before Seringapatam, whilst commanding the Bengal Artillery, in the memorable action between the English army and Tippoo Sultan, in 1799, and his remains were interred with all military honours at Seringapatam.

Here Lyeth ye Body of Edwarde Bainarde, Esq. whoe for the space of many yeares yeven to his dyinge day was Justice of Peace and Corum, and sometimes Custos Rotulorum, and Hygh Sheriffe of the Countye of Wilts. a Bountyefull Friend to his Brethren and Sisters, and to his Servants Liberall, and an enemy to noe man. He lyved to the age of 63 years and dyed, and was buried ye 21 daye of Dec. 1575.

Lett envy saye what it can,
This was an honest man,
Whoe in his Life did many good,
And to the truth firmly stode;
Religious, wise, and just, was hee,
And ever Lyved worthlie.

Arms, Quarterly, 1. and 4. S. a fess. bt. 2 chev. O. 2. and 3. o. an eagle disp. with 2 heads, G. Crest, a demi unicorn O.
1. a fess. bt. 2 chev. o. imp. O. a chev. bt. 3 fleur-de-lis, S.
2. imp. az. a chev. bt. 3 pears O.
3. az. a li. rampt. bt. 9 fleur de-lis, O.
4. az. 2 swords in saltire bt. 4 fleur-de-lis O.
5. O. a chev. bt. 3 eagles heads erased S.
6. O. a chev. bt. 3 garbs S.
7. pp. fess. imbattled O. & S. on each 3 patte chief O.

Near this place Lyeth the Body of the Honourable James Mountague, third son of Henry, Earl of Manchester, and Mary his Wife, daughter and heiress of Sir Robert Baynard, of Lacham, in the county of Wilts, Kt. who had shue, viz. Walter, James, George, Robert, Henry, Edward, Sidney, Mary, Charles, William, Katharine, Thomas, and John. Walter died young, James married Diana, daughter to Anthony Hungerford, of Farly Castle, in the county of Somerset, Esq. Mary was married unto Thos. Ewer, of the Lee, in Hartfordshire, Esq.

James, the Father,	dyed Anº Ætat.	59.
Mary, the Mother,		63.
James, the Son,		38.

James, the Son, hath left issue four sons: Edward, James, Anthony, and Robert.

Arms, Quarterly. 1 & 4. A 3 fusils conjoined G. within a bord. S. 2 & 3. O. a eagle displ. az. beak, impaling quart. 1 & 4, S. a fess. bt. 2 chev. O, 2 & 3. O. an eagle with 2 heads G.

To Frederick Augustus Courtenay Montague, Capt. of the 23d Regiment, or Royal Welch Fusileers, and Major in the Portuguese service. Adorned with the choicest gifts of heaven, Nature had wreathed the olive Branch, that so conspicuously flourished on his brow, as emblematic of his amiable and affectionate mind. Patriotism and Loyalty, that roused him to seek mortal glory, led him to volunteer his service in his Country's cause at the early age of 16. And, after displaying undaunted courage in Holland, in Martinique, in the expulsion of the French from Portugal, and lastly, at the age of 26, at the memorable battle of Albuera, in Spain, fought on the 16th of May, in the year 1811, he finished his mortal career, pierced through the heart by a musket-ball, whilst gallantly leading his men to a charge. He nobly fell, leaving the laurels so gloriously acquired to be entwined round the hearts of his afflicted parents, who in commemoration of their departed Son, erected this Monument.

Near this place are deposited the Remains of James Montagu, Esq. of Lackham, who died July 12, Anno Domini 1798, Ætatis 47.

As a small token of gratitude and respect, this is humbly erected and dedicated to him by his nephew, George Montagu, to commemorate the many virtues of his best friend and patron.

This modest stone, what few vain marbles can,
Plainly denotes, here lies an honest man,
Whom Heaven kept sacred from the proud and great:
. . . . .
Calmly he looked on either life, and here
Saw nothing to regret, or there to fear.
The friend, the comfort of the sick and poor,
Want never knock'd unheeded at his door:
All mourn his death, his virtues long they tried,
Nor knew how much they lov'd him till he died.

BENEDICTUM EST.

Against South pillar of nave.

Near this place are interred the Remains of Mrs. Catharine Passmore, who resided many years at Notton, in this Parish, universally respected. She died on the 29th day of Jan. 1805, Aged 84 years.

Near this place are deposited the Remains of Anthony Barrett, of Notton, Gent. one who by sanctity of manners, joined to genuine piety and general integrity of conduct, supported through life the character of a true Christian, and departed on the 7th day of April, 1791, Aged 63 years.

Also near this Place are deposited the Remains of Anna Barrett, wife of the abovesaid Anthony Barrett, who departed this life on the 20th day of Sept. 1803, Aged 72 years.

On Flat Stones.

Here lieth the Body of Mrs. Martha Mortimer, Wife of Mr. John Mortimer, who died January 7, 1804, Aged 68 years.

Also, here lieth the Body of Mr. John Mortimer, who died July 10, 1807, Aged 67 years.

Here lyeth the Body of George Mortimer, who died April 30, A. D. 1748, Aged 32 years.

On Flat Stones in Nave.

Here lyeth the Body of Nathaniel Gough, the Son of Nathaniel Gough and Mary his Wife, who departed this life Feb. ye 24, A. D. 172$\frac{4}{5}$, Aged 4 years.

James Spencer, son of Richard and . . . . Spencer of Notton, died November 5, 1731, in the 39th year of his age.

Also Diana, Wife of Harris Spencer, Ob. 13 Nov. 1773, Aged 76 years.

Underneath this Stone is deposited the Remains of Nicholas Barrett. He departed this life the 1st day of April, 1783, Aged 63 years.

On Flat Stones N. aisle.

In Memory of Samuel Crew, gent. He died Oct. 8, 1761, Aged 80 years.

Also, in Memory of Samuel Smith, Esq. who departed this life July the 26, 1777, Aged 67.

Also two of his Sons, Samuel, aged 37 years, and Ephraim, aged 6 years. Also Frances, Wife of Samuel Smith, who departed this life Dec. 6, 1783, Aged 63 years.

In Memory of John Pritchard, who died April the 2nd, 1757, Aged 27 years.

In Memory of John Pritchard. He died Feb. 19, 1756, Aged 56 years.

Also Emma, Wife of John Pritchard, who died Dec. the 15, 1756, Aged 51 years.

Near this Place are deposited the Remains of Richard, son of Richard and Ann Spencer, who died Dec. the 13th, 1814, Aged 28 years.

Also to the Memory of Richard Spencer, who died Nov. 26, 1808, Aged 60 years.

Also Hannah, second Wife of the above Richard Spencer, who died May the 22d, 1819, Aged 64 years.

Beneath this stone are deposited the Remains of Wm. Thresher, of this Parish, who departed this life the 7th of Feb. 1807, Aged 55 years.

Here Lyeth the Body of Samuel Michell, of Notton, Clothier, who deceased the 4th day of Feb. 1698, Aged 74 years.

Here lyeth the Body of Susannah, the Wife of Samuel Michell, who departed this life y . . . . March. Anno Domini 1699, Aged 76 years.

Underneath lieth interred the Body of Mr. Robert Ayres, Gent. of Bewley Court, in this Parish, who departed this life the 9th day of May, 1783, Aged 75 years.

In Memory of Mary, Wife of Arthur Gough, who died March the 11th, 1759, Aged 38 years.

Here lieth the Body of Jane, Wife of John Gough, who died Nov. 11, 1773, Aged 35 years.

In S. transept.

In Memory of Susannah, daughter of Thos. Colborne, gent. of this Parish, who died January 14, 1776, Aged 73 years.

Near this Place lyeth the Body of Thomas Colborne, sen. He died May the 10th, A.D. 1700, Aged 52.

Also Neare lyeth the Body of Henry Colborne, sen. Dier, who departed this Life May the 25, An° Dom̃ 1733, Aged 54 years.

Also, in Memory of Henry Colborne, Dier, who died June 20, 1764, Aged 55 years.

Sacred to the Memory of John Skotlowe, Esq. of Notton Lodge. He was born at St. Helena 28th February, 1774, Married to Sarah Pollok, daughter of the Rev. Thos. Pollok, L.L.D. 19th Feb. 1799, died 7th Sept. 1820. Decended from a long line of ancestors of Norman extraction, he supported the purity of his birth by courtesy of manners, as well as the more solid virtues of the heart. His only son, Coulson Skotlowe, a child of rare attainments, was born 16th January, 1800, and died at Gratez, in Syria, 13th of January, 1808.

Chare vale conjux, te filius urget ab alto, te uxor spe, votis jam moribunda sequor.

On Mon. in S. aisle.

To the Memory of Barnard Dickinson, Esq. of Bowden Park, who departed this life the 4th of March 1814, Aged 67 years.

Arms, O. bend engrailed G. bt. 2 li. ramp. G. over all an escutch. A. charged with a chev. bt. 3 squirrels, G. Crest, a sinister hand, pp. holding a laurel sprig.

Charles Willcox, the Son of William Willcox, of Hazland, departed this life the 8th day of July, 1680, and was buried the 10th day of the same month.

William Willcox, Son of William Willcox, of Laycock, departed this life the 29th day of April, 1681, and was buried the 2d day of May.

Samson, the son of William Willcox, hee dyed April ye 2d, Aged 86. William Willcox, he dyed April the 23d, An° Dom̃. 1689.

Heare Lyeth in this Allye, neere unto this Place, the Bodie of Robert Hellier, late one of his Majesties Cryers to the Courts of the Common Pleas in Westminster, whoe lived 63 yeares, and deceased the 9th of April, An° Dñi 1630.

To the Memory of James, late Lord Bishop of Worcester, second son of the Rev. James Johnson, M.A. many years Rector of Long Melford, in the county of Suffolk, and grandson of George Johnson, Esq. of Bowden Park, in this County.

In the year 1752, he was consecrated Bishop of Gloucester; and in the year 1759, was translated to the See of Worcester, in which Cathedral a Monument is erected to his Memory.

He died at Bath on the 27th day of Nov. 1775, and in the 70th year of his age, in consequence of a most unfortunate fall from his horse, and was buried here, in the vault of his ancestors.

This Monument may record, likewise, the unhappy fate of his elder Brother, who met with his death at Bath, by a like accident, a few years before, and was buried here.

Arms, impaling A. a bend S. on a chief S. 3 wool-packs, A.

Entrance of West End.

In Memory of Robert Edwards, who departed this life September ye 23d, 1758, Aged 83.

In Memory of Ann, Wife of Robert Edwards, who departed this life August 30, 1751, Aged 87 years and 5 months, Married 60 years and 10 months.

DONATION.

April, An° Dom̃ 1629.

At this Place, upon every Sabbath-day, after Morning Prayers are ended, Thirteen Loaves of Bread are to be distributed unto Thirteen poor People of this Parish, unto such poor as are past their labour in respect of Age or Decripitness, or poor in being overcharged with children, to be distributed unto them by the discretion of the Minister and two Churchwardens of the Parish for the time being.

Atchments.

Arms, G. a li. ramp. O. within a bord. engrailed O. impaling az. 10 billetts O. 4 3 2 1 on a chief O. a demi li. sable. Crest, an Earl's Coronet.

A. a chev. bt. 3 crossle s fitch. S. impaling G. a li. ramp. O. within a border engrailed O.

Quarterly, 1 & 4 A. 3 fusils conj. in fess G. 2 & 3 or. an eagle disp. vt. impaling, A. a chev. S. between 3 boars heads trip. sable.

The Church consists of Chancel, Nave, North and South Aisles, north and South Transepts.

A little painted glass in Chancel Window, Reg. 1559.

The Rev. Mr. Robinson late Vicar.
The Rev. John Paley present Vicar.

W. H. Fox Talbot, Esq. Lord of the Manor, succeeded his Father.

KINGTON ST. MICHAEL.

Against N. wall of Chancel.

Near this Place lies the Body of Benjamin Griffin, M. A. of New College, in Oxon, and Vicar of this Parish. His Virtues gained him the esteem and love of all that knew him. He lived as became his divine Profession. His goodness and integrity were such as ought to be patterns to the latest times: And the two Vicarage Houses he rebuilt (here and at Colem,) are ample Monuments of his publick Spirit. His life was short, but Exemplary, and he died, endeavouring and praying for the good of his Parish and the Church, in the 39th year of his age, the 26th of Nov. 1716, and could not die unlamented.

His most dear and sorrowful widow Rose, the 5th daughter of Sir William Leche, thought herself obliged from the singular piety she bore him, to erect this Stone, though not wanted to perpetuate his beloved Memory.

Also the Body of Mrs. Rose Bave, late widow of Mr. Francis Bave, Alderman, of the City of Bath, died the 24th of July, 1734, Aged 62 years.

And near this Place also lies the Body of Hester Whitelock, widow, fourth daughter of the said Sir William Leche. She died the 21st of September, 1735, Aged 71 years.

South Wall.

Under those two Stones lyeth the Bodies of Nicholas Gastrell, gent. who departed this life the 15th, and was buried the 20th day of February, in the year of our Lord 1662, Aged 83 years and 7 months.

Also, the Body of Mary his Wife, who departed this life the 22d, and was buried the 23d day of October, in the year of our Lord 1661, Aged 73 years and 5 months.

Against a Pillar on North side of Nave.

Near this Place lyes interred the Body of Wm. Coleman, of Langley in the Parish of Kington St. Michael, who departed this life March 7, 1738, Aged 63 years.

And also that of Sarah his Wife, who died 9 Dec. 1767, Aged 74.

On Flat Stones.

Here lyeth the Body of Thos. Stubbs, Esq. who departed this life March 7, 1700, Aged 55.

Jonathan Power, gent. died 29th Sept. 1748, Aged 48. In Memory of him his sister, Sarah Coleman, directed this Stone to be here placed.

Beneath this Stone lies interred the Body of Mrs. Rebecca Knott, who departed this life the 7th of June, 1760, Aged 68.

And also the Body of James Power, jun. gent. who died ye 9th of August, 1715, Aged 34 years.

Likewise the Body of James Knott, gent. who died 20th March, 1766, Aged 36.

Here lyeth the Body of ... Power, gent. Son of Nathaniel Power .... and Rebecca Gastrell, his Wife, Nephew and Sole Heire to James, son of Nicholas Gastrell, gent. and Mary his Wife, 3rd and youngest Sister and coheir to Sir Charles Snell, Kt. Lord of this Manour, Qui obiit 16 die mensis Junij, An° Dñi 1705, Aged 44.

Also here Lyeth the Body of Elizabeth Power, the Wife of James Power, sen. and daughter of Jonathan Deeke, of Langley, in this Parish, Clothier, who departed this Life, Oct. the 1st. A.D. 1726, Aged 67 years.

Beneath is interred the Body of .... Late Wife of James Barrett ... died 19th July, 1766, Aged 33.

On a Brass.

Here ly the Body of Jonathan Deeke, of Langley, clothier, and Grace his Wife, who having lived together in Matrimony above 57 years, departed this Life, He July ye 23d, Anº Ætat. 86. Anº Dom. 1699. She August ye 10, Anº Ætat. 83, 1699.

I went before, as was my place to do,
And I in mine soon followed you;
Nor Life nor death can separate us two,
We'll hand in hand to heaven go.

P. M.

Isaaci Lyte, de Easton Pierse, Geñ. Uxorem habuit Israel, filiam Thos. Browne, de Winterbourne Bassett, Geñ. Convixit illi annos 52. Obiit anno ætatis suæ octagesimo tertio, Feb. 21, 1659, Posuit Johannes Awbrey.

Arms, A chev. charged with a mullet between 3 swans, impaling, an eagle displayed.

On Monument in N. aisle.

Near the North Door of this Church lieth the Remains of Robert Glenn, gent. Obiit ye 24th December, 1775, Æt. 74.

Also, Elizabeth his Wife, who departed this life Oct. the 13, 1796, Aged 84 years.

James Gilpin was born in this Parish in 1709, and descended from the Snells, some time Lords of this Manor. He was educated in Westminster School, and chosen a King's Scholar into St. Peter's College, at Westminster in 1724, from whence he was elected to be one of the Students in Christ Church in Oxford, in 1728, and from thence he removed to the Middle Temple, London, in order to study the Common Law of the Land, which he made his profession. He was Registrar to the Dean and Chapter of Christ Church, in Oxford, and Auditor of their Accounts, and Recorder of the City of Oxford. He died the 14th day of December, in the year of our Lord, 1766, and is buried in the Church-yard, close to the North Wall of the tower of this Church.

Arms, A boar S.

Beneath a Tomb without the North door of this Church, and near to the same, lyeth interred the Body of James Gastrell, Gent. son and heir of Nicholas Gastrel, Gent. and Mary his Wife, one of the sisters and coheirs of Sir Charles Snell, Knight, Lord of this Manor. The said James Gastrell was buried the 5th day of June, 1678, Aged 54 years.

Near this Stone lies interred the Body of Sydenham Tucker, gent. who died 9th of May, 1771, in the 58th year of his age.

Arms O. a chev. G. charged with a mullet, pierced O. bt. 3 rams, passant. Guard A.

In a Vault beneath this place lies interred the Body of Francis White, of Langley, gent. who departed this Life the 4th of June 1707, Ætat. suæ 73.

As likewise the Remains of Mrs. Hannah White, first Wife of the said Francis White, by whom he had 11 children, 3 of which died young, the other 8 lived to be men and women, viz. Francis, John, Elizabeth, Grace, Ayliffe, Thomas, James, and Liddia.

Also, in the same Vault, lie interred the Bodies of Ayliffe White, gent. and Elizabeth his Wife. He died 30th Jan. 1761, Aged 90. She died the 4th Sept. 1758, Aged 59. And also Francis, their Son, who died the 18th of March, 1761, Aged 34.

In Memory of Sarah, Wife of John Provis, of Chippenham, Wilts. and daughter of James and Sarah Mascall, of this Parish, whose Remains are deposited near the North side of this Church. She died Sept. 14, 1813, in the 35th year of her age.

Sacred to the Memory of Isaac Gale, of Bulidge, Esq. who departed this Life, Feb. 26, 1792, Aged 66.

Sacred also to the dear Memory of Elizabeth, widow of Isaac Gale, Esq. and daughter of Richard Michell, of Langport, in the County of Somerset, Esq. who departed this life, after a long and painful illness, March 4, 1806, Aged 70 years.

This is erected by her affectionate son and only child. In every situation of Life, as Daughter, Wife, and Mother, she shined pre-eminent. She was indeed the best and most valued of Mothers: Her temper wes most amiable, her conduct most exemplary, combining every social and domestic virtue, with the great duty of a pure Christian.

Arms—Quarterly, 1 & 4. az. a fess. fretty A. & S. 2 & 3 S. a li. ramp. O. over all an escutch. G. charged with a chev. O. bt. 3 swans pp.

On a flat stone.

Beneath lies Bamfylde Sydenham, gent. who departed who departed this Life Feb. 20, A. D. 1696, aged 82 years.

Here also lyeth the Body of Sarah, late Wife of Sydenham Tucker, gent. who departed this life the 28th of April, A. D. 1749, Aged 40 years.

Arms—a chev. charged with a mullet between 3 rams.

On Monuments in S. aisle.

Sacred to the beloved Memory of John Hitchcock, yeoman, of this Parish, Son of Harry and Jane Hitchcock, of All Cannings, in this County, who departed this life April 18, 1820, Aged 32 years.

Daniel Yealfe, Schoolmaster of this Parish 48 years, Vestry Clerk 30 years, and Parish Clerk 16 years, was buried 15th day of April, 1779, at the south-west corner of this church porch, in the 70th year of his age. Mary, 45½ years the Wife of Daniel Yealfe, was buried 25th Oct. 1778, near the south-west corner of this church porch, in the 85th year of her age.

On Flat Stones.

H. S. E.

Ric Humphryes, hujus Ecclesiæ Vic. nec non de Dracot cerne Rector. Qui obiit Jan. 31, 1711, Æt. suæ 55.

Hic etiam jacet Corpus Annæ, uxoris, quæ obiit Feb. 22, 1727, Æt. suæ 65.

Here lyeth the Body of Anne, late Wife of May Pinchen, gent. of the Parish of Langley-Burrell, in this County, who departed this life the 14th day of February, Ano Dom. 1721, Aged 43 years. She was one of the daughters of Richard Estcourt, gent. of Swinley, in this Parish.

Here lyeth ye Body of George Pinchen, son of ye above-named Anne, who died 17th Sept. A. D. 1722.

Here lyeth the Body of Mary, Wife of Wm. Alexander, of the Parish of Great Summerford, who departed this Life March ye 22d, A. D. 1735, Aged 56 years.

Here lyes the Body of George Eastcourt, late of Swinley, in the Parish of St. Michael, who departed this Life in the 29th year of his age, in the year 1712.

DONATIONS.

1730, Dec. 6.

Mrs. Sarah Bowman, by Will of this Date, gave the sum of £5 per annum for ever, payable by the Trustees of Christ's Hospital, London, to the Schoolmaster of Kington St. Michael towards the Education of the Poor Children of that Parish.

1672, Feb. 10.

Mr. Isaac Lyte, by Will of this Date, gave the Alms Houses, and a Rent Charge of £21 per annum, issuing out of Lands in the Parish of Corston, to be paid Quarterly to Six poor Unmarried Men of the Parish of Kington St. Michael, and the Rent of a Close adjoining for the repairs of the said Houses.

1664, Sept. 1.

Mr. William Woodroffe, by Will of this Date, gave an Annuity, or Rent-Charge, of Thirty Shillings per Annum, issuing out of certain Lands in the Parish of Chippenham; viz. Ten Shillings to the Minister of Kington St. Michael for Preaching a Sermon, and Twenty Shillings to the Poor of the said Parish as shall be most in need, to be paid on the 18th day of September, O. S.

1694, Dec. 20.

Mrs. Dorothy Newman, by Deed of this Date, gave to the Poor of the Parish of Kington St. Michael above their Monthly Allowance, an Annuity, or Rent-Charge, of £6 per annum, to be paid every St. Thomas' Day, by the Trustees, in the Church Porch.

1727, Dec. 18.

Mr. Thomas Taylor, by Will of this Date, gave to the Poor of the Parish of Kington St. Michael, an Annuity, or Rent-Charge, of Twenty Shillings per Annum, issuing out of lands in that part of the Parish called Langley.

Hatchments in Chancel.

1st. S. a bend G. charged with 3 buckles O. bt. 3 phæons A. impaling S. a saltire A. Crest, a dex hand, holding a spear.

2d. Quarterly, 1 & 4. Quarterly, G. & Az. over all a cross fleury or. 2 & 3 S. a fess. O. charged with 3 negro heads of the first bt. 3 arrows of the second, pointed and feathered of the first.

The Church consists of a Chancel, Nave, North and South Aisles. At the East end of Nave is a Saxon Arch, with one moulding, in good preservation, but from its long standing, the north side have given way, and is out of its perpendicular direction.

YATTON KEYNELL.

On Mon. in Chancel against North Wall.

Under these 2. Tombe Stones lye Elizabeth, the late Wife of William Stump, Gent. Shee was buried the 16th Day of April, 1683, her Age 58. Also William Stump, theire Sonne was buried the 18th day of August, 1646. His age 22.

Here lyeth ye Body of Constant, ye Wife of William Harris, and Daughter of William Stump, Gent. who departed this life ye 3d of May, 1697, Aged 77 years.

Neere this place lieth the Body of James Tayler, Sonne of Josias Taylor, who departed this life March the 19th, 1643, being of the Age of 24 years.

Against S. wall of Chancel.

To the dear Memory of Mrs. Elizabeth Child, eldest daughter of Ephraim Westley, of Whitcliffe, in this County, gent. and Wife of George Child, M.A. and Rector of this Church, who departed this Mortall life on the 10th of August, in the Yeare 1666, and of her Age the 30, and lieth Entombed near to this Place.

Near this Stone lie the mortal Remains of Benjamin Pidding, Batchelor, 18 years Rector of this Parish, second son of James Pidding, Clerk, by Jane his Wife, sister of James Jeanes, who purchased the advowson of this Rectory 1735. He died 26th of September, 1763, Aged 53. Also in the same grave lieth the Body of Elizabeth, daughter of James Pidding, Rector of this Parish, by Elizabeth his Wife. She died 22d October, 1774, Aged 36 weeks. Also two male twins, sons of J. and E. Pidding, prematurely born on the 19th March, 1775: one died the 20th inst. the other the 4th of April following. Also Joseph, son of J. and E. Pidding, who died April 24, 1783, Aged 37 weeks. In the same Grave are deposited the earthly Remains of Elizabeth Pidding, Wife of J. Pidding, Rector and Patron of this Parish. She died March 20, 1793, Aged 44 years.

In an adjoining grave are interred the Remains of Sophia Matilda Pidding, third daughter of J. and E. Pidding. She died April 21, 1809, Aged 23.

Against N. Wall of the Nave.

Elizabeth, the mournefull Relict of James Wilde, of West Yatton, gent. who departed this life, May 25, 1702, in the XLI year of his Age, Erected this to his pious Memory.

Beneath this Place lyeth the Body of Margaret, the Wife of John Wilde, of this Parish, Gent. who died the 21st day of Nov. 1739, Aged 41 years.

Also, here lieth the Body of Elizabeth, the daughter of Edward and Britannia of the City of New Sarum, and sister to the aforesaid Margaret Wild. She died 21st of August, 1722, Aged 22.

Arms S. a chev. engrailed O.

On a Flat Stone in Nave.

Underneath are deposited the Remains of Mrs. Eliz. Kemm, who departed this life the 26th day of March, 1795, Aged 76 years.

On Monuments in S. aisle.

Here Lieth the Bodies of Ebraham Light, hee was buried under this next Tombe Stone, the 29th day of May 1651, his age 84.

And under the second Stone joyning to it, Ann his Wife was buried the 31st day of March 1652, her age 64. Under ye third Stone, Isaac Light, the Son of Abraham Light, yeoman, was buried ye 21st Day of July 1653, his age 42.

Here lyeth also the Body of Nathaniel Light, who died November the 4th, 1687, Aged 75 years.

Also, near this Place lyeth the Body of Mary the Wife of Nathaniel Light, who departed this life ye 6th day of December, 1705, Aged 81 years.

In Memory of Martha, the Wife of Richard Tayler, gent. She died Jan. 15, 1756, Aged 40 years.

Martha, their daughter died Jan, 21, 1764, Aged 16 years.

Also, of Richard Tayler, jun. gent. late of Castle Comb, who died May 6, 1797, Aged 48.

Here lyeth the Body of Josias Tayler, who departed this life, November 21, and was buried November 25, Anno Dñi 1632.

On a flat stone.

Here lyeth the Body of Isaac Taylor, who departed this life July the 12th, A. D, 1716, Aged 30 years.

On a Tomb-stone by S. Wall.

Here lyeth the Body of Thomas Clark underneath the second Tombe, who departed this life Dec. 21, in the year of our Lord God 1654, Aged 56.

The Rev. Thomas Hooper present Rector.

Register commenced 1653.

HARDENHUISH.

In orientali cæmeterii parte tandem requiescit Johannes Thorpe, A. M. S. A. S. In parochia Sanctæ Margareta, juxta civitatem Roffensem, Natus A. D. 1715, Ob. August 2° A. D. 1792, in spem Lætæ Resurrectionis, per sola Xti merita.

Arms ppale, 3 crescents in chief counterchanged. 3 loz.

Sacred to the Memory of Benjamin Colborne, of Bath, Esq. whose Remains are deposited in the Vault beneath this Church. He died October 2d, 1793, Aged 74 years, fully possessing Family Affection, and Sincerity in Friendship.

In the Vault of this Church lieth interred Henrietta, Wife of Benjamin Colborne, Esq. daughter of Thomas Nash, of the City of London, Esq. She died the 29th of January, 1783, Aged 55, much lamented by her family and friends.

Sacred to the Memory of William Colborne, Esq. of the Circus, of Bath. Having enjoyed a long life of health and happiness, the just reward of his wisdom and temperance, he died at the advanced age of 97, leaving behind him the character of a religious and upright man, a kind master, a sincere friend. Obiit July 13, 1804.

Beneath are deposited the Remains of Ann, widow of Abraham Craiesteyn, of London, Esq. and sister of Joseph Colborne, Esq. of this place. Distinguished by her tenderness as Wife, affection as Sister, sincerity as Friend, and who, having lived justly esteemed and beloved, died justly lamented, May 9th, 1764, in the 50th year of her age.

Sacred to the Memory of Col. John Hunter, of Newcastle-upon-Tyne, who died at Bath, April 5, 1791, in the 76th year of his Age. He was long an intimate friend of the Colborne Family, and requested his Remains should be deposited in the Vault of this Church.

Beneath are deposited the Remains of Elizabeth Towers, Relict of the late Rev. Samuel Towers, of Hornsey, Middlesex, and sister of Joseph Colborne, Esq. late of this place. She departed this life Feb. 24, 1803, in the 84th year of her age.

To the Memory of the sincerest Friend, the most affectionate Sister and Wife, the kindest Mother, and the most exemplary Christian, this Monument is, with the deepest gratitude, inscribed by Filial Affection.

Here Rest the Remains of Joseph Colborne, Esq. who possessed all those virtues which rendered him esteemed and beloved while living, and sincerely regretted now dead. On the 7th day of February, 1781, he departed this life, in the 66th year of his age.

This Church was Erected at his sole Expence.

Sacred to the Memory of William Pinniger, of Chippenham, in this County, gentleman, whose Remains lie interred at the East End of this Church. Obiit 4th June, 1785, Aged 56.

Hatchment.

A. a chev. S. charged with 3 mulletts A. bt. 3 bugle horns, S. stringed G. impaling S. on a fess. A. 3 catherine wheels G. bt. 6 billetts O. Crest, a stag's head pp. issuing out of a ducal coronet.

George Hawkins, Esq. Lord of the Manor.

CHRISTIAN MALFORD.

On Monuments in Chancel.

Near this Monument lyeth buried, in hopes of a glorious resurrection, the Body of Richard Burgess, who by Care and Industry acquired a plentiful Fortune. He was a constant Benefactor to the poor, a sincere Friend, and a cheerful Companion. He acted in the Commission of the Peace with great candor and impartiality, and died lamented by all his Acquaintance, the 20th of May, Anno Dom̄. 1738, Ætat. suæ 63.

Also, near this Monument Lyeth interred, in hopes of a glorious Resurrection, the Body of Sarah, the daughter of Richard Burgess, Esq. who departed this Life April the 14th, Anno Dom̄ 1740, Ætatis suæ 33. This Monument was erected by his disconsolate Daughter, Sarah Burgess.

East End.

Near this Monument, and by the side of his beloved Daughter (Eliz.-Frances, who died May 6, 1796, aged 18 years) are deposited the Mortal Remains of the Rev. William Willes, A.M. Archdeacon of Wells, and Rector of this extensive Parish, who died May 12, 1815, aged 84 years. He performed the duties of his holy Office with unexampled zeal and unaffected devotion for the space of nearly 60 years, and until the period of his decease. This Monument was erected by his sorrowing Widow and Children to the Memory of an affectionate Husband, a kind Father, a zealous Pastor, and an honest Man.

An Angel's arm can't snatch him from the Grave—
Legions of Angels can't confine him there.

In the same Vault, and by her express desire, are deposited the Remains of Mrs. Margaret Willes, Relict of the above-mentioned William Willes, who departed this life January 17, 1821, Aged 74 years.

Arms—A. a chev. S. bt. 3 mulletts, G. impaling A. a li. ramp. az. bt. 3 escal. shells of the same.

To the Blessed Memory of Sarah, the Wife of William Itchener, Rector of this Church. She was the Daughter of William Stratton, Esq. of Wanborough, and of Dorothy his Wife, daughter of Robert Hippisley, Esq. of Stanton, in the County of Wilts. She was of a weak constitution of Body, but God gave her a Soul of the most perfect kind; pious, meek, humble, just, and charitable. Her Beauties were Heavenly, and her Ornaments those which in the sight of God himself are of great price, and in these she was always incomparably lovely. In the lustre of so many Virtues, she shined even in this dark corner, and in the glories of them (through the merits of Christ) she shall shine for ever in the kingdom of God. She left two Sons, and dyed in ye year of her age 38, and of Christ, 1719, Oct. 26.

Sown in dishonour, to be raised in glory.

On Flat Stones.

Jane Bower, widow, daughter of Robert Hippesley of Stanton, near Highworth, in the County of Wilts. Unhappy in Marriage: Through much tribulation we must enter into the kingdom of God. She died May 20th, An° Dñi 1719, Aged 70 years.

Underneath are deposited the Remains of Wm. Willes, who died July 28, 1772, Aged 9 months. Likewise of Charles-Jeanes Willis, who died August 25, 1785, in his 5th year.

Of Elizabeth-Frances Willes, who died May 6, 1796, Aged 18 years.

H. S.

Henricus Margetts, A.M. hujus Ecclesiæ Rector . . . . nec non Præbendæ . . . .

Qui

Pro suo solenn . . m amoria, et Cœlestium H . . orum ardore, ad ifestum Paschatis unimo consciona Ad diem Victorio . . . . dum Cœtui Militantiu . . . dixit, et ad anniversarum Regine . . . . Ad cœtum triumphantum transmigravit octavo scilicet iduum Martii, Anno salvis 170$\frac{8}{9}$ Ætatis fuit, 61.

Cujus . . . adextra fidissima C . . . Dñi Eduardi Waterho . . Armigeri, filia Br . . . Qui quum pro . . . Virginis viduæ et . . . milias Partes . . . posites qui annum . . quod excurrit illum sequnta est. crast Martini 1706.

On a Mon. in S. aisle.

To the Memory of Mr. John Philips, of this Parish. He was a man of a warm and open spirit, but of very valuable sense and understanding, by which he made himself useful and beneficent to all his friends and neighbours round this Country, and for which he will be often desired, and cannot be soon forgotten. He died in the 64th year of his age, Feb. 21, 1723. Eleanor, his sorrowing Wife, erected for him this Monument. And also Eleanor daughter of Robert and Ann Peacock, and Wife of John Philips. She died November ye 14, 1737, Aged 75 years.

On Flat Stone.

Here lyeth the Body of Lucy Trimnell, the Wife of Wm. Trimnell, who departed this Life the 7th day of June, Anno Dom. 1702, Aged 57 years.

Here Lyeth the Body of William Trimnell, who departed this life the 24th day of February, An° Dñi 170$\frac{3}{4}$ Aged 60 years.

South Wall.

Here lieth the Bodies of John Rily, and also his Wife, who were buryed ye second day of July, Anno Dom. 1637.

On Flat Stones.

Here lieth the Body of Hester, the Wife of Robert King, of Avon, who departed this Life the 9th day of January, An° Dom. 17-- Aged 79 years.

Here lyeth the Body of Robert King, of Avon, who departed this life the 21st of September, Anno Dom. 1727, Aged 74 years.

The Church consists of Chancel, Nave, and South Aisle. In the North Window of Nave is some stained Glass, and the ancient Oak Screen is still in good preservation.

Mem. That the old Parish Register was burned in the House of Mr. John Ferris, of Furglane, where the Curate, Mr. Wm. Piggot, then lived, the House being fired by lightning, and here noted by John Stump, Curate of the Church of Christian Malford.

Register commenced 1658.—John Watson Beadon present Rector.

Lord Carnarvon Lord of the Manor.

CORSHAM.

Mon. in Chancel against North Wall.

To the Memory of John Hart, of this Parish, gent. who departed this life March 7, 1779.

Also, of Catharine Hart, his Widow, who departed this Life Sept. 25, 1808.

Hic jacet corpus Roberti Hulbert, in dies supremi expectatione, qualis erat iste dies indicabit.

Substracto tumulo corpus jacet hic repositum, Johanni Morgani, et agro Somersetensi, Arm. Chiliarchæ magnanimi, exemplaris virtute intrepidæ insignissimi, pro rege, pro patria pro segibus, nec non pro religione vere Catholica. In nuperis nefandis motibus præpotoris adversus perduelles acerrimi, nobis etsi intempestive heu nimis, at sibi exoptato feliciter, ex improvisio ad Sydera rapti, anno { ætatis 73. salutis 1684.

Fortia nunc muto requiescant ossa sepulchro,
Æterno exurgant tendem fruitura triumpho.

Quæ perfæmineum sparsa est perfectio sexum lector, in hâc una tota sepulta jacet. Edw. Rede, Arm. hoc distichon in memoria Annæ uxoris, suæ ex inclyta familia Baynardorum, de Lecham oriundæ, hic incidi curavit, quæ obiit Aug. 23, 1615.

Near this place lyeth the Body of Martha, the Wife of John Smith, of Corsham, eldest daughter of Leonard Smith of Clanfield, gen. who departed this Life the 20th day of Sept. 1669.

Against S. wall of Chancel.

In Memory of Elizabeth Harington, widow, obiit 16th June, 1817, Æt. 75. She was daughter of Abraham Chambers, Esq. of New Bond Street, London, Banker, and Married first, in September 1761, Wm. Hallett, of Canons, Middlesex, and last, on the 31st of December, 1781, the Rev. Richard Harington, of Hagley, cõ Worcester, whom she survived.

Arms, 1st. O. on a bend engrailed G. 3 bezants, a chief az.
2d. G. a chev. O. bt. 3 cinquefoils O.
3d. Az. a frett. A.

Here lieth one beneath this Brittle Tomb
Inclosed in his Father's Grave, and 's Mother's womb:
If thou a stranger be, and shalt desire
To know or who or what he was, Enquire;
The comon Country voice will, as thou passe,
But most the poore, acquaint thee what he was,
And all will Tell Thee he was one who di'd,
Except himself, too soon for all beside;
And if a Neighbour, All that thou shalt have
From me, is only this, here is the grave
Of such a one, whose name when thou shalt heare,
Thou'lt say that that's Enough, I may forbeare.

Here lieth the Body of James Hulbert, gent. who departed this life the fifth day of April, 1653, Aged 39.

Arms S. a cross O. bt. 4 leop. faces jessant fleur-de-lis O. a crescent G. impaling ermine, a bend G.

John and Thomas Hulbert, of this town of Corsham, Clothier, ye sons of James Hulbert, of Eston, within this Parish, clothier, deceased. John, the Eldest, Aged 49. happily exchanged this life ye 3d of September, 1626. Thomas, the younger, Aged 53, finished his course ye 16th Oct. 1632, of whose powerful prayers unto God, and most Christian departure, was witness wth many others that were then likewise present.

Two Brothers near Interred here doe Lye,
Whose love to each, whose trade, whose charitye,
Whose Zeale to God, whose truth to all was such,
As they seemd one of all admired much.
John was the eldest, a man Discreete and stoute,
Faithfull and Just in all he went about;
By seniority he first obtained,
The blessed Port that Thomas since hath gained.
Thomas was endow'd with such rare parts,
He no ways needed to be taught the Arts;
And though he kept him to his trade in cloth,
Yet was he divine, and a Courtyer both;
A Father strict, yet tender o'er his childe,
A loving Neighbour, and a Master Milde,
Who never did ye needy poor contemne,
And God enriched him by the hands of them;
Each like to other in ye choicest parts,
Each Brother's prayer speakes th' other his deserts,

O're whose dust doth this Monument remain,
Scarce two such Brothers hath ye world again.

Sir Edward Hungerford, Kt. of ye Honble Order of ye Bath, and ye Sherif of this County of Wilts, who hath caused this to be Erected in Memory of these Brothers, as well for their pious and profitable conversation with all, as for their constant Faithfull respect to him in particular, & Especialy for the praysworthy service that Thos. Hulbert did him in that year 1632.

Here lyeth interred Mrs. Winifred Jewks, who, with ye affection of a true and faithfull friend, spent great part of her time with the Lady Hungerford, of this Place, to whose Memory, with ye like affection, the said Lady Hungerford hath erected this Monument, the 31st day of May, 1671.

Arms, 3 falc. heads erased.

Mary, the danghter of John Kington, Esq. and of Mary his Wife, of Jaggards, in this Parish, was buried April ye 22d, 1708, Aged 11 weeks.

Arms. 10 gutle drops on a chief, 3 ducal crowns.

On Flat Stones.

Integer vitæ scelerisq. p . . us, hic jacet corpus Georgi Downes, de Interiori Templo, Arm. obiit vicessimo quarto die Januarii, Ætatis suæ 87, annoq. ære Christianæ 1738.

Here Lyeth the Body of Theodata Downes, gent. who departed this life the 22d day of April, An° Dñi 1726.

On a Brass Plate.

Here lyeth ye Body of Thomas Hulbert of this Town of Corsham, clothier, who, aged 53, Christianly finished his course, with powerful prayer to God, upon Tuesday, being ye 16th of October, 1632. He espoused Elizabeth, ye daughter of Thos. Wallis, of Trowbridge, Clothier, by whom he had issue Anne, Elizabeth, Thos. who deceased before him, Bridget married to William Sherstone, of Bromham, gent. Susan married to John Hallidaye, in the County of Gloucester, clothier, James, Elizabeth, and Mary, all five yet living to testifye their father's piety and care of them.

H. S. E.

Thos. Hulbert, Arm. de Eastonin Parochia Corsham, qui obiit decimo sexto Jan. An° Dñi 1743, Æt. suæ 63.

Sacred to the Memory of the late Mrs. Eliz. Hulbert, who died Dec. 17, 1819, Aged 73.

On Monuments in S. aisle.

Near this Place lieth interred the Body of Nathaniel Handcock, of Lipyat, who deceased the 11th of Sept. An° Dom̃ 1693, Aged 24 years.

Near this Place lie the Remains of John Hancock, sen. gent. of West Wells, in this Parish, who departed this life Feb. 20, 1732, Aged 69. And also of Ann his Wife, who departed this life June 21, 1735, Aged 64.

And also is interred in the same Vault John Hancock, gent. of West Wells, son of the above John and Ann Hancock, who departed this life the 27th of March, 1768, Aged 73. And also of Milicent, his Wife, who departed this life Nov. 6, 1781, Aged 76. Likewise of Mary, daughter of the above John and Milicent Hancock, who departed this Life the 25th of November, 1771Aged 29. Also of John, their son, who died in his infancy.

Near this Place lieth the Body of Jane Stubbs, widow, late Wife of Thomas Stubbs, of Kington St. Michael, in this County, Esq. and daughter of Wm. Duckett, late of Hartham, in this Parish, Esq. She died the 30th day of January, 1712, Aged 55 years.

Near this Marble are interred the Remains of the Rev. Richard Fowell, M.A. formerly Fellow of Exeter College, in Oxford, afterwards Rector of Hilperton, and Vicar of this Parish, where he died in the year 1750, and of his age 55. In the same Grave are deposited the Remains of Ann Fowell, his Wife, who died the 8th of Feb. 1768. Also, of James Fowell, their second Son, who died the 24th of June, 1768. Also of William Fowell, their fourth Son, who died the 14th of Jan. 1739-40. Also of John-Fowell Davis, son of Stansfield and Mary Davis, who died the 20th of August, 1768. Also of Mary the Wife of Stansfield Davis, who died May 29, 1789. Also of Stansfield Davis, who died May 20, 1801.

Arms, Az. a chev. O. in chief 3 mullets of the last.

Near this Place lieth the Body of the Rev. Mr. Edward Wells, Vicar of this Parish, and the first Master of the Free School built by the Lady Hungerford. He died July, Anno Dom. 1677, Ætatis 37.

27

Here lyes the Bodies of Mr. William Chapman, of Pickwick, gent. and Elizabeth, his Wife. She deceased May the 10, and hee died June the 1st, Anno Domini 1675.

Arms—Pp. chev. A. & S. at the fess. point a crescent counter changed, a canton G. impaling, S. a cross O. bt. 4 leop. faces, jessant, fleur-de-lis O.

Near this Place lyeth the Body of James Handcock, of Lippiat, in this Parish, gent. who departed this Life the 7th day of September, 1715, Aged 53 years.

Also near this Place Lyeth the Body of Edward Handcock, of Harpingeras, who died Jan. 13, A. D. 1733, Aged 66 years.

Here Lyeth the Body of Jane Hancocke, Daughter of Thomas Hancocke, who departed this life the 29th day of Nov. 1667.

In Memory of the Rev. Wm. Pryer, who died March the 20th, 1765.

Near this place lyeth the Body of John Hulbert of Thingley, sen. who was buried Feb. 9, Anno Dom. 1701, Aged 82 years.

Also near this Place lyeth the Body of Sarah, the Wife of John Hulbert, aforesaid, who was buried August 19, Anno Dom. 1704, Aged 74 years.

Near this place lyeth the Body of Wm. Philpot, gent. who departed this life the 1st of Jan. 1719, Aged 69 years.

Near this place lieth interred the Body of James Peirce, gent. of this Parish, clothier, who departed this Life the 18th day of June 1727, Aged 49 years. Also, near this place lieth interred the Body of John Peirce, who departed this Life the 10th day of Dec. 1785, Aged 82 years. Also near this place lieth interred the Body of John, Son of James and Sarah Peirce, who departed this Life the 3d day of August, 1790, Aged 24 years.

Erected to the Memory of the truely Religious John Salway, Son of John and Elinor Salway, who exchanged this Life April the 29th, Anno Dom. 1687.

Rich. Lewis, Arm. quod mortale super . . . hic subtus conditur, at quarti pinit, qui pietate fide hospitis charitate pares carissimos priorem, habuit neminem vir pitæ integerrimus deo Ecclesiæ, Patriæ fidissimus, filius natus tertius, Edouardi Lewis, equitis, et prænobilis Annæ Beauchamp, ab æque illustri ac antiquâ Sackvillerum, prosapiâ oriundæ hac Stirpe editus his virtutibus . . . gnis, cum bonorum luctû pauperum domno, sento confectus Cœlo maturus, obiit Octobris 7, Anno Æatis 83, salut. 1706.

Arms—S. a li. rampt. A.

On Flat Stones in S. Aisle.

Underneath are Deposited the Remains of Sarah, Wife of Benjamin Young, of Easton, who died April the 4th, 1790, Aged 72 years.

Also underneath are Deposited the Remains of Benjamin Young, who departed this life January 6, 1814, Aged 85 years.

Sacred to the Memory of John Hancock, gent. of West Wells, who died Dec. 11, 1790. Likewise Hester his Wife, who died Dec. 29, 1790. Mary-Ann, infant daughter of William and Mary-Ann Hancock, who died March 14, 1818.

In Memory of Richard Hart, of Har . . . in the County of Gloucester, who died Nov. 7, 1752, Aged 76 years.

Also of Susannah, his eldest daughter, who died Feb. 22, 1758, Aged 31 years.

Also, of Elizabeth, his Wife, who died Sept. 4, 1785, Aged 86 years.

Against N. Pillar of the Nave.

Near this Place lyeth the Body of Robert Nalder, who was here buried ye 16th day of May, 1664.

Also, near this Place lyeth the Body of Ann Nalder, Relict of Robert Nalder, who deceased ye 1st day of May, 1698.

Against South pillar of nave.

Memoriæ suavissimi juvenis Thomæ Godwin, Roberti Godwin, de Yate, in com̄ Glou. generosi, fil. natu minoris, qui post viennium in Œ. de Christi apud Oxoniensis feliciter clapsum, carnis exuvias variolarum labe fædatas, hoc loco deposuit, obiit 16° Julii, Anno Renovati Hominis 1719, Ætatis suæ 21.

Arms—a chev. erm. bt. 3 leop. heads cabossed.

On Flat Stones in Nave.

Jane Coggan died January 17, 1808, Aged 60 years.

John Stump, gent. died Oct. 21, 1804, Aged 60 years. Also Betty Stump, Relict of John Stump, died February 13, 1814.

Ann Wicks, of Heston, in the County of Middlesex, Ob. 2 May, 1786, Ætat. 53.

On Mon. in N. aisle.

Near this Place ly the Bodies of Edward Thrift, gent. and Anne, his Wife. He departed this life the 12th day of May, An° Dñi 1704, in the 63d year of his age, and Shee the 19th of Sept. A. D. 1692, in the 52d year of her age.

Underneath this Place lyeth the Body of Wm. Jarvis, who departed this life the 7th day of April, Anno Domini 1723, Aged 29 years.

Arms—a chev.

In Memory of John Leir, second Son of the Rev. Thomas Leir, of Jaggards, who died February 13, 1784, in the 17th year of his age.

Also Mary, an infant, who died Dec. 30, 1774.

North Wall.

Near this place lyeth the Body of Rebecca, Wife of Edward May, Relict of William Jarvis, who died the 28th day of October, 1743, Aged 50 years.

Also, near this Place, lyeth the Body of Rebecca. Wife of Edward Mitchell, jun. and daughter of William Jarvis, and Rebecca his Wife, who died October the 30th, 1743, Aged 23 years.

Arms—A chev.

On a Flat Stone in N. Aisle

William Hicks died March 17, 1786, Aged 87 years.

Also Ann, Wife of William Hicks, who died July 23, 1788, Aged 83 years.

In Memory of John Kington of Jaggards, in this Parish, Esq. who died Sept. 6, 1729, Aged 50 years.

Also of Mary his Relict, who died August the 13th, 1744, Aged 57 years.

Also Ann, the Daughter, who died March 28, 1720, Aged 15 years.

Interred near this Monument John Kington, Esq. who, to the Memory of his Parents and Sister, caused this inscribed Marble to be erected, who died Sept. 26, 1766, Aged 52 years, interred also near this Monument.

Sacred to the Memory of Richard Collins, Esq. Captain in His Majesty's Navy, who departed this life June the 24th, 1780, Aged 47 years.

Hatchments in South Aisle.

1st.

1. A tiger's head erased. pp.
2. A. 2 bars engrailed az. between 9 martlets, G.
3. Erm. 3 chevronells G.
4. A. a fess. G. bt. 6 annulets G.
5. A. on a saltire, engrailed S. 9 annulets O.
6. Same as the first.

2d.

1. A tiger's head erased pp.
2. A. a li. pass. az.
3. A. 2 bars engrailed, az. between 9 martlets, G.
4. Erm. 3 chevronells G.
5. Az. a chev. A. bt. 3 dolphins embowed A.
6. As the first, impaling perpale A. and az. a chev. bt. 3 talbots counter-changed on a fess. G. 3 leopards heads cabossed O.

3d.

A spread eagle S. over all on a shield A. 3 tigers heads erased pp. charged with an inescutcheon, az. a chev. A. bt. 3 dolphins emb. A. a chief O.

Arms—O. a bend engrailed G. bt. 2 li. ramp. of the last, over all an escutch. A. charged with a chev. between 3 squirrels G.

A. a li. ramp. G. debruised by a fess. O. charged with two li. ramp. combatant, holding a dex hand G. in chief 2 dex hands of the last, impaling G. on a chev. A. 3 leop. heads cabossed S. between 3 cinquefoils A.

Az. on a chief O. 2 fireballs inflamed pp. bt. 3 li. passant guard O. in chief on an escut. A. a sinister hand G. over all an escutch. Quarterly 1 & 3 G. a chev. vair A. and az. between 3 crescents A. a canton charged with an annulet O. 2 & 4 az. 4 loz. in fess. conjoined O. between 3 eagles heads erased O.

In the Chancel is a free-stone Altar Tomb, 10 ft. long, and 5½ ft. wide, with the Arms—A fess. engrailed bt. 3 griffins heads erased, impaling a chev. bt. 3 griffin's heads erased. The inscription is obliterated.

The Rev. John Methuen, Rector.

Paul Cobb Methuen, Esq. Lord of the Manor.

BIDDESTON.

Mon. in Chancel against North Wall.

H. S. E.

Mathew Mountjoy, Obiit Oct. 16th, 1787, Ætat. 36.

In Memory of William Mountjoy, of Biddeston St. Peters, gent. who died Nov. ye 21st, 1734, Aged 37. And also, Elizabeth, Relict of the above William Mountjoy, who departed this life ye 16th day of Feb. A.D. 1741, Aged 73. Also Wm. Mountjoy, gent. died February 23, 1766, Aged 73. Also Barbara, Relict of the above, died April 1, 1767, Aged 75. Also William Mountjoy died January 31, 1776, Aged 55 years. Also Elizabeth, Relict of the above, died Sept. 29, 1776, Aged 60 years. Also in Memory of William Mountjoy, gent. he departed this life the 14th April, 1787, Aged 39 years. And of Barbara, who died Oct. ye 20th, 1720, Sarah, August ye 7, 1727, daughters of William and Barbara Mountjoy, jun. and died in their infancy.

Arms—G. 3 inescutcheons O.

S. Wall of Chancel.

Near this Place lyeth the Body of Thomas, son of William Mountjoy, of this Place, gent. who deceased the 12th day of August, Anno Dom̄ 1695.

Near this Place lyeth the Body of Thomas, Son of William and Elizabeth Mountjoy, of this Place, gent. who departed this life the 6th day of February, 170$\frac{5}{6}$.

Sacred to the Memory of Mary-Ann, the Daughter of Samuel and Ann Mountjoy, who died June 19, 1807, Aged 19 years. Also Elizabeth their Daughter, who died June 4, 1812, Aged 26 years.

Against North Wall of Nave.

Neare this Place lyeth Buried the Body of Mr. Richard Wastfield, senior, who departed this life the 8th day of Nov. Anº Dñi 1652.

Also near this Place lyeth Buried the Body of Richard Wastfield, gent. ye younger, who departed this Life the 26th day of Feb. Anº Dom̄ 1682.

Margaret, Wife of James Little, died July 3d, 1761, Aged 58 years. Also James Little died Feb. 11th, 1766, Aged 66 years. Joanna, Wife of Aaron Little, died July 27, 1804, Aged 48 years. Also Aaron Little died Dec. 12, 1806, Aged 69 years.

South Wall of Nave.

Near this Place lyeth the Body of Thomas Willshire, sen. late of this Place, yeoman, who departed this Life the 26th day of March, Anno Dom. 1698.

Underneath are deposited the Remains of John Skeate, late of Slaughtenford, who died August 3, 1806, Aged 76 years.

Near this Place lyeth the Body of William Wastfield, son of Richard Wastfield, sen. gent. deceased, and Elizabeth his Wife. He died July the 21st, 1728, Aged 23 years.

William Wastfield, gent. obiit 9th Feb. 1782, Æt. 57. Also Elizabeth Wastfield his Wife Ob. 16th March, 1796, Æt. 77. Also Mary, Wife of William Edwards, Ob. 14th April, 1803, Æt. 33.

Near this Place lyes interred the Body of William Harrison, gent. Son of John and Martha Harrison, late of the City of Bristol, who departed this life the 10th day of February, 1736, Ætatis suæ 23.

Underneath lieth interred the Body of Mrs. Mary Wastfield, spinster, who departed this life the 20th day of June 1782, Aged 68 years.

Register commenced 1688.

NORTH WRAXHALL.

On Monuments against South Wall.

In Memory of Richard Oriel Singer, Esq. late of his Majesty's 32d Regt. who died Oct. 15, 1818, Aged 37 years, whose Remains are deposited in a Vault in this Church-yard.

Sacred to the Memory of Joseph Oriel, gent. of this Parish, who died the 30th of Jan. 1765, Aged 45 years. Also to the Memory of Maria, Wife of Joseph Oriel, who died the 25th of February, 1775, Aged 32 years. Likewise to the Memory of William Oriel, their son, who died Abroad, aged 40 years. Also to the Memory of Joseph Oriel, their eldest son, who died the 9th of March, 1804, Aged 54 years.

To the Memory of the Rev. Jonathan Cope, late of Christ-Church College, Oxford, only Son of Sir Jonathan Cope, Bart. of Brewern, Oxfordshire, and of Annabella his Wife, the last descendant of that Hon. and antient Family, he died March 10, 1814, at the early age of thirty-four, leaving to those, who placed all their hopes of earthly happiness on a most dutiful and affectionate Son, no other support under their heavy Loss, than that which they derive from Resignation to the Will of God. The Lord hath given, the Lord hath taken away, blessed be the name of the Lord.

Arms—A. on a chev. az. 3 fleur-de-lis A. bt. 3 roses pp.

On Flat Stones in Chancel.

Here lyes the Body of Thomas, the Son of Thomas Goddard, Rector of this Church, and Ann his Wife. He was born the 7th of August, 1702, and dyed the 14th of Oct. following.

Here lieth the Body of Anne, late Wife of John Earle, Rector, and eldest Daughter of James Goddard, of Marston, in this County, gent. who died the 24th, and was buried the 28th of November, 1681, aged 20 years and 10 months.

Hic jacet Johan. Seale, de parochiæ quondam . . . et ecclesiæ ornamentum, qui multos . . annos Xni ministri, sub . . . . mariti et patris optimi muncra integre Fingebatur, febre tando oppressus ux ima et filio uno mortuis, uxore et quatuor filiabus Relictis pie, fato concessit 20 die Augusti, An° Dñi 1697, Æt. suæ 57.

Nulli flebilior, quam mihi.

Hic jacet Resurrectionem vitam, a temam spe humilissima expectus, Gulielmus Lacy, A. M. hujus parochiæ per multo annos Rector et Incumben. Obiit 31 Decembris, Anno Salutis Nostriæ 1760, Ætat suæ 57.

Qualis eiat postrema dies, indicabit interea equie ai in ptiec precor.

Hic jacet Catherina, Gulielmi Lacy, A.M. hujus Ecclesiæ Rectoris, Uxor, Quondam non inamibilis, Obiit April 13, A. D. 1760, Ætatis suæ 50.

Here Lieth the Body of Edward Bridges, late Rector of this Parish, who departed this present life the 17th day of November, in the year of our Lord 166-.

Here Lieth the Body of . . . Wife of . . . . still, Rector of this Parish. Obiit April 25, 1760, Ætatis 47.

Against S. wall of Nave.

Heare Lyeth the Body of Alice Cullymore, Wife of Thomas Cullymore, daughter of James Hulbert, of Slaughtenford, gen. Dyed in assured hope of Eternall Lyfe by jhesus Christ, June the 11th, An° Dom̃ 1643, Ætat suæ 37.

On a Mon. in N. Aisle.

In Memory of Ezekiel Wallis, Esq. of Lucknam, near this Place, only Son and sole heir of James Wallis, Esq. from whom he inherited an ample fortune, which he employed in acts of generosity and benevolence. He died Dec. 31st, 1735, Aged 43 years. Also of Cecilia, his Wife, the youngest daughter of Isaac Selfe, Esq. of Beanacre, in this County, by Penelope his Wife, daughter and coheiress of Charles Lord Lucas, Baron of Shenfield, in Essex, who married, secondly, the Worshipful John Coxed, LL. D. Warden of Winchester College, whom she likewise survived, and departed this life January 31, 1760, Aged 60 years. Paul Methuen, Esq. her Nephew and Heir, caused this Marble to be erected.

Arms, 1st. Erm. a bend G. impaling, erm. 3. chev. G.

2d. P. fess. erm. a bend G. in base p. chev. A. & az. a chev. S. bt. 2 roses G. in base a garb O. impaling erm. 3 chev. G.

A White Marble Tomb.

Paul Methuen Esq. who lies here interred, died Jan. 22, 1795, Aged 72 years. He was the only Son of Thomas Methuen, Esq. of this County, also heir of his Mother's Family, the Selfe's, of Beanacre, and of the Right Honble Sir Paul Methuen, Kt. of the Bath. He had issue, by Christian his Wife, two Sons, Paul Cobb Methuen, Esq. his eldest Son and heir, Thomas, who died before him, and one Daughter, Christian, married to Frederick Lord Boston.

He that walketh uprightly, walketh surely.

N. Side.

In the Vault underneath are deposited the Remains of Christian, Wife of Paul Methuen, Esq. daughter and coheiress of Sir George Cobb, Bart. of Adderbury, in Oxfordshire, by Ann, his Wife, daughter and coheiress of Joseph Langton, Esq. of Ne..haven, in the County of Somerset, who died the 21st of May, 1776, Aged 56 years.

Thomas Methuen, second Son of Paul Methuen, Esq. and Christian, his Wife, died at Nice, in the dominions of Savoy, where he went for the recovery of his health, April 27, 1774, Aged 20 years, and was interred in the Vault under this Tomb the 21st of July following.

Near this place are Deposited the Remains of Anne Christian Methuen, second daughter of Paul Cobb Methuen, Esq. She died March 26, 1808, Aged 22.

Though no proud monument, or breathing bust,
With awful grandeur, guards her slumb'ring dust,
This simple Tablet shews, and shews with truth,
When Anna perished—in the bloom of youth!
How memory of her worth could love to tell,
And on her charms with grateful pleasure dwell;
How each perfection shone in her combin'd,
A feeling bosom, with a spotless mind.
But Virtue needs no record on her tomb,
And comment vain on Providence's doom:
Enough, that Heaven received her parting breath,
And mild Religion calm'd the frowns of Death.

In the north-west corner of the north aisle are two stone figures lying, perhaps a Knight Templar and his Lady: they are much defaced. At the South Porch is a Saxon Arch.

Rectors of North Wraxhall, extracted from the Register, which commenced 1677.

John Beale,	*inducted*	1697, Aug. 20.
Thos. or Wm. Goddard,		1711, Dec. 20.
John Clements,		1718, July 23.
Wm. Lacy, M. A.		{ 1732, Nov. 5. { 1761, June 3.
Henry Hill,		1804, Mar. 28.
Jonathan Cope,		{ 1804, June. { 1814, May 15.
Michael Wyatt, present Rector, who built the Rectory House, in a Gothic style, in 1819,		1814, May.

Paul Cobb Methuen, or Lord Peterborough, Lord of the Manor.

COLERN.

On Monuments against N. Wall of Chancel.

Beneath this Place lieth the Body of Mary, the daughter of Charles and Elizabeth Weston. She departed this life June the 22d, 1709, Aged 1 year and 6 weeks.

Near this place lieth interred the Body of Jane, Wife of Mr. George Drewett, and daughter of Thomas and Elizabeth Salmon, who died March 12, 1769, Aged 39.

Underneath lieth the Body of Mary, the Wife of John Browning, late of the Parish of Yatton Keynell, Wilts, who died January 10, 1801, Aged 49 years. Also the Body of Grace, the Wife of Thomas Browning, of this Place, who died May 14, 1803, Aged 31 years. Also the Body of John Browning, yeoman, of Yatton Keynell, who died February the 1st, 1811, Aged 62 years.

To the Memory of Elizabeth, daughter of John and Elizabeth Browning, who died August 25, 1771, Aged 24.

In Memory of Mrs. Elizabeth Browning, of Leigh de la Mere, and daughter of Thomas and Elizabeth Salmon, of this Parish, who died March 27, 1793, Aged 68 years.

Near this Place lyeth the Body of Susannah, Wife of Peter Drewett, of this Parish, Clothier, and Daughter of Thomas and Elizabeth Salmon, who died Dec. 26, 1758, Aged 26 years.

Johannis Houghton, antiqua Houghtonorum Famina
In Agro Lancastriensi ortus,
Huic Ecclesiæ per 21 et quod excurrit annos,
Invigilavit fidelis pecurigilisq. Pastor
Alienæ memor Salutis quia non immemor suæ
Vir erat
Probitate illustri, et integritate spectate
Aperto absq. omni fuco pectore
Primæ et Fidei tenax et Pietatis æmulus,
Obiit die Septembris 3, An° Dñi 1702, Ætat. suæ 44.

Atque juxta hoc marmor placide in Domino
Requiescit
Cujus etiam ad Latus
Obdormit dilecta ejus conjux Maria,
Fœmina præcellentissimis et corporis et animi Dotibus

Eximie culta
Prudentia candore in . . dibinque
Tam moram quam oris, ge. tusq. suavitate
Cæterisq. sui sexus ornamentis,
Summe spectabilis
Virtutis erat intactæ, pietatis plane singularis
Et Deum quem impense dilexit religiose coluit,
Rei domesticæ non indiligens,
Nec imperita erat administrata, incaruit tamen
Hospitalitate splendide charitate diffusa,
Cum longa tandem valetudine laborasset,
Desideratissimam suam animam ad altiora aspirantem,
Placide efflavit, die Aprilis 24,
Anno Dom. 1717, Ætatis suæ 59.

Filia fuit Georgii Yate, de Waltham,
in Agro Hantoniensi, generos,
Et primis Nuptiis desponsata fuit Thos. Harris, Arm
Cui unicam peperit filiolam in tenera ætate extinctam
Secundis desponsata fuit
Rev'endo Johanni Houghton, quo defuncto
Nupta fuit tandem Johanni Michell, generoso,
Prædicto Johanni Houghton, tres pepirit filios,
Johannem, Carolum, et Georgium:
Johannis, optimæ spei adolescens
Cum jam decimum septimum egebat annum
In ipso juventutis flore succisus occubuit
die Sept. 12, Anno Dom. 1712.
Carolus, tredicim tantum numeravit mensis,
Atq. hinc obiit die Junii 24, A. D. 1698.
Georgius, unice superstes,
Hoc in Parentis, et fractres,
Pii sui gratiq. animi testimonium extruxit 1722.

Arms, barry of 6, A. & az. impaling p. fess imbattled A. & vt. 3 gates counter-changed.

A BENEFACTION.

William Harris, D. D. gave to the Poor of the Parish of Cullern in manner and form following: *Item*, I will and require my executors to lay out Three Hundred Pounds in one parcel of Land, which I desire may be conveyed to such Persons as they shall think fit, in trust, that the Rents, Issues, and Profits thereof, be disposed yearly, and every year, amongst such poor persons of Cullern, where I was born, which are housekeepers, and take no alms of the Parish, to be distributed at the Feast of Easter and Christmas, by the discretion of my Executors, the Vicar, Churchwardens, and Overseers of the Poor there: But if it should happen that my Executors die without issue, then he that is the Owner, or Right Proprietor of the Farm in Cullern, shall be a Trustee, with the Vicar there, to see this charitable use honestly disposed of to such poor people as really want the same. Dated Nov. 6, 1700.

Memorandum, That Charles Savage, of Westwood, in this County, Esq. being one of Dr. Harris's Executors, has, in lieu of the said £300, settled a Rent-Charge of Twelve Pounds per annum, free from all Taxes and Payments whatsoever. For the payment of which the said Charles Savage has charged an Estate of his at Keevillwick, in the Parish of Keevill, in the County of Wilts.

This Monument was Erected in the year 1708, to the Memory of that Pious Divine, Dr. William Harris, who died Nov. 9th, 1700, and was interred in the Cathedral Church at Winchester.

Beneath this Place lyes interred the Body of Thos. Harris, Esq. late of this Parish, elder Brother to the said Dr. Harris, who departed this Life the 19th of March, Anno Dom. 1691.

Arms—Az. 3 crescents.

H. S. E.

Thomas Harris, de Colern, in com̃ Wilt. gen. qui per annos plusquam triginta, Christani, subdidit, mariti, et patris optimi munera in istâ parochia fideliter obi-nit gangreno tandem pede correptus, tribus filiabus et uno filio, defunctis, tribus filiis et unâ filia superstitibus xix die Nov. pie fato sabmisit,

Æræ Xñæ 1674,
Anno Ætat. suæ 63.

Qui bene vixit non metuit mori

Thomæ Harris, juxta sep . . . accubat, Jana, filius dilecta conjux . . . sicut mariti . . . . in animos pietatis officiis perpetua, comes ita in ejusdem vidus etiam oc . . . atac . . is . . . suit . . . . . ,
Ipsa jam . . . . sat. ut . . . .
Idem torus ea . . . pignoro, idem animi affectus, idem quoq. lapis et ipsa jungeret urna, obiit Junii xxiv. Anno Dom. 1799, aged 80.

Arms—3 crescents impaling, a cross engrailed, over all a bend.

South Wall of Chancel.

To the Memory of the Honorable Mrs. Elizabeth Forrester, daughter of Sir Thomas Tyrrell, Bart. of Thornton, in the County of Bucks, and Relict of the Honble William Forrester, a Captain in the Royal Navy. She had an only son, William Lord Forrester, who died October 21, 1762, Aged 27 years, and was interred in the Parish Church of Didmarton, in the county of Gloucester, where the Remains of his Mother were also deposited, on the 4th of Nov. 1776. Her exemplary Piety, diffusive Charity, and universal Benevolence, were continually manifested during a residence of upwards of 30 years in this Parish. She left by Will the sum of Three Hundred Pounds, for the Benefit of such poor Inhabitants of Colern as receive no Alms of the Parish. In order more firmly to secure this benefaction, Lands within the said Parish were purchased and conveyed to Trustees in such manner as fully to answer her benevolent purpose.

Zechariah Salmon, of this Parish, yeoman, died July 19, 1683, Aged 48 years.

Elinor, his Wife, dyed July 17, 1722, Aged 76 years.

Underneath lyeth ye Body of Elizabeth, ye Wife of Thos. Salmon, who died April ye 9th, 1757, Aged 62.

Also underneath lyeth ye Body of Thomas Salmon, ye only Son of Zechariah and Elinor Salmon. He died May ye 9th, 1760, Aged 70.

Underneath lieth interred the Body of Mrs. Mary Berkeley, spinster, daughter of Richard Berkeley, Esq. of Stoke-Giffard, in the County of Gloucester, who died the 13th day of January, 1727, in the 70th year of her age.

Near this Place is interred the Body of the Reverend Mr. James Mascall, M. A. late Vicar of this Parish, who departed this life March ye 22d, in the year of our Lord, 1719, Aged 35.

Here lyeth ye Body of Charles Trimlin, the Sonne of Andrew Trimlin, who deceased Nov. ye 27, 1657.

On a Flat Stone.

Here lieth ye Body of Charles, ye Son of John Houghton, Vicar, and Mary his Wife, who was born the 11th of May, 1697.

On Monument in Nave.

Sacred to the Memory of Mr. John Ford, Builder, of the City of Bath, who died the 6th of September, 1767, Aged 56 years, whose abilities and enterprise in business, in a great measure contributed to the erection of the handsome Buildings and Streets of that City.

Also to the Memory of his Son, Mr. John Ford, Statuary, who died February 23d, 1803, Aged 67 years.

West End.

Near this Place lyeth the Body of Thomas Edwards, of Slaughterford, yeoman, who died March 2, 1740, Ætatis suæ 82. Also Mary the Wife of Thomas Edwards dyed the 8th of January 1744, Aged 69 years.

Sacred to the Memory of Catharine Vincent, eldest daughter of the late Colonel Henry Vincent, of the Bengal Establishment, who died at the Hot Wells, Bristol, the 28th of June 1811, Aged 28.

Juxta reponitur quicquid mortale fuit, Rev. Josephi Needham, A. M. Qui plus triginta annos quos hujus ecclesiæ Vicarius extatit, simul ministerii munus fideliter obivit et adolescentibus erudiendis in literas humaniores sedulo incubuit, nec æstimatione tuâ, lector ideo vilescat, homo erat et nihil humani sprevit, Jesut etiam salutis auctor liberos benigne accepit et Agnos suos apostoli tutelæ commendavit. In eodem tumulo Reconditæ sunt reliquæ Lydiæ, uxoris ejus dilectæ, ex quâ unam suscepit filiam, Lydiam uxorem Zechariæ Shrapnel, de Bradfordia, in hoc agro Wiltoniensi, quæ honoris ergo Parentibus hoc monumentum posuit.

obiit { ille 20 Decem. 1759, Ætatis 67.
illa 3 August, 1735, Ætatis 31.

Vale lector vive memor mortis, et in Christo vitam æternam quæras.

On Flat Stones.

Underneath this Stone is deposited the Remains of Sarah Garland, wife of James Garland. late of the City of Bath, and daughter of James and Sarah Woodham, who departed this life the 7th day of Nov. 1808, Aged 35 years.

Eleanor Parkes born May 11, 1801, died June 26, 1809. Mary-Eleanor Parkes born August 28, 1768, died Nov. 29, 1809. Richard Parkes, Esq. born March 21, 1743, died June 11, 1810. Richard Constantine Parkes, son of the above Richard and Mary-Eleanor Parks, born 30th September, 1791, died 23d November, 1818, on his passage from Calcutta to the Cape of Good Hope, where he was proceeding for the recovery of his health.

Here lyeth the Body of Francis Edwards, junior, who departed this life the 26th of May 1692.

Here lyeth the Body of Mary Webb, late Wife of John Webb, who departed this life the 26th day of August, 1690.

On Monuments in S. aisle.

To the Memory of Mary, Wife of John Edwards, of this Parish, yeoman, who died April 22, 1772, Aged 62. Also John Edwards, who died Nov. 28, 1774, Aged 61.

Near this Place resteth the Body of Walter Edwards, of the More, in the Parish of Corsham, yeoman, who departed this life ye 28th day of January 1735, Aged 66 years. Also near this place resteth ye Body of Elizabeth, the Wife of Walter Edwards. She died the 15th day of Dec. 1746, Aged 64 years.

Near this Place lyeth the Body of Mary the Wife of Samuel Edwards, who departed this life March the 27, 1704, in the 66th year of her Age. Also near this Place lyeth the Body of Samuel Edwards, who departed this life May the 9th, 1709.

Near this Place lyeth the Body of John Edwards, of Slaughterford, who died March 30, 1767, aged 62. Also Sarah, Wife of John Edwards, who died August 31, 1788.

In Memory of Sarah, daughter of Richard and Rachel Aust, who died March 8, 1771, Aged 33 years.

Near to this Place resteth the Body of Jane, the Wife of John Webb, the younger, of this Parish, who departed this life the 18th day of October, in the 3d year of the Rayne of our Soveren Lord, James the Second, Anno Dom, 1687.

Near this Place lyeth the Body of John Edwards, of this Parish, sen. who departed this life March the 31, 1718. He having no issue, left his Nephew, Walter Edwards, his Brother's Son, his sole Executor, and he, in Memory of his Uncle, hath erected this Monument.

Here lye interred ye Bodies of Gifford Hulbert and his Wife Mary. He departed this life ye 9th of May, 1653, and She on the 24th of Feb. in the year 164$\frac{5}{6}$.

Francis Salmon of this Parish lies interred in the Parish Church of St. John, in the City of Bristoll, who departed this life the 30th of April, 1674, Aged 54 years. Mary, his Wife, daughter of Gifford Hulbert, died the 15th of March, Aged 55 years, Anno Dom. 167$\frac{8}{9}$. Alsoe ye Bodies of 2 Children of Francis Salmon, lie buried in ye Chancell of this Church, who died in their Infancy.

Near to this Place lieth the Body of Alice, the Wife of John Stokes of the Parish of Bradford, and daughter of Samuel and Mary Edwards of this Parish. She died March the 13th, 1717.

North Aisle.

Near this Place lie interred the Bodies of Thomas, Ann, and John, Sons and Daughter of Thomas and Sarah Jones.

Thomas died June the 28, 1748, Aged 1 month.
Ann died February the 14th, 1754, Aged 3 years.
John died May the 7th, 1754, Aged 2 years.

Near to this Place lyeth interred the Body of Mr. James Lewis, Vicar of this Parish, who departed this life the 8th day of January, 1725, in the 34th year of his age.

On Flat Stones in N. Aisle.

In Memory of Sarah, Wife of Thomas Jones, who died September 13, 1775, Aged 57.

Also Thomas Jones died Decem. 28, 1785, Aged 68.

In Memory of Thomas Jones, who died Aug. 21, 1693. Also in Memory of Ann, the daughter of John and Mary Jones. She died the 28th of Feb. 1757, in the 34th year of her age.

Here lyeth the Body of Daniel Jones, who died Oct. 8, 1808, Aged 75 years. Also Grace, the Wife of Daniel Jones, who died April 27, 1810, Aged 71 years.

Beneath this Stone lyeth the Body of John Jones, of this Parish, yeoman, who died January 4, 1774, Aged 81. Also Mary, his Wife, who died March 30, 1774, Aged 85.

Samuel Drewett, clothier, died May 20, 1791, Aged 46 years.

The Church consists of a Chancel, Nave, North and South Aisles.

The Rev. Aubrey-Charles Price, present Vicar.

BOX.

Mon. in Chancel against North Wall.

Juxta sepultus est Gulielmus Eyre, de Ashley, hujusæ Parochiæ, generosus. Uxorem habuit Elizabetham

Radolphi Flowerdew, de Hethersett, in comitatu Norfolk, armigeri, filiam, ex quâ septem liberos suscepit, erat pius, sobrius, pacificus, Obiit primo die Feb. Anno Domini 1699, Ætat. 82.

Arms—On a chev. 3 cinquefoils.

Near this Place, and in the same Grave with her dear late Husband, Thos. Blow, Esq. lyeth the Body of Mary Blow, widow, one of the daughters of Robert Butler, late of Great Chelsea, in the county of Middlesex, Esq. and Martha his Wife, sister of Edward Butler, Dr. of Laws, late President of Saint Mary Magdalen, in the University of Oxford, and sister to Ann Eyre, Wife of Serjeant Eyre, late of this Parish. She was a most amiable and affectionate Wife, a most tender Relation in every capacity, a warm and zealous Friend, and, above all, an exemplary Christian, adorning the Doctrine of God our Saviour in all things. She bore a long, a tedious illness, contracted probably by an over-sedulous attendance on an infirm but valuable Husband, with an evenness of temper peculiar to her, and is now gone (alas for those many whom her engaging behaviour had endeared her to, but who must for a time be separated from her) to that happy Place where there shall be no more death, neither any more pain. She died the eleventh of November, in the sixty-second year of her age, and in the year of our Lord One Thousand Seven Hundred and Fifty-five, having finished the Work which was given her to do: For in the great variety of life which fell to her share, she preserved a surprising propriety of Behaviour, and always became the Post which was assigned her, ever mindful of the one thing needful, and of so unblemished a Reputation in every station as might have done honour to better times than those she lived in. This Monument is erected to her dear Memory by her till now inseparable Niece, the most sorrowful Executrix of her last Will and Testament, Mary Herbert of Chelsea, widow.

In Memory of Charlotte Northey, daughter of the late William Northey, Esq. of Ivy-House, who, after a painful and lingering illness, which she bore with the greatest patience and resignation, died Feb. 18, 1789, Aged 28.

Here lie the Remains of William Northey, Esq. son of William Northey, Esq. of Compton Bassett, Wilts. by Abigail, daughter to Sir Thomas Webster, Bart. of Battle Abbey, Sussex, who departed this life Dec. 21, 1770, in the 49th year of his Age. He was a kind Relation, a true Friend, a warm Patriot, and a most worthy Man. He gained a complete knowledge of the Interests of Britain: at Court independent, in the Senate unbiassed. This was his true character: to add more appear ostentations, to say less not doing justice to his Memory.

Also the Remains of Lucy Northey, his youngest Daughter, who died June 11, 1785, in the 15th year of her age.

Reader!

In pity drop one kind, one tender tear,
For every virtue lies collected here;
Snatched off in all the bloom of pleasing youth,
A mind adorn'd with honour, goodness, truth.
To prove that souls angelic spurn this earth,
She raised our wonder, then resign'd her breath.

To these so mourn'd in death, so lov'd in life,
The afflicted parent, and the widowed wife,
With tears inscribes this monumental stone
That holds their ashes, and expects her own.

Arms—O on a fess az. 3 Roses A. bt. 3 tigers pp. or. O. each charged with as many mullets A. impaling S. on a chev. O. 3 roses G. bt. 3 pistols O.

South Wall of Chancel.

Near this Place lies interred the Body of Harriet Northey, Wife of William Northey. of Compton Bassett, in the County of Wilts. Esq. Daughter of Robert Vyner, of Gautby, in the County of Lincoln, Esq. who departed this life the 28th day of October, 1750, Aged 27. Also the Remains of Ann Northey eldest Daughter of the said William Northey, Esq. by Ann, daughter of Edward Hopkins, Esq. of Coventry, who died in August, 1765, Aged 12 years.

If manners gentle, void of guile and strife,
Could health prolong, and add to human life;
If manly sense, and innocence of heart
Could shield the stroke of Death's unerring dart;
Her friends would not regret Life's narrow span,
And she'd have liv'd beyond the age of man;
But gracious Heaven, who knew her virtues best,
Recall'd her placid soul to blissful Rest.

Near this Place lyeth the Body of Thomas Goddard, gent. 4th son of Edward Goddard, late of Upham, Esq. deceased February the 7th, An° Dom̄ 1691, in the 71 year of his Age. Near this Place also lyeth interred the Body of Priscilla Goddard, of Upham, Esq. and Mother of Thomas Goddard above-named, buried June the 15, An° Dñi 1681, in the 88th year of her age.

Arms—G. a chev. vair between 3 crescents, erm.

On Flat Stones in Chancel.

In Memory of Mary, the Daughter of Dr. Thomas Tenison, late Rector of Chiddingstone and Lydd, in the County of Kent, Prebendary and Chancellor of the Diocese of Oxford, by Mary his Wife, Daughter of Thomas Smith, late of Nottingham, Esq. She died the 23d day of June, A. D. 1743, aged 1 year and 19 days.

Here lyeth the Body of John Phillipps, Vicar of this Parish, who departed this life the 12th day of July, 1707, Aged 57.

Here lyeth the Body of Constantia, Wife of John Phillipps, Vicar of this Parish, who departed this life the 17th day of October, 1703, Aged 29.

Underneath are deposited the Remains of Mary Standfast, Wife of the Reverend William Standfast, LL. D. who died August 21, 1744, aged 48.

Also of Harriot Smith, spinster, her 5th and youngest daughter, by her first Husband, Thos. Smith, of Nottingham, Esq. who died June 27, 1784, aged 57.

Here lyeth the Body of Hugh Speke, of Haselbury, Esq. second Sonne of Sir George Speke, of Whitlakington, of the county of Somerset, Knight of the Bath, who deceased the Fourth day of Jan. A. D. 1624.

Here lieth the Body of Mary, the Wife of George Speke Petty, of Cheney-Court, Esq. and daughter of Sir Thomas Gore, of Barrow, in the County of Sumersett, Knight. She died the 12th day of July, in the year of our Lord 1700, Aged 31 years.

Here also lyeth the Body of George Speke Petty, late of Cheney Court, and afterwards of Haselbury, Esq. He dy'd the 27th day of March, in the year of our Lord 1719, Aged 52 years.

Here lyeth the Body of Sir Hugh Speke, Bart. deceased the 5th day of July, 1661, and the Body of his only daughter, Ann Speke.

Also, here lyes the Body of Dame Rachel Speke, eldest daughter of Sir William Wyndham, of Orchard Wyndham, in the county of Somerset, Knight and Bart. by Dame Frances, daughter of Anthony Hungerford, of Farley Castle, Esq. and Relict of Sir George Speke, of Haselbury, Bart. and afterwards Wife of Richard Musgrave, Esq. obiit Oct. 26, A. D. 1711, Ætat. 54.

Arms—Quarterly, 1 & 4. 2 bars, over a spread eagle charged with an escut. surcharged with a sinister hand; 2 & 3. 3 chev. between 3 mullets pierced.

Hic jacet
Georgius Speke, Baronettus, Filius Hugonis Speke, Baronetti, de Haselbury, in comitatu Wilton. Annaeq. filiæ unicæ et Heredis Johannis Mayne, Armigeri, de Staplehurst, in comitatu Cantii Natus 1° die Octobris, An° Dom̄ 1653, Denatus 14 die Januarii, An° Dom̄. 1685.

[BY WALLER, THE POET.]

Under this stone lyes Virtue, Youth,
Unblemisht Probity, and Truth,
Just unto all Relations known,
A worthy Patriot, Pious son,
Whom Neighbouring Towns so often sent
To give their sence in Parliament;
With lives and fortunes trusting one
Who so discreetly us'd his own.
Sober he was, wise, Temperate,
Contented with an old Estate,
Which no foul avarice did encrease,
Nor wanton luxury make lesse.
While yet but young his Father dy'd
And left him to a happy Guide:
Not Lemuel's Mother with more care
Did councell and instruct her Heir,
Or teach with more success her Son
The vices of the time to Shunn.
An Heiress she, while yett alive,
All that was her's to him did give;
And he just gratitude did show
To one that had obliged him soe;
Nothing too much for her he thought,
By whom he was so bred and taught,
So early made that path to tread,
Which did his youth to Honour lead.
His short life did a Pattern give
How neighbours, husbands, friends should live.
The virtues of a Private life
Exceed the glorious noise and strife
Of Battels wonn, in those we finde
The solid interest of Mankinde.
Approv'd by all, and lov'd so well,
The young, like fruit that's ripe, he fell.

Arms—Quarterly 1 & 4. a spread eagle, 2 & 3. 3 chevronells between 3 cinquefoils over all an escutch. charged with a sinister hand. Crest, a hedgehog.

Here lyeth the Body of Dame Ann Speke, the sole Daughter and Heiress of John Mayney, of Staplehurst, in the County of Kent. Esq. the Relict of Sir Hugh Speke, of Haselbury, in the county of Wilts. Baronet, and Mother to Sir George Speke, aforesaid, Bart. who departed this life the 13th of January, Anno Dom̄ 1685.

Here lyeth the Body of Mary, the daughter of George Speke Petty of Haselbury, Esq. She dyed March 19, A. D. 1719, Aged 20 years.

Here also lyeth the Body of Thomas, Son of George Speke Petty, of Haselbury, Esq. He dyed Nov. 13, A.D. 1725, Aged 36 years.

Arms—2 bars, over all a spread eagle, charged with a sinister hand, impaling perpa'e, 3 chevronells between 3 cinquefoils counter-changed.

Francis Speke, third Son of Hugh Speke, Esq. was borne att Haselbury ye 4th day of October, being Thursday, about 4 of ye Clock in ye Morning, in the yearr of the Reigne of our Sovereigne Lord King James, Anno Domini 1610.

Stay, passenger, and learn from hence,
How God the just doe recompence:
Unto this Gentleman were given
The Golden meen approved by Heaven;
A name unblemished, length of days,
A Greatfull friend to tell his praise
Upon his Tombe, all which aprove,
His zealous piety and love.

He dyed October the 8th, 1683, Aged 73 years.

Arms—Quarterly 1 & 4, a spread eagle, 2 & 3, 2 bars indented in chief, 3 annulets, a mullet pierced for diff.

On Monuments in Nave.

In Memory of John Neat, who died December 7, 1807, Aged 93 years.

Also Amy, Wife of the above John Neat, who died December 14, 1791, Aged 70 years.

George Neat died August 2, 1814, Aged 62 years.

And Elizabeth, Daughter of George and Ann Neat, died December 13, 1814, Aged 26 years.

To the Memory of Ann, Wife of Edward Lee, who died 30th of June, 1766, in the 32d year of her age. Also two children, John and Betty, died infants. Also Edward Lee, who died the 24th of April 1797, in the 71st year of his Age.

In Memory of Michael Coleman, Esq. He resided upwards of Thirty Years in the Island of Jamaica, and returned to his native Country for the benefit of his health, but too late. He died Feb. 2, 1816, in the 45th year of his age. In him were united the dutiful and affectionate Son, the loving Brother, and truly sincere friend.

South Wall of Nave.

To the Memory of William and Henry Redwar, only Sons of the late Henry Redwar, Esq. of Spanish Town, in the Island of Jamaica, who were in the enjoyment of perfect health only ten days before they were called to surrender their spirits to Him who gave them. William died at their Estate, Dumbarton, in St. Ann's, in the above Island, Nov. 8, 1807, in his 24th year. Henry died at Middle Hill, in this Parish, Dec. 27, 1807, in his 19th year.

To the Memory of Thomas Bowdler, Esq. formerly of Ashley, in this Parish, who died May 2, 1785, Aged 79 years. Elizabeth Stewart Bowdler, his Wife, Daughter and Coheiress of Sir John Cotton, of Conington, in the County of Huntingdon, Baronet, who died May 10, 1797, Aged 80 years. Jane Bowdler, their eldest Daughter, who died March 4, 1784, Aged 41 years. And Elizabeth-Julia Bowdler, their second Daughter, who died May 4, 1754, Aged 10 years. This Humble tribute of duty and affection is erected by John, Frances, Henrietta, Maria, and Thomas, the five surviving children of the said Thomas and Elizabeth Stuart Bowdler.

Arms—2 doves in pale, impaling, a spread eagle.

Heare lieth the Body of Anthony Longe, Esq. buried the 2d of Mai, 1578.

Arms—Quarterly 1 & 4 long. 2 & a border in chief, a roundel between 2 bucks heads cabossed, 3 pair of wings conjoined. impaling quarterly 1 & 4, barry of 5 erm. 2 & 3. a li. ramp.

On a Brass Plate.

Beneath this Plate lyeth ye Body of John Rawlings, of this Parish, sen. who departed this life the 3d day of June, 1709, Aged 75.

On Flat Stones.

Samuel Pinchin died April 7, 1751, Aged 58 years. Susanna Pinchin, his Wife, died July 22, 1775, Aged 81 years. Tobias Pinchin, their Son, died March 6, 1776, Aged 49 years. Mary Pinchin, their daughter, died April 28, 1778, Aged 53 years. George Gibbons died May 13, 1781, in the 40th year of his age. Jane Gibbons, his Wife, died September 17, 1795, Aged 64 years.

Elizabeth Pinchin, Wife of William Pinchin, died October 4, 1735, Aged 80 years. John Pinchen, son of William and Jane Pinchin, died July the 5th, 1754, Aged 31 years. Ann Pinchen, daughter of William and Jane Pinchin, Jane Pinchen, died December 19, 1789, Aged 65 years.

William Pinchin died August 23, 1694, Aged 42 years. William Pinchin, Son of the above William Pinchin, and Elizabeth his Wife, died Jan. 15, 1756, Aged 55 years. William Pinchin, Son of William and Jane Pinchin, died November 27, 1750, Aged 30. Jane Pinchin, Wife of William Pinchin, died Nov. 1, 1775, Aged 77 years.

Joseph Pinchin, Son of William and Elizabeth Pinchin, died June 27, 1768, Aged 80 years.

Mary Pinchin, Wife of John Pinchin, died Feb. 12, 1770, Aged 42 years.

Ann Burgess, Daughter of William and Elizabeth Pinchin, died August 5, 1778, Aged 80 years.

Joseph Pinchin, Son of William and Jane Pinchin, died January 29, 1797, Aged 72.

Benefactions to the Parish of Box.

1. Dame Rachel Speke, Relict of Sir George Speke, of Haselbury, Bart. and Daughter of Sir William Wyndham, of Orchard Wyndham, in the County of Somerset, Kt. and Bart. A.D. 1711, gave by Will the Interest of one Hundred Pounds for ever for teaching Poor Children to Read, and instructing them in the knowledge and practice of the Christian Religion, as professed and taught in the Church of England.

2. George Speke Petty, of Haselbury, Esq. A. D. 1719, gave to the Charity School the Interest of One Hundred Pounds for ever.

3. Thomas Speke, of Haselbury, Esq. A. D. 1725, gave to the Charity School £100.

4. Mrs. Ann Speke, Relict of Thomas Speke, A. D. 1726, gave to the Charity School £100.

5. Mr. Pancefort Miller, Merchant in Jamaica, A.D. 1727, gave to the Charity School £100.

N. B. The £500 above-mentioned were laid out in purchasing Lands and building a Barn at Foggam, which were leased out at Lady-day, A. D. 1733.

6. The Trustees of Henry Hoare, of Stourton, Esq. gave £100 towards the building a Room in the Workhouse for the Charity School, and the same was completed and fitted up by other gifts A. D. 1728.

7. The said Trustees also gave £100 towards building the Workhouse, A. D. 1728.

The Church was first built A. D. 1200, rebuilt 1713.

The Rev. Isaac-William-Webb Horllock present Vicar.

William Northey, Esq. M. P. Lord of the Manor.

GRITTLETON.

On Monuments in Chancel.

Here lyeth the Reverend Thomas Barker, M. A. late Fellow of Lincoln College, Oxon, and 30 years Rector of this Church. He died February 21, 1740, Aged 56 years.

Sacred to the Memory of the Reverend Thomas Pollock, LL. D. Rector of this Church 38 years. He died 29th September, 1801, Aged 65. Also Susanna, Relict of the Rev. Thomas Pollock, only daughter of Charles Palmer, Esq. of London. She died 11th November, 1802, Aged 58. This Monument is erected by their daughter, Mary Pollock.

On Flat Stones.

Here lyeth the Body of Margaret the Wife of Thomas Tattersal, Daughter of Mr. Nicholas Penwarne, Rector of St. Stephen's Church, in Bristol, who dyed Sept. 30, 1714.

Here lyeth the Body of Thomas Tattersal . . . . the Reverend Rector of this Church, who dyed April 12, 1719, whose good works celebrate his Memory.

Here lyeth interred the Body of Walter White. Esq. who departed this life the 2d day of January, 1678, in the 34 year of his age.

Here lieth the Body of Hester White, Wife of Walter White Esq. She was Mother to Lieut-Colonel White, who departed this life the 2d of December, 1644, Aged 50.

Here lyeth the Body of Lieutenant-Coll. Walter White, sometime Governor of Bristol Castle, for the Parliament of the Common Wealth of England, and was lord Ger . . . hlow, who departed this life the 3rd day of June, 1643, aged 26.

James, Son of the Rev. Thomas Barker, and Elizabeth his Wife, died the 14th of December, 1721, Aged 4 months. Also Betty, daughter of the Rev. Thomas Barker, and Elizabeth his Wife, died the 8th of Feb. 1736, Aged 8 years.

On Brass Plates.

In obitum maxime hij Gualteri White, generosiovi, obiit 15 Decembris, 1626, Ætatis suæ LIV.

Heu mihi quod Lachrymis congruit iste color.

He married Hester, daughter of Abraham Connam, by whom he had issue one Sonne and 4 Daughters.

White's breathless Corps which here interred doth lie,
Sad Lecture, Reader, of Manne's Mortallitye.

Arms—3 arrows in pale, impaling a chev. erm. bt. 3 signets.

Here also lyeth interred the Body of Rebecca, the Wife of Robert Wilshur, of this place, gent. She was Daughter of Nicholas Greene, of Winterborne Stoke, in this County, Esq. by Elizabeth, his Wife, Relict of Coll. Walter White. She departed this life the 14th day of April, Anno Domini 1725, Ætatis suæ 66.

Here also lyeth the Body of Rebecca Wilshure, daughter of the above Robert Wilshure, gent. who departed this life Feb. 11, 1769, Aged 76.

Here also lieth interred the Body of Walter Wilshure, gent. who departed this life the 24th of November, 1766, Aged 70.

Here lyeth the Body of Jane, second Wife of Walter Brokenbrow, of this Parish, yeoman, who died the 12th of May, 1751, Aged 46 years.

Beneath this Stone lyeth the Body of Elizabeth, the Wife of Walter Brokenbrow, of this Parish, who departed this life the 26th day of September, 1737, Aged 30 years.

On S. wall of Body.

Here lyeth the Body of Isaac Bristow, who deceased Nov. 1, 1650.

On a Brass Plate against E. end of Nave.

In obitum Gulielmi Gore, armigeri, qui
Evivis expiravit vicesimo die Aprilis,
Anno Salutis 1647.
Gaudelo juvenis pravum dum rideat ævum
Judicis adventum mente revolue tamen,
Quamuis fata trahunt finem dum spiritus adsit
Respice sic munus vita perennis erit.
Eccles. xi. 9.

Mors sola fatetur, quantula sint hominum corpuscula.

Arms—A chev. bt. 3 bulls heads cabossed.

On Brass Plates in Nave.

Ann, ye Daughter of Robert Wilshur and Rebecca his Wife, died July 30, 1742, in the 43d year of her Age, and is here interred.

Mary, the Daughter of Mr. Robert Wilshur, and Rebecca, his Wife, departed this Life in London, on the 16th day of July, 1709, in the 22d year of her age, and is here interred. Here is also interred the Body of Priscilla, the Wife of Mr. John Bennett, of the City of Bristol, and daughter of Mr. Robert and Mrs. Rebecca Wilshur, who departed this life the 12th day of March, Anno Dom. 1732, Ætatis suæ 42.

Beneath this Stone lyeth the Body of Ann, the Wife of Walter Wilshur, of this Parish, gent. who departed this life Nov. 5, 1742, Aged 43 years.

Near this place lyeth the Body of Walter, Son of Walter and Ann Wilshur, who died in his infancy.

In Memory of William Brokenbrow, who died July the 26, 1771, aged 35 years. Also of Ann, his Wife, who departed this life Feb. 14, 1799, Aged 65 years.

On a Mon. in N. Aisle.

In Memory of Nicholas Brokenbrow, who died Sept. 14, 1777, Aged 51 years. Also Frances, Wife of Nicholas Brokenbrow, who died July 22, 1788, Aged 49 years.

On Flat Stones in N. Aisle.

Here lies the Body of Nathaniel Houlton, Esq. late of Seagry, third Son of Joseph Houlton, Esq. of this Place, who for upwards of twenty years was a worthy and useful Magistrate, as one of his Majesty's Justices of the Peace for this County. He married Mary, Daughter of Francis Newton, Esq. of Taunton, in the County of Somerset, and died the 2d of May, 1754, in the Sixty-first year of his age, without issue.

Arms—Quarterly, 1 & 4. on a fess. wavy, 3 roundels between as many talbots heads erased, a mullet pierced for diff. 2 & 3. an annulet within a bord. of estoils. of 8 points, a canton charged with a li. ramp. impaling, on a chev. 3 garbs.

Here lies the Body of John Houlton, Esq. second Son of Joseph Houlton of this Place, Esq. who died the 23d of April, 1767, in the 76th year of his age.

Here also lies the Body of Joseph Houlton, eldest son of the above John Houlton, who died the 27th of November, 1765, in the 45th year of his age.

Mary, Wife of Joseph Houlton, died October the 21, 1796, Aged 74.

Josephus Houlton, armiger, Obiit decimo die Aprilis, Anno Domini 1731, Ætatis suæ 68.

Robert Houlton, Esq. fourth Son of the above Joseph Houlton, and Lord of this Manor, died the 10th of September, 1771, in the 68th year of his age.

John Houlton, Esq. Rear-Admiral of the Blue, 7th Son of John Heulton, Esq. of Bristol. He died the 26th of January, 1791, aged 62, having served in the Royal Navy with great credit for the space of sixty years, and both in his publick and private capacities was respected and beloved by all who knew him.

Arms—On a fess wavy, 3 roundels bt. 3 talbots heads erased, impaling perpale fess. in chief, 3 bucks tripping in base, an annulet within a border of estoils.

Joseph, son of Joseph and Anna Houlton, of Farleigh Castle, died April 15, 1725, Aged 7 years.

Elizabeth died in March 1731, aged 2 months. Another Son died in November, 1735, soon after his birth.

Arms—A fess between 6 fleur-de-lis addition to talbots.

Underneath lie the Remains of Joseph Houlton, of Farleigh Castle, in the County of Somerset, Esq. Lord of this Manor, who died July 8, 1750, Aged 62 years. And of Anna his Wife, sole Daughter and Heir of Abraham Hook, of Bristol, Esq. descended from an ancient family of that name in the County of Glou. who died October 24, 1754, Aged 59.

His happy temper, and amiable disposition in domestic and private life, his lenity, with the strictest uprightness, in the public administration of Justice, made his death very generally and deservedly lamented. In her a real principle of religion, with a true sense of the conjugal and parental duties, perfected the character of an affectionate Wife and tender Mother. Happy in each other, they were enabled to bear the loss of four children, Anna, interred under this Stone, who died unmarried, Nov. 18, 1735, in the 20th year of her age, the other Three, under that on the left hand. Mary, the only child who survived them, died without issue, Sept. 14, 1762, the much-loved Wife of James Frampton, of Moreton, in the County of Dorset, Esq. who laid and inscribed this Stone to their Memory, in testimony of his affectionate esteem and gratitude.

On a Brass Plate.

Robert Houlton, Esq. Lord of this Manor, who died 10th September, 1771, gave by his last Will one Annuity, or clear yearly Rent-charge of Twenty Shillings payable out of his Estate at Clapcote commonly called or known by the name of Lofts, otherwise Scropes, in this Parish, to the Minister, Churchwardens, and Lord of the Manor for the time being, to be by them from time to time, as occasion shall require, laid out in repairing and keeping repaired this Aisle belonging to the Houlton family.

Here lyeth the Body of Sarah White, who died the 27th of March, 1763, Aged 87.

In testimony of whose diligence and faithful service, through a series of 40 years in his family, this Stone was laid by Robert Houlton, Esq.

The Church consists of Chancel, Nave, and N. Aisle.

The Rev. William Bourne, present Vicar.—Robert Houlton, Esq. Lord of the Manor.

LEIGH DELAMERE.

On Monuments in Chancel.

Near this Place lyeth the Body of Henry Liles, who departed this life the 10th day of May, A. D. 1701, Aged 75 years.

Here lyeth Mr. Robert Latymer, some time Rector and Pastor of this Church, who deceased this life the second day of November Anº Dom̄ 1634.

Against North Wall of Nave.

In Memory of Sarah, Wife of Richard Browning, and Daughter of Thomas and Mary Ritchings, who died March the 11th, 1768, Aged 26. Also Mary, their Daughter, died March 17, 1766, Aged 7 months.

To the Memory of John Browning, eldest Son of John and Alice Browning, of this Parish, who died March the 20th, 1751, Aged 35 years.

Farewell my Wife and Children Dear,
The time will come then you'll be here:
Serve ye the Lord, and in him trust,
Then happy will you be, and blest.

Also James, son of John and Mary Browning, who died Jan. 22, 1787, Aged 3 years and 8 months.

Near this Place lieth ye Body of James Browning, yeoman, who departed this life ye 16th day of July, Anno Domini 1706, Æt. 62.

Also near lyeth the Body of Elizabeth, ye Wife of James Browning, who departed this life October 12, 1734, Aged 83 years.

Near this Place lyeth ye Body of Alice, Wife of John Browning, who departed this life May 22, 1763, Aged 72 years.

Also near this Place lieth the Body of John Browning, who departed this life, April 7, 1764, Aged 81 years.

Death in a very good old age
Ended our weary pilgrim stage;
It was to we an end of pain,
In hopes to enter life again.

And also near this Place lieth the Body of Sarah, Daughter of Richard and Sarah Browning, who departed this life May 2, 1764, Aged 15 weeks.

In Memory of James Browning, yeoman, who died February 24, 1781, Aged 67 years.

Also of Betty, his Wife, who died January 25, 1760, Aged 32 years.

Also of Catharine, his late Wife, who died Dec. 26, 1790, Aged 57 years.

Near this Place lieth the Remains of Sarah and Betty, Daughters of James and Betty Browning. Sarah died April 7, 1766, Aged 17 years, Betty died February 16, 1767, Aged 19 years.

Sacred to the Memory of George Browning, who died August 26, 1808, Aged 48 years.

On Monuments in S. aisle.

Near this Place lieth interred the Body of Mary Scott, spinster, who died September 12, 1775, Aged 72 years.

In Memory of Sarah Greenway, who died May 25, 1789, Aged 71 years.

Sacred to the Memory of Eleanor, Wife of James Browning, who died September 18, 1805, Aged 51 years. Also of James Browning, who died March 11, 1812, Aged 60 years.

On Flat Stones.

In Memory of Thomas Son of John and Alice Browning. He departed this life February 16, 1751, Aged 25 years.

Stande, looke downe, and behold the Stone under which was laide the Body of Elizabeth, eldest daughter of Secole Chiver, Esquier, Lord of this Mannour, the miracle of her age, for Reason, Language, and Religion, who deceased August 10, 1653, mense Ætatis suæ 33.

Here Lyeth the Body of Henry Chivers, late of Quemerford, in this County, Esq. who dyed the 30th day of April, Anno Domini 1720, Ætat. suæ 67.

Also here lyeth the Body of Bridged, the Wife of Henry Chivers, who died October 11, 1724, Aged 71 years.

Arms—Quarterly, 1 & 4, on a chev. engrailed, a crescent 2 & 3, a li. rampant, impaling on a fess. 2 mullets between 3 martlets volant.

Hatchment.

Quarterly, 1 & 4. p. fess. S. & A. a pale engrailed counterchanged, on each piece of the first, a trefoil slip. of the second, 2 & 3. p. fess. perpale, on a chief A. a chev. engrailed S. in base perpale S. & G. a li. ramp. A. over all an escut. az. charged with a fess. between 3 chess rooks O.

The same impaling az. within a bord. engrailed 3 lozenges in bend O.

Over the south entrance is a small statue, supposed to be St. Margaret, the tutelar Saint of this Church.

CASTLE COMBE.

On Monuments in Chancel.

Antecessoribus suis, ex perve tusta Scropiorum,
Baronium de Bolton, in Agro Ebor
Prosapia Recto et continue masculo stemnate oriundis
Decem scilicet gradus a Ricardo le Scrope, Milite,
Barone de Bolton,
Et regnante Ricardo Secundo Angliæ summo
Cancellario, huc usque numerantur
Quorum fere omnium
Per plures annorum centurias proxime elapsus,
Infra hujus Ecclesiæ Cancellos depositi sunt,
Cineres nullo hactenus marmore insigniti
Præsertim vero.
Avo plurimum colendo Johanni Scrope, arm̃
Parentibus admondum venerandis Ric̃ et Francisca,
Patrueli erga se suosque beneficentissimo
Georges Scrope, Armigero, et Mariæ uxori ejus,
Fratribus Johanni, Gulielmo, et Caroli,
Quorum primus ille et natu maximus S. T. Professor
Ecclesiæ de Kington Sancti Michaelis Vicarius,
Hujus Rector tandem et Patronus evasit
Vir bonus integer eruditus,
Pastor fidelis prudens indefessus
Ad perfectam sacro sanctæ Religionis Normam,
In quantum quidem mortalitati conceditur,
Voce Scriptis exemplo conformatus,
Sororibus Elizabethæ et Rachel,
Filiolo denique carissimo Johanni
Optimæ spei puero vix dum decenni
Hisce omnibus pietatis sua ac observantiæ
Hoc qualecunque Monumentum posuit
Ricardus Scrope, S. T. P. hujus Ecclesiæ Rector
et Patronus, A. D. 1778.

Arms—1 & 4, az. a bend O. 2d. A. a saltire engrai'ed G. 3d. A. a fess. cotised G.

On Flat Stones.

Here lyeth the Body of Susanna, the Wife of John Davis, of Walington, in the County of Norfolk, Esq. who died May 5, 1750.

Arms—Quarterly, 1 & 4. a griffin segrant, 2 & 3, barry of 5, in chief a crown, over all a escut. quarterly, 1 & 4. a eagle disp. 2 & 3.

Reverend Henry Southouse died July the 9th, 1811, Aged 39 years.

On Flat Stones in Nave.

Beneath this Stone lies interred the Body of Elias, the Son of William and Elizabeth Taylor, of this Parish, who departed this life the 25th of December, 1752, Aged 22 years.

Near this Stone lies interred the Bodies of Ogborne and William, Sons of William and Elizabeth Taylor. Ogborne died March 27, 1729, Aged 14 years, William died the 1st of May, 1729, Aged 1 year.

In Memory of Mary, daughter of William and Susanna Griffing, gent. who died November the 8th, 1739, Aged 21 years.

Here lyeth the Body of Mary, the Daughter of Nicholas and Rachel Pearse, who died the 1st day of November, 1741, Aged 25.

Here lie the Remains of Mr. Walter Fisher, and Mary his Wife. Also of Walter, John, Richard, and William, their sons.

Here lyeth the Body of Mary, the Wife of John Fisher, Clothier, of this Parish, who departed this life the 3d day of September, 1726, Aged 28 years and 6 months.

Here lieth the Body of John Fisher of this Parish, Clothier, who died April the 12th, in the year of our Lord 1743, Aged 48 years.

Here lyeth the Body of Mary, the daughter of John Fisher, of this Parish, Clothier, and Mary, his Wife, who departed this life the 8th of February, 1736, Aged 17 years.

Here lieth the Body of William Taylor, who died April the 20th, 1756, Aged 39 years. Also Hannah daughter of William and Ann Taylor, died June the 7, 1766, Aged 16 years. Also Ann, Wife of William Taylor, died May the 7th, 1786, Aged 78 years.

Here lies the Remains of John Willis, jun. who died September 1729, Aged 43 years.

Also in Memory of Margaret, Wife of Charles Maude. She died October 27, 1770, aged 89.

Against S. aisle.

Near this Place lies interred the Body of Aylife White, gent. who departed this life Feb. 9, 1757, in the 53rd year of his age.
Also the Remains of Hannah, his Wife, who died the 5th day of January, 1759, in the 42d year of her age.

Near this Place lieth the Body of Nancy, Wife of Francis Taylor, late currier of Bristol, and Sister to Henry Hillman, Esq. of Dinton. She died January 22, 1786, Aged 52 years.

Near this Place lyeth the Body of Mary, the Wife of Francis White, clothier, who departed this life the 22d day of May, in the year of our Lord 1734, and in the 74th year of her age. Also near this place lyeth the Body of Francis White, of this Parish, clothier, who departed this life the 21st day of November, 1736, Aged 76 years.

Near unto this Place lyeth interred the Body of Tobias Seed, of the Parish of Bitton, Gent. who, after he had lived to the Age of 77 years, departed this life the 12th day of July, 1704.

In Memory of Mr. John Lewis, of Long Dane, in this Parish, who died Sept. 1st, 1780, Aged 66.

Near this Place lyeth interred the Body of Richard Beven, sen. Yeoman, who departed this life in Castle-Combe the 5th of October, 1697, Aged 58 years.

Also Richard Beven, jun. departed this life the 7th day of January, 1768, Aged 20 years and 9 months.

Near this Place are deposited the Bodies of Mr. Walter Fisher, Clothier, and Mary his Wife, who left behind them six sons and four daughters, all decently educated and formed for the World by their industrious care and tenderness.

To the Memory of these valuable and respected Parents, Price Fisher, Esq. their youngest Son, Member in the last Parliament for Malmesbury, in this Neighbourhood, and in the present for Boroughbridge, in Yorkshire, hath caused this Monument to be erected, A. D. 1764. Walter, John, Richard, and William, sons of the said Walter and Mary Fisher, are here also interred.

Under the corner-seat before this stone is interred the Body of Daniel Nichols, of this Parish, Clothier, who departed the 31st of January, 1718, Aged 39 years.

Remedium unicum Jesus Christus.

Christ is the only Salve for everi sore,
Learne him aright, ye neade to learne no more.

Ricardus Gillus, Obiit nono die Januarij, 1588.

On Flat Stones.

Here lyeth the Body of Walter Fisher, of Blackwell, Hall, London, Factor, who departed this life the 8th day of May, 1736, Aged 47 years.

On Mon. in N. Aisle.

In Memory of Thomas Child, gent. who died July 4th, 1773, Aged 72 years. Mary his Wife died August 31, 1769, Aged 72 years.

Near to this Place lyeth the Body of Mary, the Wife of Francis Childe, Clothier, who departed this life the 21st day of August, 1703, Aged 31 years and 8 months.

Near to this Place lyeth the Body of Francis Childe, Clothier, who departed this life the 9th day of January, 1701, Ætat. suæ 36.

On Flat Stones in N. Aisle.

Here lies buried the Body of George Scrope, Esq. who departed this life December the 27th, 1744, Aged 44 years. And also the Body of Mary Scrope, his Wife who departed this life July the 13, 1774, Aged 74 years.

Arms—Az. a bend O. impaling S. 3 escut. O. charged with as many eagles disp. S. Crest, 7 ostrich feathers, az. issuing out of a ducal coronet.

In Memory of Edward Taylor, who died June 16, 1776, Aged 44 years. Also of Rebekah, his Wife, who died March 20, 1780, Aged 67 years.

In Memory of Elizabeth, daughter of Edward and Rebekah Taylor, who died Feb. 5, 1770, Aged 47 years.

A Benefaction.

Mr. WALTER PARRY, by his Will, dated the 18th day of March, 1730, (which is proved in Doctors Commons) gave to the use of the Poor of Castle Combe the sum of £100, the Interest whereof to pay the teaching of Ten Poor Children to read the Scriptures as soon as they are capable to learn, and continue till seven years old, and no longer.

The above Legacy, with £20 due for interest, was paid by Mr. Parry's Executors, to George Scrope, Esq. Lord of this Manor, who by deed dated the 25th and 26th days of March, 1741, conveyed to nine Trustees, closes or pieces of Land, containing together about 22 acres, all situate in this Parish, then known by the following names, viz. The Lower Tyning of the Down, the Tyning of the Downe, next the Lye and the Hill Side of the Ground next to the Lye, for securing payment of the yearly Sum of £5 to be used according to the intent of the said Will, the same being then reckoned to be a full satisfaction of interest money for the £120.

ELVER NEWMAN, } *Churchw.*
WM. BEALE, } 1817.

In the North Aisle is a Knight Templar, in armour, with his feet resting upon a lion. Under him are six small statues, but much mutilated.

At the east end of the Nave, is a Painted Arch ornamented with carved figures in stone.

Hatchments in Chancel.

Az. a bend O. impaling S. 3 escut. charged with as many eagles displayed S.

1. Quarterly, 1 & 4. az. a bend O.
2. A. a saltire engrailed G.
3. A. a fess cotised G. impaling az. a cross O.

The same as before quarters impaling A. a chev. S.

1. Az. a bend O.
2. O. 3 bulls heads cabossed S.
3. A. a cross crosslet G. over all a bend S.
4. A. a saltire engrailed G.
5. A. a bend cotised G.
6. A. a whirlpool az.
7. Checkey O. and az. a chev. G.
8. A. on a chief G. 3 bezants.
9. O. on 5 fusils conjoined in fess G. as many bezants.
10. G. a li. rampant erm.
11. A. a chev. S. between 3 billets ermines.
12. As first.

1. Az. a bend G.
2. A. a saltire engrailed G.
3. A. a fess. cotised G.
4. A. a whirlpool az.
5. Checkey O. & az. a chev. G.
6. A. on a chief G. 3 bezants.
7. O. on 5 fusils conjoined in fess. G. as many bezants.
8. G. a lion rampant erm.
9. A. a chev. S. between 3 billets erm.
10. As first.

1. Az. a bend O.
2. A saltire engrailed G.
3. A. a fess cotised G.
4. A. a whirlpool az.
5. Checkey O. & az. a chev. G.
6. A. on a chief. G. 3 bezants.
7. O. on 5 fusils conjoined in fess as many bezants.
8. G. a lion ramp. erm.
9. A chev. S. between 3 billets erm.
10. As first.

William Scrope Esq. Lord of the Manor.

The Reverend Thomas Hooper present Rector.

WEST KINGTON.

On Monuments against North Wall.

Memoriæ sacrum Jacobi Johannis Hume, Œdis Christi in Academiâ Oxoniensi, alumni olim, et hujusce Ecclesiæ nuperrime Rectoris, qui cum in successorum non minus quam sui ipsius usum Ædes omnes Rectori hujus Ecclesiæ proprias, subtibus suis Vetustate pene collapsas jam instauraverat, morte extinctus est.

Mærens vidua
Alias quidem virtutes,
Mariti amantissimi silentio desiderans,
Hoc saltem munificentiæ ejus documentum
Commemorari voluit,
Natus Oct. 12, 1776, obiit Oct. 30, 1816.

Natorum memoriæ quoque sacrum Jacobi Johannis Hume.

Henriettæ Franciscæ, quæ obiit 5° Februarii, 1814, infans.

Ricardo Jacobi, qui obiit Maiæ, 1815, natus annos quatuordecim.

Jacobi Johannes item, qui obiit 30mo Nov. 1817, natus octo mensis.

On Flat Stones.

Here lyeth the Body of John Curtis, yeoman, who departed this life the 14th day of October, 1721, Aged 23 years.

Here lyes a Branch just fully grown,
Then in came Death, and cut it down,
'Twas fresh and green in the morning sun,
Dry'd up and withered ere the day was gone.

Here lyeth ye Body of Jane, ye Wife of the Reverend Robert Davenant, D. D. late Rector of this Parish, who died ye 7th of August, Anno Domini 1681, Æt. suæ 59.

And also the Body of Mrs. Jane Halle, widow of of the Rev. Mr. Thomas Halle, late Rector of Chilton, deceased. She died Sept. 27, An° Dom̃ 1731, Ætatis 78.

Here lie the Remains of Louisa, daughter of the Rev. J. J. Hume and Lydia his Wife. She died the 24th day of March, in the year of our Lord 1810, Aged fourteen weeks.

Here lieth the Body of James, son of Robert Davenant, D. D, and Jane his Wife, who deceased the 4th day of June, 1674.

On Monuments in South Transept.

Near this Place lyeth the Body of Richard Terrill, of this Parish, gent. who died March 10, 1766, in the 35th year of his age. Also Betty, daughter of Richard and Sarah Terrill, who died Sept. 16, 1760, Aged 16 years.

Near unto this place Resteth the Body of Richard Terrill, who departed the 22d day of August, Anno Domini 1670. Also near this Place lyeth the Body of Ciscilica, the Wife of Richard Terrill, who died May the 5th, An° Dom̃ 1721, Ætatis suæ 99.

Also the Body of Mary, the Wife of John Terrill, who departed the 28th day of October Anno Domini 1687.

Near this place lyeth the Body of Ann, the daughter of Richard Terrill, gent. and of Ann his Wife, who died the 26th day of November, 1740, Aged 20.

On Flat Stones in S. transept.

Here lieth the Body of John Terrill, gent. who departed this life April the 18th, 1726, Aged 62.

Here lie the Bodies of John and Ann, son and daughter of Richard and Sarah Terrill, of this Parish. John died May the 4th, 1764, Aged 2 years and 7 months. Ann died August the 17th, 1759, in the 4th year of her age.

Here lyeth the Body of John Terrill, gent. who departed this life the 1st day of June, 1692.

Under this Stone lieth the Bodies of Ann and Alice, the Wife and Daughter of Richard Terrill, gent. Ann his Wife died February the 8th, 1721, Ætatis suæ 30. Alice their daughter died Dec. 16, A. D. 1717, Aged 9 hours.

Sacred to the Memory of Frances, Widow of the late Walter Post, and grand-daughter of the Rev. Dr. Burnett, who departed this life the 30th of May, 1811, Aged 83.

In the Pew below lies the Body of the Rev. Thomas Burnett, D. D late Rector of this Parish, and Prebendary of Sarum, who died May 29, 1750, Aged 80.

Also the Body of Elizabeth his Wife, daughter of Philip Bathurst, Esq. who died Feb. 27, 1747, Aged 78 years.

Oh mi dear children, marke what I say,
Our Mother's Bonns truli are wrapt here in clay,
Her Soule, no doubte, to Heaven is gone thither,
Where we most joyfulli shall meet altogether.
The Lord be your guid, the Lord be your strength,
And give you his speciall grace to die in him at length.
You, gentle Readers, remember your end,
Be tru unto such whom faythful you find,
Lett this be example, and tell it abroode,
How faithfulli this Woman died in the Lord.

[*Over the above Inscription is the statue of a woman and six children.*]

There is still remaining, in good preservation, the antient oak Pulpit, handsomely carved in the Gothic style, in which Bishop Latimer preached, *temp.* Hen. VIII.

Register commenced 1538.

Sir Bethell Codrington present Lord of the Manor.

The Reverend Edward Ravenshaw Rector.

NETTLETON.

Mon. in Chancel against North Wall.

Under the East Window without, lyeth the Body of Elizabeth Arnold, late Wife of Samuel Arnold. And near the said Window within, lie the Bodies of three Infants, children of the said Samuel and Elizabeth

Arms—G. 3 broad arrows, impaling per fess, quarterly 1 & 4 perpale, indented A. & S. 2 & 3 A. a fleur-de-lis O, in base G. a fess checkey O. and az. between 8 billets A.

Near this Place lies interred the Body of the Rev. Mr. Samuel Arnold, near 40 years Rector of this Parish, whose truly Christian piety and humility, extensive learning, and unbounded charity. are still exemplary, to those amongst whom they were constantly exercised, and will receive an ample distinction and recompense at the resurrection of the just.

In Memory of the Rev. Daniel Elliott Mills, thirty-three years Rector of this Parish, who departed this life the 18th of July, 1786, aged 69 years.

Also of Mary Mills, wife of the said Daniel Elliott Mills, who departed this life the 7th of Dec. 1777, Aged 62 years.

S. Wall of Chancel.

Beneath this place lyeth interred the Body of Catharine, the Wife of John Nickolls, of this Parish, and Daughter of John Price, late of Chepstow, in the County of Monmouth, who departed this life the 24th day of April, 1714, Aged 62.

Arms—S. a chev. A,

In Memory of Anna-Maria Denison, eldest daughter of the late Rev. William Denison, D. D. Principal of Magdalen Hall, Oxford, and Rector of Chalton and Clanfield, Hants. She died Oct. 28, 1798, Aged 37 years.

Also in Memory of Frances Denison, sister of the above, who died May 13, 1809, Aged 44 years.

On Flat Stones.

Here lyeth the Body of Mr. John Nicholls, of this Parish, who died Oct. y^o^ 31st, A. D. 1727, Aged 73.

Beneath this Stone lyeth the Body of Joyce, Wife of William Fabian, of this Parish.

Here lyeth the Body of Mrs. Barbary Fabian, the daughter of Sir William St. John, Knight, late Wife of John Fabian, gent. and mother of ten Children, who departed this life the 27th day of May, in the year 1686, Aged 67 years.

Here lyeth the Body of Mr. Joseph Rickards, late Rector of this Parish, who departed this life the 24th day of September, 1714, Aged 66 years.

Here lieth the Body of Mrs. Mary Nickols, widow of Mr. John Nickols, and Relict of the Reverend Mr. Joseph Rickards. She departed this life Sept. ye 27, A. D. 1729, Aged 71 years.

On a Brass Plate against E. end of Nave.

Here lyeth the Body of Philip Davis, of this Parish, Yeoman, who departed this life July 14, An^o^ Dom̃ 1675, Ætatis suæ 80.

Also, here lyeth the Body of Mary, Wife of Philip Davis, who departed this life the 4th of September, 1694, in the 28th year of her age.

Here lyeth the Body of Mary, daughter of Robert and Elizabeth Tylie, of Marshfield, and Wife of John Long, of this Parish, yeoman, who departed the 25th of October, Anno Dom̃ 1686, Ætatis suæ 36,

Against S. aisle.

Near this Place lie interred the Bodies of Joseph and Elizabeth, Son and Daughter of Joseph Gilmore, and of Elizabeth his Wife. Joseph died April 16, 1756, Aged 35 years. Elizabeth died April 29, 1753, Aged 36 years.

Also Elizabeth, Wife of the above-said Joseph Gilmore, sen. She died September 19, 1768, Aged 83 years,

---

Near this Place lyeth the Body of St. John Fabin, gent. who died June the 4th, 1731, Aged 51 years.

Also the Bodie of Elizabeth, Wife of the above-said St. John Fabin, and John his Son by her, who both died the 16th of Nov. 1715, the former aged 25, the latter 6 months.

Beneath this Place lyeth the Body of Elizabeth, late Wife of St. John Fabin, of this Parish, gent. who deceased August ye 4th, Anno Dom. 1691, Aged 42. Also the Body of Annette, second wife of the aforesaid Sir John Fabin, who deceased Nov. 29, Anno Dom. 1713, Aged 67. Also the Body of Love Gilmore, grandson of the said St. John Fabin, who dyed September the 12, Anno 1714, Aged 5 days. Likewise the Body of the above-said St. John Fabin, gent. who died November the 2d, 1729, Aged 85.

Arms—Erm. within a bord. engrailed G. 3 fleur-de lis, S.

Andrew Carrick, Esq. Lord of the Manor.

Henry-Frederick Bythesea, Rector.

LITTLETON DREW

South Wall of Chancel.

In Memory of William Latcham, Gent. who departed this Life the 26th day of Feb. 1796, Aged 84 years. Also of Elizabeth Latcham, his daughter, who departed this life the 20th of August, 1791, Aged 45 years.

This Tablet is erected by their affectionate relative Susannah Beake.

On Flat Stones in Body.

John Chapman, 1632, Margaret Chapman 1655.

Beneath this Stone lyeth the Body of John, the son of John Chapman, yeoman, and of Jane his Wife, who departed this life August 23, 1741, Aged 33.

Beneath this Stone lyeth the Body of Jane, the Wife of John Chapman, yeoman, who departed this life the 7th day of February, 1734, Aged 90 years.

Beneath this stone lyeth the Body of John Chapman, yeoman, who departed this life the 10th day of April, 1741, Aged 49 years.

A little painted glass in Chancel Window. On the south side of the Nave, under a small canopy, is a stone statue, much broken.

Register Commenced March 25, 1706.

The Rev. George Page late Rector.—The Rev. John Colmer present Rector.

Duke of Beaufort Lord of the Manor.

ALDRINGTON.

On a Monument in Chancel.

Here under resteth the Body of Charles Gore, Sonne and Heire of Charles Gore, Esq. who cheerfully surrendred His Soule into the Handes of his Redeemer, September 3, An° Dom. 1628, Ætatis suæ 16.

Arms—O. 3 bulls heads cab. S. a crescent S. for dif.

On a Brass Plate.

Psal. cxvi. v. 15. Precious in the sight of the Lord is the death of his Saints.

Here lie the Bodies of Charles Gore, Aged 6 years and 18 weeks, Edward Gore, aged 9 weeks, Mary Gore, aged 1 year and 14 weeks, Anna Gore, aged 12 weeks, and Elizabeth Gore, aged 4 years and one month, all children of Charles Gore, of Aldrington, Esq. and Lydia his Wife, expecting the second coming of Christ. Malachi iii. 17. They shall be mine, saith the Lord of Hosts, in that day when I make up my jewells.

Jewells of price this place contains,
As a choice cabinet, the Remaines
Of those sweet soules, all of a race,
Which now in Heaven have their place.

Parens uterq. mærens posuit, Anno Domini 1641.

M. S.

Thomæ Gore, de Aldrington, Arm̃
Cujus exumæ hic juxta sitæ
Honoris ergo posuit, filius et hæres.
ejusdem nominis,
Obiit Martii 31, Anno Salutis 1684, Ætat. suæ 51.

Virtutem exemplar cultor pietatis alumnus
Castali dum patrii fama decusq. laris
Succubuit sævis infirmo corpore fatis,
De quibus exceisa mente trophæa tulit
Plenaq. priscorum monumenta reliquit honorum
Uno cum fatis intentura die
His fruimur grati Supernus, ille æthera victor,
Non ementiti pignus honoris habet
Nam cum Cœlicolis Cœlestis præco triumphans,
Æterno celebrat laudis honore Deum.

Arms—O. 3 bulls heads cabossed S. impaling A. a li. ramp. S. gorged with a crown O.

On Flat Stones.

Expectans Expectavi. Psal. xl.

With Jacob's Rachel, I (am James his wife)
Waited full long before our married life ;
In mee it was a matchless expectation,
More tedious farre till matches consummation,
Which once enjoyed, and scarce three years in all,
A lingering sickness ridd me out of thrall.
For this my change all myne appointed daies,
I waited still, and waiting gave God praise,
That had so fitted me for heaven, where
My soul now rests, as doth my body here.

Usque quo Domine, Apocal. vi. 10.
Veni Domine Jesu, Apoc. xxii. 20.

One of her sexes worthies here doth lie,
A wife, a pattern to posterity,
To her husband loyal, courteous unto all,
Pious to God, to the poore most liberall.

Also here lyeth the Body of Mrs. Mary Gore, sister of Charles Gore, Esq. Lord of this Manour, who departed this life the 20th day of Oct. Anno Dom. 1705, Aged 20 years.

Also here lyeth the Body of Charles Gore, Esq. late Lord of this Manour of Aldrington, who departed this life the 8th day of January, A. D. 1710, Ætat. 27.

Here lyeth the Body of Charles Gore, Esq. late Lord of this Manour, who departed this life the 11th day of November, An° Dñi 1649, Ætatis suæ 56.

Here lies the Body of Mary, Relict of Thomas Gore, of Aldrington, who died August the 10, 1718, Aged 78 years.

Arms—3 balls imp. a li. ramp.

Gualteri Gore, Armigeri, Mannerii hujus Domini,
Posuit dno, Maria Gore, avia ejus piissima,
Hoc Aldringtoniæ Gororum masculus hæres,
Ultimus peu tumulum marmore tectus habet
Quem quonian a lunis cœlesti grata Parenti,
Cura fuit terris noluit esse diu
Nempe vocat primo Deus, hinc quos diligit ævo,
Et sibi sede illis dat propriore fruit,
Ergo his ter septem quum nondum impleverat annos,
Ad superas rediit venerat unde domos.
Obiit 6 Nov. A. D. 1712.

Arms—3 bulls heads cabossed.

Here lyeth the Body of Lydia Gore, daughter of Charles, Gore, Esq. who dyed the 11th of September, 1643, Aged 1 year and 9 months.

An Epitaph upon Mrs. Elizabeth Gore, daughter of Charles Gore, of Aldrington, Esq. and Lydia his Wife, who departed this life Anno Domini 1641, ætat. suæ 4.

So rare a Piece for Bewty, Grace, and witt,
Though God had shew'd us, yet he thought not fitt
For us to gaze upon too long, 'twas Hee
That took her to Himself, Himself to see.
Admired shee was by all that did behold her,
Much more shall be when God anew shall mould her.

On Brass Plates.

Of yõ charitye pr̃y for the Soule of Thomas Gore, Esquyer, late Lord of this Toune, the whych decesyd the 25th day of july, An° Dñi 1635, on whos Soule jhu have mercy, am̃e.

[Under the above is an Altar Tomb, but no inscription, the Arms are—G. a chev. A. impaling G. a fess G.]

Here lyeth the Body of Mrs. Lydia Gore, ye Wife of Charles Gore, Esq. late Lord of this Manour of Aldrington, who departed this life the 3d day of January, Ano Dom 1651.

Reader, if thou hast a tear,
Do not grudge to drop it here,
Thinke not it can fall alone,
Flouds are due unto this stone.
Here lyes (ah! how that word does pierce,
And double blacks the mournful herse!)
Vertue's faire copy, Heaven's delight,
Not fit for mens, but angels sight,
In whose pure brest, sweet innocence
Exil'd by most found such defence,
Where no black thoughts, the sire of shame,
Charm'd by her vertue, magick game,
Lov'd by the Rich, the poor did blesse
Her as their souvereigne almonesse;
Wife, Mother, Friend, better no age
Ere should be upon the world's stage,
Then reader if thou hath a teare,
Canst thou grudge but drop it here?

Against S. aisle.

Near this Place is interred the Body of Charles Gore, Esq. Uncle of Thomas Gore, Esq. the present Lord of this Manour, who changed this mortal for an immortal life on the 21st day of February, Anno Æræ Christinæ 1692, Ætat. suæ 57.

Abiit, non Obiit.

Arms—O. 3 bulls heads caboshed S.

On a Brass Plate.

Here lieth the Body of Edward Gore, gent. second Son of Thomas Gore, late Lord of this Manor of Aldrington, Esq. who departed this life Sept. 22, A. D. 1686, Aged 16 years.

On Flat Stones.

Here lyeth the Body of William James, gent. who departed this life the 28th of March, 1637, expecting a joyful Resurrection.

Here lieth buried the Body of Mrs. Anna James, Wife of Mr. William James, gent. and Mother to Mrs. Lydia Gore, Wife of Charles Gore, of Aldrington, Esq. deceased the 20th day of December, 1636, Ætat. suæ 70.

Also here lyeth the Body of Joane, the Wife of Wm. French, who departed this life the 7th day of Feb. Ano Dom. 1777, Aged 76.

On Brass Plates in South Wall of South Aisle.

An Epitaph upon the Death of that goodly and grave Matron, Mrs. Ann James, Wife of Mr. William James, Gentleman, and Mother to Mrs. Lydia Gore, Wife of Charles Gore, of Aldrington, Esq. whose Body heare lieth interred in hopes of the Resurrection. Obiit 20th Dec. Anno Salutis 1636, Ætatis suæ 70.

Dear Saint of God, to whom in life most dear,
God's house, and messengers, and servants were,
The holy things of God, most precious all,
Precious with God her death and buriall.
Her soul enlaged and set at liberty
The 70th year of its captivity.
If evidence for Heaven be truth of grace,
Then sure in Heaven this Matron hath a place.
Let after ages say, when this is gone,
Blest be the Memory of such a one.

An Epitaph upon the Death of Mr. William James, Gentleman, whose Body here lieth interred in hopes of the Resurrection, Obiit 28 Martii, Ano Dom 1637, Aged 56.

Death parteth Soule and Body, man and wife,
So as to meet againe in better life
On better termes, meane while our bodies must
To their first nothing turne, at best but dust,
Till glorified, our soules doe alwaies sing
All glory to the Everlasting King.

Surviving friends in life, see you prepare
For life in heaven where no survivors are,
That when of this short life death ends ye story,
You sharers be with us of endless glory.

Prope jacent corpora, Gulielmi Hedges, armigeri, qui obiit 24 Junii, 1757, ætatis 68.

Et Elizabethæ, uxoris ejus, filiæ et heredis Thomæ Gore, armigeri, nuper hujus Manerii Domini, quæ obiit 13 Decembris, 1743, ætatis 51.

Ac etiam Thomæ Hedges, armigeri, filii eorum et heredis, qui obiit 8 Augusti, 1782, ætatis 60.

Elinor, uxor Jacobi Montagu, armigeri, parentibus optimis et fratri carissimo, non beneficiis, ergo licet amplis receptis, sed amoris causa.

H. M. P.

Juxta etiam jacet Elizabetha, ux. secunda Gulielmi Hedges, armigeri, quæ obiit 8 Aprilis, 1788.

Arms—Az. 3 swans necks eras. A. over all a escut. O. charged with 3 bulls heads caboshed.

On Flat Stones in S. Aisle.

Here lieth the Body of Mary Combes, who died Nov. the 15th, 1765, Aged 50 years.

Here lyeth the Body of Mary, late Wife of Daniel Holborrow, who departed this life the 22d day of July, An° Dom. 1697.

Also here lyeth the Body of Daniel Holborrow, who departed this life December the 30th, A. D. 1719, Aged 78.

Arthure Virer departed this life the fourth day of December, Anno Dom. 1672.

Also Daniel, ye Son of Daniel and Mary Holborow, departed this life the 7th day of June, A. D. 1712.

Here lie the Bodies of Charles Gale, yeoman, and Elizabeth his Wife. He dyed March 8, 1702, Aged 84 years. And She, Jan. 22, 1672.

Also here lyeth the Body of Jefery Gale, Son of Charles and Elizabeth Gale, who dyed August the 28, 1736, Aged 71.

Beneath this Stone lyeth the Body of William French, of this Parish, yeoman, who departed this life the 25th of April, 1744, Aged 79 years.

Also here lyeth the Body of Joan, ye Wife of William French, who departed this life the 7th of Feb. 1733, Aged 76 years.

Hatchment.

Quarterly 1 & 4. az. 3 swans necks A. 2 & 3 O. 3 bulls heads eras. S. impaling O. a unicorn pass. S. on a chief az. 3 g. A.

In the chancel window is some painted glass, and also in the window of south aisle is part of three figures, and above them 3 dice, in stained glass. At the north entrance is a Saxon moulding.

George Montagu, Esq. Lord of the Manor.

The Rev. John Turner Rector.

LUCKINGTON.

Mon. in Chancel against North Wall.

Here lieth the Body of Dionis-Rachel Fitzherbert, daughter of Henry Fitzherbert, Rector of this Place, and Dorothy, his Wife, who died May 5, 1785, Aged 79 years. Also of Mary Fitzherbert, Sister of the above, who died Feb. 13, 1792, Aged 86 years.

Arms—G. 3 li. ramp. O.

Sacred to the Memory of the Rev. John Woodroffe, M. A. Rector of this Parish 36 years, and of Wick Rissington, in the County of Gloucester, who departed this life the 20th of January, in the year of our Lord 1795, Aged 82.

Arms—G. a chev. between 3 cinquefoils A.

Near this Place lieth the Body of the Rev. Wm. Norris, M. A. Rector of this Parish thirty-eight years. He died Nov. 7, 1758, Aged 70.

Arms—Quarterly, 1 & 4 A. 2 & 3 G. a fret. O. a fess. az. impaling O. a cross, G.

S. Wall of Chancel.

Underneath lie the Remains of Lucy Woodroffe, Wife of the Rev. Mr. John Woodroffe, M. A. Rector of this Parish, Daughter of the Honble Godfrey Boate, Esq. one of the Justices of his Majesty's Court of King's Bench, in the Kingdom of Ireland, and Cary his Wife, daughter of Alexander Denton, Esq. of Hillsden, in the County of Bucks. She died March 11, 1776, Aged 66.

On Flat Stones.

Here lieth the Body of Christian, daughter of Charles Gale, who dyed the 31st of May, 1641.

William, the Son of Nicholas Waddington, Rector, was buried the 1st of July, Anno 1643, Anno ætatis suæ 8.

Martin Waddington, M^ter^ of Arts, and Minister of Alderington, was buried the 23d of November, Anno 1642, anno ætatis suæ 31.

Here lieth the Body of Wm. Hieron, Rector of this Church, who departed this life the 22d day of December, Anno Dom. 1676.

Here lieth the Body of Sarah, Wife of William Jones, who died March 8, 1793, Aged 37. Ann, their daughter, died May 21, 1791, Aged 8 months.

Hic jacet corpus Johannis Newman, Rector, qui mortem obiit decimo die Feb. 1674, Æt. suæ 67.

Mary Scott, the daughter of Roger Scott of the Devises, who departed this life the 20th day of April, 1719, æt. 84.

In Memory of John Newman, who died the 22d of Oct. 1746, Aged 77 years.

West End of Nave.

Near this Monument are deposited the Remains of John Harford, Son of Mr. Charles Harford, of Bath, and Elizabeth his Wife, who died the 23d day of June, 1769, Aged 18 years.

Near this Place is interred the Remains of Katherine Fitzherbert, widow of Fownes Fitzherbert, Esq. who departed this life the 23d of March, 1798, Aged 88 years.

Arms—Bendy of 5 A. & S. a canton G. charged with a bend O.

On Flat Stones in Nave.

Beneath this Stone lyeth the Body of Katherine Dorothy, Jones, spinster, one of the daughters of John Jones, late of this Parish, and Elizabeth his Wife, who departed this life the 13th day of March, 1805, Aged 46 years.

In Memory of Elizabeth, Wife of John Jones (and Neice of the Miss Fitzherberts) who died Feb. 4, 1786, Aged 63. Also of John Jones, husband of the above-named Elizabeth, who departed this life the 17th day of December, 1795, Aged 76 years.

Here lieth the Body of Fownes Fitzherbert Huntley, Esq. who died July 26, 1774, Aged 49 years.

Also Mary his Wife died Dec. 18, 1775, Aged 30 years.

On Monuments in S. aisle.

To the Memory of Dorothy Fitzherbert, daughter of Henry Fitzherbert, Rector of this Place, by Dorothy, his Wife, who died Dec. 19, 1780, Aged 80.

From her charity, pain, and great suffering here, she is doubtless received with the heavenly blessed.

Arms—G. 3 li. ramp. O.

Near this place resteth the Body of Ann Fitzherbert, Daughter of Henry and Dorothy Fitzherbert, Rector of this Place, who departed this life the 3d of April, 1779, Aged 80.

Tired with pain and weakness, she wished this blessed change.

[Arms as before.]

Near this Place lie the Remains of Mary, widow of John Tyndall, Esq. of Bathford, Somersetshire, Daughter of John Fitzherbert, Esq. and Ann his Wife, who died June 4, 1736, Aged 88.

Also of Frances Fitzherbert, daughter of Henry Fitzbert, Rector of this Place, and Dorothy his Wife, who died Jan. 30, 1771, Aged 69.

She suffered a long illness with great resignation and fortitude.

[Arms as before.]

On Flat Stones.

Ann the Daughter of John Fitzherbert, Esquire, and of Ann his Wife, was buried Nov. 13, 1685. Katherine, wife of Hum. Fitzherbert, Esq. dyed 18 Aug. 1734, Aged 63.

Here resteth the Body of Ann, the Wife of John Fiizherbert, Esq. who was buried April the 2, 1682.

Also Humphrey Fitzherbert, Esq. her son, who died July the 25th, 1727, Aged 75 years.

Here resteth the mortal part of Joseph Holborrow, of this Parish, who departed this life the 30th day of Nov. 1741, aged 71.

Here also resteth the Body of Martha, the Wife of the above Joseph Holborrow, who departed this life the 26th day of December, A. D. 1746, in the 76th year of her age.

Here lyeth the Body of Fownes Fitzherbert, Esq. Son of Humphry Fitzherbert, Esq. by Katharine, his Wife, who departed this life the 21st of February, 1756, Aged 62.

Here also lyeth the Body of Humphry Fitzherbert, Esq. Son of Humphry Fitzherbert, Esq. by Katherine his Wife, who departed this life the 26th of April, 1769, Aged 71 years.

Here lyeth the Body of John Fitzherbert, Esquire, who departed this life March ye 20, 1692.

Benefactions.

Humphry Fitzherbert, Esq. new pewed this Church, and erected the Pulpit and Reading Desk at his own Expense, in the year of our Lord 1759. He also gave a silver Chalice, for the Holy Communion. Mrs. Catherine Fitzherbert, his Widow, left Twenty-five Pounds to the Reverend Mr. Woodroffe, in trust, the Interest to be distributed by him annually to the Poor of this Parish, and after his time by the then Minister and Churchwardens. She gave also a Bible and Common Prayer Book to this Church in the year of our Lord 1776.

The Rev. John Turner present Rector, and Lord of the Manor.

Register commenced 1573.

Mrs. Brook and Mr. Jones, Lord of the Manor.

In the Window of the Chancel is some painted glass.

SOPWORTH.

On Monuments against North Wall.

In a Vault underneath this Monument are deposited the Remains of Daniel Ludlow, M. D. a man no less distinguished for his medical skill than for his intellectual endowments. Anxious for a rational retirement, he had scarcely begun to enjoy a repose from the labours of his Profession, when it pleased the Almighty suddenly to call him from this sublunary state to his eternal rest, in the prime of life which had been spent in the Relief of suffering humanity. He died universally lamented, the 12th day of October, 1802, Aged 45 years.

Arms—Gules, on a fess, or, three cross patonce, sable, between three mullets, azure, a martlet for difference.

Sacred to the Memory of Betty, the Wife of the Rev. James Hardwick, LL. D. Rector of this Parish, and Daughter of the Rev. Robert Coates, late Rector of Little Sodbury, in the County of Gloucester, who died on the 26th day of January, 1808, Aged 45 years.

Having borne a severe and lingering illness with great firmness and Chrristian resignation, her mild and amiable temper, and her affectionate attachment to her Husband and Relations, have rendered her loss to them peculiarly afflicting.

Near this marble rest the Remains of Harriet Hardwick, daughter of the Rev. James Hardwick, L.L.D. Rector of this Parish, and of Betty his Wife, who departed this life the 6th day of January, 1798, in the Twelfth year of her age.

See from the earth the fragrant lily rise,
It springs, it flourishes, it fades, it dies;
So this fair flower scarce blossom'd for a day,
Sweet was the bloom, and speedy the decay.

James Hardwick, Brother to the above-named Harriet, died December 31, 1790, Aged 6 years and 7 months, and is interred in the Chancel of Chipping Sodbury Church.

There rest, sweet child, and wait the Almighty's will,
Then rise unchanged, and be an angel still.

Arms—Argent, a saltire, or, on a chief, argent, three mullets, azure.

South Wall.

Sacred to the Memory of Maria Trotman Dyer, eldest daughter of Robert Dyer, M. D. of Bristol, and Niece of the Rev. R. T. Coates, Rector of this Parish, who died 19th January, 1816, Aged 27 years.

Her amiable manners, gentle temper, and chaste mind, with her virtuous application of rare talents, her filial love, benevolence, piety, and faith, exceeded the meed of praise, and smoothed her path from earth to heaven, from blessing to be blest.

Sacred also to her beloved Brother, Samuel Dyer, Aged 16 years, lost in the BENGAL, which, with three other Indiamen, perished off the Mauritius, 14th of March, 1808.

On Flat Stones in Body.

Here lyeth the Body of Thomas Banning, Rector of this Church, and of Catharine his Wife. He died on September the 29th, An° Dñi 1688, and She died on January the 30th, An° Dñi 1692.

Hic jacet corpus . . . . . . Waterman, nuper . . . .
Ecclesiæ Rectoris, Med . . . Professoris
. . tibus et Physicis et sacri
. . . nere verbi
Manimis medicus corporibusque fuit,
. . ustamen effecit sacri . . . medicina salutis,
. . . ius obit animæ vita
perennis erit, obiit xii ivnii, anno salutis 1657,
Aged 57.

Here lieth the Body of the Rev. John Melkesham, A.M. Rector of this Parish, who died 12th March, 1742, Aged 47.

Also the Body of Levina, his Wife, second daughter of John Burgh, Esq. late of Troy, in the county of Monmouth. She died 22d of November, 1753, Aged 52. Also the Body of Lydia, their daughter, who died the 11th of February, 1741, Aged 9 weeks.

Here lyeth the Body of Thomas, the fifth Son of William Hodges, gent. and of Elizabeth his Wife, who died an infant, and was buried Feb. 13, Anno Dom. 1694.

Here lieth the Bodies of James and Samuel, the third and fourth sons of William Hodges, gent. and Elizabeth his Wife, both died infants 1686
1690
Mary, their fourth daughter, died 1680.

On Monuments in Nave.

To the Memory of John Comely, gent. late of this Parish, who departed this life the 16th day of August, 1806, in the 68th year of his age. Also of Mary his Wife, who exchanged this mortal life for a better the 24th day of May, 1797, Aged 63 years, and was interred at Withington, in the County of Gloucester. And of Thomas, Mary, and Robert, their children, who died in their infancy.

To the Memory of Mr. John Harris, who departed this life the 29th day of May, 1803, Aged 78 years.

Here lies the Body of Alice Gore, Wife of Thomas Gore, gent. Lord of Sopworth, who while . . . . Feb. 6, 1663.

Register commenced 1697.

Duke of Beaufort Lord of the Manor.

GREAT SHERSTON.

Mon. in Chancel against North Wall.

This Monument was Erected by the Executrix of Thomas Estcourt Cresswell, Esq. who, by his Will, directed the same, in Memory of Thomas Estcourt, Esq. son and heir of Sir Thomas Estcourt, Knight, Lord of this Manor, by Dame Mary his Wife, who was born about the year 1680, and departed this life in the month of November, 1704. Also of Elizabeth their youngest daughter, the sister and heiress of Thomas Estcourt, Esq. who was born in February, 1688, was married to Richard Cresswell, of Rudge, in Staffordshire, Esq. and departed this life in Feb. 1717. Also of Thomas Estcourt Cresswell, Esq. son of the said Richard and Elizabeth Cresswell, Lord of this Manor, who was born in July, 1712, and departed this life the 14th day of November, 1788.

Arms—Quarterly, 1 and 4, gules, three plates charged with as many squirrels, gules, 2 and 3, per fess, indented, gules and erm. in chief, three estoiles, or, over all an escutcheon, per fess, imbattled, argent and sable, three cross patee, counterchanged.
Crest—A bust, per pale.

Sacred to the Memory of William Jenkins, Esq. who departed this life April 22, 1803, Aged 53 years.

This Monument was Erected as a tribute of affection by his Sister.

S. Wall.

To the Memory of Ann, late Wife of William Hodges, of this Parish, Esq. and daughter of Edward Targeaunt, of Hartsburne, in the county of Gloucester, gent. who departed this life (in child-bearing) June the 23, 1676.

And to the Memory of Mary, the Relict of Thomas Hodges, of Shipton Moygne, in the County of Gloucester, Esq. daughter of Sir William Cooke, of Highnham, in the said County, Knight, and mother of the said William Hodges, who departed this life the 28th day of October, 1676.

The sayd William Hodges, out of his great affection to his deare Wife, and duty to his pious Mother, hath erected this Monument.

Arms—Azure, a chevron, argent, charged with a crescent, gules, between three crescents, argent, impaling argent, a chevron between three dolphins, embowed, sable.
Crest—The sun in full glory, or, issuing out of a crescent, argent.

H. S. E.

Richardus Weeksy, A.M. hujus Ecclesiæ Vicarius,
Istius, de Easton Grey Rector,
Scholæ etiam privitæ sed in magna
Existimatione habitæ moderator,
Qui omnibus hujus vitæ præcipue,
Clerici Marti, patris et
Ludi magistri muneribus, fideliter,
Feliciter, et summa cum laude
Per multos annos functus, fato cessit
Die 3° Junii, Anno Domini 1733, Ætatis 77.

Et juxta eum conditæ sunt,
Alicia, uxor, pietate, prudentia,
Et industria indefessa insignis,
Tali viro omino digna,
Quæ obiit die sexto Augusti, Anno Domini 1733,
Ætatis 72.
Et Maria, filia natu quarta, uxor Gulielmi Skinner A. M.
Et Ecclesiæ de Didmarton Rectoris,
Fœmina parentibus neu quam degener,
Utpote, non minus virtutum splendore,
Quam forma egregiis, et ingenio præcellenti decorata,
Quæ decessit Julii die 17, Anno Domini 1732,
Ætatis 37.

On Flat Stones.

Here lyeth the Body of Sir Thomas Estcourt, Kt. who departed this life at his house in Bath, on the 18th day of June, in the year of our Lord God 1702, Aged 59.

Arms—Ermine, on a chief, three estoiles.

Here lyeth the Body of Beata Estcourt, of this Parish, spinster, (daughter of John Estcourt, of Cranham, in the county of Gloucester, gent.) who departed this life November the 11th, Annoq. Dom. 1735, Aged 55 years.

Arms—As before.

Here lyeth the Body of Mary, the Wife of William Skinner, Rector of Didmarton, who departed this life July ye 17th, Anº Dom̃ 1752, Aged 37.

Arms—Sable, a chevron or, between three griffins' heads erased, argent impaling, on a fess, gules, 3 cinquefoils argent.

Here lyeth the Body of Jelian, the Wife of Nathaniel Watts, yeoman, who departed this life the 15th day of January, Anº Dom̃ 1670, Ætatis suæ 65. Also here lies interred the Body of Mary Brayne, spinster, who departed this life the 10th of September, 1746, Aged 74 years.

Here lies the Body of William Fifield, Clerk, late Vicar of this Parish, with the Chapel of Aldrington annexed, who died Nov. 14, 1769, Aged 56 years.

Here lies interred the Body of the Reverend Mr. Jeremiah Butt, Vicar of this Parish, with Aldrington annexed, who departed this life September 23, A. D. 1746, Ætat. 58.

Hic jacet corpus Hesteræ, vere
Piæ et Charissimæ uxoris
Jeremiæ Butt, hujus Ecclesiæ,
Cum Capella de Aldrington annexa, Vicarii,
Quæ permaguos
Dolores patientia admodum
Christiana diu passa iis morte devictis,
Die misericordia requiem, obtinuit
Vicesimo sexto die Aprilis, Anno Dom. 1740, Æt. 52.

Here lyeth the Body of Richard Weeksy, Vicar of this Parish, and of Alice his Wife, with four of their Children, who died in their infancy. Also, here lyeth the Body of Mrs. Alice Trimnell, Relict of the Rev. Charles Trimnell, and Daughter of the Rev. Richard Weeksy. She died Feb. 21, 1769, Aged 78.

On Monuments in North Transept.

In Memory of Robert Weeksy, gent. fourth and last surviving son of Richard Weeksy, M. A. sometime Vicar of this Parish, who, after a well-spent life of seventy-three years. died August 23, 1762. Also of his affectionate Sister, Mrs. Jane Weeksy, who, to the regret of all that knew her, departed this life May 1, 1761, Aged 60.

Arms—On a fesse, gules, three cinquefoils, argent.

In Memory of Mary, the Wife of Robert Holborow, who departed this life the 29th day of September, 1800, Aged 70 years. Also Robert Holborow aforesaid, who departed this life December, 8, 1816, Aged 83 years.

On an Altar Tomb.

Here Resteth the Body of Elizabeth, the Daughter of Robert Davis, who departed this life the 14th day of August Anno Dom̃ 1670, in the 20th year of her age. Here lieth also the Body of Robert Davis, the Father of the said Elizabeth, who died on July the 13th, Anno Domini 1689, Ætatis suæ 66.

On Flat Stones.

Here lyeth the Body of Giles James, gent. late whilst hee lived of Sherstone Pinckney, in the County of Wilts. who first tooke to Wife Anne, the Daughter of Edward Gore, Esq. which died without issue, and afterwards tooke to Wife Mary the daughter of John Woodelande, of Chippenham, gent. yet liveinge, by whome he had issue three children, (namelye) Woodeland his Sonne, and Mary his Daughter, both deceased, lyinge neere this place buryed. Hee departed this life the 7th day of Feb. Anº Dom̃ 1639, Annoq. Ætatis suæ 56.

Mori mihi lucrum.

Here lyeth the Body of Mr. Robert Weeksy, who departed the 23d of August, 1762, Aged 73.

Under this Stone lies the Body of Edward Hall, of this Parish, who departed this life the 23d of Feb. 1781, Aged 73. Also the Body of William-Joseph Bird, son of William and Elizabeth Bird, of the City of London, who departed this life the 23d of March, 1781.

Also the Body of Deborah Hall, Wife of the above Edward Hall, who departed this life the 14th of January, 1787, Aged 73 years.

In this transept is lying, under a small canopy, a statue of stone, in good preservation.

On Flat Stones in N. Aisle.

Here lieth the Body of Isaac Mannings, who died April the 29, 1802, Aged 68 years.

Also of Mary his wife, who died January 9, 1807, Aged 74 years.

Here lieth the Body of Elizabeth, the Wife of Robert Hambidge, who died March the 28th, 1777, Aged 66 years.

On Monuments in S. aisle.

Here lieth the Body of Dorothy James, who died January the 6th, 1802, Aged 75 years.

Near this place lyeth the Body of Thomas Davis, who died June the 2d, 1725, Aged 69.

To the Memory of Joyce Hitchings, the Wife of Giles Hitchings, who died in London September 20, 1715, Ætat. 60.

When fate cut off her slender thread of life,
A mourning husband lost a loving wife;
Children, by duty and affection led,
Deplor'd their kind and tender mother dead,
To path of virtue them she gently drew
By awfull precepts, and example too.
As time came on for silent night repose,
With fervent prayer the evening she would close;
And when soft sleep flew from refreshing eyes,
Devotion was her morning sacrifice:
She piously the sacred Sabbath spent,
Our publick worship did with zeal frequent;
And at the solemn sacramental feast,
Was constantly a reverent guest.
Why may not the glorious choir above now sing,
Their grateful anthems to the Eternal King,
And welcome one more soul to joyful rest,
In lofty regions of the ever blest?

[*Over the above is a figure kneeling.*]

On Flat Stones in S. Aisle.

In a Vault underneath this Stone lieth the Remains of Samuel Withers, late of Midway, in the County of Wilts, Esq. In him the truly affectionate husband and fond father were firmly united. He departed this life the second of March, 1785, Aged 54.

Here lieth Eleanor, the Wife of William Fifield, Clerk, Vicar of this Parish, who died the 29th of December, 1752, Aged 33 years.

Here lies Edith, the daughter of William Fifield, Clerk, Vicar of this Parish, who died the 15th day of February, 1753, Aged 14 years.

Here lieth interred the Body of Giles Hitchings, of this Parish, who departed this life the 12th day of January, 1735, Aged 81 years. Also here lieth the Body of Hester Hitchings, second Wife of Giles Hitchings, who departed this life the 20th of April 1757, Aged 68 years.

Here lieth interred the Body of Samuel Byam, of Wilsley, who departed this life the 30th of January, 1744, Aged 54.

Also here lieth the Body of Samuel, Son of Samuel and Mary Byam, who died May the 6th, 1736, Aged 15. Also here lieth the Body of Mr. Jonathan Byam, late of Wilsley, another Son of the said Samuel and Mary Byam, who died Dec. 22, 1780, Aged 64 years.

Here lieth interred the Body of Mary the wife of Samuel Byam of Wilsey, who departed this life the 22d of November, 1746, Aged 57 years.

Also here lieth the Body of Ann Byam, Wife of Jonatham Byam, of Wilsley, who departed this life January the 2d, 1785, Aged 70 years.

Underneath this Stone is deposited the Remains of Ann Byam, of Wilsley, in this Parish, Wife of William Byam, who departed this life April 15, 1801, in the 46th year of her age.

Also, underneath this Stone is deposited the Remains of William Byam, of Wilsley, in this Parish. He departed this life April the 3d, 1811, Aged 56 years.

In the north side of the Nave are four semi-arches, with a moulding ornamented in the Saxon style; also an arch in the Nave on the south side, and in the north Transept and Chancel is a lancette arch.

Against the south side of this Church is a statue carved in stone, holding in his left hand a tile to receive his bowels. It is conjectured to represent an ancient warrior, called Rattle Bones, wounded in combat, but who afterwards became the vanquisher.

Register commenced 1653.

The Rev. John Turner Vicar.

Estcourt Cresswell, Esq. Lord of the Manor.

ESTON GREY.

On Monuments against North Wall.

Underneath are interred the Mortal Remains of Mrs. Jane Harris, wife of the Rev. Mr. John Harris, M. A. Rector of this Church. She was the eldest daughter of William Parry, of this Parish, gent. and Jane his Wife, and departed this life the 27th day of August, 1752, in the 54th year of her age. Also of the abovesaid Rev. Mr. John Harris. He was eldest son of a preceding Rector, and died December 14, 1767, Aged 65.

M. S.

In proximo jacent exuviæ, viri Rev. Joannis Harris,
hujus Ecclesiæ Rectoris,
Dignissimi, qui apostemate
In stomacho laborans mortem,
Obiit Februarii 8, Anno Æræ Chiristianæ 171$\frac{8}{9}$,
Ætat suæ 60.
Nec non suæ uxoris cui nomen,
Abigail, quæ vitæ cessit Oct. 22, A. D. 1726, Æt. 47.

William Parry, gent. was buried August 9, A. D. 1684.
The East end of his grave is under this incription.

Mrs. Abigail, his Wife, was buried on April 2, A. D. 1685. Her grave is at the west end of his.

Mrs. Abigail their Daughter and sole Executrix named in both their last Wills and Testaments, caused this Monument to be erected. She died on October 18th, A. D. 1724, and is interred on the north side of her Father.

On Flat Stones.

Here lyeth Mr. Thomas Harris, second Son of the Rev. Mr. John Harris, late Rector of this Parish, and Brother of the present Rector, who departed this life August the 5th, 1742, in the 38th year of his age.

Underneath is interred John Harris, Son of the Rev. John Harris, Rector of this Parish, and Jane his Wife, who was born the 14th day of Feb. 1741, and died the 14th day of May following.

On a Monument in Body.

Near this Place lyeth the Bodies of Arthur Adye, and Mary his Wife. He died Feb. 12, 1682, and She Oct. 30, 1673.

Full of all loves, and free from discords here,
Lived and dyed this ever happy pair:
Though Death in her first fixed his cruell dart,
That but their Bodyes, not their Souls could part;
For, like a turtle, being left aloan,
He never ceas'd to sigh, or ever ceas'd to moan,
The loss of his dear consort dead and gone,
Till death at last led him the fatall way
From mortall shades to everlasting day,
Where, mixinge souls, they now in peace remain,
Fraught full of joys without alays of pain.

Against North Wall of Nave.

M. S.

Subtus jacet, nisi quod supera est, Eliz. Parry, filia primogenita, Thomæ Hodges, Armigeri, de Shipton Moigne, in com̄ Glou. nec non pia conjux Gulielmi Parry, Gent. de E. Gray, quæ cum 23 annis vixisset, obiit tandem ut in æternam viveret 8 Kal. Maij, Anno Redemp. nostræ 1680.

Noe more, poor wretched man, repine to dye,
Since cold and breathless underneath do's lye
A creature more refined and purer far,
Than thou and I, or common mortals are;
Fair, wise, and virtuous, of an upright life,
A spotless virgin, and a faithful wife.
What pity 'twas that that thus regardless fate,
To so much worth should give so short a date.

On Flat Brass Plates in Nave.

Here lieth the Body of Jane, the Daughter of William and Elizabeth Parry, who departed this life the 18th day of August, 1688.

M. S.

Johannis Parry, Gulielmo Parry, generoso, ex Elizabetha, ejus uxore, fili, qui obiit 11 Cal. Junii, A.D. 1698, Ætatis 15.

Here lyeth Michael, the Son of William and Ann Widdrington, who was born the twenty-ninth day of September, Anno Domini 1750, and died the tenth day of October following.

In the Window of the Chancel is a little painted glass.

The Rev. John Herman Hawes Rector.

Register commenced 1654.

Thomas Smith, Esq. Lord of the Manor.

Benefactions

TO THE POOR OF EASTON GREY.

JOHN ADYE, late of this Parish, gent. gave Eight Shillings annually, to be disposed of in Bread to the Poor of this Parish. The Cottages and Lands in the Parish of Sherston Pinkeney, at this time the property of Samuel Webb, Esq. of Henbury, in the County of Gloucester, are charged with this Charity.

JOHN DAY, Esq. late of Nailsworth, in the County of Gloucester, bequeathed one Pound Twelve Shillings annually, to the Poor of this Parish, the Glebe Lands and Tithes in the Parish of Sherston Pinkeney are charged with this Charity.

Mrs. ELIZABETH HODGES, late of Shipton Moigne, in the County of Gloucester, by her last Will, bequeathed Two Pounds annually for the Augmentation of a Charity School in this Parish.

ISAAC BENNETT, } *Churchw.*
March 24, 1814. }

NORTH WRAXALL CHURCH. (*Vide p.* 32.)

In the Vaulting, over Paul Methuen's *Monument, are Thirty-four Shields of Arms;*

1 of 1st. Quarterly, first and fourth azure, second and third or, a buck tripping, counterchanged.

2 2d. Argent, on a bend cottized, gules, three bezants.

3 3d. Azure, a chevron, argent, between three dolphins embowed, argent, a chief, or.

3 4th. Quarterly, first and fourth or, second and third sable, over all a bend, argent.

1 5th. Gules, three fleur-de-lis, argent.

5 6th. Argent, three tiger's heads erased, proper.

1 7th. Argent, a chevron, engrailed, gules.

2 8th. Argent, two chevrons, azure.

2 9th. Argent, two bars, engrailed azure, between nine martlets, gules.

5 10th. Ermine, three chevronells, gules.

1 11th. Ermine, a bend, gules.

2 12th. Argent, a fess, gules, between six annulets, gules.

1 13th. Or, on a bend, gules, 3 mullets, argent.

1 14th. Argent, on a saltire engrailed, azure, nine annulets, or.

1 15th. Azure, a cross engrailed, argent, between four fleur-de-lis, or.

2 16th. Ermine, on a bend, sable, two hands proper, holding a horse-shoe, or.

1 17th. Argent, on an escutcheon, azure, an eagle displayed, argent.

Quarterings in one Shield.

1. Argent, three tigers' heads, erased, proper.
2. Argent, two bars engrailed, azure, between nine martlets, gules.
3. Ermine, three chevronells, gules.
4. Azure, a chevron between three dolphins, embowed, argent, a chief, or.
5. Argent, a fess gules, between three martlets volant, sable.
6. Sable, three jugs, argent.
7. Argent. a fess gules, between six annulets, or.
8. . . . .
9. Barry of six, argent and azure, a label, gules, for difference.
10. Argent, a fess between six fleur-de-lis, gules.
11. Azure, a cross, flory, or, between four estoiles of the second.
12. Quarterly, first and fourth sable, second and third, or, over all a bend, argent.

HIGHWORTH HUNDRED.

The following Inscriptions are taken from the Churchyards of this Hundred.

HIGHWORTH.

On flat tombs in the north side.

In Memory of Francis Reason, who died April 28, 1763, Aged 62 years.

Also Hannah, the Wife of Francis Reason, who died March 19th 1783, Aged 77 years.

In Memory of Mary, daughter of Francis and Hannah Reason, who died April 22, 1762, Aged 23 years.

In Memory of John Reason, who died August 23, 1803, Aged 63 years.

Like to a dream my days are gone,
And I must rest under this tomb,
Till from above a voice shall say,
Arise, ye dead, and come away:
Then do I hope, at Christ's right hand,
Amongst God's blessed saints to stand.

Head Stones.

To the Memory of William Morse, who died Dec. 22, 1800, in the 31st year of his age.

I in this world with pain was so opprest,
That I by day and night could take no rest;
Physicians came, but all their works was vain,
Till Christ, the great Physician, eas'd my pain.

In Memory of Ann, daughter of William and Elizabeth Hughes, who died May the 1st, 1798, Aged 16 years. Also William and Jane, who died in their infancy.

To the Memory of Elizabeth, the Wife of William Hughes, who departed this life the 20th of Sept. 1801, Aged 43 years.

In Memory of William, Son of Thomas and Margaret Hughes, who died Oct. 19, 1803, Aged 31 years.

To the Memory of Joseph Powney, who died 28th May, 1792, Aged 38 years.

Also Elizabeth, Wife of Joseph Powney, who died 30th of May, 1793, Aged 46 years.

To the Memory of Ann, Wife of Joseph Powney, who died 13th Sept. 1789, Aged 73 years.

Henry Jones died Sept. 10, 1717, Aged 46.
Mary Jones died Nov. ye 6th, 1746, Aged 70.

On Flat Stones.

In Memory of Ann, daughter of Richard and Elizabeth Humphrys, who died December 23, 1769, Aged 3 years and 6 months.

In Memory of Susanna the Wife of Stephen Randal, who died Dec. the 20th, 1764, Aged 52.

In Memory of Stephen, son of Stephen and Susanna Randeel, died August ye 20, 1740, Aged 1 year and 6 months. Also Susanna their daughter died Oct. ye 30, 1747, Aged 1 year.

On Flat Tombs.

In Memory of John Gorton, who died Nov. 17, 1747, Ætatis 63. Also Sarah, his Wife, died Sept. 20th, 1765, Ætatis 77. Harry their Son died July 25, 1777. Rachell Angell, the Wife of Henry Angell, who died September 9, 1793, Aged 77 years

---

Jane, the Wife of William Chamberlen, daughter of Samuel and Jane Wing, died January 29th, 1771, Aged 47. Also Jane their daughter, and only child, died April 30th, 1769, Aged 6 years 3 months and 10 days.

Here lyeth the Body of Jane, the Wife of Samuel Wing, who departed this life, April 2d, 1758, Aged 62 years.

In Memory of Mary the Wife of Thomas Mill, of Shi . . enham, in the county of Berks. youngest daughter of Samuel and Jane Wing of this Place. She departed this life the 5th of July, 1762, Aged 27 years.

Head Stones.

Ann, the Wife of John Woodbridge, died Feb. ye 4th, 1722, Aged 61 years.

In Memory of William Stevens. He died March the 9th, 1723, Aged 75 years. Also Richard his Son, who died March 1st, 1795, Aged 82 years.

In Memory of Joane, the Wife of William Stevens. She died May the 19th, 1770, Aged 60 years.

Here lyeth ye Body of Edward Barnet, ye Husband of Ann Barnet, who was buried August ye 26, A. D. 1696.

In Memory of Elizabeth Warman, who died March 31st, 1751, Aged 69. Also Thomas, her Son, who died September 19, 1762, Aged 30 years.

Here lyeth the Body of William Tichime, who dyed May ye 9 day, 1694.

Jane Prince died March 13, 1794.

In Memory of Deborah, Wife of John Embling, who died October 2d, 1778, Aged 61 years.

In Memory of George Kates, and Elizabeth his Wife. He died 13 . . . . 1797, Aged 69 years. She died October 15, 1807, Aged 86 years. Also Maria Kates, their daughter, died April 8th, 1790, Aged 34 years.

On Flat Tombs.

Here lyeth the Body of Sarah, Wife of Michael Smith, who died September 17, 1786, Aged 43 years. Also Mary their daughter, who died November 2d, 1779, in the 3d year of her age. And also Jane their daughter, who died July ye 11th, 1794, Aged 19 years. And also Ann their daughter, who died Oct. the 26, 1801, Aged 23 years.

Here lyeth the Body of Elizabeth, the Wife of John Smith, who died February 9th, 1750, Aged 44.

Here also lyeth John Smith, her husband, who died July 18th, 1762, Aged 51.

And also Deborah, their daughter, the Wife of Thomas Saunders, who died August 1, 1805, Aged 58 years.

Here rest the Remains of John Smith of Sevenhampton, in this Parish, who died the 3d of April, 1795, Aged 55.

Dear Jesus, Saviour of mankind!
The Saviour be of me and mine.
Mortals, how few among your race
Have given this thought its weight,
That on this slender moment hangs
Your everlasting state.

In Memory of Jane the Wife of John Smith, of Sevenhampton, who departed this life June 29, 1814, Aged 72 years. Elizabeth, daughter of John and Jane Smith, of Sevenhampton, who died the 14th of January 1765, in her infancy. And of John, their Son, who died Jan. 25, 1769, Aged 2 years and 3 months. And also of Elizabeth, their daughter, who died Feb. 4, 1769, Aged 3 years and 9 months.

John Smith died May ye 14th, 1720, Aged 42.

Also Jane, ye Wife of John Smith, who died Jan. ye 18th, 1743, Aged 73 years.

To the Memory of Michael Smith, who departed this life the 12th of December, 1807, Aged 64 years.

Remember me, my children dear,
Though I am dead and gone,
Out of my pain and misery
Which I have undergone.
I was afflicted with much pain,
'Twas more than I could bear,
But the Almighty work'd his will,
And took me to his care.

Head Stones.

In Memory of William, Son of Thomas and Mary Phipp, who died Jan. 2d, 1768, Aged 11 years.

In Memory of John Darby, who died Nov. 21, 1769, Aged 56 years. Also Ann, his Wife, who died Oct. 6th, 1797, Aged 81 years.

61

Here lyeth the Body of Richard Fisher. Dyed April 8th, 1743, Aged 63.

Here lieth the Body of Margaret, Wife of John Haggard, who died March 24, 1753, Aged 72.

Here lieth the Body of John Haggard, who died Sept. 22, 1754, Aged 77.

To the Memory of Martha, Wife of John Darby, who departed this life March 15, 1797, Aged 26 years. Also three of their children, Sarah died Feb. 6, 1795, Aged 6 years. Ann died May 16, 1795, Aged 5 years. John died Jan. 22, 1795, Aged 2 years.

Elizabeth, Wife of John Darby, who departed this life April 22, 1803, Aged 44 years. Also James their Son, who died in his infancy.

To the Memory of Jane, the Wife of William Ely, who died March 19, 1789, Aged 32 years.

H. S. I.

Thomas Morse Obiit Jan. 4, 1778, Aged 75.
Jane, his Wife, Obiit April 2, 1792, Aged 88.

On the outside against North Wall of the Church.

Beneath this Spot lie the Remains of Richard Mathews, Citizen and Goldsmith of London. He died January 26, 1791, Aged 63 years. Also Richard Morgan Mathews, his Son, who died May 13, 1780, Aged 4 years. Also Deborah, Wife of William Williams, (Daughter of Richard and Ann Mathews) who died Oct. 5, 1810, Aged 43 years.

Head Stones.

To the Memory of Elizabeth, Wife of John Winning, who died April 26, 1806, Aged 66 years. Also Henry, their Son, who died April 26, 1805, Aged 29 years. Also John, Son of John and Ann Winning, who died in his infancy.

To the Memory of John Winning, who died July 15, 1796, Aged 51 years.

Long ling'ring on the borders of the grave,
From which no skill on earth had power to save,
In wasting pains I spent my daily breath,
And found no refuge, till reliev'd by death:
But now I sleep, no more by pain opprest,
And trust my Saviour for eternal rest.

To the Memory of Henry Winning, who died 12th Nov. 1782, Aged 71 years. To the Memory of Ann, Daughter of John and Elizabeth Winning, who died 23d Nov. 1782, Aged 10 years.

To the Memory of Anne, the Wife of Henry Winning, who died Dec. 5, 1752, Aged 30 years.

To the Memory of James Rodborn, who died Feb. 23, 1776, Aged 65 years.

Here lies the Body of James, the son of James and Jane Rodbourn, who died April 13th, 1767, Aged 21 years.

In Memory of Lucy, the daughter of James and Jane Rodbourn, who died April 2, 1771, Aged 14 years.

To the Memory of Joseph Rodbourn, Son of James and Filanees Rodbourn, who died 26th Nov. 1781, Aged 26 years.

Here lyeth the Body of John Smith, who died Dec. 2, 1709, Aged 34 years.

In Memory of Charles Winning, who departed this life May the 7th, 1775, Aged 65 years.

Margaret, Wife of William Winning, was buried April 2, 1740, Aged 88 years.

Mrs Rachel Ralph died 30th June, 1786, Aged 65, Elizabeth Bassett died 28th March, 1803, Aged 63 years.

On Flat Tombs.

Here lyeth ye Body of Ambrose Humphrys, who departed this life April the 26th, A. D. 1729.

To the Memory of Andrew Baden, who died May 11, 1802, Aged 23 years.

Under this tomb lyeth the Body of Richard Byrchall, jun. of Sevenhampton, who dyed the 4th of November, in the year of our Lord 1744, Aged 42 years. In Memory of Jane Byrchall, of Sevenhampton, who died Oct. 23d, 1771, Aged 71 years.

Under this Tomb lyeth the Body of Richard Byrchall, of Sevenhampton, in this Parish, who departed this life October 28th, Anº Dom̃ 1735, Ætatis 64. Here lyeth the Body of Jane, Wife of Richard Byrchall, who departed this life, Feb. 1st, 1754, Aged 80 years.

Here lyeth the Body of Thompson Packer, died March 17, 1750, Aged 68. Also Mary the Wife of Thompson Packer, died Jan. 17, 1739, Aged 50.

In Memory of Elizabeth, the Wife of Richard North. She died August 16, 1737, Aged 79 years.

In Memory of Richard North, who died Sept. 24, 1743.

Against north-west corner of Tower.

Near this place lye Thomas Allen, and Susanna his Wife. He died March 1st, 1724. She died Feb. 15, 1741.

Here lye four Children of Alexander and Elizabeth Betterton, who died young, namely, Jane died Jan. 29, 1731, Elizabeth died Dec. 5, 1739, John died Dec. 7, 1739, Ann died Oct. 7, 1741.

On Flat Stones.

Here lyeth the Body of John, the Son of Henry and Elizabeth Kilmister, who departed this life Feb. Anº Dom̃ 169· Here lieth ye Body of Henry Kilmister, who departed this life Feb. ye . . Anº Dñi 1695.

Ann, daughter of Thomas and Luci Avenall, died Dec. ye 26, 1729, in the 22d year of her age.

Here lyeth the Body of Elizabeth Hillier, formerly the Wife of Richard Batson, Gent. and afterwards of John Hillier, Clerk. She died September 16, 1773, Aged 72.

In Memory of Elizabeth, Wife of Robert Tuckey, gent. who died April 22, 1752, Aged 58 years. And also the Body of Robert Tuckey, gentleman, who died April the 20th, 1769, Aged 61.

On Head Stones.

In Memory of Arman North, who died June 7, 1755, Aged 53 years.

In Memory of John Smith, who departed this life April 29, 1776, Aged 76 years.

In Memory of William Weston, who died Nov. 7, 1763, Aged 70 years.

Also Ann, his Wife, who died Oct. 1743.

In Memory of Richard Weston, gent. late of the County of Essex. He died Sept. 2d, 1785, Aged 54 years.

Affliction sore long time I bore,
Physicians were in vain,
Till Death did seize, and God did please
To ease me of my pain.

Here lyeth the Body of William, Son of Francis and Ann Love. He died June 11, 1737, Aged 5 years.

Here lyeth the Body of Mary, daughter of Francis and Mary Love. She died January 30, 1740, Aged 13 years.

To the Memory of Penelope, Wife of Randle Pedley, who departed this life the 4th Jan. 1808, Aged 72 years.

To the Memory of John Hedges, who departed this life Nov. 25, 1795, Aged 55 years.

Also John Hedges died December 20, 1805, Aged 70.

In Memory of Mary, the Wife of Robert Moulder, who died September 30, 1784, Aged 24 years.

Severe my pain was unto me,
I pray'd the Lord to set me free.

Also Sarah, daughter of Robert and Mary Moulder, who died July 1, 1784, Aged 1 year.

Here lieth ye Body of Thomas Jacksons, of Hampton Turvill, sen. who departed this life July 1, A. D. 1703.

On Tombs, S. E. corner.

Here lyeth the Body of the Rev. James Ayscough, who died Nov. 1, 1745, Aged 60. He was 25 years Vicar of this Parish. He married Catharine, daughter of Henry Reynall Spiller, of the County of Middlesex, Esq. by whom he had issue 6 sons and 2 daughters. Catharine Ayscough died the 11th of Feb. 1775, Aged 86.

An uniform probity and an affectionate candour distinguished the Man, a truly conjugal and paternal tenderness the Husband and Father, an unwearied diligence in this laborious Cure, joined to a primitive simplicity of manners, the Clergyman. He was thankful and humble under the blessings of life, patient and resigned under his own affliction, compassionate and kind towards those of others. Thus, Reader, thou seest the most useful human virtue described in the same plain dress in which they lived in this worthy person: in others, perhaps, thou mayest find them more shining, but in few more solid, or better fitted to make men serviceable to each other, and happy in themselves.

Read and imitate.

Arms—A fess between 3 camels passant.

In Memory of Brent, son of the Rev. James and Catherine Ayscough, who died Jan. 27, 1749, Aged 21. Near this Tomb was buried Henry Reynell, and John, their sons, who died young.

Here lyeth the Body of John, son of Henry and Mary Marsh. He departed this life June . . . A. D. 1726, Ætatis . . Also Robert, ye Son of Henry and Mary Marsh. He died April 12, 1737, Aged 26 years.

Head Stones.

1664 Edward Bus deceased, June the 3d.

In Memory of John Davis, who died Oct. 18, 1756, Aged 51 years. Also Mary his Wife, who died May 4, 1810, Aged 102 years.

Here lyeth the Body of Ann, Wife of John Smith, who died March 23, 1780, Aged 63 years.

Here lyeth the Body of Grace, Wife of George Humphreys, of Sevenhampton, died Jan. ye 27, 1729, Aged 77 years.

To the Memory of Richard Lester, who died April 16, 1778, Aged 75 years. Also Elizabeth, his Wife, who died May 5th, 1797, Aged 96 years.

On a flat Tomb.

In Memory of William Underwood, who died May, 1777, Ætatis 33.

Here lyeth the Body of John Rodgerson, who died July 1, 1760, Aged 47 years.

Susanna Rodgerson, who died March 10, 1773, Aged 6· years.

Head Stones.

In Memory of Ann, Wife of William Underwood, who departed this life May the 17th, 1781, Aged 46 years.

Here lieth the Body of Sarah, the Wife of Francis Moss. She died Nov. 11, 1723, Aged 41 years.

On Flat Tombs.

In Memory of Thomas Butcher, who died Feb. 27, in the year 1743, Aged 53.

Under this Tomb lyeth the Body of Elizabeth, Wife of Thomas Butcher, who died Sept. the 9th, 1739, Aged 59.

In Memory of Charles, Son of William Butcher, who dyed August 6, in the year 1708, Aged 22 years.

In trouble, pain, and care, we run our race,
Through all our Saviour brought us by his grace,
From Sins reigning power Jesus set us free,
Yet infirmity still attending we;
By faith we hoped a pardon to obtain,
And with our Christ in endless bliss to reign.
Farewell, vain world, pain, sin, and sorrow too,
We are now at rest, and are rid of you.
Our race is run, our warfare at an end,
And now our joys all human thoughts transcend;
The praises of our God we sing on high,
His blessed face we see eternally.

To the Memory of John Lord, who died Sept. 17, 1791, Aged ·· years.

Also Susanna, his Wife, who died Feb. 5, 1801 Aged 73 years.

To the Memory of three Children of John and Susanna Lord, named, Alice, their daughter, died Feb. 16, 1767, in her infancy. William, their Son died Nov. 3, 1770, in his infancy. And Edward Goulding, their Son, died May 30, 1778, Aged 4 years.

In Memory of George Farr. He died May 23d, Anº Dñi 1731, Ætatis 62.

Susanna, the Wife of George Farr, died May the 8th, 1772, Ætatis 94.

To the Memory of Charles Farr, who died March the 7th, 1784, Aged 79.

Also Elizabeth Farr, who died Oct. 13, 1789, Aged 69 years.

In Memory of Martha Farr, who died Dec. 24, 1782, Aged 70 years.

Also Thomas Salmon, Nephew of Charles Farr, who died Feb. 7, 1789, Aged 49 years.

In Memory of Rachel Saunders, Wife of William Saunders, who died September 12, Anno Domini 1732, Aged 32 years. In Memory of William, son of William and Rachel Saunders, who died Feb. 1, 1750, Aged 20 years. William Saunders died Jan. 16, 1784, Aged 70 years.

Here lieth the Body of William Farr. He died Feb. 15, 1727, Aged 74 years.

Here lyeth the Body of Mary, Wife of John Stiff, who died March 24, 1714, Aged 107 years.

On Flat Tombs S. side of Church.

Sacred to the Memory of the Rev. John Readhead. He died May 31, 1769, in the 56th year of his age, having been Curate of this Parish 32 years.

Here lyeth the Body of John Grinnell, who died March 9, 1789, Aged 66 years.

When man hath laboured all his days,
In worldly toils, and various ways,
At length by Death's assault set free,
Lies down to rest most peaceably.

Here lieth the Body of Sarah, Austin, daughter of Thomas and Mary Grinnell, who died March 6, 1792, Aged 84 years.

Head Stones.

To the Memory of Richard Deacon, who departed this life the 11th of Nov. 1800, Aged 66 years.

In Memory of Mary, Wife of John Grinnell, who died March 20, 1772, Aged 92 years.

In Memory of James Grinnell, who departed this life April 2d, 1766, Aged 48.

To the Memory of Mary Smith, daughter of George and Hannah Davis, who died 18th June, 1786, Aged 62 years.

To the Memory of Mary, Wife of Richard Deacon, who departed this life March 26, 1811, Aged 31 years.

A loving Wife, a Mother dear,
Between her Children lieth here,
In hopes to meet in Heaven again,
And there with Christ for to remain.

To the Memory of Elizabeth, daughter of Richard and Mary Deacon, who departed this life August the 8th, 1811, Aged 6 years and 10 months.

With patience I long did bear my pain,
Great was my sufferings, and all skill was vain,
For eight long weeks afflicted sore was I,
But now I hope to live with God on high,
And there with angels for to sing,
Praises to God our heavenly King.

In Memory of Richard Dove, who died April 20, 1703, Aged 23 years.

Daniel Gibbs died Sept. 30, 1768, Aged 69.

In Memory of Stephen Cheesley, who died Nov. 3, 1804, Aged 46 years.

In Memory of Sarah, Wife of Nathanael Day. She died Jan. 28, in the year 1763, and in the 86th year of her age.

In Memory of Nathanael Day, died Nov. ye 1st. 1744, Aged 66 years.

Here lieth the Body of Sarah, Wife of Harry Edwards, who departed this life March 3, 1791, Aged 76 years.

Here lyeth the Body of Harry Edwards, who departed this life, September 3, 1773, Aged 63 years. In Memory of Ann, daughter of William and Jane Edwards, who died March 8, 1786, Aged 20 weeks. Also William, their Son, who died March 16, 1789, Aged 14 weeks. And also Maria, their daughter, who died May 3, 1795, Aged 8 months.

To the Memory of Stephen Edwards, who died 16th Nov. 1789, Aged 75 years.

To the Memory of Mary Edwards, who died 27th Dec. 1788, Aged 75 years.

In Memory of Richard Edwards, who died January 17, 1771, Aged 53 years. Also Ann, Wife of Richard Edwards, who died Feb. 9, 1769, Aged 46 years.

To the Memory of John Woodroff Edwards, Son of Richard and Mary Edwards, who died July 16, 1803, Aged 36 years. Also William, son of Richard and Mary Edwards, who died April 19, 1805, Aged 23 years. Also Thomas, Son of Richard and Mary Edwards, who died Jan. 8, 1808, Aged 16 years.

To the Memory of Richard, Son of Richard and Mary Edwards, who died Nov. 14, 1793, Aged 19 years. And also Richard their Son, who died Feb. 1794, Aged 10 weeks. And also of Lucy their daughter, who died April 4, 1794, Aged 4 years.

To the Memory of Richard Edwards, who died Jan. 31, 1794, Aged 45 years. Also Mary, Wife of Richard Edwards, who died May 4, 1793, Aged 41 years.

In Memory of Elizabeth, the Wife of Henry Edwards, who departed this life May the 26th, 1800, Aged 43 years. Also in Memory of Sarah, daughter of Henry and Elizabeth Edwards, who departed this life March 28, 1803, Aged 22 years.

To the Memory of Ann, the Wife of William Frampton, who died May 22, 1813, Aged 33 years.

In pangs of Death, O Lord, I cried to thee,
To set my soul from this frail body free,
In hopes my dearest Saviour's innocence
Would make atonement for my great offence:
The better part of me was gone before,
Whose loss, till death, I ceas'd not to deplore;
And here we lie in hopes to meet again
At that great day, in bliss for to remain.

Also Ann Edwards Frampton, their daughter, who died August 18, 1813, Aged 17 weeks.

On a tomb near the S. Porch.

Here lyeth the Body of Thomas Batson, late of Stepney, in the County of Middlesex, Esq. who departed this life the 28th day of April, Aged 69 years. And within the Church, near this Place, lyeth his Father and Mother, and several of his near Relations. Interred 26th of the same month, 1701.

On Flat Tombs.

To the Memory of Timothy Smith, who died Sept. 8, 1793, Aged 38 years.

In Memory of Joseph Cope, who died May 29, 1782, Aged 81. Also Sarah, Wife of Joseph Cope, who died May 13, 1772, Aged 82.

To the Memory of John Cope, who departed this life March 22d, 1786, Aged 56 years.

Also Mary, Wife of John Cope, who departed this life Dec. 30, 1775, Aged 49 years.

Also Sarah, the Daughter of John and Mary Cope, who departed this life Oct. 14, 1778, Aged 25 years.

Under this Tomb lyeth Mr. Henry Cullerne, who dyed Nov. 22, 1727, Aged 70.

Here also lyeth Margaret, his Wife. She dyed Jan. ye 2d, 1728, Aged 77.

Mary, daughter of Thomas and Rachel Cullerne, died Oct. ye 3d, 1728, Aged 10 years.

Thomas the Son of Thomas and Rebecca Ewer, died 7th Oct. 1763, Aged 13 weeks.

Head Stones.

Rachel, the Wife of John Dandridge, died the 22d Jan. 1757, Aged 35 years.

In Memory of Mary, Wife of Henry Simson, who died June the 3d, 1786, Aged 32 years.

Also three children died young.

Also Henry Simson died May 24, 1810, Aged 74 years.

In Memory of Susanna Fletcher, died March 7, 1736, Aged 42 years.

Here lyeth the Body of Thomas Bradley, who died March 1, 1733, Aged 59 years.

Thomas Cooke died Oct. 22, 1729.

In Memory of William Warmington, who departed this life Sept. 7, 1768, Aged 74 years.

On Flat Stones.

Here lyeth the Body of John Bayley, who departed this life April the 11th, 1771, Aged 33 years. Also John, the Son of John and Sarah Bayley, who died Nov. 22, 1778, Aged 31 years. To the Memory of Sarah Bayley, who died July 12, 1782, Aged 68 years.

Wm. Franklin, Ob. Sept. 13, 1743, Frances, his Wife, Ob. August 13, 1739. Mary Franklin, Ob. Jan. 4th, 1766. John Franklin. Ob. Oct. 1, 1773. Temperance Franklin, Ob. Feb. 13, 1774.

Head Stones.

In Memory of William Green, who died June 17, 1741.

To the Memory of Mary, Wife of William Bailey, who died 1st May, 1790, Aged 44 years.

Also Henry, their Son, who died 21st April, 1790, Aged 3 years.

Also Mary their daughter, who died 3d May, 1790, in her infancy.

In Memory of William Wo.. mington. who departed this life September 7, 1768, Aged 74 years.

Here lyeth the Body of Richard Goulding, who died December 11th, A. D. 1699.

Here lyeth the Body of William Goulding, the Son of Richard Goulding, who departed this life March 8th, A. D. 1703.

In Memory of Thomas Mathews, and Mary his Wife. He died Oct. 25, 1816, Aged 78 years. She died June 25, 1816, Aged 75 years.

Here rest the Remains of a truly honest Couple, if such a claim on earth was e'er attained; who during a long life of industry and struggle, for the support and advancement of a numerous family, the vital spark was extinguished within four months of each other, surrounded by their children, whose only hope through life is to imitate them, and in death that their end may be like theirs.

To the Memory of Susanna, Wife of Benjamin Large, youngest daughter of Thomas and Mary Mathews, who departed this life March 16, 1807, Aged 29 years.

We all know this, that Death's keen dart
Will soon the dearest couple part;
Therefore prepare (through grace divine)
Meekly each other to resign:
You'll part without much sorrow then,
Only to meet in bliss again.

To the Memory of . . . . the daughter of Edmund and Frances Howse, who departed this life the 22d of September, 1803, Aged 5 years and 5 months.

In Memory of Ann and Thomas, two children of Thomas and Mary Mathews. Ann died Nov. 12, 1770, Aged 9 years. Thomas died Oct. 24, 1773, Aged 4 years.

To the Memory of Sarah Mathews, who departed this life the 22d of April, 1788, in the 14th year of her age.

My distemper seized me so hard,
More than I could endure,
I resign'd myself unto the Lord,
To rest for evermore.

Also Sophia Mathews, who died in her infancy.

To the Memory of David Sayer, who departed this life Feb. 25, 1802, Aged 41 years.

Here lies lamented, in this silent grave,
A tender husband, and a parent brave;
Pale King of Terrors unkindly did destroy,
The widow's hope, and her dear children's joy.
Alas, he's gone! and, like a spotless dove,
To increase the number of the blest above.

Also two Daughters of David and Mary Sayer, who died in their infancy.

To the Memory of Francis Johnston, of this Parish, who departed this life May 13, 1797, Aged 53 years.

Also three of his children, John, Mary-Ann, and Jane, who died in their infancy.

Also Jane, his Wife, who died Oct. 25, 1807, Aged 48 years.

Here lieth ye Body of Mary, Wife of William Gibbs, died May 25, 1729, Aged 55 years.

In Memory of William Gibbs, who died June 13, 1728, Aged 70 years.

On Flat Tombs.

In Memory of Richard Kersill. He departed this life, Jan. 1, 1740, Aged 86. Here also lyeth Alice, the Wife of Richard Kersill. She died in the year 1714, Aged 66 years.

In Memory of Mary Kersill. She died Feb. 26, 1741, Aged 87. In Memory of William Kersill. He died Oct. the 14, 1741, Aged 61.

Here lyeth the Body of William Shermer, who departed this life, August the 3d, A.D. 1715, Aged 65 years.

Here lieth the Body of Ann, the Wife of William Shermer, who departed this life August 24, A.D. 1716.

Sacred to the Memory of Thomas Price, Surgeon, son of the Rev. Rees Price, of Burwarton, Salop. Obiit 21 July 1817, Ætatis 27 years.

Here lieth the Body of Joane Jacob, the Wife of John Jacob, late of Westrope. She departed this life August the 3d, 1675.

Head Stones.

To the Memory of Ann, the Wife of John Ansell, who departed this life the 9th of June, 1802, Aged 67 years.

To the Memory of Jane, the Wife of William Harris, who died July 13, 1815, Aged 49 years.

Remember me, my children dear,
Though I am dead and gone,
Out of my pain and misery,
Which I have undergone.
I was afflicted with much pain,
'Twas more than I could bear,
But the Almighty worked his will,
And took me to his care.

In Memory of George Davis, who died January 24, 1773, Aged 82 years.

Also George his Son, who died May 12, 1767, Aged 30 years.

Here lyeth the Body of William, Son of John and Ann Carter, who died August 22, 1720, Aged 3 years.

Here lieth the Body of William Jacob. He departed this life August the 10th, 1675.

On a flat Tomb.

Here lieth the Body of Richard Foord, who departed this life June the 27th, Anno Dom. 1744, Ætatis 49.

Like as the hart desireth the water-brooks, so longeth my soul after thee, O God.

Here lyeth the Body of Margaret, the Wife of Richard Foord, who died Jan. 5, 1767, Aged 73.

To the Memory of Mary the Wife of John Williams who died June 2d, 1815, Aged 43 years.

Also Mary-Catherine, their daughter, who died in her infancy.

To the Memory of Jane and Richard, Son and Daughter of William and Deborah Williams, who died in their infancy, 1794.

Head Stones.

Jane, daughter of John Williams, jun. and Catherine his Wife, died July 21, 1761, Aged 18 months.

Richard, their Son died Oct. 13, 1764, Aged 4 years.

Catherine, their daughter, died Oct. 30, 1764, Aged 17 months.

John Williams, sen. died April 26, 1746, Aged 66.

Jane, his Wife, died March 10th, 1740, Aged 49.

Richard, their Son, died Nov. 28, 1757, Aged 26.

To the Memory of John Williams, (who was Clerk of this Parish twenty-three years.) He departed this life the 2d day of Dec. 1778, in the 57th year of his age. Catherine, his Wife. She departed this life the 23d day of April, 1790, Aged 69 years.

Here lyeth the Body of John Angel, who departed this life Nov. 30, 1777, Aged 31 years.

All you that come my grave to see,
As I am now, so must you be.

Here lyeth the Body of Thomas, Son of Richard and Jane Watkins, who died August ye 29, 1727.

In Memory of John Jones, who departed this life the 22d day of May, in the year of our Lord 1771, Aged 61 years.

To the Memory of Mary, the Wife of John Jones, who departed this life April the 30th, 1798, Aged 82 years.

Here lieth the Body of Charles Saber, cork-cutter, in Highworth, born in Essex, and died April 25, 1735, Aged 60 years.

In Memory of Ann, the Wife of Charles Saber. She died Nov. 23d, 1737, Aged 55 years.

On Flat Stone.

Here lyeth the Body of Thomas Pickett, who departed this life July 17, 1777, Aged 73 years.

In Memory of William, Son of William and Catherine Pickett, who died July the 18th, 1741, Aged 37 years. In Memory of William Pickett, who died Feb. 16, 1773, Aged 93 years. Also Catherine his Wife died March the 6th, 1762, Aged 90 years.

On Head Stones.

John, Son of Robert and Elizabeth Lawrance, died Jan. 19, 1749, Aged 26 years. Ann, daughter of John and Martha Lawrance, died Oct. 23, 1749, Aged 1 year and 10 months.

In Memory of William Pickyett, who departed this life February 16, 1773, Aged 95 years.

Here lyeth the Body of Catharine, the Wife of William Pickyett, who died March 6, 1762, Aged 90 years.

In Memory of Jane, the Wife of Edward Carpenter, who died Oct. 12, 1751, Aged 75 years.

Here lyeth the Body of Ann Edmunds, grand-daughter of William and Catharine Pickett, died Oct. 1, 1754, Aged 16 years.

In Memory of Jemima, the daughter of Thomas and Sarah Mulcock, who died Oct. 20, 1768, Aged 1 year and 9 months.

To the Memory of Ann, the Wife of Joseph Large, who died Feb. 13, 1796, Aged 61 years.

In Memory of Mary, the Wife of Thomas Sharps. She died April 2, 1779, Aged 39 years.

Thomas Sharps. He died May 1, 1794, Aged 73 years.

Thomas, Son of Richard and Ann Sharps. He died March 26, 1790, Aged 9 months. In Memory of two Sons of Thomas and Mary Sharps. William died Jan. 22, 1771, Aged 16 years. Robert died Dec. 18, 1771, Aged 21 years.

On a flat Stone.

Here lyes the Body of John Mulcock, who departed this life Feb. 12, 1771, Aged 73 years.

Also Ann, the Wife of John Mulcock, who died Nov. 29, 1776. Also Thomas, the Son of John and Ann Mulcock, died Sept. 30, 1772, Aged 32 years. Also Jemima, the daughter of Thomas Mulcock, died young.

Sacred to the Memory of Sarah, the Wife of David Thomson, who departed this life Dec. the 31, 1819. Aged 50 years.

In Memory of Rebecca, the Wife of Anthony Major, who died Feb. 8, 1767, Aged 18 years.

In Memory of William, Son of William and Mary Ayliffe, who died April 23, 1768, Aged 22 years. Also Ann, their daughter, who died April 23, 1763, Aged 10 years.

In Memory of Jane, the Wife of William Tuff, who died June 5, 1748, Aged 54 years.

In Memory of Edmund Thatcher, who died Sept. 23d, 1761, Aged 86.

In Memory of Mary the Wife of Edmund Thatcher, who died Jan. 27, 1775, Aged 70 years.

In Memory of Edmund Thatcher. He died Sept. 23, 1742, Aged 32.

In Memory of Eleanor Thatcher, who died Nov. 14, 1745, Aged 40.

In Memory of Mary Thatcher, who departed this life May ye 25, 1774, Aged 68 years.

Also Elizabeth Thatcher, who died March ye 12, 1777, Aged 63 years.

To the Memory of Mary, Wife of Thomas Iles. She died May 3d, 1790, Aged 59 years.

Also William, Son of Francis and Mary Thatcher. He died Nov. 23, 1783, Aged 4 years and 6 months.

To the Memory of Francis Thatcher. He departed this life March 21, 1793, Aged 77 years.

To the Memory of John Tombs, who died March 20, 1798, Aged 65 years.

Also Martha, his Wife, who died Jan. 3, 1812, Aged 80 years.

Joseph, Son of Benjamin and Elizabeth Emblin, died Dec. 31, 1748, Aged 19 years.

To the Memory of Christiana, the Wife of Thomas Radway, who died 24th April, 1803, Aged 42 years.

In Memory of Elizabeth, Wife of Richard Harris, and Daughter of Philip Cook, who died 6th Oct. 1789, Aged 25 years.

In Memory of John Messenger, who departed this life April 3, 1798, Aged 87 years.

In Memory of Richard Messenger, who died July 20, 1777, Aged 63 years.

In Memory of John Messenger, jun. who died June 29, 1803, Aged 58 years.

To the Memory of Elizabeth, the Wife of John Messenger, who died 18th April, 1762, Aged 41.

In Memory of Edward Potts, who departed this life May 26, 1798, Aged 54 years.

To the Memory of John Potts, who died May 16, 1783, Aged 80 years.

Also Martha, his Wife, who died April 19, 1796.

In Memory of John, Son of John and Martha Potts, who departed this life March 19, 1763, Aged 27 years.

In Memory of Martha, Daughter of John and Martha Potts, who died September 7, 1758, Aged 19 years. Mary, their daughter, died in her infancy.

In Memory of Mary, Wife of James Reynolds, who departed this life Jan. 30, 1793, Aged 68 years.

Altar Tomb.

In Memory of Mary, Wife of John Lawrence, who died August the 11th, 1800, Aged 83 years.

In Memory of John Lawrence, who died July 5th, 1783, Aged 79 years.

Also Betty, Wife of John Lawrence, died April 6, 1751, Aged 38 years.

On a Flat Stone.

In Memory of Hester, Wife of William Morse, who died Dec. 21, 1774, Aged 85 years.

Ann, Daughter of Richard and Hester North, who died March the 3d, 1731, Aged 32 years.

Head Stones.

In Memory of Thomas Morse, sen. who died March 9, 1753, Aged 39 years.

To the Memory of Samuel Stanley, who died August 12, 1775, Aged 56 years.

In Memory of Mary, daughter of Samuel and Mary Stanley, who died Jan. 17, 1753, Aged 11 months.

Mary, the Wife of George Goodman, who died the 30th of March, 1801, Aged 66 years.

Also Ann, the daughter of Mary Goodman, who died the 9th of April, 1799, Aged 32 years.

In Memory of Luke Page, who died Dec. 7, 1798, Aged 27 years.

Here lie the Remains of Walter Jessop, who was a respectable Officer of Excise in Highworth 28 years. He died June the 3d, 1791, Aged 60 years.

In Memory of Elizabeth, Wife of the said Walter Jessop. She died Oct. the 3d, 1782, Aged 33 years.

And also Elizabeth, Daughter of the said Walter and Elizabeth Jessop, who died Oct. the 24th, 1763, Aged 3 years. And also Walter, Son of the said Walter and Elizabeth Jessop, who died Jan. the 23d, 1769, Aged 4 years and 2 months.

In Memory of Margaret, the Wife of John Grinnell, who died 5th Dec. 1762, Aged 29 years.

In Memory of Cyprus Lawrence, who died Dec. the 14th, 1773, Aged 60 years. Also Langley, Son of Cyprus and Hannah Lawrence, who died March 21, 1766, Aged 23 years.

On an Altar Tomb.

Here lyeth the Body of Virgil Parker, gent. who died April, 4, 1762, in the 81st year of his age.

Here lyeth the Body of Sarah, the Wife of Virgil Parker, gent. who died June 3, 1741, and in the 59th year of her age.

Sarah Parker, spinster, eldest Daughter of Virgil and Sarah Parker, and the last Survivor of an ancient and respectable Family, died November the 3d, 1793, in the 83d year of her age.

To the Memory of Mr. John Parker, gentleman, who died May 16, 1784, Aged 70 years.

Catherine Parker, gentlewoman, died Oct. 17, 1788, Aged 76 years.

Against E. end of Church.

Near this Place rest the Remains of Benjamin Anns, who died the 12th of March, 1807, Aged 89 years.

Also Elizabeth, the Wife of Benjamin Anns, who died the 14th of June, 1806, Aged 90 years.

Register commenced 1538, Sept. 29.

The Rev. Edward Rowden present Vicar.

HANNINGTON.

On Head Stones, S. side of the Church.

In Memory of Grachus, the Wife of Thomas Miles, who died June 3, 1780, Aged 78 years.

To the Memory of Richard Jocham, who departed this life April 5th, 1793, Aged 46 years.

In Memory of John York, who departed this life Dec. 6, 1697, Aged 77.

Also Margaret, his Wife, who departed this life Nov. 3d, 1741, Aged 76.

In Memory of William, the Son of John and Margaret York, who departed this life Nov. 2, 1744, Aged 48.

Also William York, Brother to John York, who departed this life Dec. 1702, Aged 77 years.

To the Memory of Robert Long, who died the 6th of March, 1797, Aged 84 years.

To the Memory of Sarah, Wife of Robert Long, who died the 3d of June, 1790, Aged 69 years.

Here lyeth the Body of Henry Pensom, who deceased the 1st day of Dec. 1691, Aged . . .

In Memory of Richard Pantin. He died July 26, 1757, Aged 62 years. Also Ann, his Wife, who departed this life June 10, 1766, Aged 70 years.

To the Memory of Mary, Wife of John Frampton, who died February 12, 1806, Aged 59 years.

No ling'ring sickness, or long-warning pains,
The pious want to justify their stains;
To pray forbearance from impending fate,
And urge repentance in a death-bed state:
Heaven found her fit in any hour to die,
And sudden snatch'd her kindly to its sky.

Also Michael, their Son, who died April 20, 1788, Aged 2 years and 6 months.

In Memory of Philip Cave, late of Hannington, who died April the 8th. 1803, Aged 78 years.

Also Mary his Wife, who died April 17, 1793, Aged 77 years.

With pain and sickness have our flesh consum'd,
And here our wasted bodies lay entomb'd:
Easy and open have our passage been,
From earth to heaven, from griefs to joys unseen.

In Memory of Edward Miflin, who departed this life the 14th of Sept. 1792, Aged 66 years.

In Memory of Phillis, ye Wife of Thomas Stiles, who died Dec. 9, 1729, Aged 28 years.

In Memory of Thomas Stiles, who departed this life May the 16, 1772, Aged 66 years.

In Memory of Katherine, the Wife of Thomas Stiles, who died Oct. 22, 1746, Aged 53 years.

In Memory of Francis Stiles, who died Jan. 12, 1766, Aged 52 years.

To the Memory of Toby Stiles, who died the 30th of January, 1787, Aged 78 years.

He liv'd in love, and died in peace,
And now his joys will never cease.

Also Ann, the Wife of Toby Stiles, who died the 6th of June, 1805, Aged 84 years.

Now here she sleeps within this peaceful shrine,
Till angels wake her by a sound divine.

On Flat Stones.

In Memory of John Edmond, died Nov. 3, 1722, Aged 83. Also Mary his Wife died August 30, 1721, Aged 69 years.

In Memory of Jonathan Edmond, who died Oct. 28, 1710, Aged 17.

To the Memory of Giles Edmond, who departed this life the 27th of January, 1779, Aged 81 years.

On Head Stones.

In Memory of Elizabeth Johnson, who died Feb. 4, 1771, Aged 80 years.

In Memory of Philip Ilott, who died Dec. 15, 1812, Aged 70 years.

Sigh not for me as you pass by,
For as you are, so once was I;
And as I am, so must you be,
Therefore prepare to follow me.

In Memory of Ann, Wife of Philip Ilott, who died March 6, 1802, Aged 86.

Farewell, dear Husband, I could not stay,
My time was come, I must away:
God be your guide, and give you grace,
That Heaven may be our resting place,
With those our friends that's gone before,
To live in joy for evermore.

In Memory of Henry Angel, who died 17th July, 1788, Aged 89 years.

To the Memory of John Angel, who died Jan. 8th, 1747, Aged 86.

To the Memory of Elizabeth, Wife of Henry Angel, who died Dec. 8, 1751, Aged 68.

On Flat Tombs.

In Memory of Edward Lock, who departed this life Nov. 20, 1772, Aged 45 years.

To the Memory of Joseph Gerring, who died Feb. ye 25th, 1717, Aged 50 years.

Also here lyeth Jane, his Wife. She departed this life January 31, 1764, Aged 92.

In Memory of Elizabeth Lockey, who departed this life March ye 23d, 1774, Aged 53 years.

In Memory of Charles Clarke, who was buried Sept. 27, 1737, Aged 54 years.

Also Margaret Clarke, his Sister. She died June 10, 1773, Aged 87 years.

Head Stones.

To the Memory of Thomas, Son of Jabaz, and Margaret Westall, who died August 30, 1800, Aged 34 years.

To the Memory of John Weston, who departed this life Feb. the 19th, 1803, Aged 77 years.

To the Memory of Rachel Weston, who departed this life May the 30th, 1796, Aged 72 years.

To the Memory of Elizabeth Weston. She departed this life May 24, 1790, in the 70th year of her age.

To the Memory of Thomas Weston, who died Oct. ye 26, 1780, Aged 63 years.

Also Sarah, his Wife. She died May 21, 1780, Aged 60 years.

In Memory of Catharine, the Wife of Richard Daws, who died Nov. 19, 1777, Aged 88 years.

In Memory of Edward Reason. He died Oct. 27, 1738, Aged 56 years.

In Memory of Jane Peters, who departed this life September 16, 1772, Aged 80 years.

To the Memory of Mary, daughter of Daniel and Rachel Peters, who died March 19, 1791, Aged 43 years.

In Memory of Daniel Peters, who departed this life Jan. 14, 1768, Aged 65 years.

In Memory of Rachel, Wife of Daniel Peters, who died Nov. 20, 1766, Aged 55 years.

To the Memory of Samuel, Son of Daniel and Rachel Peters, who died the 11th Sept. 1789, Aged 45 years.

Margaret, daughter of John and Ann Peters, died Jan. ye 26, 1742, Aged 22 years.

In Memory of Mary Penn, daughter of William and Mary Weston, who died May 16, 1752, Aged 37 years.

Here lyeth the Body of Rachel, daughter of William and Mary Weston. She died June ye 23d, 1722, Aged 3 years and 6 months.

In Memory of Mary, Wife of William Weston, who died April 11, 1742, Aged 58 years.

In Memory of William Weston, who died Oct. 15, 1750, Aged 67 years.

In Memory of Thomas Westell, who died Jan. ye 7th, 1763, Aged 58 years.

Also Margaret, his Wife. She died Dec. 12, 1772, Aged 70 years.

A Father kind, a Mother dear,
Two faithful friends, lies buried here,
Our days are past, our glass is run,
Our children dear prepare to come.

In Memory of Elizabeth, Wife of John Baker, who died May 13, 1781, Aged 78 years.

Also John Baker, who died 1781, Aged 79.

In Memory of Thomas, Son of William and Martha Webb, who died March 12, 1771, Aged 10 years.

Also William, Son of William and Martha Webb, who died April 4, 1771, Aged 4 years.

To the Memory of Martha, Wife of William Smith, who departed this life the 26th day of April, 1780, Aged 24 years.

To the Memory of Henry, Son of William and Martha Smith, who died in his infancy, in the year of our Lord 1780.

To the Memory of Martha, daughter of William and Martha Smith, who died in her infancy in the year of our Lord 1779.

To the Memory of Toby, Son of William and Martha Smith, who died in his infancy in the year of our Lord 1778.

In Memory of Richard Newman. He died April ye 4th, 1753, Aged 41.

In Memory of Mary Wife of George Ayliffe, who died September 14, 1794, Aged 52 years.

To the Memory of William Gregory, who departed this life the 2d of July, 1788, Aged 59 years.

In Memory of Jane, the Wife of William Gregory, sen. who departed this life April the 23d, in the year of our Lord 1751, Aged 57. In Memory of William Gregory, who departed this life August the 14th, in the year of our Lord 1777, Aged 83 years.

In Memory of Jane Plumer, who departed this life Jan. 26, 1772, Aged 49 years.

In Memory of Mary, daughter of William and Sarah Gregory, who died April 1, 1771, Aged 12 years. Also Ann, their daughter, who died April 3, 1771, Aged 10 years.

To the Memory of Mary, daughter of William and Sarah Gregory, who departed this life the 13th of March, 1794, in the 17th year of her age.

Altar Tombs.

Sacred to the Memory of Mary the Wife of John Hitchman, who departed this life the 30th of March, 1803, Aged 67 years.

Here lyeth ye Body of William York, who died Feb. ye 23d, 1772, Aged 70 years.

Here lyeth the Body of Ann, Wife of William York, who died Dec ye 2d, 1778, Aged 80 years.

Here lyeth the Body of James Haines, who departed this life April 21, A. D. 1772, Aged 29 years.

In Memory of Michael Haines, who died Sept. 5, 1753, Aged 75 years. Also Elizabeth, his Wife. She died June 9, 1764, Aged 70.

In Memory of John Haines, who died Dec. 1748, Aged 47.

On Head Stones.

Here lieth the Body of William Curtis, who died March 14, 1730, Aged 70.

In Memory of William Edmond. He died Oct. ye 5th, 1748. And also of Elizabeth his Wife. She died July 6, 1763, Aged 74 years.

On an Altar-Tomb against W. end of Church.

To the Memory of Maria Hedges, daughter of Charles and Ann Hedges, who departed this life May the 14th, 1815, Aged 17 years.

I well in health from home did go,
And met with Death, that deadly foe,
Which did prevent all things design'd,
Hope now in Christ I shall remain.

Head Stones, North Side.

In Memory of William Pound, who died July 8, 1798, Aged 50 years.

To the Memory of John Dawes, who died Feb. the 24th, 1795, Aged 73 years. Also Mary, Wife of John Dawes. who died Dec. the 10th, 1792, Aged 77 years.

Register commenced 1571.

STANTON.

On Flat Stones, West End.

In Memory of Jacob Mathews, who departed this life April 27, 1816, Aged 68 years.

By the grace of God I am what I am.

To the Memory of Henry New, who departed this life the 2d of May, 1800, Aged 87 years.

Also to the Memory of Martha, Wife of Henry New, who departed this life the 9th of Dec. 1809, Aged 84 years.

Here lyeth ye Body of Benjamin Bacon, who departed this life June the 23, Anno Dom. 1680.

Reader on me cast an Eye, as thou art
now so once was I. Though thou art
well and healthy be, Sure of this Th . .
Thou must dye. Anno Dom. 1679.

In Memory of Akerman Selby, who died July ye 2d, 1752, Aged 92 years.

Here lyeth ye Body of Akerman, Son of Akerman Selbee, who departed this life Dec. ye 28, A. D. 1777, Aged 22.

Here lyeth ye Body of Elizabeth, Wife of Akerman Selby, who died May 21, 1725, Aged 65 years.

Here lyeth ye Body of Elizabeth, Wife of Thomas Hitchman, who died April 10, 1752, Aged 40 years.

Richard Savage Desaced Nov. the 20th, 1673.

Here lyeth the Body of William, Son of John Savery, who died March 12, 1706.

His Death you see hath Parted us Twaine,
I hopee Earee long To meet againe.

Richard Orchard died March the 26, 1674.

In Memory of Thomas Stevens, who died April 24, 1756, Aged 74.

Sarah, Wife of Thomas Stephens, who died Dec. 18, 1749, Aged 63.

In Memory of John Morse, who died Jan. 3, 1762, Aged 71 years.

To the Memory of Isaac Matthews, who died Jan. 10, 1814, Aged 74 years.

Within this consecrated spot of ground
The mortal part of Isaac Matthews lays;
May he amongst the bless'd be found
Whom God to everlasting life shall raise.

This Stone was erected to the Memory of his beloved Parent, by William Mathews, as a mark of his filial Regard.

William Smith, of Upper Norton, in Oxfordshire. He died Jan. 30, 1744, Aged 71.

Lay me down with Christ to Rest,
With him I hope my soul is blest.

In Memory of Hercules, the Son of Gabriel and Sevie Underhill, who died 21st April, 1764, Aged 23 years.

In Memory of Gabriel Underhill, who died 28th Dec. 1703, Aged 70. Elizabeth their daughter, who died in her infancy.

Here lyeth the Body of Anne, the daughter of William and Mary Rime, who died March 26, 1730, Aged 13 years.

Here lyeth the Body of Jeffery Rime, who died April 2, 1730, Aged 77 years.

Also the Body of Ann, his Wife, who died March 7, 1729, Aged 63 years.

In Memory of Mary, the Wife of William Rime, who departed this life July the 6, 1782, Aged 74 years.

Also Catherine, their daughter, who departed this life the 28th of April, 1797, Aged 53 years.

Also Susanna Hunter, daughter of William and Mary Rime, who departed this life Oct. 9, 1815, Aged 75 years.

Here lyeth the Body of John Head, deceased Oct. 28, 1723, Aged 57 years.

In Memory of John Eatall, who died March 15, 1747, Aged 70 years.

In Memory of Jane, the Wife of John Eatall. She died Dec. 12, 1756, Aged 67 years.

Here lyeth the Body of John Eatall, who, by a violent distemper, departed this life Nov. 13, 1767, Aged 39 years.

Here lyeth the Body of Ann Smith, daughter of Henry and Mary Smith, who died died Jan. 13, 1767, Aged 20 years.

Israel, the Wife of Thomas Moorse, died April ye 24th, 1640, Aged 41 years.

In Memory of Hannah, the Wife of Thomas Titcombe, who died Nov. 22, 1762, Aged 41 years.

Beneath this Stone resteth the Remains of George Hooper, who departed this life April 23, 1815, Aged 70 years. Also John, Son of George and Mary Hooper, who died in his infancy.

Here lyeth the Body of Margaret Same, who departed this life June 20, A. D. 1711.

In Memory of Elizabeth, Wife of Jonathan Garlick, who died August 5, 1775, Aged 79.

Jonathan Garlick died January 29, 1778, Aged 88.

Henry Morse, Son of Thomas, lyeth here, who died Feb. 11, 1729, Aged 74 years.

To the Memory of Joseph Hiett, who departed this life the 4th of Sept. 1793, Aged 48 years.

To the Memory of Robert Hiett, who departed this life the 13th of Feb. 1795, Aged 38 years.

In Memory of Richard, Son of Robert and Mary Hiett, who died May 18, 1786, Aged 22 weeks.

In Memory of Sarah, daughter of Robert and Mary Hiett, who died 14th May 1794, in the 17th year of her age.

Here lyeth the Body of Giles Head, who departed this life June ye 10th, An° Dom̄ 1712.

Here lyeth ye Body of Thomas, ye Son of Giles Head, who died March the 21, 1729, Aged 66 years.

Also Ann, the Wife of Thomas Head, died May 25, 1721, Aged 48 years.

Here lyeth the Body of William Monday, who died March ye 3d, A. D. 1698.

Heare lieth the Body of John Burges, who deceased the second day of June 1616.

Edmond Burges buryed in Staunton ye 2d March, 1...

Here lyeth ye Body of William Bacon, who died Sept. 2, 1676. Here also lyeth the Body of Joan, ye Wife of Thomas Morse, of this Parish, and Daughter of the said William Bacon, who . . . . married to Thomas Morse, at Great Coxwell, Barks, by whom she had seven Children, six whereof living, Robert, William, John, Thomas, Richard, and Elizabeth, who purchased this Stone to perpetuate her Memory. She died June 2, 1715, Aged 63. J. M. Aged 57.

Here lieth the Body of Margery Bacon, the Wife of William Bacon, who deceased the 16th day of November, An° Dom̄ 1682.

Here lieth the Body of Elizabeth Elizabeth Crook, who departed this life the 20th day of Dec. Anno Dom̄ 1682.

Against S. side of the Church.

Beneath this Stone lyeth the Body of Elizabeth, the Daughter of William and Susanna Akers, who departed this life August the 24, 1809, Aged 20 years. Also Richard, their Son, who departed this life June the 28, 1804, Aged 2 years and 10 months. And also Thomas, their Son, who departed this life Jan. 2nd, 1812, Aged 12 years.

The Rev. John Awbrey Trenchard Vicar.

INGLESHAM.

On a Tomb, S. side of Church.

In Memory of Ann, Wife of Daniel Heming, who died Feb, 1794, Aged 68 years.

Head Stones.

In Memory of Isaac Heming, who died Feb. 15, 1765, Aged 52 years.

In Memory of Catharine, the Widow of Isaac Heming, who died June 7, 1768, Aged 47 years.

In Memory of Sarah, the daughter of Isaac and Catharine Heming, who died May 30, 1769, Aged 17 years.

In Memory of Edward Gorton, who departed this life June the 9th, 1788, Aged 77 years.

Here lyeth the Body of John Gardner. He departed this life the 25th of May, Anno 1679.

Elizabeth, Wife of Richard Yeats, of Buscott Wick, died March 6, 1805, Aged 44 years.

Also James Cheeseley Yeats, Son of Richard and Elizabeth Yeats, died May 6, 1806, Aged 27 years.

This Stone was Erected by her surviving Children.

Stop, pensive wand'rer, at this awful spot,
Reflect awhile, for this may be thy lot;
Some painful illness, or a deep decline,
May snatch thy life, as it hath done by mine:
All means were used, but human skill was vain,
Till Christ, the true Physician, eas'd my pain.

In Memory of Elizabeth, Wife of Thomas Cheesely, who departed this life May the 10th. 1785, Aged 65 years.

In Memory of Elizabeth, Wife of Thomas Budd, who died April 24, 1783, Aged 77 years.

Here lyeth the Body of Thomas Budd, who departed this life Nov. 25, 1778, Aged 75 years.

In Memory of John Budd, who died Sept. 28, 1754, Aged 10 years.

Mary, Daughter of Thomas and Elizabeth Budd, died August 16, 1744, Aged 3 years.

Here lyeth the Body of John, Son of Robert and Alice Mattinly. He died Oct. 6, A. D. 1721, Aged 2 years.

In Memory of Sarah, Wife of William Cooper, who died August 5, 1779, Aged 31 years.

A faithful Friend lye buried here,
A loving Wife, a Mother dear,
She liv'd in love, and died in peace,
I hope her joy will never cease.

In Memory of William Cooper, who died March 18, 1791, Aged 38 years.

Sincere to all, and upright in his ways,
And all his actions justly merit praise;
Possest of these, he liv'd beloved by most,
And died lamented as the greatest loss.

In Memory of Robert Woolford, who died March 12, 1781, in the 78th year of his age.

In Memory of Thomas, Son of John and Susanna Master, of this Parish, who died Feb. 3, 1786, Aged 3 years.

On an Altar Tomb, N. side of Church.

Jacent sub hoc lapide Reliquæ Richardi Triplett, hujus Parochiæ olim Curionis.

Decessit Anno { Salutis 1732.
Ætatis 30.

Qui quidem Richardus, filius erat natu maximi Richard Triplett, A. M. olim Vicari de Highworth.

Obiit Anno { Salutis 1719.
Ætatis 30.

Under lie the Remains of the Rev. John Jordan, A. M. heretofore Fellow of Catharine Hall, in Cambridge, who having cultivated a friendship with the excellent Dr. Sherlock, when Master of that Society, was called forth by him from his retirement, at Aldridge in Staffordshire, where he lived contentedly upon his patrimony, for the Cure of this Parish, refusing from the same hands a more distant benefice of much greater value. Having rebuilt the Vicarage House, he resided constantly in it twenty-eight years, conscientiously performing the duties of his calling, a faithful Minister of Christ. By his abilities as a Divine and a Preacher, he was well qualified for higher stations in the Church, but being moderate in his desires, and happy in his situation, he solicited no favours from the Great, nor envied those who claimed them. He died August 28, 1763, Aged 76.

On Altar Tombs.

In Memory of Margaret Matthews, who departed this life the 27th of January, in the year of our Lord 1814, Aged 74 years.

Harry Matthews died March 22, 1816, Aged 52 years.

On a Flat Stone.

Underneath lie the Remains of Elizabeth Master, Wife of Daniel Master, of Cirencester, and Daughter of Isaac and Catharine Heming, of this Parish, who died March 27, 1763, Aged 23 years.

Head Stone.

Katharine, Daughter of Isaac and Katharine Heming, died Nov. 6, 1763, Aged 17 years.

Register commenced 1589.

The Rev. Stanhope Bruce present Vicar, 91 years of age, inducted 1763.

BROAD BLUNSDON.

On Flat Tombs, N. side of Church.

Here lyeth the Body of John Stapler, who died December 31, 1757, Aged 57 years.

Beneath this Tomb lieth the Body of Jane, Daughter of John and Susannah Stapler, who departed this life August 6, 1818, Aged 72 years.

Sacred to the Memory of Susanna, the Wife of John Stapler, who departed this life the 11th of Dec. 1787, Aged 82 years.

To the Memory of Mary, the Wife of George Akerman, who died June 13, 1793, Aged 32 years.

To the Memory of George Akerman, who died August 10, 1790, Aged 58 years.

In Memory of Ann, Wife of John Akerman, daughter of John and Susanna Stapler. She died July 1, 1784, Aged 51 years.

In Memory of John Akerman, who died Nov. 22, 1789, Aged 66 years.

To the Memory of John Jenner, who departed this life the 22d of May, 1807, Aged 62 years.

To the Memory of Elizabeth, the Wife of John Jenner, who departed this life the 29th of April, 1804, Aged 52 years.

In Memory of Ann, daughter of John and Elizabeth Jenner, who died Nov. 23, 1796, Aged 15 years.

Also Sarah, Daughter of John and Elizabeth Jenner, who died Jan. 15, 1803, Aged 13 years.

Head Stones.

In Memory of John, Son of John and Emma Heath, who departed this life January 30, 1776, Aged 21 years.

To the Memory of Emma Heath, Wife of John Heath, who died the 7th day of March, 1779, Aged 59 years. John Heath, who died May 11, 1780, Aged 54 years.

Here lyeth the Body of John Hall, who died August 27, 1770, Aged 83 years. Also Mary, his Wife. She died March 1st, 1771, Aged 77.

In Memory of Thomas Potts, who died Sept. 25, 1794, Aged 57 years.

Dear Wife weep no more,
Nor Children shed a tear,
For I am gone but just before
Unto my Saviour dear.

In Memory of James Avery. He died March 13, 1771, Aged 64 years.

Remember, you that passeth by,
As you are now so once was I;
And as I am, so must you be,
Prepare, therefore, to follow me.

In Memory of Alice, the Wife of Robert Litten, who died Oct. 18, 1755, Aged 62 years.

On Flat Tombs.

To the Memory of Thomas Litten, who died 17th April, 1803, Aged 82 years.

Death, like a stranger, at a distance stays,
Nor, till the message sent, his visit pays;
Yet there are some, more favoured than the rest,
On whom he calls, a free and friendly guest:
Such was my happy lot, so blest my doom,
And such the useful lesson of this tomb:
Live well, and Death, though sudden, will but prove
The shorter passage to the realms above.

To the Memory of Elizabeth, the Wife of William Litten, who departed this life August 23, 1783, Aged 67 years.

To the Memory of William Litten, who departed this life July the 16th, 1811, Aged 79 years.

O what frail man observes how oft
He does from virtue fall?
O cleanse from me from my secret faults,
Thou God, that knowest them all.
The old and young must all submit,
To fatal death, when God thinks fit.

Here lyeth the Body of Robert Litten. He died Dec. 10, 1737, Aged 64 years.

In Memory of John, Son of Thomas and Susanna Potts, who died young. Also John, their second Son, who died Oct. 8, 1786, Aged 21 years.

Here lies a youth, whose chearful bloom,
Promis'd a train of years to come;
But set for e'er his morning sun,
And life exspir'd e'er scarce begun.
He was of temper sweet, of mind serene,
No vice in his conduct e're were seen.
Take warning hence, ye thoughtless, young, and gay,
Who from the paths of virtue often stray;
You cannot tell how soon your time may come,
And unprepar'd be summon'd to the tomb.

In Memory of Thomas, the son of Robert and Mary Litten, who died April 5, 1765, Aged 7 years and 7 months.

A tender branch lies buried here,
That was belov'd by parents here;
Few was his days, short was his race
From womb to grave, short was the space.
Learn parents, then, to be content,
When God requires what is but lent;
In youth and children put no trust,
For all must die, and turn to dust.

In Memory of John, the Son of Robert and Mary Litten, who died Dec. 8, 1773, Aged 29 years.

On Flat Tombs.

To the Memory of Robert Litten, who died the 2d of April, 1784, Aged 66 years.

Certain and uncertain is the state of man,
Certain of death, but yet uncertain when;
For instance, here you have before your eyes,
How soon the strongest man grows sick and dies,
Sudden from off this tiresome stage he fled,
One day in health, the next amongst the dead;
The stroke surprising to a carnal eye,
But not to one prepar'd to die.

In Memory of Thomas Puzey, Schoolmaster, who departed this life April 30th, 1769, Aged 35 years and 9 months.

To the Memory of Harriot, daughter of Joseph and Mary Jarvis, who died April 30, 1813, Aged 22 years.

Though few my days were here below,
The longer is my rest;
God call'd me hence in early life,
Because he thought it best.

Sacred to the Memory of William King, who died March 27, 1807, Aged 70 years.

To the Memory of Ann, Wife of William King, who died Jan. 20, 1781, Aged 43 years.

Head Stones.

Here lyeth the Body of Samuel Hornblow, who departed this life Sept. 7. 1767, Aged 61 years.

In Memory of Sarah, Wife of Samuel Hornblow, who died Nov. 1st, 1780, Aged 67 years.

When sickness comes,
Night you think long,
From watch to watch
The morning cometh on.
Before night comes,
Make use of precious light,
Before death enters
With ghastly sight.

In Memory of William, Son of Samuel and Sarah Hornblow, who died Nov. 7th, 1773, Aged 21 years.

Though painful sickness hath my flesh consum'd,
And here my wasted body lies intomb'd;
Easy and open hath my passage been,
From earth to heaven, from grief to joy unseen.

In Memory of James Litten, who died May 16, 1815, Aged 60 years.

To the Memory of Mary, the Wife of James Litten, who died June 10, 1800, Aged 45 years.

Reader, be sure make Christ thy friend,
Be always ready for thy end,
I in my prime was catch'd away
Therefore repent, make no delay;
Youth, health, nor strength, could not me save,
From God's decree, bar from my grave.

Also James their Son, who died young.

On Flat Tomb against S. side of the Church.

In Memory of Mary, Wife of John Stone, who died March 14, 1805, Aged 61 years.

O God to me take heed,
I help of thee require;
O Lord of Hosts, with haste and speed,
Help me I thee desire.

In Memory of Francis, Son of John and Mary Stone, who died March 28, 1802, Aged 27.

With pain I've been long oppress,
That wore my strength away,
It made me long for lasting rest,
That never shall decay.

On Head Stones.

To the Memory of Mary, Wife of Thomas Hunt, who departed this life the 5th of October, 1767, Aged 63 years.

Mary, Wife of Thomas Hunt, died 5th August 1765, Aged 49 years.

In Memory of Mary, Wife of Thomas Hunt. She died August 17, 1767, Aged 39 years.

In Memory of John Litten, who died Feb. 7, 1744, Aged 25 years.

In Memory of Ann, Wife of John Dore, who died Dec. 30, 1780, Aged 57 years.

In Memory of Thomas, Son of William and Susanna Penniger, who died Dec. 6, 1774, Aged 3 years.

Sacred to the Memory of Sarah, Daughter of John and Elizabeth Deacon, who departed this life Sept. 22, 1817, Aged 31 years.

Although Death's dart did pierce my heart
When I was in my prime,
My friends most dear to weep forbear,
'Twas God's appointed time.
For sudden death, you plainly see,
Has eas'd me of my misery.

To the Memory of Martha, daughter of James and Lizzy Deacon, who died July 29, 1809, Aged 3 years.

Parent, lament not o'er thy child,
To God's decree be reconcil'd,
The Spirit from the body fled,
Will gain a better in its stead.

Ann, the Wife of Thomas Wells, dy'd Dec. ye 21st, 1740, Aged 88.

Thomas Wells, departed this life April 3, 1732, Aged 79.

In Memory of John Perkins, who departed this life Dec. 2, 1767, Aged 75 years.

In Memory of Mary, Wife of John Perkins, who departed this life April 27, 1767, Aged 70 years.

In Memory of John, Son of John and Mary Perkins, who died July 3, 1776, Aged 50 years.

In Memory of Mary Wilkins, who died Jan 6, 1773, Aged 74 years.

In Memory of William, Son of John and Mary Perkins, who died Oct. 30, 1769, Aged 45 years.

In Memory of William Wilkins, who departed this life April 7, 1761, Aged 9 years.

Here lyeth the Body of Mary, Wife of William Wilkins, who died March 3, 1740, Aged 84.

Here lyeth ye Body of Elizabeth, Wife of Robert Straing. She died July 13, 1734, Aged 32 years.

On Flat Stones.

Here lyeth the Body of Ann, the Wife of Robert Wollford. She died June 21, 1738, Aged 27 years.

Here lyeth the Body of Humphry, Son of ye Widow Hewet, who was buried January ye 31, Anno Dom. 1691. Here lieth the Body of William Hewet, who was buried Sept. ye 3d, Anno Dom. 1691.

In Memory of William Butler, who departed this life Oct. 3, 1787, Aged 54 years.

Here lyeth ye Body of Jeffry and Mary Lockey, who departed this life Dec. 26, A. D. 1705, Aged 26 years.

Here lyeth ye Body of John Tayler, who departed this life March ye 30, Anno Dom. 1695.

Here lyeth ye Body of Elizabeth, ye daughter of Jeffery and Mary Lockey, who departed this life Oct. 25, A. D. 1703.

In Memory of Mary the Wife of John Midwinter, who died July 22, 1638, Aged 30. James, Son of John and Mary Midwinter. He died Feb. 20, 1736.

Here lieth the Body of Margaret, the Wife of Thomas Hatt, and Thomas Pinhell, his Son, who departed this life Sept. 16, Anno Dom. 1693.

Here lies interred the Body of Sarah, Wife of Thomas Hatt, who deceased Nov. 23, Anno Dom. 1693.

In Memory of Edward Drew, who departed this life May 12, 1815, Aged 42 years.

Mourn not, dear Wife, at my decease,
I hope with God I've made my peace,
In Christ alone I only trust,
To rise in number with the just.

To the Memory of William Nobes, who departed this life April 29, 1804, Aged 34 years. Also Rebecca, Wife of William Nobes, who departed this life April the 12th, 1804, Aged 35 years. Also James, Son of William and Rebecca Nobes, who died in his infancy.

Boast not, O Death! thy universal reign,
Thou, in thy turn, shalt in the end be slain.

To the Memory of Moses, Son of John and Sarah Drew, who departed this life the 25th of May, 1802, Aged 28 years.

To the Memory of Martha, Wife of Richard Tinson, who died the 11th of June, 1801, Aged 25 years.

Also Martha, their Daughter, who died the 4th of May, 1801, Aged 23 weeks.

To the Memory of John, Son of John and Sarah Drew, who departed this life Oct. 26, 1812, Aged 50 years.

Farewell, my dearest friend, I must away,
Death calls me hence, I could no longer stay,
Farewell all earthly joys, I go to prove
The endless pleasure of the saints above.
Farewell my pains, disorders, doubts, and fears,
In Heaven there's neither sickness, grief, nor tears,
All I possest below I now resign,
Vain world farewell, but welcome joys divine.

In Memory of Sarah, Daughter of John and Sarah Drew, who died Dec. 11, 1785, Aged 11 years.

Also Thomas, Son of John and Sarah Drew, who died March 21, 1788, Aged 13 months.

And also Jane their Daughter, who died April 10, 1778, Aged 5 weeks.

In Memory of Martha, daughter of John and Sarah Drew, who died Oct. 26, 1771, Aged 5 years.

In Memory of Sarah, Daughter of John and Sarah Drew, who died Sept. 17, 1771, Aged 8 years.

To the Memory of Elizabeth, the Daughter of John and Sarah Drew, who departed this life the 1st of August, 1795, Aged 31 years.

Reader, prepare to follow me,
For as I am, so shalt thou be,
Rolling in dark and silent dust,
Prepare for death, for die thou must:
Life is uncertain, death is sure,
Sin is the wound, Christ is the cure;
Praises on tombs are vainly spent,
A good name is a monument.

To the Memory of Thomas Drew, who departed this life July the 16th, 1818, Aged 35 years.

Confide not, Reader, in thy youth or strength,
But more than both, the present moment prize,
Graves here surround thee of each breadth and length,
And thou may'st be, perhaps, the next that dies.

Also Sarah and Jane, daughter of Thomas and Sarah Drew, who died in their infancy.

On Flat Tombs.

To the Memory of Sarah, Wife of John Drew, who departed this life Sept. 10, 1810, Aged 73 years.

Hail, sacred grave, be loyal to thy trust,
Till my dear Lord revives my sleeping dust,
Then as a faithful steward safe restore
That precious treasure thou canst keep no more.

To the Memory of John Drew, who died the 2d of Oct. 1802, Aged 73 years.

Farewell, my Wife and Children all,
My time was come, the Lord did call
Me to my grave, and there to lay
Until the resurrection day.

In Memory of Peter Harris, who died Feb. 10, 1802, Aged 61 years.

Though gone from hence, we hope from Him 'tis given,
To live with Christ for evermore in Heaven.

In Memory of Mary, Wife of Jonathan Barnes, sen. who died May 24, 1780, Aged 63 years.

Dear Husband, now my life is past,
My love to you so long did last;
Now I am gone no sorrow take,
But love my children for my sake.

Also to the Memory of Jonathan Barnes, sen. who died January the 6th, 1810, Aged 95 years.

Happy's the man whom God doth own,
And to the marriage-supper bidden,
Who here lays down his earthly load,
Whose blessed spirit makes in heaven.

To the Memory of Jonathan Barnes, who departed this life April 18, 1797, Aged 48 years.

In perfect health he went from home,
Not thinking that his glass was run,
All flowers grow but to fade away,
More sudden death does life decay.

To the Memory of Mary Beames Barnes, Wife of Jonathan Barnes, who departed this life Jan. 31, 1817, Aged 66 years.

In Memory of Jonathan, Son of Edward and Margery Barnes, who died Dec. 31, 1773, Aged 6 years and 3 months. In Memory of John Barnes, Son of Jonathan and Mary Barnes, who departed this life May the 11th, 1787, in the 6th year of his age. To the Memory of Edward, Son of Edward and Margery Barnes, who departed this life Oct. 16, 1794, Aged 24 years. In Memory of three children of Jonathan and Mary Barnes: Mary, their daughter, died Nov. 16, 1773, in the first year of her age: Jonathan, their Son, died Oct. 10, 1774, Aged 15 weeks: Jonathan, their second Son, died March 6, 1778, Aged 5 weeks.

To the Memory of Joseph, Son of John and Mary Adams, who departed this life the 6th day of Feb. 1776, Aged 68 years.

In Memory of John Adams, who died August ye 8th, 1747, Aged 74 years.

In Memory of Mary Adams, who died Feb. 1762, Aged 82 years.

In Memory of Betty, the Widow of William Limmer, gent. daughter of John and Elizabeth Morriell, late of Buryrown, who departed this life the 18th of July, 1746, Ætatis 50. Also the Body of Philadelphia Brook, daughter of James and Philadelphia Pinnock. She departed this life the 19th of Jan. 1774, Aged 63 years.

Here lyeth ye Body of John Strange, who died August 1, 1725, Aged 70 years.

In Memory of Samuel, Son of Richard and Joan Kenby, who died March 12, 1777, Aged 27 years.

To the Memory of John Adams, who departed this life the 24th of Dec. 1812, Aged 95 years.

In Memory of Mary, Wife of John Adams. who departed this life Dec. 24, 1777, Aged 58 years.

In Memory of Robert, Son of John and Mary Adams, who died Dec. 3, 1783, Aged 21 years.

In bloom of youth he serv'd his God,
And in the paths of virtue trod;
In other griefs a share he bore,
The needy shar'd his little store.

In Memory of William Bradley, who died Feb. 12, 1744.

To the Memory of Jane, the Wife of John Pinnock, who died 27th May, 1797, Aged 73 years.

Laden with years, by sickness prest,
This pious matron came to rest,
A fair example of good life,
She was a chaste and loving wife:
Her house did shew her prudent care,
She knew both how to spend and spare.
Mourn not, she's gone where tears do cease,
She upright liv'd, and died in peace.

To the Memory of John Pinnock, who died Nov. 13, 1804, Aged 66 years.

Here Resteth the Body of Edith, Wife of John Pinnock, who was buried Feb. 18, A. D. 1693.

And also John Pinnock, her Husband, was buried Nov. 19, 1699.

Here lyeth also the Body of John, the Son of John and Edith Pinnock, who was buried Sept. A. D. 1702.

James, Son of John and Sarah Pinnock, died July 17, 1763, Aged 79 years.

To the Memory of Francis, Son of Edward and Margery Barnes, who departed this life Nov. 1, 1813, Aged 37 years.

To the Memory of Moses, Son of Edward and Margery Barnes, who departed this life Feb. 28, 1810, Aged 77 years.

To the Memory of Margery, the Wife of Edward Barnes, who departed this life July the 2d, 1807, Aged 66 years.

To faith and charity her heart inclin'd,
Gentle, prudent, and of an easy mind,
Ready to forgive, fearful to offend,
Faithful to her husband, true to her friend:
Her course she finish'd, and resign'd her breath,
In pursuit of heaven through the vale of death.

To the Memory of Edward Barnes, who departed this life the 8th of August, 1809, Aged 69 years.

Humane and gentle, affable and kind,
A plain, but open, moral, honest, mind;
He liv'd to die, in Christ he put his trust,
To rise, through Him, triumphant with the just.

In Memory of John Wells, who departed this life April 17, 1756, Aged 48 years.

Here lyeth the Body of George Moore, who died Nov. 29, 1747, Aged 41 years.

Here lieth the Body of George Gleed Moore, who died the 10th of June, 1805, Aged 66 years.

Here lyeth the Body of Elizabeth Eldridge, who died the 17th of Nov. 1789, Aged 85 years.

To the Memory of Edward Eldridge, of Sevenhampton, in the Parish of Highworth, who was the Son of William and Mary Eldridge, of Dryfield, in the County of Gloucester. He died Oct. 31, 1767, Aged 72 years.

Here lyeth the Body of George Geeld, who departed this life Nov. 13, Anno Dom. 1729, Aged 19 years. In Memory of Richard Moore, who died Oct. 4, Anno Dom. 1711. Elizabeth, Wife of George Geeld, died Sept. 3, 1724, Aged 78.

To the Memory of Robert Hatcher, who departed this life April the 26, 1803, Aged 76 years. To the Memory of Martha, the Wife of Robert Hatcher, who departed this life Nov. 4, 1796, Aged 61 years. To the Memory of Mary Strange, who died August, 1797, Aged 53 years.

In Memory of William Eldridge, who died August 9, 1793, Aged 49 years.

In Memory of Rachel Eldridge, Wife of William Eldridge, who died April 15, 1791, Aged 46 years.

To the Memory of Alice, the Wife of John Grinnell, who departed this life, April the 27th, 1815, Aged 50 years. To the Memory of John Grinnell, who departed this life Nov. 10, 1815, Aged 54 years.

To the Memory of Alice, Wife of Joseph Shewry, who departed this life Nov. 9, 1818, Aged 20 years.

In all the bloom of youth, she met her death,
Yet calm as hoary age resign'd her breath,
Prepar'd by virtue for her blest remove;
There sure to find what's only found above,
Friendship sincere, and peace, and heavenly love.

Under this Tomb, lyeth the Body of Thomas Hitchman, who died August 11, 1760, Aged 77.

In Memory of Thomas, Son of Thomas and Jane Hitchman, who died Oct. 17, 1756, Aged 22 years.

Head Stones.

In Memory of William Martin, who died Dec. 29, 1784, Aged 81 years. Also Sarah, his Wife, who died Dec. 19, 1770, Aged 65 years.

Here lyeth the Body of Moses Akerman, who died July 22, 1760, Aged 74.

In Memory of Martha, the Wife of Moses Akerman, who died April 18, 1747, Aged 54 years.

In Memory of John, Son of Moses and Mary Akerman, who died July 7, 1770, Aged 41 years.

Here lyeth the Body of Moses Akerman, who died July the 26, 1767, Aged 39 years.

To the Memory of Thomas, Son of William and Grace Akerman, who departed this life the 23d of Sept. 1811, Aged 32 years.

Here lyeth three children of William and Grace Akerman. John, their first Son, who died an infant, also Thomas, their Son, who died April 12, 1778, Aged 1 year, also John, their second Son, who died Jan. 18, 1781, Aged 3 years.

To the Memory of William Akerman, who departed this life April the 11th, 1795, Aged 65 years.

To the Memory of Grace, the Wife of William Akerman, who departed this life the 19th of October, 1797, Aged 59 years.

To the Memory of Elizabeth, daughter of William and Grace Akerman, who departed this life the 20th of April, 1801, Aged 27 years.

To the Memory of Elizabeth, Wife of William Wiggins, who died March 2, 1789, Aged 82 years.

To the Memory of William Anger, who departed this life August the 1st, 1810, Aged 40 years.

CASTLE EATON.

Head Stones.

Sacred to the Memory of Joseph Newman, the Son of Harry and Mary Newman, who departed this life May 2d, 1817, Aged 13 years.

To the Memory of Harry Newman, who died Jan. the 5th, 1812, Aged 42 years. Also Harriet, daughter of Harry and Mary Newman, who died Feb. 19, 1812, Aged 10 weeks.

William, Son of John and Alice By, of Stow. He died June 3, 1736, Aged 21 years.

In Memory of Richard Knapp, Son of Edward and Elizabeth Knapp, who died Nov. 10, 1796, Aged 14 years.

In Memory of Susannah Kibblewhite. She died Feb. 17, 1808, Aged 85 years. In Memory of Elizabeth Morgan, Wife of Charles Morgan, and Daughter of Thomas and Susannah Kibblewhite. She died Oct. 29, 1793, Aged 30 years.

In Memory of Thomas Kibblewhite, who died Dec. the 11th, 1776, Aged 60 years.

To the Memory of John Kibblewhite, who died Nov. 28, 1817, Aged 71 years. Joanna, his Wife, died April 9, 1810, Aged 73 years.

Elizabeth, daughter of Thomas and Mary Kibblewhite, died April 22, 1745, Aged 23 years.

In Memory of William Packer, who departed this life Sept. 20, 1738.

Here lyeth ye Body of Susanna, Wife of William Packer, who died Nov. 13, 1740, Aged 67 years.

In Memory of Samuel Cook, sen. who died Nov. 10, 1730, Aged 61 years.

In Memory of Elizabeth, Wife of Samuel Cook, sen. who died Nov. 13, 1770, Aged . . .

In Memory of Amy, the daughter of John and Elizabeth Kinner, who died April 1775.

Christopher, the Son of John and Elizabeth Kinner, who died May 30, 1760, Aged 23.

On a Flat Stone.

In Memory of John Kinner, sen. who died March 30, 1770, Aged 80 years.

In Memory of Elizabeth, Wife of John Kinner, sen. who died April 14, 1777, Aged 71 years.

In Memory of John, Son of John and Elizabeth Kinner, who died July 5, 1797, Aged 63 years.

In Memory of Jane, the Wife of John Kinner, daughter of John and Elizabeth Alexander, who died April the 25, 1729, Aged 31 years.

In Memory of John Alexander, who died May 20, 1771, Aged 75 years.

In Memory of Elizabeth, the Wife of John Alexander, who died Jan. ye 26, 1734, Aged 58 years.

In Memory of John Alexander, sen. who died in the year 1747, Aged 75 years.

On Head Stones.

Here lyeth ye Body of Alice, ye Wife of John Alexander, who died May 29, 1737, Aged 59.

To the Memory of Mary, the Wife of John Alexander, who died April 28, 1758, Aged 40 years.

Mary, the Wife of Thomas Davis, died Nov. 1, 1738, Aged 72 years.

To the Memory of Thomas Harris, who died Sept. 13, 1783, Aged 67.

In Memory of Martha, the Wife of Thomas Harris. She died June 29, 1769, Aged 30 years.

Mary, daughter of John and Margaret Bennett, dy'd Dec. 12, 1743, Aged 7 years.

In Memory of two Children of Robert and Mary Bennett. Margaret died June 13, 1787, Aged 5 years. Sarah died July 3, . . .

In Memory of Elizabeth May, Daughter of Thomas and Sarah Munday, and Wife of John May, of Ampney. She died Nov. 15, 1788, Aged 79 years.

In Memory of Thomas Munday, who died Aug. 12, 1742, Aged 58 years.

In Memory of Sarah, the Wife of Thomas Munday, who died January 13, 1750, Aged 64 years.

In Memory of William, the Son of Thomas and Sarah Munday, who died July 15, 1762, Aged 47 years.

In Memory of Grace, the Wife of William Goldin, of Cirencester, who died April 19, 1760, Aged 67.

In Memory of John Kibble, who died April 10, Anno Domini 1716.

To the Memory of Hannah, Wife of William Gale, who died June 10, 1744, Aged 24 years.

Amy, Wife of William Sealey, departed this life May the 18, 1756, Aged 51 years.

In Memory of John Hughes, who died Sept. 8, 1766, Aged 62 years.

Also Elizabeth, Wife of John Hughes, who died July 4, 1753, Aged 43 years.

In Memory of Alexander Hughes, who died June 7, 1788, Aged 49 years.

Also Jane, Daughter of Alexander and Susanna Hughes, died Dec. 3, 1788.

Here lyeth ye Body of Robert, Son of Robert Simonds, who was buryed Dec. 15, 1687.

Here lieth ye Body of John, Son of Robert Simonds, who was buryed Oct. 3, 1680.

Here lyeth the Body of William, Son of Robert Simonds, who was buryed Nov. 9, 168 .

In Memory of Elizabeth, the Wife of William Sealy, who died July 13, 1762, Aged 40 years.

In Memory of Elizabeth, the Daughter of John and Mary Alexander, who died May the 29, 1766, Aged 22 years.

In Memory of Catherine, Wife of Richard Husks, daughter of Thomas and Sarah Wilkins, who died March 24, 1780, Aged 35 years.

Death is a painful way that all must tread,
Joyful to them that are by virtue led:
Then grieve not, friends, because I died so soon,
My day's journey finished at noon.

In Memory of Elizabeth, Wife of Henry Humphrys. She died July 11, 1799, Aged 53 years.

Margaret Wife of Richard Kibbell, died Feb. 2, 1740, Aged 45 years.

In Memory of Richard Kibbell, who departed this life April 11th, 1740, Aged 60 years.

Here lyeth the Body of Elizabeth, the Wife of Alan Keble, who died March the 30th, 1727, Aged 87 years.

In Memory of Mary, Wife of William Rime, died May 21, 1789.

Here lyeth the Body of Charles Jones, who died April 30, 1760, Aged 5 years.

The Rev. Henry Brent, Curate.

BLUNSDON ST. ANDREW.

Head Stones.

In Memory of Richard, Son of Richard and Phillis Smith, who died August 15, 1767, Aged 27 years.

In Memory of Adye Ayers, who departed this life August 13, 1763, Aged 67 years.

Also Jane his Wife, who departed this life Dec. 11, 1776, Aged 94 years.

In Memory of Richard Smith, who departed this life July the 9th, 1764, Aged 57 years.

In Memory of Phillis, Wife of Richard Smith, sen. who departed this life Jan. 24, 1768, Aged 52 years.

On Flat Tombs.

Near this Place lyeth the Body of Elizabeth, the Wife of Robert Payn. She died Oct. 12, 1722, Aged 34 years. Also Sarah, her infant, 8 months old.

John Ayer, who died Sept. the 3d, Anno Domini 1728, Ætatis 65.

Also here lyeth Catherine, Wife of John Ayers, who died Feb. the 14, 1745, Aged 82.

Here lyeth the Body of Mr. Thomas Ayers, who departed this life Feb. the 29, 1741, Aged 51 years.

In Memory of John, Son of Joseph and Anna Green, who died October the 26, 1752, Aged 24 years.

Head Stones.

Here lyeth the Body of John Ayer, who departed this life April 11, A. D. 1709.

Here lieth the Body of Jane Macklyn, the loving Wife of William Macklyn, by her three Children, 23d of January, 1659.

On Flat Stones.

Here lyeth the Body of Mary the Wife of Mr. Thomas Harding, who departed this life the xvii day of June, Anno Ætatis 90, et Salutis 1684.

Here lieth the Body of Seth, the Son of Thomas Harding, Gent. who departed this life the last day of Dec. in the year of our Lord 1691.

In Memory of Thomas Harding, gent. who died Jan. 1724, Ætatis 63.

Also John Harding, of Lechlade, who died Jan. 2, 1776, Aged 77 years.

Here lyeth the Body of Jane, the Wife of Anthony Taylor. She died Feb. 25, 1728, Aged 59 years.

Flat Stones. S. Side.

In Memory of Martha Ayers, who departed this life March 4, 1797, Aged 71 years. In Memory of Mr. Edward Ayers, Son of Mr. John and Mrs. Elizabeth Ayers. He died June 24, 1784, Aged 56 years.

In Memory of Mr. Thomas Ayers, who departed this life October the 3d, 1781, Aged 65 years.

To the Memory of Phyllis, Wife of Thomas Ayers, who departed this life Jan. 21st, 1814, Aged 71 years.

To the Memory of Martha, daughter of Thomas and Phyllis Ayers, who departed this life Jan. 15, 1813, Aged 38 years.

Affliction sore long time I bore,
Physicians were in vain,
Till God was pleas'd to give me ease,
To ease me of my pain.

Here lyeth the Body of John and Elizabeth Ayers, who died Feb. 9, 1770, Aged 66 years.

Here lyeth the Body of Mr. Richard Croft Ayers, Son of Mr. John and Elizabeth Ayers, who died May 3, 1762, Aged 51 years.

Head Stone.

To the Memory of Mary, Daughter of Thomas and Phyllis Ayers, who departed this life Feb. 14, 1772, Aged 1 year.

MALMESBURY HUNDRED.

CRICKLADE.

(St. Sampson's Parish.)

Mon. in Chancel against North Wall.

Sacred to the Memory of John Bristow, gent. whose Remains lie interred near this place. He departed this life the 15th Feb. 1788, Aged 48 years.

Sacred to the Memory of William Adams, Esq. whose Remains lie interred in the Family Vault in the Church-yard: Born July 1st, 1774, Died June 2d, 1812.

H. S. C.
Johannis Flood,
Hujus Ecclesiæ per xxxv annos Vicarius:
Vir optima, quæq. meritus si quod habeant meritorum,
Reda fides, castus sermo, par vita.
Miseros omnes, cognatus, largus fovit.
Amicis totus potuit,
Inimicorum odia non contempsit, sed lenitate vicit.
Duxitin Uxorem Mariam filiam unicum ultimi incumbentis.
Andræ Lynne, ex Anna conjuge,
Plurimum de illa suscepit sobolem
Mariam, Johannem, Henricum, Andream,
Unum atq. alterum
è quibus non illum reliquit supers. vitem
Quippe qui Cœlo dignos genuit tandem
Piis, laboribus, exhaustus
Infractusq. morbo male pertinace,
Quum nec sibi, nec aliis posset ulterius providere;
Vitam cujus cum primum pertæsus est,
Lubens deposuit,
ob. vii Jan: Anno Salut. MDCCIII.
Atq. ætat. suæ LVIII.
M. H.
Honoris et pietatis ergo,
V. M. P.

This is inscribed to the Memory of John Nott, eldest Son of the late Captain J. V. P. Nott, First Lieut. of His Majesty's Ship *Success*. He was carried off by the Yellow Fever, at Port-Royal, Jamaica, on the 18th of August, 1794, in the 24th year of his age.

Also to the Memory of his youngest Brother, George Nott, who fell a sacrifice to the same dreadful disorder, in November, 1795, in the West Indies, on Board His Majesty's Ship *Beaulieu*, in the 17th year of his age. Though cut off at so early a period, they promised not only to be an ornament to their profession, but to their Country. In private life, their Virtues were such as to make their loss ever to be lamented by all who knew them. The affliction of their surviving Parent, (by whom this Monument is erected) is too poignant for description.

E. Wall of Chancel.

Hoc Telum Patriam defensore strenuissimo orbavit.

To perpetuate the Memory of John Neale Pleydell Nott, Esq. Commander of his Majesties Ship *Centaur*, who lost his life off Martinique, April 29, 1781, in the 49th year of his age, gallantly supporting his Countries Cause against the French Fleet, commanded by Mons. de Grass. He married Catherine, Daughter of Robt. Andrews, Esq. by whom he left issue three Sons, John, Edward, and George, and two Daughters, Diana and Elizabeth.

Sacred to the Memory of John Nott, Esq. of Braydon, in the County of Wilts. He died June 23d, 1763, Aged 64. And of Elizabeth, the Daughter of Henry Neale, Esq. of Allesley, in Warwickshire, his Wife. She died Sept. 6th, 1746, Aged 44. They left three surviving Sons, John Neale Pleydell, Joseph, Roger, and had many other Children, who died in infancy. Joseph Nott died at Madrass, in the East India's, in 1769, without issue.

Here Lyeth the Body of Edward Nott, of Braydon Fforest, Esq. who died March ye 23d, A. D. 1712, Aged 72 years.

Anne Wife of Edward Nott, Esq. died Feb. 18th,

Anno { Dom. 1706.
Ætat. 66.

All that Remains of what to me was deare,
Of Wife in Vertue, Beauty, Love lies here.

Sacred
To the Memory of
The Rev. R. Purdy,
D. D.
Ob. Oct. 15, 1808.

Here lyeth the Body of Robert Packer, gent.
Who died the 24th of Nov. 1727,
Aged 55 years.

Here lyeth the Body of
William Packer, gent.
Who departed this life
The 5th day . . . .
Anno Do . .
Et Tu . .
And also ye . . .
Formerly . . . .
Said Mr. Packer, and
Wife of Edmond Morgan,
Gent. She was Daughter
of Edw. Pleydell,
of This Parish, Gent. and
Mary his Wife. She departed
this life the 15th of May,
Anno Dom. 1722, in ye
39th Year of her age.

. . . none Remove her Bone

Without the Rails, on Flat Stones.

Here lyeth the Body of John, Son of John and Mary Flood. He departed this life the 11th day of April, in the 21st year of his age, and in ye year 1691.

Here lyeth the Body of Henry, Son of John and Mary Flood. He departed this Life ye 3d day of July, in the 11th year of his Age, and in the year 1683.

Here Lyed ye Body of ye Rev. Mr. Andrew Lenn, sen. formerly Vicar of this Place.

Here lyeth ye Body likewise of Ann Palmergran, daughter of ye said Mr. Lenn.

Here Lyeth also ye Body of Mrs Frances Norse, who dyed Feb. ye 3d, A. D. 1712, Aged 61 years.

Here lyeth the Body of John Bristow, gent. who departed this Life Feb. the 15th, 1788, Aged 48 years.

Here Lyeth ye Body of John Bristow, who departed this life the 4th of April, A. D. 1656, Aged 47 years.

And also Jude, the Wife of John Bristow. She departed this life the 16th of August, A. D. 1681.

And also William, Son of Robert and Rebecca Bristow, who departed this life the 6th of September, A. D. 1732, Aged 39 years.

Here lyeth the Body of Robert Bristow, who departed this life Sept. 4, 1769, Aged 79 years.

Here lyeth the Body of Rebekah Lawe, daughter of William Lawe, Attorney, and Joanna his Wife, who departed this life Sept. 29th, 1711. And also Joanna Lawe, his Wife. She died May the 4th, 1728, Aged 92 years.

Here lyeth the Body of John and Robert Harper. John departed this life Aug. ye 14th, 1701, in the 44th year of his Age.

Robert departed this life March the 28th, 1728, in the 68th year of his age, and was Churchwarden with William Waine, for the Parish of Crekelade, 23 years and upwards.

My life was nothing else but pain,
Whilst here on earth I did remain,
At length the Lord, it did him please
To take me to a place of ease.

Against the North Pillar of the Tower.

Near this Place lyeth the Body of Mr. Henry Dennis, who departed this life the 27th day of July, in the year of our Lord 1742, Aged 42 years.

Taught half by Reason, half by mere Decay,
To welcome Death, and calmly pass away.

This Monument is erected to perpetuate the beloved Memory of John Pitt, jun. who died the 10th day of December, 1786, Aged 19 years.

On a Wood M. in west wall of north transept.

In Memory of Mary, Daughter of John and Mary Skillin. She departed this life July 23d, 1738, Aged 21 years.

Beautiful was I as the growing flowers,
Cut down and wither'd in few hours;
I was in health, as might be to-day,
And to-morrow at noon was called away.

Near this Place lyeth interred the Body of John Skillin, who was Clerk and Sexton of both Parishes in this town upwards of forty-two years. He was a loving Husband, a tender Father, and a social Friend. He departed this life July the 6th, 1770, Aged 78 years.

Near this Place lyeth Mary, Wife of John Skillin. She died Sept. 24, 1763, Aged 70 years. She was a loving Wife, and a tender Mother to five sons and seven daughters.

To the Memory of Thomas Skillian, who died Feb. 17th, 1816, Aged 56 years.

Also Thomas, Son of Thomas and Isabella Skillian, who died May 24th, 1815, Aged 30 years.

Near this Place lyeth ye Body of H. Nicholas Hardham, who departed this life July 26, A. D. 1799.

On Flat Stones in North Transept.

Here lieth the Body of Mrs. Catherine Hardham, Wife of Mr. Nicholas Hardham. Buried Feb. 23d, A. D. 1712.

In Memory of Sarah, Daughter of Christopher and Sarah Saunders, who died Oct. 2d, 1748, Aged 25 years.

In Memory of Christopher Saunders, who died Feb. 6, 1746, Aged 58.

Here lyeth the Body of Sarah, the Wife of Christopher Saunders, Mercer, eldest Daughter of Mr. Samuel Saunders, of Tetbury, Gloucestershire. She departed this life May the 2d, 1734, Aged 33 years.

Here lyeth the Body of Hannah, daughter of Christopher and Sarah Saunders. She died March 3d, $172\frac{5}{6}$, Aged 7 months.

Also here lyeth the Body of Christopher, the Son of Christopher and Sarah Saunders. He died March 27, 1729, Aged 6 months.

Here lyeth the Body of Ann Saunders, who departed this life the 5th day of January, Anno Dom. 1679. Let none remove her Bones.

Here lyeth the Body of William Fry, who departed this life January the 2d, Anno Dom. 16-7.

Here lieth the Body of Elizabeth, the Daughter of William and Elizabeth Fry, who departed this life March 8, A. D. 1716, Aged 22 years.

Mary Hopkins, Aged 41.

Here lyeth the Body of Elizabeth, Wife of William Ffry. She departed this life April ye 1st, A. D. 1721, Aged 66 years.

Near this Place lyeth the Body of William Ffry. He died August ye 26th, 1730, Aged 88.

Elizabeth Smith died 1752.

Here lieth the Body of Mr. Nicholas Hardham, who departed this life July 26, Anno { Dom. 1709, Ætat. 56.

Here lieth the Body of Thomas Skillin, who departed this life Feb. the 9th, 1773, Aged 51 years.

Death . . warning to me gave,
But quickly sent me to my grave;
Serve God and Christ, make no delay,
For no one knows their dying day.

In Memory of Edmund King, who died March 24th, 1798, Aged 39 years. Also Martha, his Wife, who died March 8th, 1801, Aged 67 years.

In Memory of Lodowick Packer, who died Oct. 22d, A. D. MDCCXXXV. Aged 50 years.

All men on earth are bound to die,
Therefore think on eternity;
When life is past, and death is come,
Then well is he that well hath done.

Also in Memory of Mary, the Wife of Lodowick Packer, and also Wife to Daniel Fletcher, who died January the 11th, 1770, Aged 76 years.

On Flat Stone in S. Transept.

Hic dormit corpus
Rowlandi Nicholson,
Senioris, Generosi, qui heu
Animam expiravit nono die
Octobris, Anno Dom. 1680,
Annoq. Ætatis septuagesimo secundo.

Resurgemus.

Cause the World was not worthy him to have,
The great Jehovah shut him in this grave.

Here lyeth ye Body of
Catharine, ye Wife of Rowland Nicolson,
who departed this life November ye 12th,
1704.

Here lieth the Body of Mr. Rowland Nicolson, jun. who departed this life the 25th day of Jan. 1686, in the 39th year of his age.

Who lived beloved, in faith he dy'd,
His life was desir'd, but God deny'd.

Here lyeth the Body of William Packer, who departed this life the 9th day of October, A. D. 1697.

Who lived beloved, in faith he died,
His life was desired, but God denied.

Here lieth also Mary, the Wife of William Packer. She died May the 9th, Domi. 1729, Aged 62 years.

Here lieth ye Body of Catharine, the Wife of Richard Packer. She died Dec. ye . . 0, 1723, Aged . . years.

Here lieth ye Body of William Packer, Son of William and Mary Packer, who departed this life August the 5th, Anno Dom. 1663.

Here lieth the Body of Joan, the beloved Wife of Simon Wild, who departed this life August the 16th, A. D. 1713.

Here lyeth the Body
of Simon Wild, jun.
He departed this life
February the 3d, A. D. 1710.

he Wase in Jenus for
Singing, Ringing, &
Writeing he dyed in the
21st year of his age being
much lamented.

Also Alice Haines,
Which Interred the 26
Oct. 1730.

Here lyeth the Body of Simon Wild, who departed this life Sept. ye 11th Anno Dom. 1720. He died in the 77th year of his Age.

Here lieth the Body of Mary, daughter of Richard and Ann Kinneir, jun. who died Feb. 24th, 1785, Aged 6 months.

Walter, their Son, who died Dec. 26, 1792, Aged 15 years.

In Memory of Richard Kinneir, gent. who died Nov. 19, 1784, Aged 72 years.

Richard Kinneir, jun. who died March 5, 1813, Aged 63 years.

Ann, his Wife, who died Feb. 4, 1787, Aged 39 years.

Joseph, Son of Richard and Sarah Kinneir, died March 19, 1811, Aged 8 months.

Here lyeth the Body of Charles Beris, who departed July 20th, Anno Dom. 1645.

Here lyeth the Body of Elizabeth Archard. She departed this life July the 24th, 171-.

On Flat Stones in the Tower.

In Memory of Susanna, Daughter of Richard and Susannah Kinneir, who departed this life November the 9th, 1742, Aged 12 years.

Here lyeth the Body of Ann, the Daughter of John and Anne Pitt, who departed this life December the 9, A. D. 1709, Aged almost 9 years.

Here also lyeth John, the Son of John and Mary Pitt, who dyed the 15th of Nov. 1727, Aged 11 years.

Here lyeth the Body of
Mr. John Pitt,
Who departed this life
Feb. 25, Anno 17$\frac{16}{17}$
In the 18 Yeare of
his Age.

Mary, Daughter of James and Mary Norman, died Nov. 21st, A. D. 1784, Aged 50 years.

In Memory of Christopher Pitts, gent. who died May the 10th, Anno Dom. 1730, Ætatis 42.

Here lyeth the Body of Ann, the Wife of Henry Dennis. She departed this life Nov. 29th, Anno Dom. 1713, Aged 48 years.

This Stone was laid at the charge of Mr. Edward Fettiplace.

Here lyeth the Body of Annabella, Wife of Edward Pleydell, Esq. Daughter of the Right Honble Sir John Ernſe, Kt. who was Chancellor of the Exchequer & Privi Counsell, in the Reigns of King Charles the 2d, King James, and King William and Queen Mary. She departed this life Nov. 27, Anno Dom. 1705.

Here lieth the Body of Edward Pleydell, Esq. formerly Member of Parliament for this Borough. He departed this life April 23d, Anno Dom. 1731, Æt. 76.

On a Mon. in Body of Church.

Erected to the Memory of William Maskeylne, gent. who died May 5th, 1809, Aged 81 years.

Mary, his Wife, who died June 19th, 1814, Aged 65 years.

Mary, their Daughter, who died July 14, 1789, Aged 20 years.

Elizabeth, their Daughter, who died October 23d, 1789, Aged 19 years.

On Flat Stones.

Here lyeth the Body of Elizabeth Archer. She died July the 24th, 1715, Ætatis 17.

Here lyeth the Body of Rebekah Archer. She died May 25th, 1728, Ætatis 71.

Here lyeth the Body of Mary Archer. She died March the 2d, 1729, Ætatis 79.

Here lieth the Body of Mrs. Martha Pleydell, Daughter of Edward Pleydell, of this Town, gent. She died May 23rd, Anno Dom. 1727, Ætatis 64.

She gave twenty Shillings per Annum for ever to the Poor of this Town, and a Branch for Candles to this Church.

Here lyeth Mary, the Daughter of Thomas and Mary Weston, who departed this life July 1[?]th, A. D. 1699.

Here lyeth the Body of John, Son of Thomas and Mary Weston, who died August 18th, A. D. 1700.

To the Memory of John Byrt, who departed this life September the 23d, 1796, Aged 84 years.

To the Memory of Mary Byrt, who departed this life August 18th, 1783, Aged 70 years.

Here lyeth the Body of Mary, the Wife of Richard Byrte, who departed this life May the 20th, 1713, in the 26th year of her age.

Also here lyeth Richard Byrte, who departed this life May the 31st, 1758, old stile, Aged 84 years.

Here lyeth the Body of Mary, the Daughter of Christopher and Mary Mathews, who departed this life May the 27, A. D. 1702, Aged 4 years.

Here lieth the Body of Richard Burt, junior, who departed this life March the 16, Anno Dom. 1 6 8 4.

Richard Byrt, died March 13, 1772, Aged 63.

Mary, his Daughter, died Oct. 31, 1772, Aged 36.

Here lieth ye Body of Catharine Byrt, who departed this life December ye 11th, A. D. 1702.

Here lyeth the Body of Margery, the Wife of Richard Burt, sen. who departed this life August ye 17th, A. D. 1703.

In Memory of Ann, Wife of Richard Byrt, jun. who died March 16th, 1787, Aged 83 years.

Also Ann, Daughter of Richard and Ann Byrt, died Jan. 3rd, 1784, Aged 45 years.

Here Lyeth the Body of Richard Byrt, who departed this life June the 26, Anno Dom. 1687.

On Monuments in N. Aisle.

Near this Place lyeth the Body of Margaret, Wife of Henry Brind, Goldsmith, in London, daughter of Thomas and Eleanor Carter. She died Aug. 18th, 1750, Aged 25 years.

Here lyeth ye Body of Francis Bristow. He departed this life August A. D. 1704, Aged 67 years.

Also Sesanna his Wife departed this life August the 24, A. D. 1718, Aged 64 years.

Here lyeth Ann Fluc, daughter of Francis and Susanna Bristow, who died June ye 4th, 1748, Aged 61 years.

Also here lyeth the Body of Jane, the Wife of Mills Fluce, Daughter of Francis and Susanna Bristow. She departed this life May the 26th, 1762, Aged 69 years.

Here lieth the Body of Thomas Skillin, who died July 2, 1770, Aged 71 years.

. . . Susanna, his Wife,
. . ghr of Francis &
Susanna Bristow,
who died Jan. 4, 1772,
Aged 81 years.

Here lyeth ye Body
Susanna, daugh . .
of Francis & Susan . ,
Bristow, who depar . .
this life Septem . . .
ye 20th, Anno Dom.
1 6 8 2.

Here lyeth ye Body of John Wild, who departed this life November ye 29, A. D. 1696.

Here lieth ye Body of John Wild, who departed this life March the 18th, A. D. 1708.

Here Lyeth ye Body of Mary, Wife of William Archer. She departed this life Jan. 11, 172$\frac{7}{8}$, Aged 56 years.

Also William Archer. He was Buried April ye 9th, 1729, Aged 62 years.

Here lyeth the Body of William Jones, gent. who departed this . .
April the 28 : 17 . .
Aged 70 years.

In Memory of Robert Jenner, Son of Nath. Jenner, of Widhill, gent. Departed this life May 12, A. D. 1730, Ætat. 18.

Here lyeth the Body of Richard Pannell, who lived at Cockett, in the Parish of Cricklade, and departed this life the 9th day of N° Anno Dom. 1694.

Here lyeth the Body of John, the Son of Richard Pannell, who departed this life the 5th day of June, A. D. 1694.

In Memory of John Jenner, Son of Nath. Jenner, of Widhill, gent. Departed this life July 7th, A. D. 1731, Ætat. 23.

Here lieth interred the Body of Elizabeth, the Wife of Robert Jenner, Esq. who departed this life Nov. 23, An° Dom. 1658.

On an Altar Tomb.

Here lyeth the Body of Robert Jennior, Esq. Citizen and Gouldsmith of London, who, out of his Piety & Charetie, Built the Eight Almeshouses in the Abbie of Malmsburie, and hath Allowed Fourtie Poundes Ayear for Ever for the Maintenaunce of Them: who Allsoe Built A free schoule in this Parrish & Left Twentie Poundes A yeare for the Maintenaunce of it for ever. Hee Lykewise Built the Parrish Church of Marston Maysie, in the Countie of Wilts: at his owne Proper Cost and Charge: Hee Hath Allsoe given Twentie Poundes Ayeare to St. Bartholomeues Hospitall, and Fiveteene Poundes Ayear to the Gouldsmiths for fiveteene of the Poorest Men of Theire Compaie, and five Poundes A yeare to the poore of St. John Zacharies Parrish, & five poundes Ayeare To the Poore of St. Leonards Parrish, in Foster Lane London: beeing All for ever.

Hee Deseased this Life the 7th of Decem̃ 1651, Aged 67 years.

Against S. aisle.

In Memory of Edward Pleydell, gent. who dyed the 2d of February, 1675.

Also Mary, Wife of the said Edward Pleydell, gent. who dyed the 13th of April, 1712.

And also Mrs. Elizabeth Pleydell, Daughter of the above Edward and Mary, who died 28 of July, 1737.

The said Mrs. Elizabeth Pleydell gave Twenty Shill. per Ann. to the poore of this Parish for ever.

Mrs.
Mary Morgan
died Feb. 24, 1763,
Aged 77 years.

On Flat Stones.

Here Lyeth the Body of Mrs. Elizabeth Pleydell, who died July 7, 1737, Aged 77 years.

Here Lyeth the Body of Edward, Son of Edward and Ann Meddlecott. He departed this life July the 25th, 1726, Aged 3 weeks.

Here lieth also the Body of Mary Meddlecott.

On Flat Stones in Vestry Room.

Here lyeth the Body of Rachel, the Wife of Thomas Jacob. She departed this life Nov. 23, A. D. 1695, Aged 47 years.

Also Mr. Robert, Son of Mr. Thomas and Rachel Jacob, who died July 22, 1731, Aged 47 years.

Weep not for me, it is in vain,
Weep for your sins, and them refrain,
For here I lay free from all pain.
Hoping with Christ to meet again.

John Parohurst,
Gent. died the 20th of
July, 1688.

Here lyeth the Body of Mrs. Frances Skylling, Grand Daughter to Mr. Philip Jacobson, by Frances, his Wife. She cheerfully and willingly left this world on July the 3d day, 1639, Aged years 22, and 9 months.

In Memory of Betty, daughter of Richard and Elizabeth Pleydell. She died July 18, 1736, Aged 3 years & 22 weeks.

My friends and Parents do not weep,
I am not dead, but gone to sleep;
I from this World am gone to rest,
God take to him whom he love best.

The Manor.

Benfield purchased the Manor of Knisbet, and in 1791, Lord Porchester purchased it of Benfield, and in 1811, Mr. Joseph Pitt purchased it of Lord Porchester, and the first Court held in October, 1812, and in 1814, the Town Hall was taken down, and the Members for the Borough are now elected in the Church. On the South Wall of the body of the Church is the Representation of part of two Flying Horses combatant. In the Vestry Room is the iron frame of the hour-glass which formerly the Minister preached by. April 30, 1820, The Church was furnished with an Organ, which was purchased by Subscription, value £.125, Lord Radnor subscribed the first ten guineas: bought of Mr. Robins of Malmesbury.

The Tower contains five Bells: On the Treble—Wm. Champernown & Rt. White, Churchwardens. James Wells fecit, 1803. On 2d Bell—Prosperity to Cricklade, and all our Benefactors: 1703.—3d Bell—Abra. Rudhall, cast us All, Anno Dom. 1703. 4th Bell—Peace and Good Neighbourhood. A. R. 5th Bell—Mr. John Flood Minister, & Henry Dennis Robert Bristow: C. W. A. R. 1703.

Over a Porch at the back side of the House of Industry is this Inscription:—'This School was erected: 20 Pounds yearely settled on the Master by the Bounty of Robert Jenner, Esq. 1652.' This was formerly the School, but now converted into the House of Industry, which contains twenty-six persons, the £20 that was left by Robert Jenner being entirely lost, by reason of its not being explained where it was to be paid from. There is, however, a Parish School, supported by subscription from the inhabitants, for 70 boys and 60 girls.

Swindon Canal finished and made navigable on the 1st of May, 1810, the Tunnel running about 150 yards over the ground belonging to Mr. Cuss, of Cricklade.

There are two Chapels in St. Sampson's Parish: one Methodist, the other Independent.—The Parsonage is a plain modern building.

1819, May 7, Stephen Rodway was robbed and murdered by Robert Turner Watkins, on the road leading from Cricklade to Purton, (about 2¼ miles from Cricklade;) and on July 30 following, Watkins was executed at the same place.

St. Mary's.

On Flat Stones within the Rails.

Here lyeth ye Body of Mary, Wife of Richard Painter, sen. who departed this life Sept. ye 26, A. D. 1706.

Here lyeth the Body of Elizabeth, the Wife of Henry Cartwright. She departed this life December 25, 1729, Aged 76 years.

Here lieth ye Body of Richard Painter, who departed this life May 23, A. D. 1713, Aged 94 years.

Here lieth the Body of Henry Cartwright, who departed this life the 20th day of November, 1728, Aged 79 years.

R. P.

Here lyeth ye Body of Richard Painter, who departed this life, Decem. 2d. 1717, Aged 65 years.

Oh Death why was that so unkind to take my only Friend on Earth and leave me behind the best of Husbands was to me and ye most indulgent Father to his Children underneath this stone here lyes his life was much desired if god thought fit but death We must all submit Through God's mercy & the Mercy of Jesus Christ our Saviour you now sleep free from paine till you and I shall meet again

Eliz. Painter, &
Mary Cox. 1728.

Here lyeth the Body of Mary, the Wife of Rtchard Painter, jun. who departed this life August ye 7th, A. D. 1720, Aged 44 years.

Two Children have left behind one underneath
This Tombe I hope yt they mercy Find
I left them in their bloom to providence For to
take care while wee sleep in the dust yt they &
wee one day may meet to sit among ye just.

On a Flat Stone in the Body of the Church.

Here lyeth the Body of William Leetch, who departed this life Dec. ye 15th, Anno Dom. MDCCXXVII. Ætatis 49.

On a wood frame in West end of South Aisle.

Near this Place Lyeth Ann, the Wife of Richard Skillin, a loving Mother to 7 Sons and 4 Daughters, who departed this life Oct. 14, 1712, Aged 50 years. And also the Body of Mary, the Daughter of Richard and Anne Skillin, who departed this life Jan. 15, A. D. 1714.

How happy blest in Christ was I
That in this World no longer for to stay
For Death's a debt all must pay
He'll give no time no not one day
Experience to me the truth
For I did pay it in my youth
So yearnest was he in his rage
Took me away from off ye stage
Before I was 8 years of age
You yt are young prepare to dye
I was young & near this place to lye.

Richard Skillin, Carpendr dyed Jan. 27, 1738.
A Tender Father to 7 Sons and 6 Daughters.

Against the North Wall inside the Tower.

The Bells in this Tower were Recast and New Hung in the year of our Lord 1780, at the expense of the underwritten Subscribers :

	£	s.	d.
John Nesbitt, Esq.	1	0	0
Lord of the Manor	10	10	0
The Hon. Henry Herbert, Esq.	10	10	0
William Hall	2	2	0
Olive Mills	2	2	0
James Akerman	2	2	0
Maurice Vincent	2	2	0
The Rev. Dr. Froome	1	1	0
William Jones, Esq.	1	1	0
William King	1	1	0
Richard Kinner	1	1	0
James Young	1	1	0
Crook Godby	1	1	0
James Jackson	1	1	0
John Hinton	0	10	6
Henry Lawe	0	10	6
Thomas Pike	0	10	6
William Hill	0	10	6
Wilkins Ellis	0	5	0
John Habgood	0	5	0
John Slatter	0	5	0

Mr. John Hinton,
Mr. James Akerman, } *Churchwardens.*

Inscriptions on the Bells:

First Bell—Peace and Good Neighbourhood. 1779.

Second Bell—Thomas Rudhall, Gloucester, January, 1779.

Third Bell—Prosperity to this Town.
On the Tingtang,
Come away, make no delay.

On the Communion Table.

C W Z M T B 1627 On the Pulpit R G W T.

MALMESBURY.

In the East End of the Body of the Abbey on a plain Stone.

Near this Place rest the Remains of the Rev. Henry Strong, late Vicar of this Parish, who departed this life on the 22d day of October, 1793, in the 40th year of his age.

Also Mary, Daughter of Henry and Hannah Strong, who died Nov. 24th, 1804, Aged 25 years.

Underneath this Place lyeth the Body of Mrs. Elizabeth George, of ye Parish of Steepple Ashton; who departed this life June 28th, A. D. 1734, Aged 65.

Underneath lyeth ye Body of Rebecca, ye Beloved Wife of Mr. George Gilespy, of this Town, who changed a Mortall for an immortall Being August ye 31st, 1697.

Juxta sepultus est,
Vir Revrendus
Robertus Greenway,
A. M.
Obijt . mo die Dec.bris
Anno { Dom. 1751.
Ætatis 51.

In Memory of Anastacia, Wife of Benjamin Garlike.
She dyed December ye 4th, 1752, Aged 49 years.

On a Monument against the first Pillar, north side of the Abbey.

The Blessed Memorials
of
Mrs. Elizabeth Warneford, who was Daughter
& Heire of Thos. Godwyn, Esq.
. . . . .
By whom Shee had Issue onely a Daughter,
Married to Sir John Hervey, Knight. By her
Second Husband, John Stumpe, of Malmesbury,
in the County of Wilts. Esq.
Heire Male to Sir James Stump, Kt.
Whose Heires Generall were maryed
To several Honorable Families Heere
Delyneated by their Arms and Coronetts,
Shee had Issue 3 Daughters and Heires,
That is to say, Elizabeth, maryed to ye
Hoble Kt. Sir John Powlett, of Hyde, Neere
Wynton. Katheryne maried to Foulke
Buttery, of the County of Northampton,
Esq. And Anne, Maryed to William Plumer,
of Bedfordshire, Esq.
She departed this Mortall Life upon
The 12th day of April, 1651,
To whose remembrance Lady Powlett,
Her Loveing and most beloved Daughter,
hath consecrated this
Monument.

Against the second Pillar.

Subter jacet
Johannis Willis,
Unus E. L. X^ia Clericis
In Alma Curia Cancellarii
Vir integer, probus, pius
Qui fratrum suum et sororem
Custodiæ suæ relictus
Et curâ sustinuit
Et amore prosecutus est
Non Fraterno tantum, sed etiam Parentali
Benevolent am Exercuit
Cum in omnes, quam maxime effusam
Tum in Pauperes vere Christianam
Abi Lector
Et illius mores imitanto effice,
Ut qui dum vixit id unice studuit
Ut quam plurimis prodesse posset,
Tibi prosit etiam defunctus
Natus est viii° die Febii A. D. MDCC.
Obiit xiii° die Sept. A. D. MDCCXLIV.

On the Third Pillar.

In Memory of Mary, the Wife of Captain Samuel Spencer, interred in the North Aisle of this Abbey, Ob. 16th Sept. 1782, ÆT. 61.

Also the Remains of the above Capt. Samuel Spencer, interred in the same Grave, Ob. 20 Jan. 1796, ÆT. 78.

Against the Fourth Pillar.

In Memory of
Edmund Wilkins, Esq.
who was for the space of nearly forty years
Receiver-General
and an Active Magistrate for the County of Wilts.
and High Steward
of the Borough of Malmesbury.
He fulfilled these Stations
with Honour, Fidelity, and Humanity,
Zealous and Punctual in his Service to his County,
Uniformly steady to the Interests of this Borough,
Impartial and Benevolent in Justice.
He died April 17th, 1804.
Aged 77.

Sacred
To the Memory of
Sarah Gale, Wife of the
Rev. Edmund Estcourt Gale,
Late Rector of Newnton,
who died July 31st, 1810,
Aged 85 years.

Also Jane Gale,
Daughter of the above
Edmund Estcourt
and Sarah Gale,
who died Nov. 26th, 1817,
Aged 62 years.

Near this Place lyes the Body of Joseph Hancock, ye Elder, and Elizabeth his Wife.
He dyed September 18th, A. Dom. 1723, Æt. 74.
She dyed Nov. 30th.
Also Elizabeth, ye Wife of Thomas Hancock, who dy'd Feb. ye 17th, 1751, Aged 36 years.
And Thomas, Above menchand, who dy'd Feb. ye 1st, 1751, Aged 32 years.

Jane Dewell,
Obiit die Decembris 27, A. D. 1803,
Erigit hoc Conjux marmor tibi munus inane,
Et paulum fractas plorat amicitias,
Donec tempus erit,
Cum nubila cuncta recedent,
Nosq. iterum œterno fœdere junget amor.
Elizabeth Dewell, Obiit May 11, 1805, Anno æt. 57.
Mary Dewell, Ob. Oct, 8th, 1817, Anno æt. 72.
non omnia terræ obrutu :
vivit amor, vivit dolor, ora negatur dulcia conspicere,
at flere et meminisse relictum est.

On North Side of the Third Pillar.

In Memory of Timothy Dewell, M. D.
who died the 29th day of July, 1792,
Aged 51 years.
Also of Mary Dewell, his Mother,
who died the 24th day of August, 1803,
Aged 86 years.

In Memory of Mr. Charles Spencer, Mercer,
who departed this life ye 5th of Feb. 1732,
Aged 58 years.

On Flat Stones within the Communion Rails.

Here Resteth the Body of Mr. William Harding,
who was intered the 12th day of August,
in the year of our Lord 1667.

Here Lyeth the Body of *William*,
Wife of Thomas Webb, who departed this life
the 7th of January, 1654.

Here lyeth the Body of Mrs.
Mary Grayle, late Wife of
Mr. Henry Grayle, of Malmesbury,
who resigned up her spirit To
God · Who · Gave it The · xx Day
of March · Anno Doni · 1650.

A Prisoner of hope lyes herein below,
What she by sin receiv d the Fatall Blow
Of Death his impartial hand, But Gods decree
Must stand and Befullfilled, Therefore she
waits for yt Blessed Time, when Shee may cry,
Death where's thy sting, o grave Thy victory,
This was her hope before Shee Turnd to dust,
To praise the Lord in Glory wth the just.

In Memory of
. . Rooke, late . . . Church,
. . parted this Life Nov. ye 13th,
Anno { Dom. 1706, Ætatis sua 72.

And of
. . . elder Daughter of
Thomas Rooke,
. . . . who deceased
Anno { Dom. 1706, Ætatis suæ

On Brass Plates in Body.

Here Resteth the Body of Robert Arch, som Time Burgesse of this Town, who deceased the Seaventeenth day of March, Anno Domini 1660, Expecting the Generall resurecton.

Here Resteth the Body of Edmond Hobbes, some Tyme A Burges of This Town, who Deceased the 22 day of April, Ano Domini 1606, Expectinge The Generall Resurrection.

Here lyeth the Body of Mrs. Rebekah Davies, late Wife of Thomas Davis, and Daughter of Henry Grayle of Malmesbury, who deceased December 23, Anno Dom. 1650.

In Memory of Mary,
Wife of Mr. Edward Lyne,
who departed this life the
Eighteenth day of February, in
the year of our Lord 1767,
Aged 48 years.

Also three of her children, who died in their infancy.

Also of Mr. Edward Lyne, who died April the 30th, 1771, Aged 52 years.

Phebe, the Wife of Edmund Lyne, died February the 7th, 1793.

In Memory of Alice Uncles, Wife of John Uncles of Stroud, Daughter of Henry and Ann Williams, who departed this life August the 31st, 1761, Ætatis 44.

Also of Ann, Daughter of the said John and Alice Uncles, who departed this life, October the 28th, 1764, Aged 17 years.

In Memory of Ann Williams, Relict of Henry Williams, of this Town, who died the 10th of Feb. 1763, Ætatis 82.

In Memory of Elizabeth, the Wife of Henry Williams of this Town.
And also of Henry, their Son.
She dy'd the 3 of }
And he dy'd the 4 of } October, A.D. 1712.

In Memory of Henry Williams, a Capital Burgess of this Borough, who departed this life the 8th day of April, 1737.

Also in Memory of Philip Williams, Son of the said Henry Williams, who departed this life the 28th day of March, 1740.

In Memory of Ann, Wife of Jeremiah Rowles, who departed this life Sept. 12, 1776, Aged 66 years.

In Memory of the Reverend Mr. James Webb, A. M. Rector of Broughton-Gifford, in this County, who died August 1, 1742, in the 46th year of his age.

Also Mary Webb, Wife of the above Rev. Mr. James Webb, who died January 2, 1774, Aged 71 years.

Hester, Wife of Robert Peers, gent. died Feb. 26, 1749, Aged 36 years.

Lo here in grave my loving Wife is Laid,
Had God so pleas'd she'd longer wth me stay'd,
. . . at mine Eyes with her's had closed been,
. . ad not this time of sorrow seen.

In Memory of Robert Peers, who died Feb. 2d . . . .

Here lyeth the Body of William Wayte, gent. who departed this life the 28th of August, 1670.

Here lyeth the Body also of Sarah, the Wife of William Wayte, who departed this life . . 1698.

Sacred to the Memory of Elizabeth, Wife of John Smith, who departed this life Dec. 17th, 1790, Aged 62 years.

In Memory of Robert Huckings Player, gent. who departed this life Sept. 13th, 1780, Aged 60 years.

Sacred to the Memory of Elizabeth, Wife of Richard Peers Player, who departed this life October 1, 1817, Aged 32 years.

Here lyeth the Body of Mary, the Wife of Richard Player, late of this town, Mercer. She died the 14th of September, 1721. And also the Body of Elizabeth, the Wife of Robert Huckings Player, gent. She dyed June the 1st, 1755, Aged 40 years.

This stroke of Death did end my time,
And cut me off just in my prime;
Therefore prepare, make no delay,
For time and tide for no man stay.

Mary, their daughter dy'd October the 23rd, 1756, Aged 13 years.

Richard Player, gent. died July 30th, 1769, Aged 30 years.

In this Vault are deposited the Remains of Betty Lyne. Obiit 4th Nov. 1776, Ætat. 78.

Blessed are the dead which die in the Lord.

In Memory of John Lyne, who departed this Life April the 27th, 1775, Aged 72 years.

Also of John, the Son of the above John Lyne, by Esther, his Wife, who was Born March the 26th, 1771, and died the 8th of April, following.

Underneath this Stone resteth the Remains of Ann, the Wife of Samwell Ody, who departed this life December 15, 1810, Aged 30 years.

. . er this Stone
. . . the Body of
. . d Wilkins,
. . ed this Life
April, 1804,
. . 78th year
Age.

Underneath is deposited the Remains of Mary King, spinster, who departed this life . . . 28th, 1781, Aged 64 years.

On a small plain Stone against third Pillar in Body.

Sacred to the Memory of Ann, the Wife of William Fry, who died April 19, 1799, Aged 75 years. Remember a Christian.

Also William Fry, who died May the 4th, 1805, Aged 64 years.

In hopes of the general Resurrection, what sort of Man he was, on that Day will appear.

On Mon. against the fourth Pillar.

In hope of a happy resurrection, near this Place lie the Remains of Joseph Cullurne, of Burton-hill, in this Parish, gent. who departed this life November the 28th, 1764, in the 79th year of his Age.

And of Elizabeth Cullurne, his Wife, who died on the 13th of October, 1763, Aged 71 years.

And likewise of Robert Cullurne, the only Son of the said Joseph and Elizabeth Cullurne, who died May the 15th, 1751, in the 22d year of his Age.

N. B. The above-named Joseph Cullerne, at the earnest request of the said Robert Cullurne, left an Estate at Cleverton, near this Town, chargeable with the neat payments of Twenty Pounds per Annum for ever for the following purposes; viz. Ten Pounds to the Poor of Malmesbury, Five Pounds to the Poor of Westport, and Twenty Shillings to the poor of the Tithing of Burton-hill, to be distributed on the First day of January every year, in sums not exceeding Five Shillings to each Family, Twenty Shillings for a Sermon to be preached annually on the 12th day of March, in this Church, Twenty Shillings for a Dinner to the Trustees on the same day, Ten Shillings to the annual Distributor of this Benefaction, Thirty Shillings a year to Sarah Hughes, his faithful Servant, during her natural life, and after her death to be divided in equal portions according to the respective Donations above specified to the Poor of Malmsbury, Westport, and Burton-hill aforesaid. Blessed be the man who provided for sick and needy.

Ann Cullurne ob. Feb. 22d, 1778, Æt. 21 years.

Against the fifth Pillar of the South side.

Sacred to the Memory of Thomas Pinnell, who died May 25, 1787, Aged 58 years.

Also John Hanks, who died Dec. 30, 1800, Aged 47 years.

Also Mary Hanks, who died Nov, 4, 1811, Aged 52 years.

To ye Memory
of

Thomas Arnold,		who Dy'd	13th Feb. 1705,
Eliz. his Wife,			26th Sept. 1728,
John &	their sons		25th Jan. 1710,
William			22d April 1712,
&			
Mary, yeir Dãter,			5th May, 1737.

wife of H. Hancock, Aged 61 years.

Arms—Sable, on a chev. engrailed, 3 escalops, gules.

Near this Monument are deposited the Remains of Edmund Cullurne, Apothecary, of Bath, who died Sept. 25th, 1765, Aged 44.

Against the sixth Pillar.

Near Lyeth the Body of Mary, Wife of Absalom Thomson, who died June 30th, A. D. 1723, Aged 50 years.

Here also lyeth the Body of Absalom Thomson, who died Nov. 24th, A. D. 1726, Aged 66 years.

Also here lieth the Body of Daniel, Son of Absalom and Mary Thomson. He dyed Sept. 11th, 1749, Aged 42 years.

Beneath this Place lyeth the Body of Richard Thomson. He died Oct. 13, 1769, Aged 66 years.

Underneath that Stone resteth the Body of William Robence of the Abbey, Gent. who ended this life Nov. the 5th, A. Di. 1700, Ætatis suæ 57.

On a plain Stone S. Wall of S. Aisle.

Near this Place lyeth interred the Body of Sarah, Daughter of John and Mary Rogers, who departed this life Oct. the 8th, 1744, Aged 21 years.

In love she lived, in peace she dy'd,
Her life was desir'd, but God deny'd.

Also near this Place lyeth the Body of Mary, the Wife of John Rogers, who departed this life the 1st of March, 1749, Aged 7[illegible] years.

On Flat Stones in S. Aisle.

In Memory of Thomas Iddols, who died Nov. 21, 1812, Aged 89 years.

Also Ann, his Wife, who died July 31st, 1769, Aged 43 years.

Also John, their Son, who died Feb. 9th, 1801, Aged 37 years.

Under this Stone Lieth the Body of William Robins, Son of William Robins, of the Abbey, who was Interred the 24th of April, Anno Dom. [illegible].

Richard B. Robins, sen. Ob. 21st June, 17[illegible], Aged 57 years.

Also

Richard Robins, jun. Ob. 21st Dec. 1816, Aged 83 years.

In Memory of John Legg, who departed this life July 27, 1771, Aged 23 years.

Here Lyeth the Body of Henry Robins, of Malmesbury Abbey, gent. who died June the 19th, A. D. 1728. Aged 54 years.

On Flat Stones in N. Aisle.

In Memory of John Lewis, Surgeon, who departed this life December the 28th, 1780, Aged 62.

In Memory of Isaac Watts, who died Dec. 15th, 1789, Aged 65 years.

William Watts died June 2, 1793, Aged 71 years.

Elizabeth, their Sister, and Wife of John Garlick, died March 26, 1798, Aged 65 years.

Also John Garlick, who died May 6th, 1802, Aged 72 years.

In Memory of Alice, late Wife of Thomas Newth. She died 28th April, 1767, in the 56th year of her age.

Also Thomas Newth. He died Dec. 10, 1776, Aged 69 years.

Also Mary, Wife of Mark Newth, who died May 21, 1785, Aged 81 years.

In Memory of Ann, late Wife of James Dyer. She died the 11th. Dec. 1770, in the 26th year of her age.

And also that of William Norris Dyer, and James Dyer, their Sons. James died 19th August, 1770, Aged 3 years and 6 months, William Norris died 10th August 1770, Aged 1 year and 6 months. Also Charles, Son of James and Mary Dyer, who died August 30th, 1781, Aged 2 years and 8 months.

Near this Place lyeth the Body of
Thomas Stump, gent. who departed
this life the 6th day of April,
Anno Dom. 1698,
Ætatis suæ 79.

O Death, how cruel is thy dart,
To strike this Captaine to the Heart,
Too good he was here to remain,
Jehovah tooke him for to traine :
In Grave his Body doth remain,
Till Christ himself doth come again.

On a Flat Stone in North Chapel.

Here Lyeth ye Body of John Stump, sen. of Charlton, who died Jan. 22d, 1798, Aged 62 years.

On Flat Stones in N. Aisle.

Here Lyeth the Body of Thomas Estcourt of Burton-hill, in this Parish, Esq. who departed this life the 13th day of April, in the year of our Lord, 1723, Aged 70 years.

Underneath this Stone Resteth the Body of Mary Spencer, Wife of Captain Samuel Spencer, who departed this life the 16th of September, 1782, in the 62 year of her Age, and 38th of her Marriage. As her life was innocence, so her hope was confident, that she should attain the Resurrection of the just, through Jesus Christ our Lord.

Also the above Captain Samuel Spencer, Ob. 20th January, 1796, ÆT. 78.

His confidence resteth in a Resurrection to Eternal Life, his hope to be saved with the Blessed Elect in and through the merits and mediation of his Lord and Saviour Jesus Christ.

On a Brass Plate.

Here lyeth the Body of Capt. William Ivye, Esq. one of [illegible]e's Justices of the Peace for this County, [illegible] 67 years. He departed this life the 16 of Au[illegible]t, Anno Dom. 1680.

On Monuments in King Athelstan's Chapel.

Sub hoc Marmor
Reponuntur exuviæ Mortales
Johannis Harvey, de Cole Park,
In Paroch. Malmesb. Armigeri.
Nati Cantabrigiæ, de Famlia
Ejusdem Nominis in Agro
Bedfordienii, non minus
Antiquâ quam Honorabili.
Denati Ædibus in suis in magnum,
Et suorum, et proximorum omnium
Mœrorem, 27° die Februarii,
Anno { Dom. 171$\frac{2}{3}$,
Ætat. suæ 44.

Arms—A chev. or. between 3 leopards heads, caboshed argent.

In Memory of Bartholomew Hiren, gent. late of Shipton-under-Whitchwood, in the County of Oxford, Father-in-law to Thomas Rooke, of Whitchurch, gent. and to James Groome, of Neunton-supra-Loe, Rector, who departed this life the 26th of October, 1703.

In Vestry-Room.

John Samwell Ody, gent. Ob. 17 September, 1813, Aged 69.

Martha his Wife, Ob. 24 March, 1810, Aged 67.

Cath. Prichard, spinster, Ob. 17th October, 1816.

Against the south entrance.

In Memory of James Pope, who died Feb. 8th, 1759, Aged 70.

Also Frances, his Wife, died April 1st, 1769, Aged 80 years.

Also Bartholomew King, died Feb. the 3rd, 1787, Aged 72 years.

And also Ann, his Wife, died June 1st, 1766, Aged 48 years.

In Memory of Ann, the Wife of William Rimell, who died June 19th, 1798, Aged 68 years.

Also Thomas Rimell, their Son, who died May 14th, 1810, Aged 47 years.

Beneath this place lyeth the Body of Ann, the Wife of Daniel Rimell, who departed this life Nov. 14th, 1745, Aged 77 years.

On Monument in South Porch.

Sacred
To the Memory of
G. I. Saunders, who departed this life
Sept. 23, A. D. 1806,
Aged 21 years.

Psalm 73, 26. My flesh and my heart faileth, but God is the strength of my heart, and my portion for ever.

Isa. 26. 4. Trust ye in the Lord for ever; for in the Lord Jehovah is everlasting strength.

Also Mary Saunders,
Mother of the above
G. I. Saunders,
who died Jan. 21st, 1818, Aged 63.

Be ye also Ready.

Underneath Resteth ye Body of John Turner, of Malmsbury, who departed this life 13th of July, 1-89.

You that survive, with one accord
Be always ready for your Lord:
Expecting Death at home, abroad
It seized me upon the road.

Benefactions.

Against east end.

Robert Jenner of Widhill, in the County of Wilts. Esq. about the year 1622, did erect an Almeshouse for the poor People of the Town of Malmesbury, and Endowed it with £.40 a-year for ever to be paid out of the Manor and Lordship of Widhill.

Mr. Henry Grayle, one of the Capital Burgesses of Malmesbury, died April 6, 1661, and by Will bequeathed to pay for ever, to be paid yearly out of his Estate, iu Summerford Magna, to the Churchwardens Overseers of the Town of Malmesbury, for the Apprenticing of poor Children of the said Town.

Mr. Edmund Wayte, one of the Capital Burgesses of Malmesbury, dyed in June, 1661, and by Will bequeathed 40*s*. to the Poor of Malmesbury, 20*s*. to the Poor of Burton-hill, and 20*s*. to the Poor of Westport, yearly, to be paid out of Canopps Mill, into the hands of the Church Wardens of the Respective places, and by them to be distributed on each Good Friday for ever.

Manor.

In 1700, the Manor belonged to Thomas Lord Wharton, afterwards Marquis of Wharton and Malmesbury. He died in 1715, and Philip, who, in 1718, was created Duke of Wharton, succeeded to it. The next proprietors appear to have been Maria Theresa, Dutchess Dowager of Wharton, Sir Charles Keymes, and Sir Christopher Musgrave, Baronets; who about the year 1750, sold it to Sir John Rushout, Baronet, one of his Majesty's most honorable Privy Council. In 1760, Sir John gave it to his son, the late Lord Northwick, on his coming of age, a gift which he afterwards confirmed by his Will. He died in 1775. The late Lord enjoyed the Manor till the time of his Death, which happened in 1800, and by his Will devised the same to his widow, the Right Hon. Lady Northwick. Sir George Rushout is the present Lord.

In King Athelstan's Chapel is the following Epitaph on Lady Marshall:

Stay, gentle passenger, and read thy dome—
I am, thou must be, dead.

In assured hope of a joyfull resurreccon, here rests deposited all that was mortall of the religious and virtuous Lady Dame Cyscely Marshall, daughter of the Honourable Sir Owen Hopton, Kt. late lieftenant of the Towre Royal, the faythful, modist, and loyall wife of Sir George Marshall, Knight. Whether transcended in her more the ornaments that beautified a wife, a mother, a matrone, is still a question betwixte her all disconsolate husband, daughter, servants: Onely this is agreed upon all hands, such were her perfections in each state, that in vayne will any epitaph endeavour to delyneate them. What her fayth, hope, charity, temperance, piety, patience, may (to better purpose) be expected from the trump of an archangell in the Day of God's generall retribuccon, than from the faynte and flagging attribucons of any particular penn. To close all, with her close theis two spirituall eiaculacons, Miserere mei, Deus; et Domine recipe animam meam, (have mercy upon me, O God, and receive my soul, O Lord,) were the wings whereon the last breath of this turtle mounted towards heaven: To whose sweete memory her sad mate hath devoted this poor Monument, which Oh let no prophane hand violate.

Emigravit 23 Apryll, Anno Salvat. 1625.

The Abbey Register contains a curious memorandum relating to one whose Remains were also deposited in this Chapel.

"John Buclle, reputed to be a gypsie, deceased September 21st, 1757, at John Peryn's house, upon the Ffosse, in Shipton Parish, in Gloucestershire, and was buried in King Athelstone's Chapell, by King Athelstone and Lady Marshall, within the abbie church, at Malmesbury. This buriall was Sept. 23, 1657. Howbeit, he was taken up again by the meanes of Thomas Ivye, esq. who then lived at the abbie, and by the desires and endeavours of others out of the said chappell, was removed into the church-yarde, and was there re-buried neere the east side of the church poorch, October 7, 1657, in the presence of Thomas Ivye, of the abbie, esq[r]. Pleadwell, of Mudgell, esq[r]. Richard Whitmore, of Slaughter, in the Countie of Glocester, and Dr. Qui, of Malmesbury, with very many others."

"Simon Gawen, sometime Vicar of this parish, but put out and expelled because a Nonconformist, was buried 22d Jan. 1671."—*Par. Reg.* Mr. Gawen was Vicar of Malmesbury in 1629, as appears by the Register.

Arms of the Abbey of Malmesbury :

Upon a chief, argent, a mitre, or, between two crosiers, azure ; on the fesse and nombril points two lions passant guardant, or : the base gules.

In the parish of Westport is a Presbyterian Chapel: in St. Mary's an Anabaptist: and in that part of the town called Hollway a Moravian.

A DESCRIPTION OF THE REMAINS OF THE ABBEY CHURCH.

"What exists of the Abbey Church may be considered as about one-fourth of the building in its perfect state. On approaching the eastern side of the ruin, the first part we come to is the centre of the transept, where formerly stood the lofty spire. It was supported by four circular arches, two of them are yet complete, viz. the arch which leads into the northern side of the transept, and the arch which opened into the nave. These arches are about 60 feet in height, and 21 in width. The Abbey Church, at present, consists only of a part of the nave and side aisles : it is 60 feet in height, 110 in length, and 68 in breadth, or eighty, the thickness of the walls included. The several parts appear to have been constructed at periods very distant from each other. From the outside of the nave down to the aisle rise ornamented pinnacles, from which spring flying buttresses, as also from the walls. There is a relic of the circular arch of the grand western entrance. The pillars are round and plain, from the base to the capital, on which are specimens of elegant sculpture. There are a few bass-reliefs remaining, in very good preservation. One of the figures, a sagittary, has been particularly admired by the antiquarian. On the southern side of the nave are two porches, the outer is a deep Saxon arch, measuring from the centre of its front to the inner porch eleven feet, its width twenty, and its height about eighteen. This porch is very magnificent, it has eight mouldings, ornamented with a variety of sculpture, which begins at the base, and continues round in a regular sweep to the opposite pedestal, without capital or any interruption. These mouldings vary in breadth; some are about ten inches, and others a foot and upwards. The first moulding (which is contiguous to the door) has a waving branch, with lateral tendrils; the second is covered with lozenges : the third exhibits histories from the Old Testament; on the fourth the branch and tendril are repeated, but of a smaller size; the fifth is a continuation of histories from the Old Testament; the sixth have lozenges and tendrils interwoven ; on the seventh are exhibited pieces from the New Testament;* and the eighth is adorned with tendrils. The celebrated Mr. Addison, who was one of the Members in Parliament for the Borough of Malmesbury, on viewing the Porch, declared, that it was the most complete work of the kind he had ever seen. The inner Porch is also a Saxon arch : it is seventeen feet in length, twelve in width, and sixteen in height : on the sides of this porch are some small Saxon arches : above these are placed stone statues of the twelve apostles, six on each side, having an angel stretched over their heads. There is a room above the porches, said to have been the school-room belonging to the abbey. The immediate entrance into the Church is nine feet in height, and five in width. It has three mouldings, similar to those in the outer porch, and above this portal seems to be a representation of the Deity on a throne, supported by angels. Just within this entrance (fixed in the wall to the left) is a head with a crown on it, supposed to represent our Saviour wearing the crown of thorns. On advancing, we perceive the nave to be separated from the side aisles by massive round columns, with plain capitals, six on each side. These columns support three rows of arches, the lowest and the highest somewhat pointed, and the central proper Saxon. Over one of the rows on the southern side is a small stone structure, projecting from the wall, with a grated opening towards the body of the church. It is supposed by some to have been a kind of prison for the monks, or the place where they performed public penance; by others it is thought that it was intended

" * Some of the scriptural subjects are—'The creation of Adam and Eve : their trespass and expulsion from Paradise'—'Christ and his disciples eating the Paschal Supper,'—'The Crucifixion of Christ, his burial, resurrection, and ascension; and the descent of the Holy Spirit on the apostles.' The historical sculpture consists of about eight bass-reliefs, some of them in good condition, others much defaced, especially those towards the base of the arch : it may, therefore, be conjectured that these begin at the left of the spectator."

102

for the abbot's household, from whence to view the procession, or perhaps appropriated to the use of the abbot himself. The ribs of the groins in the vaulting of the church are ornamented with foliage and heads, accounted very elegant. The heads are supposed by some to represent the benefactors to this monastery. The lower part of the altar-piece is a solid wall, witb a cornice, ornamented with griffins, dragons, and other figures. This wall, probably, was the screen, which formerly separated the nave from the transept; in the centre is a trace of the door-way which led into it. The seats in the chancel, on each side of the communion table, seem to be those ouce belonging to the choir. In a small inclosure, in the south aisle of the church, is a tomb, with an effigy of a man in royal robes, and a lion at his feet, lying upon it. It is called 'KING ATHELSTAN'S TOMB:' but we must not infer from thence that Athelstan was interred in this part of the church. William of Malmesbury affirms to the contrary; and agreeably to the testimony of this early historian, I am informed by the Rev. Mr. Bisset, the present Vicar of Malmesbury, that some years ago he was present when what is called Athelstan's Tomb was opened, and appearances indicated that it was only a cenotaph. The late Dr. Mapson, of Tetbury, conjectured, that when the place of King Athelstan's interment, under the high altar, became ruinous, his monument might have been removed into that part of the church where it now stands, in order to preserve it from the inclemency of the weather. The doctor's conjecture is rendered the more probable by what Mr. Warner has remarked: 'There is,' says he, 'a considerable resemblance between the sculpture on this tomb, and the figure of that monarch on the reverse of his famous seal, of which I have seen a cast from the original, in the possession of the late Gustavus Branden, esq.' Mr. Evelyn, son to the celebrated Evelyn, made drawings of King Athelstan's tomb, which were some time since shewed by Mr. Bryan to to the Society of Antiquaries."

WESTPORT.

Mon. in Chancel against North Wall.

In Memory of Mariah, Wife of Richard Stump, who died Sept. 28, 1788, Aged 32 years.

Also Richard Stump died Oct. 21st, 1788, Aged 43 years.

To the Memory of Sarah, the Daughter of William and Ann Stump, of Colepark, in the Parish of Malmesbury. She died April 16, 1788, Aged 1 year and 6 months.

Near hereunto are interred ye Bodys of Symon Oateridge, of Hyem Park, in this Parish, who dy'd April 21st, 1685, Aged 63.

Symon, eldest son of Symon and Sisley, his Wife, who dyed in ye yeare 1688, Sept. 15. Aged 33.

Nathaniel, their younger Son, who departed this life ye 12th of Dec. next following, Aged 22.

In Memorie of Cicely, ye Wife of Simon Oateridge, of Hyem Park, who died November 22, 1703, Aged 71,

Near this Place also lyeth the Body of Harry, Son of Simon and Cicely Oatridge. He died May the 31, 1723, Aged 65.

In east end of Chancel.

In Memory of Memory of Thomas Hulbert, grandson of Thomas Hulbert, of Prickwick, in this County, who died March the 29th, 1776, Aged 13 years.

Under this Stone Resteth the Body of Elizabeth, Wife of Jeremiah Sifford, of this Parish, who died Nov. ye 13th, A. D. 1733, Ætat. suæ 62.

Near this place are deposited the Remains of Daniel Bennett, late of this Parish, who departed this life ye 24th day of Oct. 1779, in the 85th year of his age.

Also Mary Bennett, his Wife, who departed this life the 22d of January . . Aged . . years.

Also Edith Arman, Widow, Sister of the above-named Daniel Bennett, who departed this life the 26th day of April, 1778, in the 78th year of her age.

Also Giles Bennett, of Malmesbury, eldest Son of the above-named Daniel Bennett, who departed this life the 27th of March, 1795, in ye 75th year of his age.

Also Mary Bennett, his Wife, who departed this life the 15th of Sept. 1782, Aged 51.

Also Daniel Bennett, youngest Son of the above named Daniel Bennett, who departed this life the 30th of March, 1795, Aged 65.

Also Giles Bailey Bennett, Son of the above-named Giles Bennett, who departed this life the 10th of Nov. 1816, Aged 47 years.

Under that tombe resteth the Body of Ann, ye Wife of Mr. John Wayte, of Westport, who departed this this life the 26th of September, Anno Dom̄. 1690, in the 39th year of her age.

I life to nine, ye tenth brought death to me;
When Christ shall come deliverance shall be;
My child in me, we both in dust do lie,
Dea h where's thy sting, Christ will give victorie.

South Wall.

Hic jacet exuviæ mortales illius Reverendi Johannis Fisher, cujus mors suis damnum sibi vero maximum lucri attulit; qui e vivis excessit mensis Decem. 4° die Anno Salutis 1710, Ætatis suæ 51.

Underneath also lyeth ye Body of Abigail Ballinger, Wife of John Ballinger, of Bristol, Daughter of John and Ann Fisher, who departed this life Jan. 30, A. D. 1734.

Mors est Lucrum.

As you are now, so once were wee,
And as wee are, so shall you bee.

Near unto this place Resteth the Body of Thomas Brown, Son of Edmund Brown, of Westport, late Minister at Pucklechurch, in ye County of Glocester, who departed this life the 16th day of November, Anno Domini 1672, et ætatis suæ 25.

And also the Body of Elizabeth Browne, Daughter of the sayd Edmund Browne, who deceased the 8th day of August, 1673. Here Resteth the Body of Mary Browne, late Wife of Edward Browne, jun. who departed this life ye 31st day of March, 1676.

Here lyeth ye Body of William Conway, a faithfull steward in the house of God, who when he had fulfilled his ministry, resteth from all his labours, June the 3rd, Anno Dom. 1694, Ætatis que suæ 60. Here lyeth also the Body of Hannah, Wife of William Conway, who departed this life Oct 22, A. D. 1711.

On a Flat Stone in a Pew in Chancel.

Also here Lyeth the Body of Edye Gillmoor. Who was buryed ye 13th of November, 1691.

Here Resteth the Body of Thomas Walk . . ho departed this life the . . . ay of August 16 . .

Edward Hale Aged 68, 1751.

Eliz. Hale died May 3d, 1777, Aged 96 years.

Martha Hale, died Jan. 6th, 1788, Aged 62 years.

Here lieth the Body of Sarah, Wife of Robert Stump, late of Whitchurch, in the Parish of Malmesbury, who departed this life January ye 19th, 1783, Aged 65 years.

Also Robert Stump, of Whitchurch, died Jan. 9th, 1766, Aged 70 years.

On Monuments in Body on N. Wall.

All flesh is grass, and all the glory of man as the flower of grass: the grass withereth, and the flower thereof falleth away.

Near this Place lie the Remains of Thomas Tugwell, and of Ann, his Wife. She died August 12th, 1723, Aged 43. He died Oct. 11th, 1727.

Also of Alice, their daughter, Wife of Robert Stent, who died Sept. 27th, 1731.

And of William Tugwell, their Son, who died Aug. 26, 1782, Aged 77.

And also of Thomas, their Son, who died the 25th day of March, 1800, Aged 90.

Come unto me all ye that labour and are heavy laden, and I will give you rest.

Near this Place lyeth the Bodys of Richard Garlick, of Hyam Park, and Beate, his Wife. He died May the 29th, 1742, Ætat. 83. She died Dec. 13, 1746, Ætat. 69.

Also Mary, Daughter of George and Mary Garlick. She died Nov. 17, 1768, Aged 14 years.

And also Thomas Garlick. He died June the 17th, 1770, Aged 57 years.

Sacred to the Memory of Elizabeth, the Wife of George Garlick, who died June 15th, 1797, Aged 31 years.

Sacred to the Memory of Giles Garlick, who died May 30, 1814, Aged 66 years.

Sacred to the Memory of Ann, Wife of John Garlick, who died April 7, 1779, Aged 60 years.

Daniel, their Son, died Sept. 25, 1770, Aged 11 years.

John Garlick died Jan. 2d, 1792, Aged 75 years.

Richard, Son of Thomas and Susanna Garlick, died January 28, 1778, Aged 8 months.

George, their Son, died Feb. 5, 1785, Aged 2 years and 6 months.

John, their Son, died August 30, 1786, Aged 7 years.

William, their Son, died Nov. 29, 1793, Aged 7 years.

Susanna, Wife of Thomas Garlick, died May 11th, 1793, Aged 44 years.

Thomas Garlick died Feb. 24, 1794, Aged 45 years.

John, Son of John and Ann Garlick, died August 25, 1792, Aged 38 years.

George, Son of George and Elizabeth Garlick, died Sept. 18th, 1785, Aged 11 weeks.

Joseph, their Son, died March 16, 1797, Aged 7 weeks.

In north Wall under the Gallery.

Underneath lyeth the Body of Mary, the Wife of Nathaniel Smith, who ended this life May the 29th, A. D. 1699.

Th' awakened Soul Christ likeness doth delight,
His angels guard her dust thro'out Deaths night:
The man approaches when it wak'd & dress'd,
By Heaven's Bright company shall be caress'd.

Underneath lieth ye Body of Abigail, Wife of Mr. Moses Price, who departed this life on the 21st of August, 1729.

A pious Woman, faithfull friend,
And loving Wife unto the end.

Underneath lieth the Body of the Reverend Mr. Moses Price, of this Parish, who departed this life Nov. 23, A. D. 1736, Aged 56.

Also Abigail, second Wife of Mr. Moses Price. She died Oct. 24th, 1751, Aged 79 years.

In Memory of Abigail Godwin, the Wife of Nathanael Godwin, who departed this life June 18, 1762, Aged 60 years.

On a plain Stone.

In Memory of Nathanael Godwin, who departed this life Dec. 8th, 1744, Aged 34 years.

Also in Memory of Moses Godwin, the Son of Nathanael and Abigail Godwin, who departed this life June the 14th, 1759, in the 23d year of his age.

Also in Memory of Nathanael, Son of Robert and Anne Godwin, who died Sept. 11th, 1766, Aged 13 weeks.

In West End.

Underneath lieth the Body of Robert Rumsey, who departed this life February the 23d, A. D. 170$^{10}_{9}$.

Also ye Bodys of Nathanael, two Samuels, and Giles, Sons of Robert and Ann Rumsey, ye first Samuel died May ye 18th, 1708, ye other Samuel May 30, & June ye 6th & 7th, 1712.

Underneath lyeth ye Body of Hester Rumsey, daughter of Robert and Ann Rumsey. She died August ye 7th, A. D. 1735.

Also underneath lyeth interred Anna, Wife of Robert Rumsey, who dyed Oct. ye 11th, 1749, Aged 73.

Underneath Resteth the Body of Nathaniel Smith, of Westpurte, who departed this life the 19th of November, 1688.

Can we be just in silence to conceal
Thy fervent praying and thy pious Zeal
With Holy violence pressing to the Mark
Safe now Ariu'd into thy Heavenly Ark
Oh Blessed soul to such estate art Rais'd
Whilst we are weeping thou art singing praise
Lord Jesus doubel his spirit yt did proceed from thyn
And Lett it rest on some yt are now left behind.

Underneath Resteth also the Body of Samuel, the Sonne of Nathaniel and Mary Smith, who departed this life the 24th of January, 1688.

Besides Creation's Right devoted to was I
To the Creator's seruis of the Ministry
The Great Jehovah who is only Wise
Discharged me of this Worke to Glorious imployes
Let earth be silent what the Lord hath done
hath taken but his owne then Wher' ye Wrong.

S. Wall.

Near this place lyeth the Body of Isaac Exton, Malster, of this Parish. He died Jan. 15, 1744, Aged 71 years.

Also here lyeth the Body of Hannah, the Wife of Isaac Exton. She died May the 5th, 1750, Aged 73 years.

Also here lieth the Body of their three children, Edmund, Isaac, and Elizabeth. Edmund died October the 2d, 1713, Aged 2 years, Isaac died March the 10th, 1720, Aged 10 days, and Elizabeth died Aged 14 days, for they was twins.

Also here lyeth the Body of Rebecca, the daughter of Charles and Ann Exton. She died Feb. 12, 1747, Aged one year and 5 weeks.

Also Mary, their Daughter, dy'd Sept. 19th, 1757, Aged 26 years.

Near this Place lyeth the Body of Charles Axton, who was buried the 20th of Oct. 1689.

Also near this Place lyeth the Body of Joan Axton, Daughter of Charles and Joan his Wife, who was buried the 31st of January, 1696.

Also near this Place lyeth the Body of Joan Axton, daughter of Edmund Axton, and of Margaret, his Wife, who was buried the 10th of August, 1704.

Near this Place is interred the Body of Ann, ye Wife of Charles Exton. She departed this life June 14th, 1759, in the 57th year of her age.

Also Hannah, the daughter of Charles and Ann Exton. She died April 13th, 1775, Aged 40 years.

And also of Mary, the Wife of Thomas Exton. She died July 31, 1779, Aged 38 years.

And also the above Charles Exton. He died May the 6th, 1787, Aged 81 years.

Also Thomas Exton, died August the 17th, 1789, Aged 48 years.

Underneath lieth ye Body of Edmund Extone, who departed this life December ye 29th, A. D. 1711.

Also in Memory of Margaret, Wife of James Exton, who died December the 11th, A. D. 1734, Aged 36 years.

On Flat Stones in Body.

John, the Son of Henry and Rachel Hankes, died Oct. 5th, 1732, Aged 1 year and 10 months.

Also Rachel, their daughter, died Feb. 10, 1739, Aged 1 year and 3 months.

Also in Memory of Henry Hanks, who died August the 1st, 1753, Aged 60 years.

Also Ann, their Daughter, who died Oct. 11th. 1751, Aged 8 years and 3 weeks.

Here lyeth the Body of John Giles, who departed this life February the 18th, 1783, Aged 24 years.

Short was the warning that death gave,
When I was summon'd to the grave:
The like, or worse, he may serve on thee,
Therefore always prepared be.

Isaac Giles died the 26th of July, 1787, Aged 71 years.

Also Mary, his Wife, who died the 6th of September, 1787, Aged 68 years.

In Memory of four children of Miles and Mary Martin, gent. three daughters and one Son. Mary, the first, buried April the 18th, 1719, Ætat. 1 year and 3 quarters. Martha, the second, buried May ye 29th, 1724, Ætat. 3. Mary the third, buried Nov. ye 6th, 1728, Ætat. 5. Miles, their Son, buried August the 17th, 1729, Ætat. 10.

With innocence we have run our race,
Kind death hath set us free;
But we was born for a better place,
This world was not for wee.

On an oak chest, at the west end of the church is this inscription:

WILLIAM	THOMAS	ANNO DO
ALLEXAM	DAUIS	MI · NI
DER	C W	1639

The Rev. D. Nichoals Rector.

DAUNTSEY.

On a Monument in Chancel.

Sacred to the Memory of
Charles West, Aged 16 months
died May, 1760.
Milborn West, Aged 4 years,
died March, 1769.
Mary-Ann West Aged 15 years and 4 months,
died Jan. 1770.
Sons and Daughters of the Rev. Francis Maria West, and Sarah his Wife.
Also another Daughter,
Susanna, the Wife of
Henry Blachford Scudamore, Esq.
died 1st Nov. 1798,
Aged 32 years.

C. W. 1760.
M. W. 1769.
M. A. W. 1770.

On Flat Stone within the Rails.

Here lieth interred the Body of the Honble Lieut. General Harry Mordaunt, Son of the Right Honble the Lord Viscount Mordaunt, who departed this life the 5th day of January, 1719, Aged 56.

Without the Rails.

Sacred to the Memory of
Susanna, the affectionate
and beloved Wife of
Henry Blachford Scudamore,
of St. James's Square, Bath, Esq.
who died
the 1st of November, 1798,
and left a disconsolate Husband, one son,
and three daughters,
to lament her loss.

106

Here lyeth the Body of the Rev. Mr. Peter Rival, Rector of this Parish, who departed this life July 16, Anno Dom. 1730, Ætatis 68.

On a Brass Plate.

Richard Cheffneare, Doctor in Divinity, departed this life April 7th, 1763.
Resurgam.

P. P. 1790.
Aged 2 years.

On a Mon. in S. Aisle.

This Monument is erected to the Memory of Ann, Wife of Jonathan Creed, yeoman, daughter of John Reeve, late of this Parish, schoolmaster. She departed this life the 7th of Jan. 1772, Aged 64.

Also to the Memory of Jonathan Creed, who departed this life Feb. 13, 1811, Aged 89.

Over south door.

Keep thy foot when thou goest
into the house of God. Eccl. c. 1st.

In West End of South Aisle.

William Bartlett,
and
Anthony Rogers
Church Wardens, 1726.
John Fox, Ancestor.

On a Monument in south wall of the Body.

This Monument is Erected to perpetuate the Memory of John Mulcock, yeoman, who depated this life the 20th day of September, 1790, Aged 66 years.

Go home, my friends, and cease from tears.
I must sleep here till Christ appears.
Spectators all, as you pass by,
As you are now, so once was I;
But as I am, so must you be,
Prepare for death, and follow me.

Also Martha, Wife of the above-said John Mulcock, who departed this life the 3rd day of February, 1801, Aged 82 years.

Preserve, O Vault, inviolate thy Trust,
Till Heaven's high Mandate claims the sacred dust.
When the last trump th' awak'ning sound shall give
Rise ye that sleep, your Saviour bids you live.

On Flat Stones in S. Aisle.

Here lyeth the Body of John Reeve, Schoolmaster, of this Parish, who departed this life June the 26th, A. D. 1713, Aged 46.

Here lyeth the Body of John Reeve, jun. who departed this life August ye 10th, 1765, Aged 59 years.

A. C. 1772.

H. S. T.

Anna, eldest daughter of Nathan Cooper, Obiit 19th May, 1732, Ala. 25.

H. S. T.

Sarah, the Wife of Nathan Cooper, Ob. 29th Dec. 1733, Ala. 51.

On a Monument in North Aisle.

This small tribute of respect to the Memory of
Mrs. Alice Wayte, (the best of Mothers) is erected
at the request of her youngest Son,
Simon Wayte, Esq.
late of Groundwell, in this County.
She died universally regretted
at the age of 82 years, A. D. 1768.
In the same Vault are deposited
the Remains of her two Daughters,
Mary and Elizabeth,
who died single.

On Flat Stones in Body.

Here Lyeth the Body of John Oven, of Whitlands, Desessed the 27th day of June, being Aged 52, Anno Dom. 1647.

Here Resteth the Body of William Rich, deceased the 15th of November, Anno Domini 1647.

Here lyeth the Body of Simon Allin, who departed this life Sept. ye 8th, 1727, Aged 77 years.

Here lyeth also the Body of Alline Wayte, Son of William and Allice Wayte, who departed this life March 18th, A. D. 1727, Aged 6 years.

Here lyeth the Body of Richard Kendall, who departed this life the 25th day of Oct. A. D. 1686.

Here lyeth also the Body of Mary the Wife of Simon Alline, and daughter of Richard Kendall, who departed this life March the 14th, 1720, Aged 70 years and 8 months.

Here lieth the Body of Thomas Lea. He died May ye 6, A.D. 1718, Aged 42 years.

Here lyeth the Body of Mrs. Barbon Lawrence, who departed this life June ye 30th, 1739, Aged 51 years.

Here lyeth the Body of Mary Lawrence. She departed this life Aug. 2d, A.D. 1729, Ætat. 64 years.

Jane, daughter of John and Everist Reeks, died Oct. ye 12th, 1809, Aged 14 years.
Also of their children died infants. Also Everist, Wife of Thos. Reeks, died Oct. 14th, 1815, Aged 59 years.
Also John Reeks died May 12, 1816, Aged 60 years.

On Flat Stones in N. Aisle.

Here lyeth the Body of Margaret, the Wife of Edmund Wayte, the elder, who departed this life the 25th day of November, Anno Dom. 1685.

Here lieth the Body of Edmund Wayte, the elder, who departed this life the . . Dec. Anno Dom. 16.2.

Memoriæ
Viri optimi nō intermoriture,
Sacrum
Hoc tumulo conduntur
Minutæ viri magni reliquiæ
Dn[i] Actonis Drake, Armigeri,
Illustrissimo Comiti de Danby, A. cubiclo, et Forestæ olim regiæ de Whitchwood, in agro Oxiensi, custodis, Famæ pariter
Et fidei illi vatæ, qui diu superstes
Gentis suæ erat ingens ornamenta.
Defunctus triste
Desidera
Fatis cessit prid. non. Maij, Ann. CIↃIↃCLI.

On an Altar Tomb of White Marble in the north transept.

[On the north side of the Tomb.]

Here was
Partly bred-up in the Lowe-Countrey warres under Maurice Earle of ; Nassaw, Afterwards Prince of Orange ; And in many other Milita[ry] Accons ; of Those Times Both by Sea and Land. Hee was made A Cap[tn] in the Warres ; of France and There Knighted for his good service under Henry ye IV ; Then French King. Hee was imployed as Lieutenant · Generall of the ; Horse and Sergjeant Maj[h] of the whole Army in Ireland ; Under Robert Earle of Essex and Charles Baron of Mountioy ; in the Raigne of Queene Elizabeth.

[South side.]

Hee was made Baron of Dauntsey and Peere of this Realme by King James ; the first, and by him made Lord President of Munster and Governour ; of Garnsey By King Charles the first hee was created Earle of Danby ; made one of his Privie Councell, and Kinght of the most noble order of the ; Garter, But declyning more active imployments in his latter time ; (by reason of imperfect health) Full of honour woundes and scars Hee dyed at his howse in Cornb[ry] Park in the County of Oxford, in the 71 year of his age.

LAVS DEO.

[On the East end.]

Sacred Marble safely Keepe
His dust, who under thee must Sleepe
Untill the graves againe restore
Their dead, and Time shall be no more
Meane while, if he (w[ch] all thinges weares)
Doe ruin thee, or if the teares
Are shed for him, Dissolve thy frame
Thou art requited, for his Fame
His Vertues, and his Worth shal bee
Another Monument for thee. G. Herbert.

[Round the edges of the Tomb.]

Henry Earl of Danby. 2[d] Sonne to S[r] John Danvers K[t] and Dame Elizabeth Daught[r] & Co-heyre to Nevill L[d] Latimer : Borne at Dauntsey in the County of Wilts. the 28th day of June, An° Dñi. 1573, and Baptized in this Church the first of July Following being Sunday, hee Departed this Life on the 28th of Jan. A° Dñi 1643, & Lyeth here Interred.

Length of the Slab 8ft. 10in. width 4ft. 8 in.

On a Brass Plate S. Aisle.

Now Richard Hunt, A Servant true
to the Earle of Danby here
Ruled 18 years his Wilts. Estate
Lyeth Buried underneath
this Marble Stone, whose desire was
All ages yet to Come
Would not disturbe his Body's rest
but lett his Bones alone
Till Jesus Christ (in whome only
was All his hope and trust)
Shall Glorifye his sinfull Corpes
Which here have Layne in Dust.

Hee was born ye 11th of Aprill An° 1581 And departed this Life ye 30th of Aug. 1647.

On the Arch between the Body and Tower.

This Tower was begun to be built April 21st, 1630. Also this Church repaired, enlarged, and the whole work fully ended Sept. 17, 1632.

The Rev. Mr. G. Bissett, present Vicar.

SOMERFORD PARVA.

South Wall.

Here Lyeth the Body of George Wroton, Esquire, who deceased at Mandish House the 29th day of January, in the year of our Lord God 1627.

On Flat Stones.

Here lyeth the Body of Sarah, the Wife of John Godwin, who departed this life the 26th of October, 1748, Aged 40 years.

Also here Lyeth their two Children, Mary Aged 7 years, and Sarah 21 days.

On Brass Plates.

Here lyeth the Body of Mary, the Wife of Francis Baskerville, gent. who departed this life the 14th day of Feb. 170$\frac{9}{10}$ Aged 56 years.

Here Lyeth the Body of Mary, ye Wife of John Paumer, Rector of this Parish, who deceased ye 13th day of May, in the year 1690.

If Vertue it selfe did with Vertuous Woman die,
Reader, Thou Then mights say here it doth Lie.

Here Lyeth ye Body of Francis Baskerville, who departed this Life July ye 4th, A.D. 1723, Aged 77 years.

On a Monument in S. Wall of Body.

Near this Place lyeth the Body of Elizabeth Langton, Wife of John Langton, of Pirton, in this County, Gent. (eldest Daughter of Francis Goddard, of the same place, Esq. and Elizabeth, his Wife,) who dyed in London, of the small pox, the 25th of January, 1701, in the 25th year of her age, very much lamented, being a true Friend, charitable Neighbour, a pious, Virtuous, good Wife.

On Flat Stones in Body.

Here Lyeth the Body of John Blicke, who departed this Life the 9th of July, 1634.

Here Lyeth the Body of Robert Blicke, Son of John Blicke, who was buried 29th of September, 1667.

Here lieth the Body of Robert Blicke, Son of Robert Blicke, who was Buried 26 of March, 1683.

Death thy sting is Blunt, grave Boast no more,
. . e Soules now free who was a slave before;
Therefere oh bones, lye quiet in the dust
Untill the resurrection of the just.

Also here lieth the Body of Mary, the Wife of Lucian Brown, and Daughter of Robert Blicke, who dyed February ye 2d. 172$\frac{2}{3}$.

Here lyeth ye Body of Ann, ye Daughter of Lucian and Mary Browne, who was buried June ye 3d.

Under Lyeth the Body of John, the Son of Lucian Browne, and Anne, his Wife, Daughter to John Mayer of Somerford Magna. He departed this life the 12th of February, Anno Dom. 17$\frac{11}{12}$ Ætatis 42.

In Memory of John Collingborne, who died Jan, 7th, 1733, Aged 85.

And also of Joan his Wife, who died Sept. 13th, 1733, Aged 79.

In good old age he laid us down
To rest untill tho Trumpet sound;
And then raised again shall be,
To live with Christ eternally.

Here Lyeth ye Body of Ann, Wife of Andrew Heath. She departed this Life Nov. 3, Anno Dom. 1731, Aged 27 years.

Her merry life with me was short,
She was Quickly gone,
Her Labour o'er,
Her Glass is run.

In Memory of Andrew Heath, of Clack, who departed this Life May the 3, Anno Dom. . . . Aged 41 years.

Since 'tis ordained all men must die,
Reader, contemplate Eternity.

Emma, the Wife of Richard Thomas Gent. dyed the 29th, and was buried the 31st day of December, 1675.

Francis Goddard, de Pirton, in Comitatu Wilts. Armigeri, et Elizabeth uxoris ejus, quorum cineres sub hoc marmore teguntur. Elizabeth mortem obiit 17 die Septem. Ætatis suæ 61. Excessit Franciscus 22 die Octobris 1701, Ætatis suæ 62.

Resurgamus.

Here Lyeth ye Body of Charles, Son of Charles and Sarah Spencer, Mercer in Malmesbury, who died Feb. 21, A. D. 1716, Aged 1 year.

Elizabeth White, . .
spinster, Daughter of .
White, of Exon, Merchant
of William White little .
Esq. dyed ye 25th day of .
1694.

Extent of Somerford Parva 1086 acres.

CHARLTON.

On a Monument in Chancel.

To the Memory of the Rev. John Hollingworth, A. M. Curate and Vicar of this Parish for thirty-two years. He died Feb. 17th, 1800, Aged 63 years. Also of Sarah, his Wife, who died Dec. 27, 1803, Aged 57 years.

Do justly, love mercy, and walk humbly with thy God.

On a Flat Stone within the Rails.

Here Lyeth interred the Body of Mr. Mathew Whitly, late Vicar of this Parish, who departed this life on the 9th day of September, Anno Dni 1670.

On a Monument in N. Aisle.

The Honourable James Grahme, second Son to Sir George Grahme, Baronet, of Netherby, in Cumberland, Born at Norton Conyers, in Yorkshire, in March, Sixteen Hundred and Forty Nine, Servant to King Charles and King James the Second, Lived and Died an unworthy but true Member of the Church of England, Faithful to both his Masters, and a sincere Lover of Monarchy, Died Jan. the Twenty Sixth, And was Buried Monday, the second of February, 17 29/30

In West End of Body.

To the Memory of Elizabeth, daughter of John and Jane Brooks, who died September 25, 1816, Aged 15 years.

On a Brass Plate against the first Pillar.

Neare to this Place Lyeth interred the Body of that truley virtuous Matron, Josuan Pitman, Formerly the Loving and Faithfull Wife of Robert Tayler, of this Parish. Shee dyed the Relict and Widdow of Richard Pitman, Gent. in the Month of January, 1647. As alsoe the Body of John Tayler, her Sonn, who was deprived of this Life by impartial Death in the Month of September, 1673, in the 30th year of his age.

On Brass Plates in Body.

Here Resteth ye Body of Jeane Gastrell, who departed this Life ye 3d day of February, in the yeare of our Lord 1700. & Giles, ye Son of John Gastrell, who departed this life June ye 15th, 1727.

Here Resteth ye Body of John Gastrell, Gent. who departed this life ye 28th day of September, in ye year of our Lord 1694. & Joane, ye Wife of the above sayd John Gastrell, who departed this Life Feb. 18th, 1724.

Here lieth the Body of Hester, the Wife of Henry Martyn, Gent. Aged 37, who departed this life the 17th day of June, A. D. 1667.

If women all would live like thee,
Then Men with Wives might happy be.

Here Lyeth interred the Body of Anne Hackwell, Late Wife of Thomas Hackwell, of London, and eldest Daughter of Mr. John Raymond, Late of Cirencester, Aged 38 years, who departed this life the 2d day of January, Anno 1664, Expecting a happie Resurrection.

Here under Lyeth ye Body of Mary, the Wife of John Phelps, of Ambury, in this County, Daughter and only child of John Thick, and Hester, his Wife, of this Parish. She departed this Life ye first day of November, in ye year of our Lord 1703, Aged 50 years.

Here Lyeth interred the Body of Elizabeth Sa . . who departed this Life the 5th day of December, Anno 1712.

Here lieth the Body of Mary, Wife of William Johnson, who departed this Life December 9th, A.D. 1726.

In the South Porch.

Here under lyeth the Body of John Waters, gent. who departed this life the 9th day of December, 1676.

On a Flat Stone in Chaucel.

Richard Beswick, M. A. hujus Ecclesia
Oniensis Vicarus. Primo die mensis Novembris 1670,
A. D. vicesimum secundum . . 1700.

Outside of Chancel.

Near this Place Lyes the Body of George Harvey, who was Buried the 14th of June, 1607.

On an ancient oak Pulpit against the North Wall.

WO · BE · VNTO · ME · IF · I
PREACH · NOT · THE
GOSPEL · ANNO · DOMINI
1630.

On an Altar Tomb in the Chancel are the Effigies of a Man and Woman lying, with five small figures kneeling, three on the right, and two on the left, formerly there were six, three on each side. The Male figure is in armour, his head resting on his helmet, with his hands meeting over his breast. There is no inscription, but it is thought to be the tomb of Sir Henry Knyvett and his Lady.

The Church consists of two Chancels and a Nave. Under the North Chancell is the Family Vault of the Right Hon[ble] Thomas Howard. The Tower contains five Bells; on the second—Humphrey Woodcock, Churchwarden. Rudwell, Glocester, 1734.

In 1817, the Church was entirely new Pewed, at the expense of the Right Hon. Thos. Howard.

Round the family Pew of the Earl of Suffolk is some ancient carving, representing human figures.

The Right Hon. Thomas Howard, in 1807, inclosed about 300 acres of Breadon Forest, 200 of which he have already planted.

Benefactions.

On a Wood Frame.

The Gift of Lady Winchcomb, Anno Domino 1706, Twenty Shillings to be paid Annually for Ever out of certain Lands in Hankerton, to buy Books for the Instruction of the Poor Children of the Parish of Charlton.

Lady Winchcomb's Sister by Will gave a field in the Parish of Brokenborough, containing by Survey 7 acres, 3 Rod, 35 perch, Adjoining to Lands of the Earl of Suffolk, Earl Radnor, and Lord John Sparrow, to the Poor of this Parish for ever.

There is a School in this Parish, in which are about 80 boys and girls, supported by the Right Hon[ble] Thomas, and Elizabeth Jane Howard.

GARSDEN.

Mon. in Chancel against North Wall.

To the Memory of Sir Laurence Washington, Kt Lately Chiefe Register of the Chancery, of Known Pyety, of Charitye exemplarye, a Loving Husband, A Tender Father, A Bountifull Master, A Constant Reliever of the poore, and to those of the Pasish A Perpetuall Benefactor, Whom it pleased God to take into his peace, from the fury of the insuing Warrs, Oxon, May 14, here interred 24, Anno Dom. 1643, Ætatis suæ 64. Where also Lyeth Dame Anne, his Wife, who deceased June 13th, and was buried 16, Anno Dom. 1645.

Hic Patrios cineres curavit filius urna
Condere, qui tumulo nunc jacet ille pius.

The pious son his parents here interred,
Who hath his share in Urne for them prepared.

On Flat Stones in Chancel.

Sacrum Memoriæ Anna, Filiæ
Laurintij Washington, Esquitis,
et uxoris Christopheri Gise,
Hic sepultæ, Junii 4°, Anno Dom.
1642, Ætat. suæ 20.

Here Lyeth the Body of Lawrence
Washington, Esq. the only Son
of Sir Lawrence Washington, who
Departed this Life Jan. 17, was
buried Feb. 11, Anno Dom. 1661, and
inclosed by Elinor, his Wife,
April 16, Anno Dom. 1663,
Ætat. suæ 39.

En mercede virum pensatum mune . .
Prospicit ille suis dina supersta sibi . .

Behold, how duty well performed is paide,
Sure he him here his dust hath Laide.

Here Lyeth ye Body of Dame Elienor Pargiter, 2d Daughter of William Guise, of Elmore, in ye County of Gloucester, Esq. first married to Lawrence Washingt n, Esq. afterwards Sir William Pargiter, of Grittleworth, in ye County of Northampton, Kt. who departed this Life the 19th day of July, in the year of our Lord 1685. Ordered her remains to be deposited here in hopes of a Blessed Resurrection.

On Flat Stones in Body.

Here Lyeth the Bo
of Roger Gantlet,
who Departed this Li
the 13th day of March,
Anno Domini 1680.

Under this Stone Lyeth the Body of Roger Gan . .
He died June the . . 1727, Ætat. suæ . .

Also in Memory of Sarah, Wife of Roger Gantlet, aforesaid. She died Feb. 8, 1729, Ætatis suæ 74.

In the outside, against the south Wall.

Here under lyeth the Body of Henry Drinkwater, who was buried the 3d day of April, 1693.

On a Head Stone in the Churchyard.

In Memory of Sarah, the Daughter of John and Ann Ellison, who departed this life May 28th, A. D. 1744.

Near five foot long, and three foot round,
A Girl near nine years old,
Now lays interred within the ground,
A wonder to be told.

Young men and maids serve God betimes,
For Death took me just in my prime,
So it may you, therefore I pray,
Make use of time whilst you may;
Therefore repent, live Godly still,
Then welcome Death, come when it will.

The Church consist of Chancel and Nave. Round the pulpit is some ancient carved work, and a few small pieces of painted glass in the south windows, and part of two heads in the east window of the chancel.

There are five Bells in the Tower; with these inscriptions on them:

First—God bless Queen Ann. Robt. Cor, 1703.
Second—1703.
Third—Come when wee Call, and serve God All: Robt. Cor, 1703.
Fourth—1703.
Fifth—Robt. Cor, 1704.

The Manor

Formerly belonged to Earl Ferrers, who was executed in 1760, for the murder of his steward either at the Manor House of Garsden, or at his seat in Hampshire. Paul Methuen, Esq. succeeded Earl Ferrers, and the present Lord of the Manor is Paul Cobb Methuen, of Corsham, Esq. The Manor House is an ancient stone building, now occupied by a farmer. The extent of the parish is about 1200 acres, chiefly pasture.

The Parsonage House was re-built in 1818. There is a Sunday School, supported by subscription, in which are about 20 children.

The Rev. Thomas Anthony Methuen, Rector.

L E A.

On Flat Stones in Body.

In Memory of the Rev. Leolin Edwards, who departed this Life September the 1st, 1762, Aged 86.

V. D. M.

The Soul that once inform'd this dust
To publish Heaven as envoy here,
Was call'd at length to leave this trust,
In hope to serve in nobler sphere.

Ann, the Wife of Leolin Edwards, departed this Life September the 12th, 1778, Aged 75 years.

Joanna, the Wife of John Reynolds, departed this life August the 7th, 1783, Aged 48 years.

On a Brass Plate.

In Memory of Joseph Mills who died July 5th, 1760, Aged 78.

Also of Mary, his Wife, who died Jan. 13th, 1732, Aged 35.

In Memory of John Weeks, of Cleaverton, who departed this life February 13, 1796, Aged 47 years.

In Memory of Mary, Wife of John Weeks, of Cleverton, who departed this life October 11th, 1789, Aged 36 years.

Also Amy, Daughter of John and Mary Weeks, who departed this life January 7th, 1786, Aged 1 year.

The Pulpit, which is very ancient, stands against the north wall, and on it is a little carving in the Gothic style.

The Church is a plain building, consisting only of a Chancel and Nave, both under one roof. The Tower contains five bells, each having an inscription. On the

First—Anno Domini 1670.
Second—Simpkins and John Young, Ch. Wardens, 1663.
Third—Idem.
Fourth—R. P. Anno Domini 1622.
Fifth—Idem.

The Registers of the Churches of Garsden and Lea were formerly kept in the House of the . . . . who performed the duty of both Parishes. But in 1752, the house taking fire, both the Registers were burnt, and the Plate belonging to this Church destroyed. Pewter is now used.

Lord Wharton formerly was Lord of this Manor, — Boucher, Esq. succeeded him, afterwards Fitz-William, who married in the Boucher family. The Earl of Pembroke is the present Lord, having lately purchased it.

The Rev. Thomas Anthony Methuen, Rector.

BROKENBOROUGH.

On Monuments aginst S. Wall of Chancel.

Here Lyeth ye Body of Margarett, the Daughter of William Robins, gent. and Mary his Wife, who was buried the 25th day of December, Anno Dom̃ 1675.

Neere under this Wall was the Body of Joana Robins, Daughter of William Robins, gent. and Mary his Wife, Interred, the 22d of December, 1668.

Here Lyeth the Body of Nicholas Robins, the Sone of Richard Robins, and Joanna his Wife, Gent. who departed this life the 13th of Jan. 1665.

On a Monument in North Aisle.

Here
Lieth the Body of Roger Andres,
Departed this Life the 20th day of March, 1638.

On a Flat Stone in Body.

Here Lyeth the Body
of T · AS · ADY, Gñt
WHO DECEASED · IRS ·
DAY of October, Anno Dom. 1637.

Here Lyeth the Body of Willm Gease, of this Parish. He departed this Life June the 5th, 1743, Aged 84 years.

On the Pulpit against the South Wall:

ROGER · ANDROS · AND
ISAC · PUNTAR · BOTH
CHURCH · WARDENS · 1641.

The Church consists of a Chancel, Nave, and North Aisle. The north wall of the Nave is supported by four plain semi arches.

The Manor have long been in the possession of the Howard family, now Earl of Suffolk.

The Rev. J. Nicholeſs preſent Rector.

BRINKWORTH.

On Flat Stones in Chancel.

Here Lyeth that which was Maortall of Doctter
William Dowdeswell, Rector
of this Church hee Departed
This Life the 20th Day of May,
Anno Domini 1671.

Here Lyeth ye Body of Richard Copson, A. M. Rector of Brinkworth, who died May the 24th,

Anno { Doml 1732,
{ Ætat. 46.

Quales fuerunt dies indicabit Supremus.

Here Lyeth the Body of Mary, the Wife of Richard Copson, M. A. Rector of Brinkworth, who died on

New Year's Day, Anno { Dom. . .
{ Ætat. 30.

William Thornton, Rector of Brinkworth, died 15th Feb. 1760, Aged 75 years.

Repentance towards God, faith towards our Lord Jesus Christ.

Ann Thornton, died 29th March, 1750, Aged 65 years.

That when He who is our Life shall appear, we may also appear with him in glory.

On a Monument in S. aisle.

In Memory of John Stratton, gent. who died Feb. 25,

Anno { Salutis 1718,
{ Ætatis 49.

Also Mary, his Wife. She died Dec. ye 26th,

Anno { Dom. 1723,
{ Ætatis 53.

On a Brass Plate in North Wall of North Aisle.

In Memory of John Weeks, Gent.
who dyed July 24, 1745, Aged 72.
He was Grandson to ye very worthy John Weeks,
A Gentleman no less respectable
For his good Economy, and other private Virtues,
Than Memorable
For his publick Charities and Benefactions,
Especially to this his native Place,
To the poor whereof he left Ten Pounds per Annum,
And for the Instructing Ten poor Children,
To the Schoolmaster Five Pounds per Annum
for Ever.
His Wife Elizabeth,
Descended from a reputable and worthy family
in Gloucestershire,
Survived him not long.
She was a Daughter of Mr. Edmund Morgan,
of Fairford.
Was Baptized June 23, 1668,
And died March 20, 1747.

This Monument was erected as a Testimony
Of the Reverence and filial Piety
Of their ever Dutiful Son,
John Weeks, 1748.

On a Monument against North Wall.

Near this Place Lyeth the Body of Richard Stratton, gent. who departed this Life the 26th of June, 1782, in the 86th year of his age.

Also of Mary, Wife of Richard Stratton, gent. who departed this Life the 26th of August, 1740, Aged 36 years.

Out of a dutiful regard to their Memory, this Monument was erected by William Stratton, their Son.

On Flat Stones in Body.

Richard Stratton, Jun. died July the 6th, 1780, Aged 54 years.

Susanna, his Wife, died April the 4th, 1755, Aged 30 years.

Here Lyeth the Body of William Beale, who died the 2d day of March, 1626.

Jasper Stratton died Jan. 19th, 1798, Aged 70 years.

Grace, his Wife, died Dec. the 19th, 1773, Aged 50 years.

Here lyes the Body of Thomas Eaton, gent. Hee departed this Life the 29th Day of May, Anno Domini 1671.

Here Resteth the Body of John Weeks, gent. who departed this Life Nov. 25th, 1762, Aged 67.

On a Brass Plate.

Here Lyeth the Body of John Weeks, gent. who departed this Life July 24th, 1745, Ætat. suæ 72.

Also here Lyeth the Body of Elizabeth, his Wife. who departed this Life March 20th, 1747, Ætat. suæ 80.

Here Lyeth ye Body of John Crips, Son of Edward and Ann Crips, A. B. of Pembroke Coll. Oxon. and Late Master of Dauntsey School, who died Oct. 2d,

Anno { Ætat. 31,
{ Dom. 1782.

Here Lyeth the Body of Ann Crips, Daughter of Ed. and Ann Crips. She died April 18th, Anno Dom. 1725. Aged 43 years.

Here Lyeth Anne, Daughter of Moses and Elizabeth Sarrande, of Dauntsey. She died July 16, 1723, Aged 14 years.

In Memory of Elizabeth, the Wife of Moses Sarrande, of Dauntsey. She died June 8th, A. D. 1723, Aged 41 years.

Also two Children. Eliz. She died June 30, 1723, Aged 7 years.

Charles died Dec. 7, 1723, Aged 18 weeks.

Here Lyeth ye Body of Edward Crips, sen. who died August 18, Anno Dom. 1770, Aged 68.

Ann, Wife of Edward Crips, was buried Nov. ye 13th, 1730.

On Flat Stones in S. Aisle.

Here Lyeth the Body of Ann Phelps Stratton, Daughter of John and Mary Stratton, who died Nov. the 10th, 1730, Aged 28.

In Memory of Undecimus Stratton, who died Nov. 29th, 1807, Aged 74 years.

In Memory of Thomas Stratton, who died Jan. 19th, 1802, Aged 72 years.

On Flat Stones in N. Aisle.

Here Lyeth the Body of Ann Weekes, who departed this life the 1st of May, 1692.

Here Lyeth the Body of John, ye Son of Richard and Susanna Weekes, who departed this Life Jan. ye 17th, A. D. 1692.

Also here Lyeth . . . their Daughter, who departed this life March ye 30th, A. D. 1696.

Near this Place Lyeth Ann, ye Daughter of Richard and Susanna Weeks. He was Buried August ye 8th, 1701.

Inscription on an ancient oak chest.

JOHN . BEALE · GEFRI . HINIL .
CHURCH · WARDENS.
WO · BE · UNTO · ME · IF · I · PREACH
NOT . THE . GOSPEL · 1630

The Communion Table is of oak, very handsomely carved. On one end is the date 1630, and on the other the initials A. B.

The Rev. James Sparrow succeeded to the Rectorship of Brinkworth on the death of the Rev. W. Thornton, who lies buried in the Chancel; John Penton was the late Rector, the Rev. Matthew Marsh present Rector.

The Manor of Brinkworth belongs to the Earl of Suffolk.

John Weeks gave for ever five Pounds per Annum to the Schoolmaster for the support of a Charity School, which with about £.20 subscribed, nearly 60 children are educated.

The Church consists of Chancel, Nave, North and South Aisles. The Nave is supported by five plain round pillars on each side, and five pointed arches. In the roof of the North and South Aisles is some small ancient carving, in foliage. In the South Aisle is an ancient oak chest, strongly bound with iron. The Tower contains five Bells :—

On the First—

Thomas Lewen, John Oliffe, Church Wardens. 1663.

I am the first, although but small,
My voice is heard above you all.

Second—

Thomas Lewen, John Oliffe, Church Wardens. 1663.
William Perdue, and Richard Perdue. R C * I S

Third—

Thomas Lewin, John Oliffe, Church Wardens. 1663.

Fourth—

Idem.

Fifth—

I sound to make the sick repent,
In hopes of Life when Breath is spent:
Come when I call, to serve God all,
To sing Alleluia unto the King of Saints.

Thomas Lewen, John Ayliffe, Church Wardens.
William Perdue, and Richard Purdue. 1663.

CORSTON,

On Monuments against E. Wall of Chancel.

Near this Place lies interred the Bodys of William ye Eldest Son of Isaac and Grace Gale, who dyed ye 23rd of December, 1691, Aged 12 years.

And Edmund, their second Son, dyed July ye 17th, 1685, Aged 19 months.

Under also Lyeth the Body of Isaac Grace, gent. who always lived on earth as a true disciple of Jesus Christ, in all humility, in Patience, in Wisdom, in Goodness, and in Love and Charity with all men. He departed this Life the 24th day of June, in the year of our Lord 1726, in the 81st year of his age.

Sacred to the Memory of Mrs. Grace Gale, Widow of Isaac Gale, Gent, youngest Daughter of George Estcourt, of Swinly, D. D. She dyed April 18th, 1734, in the eighty-second year of her age. In every station of her life she was truly Christian and Charitable, Loving & beloved of all.

Mors est janua vitæ. J. H. S.

Beneath this Place lie interred ye Bodies of Nathanael and Elizabeth Power, and Elizabeth their Daughter. Nathanael died July the 2d, 1761, Aged 71. Elizabeth, his Wife, died the 29th of May, 1755, Aged 66. And Elizabeth, their Daughter, died Sept. the 12th, 1743, Aged 4 years.

Weep not for us who goes before,
For Christ has quit our sinful score:
O happy change for us to die,
To live with Christ Eternally.

William Power died Sept. 22d, 1773, Aged 47.

I pin'd away through pain and grief,
In faithless friends is no belief;
But now my Corps from man is free,
No man that's left can arrest me.
Gold cannot bring man lasting rest;
Without mercy none is blest.

In Memory of Arch, Son of William and Ann Gale. He Died Jan. 29th, 1748, Aged 28 years.

Also William Gale. He died June 17th, 1751, Aged 72 years.

Also Ann, his Wife, died April 22d, 1762, Aged 82.

And Also Ann, Wife of William Gale, died Oct. 4, 1766, Aged 33 years.

Also William Gale, died August 25, 1793, Aged 73 years.

On Flat Stones.

To the Memory of John Smith, who died Nov. 20th, 1807, Aged 82 years.

On a Monument in the N. Wall of the Body.

In Memory of Giles Punter, who departed this life the 11th of July, 1745, Aged 73 years.

All the paths of the Lord are mercy and truth unto such as keep his covenant and his testimonies. Psal. xxv. v. 10.

On a plain Stone in North Wall of Chancel.

In Memory of William Earle. He died December ye 18th, 1737, Aged 72 years.

Also in Memory of John Drew. He died Nov. 30th, 1747, Aged 75 years.

And also in Memory of Jane, the Wife of William Earle, who departed this life the 30th of August 1749, Aged 67 years.

To wait on God is not in vain,
For he restores to Life again.

Mon. in Chancel against North Wall.

To the Memory of Thomas Bromsgrove, who departed this Life April 7th, 1785, Aged 45 years.

Also Ann, his Wife, who departed this life May 15th, 1804, Aged 61 years.

A worthy Father, and a tender and Affectionate Mother, and a sincere Friend, Beloved, Respected, and sincerely Lamented.

In Memory of James, Son of William and Margaret Godwin, who died June the 8th, 1770, Aged 1 year and 1 month.

A loving Child, both meek and mild,
Lies near unto this Place;
Its hoped its Soul, without controul,
Will attend the throne of grace.

South Wall of Chancel.

In Memory of Charles Smith, who departed this life the 18th of October, 1745, Ætat. 64.

Also in Memory of John, his Son, who departed this Life the 26th of October, 1746, Ætat. 28.

Our work is done, our Glass is run,
And here we must remain,
A lump of Clay, till judgment day,
And then shall rise again.

In Memory of John Sealy, who died May 10, 1791, Aged 46 years.

Also of Alexander and Richard, Sons of John and Martha Sealy, who both died July 13th, 1779, Alexander aged 4 years, Richard aged 2 years.

Also of John, their Son, who died Jan. 25, 1804, Aged 31 years.

Also of Richard, their Son, who died June 16th, 1807, Aged 27 years.

Sacred to the Memory of William Sealy, who died Sept. 23, 1816, Aged 34 years.

Be ye also ready, for in such an hour as ye think not, the Son of Man cometh. Matt. xxiv. 44.

The Screen, which parts the nave from the chancel, is ornamented with a little ancient carving, in the Gothic style.

The Rev. John Strong late Vicar, succeeded by the Rev. D. Bisset.

The Earl of Radnor, Lord of the Manor.

RODBORNE.

On Monuments in Chancel.

In Memory of Thomas Kaynes, who died August 6th, 1773, Aged 63 years.

Also Ann, Daughter of the above Thomas Kaynes. She died June ye 10th, 1779, Aged 26 years.

Also Mary, Wife of the above Thomas Kaynes, died Jan. 25, 1794, Aged 75 years.

Sacred to the Memory of John Kaynes, who died April 4th, 1813, Aged 65 years.

Also Mary, his Wife, who died May 31st, 1814, Aged 51 years.

Beneath this Place Lyeth the Body of Charles Palmer, of this Parish, who departed this life the 9th day of September, 1722, Aged 56 years.

O reader, stay one moment with ye Dead,
Have one good thought when on ye graves you tread.
Go, reader, learn to live and die like men
That have immortall souls, and then come here again.

Arms.—Sable, a chevron or.

To the Memory of Joan, Daughter of William Shipton, and of Joan his Wife, who departed this life ye 5th day of July, A. D. 1699, Aged 19 years and 6 months.

Virtuous though young soo good were apt to say
Too soon too soon she was taken hence away
Yet yearly . . . the sooner called on high
To glory though her Body in dust doth ly
Tis to resine grow pure fit to unite
The soul at the latter day in endless light.

In Memory of Sarah, Wife of John Handy, who died May the 2d, 1773, Aged 34 years.

Also two Sons, died infants.

In Memory of Elizabeth, Wife of John Rogers, Daughter of John and Sarah Godwin, who died May 14th, 1772, Aged 28 years.

Also here Lieth Jane and Sarah, their 2 Daughters, Died infants.

Dear Husband, now my life is past,
My love to you so long did last,
But now for me no trouble take,
But love my children for my sake.

In Memory of John Godwin, gent. who died Dec. 21st, 1760, Aged 56 years.

Edith, his Wife, died Dec. 10th, 1789, Aged 78 years.

And John, their Son, died April 8th, 1795, Aged 43 years.

Underneath Lyeth the Bodys of William Shippen, and of Joan his Wife, dyed May ye 3d, A. D. 1731, Aged 78 years.

She dyed July ye 11th, A. D. 1728, Aged 83 years.

Death, in a very good old age,
Did end yt weary pilgrimage,
And was to them an end of pain,
The only way to life again.

Also in Memory of John, their Son. He dyed March the 16th, 1733, Aged 48 years.

Also, in Memory of Mary Godwin, the Daughter of William and Joan Shippen. She dyed June ye 30th, A. D. 1742, Aged 66 years.

Underneath Lye the Bodyes of Jacob and John Godwin, Sons of Jeremie Godwin, and of Frances his Wife. Jacob died Nov. ye 14th, A. D. 1694, aged 2 weeks and 2 days, John died Feb. ye 19th, 169$\frac{8}{9}$ Aged 4 weeks.

Lovely to look on were these Babes, but they
Came, saw ys world, dislik'd, and went away,
As flowers new blown, soe fair, it seem'd no less,
Than forms too sweet to joyne wth rottenness:
In Baptizem wash'd from sin, their souls so pure,
Wth their Redeemer Christ are now secure,
Call'd hence by God, in peace of ym may sing,
The grave noe Conquest gets, Death hath noe Sting.

To the Memory of John Alexander, who departed this Life the 6th of Nov. 1726, Aged 78 years.

A faithful friend, a Father dear,
A loving Husband resteth here:
The loss is great which we sustain,
But Christ hath made our loss his gain.

Also to the Memory of David, Son of the above John Alexander, who departed this life the 7th of March, 1746, Aged 56 years.

Gentle and Easy, void of Debate and strife,
Alwais doing good, to this he spent his Life,
Even to the grave, wherein he now doth rest,
Whose soul, God grant, to sit in heaven with the just.

And also to the Memory of Joyce, Daughter of the above John Alexander, who departed this life the 12th of April, 1749, Aged 51 years.

Christ, my Redeemer, knew which way was best
To ease my pain, and take my soul to rest.

In Memory of Margaret, Wife of John Alexander, who died the 3d of May, 1750, Aged 86 years.

A Righteous Life I ever led,
Preparing for my earthly Bed;
Sorrow and pain I've undergone,
Till Christ in mercy took me home.

Mary Alexander, Aged 81 years.

Arms.—Sable, a chevron or.

On Monuments in the Body, on South Wall.

In Memory of John Handy, who died Dec. 14th, 1788, Aged 83 years.

In Memory of Margaret, Wife of John Handy. She departed this Life May 18, 1780, Aged 77 years.

Sacred to the Memory of Mary, Wife of Thomas Handy, who departed this life Sept. 3d, 1813, Aged 70 years.

On a Monument against North Wall.

Near this Place Lieth the Bodys of John, Mary, and Elizabeth, Son and Daughters of Thomas and Mary Handy. John died May ye 22d, 1779, Aged 5 years. Mary died May ye 29th, 1779, Aged 6 years. Elizabeth died May ye 23d, 1779, Aged 4 months.

Also Elizabeth, their Daughter, dyed Jan. 30, 1786, Aged 2 years. Mary Ann, their Daughter, died March 6, 1805, Aged 16 years.

Here Innocence and Beauty lies, whose breath
Was snatch'd by early, not untimely death:
Hence did she go just as she did begin
Sorrow to know before she knew to sin.
Death, that does sin and sorrow thns prevent,
Is the next blessing to a life well spent.

The Tower has but one bell.

Robert Pollen, Esq. Lord of the Manor, succeeded Lady Hungerford.

The Rev. Mr. Strong, late Vicar, the Rev. G. Bissett the present one.

HULLHAVINGTON.

On Monuments in Chancel.

Oliver Ivie,
Sonne And Hier of George
Ivie, Esq. of Hullavington, in ye
County of Wilts. who Married Anne
Finet in ye Year of our Lord 1649
one of ye Daughters of Sr John Finet Kt
Master of ye ceremonies To King
Charles ye First & of ye Lady Finet his
Wife Sister to ye Earl of Cleveland
this said Oliver Ivie Deceased in
November 1650 Leaveing his said Wife
Wth Child who was on ye 14 of April
1651 Delivered of a Daughter wch was
named Jane wch said Jane Ivie Deceased on ye 23
Of October 1654 wth her said Father
Lyeth under this place.
Anne Ivie his Widdow
In Memory of her Dear Husband &
Child hath erected this Monument
in ye year of our Lord God 1663.

To the Memory of George, Eldest Son
of Thomas Ivie, Esq. ye Father of 20 Children.
George Married the heiress of Oliv. . . .
She was Buried Sept. 29th, 1664.
They had Issue Oliv. Thomas Elizth Mary Ann
Catharine and Lydia.
The said G. Ivie was Lord of this Manor,
& Justice of Peace and Quorum 53 years.
He was a pious man, a grave Magistrate,
good to the poor hospitable to all and a
Lover of his Country. Buried Nov. 28, 1676,
Aged 80 years and 9 weeks.
Here also Lyes Coll. Thomas Ivye, in his Mother's
Grave, who Married Margret, Daughter of
John Whittington, Esq. he left
Sr John Ivye, Esq. Geor. Thos. Oliv. Margr.
& Catharine. he was Buried June 1681.

Erected by Ch. Atkins,
To ye Memory of her Honble Father, ye said
G. Ivye, &c.

Against the North Wall.

O man Repent this World Defie
Remember well That Thou must di
For as I am so shalt thou be
Dust and Ashes as Thou maist see
Serve God therefore wilst Thou hast Time
That Thou to Blisse at Length maist Clime
Every Estate Lord Duke and King
Rich men and poor marke well this Thing.

Simon James Gent. Buried
the 25 Day of Aprell, 1616.

Gulielmo Cole, de Bradfield, Gen.
Qui ob. iii Cal. Sept. A. D. 1701.
Anna, Gilberti Cole, Gen. E
Avo Materno . B. M. P.

On a Flat Stone.

Here Lyeth the Body of Ann, Daughter of Thomas Spencer. She Dyed the 12th Day of July, 1740, Aged 14 years.

1703. To the Memory of Hannah Twinnoy.

She was a servant at the White Lion Inn, where was an Exhibition of Wild Beasts, and amongst the rest a very fierce tyger, which she imprudently took a pleasure in teazing, notwithstanding the repeated remonstrance of its keeper. One day, whilst amusing herself with this dangerous diversion, the enraged animal, by an extraordinary effort, drew out the staple, sprang towards the unhappy Girl, caught hold of her gown, and tore her to pieces.

EPITAPH.

In bloom of youth, she is snatch'd from hence,
She had no time to make defence;
For tyger fierce snatch'd Life away,
And now she lies in a bed of clay
Until the Resurrection Day.

Who is interred in the Abbey Churchyard.

South Wall.

Near this Place Lyeth the Body of John Jacob, Esq. Son of Thomas Jacob, Esq. He married Ann, Daughter of Nathaniel Stephens, of Eastington, in the County of Gloucester, Esq. He died Sept. 2nd, 1742, Aged 47.

Near this Place also lieth the Body of the said Anne, Wife of the above-mentioned John Jacob. She died the 20th day of May, 1762.

Sacred to the Memory of Thomas Chandler, Esq. of Ash Croft House, in the County of Gloucester, who died Oct. 30th, 1800, Aged 67 years.

Near unto this Place lies the Body of Lydia Ivye, daughter to George Ivye, of Hullavington, Esq. who departed this Life the 15th day of July, 1674.

Stay, gentle passenger, and cast thine eye,
Upon this spectacle of mortallity:
Here doth the Body of a virgin rest,
Whose soul in Heaven is with her Saviour blest.
She blessed was with nature's guifts, but shin'd,
Far more with gifts and graces of the minde;
Meek, Hymble, chast, religious, and Devout,
She holy was, and happy is, no doubt.
We all must follow her in mortal state,
O that we could her virtues imitate!
Deserved prayses might, perhaps, have mist her,
Had not these lines been fixt here by her Sister.

Against North Wall of Body.

Near this place lieth the Body of John Dixon, late Minister of this Place, who deceased the 20th day of August, 1675.

If Death doe passe on all because of sin,
Then good as well as bad men share therein;
But, cruel Death, why wast thou not more kind
To him that whilste . . . he scarce came behind.

Sir Robert John Buxton was Lord of this Ma o r, William Chandler, Esq. who is lately deceased, succeeded him: at present in the hands of trustees.

The Church has a Chancel, Nave, North and South Aisles: the Chancel is divided by two small pointed arches, forming a North and South Chancel. The Nave is supported on the north side by three plain semi arches, and on the south side by three pointed ones. Most of the old pews, and the greatest part of the ancient screen, are still remaining. In the North Chancel are three Gothic arches. The tower formerly contained four bells, but from its ruinous state, two were taken down, and sold. On the tenor is this inscription—'John Stowell, Giles Minchen, Churchwardens. A. R. 1705.'

The Parsonage is a plain ancient building.

FOXLEY.

Monuments in Chancel.

M. S. Filiæ, Sororis, Conjugis, Materno vix nomine ornatæ, amantissimæ, blandæ, benevolæ, cultæ, mitis, matronalis, modestæ, puræ, patientis, piæ. Nat. prid. non. Maii, A. D. 1784; Ob. sext. Cal. Julii, A. D. 1810. Nomen in Cœlis quære, cujus ad fata accesit infans, quinto mense composita, prid. non. Novembr. A. D. 1810.

North Wall of Chancel.

This Chancel was Paved by John Stump, Rector here, June the 29th, 1708.

Underneath lieth the Body of his Son Robert, aged one year and about 8 months. He died March the 19th, A. D. 1688.

On a Flat Stone in Body.

In Memory of William Geast, who died June the 7th, 1760, Aged 63 years.

Also Mary, his Wife. She died Sept. the 17th, 1769, Aged 68 years.

On a White Marble Monument in North Aisle.

In a Vault near this Place lies the Body of
George Ayliffe, of this Place, Esq.
He married Judith Strangways, of Malbury Sandford,
in the County of Dorsett, Esq.
By whom he had 5 Children, 2 Sons & 3 Daughters,
Viz. John, George, Susanna, Catharine, and Judith.
He Died March the 3d, 1712, Aged 71.

Also Judith, his Wife,
who died June the 3d, 1710, Aged 75.

And likewise John, son of the aforesaid
George and Judith Ayliffe, died March 11th, 1721,
Aged 47.

Mine eye also is dim by reason of sorrow,
and all my members are as a shadow.
Job 17th, & 7.

O Death, where is thy sting? O Grave,
where is thy victory?

The sting of Death is sin, and the strength
of sin is the Law.
1 Corinthians 15 chap. 55 & 56 verses.

This Tomb was Erected by his Daughters,
Susanna and Judith, 1722.

This Church consists of a Chancel, Nave, and North Aisle. The Nave is separated from the latter by two pointed arches. Against the north wall of north Aisle is a helmet, for the crest crown and laurel, belonging to the family of the Ayliffes.

Inscription on the Bell—

'Mrs. Jvdith Ayliffe, Benefactor. A. R. 1729.'

The Parsonage is a neat modern building, at present occupied by Mr. Richard Carter.

The extent of the Parish is about 760 acres.

NORTON.

On Flat Stones in Chancel.

Here lies interred the Body of Esther, the Wife of Samuel Hillier, jun. of this Place, and Daughter of George and Elizabeth Evans, of London, Hosier. Also the Body of George, ye Son of Samuel and Esther Hillier. The Mother died Jan. 5, 1772, Aged 31 years. The Son died the 7th, Aged 1 year and 9 months.

Date on the Pulpit—'Anno Domini 1631.'

Edward Thornton Gold, Esq. Late Lord of the Manor, who sold it to Mr. Samuel Williams, of Bristol.

The Rev. Dr. Hornage, late Vicar.
The Rev. John Green the present one.

The Church is very small and plain, under one roof, and has but one bell.—The Parsonage is but a small cottage.—Extent of the Parish about 450 acres, half arable, and the other pasture.

BREMILHAM CHURCH

Is a small structure, standing about half a mile N. E. from Foxley, where divine service is performed but once a month. This Church is not inserted in the Maps of Wilts. The extent of the Parish is about 400 acres. Robert Holford, Esq. Lord of the Manor. The Rev. J. Nicholass Vicar.

SOMERFORD MAGNA.

On a Monument against E. Wall of Chancel.

Underneath Lyeth the Body of Mr. Richard Browne, late Rector of this Parish, who died the 24th of May, Anno Domini 1687, Aged 35 years.

South Wall of Chancel.

Here underneath Lyeth the Body of John Palmer, of Hardyedyeth, in the parish of Sandon, in the County of Stafford, gent. who married Elizabeth, the Daughter of Sir Robert Hanson, Kt. who was Lord Mayor of London in Ani 1672 & 1673, by whom he had Robert, Elizabeth, John, Hanson, and Rachel. Elizabeth was married to Mr. Richard Browne, Rector of this Place, by whom she had Richard, Elizabeth, Robert, and Hanson. She was afterwards married to Mr. Edmund Wayte, Rector of this Place, by whom she had Edmund, Ayliffe, John, Henry, and Elizabeth. He died the 5th of Oct. Anno 1719, Aged 90 years, 2 months, and 5 days.

In spe Resurrectionis.

In East Wall of Chancel.

To the Memory of
the Rev. Thomas Seale,
Late Rector of this Parish.
He Died the 23rd of June, 1771,
Aged 80 Years and 10 Months,
And he is buried the outside of this Chancel.
He was
Pious, Benevolent, Humane, Charitable:
during the space of 43 years
in which he served this Parish.
He was
diligent in the performance of all the duties
of his function.
Complacency of Manners, regularity of Life,
forgiveness of Injuries,
Gave him the Esteem of all who knew him.
He was
Loved whilst Living, Regretted when Dead.

On Flat Stones within the Communion Rails.

In Memory of Ayliffe, the Son of Edmund and Eliz. Wayte, who dyed Dec. 24th, Anno Domini 1721, Aged 32 years.

Here also Lyeth the Body of Rebecca, Daughter of Henry Wichtwick, M. A. and Elizabeth, his Wife, who dyed June the 2d, 1736, Aged 6 years, and 6 months.

Here Lyeth ye Body of Mr.
Edmund Wayte, Late . .
of this Parish, who . .
21 of October, Anno
Domini 1702 . . 47 years.

Here Lyeth also the
Body of John, the Son of
Edmund Wayte, who
Departed this Life
the 28th of June, 1716, Aged 18 years.

On Flat Stones without the Rails.

Here Lyeth the Body of Mr. Samuel Kinaston, once Rector of this Parish. He departed this Life the 5th Day of Jan. 1667, Aged 63 years.

Also ye Body of Mrs. Mary Reeve, 2d Wife of Samuel Kinaston, who departed this Life the 6th day of X^{b} 1698, Aged 70 years, & 6 months.

Nathaniel Aske, Rector of this Place, Diad Oct. 22, Buried Nov. the 5th, 1675.

Richard Aske, his Son, Diad Nov. 3, Buryed Novem. ye 5th, 1681.

Isaacus Reeks, A. M.
hujus Ecclesiæ
per xxiv annos Rector,
Ob. April,
Anno { Salut. 1728.
{ Ætat. 52.

On Monuments in Body of the Church.

Underneath rest the Bodies of John Smith, and Elizabeth, his Widow, of this Place, waiting for a joyful resurrection, through Christ. He departed June 22, 1765, Aged 55 years. She died March 19th, 1790, Aged 73 years. Also two of their Sons, who died in their infancy.

This Monument was erected out of gratitude and affection by their only surviving Child, Elizabeth Smith.

Sacred to the Memory of Elizabeth Smith, of this Place. After a long and painful affliction, which she was enabled to bear with patient submission to the will of her Creator, she resigned her soul in his hands, in humble hope of a joyful Resurrection, through the merits and mediation of her Redeemer. She was born Jan. 27, 1754, and died Feb. 22, 1798.

Underneath lie the Remains of John Smith, the last surviving Son of John and Elizabeth Smith, of this Parish. He was born on the 20th day of April, 1756, and died on the 17th day of May, 1772.

Of manners gentle, of judgement sound,
This tender plant in early youth was found:
But ah! too ven'trous he, through human art,
Was too soon smitten by Death's fatal dart:
Yet mourn not, friends, o'er his untimely grave,
The Lord who took him was the Lord who gave;
He, high in bliss, is ever freed from pain,
Your transient loss is his eternal gain.

A mournful Mother, and a loving Sister, caused this Monument to be erected to his Memory.

Sacred to the Memory of William Pyke, Son of John and Mary Pike, of this Parish, who died 21st December, 1794, Aged 37.

And also of Mary Pike, who died 19th of February, 1797, Aged 36 years.

And of Elizabeth Pyke, who died 11th of September, 1797, Aged 37 years.

On Flat Stones and Brass Plates in Body.

Here Lyeth the Body of William Knap, who departed this life August the 5th, A. D. 1698.

Brass Plate.

Rebecca, Relict of John Smith, Gent. interred March ye 2d, 1754, Aged 77 years.

On Flat Stones.

Here Lyeth buried the Body of Ann, the Wife of Lucian Browne, of Letel Somerford, and the Daughter of John and Ann Mayo, of the Parish, who Departed this Life the 24th Day of April, 1694.

Here Lyeth ye Body of Ann, ye Wife of John Mayo, who departed this Life the 9th of Feb. 1663.

Also here Lyeth the Body of Hellen, the Wife of William Alexander, who departed this Life ye 13th day of Januer Aged 84.

Also here Lyeth ye Body of Joan, ye Wife of William Alexander, who departed this Life ye 17th Day of July, 1724, Aged 84 years.

Also Here Lyeth ye Body of William Alexander, who Departed this Life the 12th of July, 1724.

Also here Lyeth the Body of Martha, Daughter of William and Joan Alexander, who departed this Life the 30th of October, Anno Domini 1742, Aged 47 years.

On Brass Plates.

Here Lyeth the Body of John Smith, who departed this Life the 28th day of November, Aged 57 years.

And also the Body of Thomas Smith, his Son, Aged 16 years, who Died the 29th day of November, and were both buried the First Day of December, Anno Domini 1724.

Eleonora, Relict of Henry Aland, interred May ye 27, 1757.

William Alexander died May 27, 1716, Aged 31 years.

Robert Alexander, died April 20th, 1738, Aged 41 years.

Here lies the Body of
MARTHA,
The Wife of William Alexander,
and Daughter of Jonas and Mary Lawrence,
all of this Parish,
Who Departed this Life ye third Day of May,
1691.

She left us young, yet her small span of Life,
Shew'd a good Daughter, Mother, Friend, and Wife.
Her Parents found her an obedient Child,
Her Children tender, and her Husband mild;
So mild, his Will she never did reprove,
One half Submission, t'other half was Love:
To all obliging, piteous of the poor,
Sparing of Speed, but liberal of her Store.
Thus true Religion her whole life did sway,
Ah! why so virtuous, and so short her stay?
Many may run a longer race of days,
But who will leave us such a Theme for praise?

On a Monument against North Aisle.

Sacred to the Memory of Lucia, the Daughter of Thomas and Winifred Pyke, who died Sept. 23rd, 1813, Aged 14 years.

Sacred to the Memory of Thomas Pyke, who died Nov. 8th, 1815, Aged 51 years.

Sacred to the Memory of Mary, Daughter of Alexander and Sarah Parsloe, of this Parish. She died July 18, 1788, Aged 13 years.

Also Elizabeth, their Daughter. She died November 3d, 1792, Aged 10 years.

Also Sarah, Wife of Alexander Parsloe. She died April 16th, 1800, Aged 53 years.

Also Alexander, Husband to the above Sarah Parsloe, Died Feb. 14th, 1808, Aged 62 years.

Near this Place Lieth the Body of Mary, Wife of John Pike, Gent. She died July 24, 1788, Aged 63 years.

Frances, their Daughter, died May 22nd, 1786, Aged 20 years.

Also John, their Son, died October 24th, 1790, Aged 34 years.

To the Memory of John Pike, who died Decem. 13th, 1779, Aged 57 years.

The greif and pain which i did bare
Unto god my heart draw'd near.

Also Ruth, Daughter of John and Mary Pike, Died June ye 10th, 1780, Aged 17 years.

Harry, their Son, died an Infant.

This Church consists of a Chancel, Nave, and North Aisle. The north wall of the Nave is supported by four shafted pillars, and four pointed arches. A great many of the old pews are still left, likewise the ancient pulpit and screen, which separate the Chancel from the Nave. On the outside of the north-east corner of the Nave, is a projection, about 4 ft. by 8 ft. of an octangular form upon a square base. It is about 12 ft. high, and appears to have been a winding passage to a gallery, the steps and the door-way may still be seen. In the east window are some small pieces of painted glass, at the bottom is a human figure, nearly perfect, with the head argent, and body azure. In two of the windows in the south wall are representations of human figures, but nearly erased. There are 4 bells in the Tower: on the *First*—' 1634.' *Second*—' Peace and Good Neighbourhood. 1731.' *Third*—' the Odore Chelton, John Brind, Churchwardens. 1663.'

HANKERTON AND CLOATLY.

On a Monument in N. Aisle.

In a Vault opposite to this Marble are deposited the remains of Giles Earle, of Eastcourt, in this County, Esq. He died the 20th of August, 1758, Aged 80. Margaret, his second Wife, and their infant Son, are interred with him. By Elizabeth, his first Wife, Daughter and coheir of Sir William Rawlinson, Knt, he had Eleanor, who died unmarried, and William Rawlinson Earle, Esq. who departed this life the 10th of August, 1774, in the 72d year of his age, was buried by his own request near the ashes of his Sister, in the Vault of their Grandfather, Sir William Rawlinson, at Hendon, in the County of Middlesex. William Rawlinson Earle married Susanna, the Daughter and sole heiress of William White, of Somerford, in the County of Wiltshire, Esq. Of four Children, only Giles and Eleanor survived him, Elizabeth and Susanna, dying young, were interred in the Vault of their Great Grandfather at Hendon.

This monument, sacred to the Memory of his Family, was erected pursuant to the last will and testament of William Rawlinson Earle, Esq. by his Widow and Executrix, in the year of our Lord 1775.

Against North Wall of Body.

Near this Place Lyeth the Body of Thomas Ludlow, and Ann his Wife. He died March 31st, 1741, Aged 71. She died January 15th, 1719, Aged 54.

Near this Place lieth the Body of Henry Ludlow, their Son, who died August 30th, 1744, Aged 55.

Grieve not for me because I've lost my breath,
My pain was such as made me wish for death:
Christ, my Redeemer, knew which way was best
To ease my pain, and set my soul at rest.

Donation Tablet in North Aisle.

1775. HANKERTON AND CLOATLY.

The several sums of Money heretofore charitably given for the Benefit of the Poor of this Parish were collected together, and amounted to the sum of Fifty-two Pounds, which, by order of a Public Vestry, was laid out and invested in the Public Funds, in the Purchase of Fifty-nine Pounds three Shillings and Sixpence, Old South Sea Annuities, in the Names of Giles Earle, Esq. the Rev. James Gyles, Vicar, William Hall, John White, and John Stagg, all of this Parish, as Trustees for the Benefit of the Poor of this Parish: And they are to take care that the interest and Dividends thereof are received and applied for the use and Benefit of the said poor according to the charitable and benevolent intent of the several Donors.

Lady Winchcome,

Daughter of Lord Thomas Howard, Earl of Berkshire, Left, by Will, to the second poor of Hankerton and Cloatly, Twenty Shillings a year yearly for ever,

Charged, and Chargeable to be paid out of an Estate in the Parish of Hankerton, formerly Wanfords, and now in the family of the Whites, the same to be paid out by the Minister on Family Bibles, first mentioned, next Prayer Books, Whole Duties of Man, and other pious books, and when furnished with those Books, if any money in hand, the same to be laid out in schooling poor Children. 1735.

The Church consists of a Nave and North Aisle; the north wall of the Nave is supported by four plain pointed Arches; at the east end of which is some ancient carving, and many of the old pews are still left. The Tower has four bells, on the north-east point is a dragon sleeping.

The Earl of Suffolk, Lord of the Manor.

James Waggett, Rector.

CRUDWELL.

On a Brass in South Wall of Chancel.

Obdormiunt in Domino placide, Maria Shewring, Virgo, Uxor, Mater, amabilis. Ob. 14 Aug. 1711.

Maria, optomiæ spei Filia, Ob. Londini, Sep. 3, 1713.

Thomas Shewring, A.M. Rector de Crudwell, Vic. de Hankerton, & Bal. Coll. Oxon. olim locuis dignissimus. Qui uñature omnibus nisi sibi moriebatur, Oct. 18, 1718.

Jana, Conjux ultima, spectatissimæ virtutis fœmina, noverca desideratissima. Ob. 27 Septembris, A. D. 1720.

On Flat Stones within the Rails.

Here Lyeth the Body of Daniel Hartford, Batchelor of Divinity, Late Rector of this Parish, who Departed this Life the 24th day of November, Anno Dom. 1679.

Here Lyeth the Body of John Bradshaw, Minister of God's word, who deceased the 3d day of June, Anno Dom. 1645.

Here Lyeth the Body of Thomas Earle, jun. merchant, who died August ye 13, A. D. 1702.

Here Lyeth the Body of Thomas Earle, gent. who departed this Life the 16th day of November, 1657, in full assurance of an Everlasting Resurrection of Eternal Life.

Here Lyeth ye Body of Elizabeth, Daughter of John and Elizabeth Oatridge, Gent. who departed this Life April ye 24, A. D. 1696.

Here Lyeth Also ye Body of Elizebeth, wife of John Oatridge, Gent. who departed this Life Feb. the 1st, A. D. 1728, Aged 76 years.

Here Lyeth ye Body of John, Sonne of John Newman, Gent. who Departed this Life the 16 of December, 1655, Aged 19 years and 5 months.

Here Lyeth the Body of Thomas Earle, The Eldest Sonne of William Earle, and Bridget his Wiffe. Thomas Deceased the 12 Daie of Februarie, Anno 1617, And Bridget Deceased the 15th Day of Ap[l], Anno Dñi 1626.

Here Lyeth the Body of Margaret, Daughter of John Oatridge, Gent. who Departed this Life April 23, 1696.

Here Lieth the Body of John Oatridge, Gent. who died June ye 23, 1720.

Here Lyeth the Body of John, the Son of John Oatridge, who Departed this Life August the 29th, Anno Dom. 1699.

Here Lyeth the Body of Henry, Son of John Oatridge, Gent. who Departed this Life, the 3d Day of October, 1747, Aged 61 years.

Here Lyeth the Body of Samuell Oatridge, who departed this Life May the 19th, An. Dom. 1693.

Here Lyeth ye Body of Edward Oatridge, Son of John Oatridge, of Oakesey, Gent. who died April ye 28, A. D. 1725, Aged 8 years.

William Oatridge Died October 27, 1685.

Death and the grave hath here beguil'd
his Parents of this Lovly Child.

Here Lies interred the Body of Henry Oatridge, Gent. who Departed this Life the 4 day of Nov. 1730, Aged 85 years.

Here lieth the Body of J. Jenner, who Deceased the seaventh Day of July, A. Dom. 1650.

Here Lyeth ye Body of Daniel Oatridge, Gent. who Departed this Life Dec. ye 3, 1705.

Here Also Lyeth ye Body of Margaret, Wife of Daniel Oatridge, who departed this Life Januy ye 19th, A. D. 1727, Aged 63 years.

On Monuments in North Chancel against North Wall.

Thomas Earle, A. M. and Vic. of Malmesbury, the only Child of Thomas Earle, Late of Crudwell, Mercer, and Elizabeth his Wife, Erects this Monument, in Dutifull Regard to the Memory of those his deserving Parents, who put on Immortality. He died Feb. 25, 1715, Aged 72. She Died Jan. 8th, 1706, Aged 60.

If Father, Husband, Friend, or Brother, ever claimed a tear,
Stranger, shed it over the grave of
WILLIAM PEACY,
Late of this Place, Gent.
An active enterprising mind, a resolute perseverance,
carried him far beyond his Predecessors
in the science of Agriculture.
The strictest integrity, a noble Liberality,
& true Christian Charity,
endeared him to every class of men.
In enriching his Country, he elevated his Family;
In giving happiness to Hundreds, he founded his own.
His science was sought for in the Wilds of America.
His exertions to save an Innocent Condemned
were repaid by mercy from the Throne.
After a lingering illness, in pious resignation,
And with confident, though humble hope,
He departed this Life
On the 26 of February, 1815, Aged 66.

Go, and do thou Likewise.

On Flat Stones in Chancel.

S. H. L. P.
Isaacus Turner,
Generosus.
Obiit Junij 27,
Ano { Salutis 1746,
{ Ætat. 57.

Here lyeth the Body of
Hanson Palmer, who died August the 17th, A. D. 1721,
Aged 57 years.

Here also Lyeth the Body of
John Palmer, the Son of the said Hanson Palmer,
who departed this Life the 14th day of July,
in the year of our Lord 1731,
Aged 46 years.

George Harewell, junr. Died Novr. 16th, 1741,
Aged 12 years.

Charles Harewell died of ye small pox, Nov. 22, 1757.
Aged 23.

Here Lieth the Body
of Susanna,
Relict of the Revd. George Harewell, Clerk,
who died July ye 21st, 1775,
Aged 74.

Elizabeth Harewell,
Daughter of the Late Revd George Harewell,
and Susanna his Wife,
Died May 12, 1798,
Aged 66.

To the Memory of Susannah, the Daughter of William and Susannah Peacey, of this Parish, who died July 15, 1812, Aged 15 years.

On Flat Stones in Nave.

Here Lieth the Body of
Mrs. Elizabeth Browne, who
Departed this Life the 21st day of February,
Ano Dom 1705.

Here Lyeth the Body of Mary, the Widow of the Revd Thomas Morgan, Rector of Swindon, Glour, and Daughter of John and Elizth Oatridge, of Estcort, Gent. Obiit Novr 21, 1758, Aged 80.

Here Lyeth the Body of
Ann, Daughter of Sr Thos Earle, Knt,
And Wife of Henry Creswick, Esq. She
Departed this Life the 18 Day of January, in the
63 Year of her Age, and of our Lord 1728.

Here Lyeth ye Body of Mary, Wife of William Weeb, who died December ye 8, A. D. 1722, Aged 29 years.

Here Lyeth the Body of John Archard, Senr. who Departed this life the 12 day of February, Anno Domini, 1674.

Here Lyeth Also ye Body of Mary, his wife, who departed this Life the 25th day of March, 1763.

Here Lyeth the Body of John Archard, who departed this Life October ye 12, 1732.

Harry Hays died March 3d, 1789, Aged 50 years.

Also of John, his Brother, who died Sept. 8th, 1790, Aged 59 years.

And likewise Mary Bell, died April 29, 1803, Aged 72 years.

Here Lyeth ye Body of William, Son of John Archard, who died Oct. 7, A. D. 1727, Aged 32 years.

Here Lyeth also the Body of John, ye Son of John and Catharine Archard

Elizabeth Hays, Daughter of the said Wm. and Elizabeth Hays, who died May 4, 1803, Aged 19 years.

John, Son of William and Elizabeth Hays, died August 14, 1794, Aged 11 years.

Elizabeth Hays, died Nov. 15, 1800, Aged 33 years.

Here lyeth the Body of Robert Son of Samuel Oatridge, who died July ye 16, 1683.

Here Lieth the Body of Margaret, Wife of Giles Driver, Daughter of Samuel Oatridge, who deceased April ye 27, 1705.

Here Lieth the Body of
Ann Estcourt,
Eldest Daughter of Giles Estcourt, Gent.
On earth esteemed, yea, Christ above
hath her Redeem'd, and shew'd his Love.
Here . . . was milde, She . . . oh
Happy Childe The . . . Excell exutus
m . . undecimo Die March 1669,
Ætatis suæ jo. hic licet in occiduo cimera aspirit
evm cvivs nomen est omnis.

North Aisle.

M. S. Thomæ Earle, Clerici, & Annæ Uxoris, hanc subter Tabulam simul jacentium.
Ille Præcessit Anno Domini 1664, Ætatis 52.
Ille sequunta est, Anno Domini 1693, Ætatis 74.
Tuba dum sonet ultima.

Benefactions to the Poor of Crudwell and Estcourt.

Mrs Walton, widow, gave	£.20	
Thos. Earle, gent. gave	£.20	1617.
Bridget, wife of Thos. Earle, gave	£. 5	1620.
Richard Harding gave	£. 5	
Thomas Browning gave	£. 5	

Thomas Earle, Gent. Son of Thomas and Bridget, gave £. x. and £.103 . . . recovered pr Will Earle, out of an Estate to the same use, 1637.

Joane Harding, Widw gave £.6 : 13*s.* 4*d.*

All which sums are improved to £.250, May 27, 1683, and the benefit thereof to the Poor for ever.

Giles Earl, Gent. gave £.100, the profit thereof in Bread every Lord's Day for ever.

For Giles Earle, Esq. eldest Son of Sir Thos. Earle, Kt. who died at Vittoria, in Spain, Nov. 8, 1677, Aged 20 years, is given £.50 the profit thereof in bread every Lord's Day for ever.

Mrs. Dorothy Calthrope gave £.22.

Thos. Earl, Gent. gave £.50 to the poor of Estcourt, the interest thereof in bread to be given every Lord's Day for ever.

1775. CRUDWELL AND ESTCOURT.

The sums of money heretofore Charitably Given for the Benefit of the Poor of this Parish were collected together, and amounted to the Sum of four Hundred and Sixty-two Pounds; And Goodenough Earle, Esq. Son and Heir of William Earle, Esq. Serjeant at Law, Long since deceased, having added a further sum of one Hundred and Twenty Pounds thereto, by paying a Legacy of Fifty Pounds, formerly Given by his Father's Will, and seventy Pounds for Thirty-five years Intrest thereof, The whole amounts to the sum of Five Hundred and Eighty-two Pounds; and the said sum of Five Hundred and Eighty-two Pounds was, by order of a Public Vestry, laid out and invested in the Public Funds, in the Purchase of Six Hundred and Sixty-two Pounds Six Shillings, Old South Sea Annuities, in the names of Giles Earle, Esq. the Rev. James Giles, Rector, Mathew Robertson, William Robertson, and John Mill, all of this Parish, as Trustees for the benefit of the poor of this Parish, and they are to take care that the Intrest and Dividend thereof are Received and Applied for the use and Benefit of the said poor According to the Charitable and Benevolent Intent of the several Donors.

The Church consists of two Chancels, Nave, and North and South Aisle: the ancient Screen that separates the Chancel from the Nave, is very entire, and many of the old pews are still remaining, some of them are ornamented with carved figures of different kinds of birds and fishes, and on one opposite the pulpit, are the royal arms. In a window in the north wall of the north aisle is a considerable quantity of painted glass, representing the heads of human figures. They have been taken from the other windows of the Church, and glazed altogether.

There are five bells in the Tower. On the *First*—'A Gift, by Tho. Earle and John Jenar. 1633.' *Second*—'Ano Domini 1633.' *Fifth*—'Edward Neale, John Oatridge, and Henry Pitts, Church-wardens.'

The Manor belongs to Lady Lucas.

James Weggett, Rector.

SEAGREY.

On an Altar Tomb in Chancel.

Here Lieth the Body of Edward Ayde, the Elder, Gent. who departed this Life the 18th day of April, in the year of our Lord God 1663. Memento mori.

On a wood frame in chancel.

In this Chancel Lyeth the Body of Henry Richmond, Clerk, Late Rector of Hornblotton, in the County of Somersett, eldest son of Oliffe Richmond, of Ashton Keynes, in this County, Gent. He died January 16th, 1723, Aged 63.
He Married Katharine, the Daughter of Edward Adye, of this Parish, gent. he left two sons, Ayloffe Henry, and George.
Katharine Richmond, died Sept. the 1st, 1739, Aged 81.
Also near this place Lieth the Body of Ayloffe Henry Richmond, Son of the above-named Henry Richmond, who died February ye 10th 1761, Aged 71 years.

On Flat Stones.

Elizth Russel died Oct. 31st, 1798, Aged 93 years.

George Searle Bayliffe, Esq. died May 3d, 1813, Aged 78 years.

On a Monument in N. Wall of the Body.

Carolus Bayliffe, Armiger,
Obiit 8 Julii, 1735, Anno Ætat. 29.

Maria Bayliffe, soror ejus,
Obiit 3° Junii, 1760, Ætat. 60°.

Maria, Uxor Georgii Searle, Bayliffe,
eorum maximus natu Filius
perquam et merito dilectus
28° Feb. 1784, Anno Ætat. 22°.
Placide compostus morte quievit.

Arms—Sable, a chev. between 3 harts, or, 2 in chief, 1 in base.

Upon the North Wall.

Under this seat lieth ye Body of Jeremiah, Son of Charles & Ann Jenkins, of this Parish, who departed this Life, June 14, 1764, Aged 5 years and 3 months.

Also Ann, Wife of Charles
Jenkins, Formerly of this Parish,
but late of St. Leonard's, in the Liberty of the Tower,
in the City of London.
She departed this Life Dec. 29, 1790,
Aged 72 years.

She was brought from London, and
buried under this Seat, according to her
own desire.

Also of Charles Jenkins,
Of the Parish of St. Leonard's,
Shoreditch, London,
who died June 24th, 1800, Aged 69 years.

On Flat Stones in Body.

Here lyeth the Body of Brudgett, the Daughter of Henry Richmond, Clerk, and Katharine, his Wife, who Departed this Life, the 6th Day of Jan. in the year 1668.

Here lyeth the Body of Oliffee Richmond, Son of Henry Richmond Gent. who Departed this Life 20 Day of June, Anno Domini 1664, Aged 6 weeks.

Charles Bayliffe died July the 8th, 17..

Under these two Seats
was buried the Body of Rachel Long,
the Daughter of Mr. Long,
Late of Calleway, Gent. April the 7th, Anno
Domini 1700.

127

On an Altar Tomb in South Transept.

Here Lies the Body of Rebekah, Wife of Henry Stratton, who Departed this Life the 12th day of June, 1678, Aged 84.

Against the East Wall.

Near this Place lies the Body of Robt. Stratton, Gent. Obiit Oct. 9th, 1758, Ætat. 75.

On Flat Stones.

Ann, Daughter of T. & R. Stratton, was here interred July the 5th. Anno Dom. 1707, Aged 4 months.

Near this Place Lyeth the Body of Robt. Stratton, Sen. Gent. who deceased Oct. 11th, 1700. Resurgam.

Here Lyeth the Body of Rebecca, ye Wife of George Richmond, Gent. who departed this Life March 15, A. D. 1725, in the 30th year of her age, Daughter of Thomas Stratton, gent. and Grace his Wife.

Husband farewell, & babes likewise,
I must be gon, then dry your eyes,
'Tis but in vain to weep and cry,
Death gave his stroke, therefor farewell.
To God alone resign'd my Breath,
And pay my debt by Child bed dead.

Here Lyeth the Body of Ann Wells, the Daughter of John and Rebecca Stratton, who departed this Life January the 7th, Anno Dom. 1714, Aged 61.

In this transept is the effigy of a man, with his sword in the scabbard, and his feet resting upon a lion. There is no inscription, but supposed to be Mr. Stratton.

The Rev. Wm. Pulsford, Vicar, 1735.
Christopher Simons, Vicar, died 31 July, 1724.
The Rev. Benj. Rogers, Vicar, 1763.
The Rev. David Middleton, present Vicar.

In a Gothic Canopy in the north wall of the body of the Church, is a male figure, lying in robes, with a dog at his feet. It is nearly hid by the pews. There is no inscription.

SUTTON.

On a Monument in South Wall of Chancel.

Near this Monument Lyeth the Body of Peter Kinton, of Bristoll, Merchant, who Departed this Life Feb, 24, Anno Dom. 1733, Ætatis suæ 82.

The long'st Life at Last must yield,
And to pale death resigne the field;
But yet death hath no conquest gain'd,
I haveng Lasting rest obtain'd.

S. Wall.

Near this Place lieth the Body of Henrietta, Wife of James Green, who died Nov. 15th, 1773, Aged 77 years.

Also Margaret, Wife of James Green, died December 10th, 1777, Aged 41 years.

Against the North Wall.

Near this Place Lyeth ye Body of James Green, who died March 24th, 1782, Aged 66 years.

On Flat Stones in Chancel.

Mary Russ died Nov. 6, 1797, Aged 17 years.

Hic jacet Corpus Avern Thomson, M. A. Obiit Nov. 29, 1729, Ætat. 31.

Brass Plate on the second Pillar from the east end in Body.

Underneath ye three uppermost seats next ye Chancell, lies the Body of Cath. Wells, late Wife of Joseph Wells, of ye Devizes. She was the Daughter of Jasper Gale, and Mary his Wife, late of Sutton. She was First Married to John Middleton, Citizen of London, by whom she left Issue two Sons, Jaspr Gale Middleton, and Loyde Middleton. She departed this Life ye 10th of October, 1745.

On a plain Stone at the west end of Body.

Near this Place lyeth the Body of Joan, Wife of John Smart, who departed this Life Jan. the 2nd, 1759, Aged 38 years.

Also near this place lyeth the Body of Ann, Wife of John Smart, who departed this Life August the 11th, 1712, Aged 33 years.

Also near this place lyeth two of their Children, who died in their Infancy.

And also William, Son of John and Joan Smart, who died ye 21 of October, 1765, Aged 8 years.

Also near this place Lyeth ye Body of John Smart, sen. who died July the 30th, A.D. 1778, Aged 55 years.

On South Wall of South Aisle.

This in Memory of John Barnard, and Hannah his Wife. He died March the 14th, 1703, Aged 84 years, and She died March the 19th, 1771, Aged 83.

Also Ann Jones, their Daughter. She died May the 12, 1715, Aged 61 years.

And Elizabeth, their Daughter. She died Sept. 20, 1718, Aged 54.

Also James, their Grandson, and Son of Ralph and Jane Barnard. He died May the 11th, 1720, Aged 6 years.

All Buried under these five tombs.

Also Mary, their Daughter, She died ye 6, 1716, Aged 76 years.

Near this Place lies interred the Body of Hannah Jones, who died April ye 6, 1753, Aged 66 years.

Also near this place lieth interred the Body of Edward Barnard, who died June the 14th, 1782, Aged 78 years.

Heare Lyeth under these Fower tombes
the Bodys of John Barnard, and Joane
his weife, and John, their Sonne, and
Mary their Grand Child, whoe Deceased the
11th Day of january, Aõ Dñi 1637.

On Monuments in the West End of South Aisle.

Near this Place lies interred the Body of Joanna, Wife of John Hopkins, who died October the 16th, 1758, Aged 49 years.

Beloved while she lived,
Her life was much desired,
Her death was much lamented,
But God her soul required.

Also near this place lieth the Body of John Hopkins, who died March 30, 1794, Aged 68.

Also Ann, his Wife, who Died Octor 2nd, 1794, Aged 68 years.

West end of south aisle.

Near this Place lies interred the Bodies of Elizabeth and Sarah, Daughters of William and Mary Bryant, of this Parish. Eliz. died May the 10th, 1744, Aged 8 weeks. Sarah died May 10th, 1752, Aged 1 year & 7 months. Also Sarah Groom died the 14th of January, 1760, Aged 74.

Also in Memory of Mary, Wife of William Bryant, Yeoman. She Died Dec. 5th, 1765, Aged 52.

On a Flat Stone in S. Aisle.

Underneath are Deposited the Remains of Henry Gatler, who died August 20th, 1762, Aged 53 years. Also of Frances his Wife, who died April 21, 1792, Aged 85 years.

On a Brass Plate that is taken up.

Underneath this tomb stone that joyneth unto the three uppermost seats, Resteth the Body of Robert Atkins, Gent. who deceased the 19th Day of February, 1670.

Next unto this side Resteth the Body of Joan, his Wife, who Deceased the 20th Day of December, 1672.

Near unto this Place under the three uppermost seats Resteth the Body of Richard Atkins, Gent. their Son, who deceased the 14th Day of Feb. 1677, his age 40 years.

In the south window is some painted glass. The Tower contains five Bells: on the 2d—'An. Do. 1638.' 3d—'Ano Do. 1631.' 5th—'Robt. . . . . James Hatherell, Ch. Wardens, 1706.'

The Rev. Charles Davis Vicar.
The Dean of Sarum V.
Rev. Henry Kett, V.
Rev. Servington Savory V.
Rev. Christopher Lipscomb.

DRAYCOT.

On Flat Stones within the Rails.

Here Lyeth the Body of the Rev. Thomas Smith, Late Rector of this Parish, who died March 5th, 1779, Aged 52 years.

ere Lyeth the Body of the Rev. John Bushell, ector of Draycot, who dyed Oct. ye 9th, A. D. 1746, the 30th year of his Age.

On Monuments in the East side of South Aisle.

Sacred to the Memory of
Sir James Tylney Long, Bart.
The Late Male heir of his Family,
Of great Note and Antiquity
In this County,
No less Distinguished
For the disinterested and independent discharge
of those Duties
To which their public Situations
Called them,
han for their more private and domestic Virtues,
Their Liberal Hospitality,
Their Loyalty to their King,
And
Their Piety towards God.
His Remains are beneath deposited
with those of his Ancestors,
who
For many Centuries
Resided at their Mansion,
In this Parish.
He died September the 14, 1805,
In the 11 year of his Age.

Sacred to the Memory
Of Sir Robert Long,
Late of this Parish, Bart.
and many years one of the Representatives of this
County in Parliament,
Whose inviolable Uprightness as a Senator,
Whose impartial Equity as a Magistrate,
Whose affable condescension as a Neighbour,
& whose exemplary conduct as a Christian,
need not, among those who knew his Virtues,
the Eulogium of this Inscription,
which yet may serve, with due honour, to transmit
his Character to Posterity,
as highly worthy of their studious Imitation.
He married the Right Honble Emma,
Daughter of Richard Earl Tylney,
who departed this Life March 8, A. D. 1758,
Leaving Issue two Sons and two Daughters.
He died Feb. 10, A. D. 1767,
Aged 62 years.

Near this Place lie the Remains of the
Honble Harriot Tylney Long,
Wife of James Tylney Long, Bart.
And youngest Daughter of
Jacob Vince, of Folkestone,
Of Longford Castle, in this County.
To whose Memory both truth and Justice
Are engaged to pay
This Comprehensive Tribute of Respect,
That no Language can too highley
Extol her Virtues, no Tears can
Sufficiently bewail her Loss.
She Died Nov. 13, 1777, Aged 41.

Here also lie the Remains
of
Sir James Tylney Long, Bart.
who died Nov. 28, 1794, in the 58th year of his age.
On this Monument,
(erected by his particular desire,)
His afflicted Widow records the Name
Of her affectionate and lamented Husband,
Who, both in public and private Life,
Uniformly practised those Virtues
To which, on the adjoyning Tablet,
He so justly bore Testimony
In his amiable and respected Father.
He married, secondly, the Right Honble Catherine,
Eldest Daughter of Other, Fourth Earl of Plymouth,
By whom he had one Son,
James,
And three Daughters,
Catherine, Dorothy, and Emma.

In West Wall of Chancel.

M. S.

Jacobi Long, Bartt

Qui Viginta duos annos continuos Senator Inferioris Ordinis, integerrimus et laudantissimus fuit; Patriæ studiosissimus, nec minus a factione alienus, notis et familiaribus amicissimus, fidissimus, et amantissimus conjux, providus et indulgens pater, patronus incorruptus et liberalis, herus clemens et beneficus terris exhibitus, ut aliis exemplum preluceret, præproperè raptus quo maturius gloriæ particeps fierat, ingenii acumen judicium limatum et grave, larga hospitalitis minime fucata caritus, veracitas mendacii impatiens, justicia et æquitas accurata morum suavis, comitas prudentia singularis, egregia plane ornamenta, ut ab omnibus coleretur, et maximi haberetur effecerunt, honorem et benevolentiam apud summos æque, ac insimos ordines hominum conciliaverunt, cujus defuncti triste desiderium, nihil lenire posserit nisi si tantarum virtutum, vestigiis ejus fideliter insistant posteri, ex uxore unica, prastantissima et honoratissima fœmina, Henrietta, filia noblissimi Fulconis Greville, Baronis de Broke, quæ hoc marmor mœrens posuit, septem suscepit liberos quinque superstites, nempe, filios duos, Robertum, census dignitatis equestris et virtutum hæridem, Jacobum, eximia indole puerum; filias tres, Dorotheam, Rachelem, et Susannam, venustate et virtutibus conspicuas, qui omnes amplo patrimonio perfruuntur ut, et bonorum pretiosissima recta et diligenti institutione, ad exemplum tam nobile examussim accurata, Obiit xvii kal. Aprilis, Anº Dñi 1728, Ætat. suæ 47.

In the north wall of Chancel, under a canopy, is an effigy, carved in stone, with his right leg across the left. His sword is in its scabbard, and his right hand upon the hilt, as if drawing it. On the north side of Chancel is an altar tomb, of curious sculpture, but no inscription. On the south wall hang two helmets, spurs, dagger, and gauntlets. On one of the helmets the crest is the same as the family of the Longs.

Rev. Rich. Humphrys, Rector, died 1691.
Rev. John Bushell 1746.
Rev. Thomas Smith 1779.
The Right Hon. Andrews Windsor, late Rector.
Rev. Henry Berry, present Rector.

STANTON.

On a Monument against E. Wall of Chancel.

Here lyeth the Body of Mary, ye Wife of William Charmbury, Rector of this Church, who Departed this Life the 30th day of May, 1676, her age 86.

Hic licet in occiduo cinere.
Aspicit eum,
Cujus nomen est oriens
Nihil sic revocat a peccato quam frequens
Mortis meditatio. Aug.

On a Monument in South Wall of Chancel.

William Twentyman, M.A. Rector of this Church
15 years,
Dy'd Dec. 20th, 1732, Aged 32 years.
He was Chaplain of the Embassy
To the Lord Lexington in Spain,
Of a most Pious, Sincere, and Generous Temper,
Endowed with those Graces and Virtues
that made him in favour with God and man.

On Flat Stones in Chancel.

Elizabeth Smith, Wife of the Rev. Samuel Smith, Rector of this Church, died May 18, 1789, Aged 39.

Beneath this Stone lyeth ye Body of Thomas Power, Late of Sheldon, in ye Parish of Chippenham, Yeoman, who died March 14th, Anno Domini 1733, Æt. 45. His only Daughter, Wife of John Taylor, of Yeaton Keynell, Gent. hath caused this Stone to be laid over his mortal part.

Beneath lies interred the Body of Elizabeth, Late Wife of William Latcham, gent. who departed this Life the 30th of July, 1754, Ætatis 45.

Also William, the Son of William and Elizabeth Latcham, lies interred here. Deceased the 17th of February, 1766, in the 24th year of his Age.

The Church consists of a Chancel, Nave, and South Aisle. The arch which separates the Chancel from the Nave is Saxon, as are also the two that support the south wall of the Nave, and adorned with Saxon mouldings. The porch entrance on the south side is Saxon, with a representation of the Virgin Mary over it.

There are but two bells in the Tower. On the outside, carved in stone, is the representation of St. George and the Dragon, On the west, near the Church, is an ancient farm house, with some Gothic windows, and at the south-east corner are two curious figures in stone. It has, most probably, been some religious foundation.

The Rev. Samuel Smith Rector.

Earl Radnor Lord of Manor, in whose family it has long been in the possession.

NEWNTON.

On a Monument against South Wall.

In Memory
of James Vaughan, Gent,
who Departed this Life March 13, 1754,
Aged 62.

And also
Of Elizabeth, his Daughter,
who dyed Feb. 12, 1744, Aged 16.

And also
of Elizabeth, his Relict,
who dyed April 27th, 1773.
Aged 77.

131

On a Monument in Chancel.

Sacred to the Memory of Edward Estcourt, L. L. D. Rector of the Parish of Long Newnton and Didmarton. This Stone is placed here by those who knew him best, and loved him most, as a Record of that warm Benevolence of heart, and firm Integrity of mind, which endeared him to those connected with him as a Relation, a Friend, and a Minister. He died September the 17th, 1802, Aged 52 years.

On Flat Stones in Chancel.

Here Lieth the Body of Robert Bodington, of London, gent. He died at Tetbury, in the County of Gloucester, Dec. 14, 1764, Aged 62 years.

Nathaniel Brewer, M. A.
Rector of this Church twenty and two years,
And Mary his Wife, were interred underneath,
in the year 1749.
What manner of persons they were,
At the judgment will appear.

Brass Plate.

Here Lyeth the Body of George
Estcourt, D[r] in Divinity, And
Grande Compounder, who Departed
This Life the Sixth Day of August,
Anno Domini 1664.

The Rev. Mr. Edmund Estcourt Gale, A. M. Rector of this Church, died July 20th, 1770, Æt. 49.

Sarah, his Daughter, died Feb. 24, 1759, Aged 10 months.

On a Brass Plate.

Here Lyeth the Body of Agnes Escourt, Wife of Richard Escourt, Gent. who Departed this Life on the 14th Day of June, Anno Dni 1605, Beeing Aged 70 years.

Here also Lyeth the Body of Grace, Daughter of the Rev. Mr. John Giles, Rector of this Place, and Wife of Jonathan Griffin. She died July 19th, 1755, Aged 55 years.

Here Resteth the Body of John Trotman, Gent. M[r] of Arts, and Rector of this Church, who marryed An, the Daughter of William . . . . of Hardwick, in Gloccst[r], Esq. And Departed this Life Feb. 1656.

In Memory of Charles Farmer,
who died Jan. 10th, 1768,
Aged 60.

Here Lyeth Richard Estcourt Esq. Bencher of Lincoln's Inn, &c. A man Learned in his Profession, Charitable, and Extreamly Usefull To his Relations, Neighbours, and Dependants. He died An° Dom. 1674.

Juxta jacet
Timotheus Millechamp,
Rector de Newnton Longa;
subtus positæ sunt exuviæ Rev[di].
Thomæ Millechamp, A. B.
Quem in SS[tum] Diaconatus ordinem
modo admissum, vis innata mores
suaves, et Literæ Politores, Ecclesiæ
Anglicanæ, et Fidei Christianæ,
spondebant propugnaculum,
decus et ornamentum;
Ast, proh! dolor nimis propere
. . . nisi pulmonali,
prædisponenti corporis crasi
confectus animam
Deo effsavit.

Hic etiam jacet
Rev[dus] Richardus Millechamp, A. M.
prædicti Timothei Filius,
natu minimus.
Qui Jan[rii] 19, A. D. 1736,
Ætatis 23[tio] Ad Mortuos migravit.

On a Brass Plate.

Here Lyeth ye Body of Richard Estcourt, Gent. who Departed this Life on the . . Day of . . Anno Dom. 1612, Being Aged 80 years.

Here Likewise Lieth the Body of Elizabeth Giles, Gentlewoman, Daughter of Giles Estcourt, Esq. and Relict of the Rev. Mr. John Giles, formerly Rector of this Place. She died Feb. y[e] 10th, 1745, Aged 80 years.

Here Lyeth Grace Estcourt, the vertuous and Truly Religious Wife of Richard Estcourt, Esq. who also Dyed An° Dom. 1674.

Here Likewise Lyeth the Body
of Richard Estcourt, Gent.
Son of Giles Estcourt, Esq.
who died Feb. 16th, 1745,
Aged 78 years.

On a Monument in Body.

Anna Millechamp,
Filia Thomæ Veel, de Symondshalt,
in Agro Gloucest. Arm̄ Ob. 7mo Junii,
A.D. 1719.
Virgo, uxor, mater, amabilis,
Rev[dus] Timotheus Millechamp,
hujus Ecc. Rector, ob. April 30°, 1727°,
A° Ætat. 51°.
Rev[dus] Thomas Millechamp,
Timothei et Annæ, præd. Filius,
natu secundus, obiit 26 Feb.
1732, A° Ætat. 22°.
R. Millechamp, A. M. ob.
Jan. 19°, 1736.

On a Flat Stone in Body.

Here Resteth the Body of Edithiate, the wife of Richard Poole, of Newnton, formerly of William Byrd, of Wotton Underedge, in the County of Glou[tr] Gent. who Departed this Life the 31st Day of March, Anno Dñi 1677.

On a Monument in South wall of S. aisle.

In Memory of Mary, the Wife of William Vaughan, of Brampton, in the County of Hereford, Esq. and Daughter of Richard Pool, Late of this Parish, gent. who died Feb. 11th, 1717, in the 21st year of her Age.

Also here Lyeth the Body of William Vaughan, Esq. Esq. who dyed Nov. 20th, 1733, Aged 42.

Arms.—Party per pale, sinister, a lion rampant between seven fleur-de-lis, dex. three lions rampant, two in chief, one in base.

Against S. aisle.

Aliciæ Poole,
Virginis præclaræ castitatis prudentia,
Id quantum morti cessit.
Juxta jacet
Richardum patrem omnibus bene merentem, generosum
Matrem, Aliciam spectatissimæ virtutis fœminam.
Habuit
Quorum paternitate, fuit fatis immature orbatæ,
Ingenii tamen ornamentis quasi innatis,
Adeo claruit,
Ut omnibus, tum pietatis, tum charitatis,
Officiis religiose perfungi,
Animo parato puit
In egenos misericordia maxime enituit,
In republica aliena minime curiosa,
In opere Dei indefesse sedula,
Vicens omnibus cara
Co nunc carior
Quoniam morte repentina longum et deflenda
nobis abrepta
23 die Julii,
A.D. 1714,
Ætatis 24.

East end of south aisle.

In Memory of
George White, late of this Parish, Gent.
who died Feb. 9, 1783, Aged 52 years.
Also of Mary, his Wife,
who died April 16, 1788, Aged 65 years.
George, their Son,
died Feb. 24th, 1763, Aged 13 months.
Elizabeth, their Daughter,
died March 26, 1767, Aged 7 years.

Dom.
Sacrum, et
Memoriæ Janæ, uxoris
Chr. Hanlcii, Cler: A. M. ex Antiquâ et
Generosâ, pulchrum stirpe prognatæ
Fœminæ Eximiæ,
Qui quidem duo iis auspiciis, iis utrinque animis,
ad nuptias venerant primo ita, deinde affectibus
mutuis, et rata fide mansere ut hoc Consortis,
beatius in terris, nihil nulli Conjuges
spes suas felicius inchocirint,
verum ah! caducas spes mortalium,
et vota cassa;
ah non insolitam in magnis virtutibus,
Rerum vicissitudinem,
Quippe, illa gravide facta cum suavissima filiola,
cognomine virum auxisset, et tam matris quam
Infantulæ salus in dubio versari minime crederetur,
Ambæ ad tres tantum menses superstites,
Mariti vota spes patris omnes confudere corrapere
abrepta, nempe, Parvula Apr. 4°, 1697.
Cujus cineres nondum sopilos suo quoq. funere
cumulavit infœlix mater, uxor desideralissima
ejusdem Apr. die 7mo in ipso flote Ætatis,
Anno supra vicesimum quinto.
Porro, intra mensem a tædis nuptialibus 14[um]
Hæ ferales accensæ, ut vel hoc exemplo
spes hominum pulcherrimæ, quam sint
fluxæ quam instibiles discant,
Qui nondum experti.
Quin potius ut Divini numinis optimum,
quemque in illam lucem suam ocyus evocantis,
tum his dispositionis
sua, arcanis eos, qui super sunt exercentis consilia
odoremus omnes SS[tæ] ejus voluntali in rebus ut
luctuosis acquiescamus Alq. ita Conjunx Reliquus
Officii sui hanc partem sane quam lacrymosam,
Longe tamen præcipuam agnoscit,
et hoc marmore testatum voluit.

Gulielmus Poole, Civis et Mercator Lond. Filius et Hæres-Apparens Richardi Poole, de Newnton, Gen. Obiit 18 die Januarii, Anno Dom. 1672. Requiescit.

Underneath also is Entombed the Daughter of this Mr. William Poole, the most Excellent among Women, Jane, Wife of Mr. Hanley, A. M. April 9th, 1697.

Ad pedes jacet Infans Jana.

Here Lieth the Body of Ann, the Wife of Richard Neubry, and Daughter of William Poole, who Deceased the Last Day of July, Anno Dom. 1648.

John Mills, died Jan. 18th, 1768,
in the 73d year of his Age.
Mary, his Wife, Died Dec. 28, 1762,
in the 78 year of her Age.

Here Lieth the Body of Jane, Daughter of Giles Estcourt, Gent. who Departed this Life March, Anno Dom. 1676.

Donations.

Mrs. Amy Haddon, by her Will, dated in the Year of our Lord 1696, left £10 yearly to the Rector of this Parish, to be continued to his Widow during her Widowhood, having one or more Children living at the time of his Decease. Also £4 yearly towards Apprenticeing one Boy and one Girl born in this Parish. Also 6 Quarters of Coals yearly for the use of the Charity School.

Mrs. Elizabeth Hodges, by her Will, Dated in the Year of our Lord, 1723, Left £2 yearly towards teaching Poor Children of this Parish to Read.

Mrs. Ann Estcourt, by her Will, Dated in the year of our Lord 1704, Left £10 yearly to the Poor of this Parish. Also £30 yearly for Apprenticeing six poor Boys, to be chosen out of this Parish, and the Parishes of Rolston and Shrewton.

The Church has a Chancel, Nave, and South Aisle: the south wall of the nave is supported by four plain pointed arches. The Tower contains four Bells; on the 3d is this inscription—' William Purdue Cast me. Anno Dom. 1628.' On the 1st, 2d, 4th, } Anno Dom. 1637.

Thomas Grimston Estcourt, Esq. Lord of the Manor, whose family have long held possession of it.

Rev. Edmund William Estcourt, Rector.

Formerly the Glebe Land of this Parish was about 12 acres, it is now nearly 16.

ASHLEY.

On Flat Stones in Chancel.

Here lyeth the Body of John Barratt, M. A. Rector of this Parish, who Deceased the 29th Day of August, 1667.

Here lyeth the Body of Margaret, Wife of John Barratt, Rector, who Deceased the 24 Day of April, 1666.

Here Lyeth the Body of Mr. Benjamin Cooper, who Departed this Life May the 1st, A. D. 1752, Aged 33.

Here Lyeth the Body of Mr. Stephen Collier, Son of the Rev. Mr. Stephen Collier, Late Rector of Rodemerton, who died suddenly March ye 15th, 1729, Aged 45 years.

Here Also Lyeth the Body of Mrs. Mary Wightwick, who Departed this Life May 20, 1756, Aged 37 years.

Heare lyeth the Body of Robert Price, Late Minister of this Place, who Departed this Life the 20 of April, Anno Domini 1638.

I have fought a good fight, I have finished my course, I have kept the faith. Henceforth is laide up for me a croune of Righteousness, which the Lord, the righteous judge, shall give me at the last day, &c. 2 Tim. 4.

Also Here Lyeth the Body of the Rev. Mr. Richard Monday, 15 years Rector of this Parish, who Departed this Life Feb. the 26, 1740, Aged 56 years.

Also Here Lyeth the Body of Mary, Wife of the Rev. Richard Monday. She Departed this Life August 19, 1749, Aged 67 years.

Against the west end of the Body.

Near this place lie the Remains of Mr. Simon Seek, and Ann, his Wife. He died the 31st of October, 1771, Aged 52. She died the 19th of April, 1760, in the 42 Year of her Age. Also of John and Simon, two of their Sons, John Died the 25th of August, 1759, Aged 13. Simon died 18 Feb. 1772, Aged 27.

Against S. Wall of S. Aisle.

In Memory of John Weake, Gent. who Departed this Life May 3, 1750, Aged 75.

Δοξα Τος Θεῶ.

Near this place Lyeth ye Body of Ferdinando Gorges, late of Westminster, Esq. Sometime Governor of ye Province of Maine, in New England. He was Born at Loftes, in Essex, Grandson and Heir to Sir Ferdinando Gorges, of Ashton Phillips, in the County of Somerset, Knight.

He Married Mary, the Eldest Daughter of Thomas Arghdale, of Loaks, in Chipping Wycomb, in ye County of Bucks, Esq.

They were very Eminent Examples of Virtue, and intirely happy in their mutual affections, and had many Children, of whom only two survived their indulgent and tender Parents.

He was Charitable and Patient, Courteous and Beneficent, Zealous and Constant to the Church, and a great Admirer of Learning.

He is interred in the same Grave in which Sr Theobald Gorges was buried Anno Dom. 1647, second Son of the Marchioness of Northampton, and Uncle to the Right Honble Richard Lord Gorges. Obiit XIV January, Anno Domini 1718, Ætat. 89.

Virtus post Funera Vivit.

On a Brass Plate.

Intombed Here Lyes,
Within This Halloed Earth,
Shee that liued Allmost
Twelve years From her Birth;
Her Tender years
To vertu was Inclin'd,
But Death too Soone
Her Body hath inshrined,
Ann Hawers Lyes
Now in Her coffin Dark,
Till wee shall meet
In God's Eternall Ark.

On Flat Stones in S. Aisle.

Here Lyeth the Body of Mrs. Cecilie Kingham, who who Departed this Life the 11th Day of March, Anno Domini 1743, Aged 75.

Here Lyeth the Body of Ferdinando Gorges, Esq. who Departed this Life the 13th Day of February, Anno Dom. 1738, Aged 76.

Here Lyeth the Body of Ferdinando Gorges, Esq. who Departed this Life the 14th Day of Jan. Anno Dom. 1718, Aged 89.

Here Lyeth the Body of John Beresford, Esq. who Departed this Life the 20th Day of April, Anno Dom. 1742, Aged 29.

Here Lyeth the Body of Alice Sherborne, Widdow, who Departed this Life the 22d Day of April, 1664.

Here Lyeth the Body of Richard Sherborne, who Departed this Life the 15th Day of July, Anno Dom. 1662.

Here Lyeth the Body of Michael Hadden, Gent. who Departed this Life Dec. 20, 1739, in the 17 year of his Age.

Also the Body of Mrs. Mary Horne, his Mother, who died May 5, 1740, Aged 68 years.

On Flat Stones in Body.

Underneath lie the Remains of William, the Son of Simon and Ann Seek, who Departed this Life Oct. 6, 1751, Aged 20 weeks.

Sleep soft in Dust,
Wait the Almighty's will,
Then rise unchanged,
And be an Angel still.

Here Lyeth interred the Body of John Wake, who Departed this Life the 10th Day of February, 1651.

Peter John Barrett Rector 1665.

John Giles in 1692.

The Rev. G. Wyatt present Rector.

The Church consists of a Chancel, Nave, and South Aisle: the south side of the Nave is supported by three pointed arches. At the entrance door on the south side is a little ancient sculpture. There are two Bells.

Extent of the Parish 940 acres, Glebe Land 27.

The Manor formerly belonged to Ferdinando Gorges, Esq. who died in 1647, in whose family it remained till 1738, when it came into the possession of John Beresford, who sold it to Sir George Paul, Knight, of Hill House, Gloucestershire: Thomas G. Estcourt Esq. who purchased it of Sir George Paul, is now the present owner.

OAKSEY.

On a Monument against the East Wall of the Chancel.

Hic
Subtus jacent Reliquiæ
Roberti Dalton,
Qui Collegii Regin. Oxon.
Alumnus olim et Socius, A.M.
Et quod majus est, antiquæ
pietatis cultor strenuus, Ecclesiæ
hujus per xvii annos Rector.
Paucis Notus
Corpore debilis, Mente vegetus
Virtutum Ferax, Ecclesiæ ornamentum,
Vitâ et Voce præco, nullo non Dignus
Elogio, eo Vero Dignior, quod nullo se
Dignum Existimaverit, fatis cessit
xvii Augusti, 1687.

On Flat Stones in Chancel.

In Memory of George Lawrence, Late Rector of this Parish, who Died Nov. the 21, 1764, Aged 38.

Here Lyeth the Body of Elizabeth Atkinson, Daughter of William and Rachel Atkinson, of William Fryers, in the County of Somerset, who was Buried 11 Feb. 1694, Aged 21 years.

Hic Jacent
Jeremiah Hewer, L. L. B.
Resurrectionem expectans Beatam.
Natus Cirencestriæ,
apud Glocestrensis,
Oxonii literis imbutus,
Hujus Parochiæ Rector,
In Kemble Vicarius:
Pius Probus
Ecclesiæ Anglicanæ
Filius obsequentissimus,
Vicinis vere Amicus,
Omnibus Humanus.
Annorum Satur
Morte Obiit April 10, 1760,
Ætatis 81.

On a Monument against the North Wall of the Body.

Near this Stone are deposited the remains of William Butt, Late of Bradford, in the County of Wilts. Gent. who Departed this Life the 24 Day of April, 1777, Aged 30.

North Wall.

Sacred to the Memory of William Goddard, whose remains are deposited in the east end of this Church yard. He died Dec. 29th, 1795, Aged 64 years.

On a Monument against south wall of south aisle.

Here rests the Body of Elizabeth, Daughter of Maximilian Bard, of London, Esq. Wife of Nevil Pool, of this Parish, Esq. and after his decease, of John Strange, of London, Gent. She departed this Life the 12 of March, in the year of our Lord 1706, Aged 58 years.

Rev. Ralph Smith, late Rector.
Rev. Edward Ryder the present one.

The Church consists of a Nave and South Aisle: in the North Wall of Chancel is a small Canopy. Round the ancient pew belonging to the Manor House is some small figures carved in oak. In the east Window of the south aisle is a representation of the Virgin Mary, with our Saviour in her arms: at the upper part of the window is a pelican, or, and two other figures: in the north window of the nave, also, is the representation of many human heads. On each side of the Nave are carved figures, projecting from the wall, by position bearing the beams or vaulting of the roof. Over the porch entrance of the north side is carved statue, but much defaced.

The Tower contains six Bells, with the following inscriptions:

1.—Peace and good Neighbourhood. 1773.
2.—The Gift of Benjamin Adamson, Esq. the Day of his Son coming of Age 21 years. Nov. 1773.
3.—Prosperity to this Parish.
4.—Thomas Rudhall, Glocester, founder. 1773.
5.—Mr. John Miles, Mr. John Johnson, Churchwardens. 1773.
6.—Come at my call, serve God all. 1773.

Extent of the Parish 2000 acres, four-fifths of which are pasture. Glebe Land about 24 acres.

In 1740, the Manor was in the possession of Benjamin Adamson, Esq. from whom it devolved to his Son: at his decease Lord Malmesbury became the possessor, who sold it to Francis Webb, Esq. at whose death it came to Frances Salisbury, his daughter, to whom it now belongs. William Masklyne Rents the Royalty and Manor-house, with about fifteen acres of Land.

POOLE.

Against the North Wall of Chancel.

Here Lyeth the Body of Frances Poole, Daughter of Edward Poole, Esq. Died at Poole, at 3 years of Age, the 11th of June, in the yeare 1644.

South Wall.

M. S.

Subtus requiescit Corpus Thomæ Myles, Artium Magistri, hujus Ecclesiæ Pastoris, qui obiit 6to die Novem. A° Dom. 1683.

Near this place lyeth the Body of Joseph Myles, Vicar of Prescot, who died May ye 30th, A. D. 1685. Also Mary, ye Daughter of Thomas and Ann Myles, who died May ye 5th, A. D. 1686. Also Thomas Myles, Gent. who died April ye 22d, A. D. 1715, Sons and Grand daughter to Thomas Myles, late Minister of this place. Also Ann, Wife of Thomas Myles, Gent. who died September ye 14, A. D. 1750, Aged 88.

Flat Stones.

The Rev. John Ferrebee, Rector of this Parish, died April 28th, 1662, Aged 88.

Also Margaret Ferrabee, his late Wife, died April 8th, 1665, Aged 87.

Here Lyeth the Body of Mary Myles, Late Wife of Thomas Myles, Rector of this Parish, who Departed this Life the 28 Day of April Anno Dom. 1702, Aged 87.

Hic jacet corpus Edwardi Poli, Armigeri, Qui in hoc mortali ævo vixit An. 48, et exhac arumnosa vita ad Dominum migravit, 28 die Aprilis, Anno . . . 1577. Elizabethæ 20

R N
1686.

On a brass plate against the north wall of the body.

Near this Place Lyeth the Body of Jonathan Fisher, many years Clerk of this Parish, who died Feb. 9th, 1795, Aged 62 years.

This Church was opened May ye 4th, 1777. The Parsonage-house is a small Cottage.

Register commenced 1632.

Dr. George Green Rector, 1761
John Hartley Green Late Rector.
The Rev. Mr. Dewell, present Rector.
Robt. Gording, Esq. Lord of the Manor.
Extent of the Parish 1100 acres, Glebe 230.

KEMBLE.

On Monuments against the north wall of Chancel.

Sacred to Posterity
Be the Virtues of Richard Digges, Gent.
He died 22 Nov. 1742, Aged 70.

Obscure, yet known to God, a soul sincere,
A heart unsully'd, and a conscience clear,
Who knew no ill, nor ere betray'd his trust,
True to his Friend, and obstinately just.

Also
Mrs. Martha, his Wife, died 9 Feb. 1739,
Aged 65 years.
And
William Diggs, Gent.
Son of Richard Diggs, Gent. and Martha, his Wife,
Died 7 Feb. 1742, Aged 45.

This is erected by Mrs. Sarah Diggs, Widow of William Diggs, Gent. She is the only surviving

Also Mrs. Sarah,
The Wife of William Digges. She
Died March the 27, 1750, Aged 60.

Arms—Argent, on a cross, gules, five eagles displayed, sable.

Near this Place Lyeth the Body of Henry, Son of Henry and Beata Stevens, who died Feb. the 14th, A. D. 1724, Aged 24 years.

Near this place also Lyeth the Body of Henry Stephens, Father of the above-said Henry, who was Buried the 2d Day of Sept. 1731, Aged 72 years.

Against the South Wall.

Sacred
To the Beloved Memory of
Mary, Wife of John Winstone,
who died Feb. 17, 1811.
She was an affectionate
Wife, and most tender parent.

Religion's narrow path with care she trod,
She serv'd her neighbour, and she serv'd her God:
Full eighty years she sojourn'd here below,
Gained many friends, and died without a foe.

137

M. S.
Pastoris hujus Ecclesiæ fidissimi,
Thomæ Holloway, A. M.
Qui Cœlebs Post vitâ lii annorum sedula,
In studiis suis ad Dom. gloria promovendis,
Et in Pauperib. opitulandis,
Feliciter actam
Singulari suâ Charitate,
Numerosa præ semet ditavit,
In Cœlum ascendit pars Cœlestis,
In Terrâ Terrestris,
S. B. R.
Infra Requies est.
Obiit Xbris XII. Anno
Ætat. 84,
Salut. 1705.

On Flat Stones in Chancel.

In Memory of Robert Timbrell, of Ewen Green, who was a person of great Piety, Temperance, and Integrity. He lived beloved, and died lamented, of all his friends, May 21, Anno Dom. 1713, in the 60th year of his Age.

Also Amy, his Wife, Daughter of Thos. Grayle, Rector of Lassington, near Gloucester, who departed this Life the 24th of December, 1738, Aged 63 years.

Here Resteth the Body of Mary Timbrell, who Departed this Life the 22 Day of July, Anno Dom. 1685.

And also the Body of Robt. the Son of Robt. Timbrell, was here Buried the 4 day of October, 1684.

Here Lieth the Body of Henry Stevens, who died Jan. 26, Anno Dom. 1737, Aged 70 years.

Also Mrs. Anna, the Wife of Mr. Henry Stevens, who died June the 29, Aged 77.

Also of Thos. Stevens, who died 7 Day of March, 1759, Aged 63 years.

Near this place lieth the Body of Anna, the Daughter of Henry Stevens, and Wife of Richard Selling, who Died October the 24, 1741, Aged 43.

Near this place lieth the Body of Richard Selling, who Departed this Life August 9, 1762, Aged 78 years.

Here resteth the Body of Joseph Stevens, who died April the 16th, 1779, Aged 70 years.

Elizabeth, Relict of Richard Stevens, and Wife of John Freeman, died January 19th, 1777, Aged 39 years.

Whilst thou art living, call for grace,
Thy Life is like a fading Flower,
Death cometh stealing on apace,
Thou knowest not the day nor hour.

Also of the above-named John Freeman, who died Dec. 3, 1791, Aged 59 years.

In Memory of William, Son of Henry and Mary Stevens, who Departed this Life the 3d Day of August, 1771, Aged 33 years.

In Memory of Richard, Son of Henry and Mary Stevens, who Departed this life the 2d day of June, 1771, Aged 43 years.

In Memory of Thos. Stevens, who was Buried April 6, 1713, Aged 40 years.

And of Elizabeth, Wife of Thomas Stevens, who was buried August 25th, 1745, Aged 67 years.

Also Henry, Son of Thos. and Elizabeth Stevens, who was buried July 25, 1772, Aged 72 years.

Against South Wall of the Body.

Near this place Lyeth ye Body of Thomas Major, who died October ye 5, A. D. 1718, Aged 69 years.

On a monument against the north wall of the Body.

Near this Place Lieth the Body of
Sir Robert Westley, Kt.
Alderman of the City of London:
A Person of unblemished Integrity.
He was one of the Sheriffs of that City
In the year 1734,
And in the year 1744, Lord Mayor.
He filled up these eminent Stations
With unquestioned Ability & Honour:
And, during his Mayoralty,
was, for his known Loyalty and Steadiness
To the true Interest of his King and Country,
Knighted by his Majesty.
Having acted wisely, unblameably, and virtuously,
In every Character and Relation,
He Departed this Life Sept. 24, in the
Year of our Lord 1745,
And the 75 year of his Age.
Also
In the same Vault Lies the Body of
Dame Elizabeth Westley, third
Wife to the said Sir Robt.
who Departed this Life 1st June, 1746, Aged 58.
Also
The Body of John Westley, Esq.
Son of the said Sir Robt. Westley,
who Departed this Life the 10 of June, 1748,
Aged 39 years.

On a Monument in the North Aisle.

Erected to the Memory of Ann Cox,
by her disconsolate Husband,
Charles Westley Cox.

Dormit non Mortua est.

Edward Poole, second Sonne of Edward Poole, Esquier, Being but two years of Age, was here Buryed the 4th Day of March, 1651.

In a Vault near this Place
Resteth the Body of Elizabeth Cox,
Wife of Charles Cox, Esq.
and youngest Daughter of Sir Robt. Westley, Kt.
A Lady of unblemished Virtue,
Properly attentive to her Family Concerns,
and yet not unmindful of the
Public and private duties
Of a Christian.
She Departed this Life Dec. 10,
In the 67 year of her Age,
and in the year of our Lord 1783.
In Testimony of her Virtues,
and his sincere esteem,
This Monument is erected
by her Affectionate Husband.

Against South Wall of S. Aisle.

Dedicated to the Memory of Beata and Edward, the Deare Wife and Son of Mr. Richard Pitt, both interred within these walls. Shee the 26th Day of April, 1650, hee the 29 Day of March, 1656,

who { conflicted / were buried / do reigne } in ye Church { militant, / materiall, / triumphant. }

She died ith noone, he in the morne of Age,
Yet Virtue (though not yeres) fild their ~~sines~~ lives page.
Resurgemus.

Posuit maritus mœstissimus, paterque plorans.

In a canopy under the above inscription is a knight templar, with his right leg across his left, a dog at his feet, with the point of the sword in the dog's mouth.

The Church consists of a Chancel, Nave, and North and South Transepts. The Tower contains five Bells, with the following inscriptions—

First—Henry Evans, Richd Timbrell, 1740.
Second—John Rudhall, 1790.
Third—
Fourth—1696.
Fifth—Thos. Mayor, Thos. Cone, Ch. wardens.

John Copson, Late Vicar.
John Froud, present Vicar.

Robert Gordon, Esq. Lord of the Manor.

BISHOPSTON.

On a Monument against the east wall of Chancel.

Hic
Obdormiscit in pace
Edetha,
Christ. Willoughby, Armig. Lond.
Conjux Charissima;
Apud Alvington in Agro Glocest. nata, an. 1607,
Ubi libras annuatim solvend. pauperibus
Ligavit
Lond. Translata matrimonium contraxat
1634,
Desponsum absentem apud exteros,
Negotiis Mercatoriis versantem
æquo tulit animo pan.
Matrimonium contractum tunc sacrum consummavit
1640.
Maritum inde ad Indos Navigantem,
Sumo expectavit desiderio P an 6¼.
Redeuntem tandem, sorte sua contentum
Mutuo conjugali fruuntur solatio,
in vicem fœlices
Fœmina,
Erga Deum pia, egenos benigna,
Voti conjugalis semper observantissima,
Amicis, fidelis, omnibus dilecta.
Obiit { Æræ Christianæ 1670, / Ætatis suæ 63.
Cujus Memoriæ hoc sacravit
Maritus mœrens.

On Flat Stones in Chancel.

Hic jacet Christopheri Willoughby, quod reliquum est, una cum prima Uxore, cum qua fœlicissimus vixerat, infœlix tamen in secundis nuptiis. Obiit 26 Jan. 1680.

Here Rests the Body of Edeth, Wife of Christopher Willoughby, of London, Merchant, Late Sheriffe of this County, who deceased this Life the 13th August, 1670.

Beneath this Stone Lye the Remains of Mary Cheeke, Relict of William Cheeke, and Daughter of Henry Willoughby, Esq. Late Lord of this Manor, who Departed this Life the 25th Day of April, 1803, Aged 52 years.

Beneath this Stone Lye the Remains of
Jane Willoughby,
Daughter of the Hon[ble] Col. Staples,
and Relick of George Willoughby, Esq.
By whom she had Eight Children,
three of them are buried near her.
She died 11 Aug[st] 1769.

On Flat Stones in Body.

Here Lyeth the Body of William Hunt, who Deceased the 27th Day of February, 1685, who gave to the poor £50, to be paid £5 yearly for ten years next after his Decease, the first pay to begin in December, 1686.

Here Lyeth ye Wife of John Rowland, minister of this Parish, was buried April 15th, Anno Dom. 1695, Aged 52 years.

Here Lyeth the Body of Cœcilia Kent, who Departed this Life April 21, Anno Dom. 1682.

In Memory of Jone, ye Wife of William Kent, Grandson of the above-named Cicely Kent, who died March ye 4th, A. D. 1727, Aged 72 years.

Here Under Rests the Body of Katherine Kent, the wife of Samuel Kent, who Deceased the 4th Day of October, 1680, Aged 26.

Under this Stone doth Lye
Two subjects of Death's Tyranny :
The Mother who, in this close tomb,
Sleeps with the Issue of her womb.
Here Death deals cruelly, as you may see,
That with the fruite cuts down the tree;
Yet is his malice all but vain,
Both tree and fruit shall spring again.

Here Lyeth the Body of Samuel Kent, who Departed this Life the 21st Day of September, Anno Dom. 1686, Aged 36.

In Memory of Richard Rudman, who died May 16, 1762, Aged 80 years.

In Memory of Elizabeth, the Wife of Richard Rudman, who died March 25, 1754, Aged 71 years.

Here Resteth the Body of Susanna, Wife of Henry Phillipps, of Wanbrough, who deceased this Life the 11th day of May, 1678, Aged 32.

Here Lyeth the Body of Margaret, Wife of John Kent, who departed this Life May ye first, A. D. 1712, Aged 60 years.

Here Lyeth the Body of Susanna Hull, of Bishopston, who Departed this Life Aug. 20, Anno Dom. 1696, Aged 81.

In Memory of John Withers, who Departed this Life Feb. 23, 1780, Aged 86 years.

Also Susanna, his Wife, who was Buried June the 20, in the year 1728, Aged 30 years.

In Memory of Mary Withers, Daughter of John and Susanna Withers, who Departed this Life December the 22d, 1798, Aged 76 years.

In Memory of Ralph Withers, Son of John and Susanna Withers, who Departed this Life December the 17, 1799, Aged 78 years.

Against the west end of south aisle.

Sacred to the Memory of Mary Wakeman, Wife of the Rev. George Wakeman, Born April 16, 1750, Died July 24, 1813.

Also to the Memory of the Rev. George Wakeman, Vicar of this Parish 27 years, Born June 20, 1760, Died June 29, 1816.

On Flat Stones in S. Aisle.

In Memory of Anne, Wife of John Smyth, Vicar of this Parish. She died March 22, Anno Dom. 1723, Aged 37.

In Memory of John Smith, Vicar of this Parish, who Died Dec. ye 28, Anno Dom. 1730, Aged 67.

Here Lyeth the Body of Elizabeth Purton, who departed this Life the 30 day of April, Anno Dom. 1685, Aged 53.

On Flat Stones in North Aisle.

Here Lyeth Elizabeth, Wife of William Harding. She died April ye 5th, 1730, Aged 28.

Here Lyeth ye Body of William Harding, who Departed this Life January ye 28, Anno Dom. 1695, Aged 51 years.

140

Donations.

Bequest of the Rev. Thomas Coker.

The Rent of Six Acres of Land to be expended as follows: £.1 per annum to the Rector of Hinton, 1.£ per An. to the Vicar of Bishopston, for the Management of the Accounts of Hinton and Bishopston Schools, Remainder for the Master of Bishopston School. The Interest of £.300, 3 per cents. for the Education of twelve poor Children.

Bequest of Christopher Willoughby, Esq.

Part of the Tythe of the Hamlet of Clynch, in the Parish of Milton, Wilts. From which £.3 10*s*. for Dowries for two poor Women, the remainder for Annuities for four poor Men of Bishopston Parish.

Bequest of Gilbert Keats, Esq.

£.16 P^r An. for Annuities for four poor People of Bishopston Parish.

1796. Mr. Thomas Goddard bequeathed to the Parish of Bishopston as follows:

£.600 to be invested in the Stock of 3 per cent Consols, in the Names of the Rector of Hinton, and Vicar of Bishopstone; from the Interest of which, £.4 10*s*. P^r An. is to be expended for Books for a School, and the remainder of the Interest for a Salary for a Schoolmaster, for the purpose of teaching all the poor Children of Parishioners, or certificated Persons: of Persons renting under 20*l*. P^r An. and of Mr. Goddard's Relations:

£.300 to be invested in like manner. The Interest to be expended partly in the payment of Ringers on certain occasions, and in keeping Bells and Tower, and the Testator's Monument, in repair, and the Remainder in beautifying, new pewing, and paving the Church.

£.139. The Interest to be expended in paving the Walks about the Church Yard.

In the east window of the Chancel, and also in the east window of the south Aisle, is a little painted glass.

The Church consists of a Chancel, Nave, North and South Aisles: the south wall is supported by three pointed arches, and the north wall by two.— There are eight Bells in the Tower.

BAYDON.

Flat Stones.

In Memory of Mary, Wife of Mr. John Williams, who Departed this Life the 12th of March, 1780, Aged 26 years.

Here Lyeth the Body of Thomas Stroud, Sen. who Died Dec. ye 20, 1709, Aged 63 years.

In Memory of Joanna, Wife of Mr. Gideon Williams, who Departed this Life Nov. ye 27, 1730, Aged 50 years.

In Memory of Mr. Gideon Williams, who Departed this Life April ye 25th, 1737, Aged 86 years.

Here Lyeth ye Body of Master Henry Smyth, who was ye Son of Master Henry Smythe, Brother to Thomas Smythe, Esq. Master of ye Custome House of London, under Queen Elizabeth of Blessed Memory, which said Henry Smythe Dyed A. D. 1631.

Here Lies William, the Son of Anthony and Mary Stroud, who died Nov. 13, 1744.

Also William, his Brother, who died March 30, 1746.

Here Lyeth the Body of Anthony Stroud, Sen. who Departed this Life July ye 16, Anno Dom. 1694.

Also Elenor, ye Wife of Anthony Stroud, Sen. who departed this Life July ye 5, 1672, his Age 68, her Age 46 years.

Catharine, the Wife of John Marshall, of Ramsbury, Daughter of Anthony and Elizabeth Stroud, Died August 24, 1745, Aged 29 years.

Also Catherine, their Daughter, Died in her Infancy.

The Rev. William Mitchell, Vicar.
Sir Francis Burdett, Lord of the Manor.

RAMSBURY.

On Monuments against the north wall of Chancel.

Here
Lies the Body of
Robert Hillman, Gent.
who departed this Life July 8, 1694,
In the Forty-ninth Year of his Age.

Underneath are Interred the Remains of Wm. Jones, Esq. He was the Eldest Son, and the last of the Male Line of the Family of William Jones, Esq. of Ramsbury Manor, by Eleonora, his Wife, youngest Daughter of Edward Ernle, Esq. of Brimslade Park, in this County. From his Piety, Modesty, Integrity, and natural sweetness of Disposition, from his Benevolence, Generosity, and strict regard to Truth, from a Quickness of Parts, join'd to a sound Judgement, from the Duty and tender Affection he ever shew'd to those of his nearest Alliance, from his engaging Behaviour to all, as well as his warm, steady Friendship to those of his more intimate Acquaintance, (so fair was his Spring of Life,) what might not have been expected from his maturer age? But in the midst of Affluence, Youth, and Health, of every flattering Prospect this World can afford, after an illness of a few Days, it pleas'd the Almighty to blast the Hopes of his Friends, by cutting him off at the early age of 22, on the 7 of April, 1766, whilst on his Travels at Besançon, in France. In Remembrance of their mutual Affection, and as a small Testimony of her Heartfelt concern for the Loss of one so justly dear to her, His eldest Sister Elizabeth, the Wife of William Langham, Esq. now Sir William Jones, Bart. has caused this Monument to be Erected, June, 1775.

On a Monument by the East Wall of Chancel.

To the beloved Memory
of
Mary Eleonora Burdett,
Eldest Daughter of the Late
Francis Burdett, Esq.
By Mary Eleonora,
Youngest Sister and Coheiress
of William Jones, Esq. of Ramsbury Manor.
This Tablet is inscribed by her Brother,
Sir Francis Burdett, Bart.
She died November 27,
1797, Aged 26.

Not formal duty prompts these mournful Lays,
No painted shew of Grief these Lines impart;
No cold, unfeeling, stale, insipid Praise,
But sorrow flowing from the o'er-fraught heart.

No need hast thou of Monumental Verse,
Lamented Maid, to prove thy worth was high;
The Widow's tear adorns thy modest hearse,
Thy name is honored with the poor Man's sigh.

Alas! they cry, that feeling heart is cold,
That lib'ral hand, which gave to all relief,
That tongue, whose sweetness never can be told,
Which charm'd our ears, and sooth'd our sharpest grief.

If thou canst look, bright Angel, from above,
As to thy God thou bend'st th' adoring knee,
Accept this tribute of a Brother's Love,
And in thy Orisons remember me.

On Monument against South Wall of Chancel.

Hic mortalitatis suæ reliquias deposuit Gulielmus Jones, eques Auratus, Serenissimi Regis Caroli Secundi Attornatus Generalis; Vir acerrimi Judicij Summæq. probitatis ac legum Anglicanarum vel omnium consensu longe Peritissimus, obijt vi nonas Mais, Anno Dom. 1682, Ætatis suæ 51.

Richardum, Filium unicum reliquit, non diu sibi superstitem, qui, maxima Galliæ parte peragrata, Tolosæ febri oppressus occubuit, nonis April, An. Dom. 1685, Ætat. suæ 17.

Cujus cineres huc relati eodem hoc conduntur tumulo.

Samuel Jones, Armiger, Domini Gulielmi, supra laudati, frater; vitâ cessit pridie idus Martias, Anno Dom. 1686, Ætatis suæ 47.

Eliz. prædicti Samuelis, filia. Obijt 9° Decembis, 1689, Ætatis suæ 4°.

Flat Stones in Chancel.

Depositum Roberti Gillmore, Armigeri, Qui objit vicesimo quinto die mensis Septembris, Anno Domini 1693, Aged 45.

Here lieth the Body of Edward Gillmore, Gent. who departed this life in or about the 31 year of his Age, and was Buried the 11 Day of September, Ano Dom. 1654.

And Agatha, his Wife, who departed this Life the 56 year of her Age, and was Buried the 21 Day of July, Anno Dom. 1680.

To the Memory of Sarah, the Wife of John Biggs, of Axford-Farm, Gent. who died Feb. 18, 1747, Aged 46 years.

On a Monument against the north wall of Chancel.

Here lies the Body of Robert Hillman Gent. who departed this Life July 8, 1694, In the Forty Ninth Year of his Age.

Monument on the second Pillar in the Body on the N. side.

Near this Place Lyeth the Body of Henry Read, of Crowood, Gent. who departed this Life ye 27 Day of January, Anno Domini $170\frac{5}{6}$ in ye 68 year of his Age.

And also ye Body of Johanna, his first Wife, who departed this life ye 11th Day of April, Anno Domini 1676, in ye 33d year of her Age.

And Likewise the Body of Banks, their Eldest Son, who departed this Life ye 2d of March, An° Dom. 1682, in ye 17 year of his Age.

On a Flat Stone in Body.

Here Lyeth the Body of John Cox, who died June 23, 1733, Aged 38 years.

On a Monument in East Wall of N. Aisle.

In Memory of Jonathan Knackstone, Gent. whose eminent virtues endeared him to all good men while living, and whose death cannot be sufficiently Lamented in his degenerate Age. He was never known to murmur, though deprived by nature of the Organs of Hearing and Speaking. Piety, Justice, Paternal Affection, Humanity, Benevolence, (which are singly admired in other men) were practised by him with an undeviating constancy. He died March 18, 1745, Aged 63.

This Marble is also inscribed to Stephen Knackstone, Geñt. and joane his Wife. He died May ye 19th, 1728, Aged 75.

She died Jan. 28, 1714, Aged 68.

Sarah, his Daughter, died August 26th, 1710, Aged 36 years.

And also Ann Knackstone. She Died Dec. ye 3d, 1740, Aged 22 years.

On a Flat Stone in North Aisle.

M. S.
Georgij Moore,
Obijt XIX die Maij,
Anno { Dom. 1729,
Ætat. 60.

Arms—A chevron ingrailed between three doves, two in chief, one in base.

Monument in the South Wall of South Aisle.

To the Memory of Henry Read, of Crowood, Esq. who died at Toulouse, in France, on the first Day of May, 1786, in the Sixty-Fourth year of his Age.

Vain are the Duties Partial Fondness Pays,
If Virtue's Plaudits Sanction not the Lays;
O'er thee, O Read! no Fading Wreaths are Hung,
No Requiems breath'd by Flattery's soothing Tongue:
Thy worth and truth, in ev'ry Act display'd,
Disdain to Borrow Adulation's Aid;
Nuptial and Filial Love, with grief sincere,
Pour o'er thy Tomb the unavailing Tear.

In a Vault near this place Lieth Mary, the Wife of Major Henry Read, of Crowood, and Daughter of John Jacob, of Salisbury, M. D. She died May, 1783, Aged 25 years.

Her Disposition, and Sincere Affection, endeared her to her Husband; a Sincerity of Attachment, to her Friends; and the Gentleness of her Manners, to all who knew her.

Near this Place are Deposited, in the family Vault, the Remains of Frances Read, Relick of Henry Read of Crowood, Esq.

To enumerate her various good Actions would be as unnecessary to those who knew her, as it would be unjust to her Character not to notice, how uniformly she exemplified, through a length of years, all those Virtues which distinguish and adorn the different Periods of female Life, while the Greatness of her Mind, during the last Struggles of Nature, added Dignity to her unsullied Virtues.

Her much Loved Children, in Testimony of their Affection and Respect, dedicate this Monument to her Memory. Ob. May, 1801, Aged 73.

On a Monument against the East Wall of South Aisle.

To the Memory of Elizabeth, Widow of Thomas Batson, Esq. Buried near her Husband in the family aisle of Highworth. Chearfulness and Temperance Prolonged her Beneficent Life to the Advanced Period of Ninety-two years, when she Departed without a struggle, on the 22 of January, 1808, Grateful for the Blessings She had experienced, and in humble Hope of a Glorious Resurrection to eternal felicity through the merits of her Redeemer.

She was of the ancient family of Lascelles, of the County of York, First Cousin by the whole Blood to the Last, and by the half Blood to the present Lord Harewood.

On the second Pillar S. side from the E. end of Body.

Sacred to the Memory of Henry Read, of Crowood, Esq. who died Jan. 9th, 1756, Aged 89.

Likewise Ann, his Affectionate Wife, who (aged 63) Survived only to ye succeeding Ninth Day of August.

On Flat Stones in South Aisle.

Here Lieth the Body of Mister Edward Keatt, of Weselcourt, in the Parish of Roughton, in the County of Wilts. who Deceased the 7 Day of Jan. An° Dom. 1677.

Here Lyeth ye Body of John Roffley, who Died Octor. An° Dom. 1720, Aged 39 years.

Here Lyeth ye Body of Thomas Hill, who Departed this Life July ye 29, A. D. 1702, Aged 49 years.

Come hither, Mortals, cast an eye,
Whilst thou hast time prepare to die;
Consider well, for die thou must,
And as I am be turn'd to dust.

In Memory of Joseph Fowles, Gent. who died July ye 21, 1731, Aged 60 years.

The Church consists of a Chancel, Nave, North and South Aisles. The Nave is supported by four massive pillars, and four pointed arches.

Sir Francis Burdett is the Lord of the Manor.

TROWBRIDGE.

On Monuments against the north wall of Chancel.

Near this Place are Deposited the Remains of Mr. John Wats, a Native of this Town, who died without Issue the 19th of December, 1741, in the 65 year of his Age.

In the year 1692, he went to Sevill, in Spain, where he resided till the breaking out of the Confederate War, when he removed to Lisbon in Portugal, and there acquired a large Fortune, a fair Character, and the Approbation of his principalls. To the World, he gave strong testimonies of the Forte of Industry, Application, and Economy; To the Rich, of the Civility and Politeness acquired by Travel; To the Poor, of Charity; to Mankind, of Benevolence; to his Patrons, of Gratitude; to his Intimates, of Friendship; to his Relations, of Beneficence; and to his Relict, of Conjugal Affection; who, as a Proof of the Tenderness she bore to him living, and the Honour she pays to his Memory now dead, Erected this Monument.

In the same Vault are Deposited the Remains of Mrs. Mary Watts, Relict of the said Mr. John Watts, who died July 13th, 1765, in the 64 year of her Age.

Robert Hawkins, S. T. B. Quondam Ecclesiæ hujus Rector, Sarisburiensis Præbendarius, utriusq. Ornamentum, altari fœliciter admotus, jam altare juxta, suaviter abdormiscit, denatus Ætatis suæ 43, Salutis 1672, cujus memoriæ hoc sacravit, in lacrymis Relicta, Elizabeth Hawkins.

Arms—Argent, on a saltire, sable, five fleur-de-lis or, a crescent of the second for difference.

H. S. E.

Abigail, Uxor Gulielmi Brewer, Arm. Tho. Strode, de Bowless, in Com. Somerset, Armig. Filia; Quam probitas, non fucata, pietas, non superba, eleemosynæ, non negotiantes, terris dilectam, Cœlo maturam reddiderunt, liberis dives, ditior operibus, multiplicem (favente Deo) in utrisq. edidit progeniem, ex his Gulielmus Pembrokia, et Maria, juxta sepulta, ex illis n Domino morientum nulla non sequntur,

Obiit Julii 25, Anno { Dom̃ 1691, Ætat. 62.

Arms—Gu'es, two bends wavy or, in chief vair, argent, and azure: impaling ermine, on a canton, sable, a crescent, ermine.

Underneath lyeth the Remains of Ann, Daughter of John & Eliz. Ching, who died April 7th, 1806, Aged 13 years.

Spe certâ resuscitandi in Christo, hic subter sacri requiescunt cineres Gul. Brewer, Armigeri, multosq. per annos ad Pacem Justitiarii, Prudentis et Integri, Literaturâ tam sacrâ quam profanâ normediocriter versati; intellectus et penetratione ingenijq.; præpollentis acumine; quod verò visce majus, pietate probitate et Charitate, insignis quippe, qui benefactis in Ecclesiam, et mopes adoratum ac perenne nomen adeptus, est in terris, et laudum gloriamq. immortalem in Cœlis quo, satur annorum famæ ac divinarum, Maii 17°, Anno { Christi 1707°, Ætatis 81.

Marmora hæc pariter, memoriæ sacra Jonathan, prædicti Gulielmi, Filij, qui sæpius mercaturæ, ergo peregre profectus, tandem apud Sinas, florente etate ac Virtute, sub idem tempus fatis concessit, eatenùs peregrinus, nunc vero Dom.

Etiam Eliz. Monck, fil. prædicti, quæ relicto marito tribusq. filijs, Tho. Jana, et Will. Obiit Lond: 5 Junij, 1707.

Arms—The same as the preceding.

M. S.

Elizabethæ, sub marmoreo eo juxta positæ, Roberti Houlton, dilectiss. Uxoris; quæ Ob. Apr. A. Dñi 1707, Ætat. suæ 20.

Etiam Elizab. filiæ, qu. ob. Apr. 16.

Arms—Argent, on a fess azure, three bezants between three talbots heads erased of the second, crescent for difference: impaling argent, three lions rampant azure, a chief of the last.

James Wereat died May 5, 1767, Aged 19.
James Wereat died July 28, 1769, Aged 89.
John Wereat died Feb. 22, 1780, Aged 67.

Flat Stones.

Hic situs est, in spe beatæ resurrectionis, Thomas Brimsdon, Generosus, obijt 16 die Junij, Anno Salutis 1691, Ætatis suæ 33.

Here also lieth the Body of Jane Long, Widdow, who Departed this life the . . . Day of Decem. 1667.

. . . . the Body . .
. . es Huish,
. . . ser of Physicke,
. . he time of Martin,
Coll. in Oxon, he fell
A sleep the 4 Day of
April An. Dom. 1640,
M. D. S.

144

Brass Plate.

Here lie the Remains of Mrs. Eliz. Brewer, who Departed this life May 28, 1761, Aged 84.

Here lies also the Remains of William Brewer, who Departed this life June 19, 1766, Aged 64.

Against North-East Pillar of Nave.

D. O. M. S.

Henrici Wallis, Armigeri, quod mortale fuit, prope sub jacet, anima superis fruente, famâ et exemplo superstitibus. Natus fuit Anno Dom. 1629, Anno 1691. Vicecomitis Wilton officio, quarto non. Sept. anni sequentis Climacterici fui magni vitâ functus est, nunc Cœli gaudiis. Marito optime merenti, et liberis Annæ, Nevillo, Henrico, et Saræ, Anna uxor et mater mœstissima. H. M. P C.

Arms—Ermine, a bend, gules; impaling sable, a fess ingrailed or, between three escallops argent.

Non procul ab hac columna, occidentem versus, requiescit Corpus Revdi et in primis eruditi viri Dom. Thomæ Lucas, Theologi vere Christiani, qui hoc in oppido annos complures Religionem puram et intaminatam, non conscionibus solum suavissimis, sed et moribus integerrimis, et charitate cœlesti incolis commendavit, levi demum valetudine, inter concionandum correptus decem fere dies decubuit, doloris penitus expers, speique lætissimæ plenus, tumque amicis, non sibi cito nimis, placidâ piorum morte, et terris excessit pridie Idus Martias, 1741.

Conjugem habuit Dom. Eliz. Coleman, lectissimam Fœminam, qua eum amantissime vixit, quam præmaturâ morte mœrens amisit xv kalendas Decem. 1732.

Cujus etiam Reliquiæ juxta sunt positæ, in memoriam parentum optime meritorum, utque posteris utile proponatur exemplar, hoc monumentum posuit solus hodie superstes Filius, Mercator Londinensis. 1758.

Arms—Argent, a fess between six annulets, gules, bar-wise: impaling azure, a cross-flory, or, between four mullets, argent. *Crest*—A wyvern's head, gules, issuing out of a ducal coronet or.

P. M. E. D. S.

Juxta jacet filiorum, Dei manumissionem manens quod mori potuit, Eduardi, filii Eduardi Davis, hujus oppidi, nec inutilis, nec indigni, incola, talis erat qualem laude prosequunter cuncti pauci æmulentur, ornate simplex, rite probus, vitæ integer ejusq. nec tenax, nec pertæsus vivendi finem, non frustrari unice solicitus comitate mansuetudine charitate, nulli secundus. Jesu nostri sacro sancti salvatoris Religionem, non tam præ se tulit quam coluit exhibuit ornavit, post hæc nil mirum se præluisse, amantissimum, suavissimum, probatissimum, maritum, patrem, amicum, Uxorem duxit, Marcam Benger, de Ogbourn, dignam tali Viro, sed cito nimis ereptam, non prius tamen quam ab illa, chara sui invicem amoris pignora susceperat, Eduardum, filium, deasq. natas Annam et Saram, quos superstites reliquitat mœrentes Vita tandem bene functa mortem, non immaturam obiit, illius nec cupidus, nec timidus, quippe qui novit eam terrorum licet aliter Reginam, aculeo dempto esse inermem, sic placidè e vivis (morientibus potius) ad Cœlitus abiit Anno Salutis 1718, Ætatis suæ 77°.

Quod fieri fas est in memors invida fecit, exuvias rapuit (bella rapina) meas, ut super inducreni æternæ regalia vitæ, quis vicit tandem dicite vivo cano.

Underneath this Stone Lyeth ye Body of William Jordan. He died August ye 5th, A. D. 1735, Aged 45 years.

Also Here lieth the Body of Elizabeth Huet, who Died November ye 8th, A. D. 1734, Aged 23 years.

Also Here lyeth ye Body of Abigail Jordan, who Departed this life the 16th of Novem. 1751, Aged 57 years.

In Memory of Elizabeth, Wife of Thomas Burgess, who dy'd June the 8th, A. D. 1727, Aged 27 years.

Also, in Memory of Wm. Son of Thomas and Constance Burgess, dy'd August ye 21, 1734, Aged 2 years.

On Flat Stones in Nave.

Thos. Dundee, Gent. died the 14th April, 1806, Aged 74 years.

In Memory of Mr. Richard Arthur, of Bristol, Druggist, who died the first of April, 1805, Aged 49 years.

On Monuments in the North Aisle.

Near this Place lieth the Body of Margaret, the Wife of Richard Shrapnell, who departed this life April ye 20th, Anno Christi 1718, Ætatis 63.

Also Lyeth the Body of Richard, the Son of Richard and of Margaret Shrapnell, who died July ye 22, 1715, Ætat. suæ 28.

Also lyeth the Body of Philip, the Son of Richard and of Margaret Shrapnell, who departed this life May the 4th, Anno Christi 1719, Ætatis suæ 29.

Also lyeth the Body of Richard Shrapnell, sen. who Dy'd April the 13, A. D. 1730, Aged 75 years.

Also near this Place lyeth the Body of Edward Shrapnell, Departed this life December the 15, Anno Domini 1732, Aged 33 years.

Sacred to the Memory of Edward Horlock Mortimer, Esq. a Deputy Lieutenant for Wilts, and Justice of the Peace for that County and Somerset, who died the 16th December, 1803, Aged 51 years.

Arms—Or, three bars azure, on a chief of the same two pales between two pikes or, in fess point an escutcheon, ermine: impaling argent, a chevron ingrailed between three crabfish, gules. *Crest*—A demi wyvern, proper, on a military helmet.

In Memory of Benjamin, the Son of Benjamin and Elizth Cottle, who Departed this life ye 9th of August, 1749, Aged 2 months.

Also in Memory of Mrs. Elizabeth Cottle, Wife of the said Benjamin, who died ye 16th of April, 1752, Aged 35 years.

Also in Memory of Mr. Benjamin Cottle, who departed this Life the 11th of December, 1753, Aged 33 years.

Here lyeth the Body of Margery Clark, the Daughter of John and Elizabeth Clark, who died Jan. ye 22, Anno Dom. 1722, Aged 46 years.

In Memory of Elizth, ye Wife of Thos. Clarke. She Dy'd ye 20 March, 1733, Aged 41 years.

Also in Memory of Thos. Clarke. He Dy'd 18 Dec. 1739, Aged 54 years.

Beneath this Stone lyeth ye Body of John Clarke, Joyner, who Departed this life ye 25 day of Februar...

Also Beneath this Stone lyeth ye Body of Robt. ye Son of John Clarke, and of Elizth his Wife, who Dy'd May ye 7, An° Dom. 169..

In Memory of Wm. Son of Thos. and Ann Clarke. He died in July, 1748, Aged 2 years.

Also in Memory of Ann, Wife of Thos. Clarke, who died ye 26 of October 1750, Aged 33 years.

Also in Memory of Ann, Daughter of Thomas and Ann Clarke, who Dy'd ye 5 Feb. 1752, Aged 4 years & 3 months.

In Memory of Elizth, the Wife of Richard Little, who died the 4th of February, 1730, Aged 25 years.

Also in Memory of Mary Ann and John, Son and Daughter of Richard & Elizabeth Little, who died in their Youth.

In Memory of John Ghey, who departed this life July the 16, 1792, Aged 78 years.

A loving Husband, a Father Dear,
A Faithful friend, do now lie here;
In love he liv'd, in peace he dy'd,
His life desir'd, but God deny'd.

Also underneath Lieth five Children of John and Martha Ghey.

Also in Memory of Mrs. Ann Ghey, Wife of Joseph Ghey, who Departed this life May 2d, 1818, Aged 60 years.

Also in Memory of Samuel Ghey, Sen. who Departed this life Dec. the 26th, 1735.

Also in Memory of Eleanor, the Wife of Samuel Ghey, Sen. who departed this life February the 10th, 1740, Aged 58 years.

Also in Memory of Mary, Wife of John Ghey, who died Sept. 19, 1814, Aged 23 years.

Also 2 of their Children, who died in their Infancy.

Also in Memory of Samuel and Mary, Son and Daughter of Samuel Ghey, Sen. Samuel Dyed 17 Sept. 1731, Mary Died 16th May, 1729.

Also in Memory of Betty, Daughter of Samuel and Eleanor Ghey, who Departed this life Feb. the 24, 1740, Aged 28 years.

Also in Memory of Joseph Ghey, who departed this life Dec. 1, 1820, Aged 66 years.

Flat Stones.

In Memory of Ann, Daughter of James and Sarah Edgell, who died July 17, 1817, Aged 18 years.

Underneath are deposited the Remains of Thomas Clark, Esq. who died the 25 day of July, 1786, Aged 48 years.

Also of John Clarke, Esq. who died the 8 day of Feb. 1804, Aged 64 years.

Brass Plate.

Here lyeth the Body of Joseph Lewis, who Departed this life the last day of December, 1738, Aged 55.

In Memory of Elizabeth, Daughter of Wm. & Ann Crowter, who died March ye 24, 1734, Aged 3 years.

Also Ann, the Wife of Wm. Crowter, died Oct. 18, 1739, Aged 31 years.

Also in Memory of John, Son of William & Ann Crowter, who died ye 28 Jan. 1750, Aged 23 years.

On a Monuments in S. Aisle.

M. S.

Venerabilis Viri Eduardi Yerbury, Arm. Qui flagranti nuper Civili Bello, Pro Fide Carolo Martyri præstitâ Lare profugus, plimuthi obijt; ibiq. Dormitorium invenit. Nec non Annæ, Viduæ ejusdem mœstissimæ, antiquâ, stirpe inter Atrebatios oriundæ, Et utrisq. Parentis liberorum Eduardi, Annæ, Johannis, posuit Jonis Filius Eduardus, Biennio ante obitum, Oct. sc: 26, 92. Qui subtus requiescunt, in spe beatæ Resurrectionis, A° Dni CIↃ IↃC XC.

Arms—Or, a lion rampant argent; impaling or, a chevron between three gules.

M. S.

Gulielmi Yerbury, Gen. et Henrici, Coll: Magd: Soc: Med: Doc: Fratrum Cœlibum integrorumq. vitæ, quorum munificentia supremis illuxit tabulis, quibus uterq. nostris, Ille et vicinis Bradfordiæ, Rhodiæ, et Beckingtoniæ, prospexit egenis.

Obie: { Gulielm. Bathoniæ, } An° { LXXIX oct. 9, MDCXCVIII. et subtus jacet.
Runt { Henric Oxoniæ, } Ætã { LIX. mar. 25, MDCLXXXVI. Ibidemq. sepultus.

Near this Monument are deposited the Remains of Esau Reynolds, Esq. who lost his life by a fall from his horse, on the 29th Day of September, 1778, Aged 53 years.

Farewell, blest Shade! Alas! too early fled,
Who knew thee living, but laments thee Dead.
No more, no more, far better would it be
To lay sepulcher'd than remember thee.

Also are Deposited the remains of Betty Reynolds, who Departed this life the 20th Day of October, 1783, Aged 77 years,
Mother of the above-named Esau Reynolds, and Wife of the under-mentioned Jonathan Reynolds.

Also are deposited the Remains of Jonathan Reynolds, who Departed this life the 17th day of March, 1786, Aged 94 years.

Arms—Argent, a chevron checky argent and gules, between three crosslets fitchy sable.

West End of South Aisle.

To the Memory of Mr. James Coles, who Departed this life Aug. 3d, 1761, Aged 42 years.

Of Hester, his Wife, who died June 3d, 1769, Aged 40 years.

Of Five of their Daughters, who all died in their Infancy.

Of Richard, their Son, who was killed at Sea, Oct. 16th, 1782, Aged 24 years.

And of Hester, their Daughter, Wife of Thomas Jefferys, Esq. who died April 12th, 1783, Aged 37 years.

Also of Elizabeth Stratton Coles, Daughter of James Coles, Esq. of Parrocks Lodge, Somerset, who died June 10th, 1816, Aged 36 years.

Near this Pillar Lyeth the Body of Hannah, the Wife of Thomas Nutt, who Departed this life the 22 Day of March, Anno Dom. 17$^{16}_{-}$ Aged 35 years.

Stay, Reader; stand, and lend an ear
Unto the dust that slumber here;
And while that thou does read of me,
Think on the glass that runs for thee.

On Flat Stones.

Francis Hooper died 24th March, 1764, Aged 82 years.

Brass Plate.

In Memory of Nicholas Greene, Gent. who died October 22d, 1771, Aged 61.

Also Rachel, Wife of the above Nicholas Greene, who died Oct. 8, 1780, Aged 69.

Also Nicholas, their Son, who died June 22, 1806, Aged 61.

In the Vault beneath are deposited the Remains of Samuel Watton, Brazier, of this Town, who Departed this life April 21st, 1818, Aged 53 years.

Also of Freelove Watton, wife of the above-mentioned Samuel Watton, who departed this life August 23d, 1819, Aged 58 years.

Also of Freelove Watton, their daughter, who departed this life June 20th, 1808, Aged 17 years.

Also of Edward Wynne Watton, their Son, who died in Infancy.

Against South Wall of South Aisle.

A Table of the Benefactors to the Poor of the Liberty of Trowbridge.

		£.
1611.	Mr. John Hawkins gave	20.
	Mr. Wm. Wallis, of London, gave	20.
	Mr. Edward Wallis gave	10.
1661.	Mr. Ezekiel Wallis gave	10.
	Mr. Anthony Shephard gave	5.
	Mr. Robert Whitchel gave	5.
	Mrs. Ann Whitchel gave	5.
	Mrs. Langford gave	10.
	Mrs. Mary Langford gave	3.
	Mr. Buckel gave	2.
	Mr. Edward Davis gave	40.
1687.	Mrs. Margaret Davis gave	10.

1692. Henry Wallis, Esq. gave £.50, the Profits thereof to 12 poor Housekeepers having no Relief (regard being had to his name & Relations) to be disposed of at the Nativity of our Saviour yearly for ever.

1700. Mr. John Davis gave £.10, the Profits thereof, together with the several sums above said, are to be distributed to the Poor of this Parish at the Nativity of our Saviour yearly for ever.

Mr. Robert Pinchen gave £.100, the profits thereof to 24 poor people, having no relief, to be distributed in Bread weekly for ever.

1753.

A Table of the Benefactions to the Poor of this Parish of Trowbridge.

1731. Thos. Cooper, of Stowford, Gent. gave £.50 to the Poor of this Parish, the Profits thereof to be distributed yearly of the feast of St. Thomas the Apostle for ever.

1736. Mr. Wm. Temple gave £.20 to the Poor of the Parish of Trowbridge, the Profits to be distributed yearly on the Twelfth Day for Ever.

1773. Wm. Temple, Gent. Son to the preceding, bequeathed to the Poor of the Parish of Trowbridge Twenty Pounds, the Profits whereof are to be Distributed annually according to the Discretion of the Parish Officers and principal Inhabitants among such as receive no parochial relief, at Christmas for ever.

A Table of the Benefactors to the Poor of the Liberty of Trowbridge.

Mrs. Ann Wallis gave £.20, the Profits thereof to be disposed of as the Gift of her Father. 1693.

1698. Mr. Henry, Mr. Edward, & Mr. William Yerbury, Erected an Alms-House in this Parish for the support of Six poor Widdows having no Relief, and Endowed it with £.22 Yearly for Ever.

1704. Mr. Richard Singer gave £.120, the Profits thereof to Six poor Housekeepers constantly frequenting this Church, having no relief, to be disposed of in Bread weekly for ever.

1721. Mrs. Ann Wallis, Relict of Henry Wallis, Esq. gave £.30 to the Poor of this Parish, the Profits thereof to be disposed of in the same manner as that given by her Husband.

1724. Mr. James Singer gave £.200, the yearly Interest whereof is to pay for the education of Ten poor Boys of this Parish for ever.

1730. Mr. Richard Shrapnell gave £.20 the yearly Interest whereof is to pay for the Education of one poor Boy of this Parish for ever.

1752.

In the south window is some painted glass.

North Aisle.

1802, Jan. 7. John Clarke, of this Town, Esq. by his Will of this Date gave Fifty Guineas, the Interest thereof to be given away in Bread Annually on Christmas Day to such poor persons as the Churchwardens and Overseers shall think most deserving of the same.

He also gave one Hundred Guineas towards the erection of an Organ in this Church, and (as soon as the Organ shall be erected) he directed that his Executors should transfer to the Churchwardens four hundred pounds, Five per Cent. Stock, the Dividends to be by them Annually paid to an Organist.

Thos. Dundee,
Of this Town, Gentleman, who gave Two Hundred pounds to compleat the above Organ.

The Church consists of Chancel, Nave, and North and South Aisles. The Nave on each side is supported by five pointed arches, resting on light pillars.

Trowbridge Register began 30 Oct. 1538.
The Rev. George Crabbe, Rector.
Thos. Timbrell, Esq. Lord of the Manor.

HILPERTON.

On a Monument against the north wall of Chancel.

To the Memory of Mrs. Elizabeth Chapman, who Departed this life July 17th, 1780, Aged 66 years.

Also of James Chapman, Gent. many years of this Parish, who Departed this life June 21, 1785, Aged 52 years.

He was an affectionate Husband, a tender Parent, and a sincere Friend.

Also to the Memory of Sarah, his Wife, who, after many years painful illness, which she bore with Christian Fortitude and Resignation, exchanged this mortal life for Immortality Jan. 29, 1801, Aged 55 years.

East End of the Church.

Near this Place lyeth the Body of John Slade, who departed this life Sept. 17, 1669.

148

Flat Stone.

Here lies Mr. John Palmer.
Mrs. B. P. N. and Child.

Mr. John P. died June 13, 1776, Aged 74.
Julia died in her 7 year.
Mrs. died March 16, 1793, Aged 69.
Peace in Christ, &c. 1793.

On a Brass Plate.

Here lieth interred the Body of Mr. John Fido, Rector of this Parish, who Departed this life 24 Day of June, 1723, in the 52 year of his Age.

Be ye also ready, for in such an hour as ye think not the Son of man cometh. St. Mat. xxiv. 44.

Register began in 1694.—Rev. Mr. Innes Rector.

STAVERTON.

Against the South Wall of Nave.

Near this small but sacred Monument resteth Jane, the beloved Wife of Stephen Smith, who Departed this Life Jan. 18, 1778, Aged 32 years.

A faithful Friend, a Wife most dear,
A tender Mother buried here;
Great is the loss that we sustain,
But Christ hath made our loss her gain.

Here also lyeth two of her Children, who died in their Infancy.

Also Jane, Daughter of the above, who died Sept. 1st, 1778, Aged 7 years.

Also Mary, Daughter of the above, who died March 20th, 1798, Aged 24 years.

Also Stephen Smith, who died April the 18, 1801, Aged 63 years.

Blessed are the Dead which die in the Lord. Revelations, Chap. xiv. Verse 13.

Also in the same Vault resteth the Remains of Sarah, the Wife of James Smith, (and Daughter of Richard and Sarah Pocock, of Allington) who Departed this life March the 28, 1804, Aged 36 years.

The bloom of her days, and the vigour of her life, She always directed to her best, her everlasting interest.

WINSLEY.

On Flat Stones in Chancel.

Under this Tomb lies the Remains of Martha and William Percy, they both died Children.

.... Body of ...... Clarke, who departed this life the 12 day of August, 1677.

Also Here lyeth the Body Henry Redman, Juner, who Departed this life the 8 Day of April, 1692.

Here Lyeth the Body of Elisabeth Parker, who Departed this life April 27th, 1752, Aged 55.

In Memory of Joseph, Son of Joseph and Jane Viles, who died July the 19th, 1775, Aged 8 years.

In Memory of Mary, Wife of William Morris. She Departed this life January ye 2nd, 1773, Aged 82 years.

Also in Memory of William Morris, Yeoman. He Departed this life July ye 8th, in the year of our Lord 1773, Aged 83 years.

Both in full age wee here doth lie,
If thou art ould prepare to die;
If thou art young prepare also,
When death do come, then thou must go.

Also in Memory of Mary, Wife of Isaac Alland, and Daughter of William and Mary Morris. She Departed this life January 9, 1791, Aged 67 years.

Against the North Wall of Nave.

In Memory of John Wilshere, who died March the 9th, 1734, Aged 46 years.

In bed of Clay I sleep with joy,
From care and labour free;
When Christ doth call, arise I shall,
And Death no more shall see.

Also near this Monument is Interr'd ye Body of Jane, Relict of the aforesaid John Wilshere, who died July 5th, 1753, Aged 66 years.

To the Deare Memory of Michael Tidcombe, Jane his Wife, and Jane his Daughter. Michael was buried January the 28, 1658; Jane, his Wife, Departed the 31 of March, 1658; Jane, his Daughter, was buried February the 10th, 1663.

These near related Friends whom death did sever,
By death Jehovah now hath brought together;
These near this place shall rest, till all returne
Their borrowed dust back to the fatall urne.

South Wall.

To the Memory of Thomas Baker, Yeoman. He Dy'd October ye 13th, A. D. 1727, Aged 41 years.

Remember, you that passeth by,
That you one day must surely dy;
Therefore with speed prepare for death
Before ye Lord demands your breath.

To the Memory of Jane, ye Wife of Thomas Baker, Yeoman, who Departed this life February the 19th, A° 17$\frac{21}{22}$, Ætatis suæ 39.

As day doth pass, and night do come,
Our lives do fade away ;
Let every one think on the Lord
While they on Earth do stay.

On a Flat Stone in Nave.

Here lyeth the Body of Richard Druce, who was buried the 30th Day of May, . . Dom. 1708.

Hatchments.

Argent, a chevron, gules, between three crosslets fitchy of the same, issuing out of as many . . . . heads couped, vert: impaling, Long.

The same as the preceding—impaling quarterly, first and fourth sable, a lion rampant between eight crosslets fitchey, argent: second and third per pale, 1st, paly of five, argent and sable, 2d, azure.

Crest—A demi buck, erect and regardant, argent, on an esquire's helmet.

Register began in 1724.

Rev. Mr. Blumsberg present Rector.

LIMPLEY STOKE.

On Monuments against North Wall of Chancel.

In Memory of Susanna, Wife of John Cooper, and Daughter of George Dike, Gent. She died 25th April, 1720, Aged 27.

Near this Place lie the Remains of Henry Fisher, Esq. who died July 10, 1795, Aged 41 years.

Also the Remains of Mary, Wife of the above Henry Fisher, Esq. and Mother to the under-named Children, who Departed this life Nov. 16th, 1816, Aged 57.

She was a kind and Affectionate Wife, a fond and most tender Parent, a good Christian, and a sincere Friend.

In the same Grave lie the Remains of George Robert Dyke Fisher, Son of the above-named Henry Fisher, and Mary, his Wife, who died June 11th, 1800, Aged 5 years.

Also of their Daughter Mary Susannah Fisher, who died Feb. 10th, 1806, Aged 23 years.

Also of their Daughter Elizabeth Fisher, who died August 4th, 1814, Aged 24 years.

Arms—A chevron between three birds.

East End.

The other Side of this Wall lyeth the Body of John Morgan, who died Oct. 28th, 1764, Aged 78 years. Clark of this Parish 46 years.

Also Eleanor, Wife of John Morgan, who died March the 27th, 1757, Aged 65 years.

In the Churchyard, behind this Wall, lie the Remains of John Morgan, who Departed this life Dec. 21st, 1788, Aged 35 years.

He was a Dutiful Son, an Affectionate Husband, A tender Father, and a Sincere Friend.

South Wall.

Near this Place lieth Ann Dike, Daughter of Thomas and Mary Dike, of Limpley Stoke, Gent. and Wife of George Dike, Esq. died July the 5th, 1776, Aged 61 years.

Also George Dike, Esq. Son of Richard and Ann Dike, of Water House, Gent. died Nov. 16th, 1783, Aged 73 years.

On a Flat Stone in Chancel.

Underneath lies the Body of Susanna Langley, Daughter of Robert and Mary Langley, of Water House, who died the 13th Day of December, 1786, Aged 17 months.

Robert Langley, Esq. died August 29th, 1815, Aged 67 years.

Mary Langley, who died Feb. 26th, 1820, Aged 73 years.

On a Brass Plate.

Here lyeth the Body of Ann Dike, the most loving and Beloved Wife of George Dike, Esq. Daughter and Heiress of Thomas Dike, Esq. and Mary, his Wife. She died 5th July, 1776, in the 61 year of her Age.

Also George Dike, Esq. Son and Heire of Richard Dike, Esq. and Ann, his Wife, of Water House. He died 16th Nov. 1783, Aged 73 years.

Against the North Wall of Nave.

Against ye foundation lyeth ye Body of John Dike, Son of George Dike, Gent. and Ann, his Wife, who Departed Feb. ye 22d, 1708.

Also ye Body of Ann Dike, Wife of George Dike, Gent. who Dyed Oct. ye 23, 1718.

Pray let not our Bones be removed.

South Wall of Nave.

Sacred to the Memory of Sarah, Wife of John Heals, who died December 19th, 1812, Aged 64 years.

Also Mr. John Heals, of. Lymply Stoke, who died May 7th, 1816, Aged 71.

The Rev. Mr. Blumberg Rector.

George Dike Fisher, Esq. Lord of the Manor.

WINKFIELD.

On Monuments against the north wall of Chancel.

Near this Place lie the Bodies of Mr. Thomas Cooper, and Ann, his beloved Wife. He was an eminent Clothier, first at Trowbridge, and afterwards at Stowford, in this Parish, where he lived many years retired from Business. They lived vertuously, and died piously: the former the 2d day of May, 1731, Aged 80 years, the Latter the 5th Day of June, 1707, Aged 55 years.

Also of John, their Grand Child, second Son of John Cooper, of Trowbridge, Esq. who died the 1st Day of July, 1714, Aged 3 months.

They had three Sons, Thomas, John, and Thomas; the first died very young, the last, Aged 22 years, at Oriel Colledge, in Oxford, in the year 1706, where he lies Interred.

John, the Survivor, erected this Monument, as a pious testimony of his Gratitude to his well-beloved Parents, and Affection to his dear Child and Brothers.

Arms—Or, a saltire azure, on a chief of the last three leopards' heads caboshed or, crowned argent.

Sacred to the Memory of Jane, Wife of Thos. Morris, Esq. of this Parish, who Departed this life January 11th, 1818, in the 71st year of her Age.

Against south wall of Chancel.

Sacred to the Memory of the Rev. Edward Spencer, who, during 56 years, (43 years of which were spent by him as Rector of this Parish) sustained the Character of a faithful and enlightened Minister of Jesus Christ. In the bosom of his Family, and among those who had the happiness to share with that Family the benefit of his Instruction and Example, the Remembrance of his amiable Virtues, his Piety, his Integrity, his Benevolence, his Humility, and his Resignation, will be long and affectionately cherished; supported to the last by that Redeemer whose Grace, through life, it was his Constant exertion to display. He died February 9th, 1819, in the 80th year of his Age.

As a Testimony of Respect and gratitude to the Guide and Friend of their early years, his Pupils have caused this Tablet to be erected.

Beneath this Monument are deposited the Remains of John Cooper, of Comberwell, in the County of Wilts. Esq. a Gentleman many years in the Commission of the Peace, who, by great Experience, and constant Application, was, in the Discharge of his Office, Inferior to few, Superior to many, and to his Country a most useful Magistrate.

In the same Vault lies Interred Sarah, the Wife of the said John Cooper, Esq. She was Daughter and Sole Heiress of Thomas Roberts, of Cirencester, in the County of Gloucester, Gent. She died 24th June, 1741, Aged 50. He February 1st, 1748, Aged 69.

Arms—Or, a saltire, azure, on a chief of the same, three leopards' heads caboshed or, crowned argent.

Crest—A demi leopard rampant proper, holding in his paw a trefoil argent, crowned or.

Against the North Wall of Nave.

Here under lieth the Body of Christopher Baylie, Esquire, who deceased ye 2th Day of April, An. Dõ 1663.

H. R. I. P.

Hic requiescit in pace

D. M. S.

Dormivnt Mortui Securi.

Arms—Three horses' heads couped: impaling three battle-axes.

Against the South Wall of Nave.

Neare unto this Place Lyeth the Body of John Bayley, of Phillipps Norton, in ye County of Somerset, Gentleman, who Deceased this life ye 24 Day of October, Anõ Dñi 1665, And Youngest Sonn to Robert Bayley, of Winckfield, in the County of Wilts. Gent. and of Christian, his Wife, who was Daughter to John Arnall, of the Parrish of Ilsington, in ye County of Dorset, Esq.

Arms—Or, on a fess ingrailed azure three fleur-de-lis or, between as many horses' heads couped sable, martlet for difference, or.

Huic vicina marmori terrâ conduntur reliquiæ Eduardi Wadman, nuper hujus Parochiæ incolæ; fuit eximæ morum suavitatis, benevolentiæ, probitatis vir, talibus insignitis virtutibus humanum genus, et fovit, et ornavit, suis precipuè carus, nulli non flebilis, naturæ concessit die vicesimo 2do Febr: A. D. 1742, Annos Natus quinquaginta et duos.

In Memory of Captain John Wadman, of this Parish, who died the 2d day of August, 1806, Aged 75 years.

On Flat Stone in Nave.

Here Lyeth the Body of Henry Noble, who Departed this life December the 1st, A. D. 1732, Aged 60 years.

Also neare this Place lyeth the Body of Ann, the Wife of Henry Noble, who Departed this life May the 21st, A. D. 1738, Aged about 30 years.

Against the Gallery.

Mr. Richard Bissie, of Pumbery, gave four Pounds yearly for Putting out a Poor Boy, an Apprentice, belonging to this Parish.

Mr. Thomas Cooper, of Stowford, Gave two Pounds yearly to the Poor of this Parish, not receiving Alms, to be paid every St. Thomas Day.

Hatchment under the Tower.

Or, a saltire azure, on a chief of the last three leopards' heads caboshed or, crowned argent; impaling sable, two bars ermine, on a chief sable, three cross pattee, or.

Over the South Entrance.

Under the Stone, as you enter ye Porch, lyeth ye Body of John Bissie, the Sonne of John Bissie, and Edith his Wife, who ended this life the 25th of October, An° 1622, Ætat. 24.

Outside, on the south wall.

Erected Anno Dom̃ 1687, By Sr James Tillie, Kt, to the Memory of his Ancestours, who, in this Parish, lived Vertuously, & died Piously, and lie Interred under the Two Opposite Tombe Stones, Viz. Under the nearest Stone John Tillie the Elder, and Mary his Wife, and Severall of their Children; And under the remotest Stone, John Tillie the Younger, and Susanna his Wife, and Severall of their Children.

Register commenced in the year 1654.

The Rev. Thomas Spencer Rector.

EDINGTON.

On Flat Stones in Chancel.

M. S.

Dni Jacobi Lewis, Richardi Lewis, Armigeri, Et Mariæ Uxoris, Optimæ Spei Filij, qui fato concessit 20° die mar. A° Dñi 1680, Æt. 9°.

Ingenio qui vicit avos vernante parentum, deliciæ generis spes, stupor astq. decvs, Parcarum inuidia teneris hic conditur annis, raro fit vir, qui noluit esse puer, non quantus, sed qualis erat deposæ, Viator, Corpore si parvus, maximus ingenio.

In Memoriam suavissimi ingenii Speiq. eximiæ pueri è nobili prosapia Eduardi, filii Ricardi Lewis, Armigeri, et Mariæ, uxoris ejus, parentes hoc posuerunt mœrentes, qui natus Apr: die 23, 1668, Denatus Feb: 13, 1670.

Dormit in hoc pulcher puer ore et mente Cubili,
Dum Sol justitia suscitet ortus eum.

Here Lyeth the Body of Anne Lewis, Daughter of Richard Lewis, Esq. & Mary His Wife, who was Borne the 8th of Octob. in the yeare of our Lord 1672, And Departed this life the 21st of September, 1673.

Here lyeth ye Body of Elizabeth Lewis, Daughter of Richard Lewis, Esq. and Mary, his Wife, who was born the 6th of Dec̃ in ye yeare of our Lord 1675, & Departed this life ye 11th of February, 1676.

Here Lyeth the Body of Lady Catharine Powlett, Wife of the Rt. Honble Lord Harry Powlett, who died April 23d, 1744, Aged 49 years.

C. L. Roots, July 12th, 1795.

On a Monument in Chancel.

Heere lye the Bodyes of the Right Wor: Sr Edward Lewys, late of the Vane, in the Countie of Glamorgan, Knt, one of the Gentlemen of the privie Chamber to Prince Henry, and after to King Charles, And of the Right Honble Anne, Lady Beauchampe, his Wife, the Widowe of Edward Lorde Beauchampe, Daughter of Robert, Earl of Dorset, by the Lady Margaret Howard, sole daughter of Thomas, Duke of Norfolke. They had Issue lyving fower Sonnes, Edward, William, Richard, and Robert, and one Daughter, Anne Lewys.

He departed this Life the 10th of October, 1630, in Memorie of Whome his Mournefull Lady Erected this Monument for him and her Selfe, whoe Deceased the 25th of September, 1664.

Round the edges of the Tomb.

Since Children are the living Corner-Stone
Where Marriage built on both sides meetes in one,
Whilst they survive, our life's shall have extent
Upon record in them, our Monument.

[On this Monument are lying the statues of the Knight and his Lady: the former is in armour, his hands meeting on his breast, a pillow under his head, and his feet resting on a lion; his Lady lying beside him, a leopard at her feet. On the north side of this Tomb are the figures of three males and two females, kneeling.]

Arms—Quarterly, first sable, a lion rampant argent, armed gules: second sable, a chevron between three fleur-de-lis argent; third gules, three chevrons argent; fourth sable, a chevron between three spear heads argent, pointed gules: impaling quarterly, first and fourth or, second and third gules, over all a bend vair, argent, and azure.

152

On a Brass Plate without the Rails.

Here lyeth ye Body of Mrs. Elizth Bayley, Daughter of Thos. Bayley, Gen. of ye Mieth, in ye Par. of Atherston, in ye County of Leicester, & Servant to Madã Lewis, who Departed this life ye 9th of August, Anno Domi 1691.

Here lyeth the Body of John Allambrigge, sometime Chaplaine to the right honorable Anne, Lady Beauchamp, who dyed June ye 15th, 1663.

On Monuments against the south-west Pillar of the Tower.

Near this Place Lieth the Remains of George Tayler, Esq. and Ann his Wife. She died March 3d, 1808, Aged 60 years, He died Feb. 14th, 1816, in the 74th year of his Age.

This Monument is erected to the Memory of William Long, Esq. who Departed this life at Baynton House June the 10th, 1807, Aged 73 years.

Arms—Long: impaling a fess between three fleur-de-lis.

N. E. Pillar.

Sacred to the Memory of Emma Long, only Child of William Long, of Baynton, Esq. and Mary, his Wife. She was born May 7th, 1794, and departed this life January 6th, 1796.

Sweet Innocent, of fondest hope, thus early taken from thy disconsolate parents, leaving them to lament a blessing that promised every future excellence.

Near this Place lieth the Body of John Long, late of Baynton, in this Parish, Esq. who departed this life the 19th day of May, in the year of our Lord 1746, Aged 54 years.

Arms—Quarterly, first and fourth Long: second and third quarterly, first and fourth argent, second and third gules, over the whole a

---

Against S. Wall of Nave.

To the Memories of Richard, James, and Ann, Sons and Daughter of Richard and Argentine Ellis, of Hurst, in this Parish. Richard died Sept. 3d, 1779, Aged 10 years; James died March 20th, 1775, Aged 8 months; Ann died Sept. 23d, 1777, Aged 18 months.

Also to the Memory of Richard Ellis, who died Sept. ye 25, 1780, Aged 53 years.

For whom the Lord loveth he chasteneth, and scourgeth every son whom he receiveth. Hebrews 12th, V. 6th.

Also to the Memory of Mr. Roger Mattick, Gent. Obiit Jan. 11th, 1788, Ætatis 84.

West End of Nave.

Near this Place lyeth the Body of James Baldwin, of Edington, who died the 1st of March, 1764, Aged 35 years.

Also in Memory of Elizabeth, Wife of James Baldwin, who Departed this life the 11th Day of Nov. 1786, in the 77 year of her Age.

Near this Place lieth the Body of Mary Eliz. Wife of Roger Carter, who died June 20, 1769, Aged 69 years.

Also in Memory of Roger Carter, who died April 14th, 1787, in the 82 year of his Age.

Near this Place lyeth the Bodies of Wm. Tayler, Yeoman, and also Robert, his Son. Robert died Feb. ye 20th, 1762, Aged 31 years.

William Tayler, died Sept. ye 13th, 1762, Aged 66 years.

Also underneath in the same Grave Lyeth the remains of Mary, Wife of William Tayler, who departed this life June the 16th, 1781, in the 77 year of her Age. Also underneath Lyeth the Remains of Susanna, Daughter of William and Mary Tayler, who Departed this life Dec. the 16th, 1810, Aged 62 years.

On Flat Stones in Nave.

In Memory of Richard Ellis, Sen. of Hurst, in this Parish. He Departed this life June ye 28, 1769, Aged 72.

Also in Memory of Sarah, his Wife, Richard Ellis, who departed this life ye 16th, 1775, Aged 75 years.

In Memory of John Hooper, and Elizth his Wife. He died . . . . . 1749, Aged 78, She died . . . . 1762, Aged 88.

Here lyeth the Body of Hanna, Wife of Thomas Wells, who Departed this life the . . . . of June, 1713.

Under this Stone lies the Remains of Edward Froud, who departed this life Feb. the 13th, 1756, in the 32 year of his Age.

Here lies ye Body of Robert, ye 4th Son of Edward Froud, Gent. and Eliz. his Wife. He dy'd January ye 4th, 171 $\frac{4}{5}$, Aged 29.

In Memory of Thomas Froud, who died Sep. ye 9th, 1733, Aged 52.

Also in Memory of Sarah, his Wife, who died June ye 8th, 1749, Aged 67.

In Memory of Elizabeth Froud, who Departed this life May the 18th, 1760, Aged 45 years.

Also in Memory of Thomas Hurn Froud, who departed this life January the 28th, 1762, Aged 17 years.

Sub hoc lapide Corpus Johannis, Eduardi Froud, Generosi, et Elizabethæ, uxoris ejus, Filii Secundi, tumulatum jacet. Qui obijt die Novembris 17°, Anno Dom̄ 1712°, Ætat. suæ 35°.

In Memory of Ann, Wife of John Froud, who died Sept. ye 18, 1765, Aged 48 years.

Also in Memory of Betty, Second Wife of John Froud, who died July the 13th, 1786, Aged 47 years.

Siste, Vistor,
Et sub hoc lapide
Qui . . . l mortale habuit depositu dilectus
Viri, . . . re reverendi Eduardi Froud:
Qualis fuit si quæras
Eximi . . . . Deum pietate,
Amore in Conjugem,
In Liberos Charitate,
In Amic . . Fide,
In cunctos B . . . . . . Humanita
Clarum . . . to
et Exemplar imitare,
. . . ter vivos esse desiit 10
Calandas Decembris, A. D. 1714, Ætat. suæ 69.

In Memory of John Froud, who died June ye 11th, 1777, Aged 66 years.

In Memory of John, Son of Ralph Hooper, who died July 8, 1752.

Here Lyeth ye Body of John, Son of John and Jane Pryor, who died Jan. ye 19th, 1760, Aged 92.

Here lyeth ye Body of Mrs. Elizabeth Grey, who Departed this life Decem. 17th, 1697, Aged 34 years.

Also here lyeth ye Body of Mr. John Grey, who Departed this life May 21, 172· Aged 67 years.

M. S.

Here lie Interred the Body of Susanna Pencutt, who died Feb. the 19th, 1798, Aged 12 years.

Here Lyeth ye Body of George Gilbert, who dyed January ye 1, 1710.

In Memory of Thomas Read, who died Jan. ye 30th, 1749, Aged 62.

Also in Memory of Mary, his Wife, who died Feb. 4th, 1749, Aged 52.

M. S.

Here lies Interred the Body of Thos. Nash, who died Oct. 4th, 1787, Aged 62 years.

Also of Mary, the Wife of Thos. Nash, who died January 1st, 1806, Aged 82 years.

In Memory of Mr. Stephen Webb, and his Daughter Betty, who died in her Infancy.

Also Elizabeth, his Wife, who Departed this life ye 2d day of April, 1754, Ætat. 60 years.

West End of North Aisle.

In Memory of Mary, Daughter of Martin, and Anamoriah Tayler, who died Sep. ye 13th, 1769, Aged 1 year 2 months.

Brass Plate.

John Long, Esq. Ob. 24 June, 1721, Ætatis 57.

Here lyeth ye Body of Thomas Woollam, Gent. who Departed this life the 15th of March, in ye Year of or Lord 1708, Aged 67 years.

On a Monument in North Transept.

Near this Place are deposited the Remains of Sarah Price, only Daugh of Edward Price, of Tinhead-Court, in this Parish.

Come, Resignation! wipe the human tear;
Domestick, anguish droops o'er virtue's bier:
Bid selfish sorrow hush the fond complaint,
Nor from the God she lov'd detain the saint.
Truth, Meekness, Patience, honor'd Shade! were thine,
And holy Hope, and Charity divine;
Tho' these thy forfeit being could not save,
Thy Faith subdu'd the terrors of the grave.
Oh! if thy living Excellence could teach,
Death has a loftier Emphasis of Speech;
In Death thy last best lesson still impart,
And write, Prepare to die, on every Heart.

She died March the 23d, 1799, Aged 27 years.

She being dead, yet speaketh. Heb. xi. 4.

Also near this place are deposited the Remains of Edward Price, who died March 30th, 1806, in the 63 year of his Age.

The Lord gave, and the Lord hath taken away, blessed be the name of the Lord.

Arms—Gules, a griffin sejant or, between three fleur-de lis, argent.

Flat Stones in North Transept.

Here lyeth the Body of Robert Bisse, Gent. He departed this life the 31st day of July, in the year of our Lord God 1690.

Mr. Christopher Gardiner was buried March the 2, 1666.

. . . avis, his Wife was buried Sept. the 25, 1693.

Here lyeth ye Body of Bridgeat, wife of John Gardiner, Gent. who Departed May 10, 1689.

Also here lyeth ye Body of John Gardiner, late of Tinhead, Gent. who Departed Oct. ye 5, 1720, Ætat. suæ 76.

Here lyeth the Body of Wm. Tubb, sometime Servant to the Right Honourable Lady Ann Beauchamp, who Gave to the Poor of this Parish Fifty Pounds. Out of a Gratefull Respect to whose Memory, the Church Wardens, J. H. and W. E. have laid this Stone on his dust and ashes. He departed this life June ye 20, An. Dō 1650.

Here lyeth ye Body of Charles Read, who was Interred ye 9th day of Jan. 1722, Aged 21 years.

James, the Son of Thomas Read, Jun. was interred ye 27th of April, 1719, Aged 22 years.

In Memory of John Nash, who died Jan. ye 19th, 1764, Aged 71 years.

Here lyeth ye Body of Thomas, ye Sonn of John Gardiner, who depd this life ye 2d day of March 1688.

On Flat Stones in South Transept.

In Memory of Jinneverah, Daur of James and Jane Pepler, who died Decem. 6, 1769, Aged 6 years.

In Memory of Ann, Daughter of James and Jane Pepler, who died Feb. 24th, 1722, Aged 1 year.

Also underneath are deposited the Remains of James Pepler, who died August 13th, 1789, Aged 62 years.

Underneath this Stone lyeth the Remains of Mary Pepler Spencer, Daughter of James and Jane Pepler. She died May 16, 1791, Aged 34 years.

Here lyeth the Body of Stephen Mills, who died September the 2d, A. D. 1729, in the 87 year of his Age.

In this Transept, on an altar-tomb of free stone, is a statue lying, with his feet resting against a small barrel. There is no inscription.

The Church consists of Chancel, Nave, North and South Aisles, and North and South Transepts. The Nave is supported on each side by six pointed arches.

Between the first and second pillars from the east end of the Nave, on the south side, is an Altar Tomb, there is no inscription, and the brass figures taken out.

Arms—Quarterly, first and fourth in fess five fusils charged with as many escallop shells; second and third a cross moline.

G. W. Tayler, Esq. Lord of the Manor.

STRATTON ST. MARGARET.

In the Churchyard, East End.

Head Stones.

To the Memory of Richard Lester, Sen. who died August 17th, 1789, Aged 44 years.

Also Elizth his Wife, who died July 27th, 1789, Aged 71 years.

To the Memory of Richard Lester, jun. who died Feb. 27th, 1814, Aged 67 years.

Thy Pains are ended, and thy sorrow's o'er,
But joy shall visit my sad heart no more:
Man's life! what is it? 'Tis a Flower,
Looks fresh, and dies within an Hour:
How frail is Man, how short his breath,
In Midst of life we are in death;
Here is a Proof, here he doth lie,
May Grace prepare, and then we're fit to die.

Mary-Artiax Highett, Daughter of Philip and Sarah Highett, died 29th of June, 1773, Aged 1 year.

Flat Tomb.

To the Memory of John, Son of John and Mary Lea, who died March 17th, 1765, Aged 17 years.

To the Memory of John Lea, who died December 18, 1781, Aged 69 years.

Also Mary, his Wife, who died Feb. 16th, 1782, Aged 63 years.

Head Stones.

To the Memory of John Fairthorn, who departed this life the 1st of Dec. 1811, Aged 66.

Also Mary, his Wife, who Departed this life the 13th of Jan. 1792, Aged 38 years.

Here lyeth Mary, Daughter of Richard and Hannah Hyde. She died July 10th, 1744.

To the Memory of Gabriel Hyde, who died June 1st, 1745, Aged 63 years.

Also Sarah, his Wife, who died Sept. 9th, 1747, Aged 63 years.

In Memory of Mary, Daughter of Wm. & Ann Jones, who died July 15, 1741, Aged 7 years.

Flat Tombs.

To the Memory of Mary, Daughter of John and Sarah Iles, who died June 8, 1811, Aged 14 years.

With Patience to the last she did submit,
And murmured not at what the Lord thought fit;
She, with a Christian courage, did resign
Her Soul to God at his appointed time.

To the Memory of John Isles, who died Dec. 21st, 1802, Aged 40 years.

May my Dear Wife and Children
This Path of Virtue tread,
May Heavenly Grace protect them
Whilst I lay Sleeping with the Dead.

To the Memory of John Jones, who died Nov. 17th, 1788, Aged 57 years.

Also James, the Son of John and Martha Jones, who died in his Infancy.

To the Memory of Martha, Wife of John Jones, eldest Daughter of John and Mary Lea, who died August 21st, 1796, Aged 52 years.

To the Memory of Jane, the Wife of Wm. Dore, who Departed this life the 22 of August, 1810, Aged 28 years.

Head Stones.

In Memory of Sarah, Wife of Morris Toms, who died August 23rd, 1745, Aged 66.

In Memory of Morris Toms, who died June 27, 1746, Aged 66.

Sarah, the Wife of Robert Panting, and Daughter of Morris and Sarah Toms, who died June 7th, 1747, Aged 36 years.

Elizabeth, Wife of John Edmonds, died Dec. ye 21st, 1726, Aged 58 years.

Flat Tomb.

In Memory of John Edmonds, Sen. who died Oct. ye 11th, 1738, Aged 64 years.

Also Elizabeth, Wife of John Edmonds, who died Dec. ye 21st. 1726, Aged 58 years.

Head Stones.

To the Memory of Elizabeth, Wife of Edward Wakefield, who died May 8th, 1751, Aged 59 years.

In Memory of Mary, Daughter of Edward and Eliz. Wakefield, who died May 31, 1754, Aged 19 years.

In Memory of Edward Wakefield, who died April 25th, 1771, Aged 84 years.

In Memory of Sarah, the Wife of Wm. Wakefield, who died June 20th, 1767, Aged 27 years.

Here Lyeth the Body of Mary, the Wife of Robert Panting, who died April ye 8th, 1750, Aged 50 years.

Richard Humphreys his Body lyeth near this Place.

Here lyeth ye Body of Richard Jay, who died Feb. 16, 1706, Aged 22 years.

In Memory of Wm. Angell, who died Oct. 25th, 1792, Aged 79 years.

Also Sarah, Wife of Wm. Angell, who died June 9th, 1784, Aged 70 years.

To the Memory of Martha Bizley, Widow of John Bizley, who Departed this life July 31st, 1786, Aged 67 years.

In Memory of John Bizley, who died April 20, 1763, Aged 42 years.

In Memory of Mary, Daughter of Thos. and Mary Bizley, who died Sept. 14th, 1791, Aged 36 years.

Frances, Wife of Richard Savage, died Jan. ye 8th, 1750, Aged 25 years.

Here lyeth ye Body of John Poynton, who departed this life September ye 3d, A.D. 1669.

Nathaniel Bizley died Dec. ye 8th, 1750, Aged 65 years.

In Memory of Ann, Wife of Nathaniel Bizley, who died Sept, 5th, 1770, Aged 74 years.

Here Lyeth the Body of James Avrey, who departed this life July ye 20th, 1723. Aged 38 years.

Also of Mary, his Wife, who Departed this life Jan. 2, 1768, Aged 86 years.

In Memory of Mr. Richard Avery, who died Dec. 20th, 1770.

Here lyeth ye Body of Catharine, Wife of John Avery, who Departed this life Feb. ye 13th, A. D. 1718, Aged 71 years.

In Memory of Robt. Avery, who died August 25th, 1733, Aged 65 years.

Here lieth ye Body of John Avery, who was Buried August 24, 1775, Aged 75 years.

Also Mary, his Wife, who was buried Feb, 15, 1774, Aged 70 years.

Flat Tomb.

Elizth, Wife of Tobias Salt, sen. died Feb. 24th, 1727, Aged 75 years.

Ann, the Wife of Robert Salt, died Feb. the 12, 1743, Aged 53 years.

In Memory of Robert Salt, who died Jan. 11th, 1753, Aged 59 years.

Tobias, Son of Robert & Ann Salt, who died Jan. 29th, 1753, Aged 35 years.

In Memory of Tobias Salt, who Died Oct. ye 16, A. D. 1719, Aged 75 years.

Tobias, ye Son of Tobias Salt. He died Nov. ye 5th, A. D. 1719, Aged 37 years.

Joon, ye Son of Tobias Salt. He died Nov. ye 12, A. D. 1719, Aged 39 years.

In Memory of Joseph and Susanna, Children of Francis and Elizabeth Smith. Joseph died March 11th, 1739, Aged 1 year. Susannah dy'd May 7th, 1747, Aged 6 years.

Here lyeth ye Body of Richard Baker, who dyed the 8th Day of September, Anno Dom. 1686.

Here lyeth the Body of Robert Copland, he departed this life the 5th of December, 1674.

In Memory of William Copland, who departed this life Feb. 1st, 1761, Aged 97 years.

Here lyeth Wm. Son of Wm. & Eliz. Copland. He died August ye 11th, 1720, Aged 26 years.

Robt. Son of Wm. & Eliz. Copland died March 16, 1727, Aged 2 years.

Here lyeth ye Body of Eliz. Wife of Wm. Copland, who died April ye 14, 1730.

In Memory of Anthony Copland, who died May ye 1, 1738, Aged 35 years.

Here lyeth two Children of Anthony and Sarah Copland. Elizabeth died Aug. ye 8, 1741, Aged 4 years, Mary died Nov. ye 25th, 1741, Aged 3 years.

In Memory of Jemima, Daughter of John and Mary Brind, who died Nov. 4th, 1786, Aged 9 weeks.

In Memory of John Adams, who departed this life Aug. 4, 1762, Aged 65 years.

To the Memory of Sarah, Wife of Robert Hyde, who departed this life May the 22nd, 1809, Aged 37 years.

I was so long with pain opprest,
That wore my strength away,
It made me long for Endless Rest,
Which never can decay.
A kind good Wife, true Friend, and tender Mother,
What else the last Day clearly will discover.

In Memory of Ann, the Wife of Francis Panting, who died April 6th, 1769, Aged 68 years.

Francis Panting departed this life August ye 21, 1749, Aged 53 years.

Francis, Son of Francis and Ann Panting, dy'd August 15, 1749, Aged 22.

Here lyeth ye Body of Robt. ye Son of Robt. Copland, who died Sept. ye 2, 1728, Aged 74 years.

Here lyeth ye Body of John Herring, who Depd this life July ye 30th, 1725, Aged 70 years.

Head Stones.

Here lyeth ye Body of Thomas Jacksones, Sen. He Depd this life June the 17 Day, 1680.

Eliz. ye Wife of Thos. Archard, who died June ye 3d, 1722, Aged 62.

Here lyeth ye Body of John Herring. He died Oct. ye 6th, 1714, Aged 61 years.

Flat Tomb.

Here lyeth Margaret, Wife of Thos. Gray, who died Oct. 19, 1739, Aged 52 years.

Head Stones.

Here Lyeth ye Body of Mary, Wife of John Williams. She Departed this life Oct. ye 13th, 1722, Aged 58 years.

Here lyeth ye Body of Catharine, the Wife of Nicholas Smith, who departed this life Sept. 30, 1719.

In Memory of Richard More, who died May 5th, 1784, Aged 64 years.

A Friend so true, there were but few,
And difficult to find;
A man more just, & true to trust,
There is but few behind.

Hic jacet Joannæ, Uxor Henrici Munday, Filia Christopheri Joce, hujus parochiæ olim Vicari. Obijt 29no die Augustus, Anno Dom. 1694.

To the Memory of John Munday, who departed this life Feb. 10th, 1813, Aged 50 years.

Honest men we Seldom meet,
Here lies one beneath your feet:
Let it to the world be known
Thou art one who read'st this Stone.

Here lyeth ye Body of Thos. Butler, who died Dec. ye 24, 1712, Aged 48 years.

Here lyeth Hannah ye Wife of Roger Butler. She died May ye 31st, 1724, Aged 39 years.

Susanna, the Daughter of Roger Butler, was Buried Feb. 28, 1717, Aged 2 years and 3 months.

Mary, Daughter of Roger Butler, was Buried Nov. ye 22d, 1708, Aged 13 years.

In Memory of Thos. Smith, who died Nov. 21st, 1773, Aged 65 years.

Here lyeth the Body of Jane, ye Wife of Thomas Tomes. She died Feb. 2, 1710, Aged 59 years.

Here lyeth ye Body of Daniel, Son of Thos. Tomes, who died May 21, 1719, Aged 27 years.

In Memory of Richard Savage. Died March 6th, 1750, Aged 80.

Elizabeth, Wife of Thos. Cook, died Sept. ye 22, 1734, Aged 73 years.

Wm. Son of Thos. & Edith Cook, was buried Dec. ye 3, 1734, Aged 45 years.

Anna, Wife of William Archard, died July ye 9, 1736, Aged 40 years.

Martha, the Wife of Akerman Selby, Daughter of Thos. and Edey Cook, died March 7th, 1785, Aged 66.

In Memory of Curtis Lester, who died July 11th, 1765, Aged 51 years.

And also Sarah, his Wife, who died August 3d, 1766, Aged 51 years.

In Memory of Charles Tye, who died March 25, 1787, Aged 59 years.

Hear, Reader, be thy Age,
Or Station, what it may,
Improve thy precious time
Whilst it is call'd to-day:
Let not thy Soul now rest,
Nor do thou entertain
The pleasing hope of rest,
Till thou be born again.

Also Martha, Daughter of Charles and Mary Tye, who died April 25, 1771, Aged 17 years.

In Memory of Charles Tye, who died April 5th, 1801, Aged 75 years.

In Memory of Elizabeth, Wife of John Wilkins, who died Oct. 12, 1780, Aged 55 years.

A tender Mother, a faithful Consort here,
Lamented by her Friends and Children dear;
She died, but is not dead, for yet she lives
With God and Christ, Eternal life who gives;
Mourn not her loss, she's only gone before,
And strive to follow her to part no more.

To the Memory of Richard, Son of Richard and Ann Woolford, who died June 4, 1813, Aged 22 years.

To the Memory of Richard, Son of Richard and Ann Woolford, who Departed this life April 4th, 1790, Aged 2 years and 3 months.

Sacred to the Memory of Ann, Wife of Richard Woolford, who died Oct. 16th, 1793, Aged 34 years.

In Bloom the tender faithful Wife
Expir'd in bringing forth a Son,
In the same moment gave up life,
And lie lamented in this Tomb.

To the Memory of Richard, Son of Wm. and Susannah Jeeves, who died Jan. 7th, 1802, Aged 21 weeks, 5 days.

Also Ann, their Daughter, who died May 13, 1803, Aged 7 weeks.

When Children die in Infancy,
Like Flowers newly blown,
God that sent them, only Lent them,
And takes but what's his own.

Here lyeth ye Body of Moses Sadler. He died May ye 18, 1730, Aged 21 years.

Ann, Daughter of John and Mary Major, died Oct. 23, 1761, Aged 14 years.

Also three Children died young.

In Memory of Hannah, Daughter of Henry and Margaret Munday. She died Dec. 18, 1751, Aged 8 years.

In Memory of Henry Mundy, who died April 10th, 1765, Aged 59 years.

In Memory of Margaret, the Wife of Henry Mundy, who died Nov. 30th, 1758, Aged 52 years.

Wm. Son of John and Lydia Mundy, died Sep. 23, 1765, Aged 3 months.

To the Memory of Jonathan Baldwin, who Departed this life May the 30th, 1807, Aged 60 years.

To the Memory of John, Son of Jonathan and Margaret Baldwin, who died April the 24th, 1803, Aged 29 years.

Also Henry, their Son, who died Dec. the 7, 1800, Aged 18 years.

And also James, their Son, who died June the 27, 1793, Aged 10 years.

And three of their Children who died in their Infancy.

In Memory of John Gay, who died March 7th, 1784, Aged 70 years.

Also Mary Kemble, who died March 15th, 1784, Aged 70 years.

Also Hannah, Wife of John Gay, who died May 12, 1786, Aged 62 years.

Henry, Son of Jonathan and Margaret Baldwin, died July 8th, 1778, Aged 5 years.

To the Memory of Edward Carpenter, who Married Eliz. the Eldest Daughter of Henry and Margaret Mundy. He died Jan. 1st, 1755, Aged 27 years.

Sacred to the Memory of Hannah, wife of Edward Curtis, who Departed this life Sept. the 6, 1815, Aged 48 years.

The Frowns of the world are with her at an End,
Exchang'd for the Smiles of her Saviour and Friend,
Escap'd from the Regions of Sorrow and woe,
Affliction and Trouble no more she shall know.

In Memory of Edward Prior, who died Dec. 15, 1766, Aged 66 years.

Also Ann, his Wife, who died August 28, 1781, Aged 84 years.

North Side.

In Memory of Hannah, Wife of Robert Hyde, and Grandaughter of Henry Munday, late of South Marston, Gent. She died March 4, 1787, in the 70 year of her Age.

She liv'd a Christian, from her Birth
Near Seventy years upon the Earth,
Full Fifty years did in this Church
Sing forth God's praise in faith and works:
Her voice by nature was so wrought,
To shake in D, a fourth above Alt;
She'd strike three Octaves perfect clear,
Now Gone to Sing with Christ in Air.

In Memory of Robert Hyde, Wheelwright, who died January 6, 1788, In the 75 year of his Age.

When Man hath labour'd all his days
In worldly Toils, and various ways,
At Length by Death's Assault set free
Lies down to rest most peaceably.

Here lyeth the Body of Sarah, Wife of Thomas Godwin, who died Jan. 2nd, 1724, Aged 28 years.

SOUTH MARSTON.

In the West End of the Churchyard.

Head Stones.

To the Memory of Thomas Titcombe, who died March 7th, 1820, Aged 89 years.

Also Mary, his Wife, who died July 8, 1818, Aged 78 years.

Also Richard King, their Grandson, who died June 20th, 1819, Aged 25 years.

In Memory of Wm. Son of Thomas and Mary Titcombe, who died Dec. 2, 1793, Aged 21 years.

A sudden Change, in a moment fell,
I had not time to bid my friends Farewell;
My life was Short, yet hope to see
A Heavenly Place prepared for me.

To the Memory of James Wilkins, who died 28 of October, 1796, Aged 74 years.

Reader, farewell, prepare thyself to die,
Whom death hath Conquer'd, here in dust must lie
Until thy Saviour in the Clouds does come,
With saints and angels brighter than the sun,
To judge the World, and give eternal Rest
To those who feared here on Earth the best,
All which believ'd, when living here like thee,
Therefore prepare thyself to follow me,
Where saints and Angels Hallelujah sing
Holy, Great God, and Praises to the King.

And also Jemima, Daughter of Ralph and Susannah Titcombe, who died 8th of July, 1795, in the 8 year of her Age.

To the Memory of Elizabeth, Daughter of William and Hannah Seymour, who died July 23d, 1777, Aged 17 years.

Also Martha, Daughter of Wm. and Hannah Seymour, who died Sept. 6, 1777, Aged 21 years.

Henry, Son of William and Hannah Seymour, who died Feb. 13, 1746, Aged 35 years.

William Wilkins, the Elder, died Feb. 28th, 1742, Aged 60 years.

William Wilkins, the Younger, died March ye 2d, 1742, Aged 28 years.

In Memory of Ruth, Wife of Henry Pinneger, who departed this life the 13th March, 1799, Aged 62 years.

To the Memory of Mary Pinneger, Daughter of Henry Pinneger, and Ann, his Wife, who died 29th April 1781, Aged 34 years.

My wedding Bed is in the Dust,
And Christ my Bride in whom I trust;
My Bride he call'd, I must away,
And here to lay till judgement day:
My race was short, but longer is my rest,
God call'd me hence, because it pleas'd him best.

To the Memory of John Pinneger, who departed this life Nov. the 13th, 1820, Aged 71 years.

To the Memory of Henry Pinneger, who departed this life the 19th Feb. 1799, Aged 77 years.

In Memory of Elizabeth, the Wife of Henry Pinneger, who died 6 Nov. 1763, Aged 36 years.

To the Memory of Henry, Son of Henry and Elizth Pinneger, who died 16 July, 1777, Aged 22 years.

To the Memory of James, Son of Henry and Eliz. Pinnegar, who Departed this life March 27, 1795, Aged 38 years.

To the Memory of Wm. Son of Richard and Jane Collins, who Departed this life August 5th, 1808, Aged 24 years.

The Earth is nothing, Heaven is all,
Death has not hurt me, but my fall;
Tho' short my days, yet hope to see
A Heavenly place prepar'd for me.
Dear Friend, pray weep for me no more,
I am not lost, but gone before.
The God of Mercy an Angel bright did send,
To take this Youth to joys that never will end.

To the Memory of Mary, Wife of Richard Midwinter, who Departed this life Jan. 4, 1817, Aged 84 years.

In Memory of Richard Midwinter, who departed this life in full hopes of a blessed Immortality, Sept. 2d, 1793, Aged 58 years.

In Memory of Ann, Daughter of Edward and Jane Head, who died March 10th, 1797, Aged 44 years.

My Distemper seiz'd me so hard,
More than I could endure,
I resign'd myself unto the lord
To rest for evermore.

In Memory of Mary, Wife of Walter Edwards, who died Dec. 22, 1787, Aged 22 years.

The end of She is peace.

To the Memory of James White, who departed this life Dec. 10th, 1808, Aged 81 years.

When Man hath labour'd all his Days
In worldly Toils and various Ways,
At length, by Death's Assault set free,
Lies down to rest most peaceably.

To the Memory of Elizabeth, Wife of James White, who died Aug. 1781, Aged 58 years.

With patience to the last she did submit,
And murmur'd not at what the Lord thought fit;
She with a Christian Courage did resign
Her Soul to God at his appointed time.

In Memory of Thos. Walington, who died Feb. ye 4th, 1749, Aged 66 years.

Weep not for me, my Children Dear,
You see my Glass is run;
It was the lord that Brought me here,
So let his will be done.

Here lyeth ye Body of Wm. Walington, who Died Dec. ye 7th, 1727, Aged 85 years.

Also Ann, Wife of William Wallington, Died May ye 29th, 1719, Aged 67 years.

Wm. Son of Thos. and Ann Walington, who died April ye 16, 1726.

Here lyeth ye Body of John Stevens, who Departed this life March ye 9th, A. D. 1708.

Also here lyeth the Body of Mary, ye Wife of John Stevens, who departed this life Dec. 30th, 1708.

Flat Tomb.

In Memory of Ann, Wife of Thos. Kempster, Eldest Daughter of the Rev. John and Eliz. Head, of this Place, who died May the 15th, 1767, Aged 34 years.

In Memory of John, Son of Thos. and Ann Kempster, who died Oct. 7th, 1775, Aged 18 years.

In Memory of Thomas Kempster, who died 16 May, 1785, Aged 61 years.

In Memory of Ann, Daughter of Thos. and Ann Kempster, who died June 26, 1780, Aged 21 years.

To the Memory of Walter Edwards, who Departed this life the 19th of April, in the year of our Lord 1800, Aged 43 years.

The best of Husbands, and a Father Dear,
A loving Brother, and a Friend lies here:
Death can't disjoin what Christ hath join'd in love,
Life leads to Death, and Death to life Above:
In Heaven's a Happier Place, frail things despise,
Live well to gain of future things the Prize.

Flat Tombs.

To the Memory of Ann, Wife of Joseph Smith, who Departed this life May 25, 1813, Aged 70 years.

Dear, loving, faithful Partner, now farewell,
With whom it was my Happiness to dwell,
With whom it was united heart with heart,
From whom it was so painful then to part.

To the Memory of Wm. Smith, who died Sept. 17, 1777, Aged 68 years.

To the Memory of Sarah, Wife of Wm. Smith, who died Feb. 2, 1784, Aged 69 years.

Sacred to the Memory of Wm. and Ann Pinneger, who died Aug. 14, 1802, Aged 4 years and 6 months.

Also James, their Son, who died May 12, 1803, in his Infancy.

Also Enos-John, their Son, who died July 25, 1815, Aged 7 years.

Also Eliza, their Daughter, who died Sept. 16, 1815, Aged 13 years.

The Lord who gave hath taken away,
We will with Resignation say;
He hath a Right his Gifts to Claim,
And blessed be his holy Name;
His will be done, His will his best,
Come life or Death, our Children's blest.

Head Stones.

In Memory of Thomas, Son of John and Mary Wilkins, who died March 12, 1759, Aged 1 year and 11 months.

Also Sarah, their Daughter, who died Sept. 15, 1761, Aged 16 weeks.

Also Hannah, their Daughter, who died Sept. 21, 1761, Aged 17 weeks.

Ann, ye Wife of Edward Prier, died March ye 7th, 1720, Aged 50 years.

Here lyeth the Body of Nehemiah Cole, who was buried the 6 day of February . . .

To the Memory of Mary, Wife of Thos. Ansell, who Departed this life Oct. 13th, 1806, Aged 61 years.

In Memory of Thos. Ansell, who died July 25th, 1778, Aged 41 years.

Mark the perfect man, and behold the upright, for the end of that man is peace.

In Memory of Lucy, Daughter of Thos. and Mary Ansell, who Departed this life Jan. 24, 1777, Aged 15 months.

In Memory of Mary, the Wife of Richard Harvey, who Departed this life March the 3, 1771, Aged 69 years.

In Memory of Richard Harvey, who departed this life May the 27, 1758, Aged 59 years.

In Memory of Hannah, the Wife of John Harvy, who died Feb. 23, 1755, Aged 97 years.

Here lyeth ye Body of John Harvy, who died June 2, 1730, Aged 63 years.

Flat Tomb.

In Memory of Hannah, Wife of John Large, who died July 14, 1809, Aged 36 years.

In Memory of Maria, Daughter of John and Hannah Large, who died Nov. 16th, 1815, Aged 16 years.

Head Stones.

To the Memory of Edward Ansell, who departed this life October the 18th, in the year of our Lord 1784, Aged 70 years.

Also Eliz. his Wife, who Departed this life May the 14th, in the year of our Lord, 1785, Aged 69 years.

Mary, Daughter of John and Sarah Edwards, died Feb. ye 8, 1725, Aged near 3 years.

Here lyeth John Beeli. He died May ye 22, 1724, Aged 71 years.

Also Elizabeth, his Wife. She died Jan. ye 31, 1724, Aged 56 years.

Sacred to the Memory of Sarah, Daughter of Thomas and Harriot White, who died July the 21st, 1818, Aged 19 years.

In Bloom of Years a Maiden here doth lie,
Then drop a tear in gentle sympathy,
And Think how soon the fairest Flow'r may die.
Long sickness She with patience bore,
Singular in person, but in virtue more;
Death's dart she ne'er dreaded, nor did her hopes prove vain,
She died rejoycing in her Saviour's name.

To the Memory of John Kempster, who Departed this life January 22, 1807, Aged 85 years.

Also Elizabeth, his Wife, who Departed this life Jan. 1st, 1819, Aged 75 years.

Here lyeth the Body of Wm. Bayley, Physician. He Departed this life, August ye 6, 1703.

In Memory of Anthony Waldron, who died Nov. 10, 1776, Aged 84 years.

Also Henry, the Son of Anthony and Susanna Waldron, who died April 24, 1760, Aged 14 years.

Martha, Wife of Wm. Waldron. She departed this life June ye 1, 1727, Aged 81 years.

Here lyeth ye Body of Wm. Waldron. He died August ye 18, A. D. 1721, Aged 76 years.

In Memory of Jane, ye Wife of Francis Smith, and Daughter of George and Mary Humphris. She died Jan. 19, 1735, Aged 21 years.

Ann, Daughter of John and Elizabeth Kempster, died March 20, 1746, Aged 4 years.

Here lyeth ye Body of Edith, Wife of John Curtis. She died March 16, 1718, Aged 60 years.

Here lyeth ye Body of John Curtis, who departed this life Oct. 15, 1730.

In Memory of Mary, Wife of John Woodroof, who Died July 14, 1776, Aged 62 years.

In Memory of Katharine Sessions, who Departed this life Aug. 17, 1780, Aged 58 years.

Here lyeth ye Body of Hannah, the Wife of Joseph Woodroof, who died Nov. 14, 1745, Aged 58.

Also John Woodroof, Son of Joseph and Hannah, who died July 25, 1775, Aged 58 years.

In Memory of Sarah, Daughter of Richard and Mary Edwards, who died April ye 9, 1781, Aged 5 years.

Here Lyeth ye Body of Ralph Butler, who departed this life Ap. ye 11, Anno Dom. 1676.

James Mundy was Buried Jan. ye 7, A. D. 1712.
James, Son of James Mundy, died Dec. ye 21, 1712.

In Memory of Lydia Mundy, who died June 14, 1751, Aged 40 years.

In Memory of Elizabeth, Wife of Thos. Smart, who died the 6 April, 1787, Aged 89 years.

In Memory of Robert Stone, who departed this life May the 25, 1778, Aged 63 years.

Whilst in the world I did remain,
My life to me was Grief and Pain;
But when the Lord he thought it best
He took me to a place of rest.

To the Memory of Catharine, the Wife of Robert Stone, who departed this life the 16th of May, 1808, Aged 73 years.

I was so long with pain opprest,
That wore my strength away,
It made me long for endless rest,
That never can decay.

In Memory of James, Son of Robt. and Catharine Stone, who died May 28, 1783, Aged 26 years.

Underneath this Stone doth lie
As much virtue as could die;
Approv'd by all, and lov'd so well,
Tho' young, like fruit that's ripe, he fell.

To the Memory of Wm. Stone, who died July 3, 1809, Aged 48 years.

Also Sarah, Wife of Wm. Stone, who died August 22, 1809, Aged 58 years.

Also Henry, Son of Wm. and Sarah Stone, who died Dec. 11, 1800, Aged 8 weeks.

Here lyeth the Body of John Gleed, who Died Dec. 21, A. D. 1711, Aged 90 years.

Here lyeth ye Body of Elizabeth, ye dearly beloved Daughter of John Bryant, & of Ann, his Wife, who departed this life Nov. the 11, A. D. 1689.

Here I lye, wrapt up in Clay,
Untill the Resurrection Day.

John Mundie, Senior, Deceased December, 1665.

Joane Gleed was buried August 20, 1681.

Hannah, Daughter of John and Mary Woodroof, who Died Nov. 12, 1758, Aged 16 years.

John, Son of John and Mary Woodroof, died Nov. 6, 1757, Aged 10 months.

On a Flat Stone near the South Porch.

Here lieth ye Body of Elinor, ye Wife of Richard Turner, who was buried ye 9 day of Dec. in the year of our Lord 1684.

Here lyeth ye Body of Sarah, ye Dearly Beloved Daughter of William Bayly, & of Margaret, his Wife. She was Borne ye second Day of July, 1668, and was Buried ye 17 Day of May, 1673.

Here lieth ye Body of Wm. Son of John and Ann Beel. He died March ye 24, 1724, Aged 31 years.

Humfrey, Son of John and Mary Cook, died Feb. ye 21, 1746, Aged 16 years.

WANBOROUGH.

In the West End of the Churchyard.

Flat Tombs.

In Memory of John Smith, Soap Boiler and Tallow Chandler, of this Parish. Born July 5, 1751, O.S. died Jan. 6, 1815.

Reader, set thy House in Order, for thou shalt die.

To the Memory of Thos. Hilliar, late of Badbury, who Departed this life the 30th Day of Dec. 1803, Aged 69 years.

When I was young, and in my prime,
The lord did prosper me and mine,
Whilst in my Sunshine of Success,
No low'ring Clouds did me distress:

My latter End was Grief and Pain,
Physician's Skill was but in Vain,
The lord was pleas'd me to release,
And take me to a better Place.
This World and wife I leave behind,
In hopes with her a better for to find,
Thro' Christ, who died for me and all mankind.

To the Memory of Elizabeth, Wife of Thos. Hilliar, who Departed this life the 31 of Dec. 1811, Aged 69 years.

You that pass by, and say of me,
Alas! her life is done,
Be it well known unto you all,
My life is now begun.
The life I liv'd, while on the Earth,
Was Sorrow, Grief, and Pain,
But now I have a life indeed,
Of pleasure, joy, and Gain.

Flat Stone.

To the Memory of Elizabeth, Wife of Benjamin Kent, who departed this life June 2, 1815, Aged 75 years.

Let no Tears of Sorrow Be,
Dear Relations, shed for me;
Tho' my Earthly life is gone,
I have found a Heavenly one.

Flat Tombs.

To the Memory of Wm. Son of Benjamin and Eliz. Kent, who departed this life June the 15th, 1810, Aged 31 years.

While pale disease upon his vitals prey'd,
His Frame exhausted, and his Strength decay'd,
With painful steps life lingering to the Grave,
Where human skill had lost the power to save;
Yet still kind Heaven disposed his virtuous mind
To live in patience, and to Die resign'd.

To the Memory of Benjamin Kent, who Departed this life August the 27, 1813, Aged 80 years.

Farewell, my pains, disorders, doubts, and fears,
In Heaven there's neither sickness, grief, nor tears.
Here to the wise and good dis, ised by none,
Sleepeth in peace the Father and Son.

To the Memory of Martha Naish, who Departed this life July 3, 1806, Aged 74 years.

To the Memory of Ann, the Wife of Thos. Simmons, who departed this life June the 5th, 1793, Aged 82 years.

To the Memory of John Simmons, who departed this life the 29th of Sept. 1790, in the 88 year of his Age.

To the Memory of Thos. Naish, who departed this life Sept. 4, 1814, Aged 79 years.

Head Stones.

To the Memory of Ann Naish, who Departed this life March 23, 1794, Aged 52 years.

In Memory of Wm. Carpenter, who departed this life March 17, 1819, Aged 30 years.

Fair was his form, more fair his Gentle mind,
Where virtue, sense, and piety combined,
To wedded love gave friendship's highest zest,
Endear'd the Husband, and made the Wife blest:
Now widow's grief Erects this sacred Stone
To make his virtues and her sorrows known;
Reader, if thine's the sympathetic tear,
O stop, and drop the tender tribute here.

Flat Tombs.

In Memory of Edward Smith, who died Nov. 12, 1797, Aged 61 years.

Keep death and judgement always in your eye,
None are fit to live, who are not fit to die;
Make use of present time, because you must
Take up your Lodging shortly in the Dust,
'Tis dreadful to behold the setting Sun,
And Night approaching, ere your work is done.

Sacred to the Memory of Edward Smith, who departed this life May the 1st, 1803, Aged 40 years.

A sudden Change, in a moment fell,
I had not time to bid my friends farewell;
Think nothing strange that happens unto all,
My Lot's to-day, to-morrow thine might fall.

To the Memory of William Barrett, who Dep[d] this life Nov. the 27, 1808, Aged 33 years.

To the Memory of John Lea, who Departed this life the 11 of October, 1799, Aged 40 years.

Stand, Reader, and Spend a Tear,
And think on me, who now lye here,
And whilst you read the state of me,
Think on the Glass that runs for thee;
Let not this world your thoughts betray,
But think upon your dying day:
In Christ alone I only trust
To rise in number of the just.

In Memory of Wm. Lea, who died July 17th, 1786, Aged 70 years.

Man, in his best Estate, is but a bubble,
Labours, cares, and never free from Trouble;
Therefore from this vain world your thoughts employ,
And ever fix them on Eternal joy.

In Memory of Hannah, Wife of Wm. Lea, who died Dec. ye 6, 1781, Aged 61 years.

Dear Husband, pray weep for me no more,
Nor Children shed a Tear,
For I am Gone but just before,
Unto my Saviour Dear.

To the Memory of Thos. Son of Wm. and Alice Lea, who died August 4, 1787, Aged 8 months.

In Memory of Wm. Son of Wm. and Hannah Lea, who died Feb. 2, 1791, Aged 48 years.

God's love and Favour is not seen always
By worldly Comforts, or by length of Days,
Long life on earth doth but prolong our pain,
A happy Death sure is the greatest gain.

In Memory of Mary, Daughter of Wm. & Hannah Lea, who died Oct. 8, 1786, Aged 42 years.

My Glass is run, my Days are spent,
My life is gone, it was but lent;
And as I am so must you be,
Therefore prepare to follow me.

To the Memory of George Lea, Son of Wm. and Alice Lea, who Departed this life 16 of June, 1819, in the 44 year of his Age.

Praises on Tombs are vainly Spent,
A good name is a Monument.

In Memory of Martha, Wife of Ralph May, who Departed this life July 11, 1798, Aged 79 years.

To the Memory of Ralph May, who Departed this life the 13th of May, 1805, Aged 90 years.

Head Stones.

To the Memory of John Gilbert, who died Oct. the 14, 1802, Aged 59 years.

I have been Industrious all my time,
And to serve my God it was my mind,
Till God was pleas'd to call me home,
To Jesus Christ his only Son.

To the Memory of Wm. Gilbert, who Departed this life June the 1, 1805, Aged 72 years.

To the Memory of John, the Son of John and Martha Wilkins, who died June 5, 1819, Aged 14 months.

To the Memory of Thos. Eyles, who died Feb. 18, 1784, Aged 79 years.

To the Memory of Steven, Son of Theophilus and Mary Smith, who died July 18, 1807, Aged 20 years.

The old and young must all submit
To fatal death when God thinks fit;
So, Reader, be sure make Christ thy Friend,
Be always ready for thy End,
I in my bloom was took away,
Therefore prepare, make no delay,
Youth, Health, and Strength, could not me save,
Nor free my Body from the Grave.

To the Memory of Esther, Wife of James Grist, who died June 4, 1806, Aged 75 years.

With patience to the last she did submit,
And murmur'd not at what the lord thought fit,
She, with a Christian Courage, did resign
Her Soul to God at his Appointed Time.

Also Sophia, their Daughter, who Died April 18, 1794, Aged 15 years.

To the Memory of Esther Hilliar Grist, Daughter of James and Esther Grist, who died Jan. 1789, Aged 15 years.

Flat Tombs.

In Memory of Jane, the Daughter of John and Jane Bendery, who died Ap. ye 1, 1765, Aged 26 years.

To the Memory of John Bendery, Late of Elcombe, Gentleman, who died the 16 day of March, 1776, Aged 76 years.

In Memory of Mary, the Daughter of John and Jane Bendery, who died Feb. 22, 1768, Aged 28.

Within iron palisades.

In Memory of Elizth, Wife of George Lea, who died Sept. 17, 1815, Aged 63 years.

With patience to the last she did submit,
And murmur'd not at what the lord thought fit.

Head Stones.

In Memory of Thomas Robins, who died Feb. 28, 1760, Aged 68 years.

God works wonders now and then,
Here lies a Millar—an honest Man!
This world's glory he did not mind,
Nor was his heart to pride inclin'd;
Vile enemies him oft oppress'd,
God set him free as he thought best.

In Memory of Wm. Son of George and Elizabeth Lea, who died May 7th, 1782, in his Infancy.

In Memory of Wm. Son of Wm. and Alice Lea. Died March 31, 1781, Aged 2 years.

Also Hannah and John, twins of Wm. and Alice Lea. Hannah died April 13th, 1781; John Died April ye 15, 1781, And was both Buried in one Coffin, April ye 18, 1781, Aged 11 months.

Weep not for Children,
For they are Blest,
And in Christ's Arms
They take their rest.

In Memory of Rachael Preedy, Wife of John Preedy, of Lambourn, who died 18 July, 1783, Aged 40 years.

To the Memory of Mary, Wife of Robert Cuthbert, who Departed this life Feb. 1st, 1786, Aged 66 years.

In Memory of Sarah, Wife of Joseph Prince, who departed this life May 22, 1790, Aged 49,

Sincerely Lamented by her Husband and Children. She was Pious without Ostentation, Charitable without boasting, Friendly without deceit; Conscious a long Time of her speedy dissolution, yet unshaken; Calm and serene, the lamp of life becoming quite exhausted, She departed, resigning her Soul into the hands of her Maker, with a full assurance of a resurrection to eternal Happiness, being the sure reward of a well Spent life.

South Side of the Churchyard.

To the Memory of Wm.-Edward, Son of Edward and Sarah Darted, who Died Nov. 4, 1814, in the 12 year of his Age.

Now he in Rest and Quiet lay
Waiting for the Resurrection Day,
Then may he wake with sweet surprize,
And in his Saviour's Image rise.

To the Memory of Daniel Long. He died May 25, 1793, Aged 34 years.

Since God thought fit to take what was his due,
The best of Husbands and of Fathers too,
My wife and Children dear I leave behind,
Hoping a Crown of Glory they will find.

Also Elizth Daughter of Daniel and Christian Long. She died August 1st, 1798, Aged 7 years and 11 months.

In Memory of Thomas, Son of John and Mary Chivers, who died March 30, 1773, Aged 6 weeks.

Also Richard, their Son, who died April 6, 1775, Aged 7 weeks.

In Memory of Thos. Mills. Departed this life August 2, 1751, Aged 87.

Sacred to the Memory of Sarah Kempester, who Departed this life Sept. the 12th, 1810, Aged 56 years.

Why should we mourn departing Friends,
Or shake at Death's alarms,
'Tis but the voice that Jesus sends
To call them to his Arms.

In Memory of John Pinegar. He died May ye 3d, 1741, Aged 53.

Sarah, Daughter of John and Sarah Pinniger, died April ye 29, 1734, Aged 2 years.

Here lyeth ye Body of Ann, ye Wife of Wm. Warman, of Middlesex. She died Oct. ye 18, 1743, Aged 52 years.

In Memory of Joanna, Wife of Edward Warman, who died May 12, 1762, Aged 80 years.

In Memory of Thos. Son of Robt. and Ann Sharps, who was buried August ye 3, 1764, Aged 12 years.

In Memory of Hannah Warman, who Departed this life May ye 7, 1779, Aged 68 years.

In Memory of Robert Sharps, who Departed this life April the 10, 1757, Aged 42.

To the Memory of Ann, Wife of Robt. Sharps, who died April 8, 1786, Aged 74 years.

In Memory of Robt. Sharps, who died May the 6, in the year of our Lord 1790, Aged 45 years.

In Memory of Mary, Wife of Robt. Sharps, who died Sept. 1, 1791, Aged 42 years.

To the Memory of John, Son of John and Sarah Smith, who died the 15 Jan. 1796, Aged 4 years and 3 months.

To the Memory of Thos. Son of Wm. and Elizth Smith, who died in his Infancy.

In Memory of Mary, Daughter of Wm. and Elizth Smith, who died Jan. ye 28, 1771, Aged 6 years.

Now in my Glory I remain,
My life was short and full of Pain;
But now the lord he thought it best
To take me to a place of Rest.

To the Memory of Rebecca, Daughter of Wm. and Elizabeth Smith, who Departed this life the 8 of Nov. 1799, Aged 22 years.

To the Memory of Henry Smith, Son of Wm. & Eliz. Smith, who died August the 21, 1806, Aged 35 years.

If ever Parent ever Children was dear,
Here as you stop, you'll drop the tender tear;
Here mourn, whom blest with sense, good nature, truth,
Death seiz'd, too early seiz'd, in bloom of youth,
Religion guided, with her brightest rays,
And Virtue guarded to the throne of Grace.
Mother dear, from weeping now refrain,
And join with me salvation to obtain.

To the Memory of Sarah-Ann Smith, Wife of Charles Smith, who died March the 21, 1806, Aged 33 years.

To faith and charity her heart inclin'd,
Gentle, prudent, and of an easy mind;
Ready to forgive, fearful to offend,
Faithful to her Husband, true to her Friend;
Her Course she finish'd, and resign'd her breath,
In pursuit of Heaven thro' the vale of death;
And now in triumph she joyful sing,
Glory and Praise to our Heavenly King.

To the Memory of Thos. Smith, Son of Wm. and Susanna Smith, who died 12 Dec. 1802, Aged 2 years.

To the Memory of Charles Smith, Son of Wm. and Susanna Smith, who died 25 Oct. 1802, Aged 3 years and 6 months.

Flat Tomb.

To the Memory of Wm. Smith, who Departed this life the 9 of Dec. 1804, Aged 72 years.

Reader, farewell; prepare thyself to die,
Whom death hath conquer'd, here in dust must lie
Until thy Saviour in the Clouds does come,
With Saints and Angels brighter than the Sun,
To judge the world, and give Eternal Rest
To those who feared here on earth the best,
All which believ'd, when living here like thee
Therefore prepare thyself, and follow me,
Where Saints and Angels Hallelujah sing,
Holy Great God, and Praises to the King.

To the Memory of Elizabeth, the Wife of Wm. Smith, who Departed this life the 18 of Jan. 1809, Aged 69 years.

Farewell, my dearest Children, I must away,
Death calls me hence, I could no longer stay;
Farewell, all earthly joys, I go to prove
The endless pleasures of the Saints above;
Farewell, my pains, disorders, doubts, and fears,
In Heaven there's neither sickness, grief, nor tears:
All I possess'd below, I now resign,
Vain world farewell, but welcome joys divine.

In Memory of Mary, Daughter of John and Mary Stout, who died Feb. 14, 1774, Aged 35 years.

In Memory of Mary, Wife of John Stout, who Departed this life Sept. the 3, 1776, Aged 72 years.

Here lyeth ye Body of John Stout, who Departed this life Jan. 6, 1776, Aged 71 years.

In Memory of Thos. Reeves, who Departed this life Nov. ye 29, 1779, Aged 68 years.

Also Sarah, his Wife, who Departed this life June ye 24, 1778, Aged 64 years.

To the Memory of John Reeves, who Departed this life the 12 of Jan. 1799, Aged 43 years.

Flat Tomb.

To the Memory of Wm. Stout, who Departed this life April 24, 1783, Aged 53 years.

The ties of Humanity, the Social efforts of the Mind, The virtues of the kindred Soul, touched by the cold hand of Death, may droop like an Evening Flower; But the gloomy night, and Darkness of the grave, shall quickly pass, The Morning of the Resurrection shall arrive, then shall they re-expand their Forms Beneath the Glorious Influence of the Almighty, Rejoycing in the Possession of an Eternal Day.

Head Stones.

In Memory of Mary, the Daughter of Isaac and Mary Ricks, who died Dec. 18, 1768, Aged 7 years and 6 months.

In Memory of Hannah, Daughter of Isaac and Mary Ricks, who Died August 12, 1788.

In Memory of Isaac Ricks, who Died the 14 of Sept. 1806, Aged 72 years.

In Memory of Mary, the Wife of Isaac Ricks, who died June 19, 1789, Aged 65 years.

To the Memory of Lizzy, Daughter of Nathaniel and Elizabeth Ricks, who Departed this life March the 3, 1816, Aged 17 years.

In Memory of Mary, Wife of Nathaniel May, who departed this life August 3, 1780, Aged 49 years. Also Seven Children, who died in their Infancy.

To the Memory of Edward Warren, who died August 11, 1797, Aged 78 years.

To the Memory of John Warren, who departed this life April 5, 1795, Aged 72 years.

In Memory of Stephen Warren, who departed this life Dec. 18, A. D. 1707.

To the Memory of Mary, Wife of Joseph Sheppard, who Died Oct. 12, 1796, Aged 31 years.

Also to the Memory of Joseph Sheppard, who died Sept. 18, 1807, Aged 42 years.

To the Memory of Edwd Smith, who Departed this life Jan. 6, 1790, Aged 82 years.

In Memory of Margaret, Wife of Edward Smith, who departed this life April 8, 1774.

To the Memory of Ann, the Wife of John Harding, who departed this life 3 Sept. 1796, Aged 29 years.

A virtuous Wife, in Prime of life,
By Death is snatch'd away,
Her Soul is Blest, and gone to Rest,
Tho' flesh is gone to Clay :
She left behind, a Husband kind,
And a beloved Son,
May they prepare to meet her where
True love will ne'er be done.

In Memory of Thos. Son of Robt. and Mary Harding, who died April 12, 1774, Aged 1 year.

Flat Tomb.

In Memory of John Harding, he died Sept. 16, 1764, Aged 70.

Also Ursula, his Wife. She died June 15, 1770, Aged 75.

To the Memory of Thomas Woodam, who died Nov. 2, 1806, Aged 84 years.

To the Memory of Martha, Wife of Thos. Woodam, who died July 6, 1809, Aged 85 years.

In Memory of Joseph Godman, who died May ye 26, 1729, Aged 59.

Also Alice, his Wife. She died Sept. ye 7, 1722, Aged 55 years.

In Memory of Ann, the Wife of Wm. Woolford, who Died Nov. 7, 1754, Aged 65 years.

To the Memory of Wm. the Son of Wm. and Mary Woolford, who Died Feb. 5, 1798, Aged 8 years.

Also Wm. their Son, who died August 10, 1814, Aged 10 years.

And also Thos. their Son, who died April 9th, 1817, Aged 23 years.

To the Memory of Wm. Woolford, who Died June 24, 1814, Aged 59 years.

Flat Stones.

In Memory of Elizabeth, Wife of William Herring, who died Oct. 1728, Aged 70 years.

Here lyeth ye Body of Wm. Herring, who Departed this life Sept. 17, A. D. 1720, Aged 72 years.

Martha, Wife of Thos. Herring, died Feb. ye 20, 1723.

Head Stones.

In Memory of Sarah, the Wife of Wm. Woolford, who Departed this life March 10, 1784, Aged 68 years.

In Memory of Wm. Woolford, who departed this life March 14, 1781, Aged 65 years.

Here lyeth Son and Daughter of Wm. and Dorothy Edwards. John died Nov. 17, 1734, Aged 4 years, Eliz. died Nov. 15, 1734, Aged 14 years.

Flat Tombs.

To the Memory of Mary, the Wife of Thos. Edwards, who departed this life the 4 of Oct. 1789, Aged 45 years.

She was all that chears and softens Life,
The tender Mother, Christian, Friend, and Wife :
And now She's gone to reign with Christ above,
Where all is joy, Grace, Harmony, and Love.

To the Memory of Thos. Edwards, who departed this life the 28 of March, 1800, Aged 79 years.

In Memory of Thos. Baker, who departed this life Jan. 10, 1732, Aged 68.

Also Eliz. Wife of Thos. Baker. She departed this life Sept. ye 10, 1736, Æt. 66.

In Memory of Wm. Edwards, who died May ye 19th, Anno Domini 1746, Aged 52.

In Memory of Dorothy, Wife of Wm. Edwards, who Died Aug. 3, 1785, Aged 90 years.

Head Stones.

To the Memory of Elizabeth, Wife of John Warren, who died May 22, 1797, Aged 82 years.

Here lyeth ye Body of John Ockwell, who Departed this Life Decem. the 7, 1753, Aged 57 years.

Here Lyeth ye Body of Wm. Edwards, who Died May 22, 1760, Aged 45 years.

Here lieth ye Body of John Edwards, who Died Sept. 25, 1758, Aged 76 years.

Martha, Wife of Wm. Woodard. She died June 30, 1745, Aged 74 years.

In Memory of Wm. Woodard, who Departed this life Dec. 15, 1737, Aged 63 years.

Here lyeth ye Body of Henry Iles, who died June 18th, 1746, Aged 51 years.

In Memory of Michael Tombs. He died June 27, 1754, Aged 36 years.

In Memory of Margaret, Wife of Francis Haines, who Departed this life Jan. ye 28, 1770, Aged 70 years.

In Memory of Bartholomew Tombs, who Died June 24, 1782, Aged 78.

Michael Hankes died Oct. 5, 1720, Aged 82 years.

Also Mary, his Wife. She died Feb. ye 14, 1703.

In Memory of Hannah, Wife of Bartholomew Tombs, who Died Oct. ye 8, 1773, Aged 61 years.

Here Lyeth ye Body of Wm. Edwards, who departed this life Dec. ye 21, A. Dom. 1723.

Here lieth ye Body of John Berry, Died March 29, 1749, Aged 83 years.

In Memory of Martha, Wife of John Berry, who Died March 10, 1742, Aged 74 years.

Here lyeth the Body of Elizth, Wife of Henry Avenell. She died Sept. ye 1, 1732, Aged 36.

Here lyeth ye Body of Henry Avenell. He died Jan. 20, 1744, Aged 70.

Here lyeth ye Body of Mary, ye Wife of Nathaniel May, who died 15 Oct. 1750, Aged 44 years.

Flat Stone.

Here lyeth ye Body of Martha, ye Wife of Thomas Edwards. She Departed this life Sept. ye 6, 1726, Aged 55 years.

Here lyeth ye Body of Thos. Smith, who Departed this life Oct. the 20th, 1740, Aged 78 years.

Martha, Wife of Thos. Smith, died May ye 8, 1725-6.

John Smith Departed this life Oct. ye 31, 1732, Aged 32 years.

Here lyeth the Body of Thos. Smith, Son of Wm. Smith, who died Sept. 26, 1770.

On a Flat Stone.

In Memory of Thos. Edwards, Gent. who Departed this life June ye 1, 1728, in the 82 year of his Age. He married Elizabeth, Daughter of Mr. John Read, of Wanbrough, and lived with her in ye state of matrimony more than 58 years, by whom he had 5 Sons and three Daughters, and they, in his life-time, were multiplied to 52 Grand Children.

In Memory of Charles Avenell, who Departed this life Oct. 10, 1780, Aged 70 years.

Also Mary, the Daughter of John and Mary Avenall, who departed this life July 10, 1781, Aged 3 weeks.

To the Memory of Eliz. the Wife of Charles Avenell, who departed this life the 30 of Oct. 1803, Aged 84 years.

When Death takes Husband, Wife, or Son,
Content thyself, and say God's will be done;
Trust in thy blessed Saviour, and expect
To meet them all again with his elect.

To the Memory of Ann, Daughter of John and Mary Avenell, who died April 16, 1790, Aged 8 months.

My Plant did flourish fair,
Like to a Rose in June,
But Death, with his cold blasting air,
Has cropt my tender Bloom.

To the Memory of Eliz^th^, Daughter of John and Mary Avenell. She Died 19 May, 1792, in the 15 year of her Age.

A tender Branch lies Buried here,
That was belov'd by Parent Dear,
Few was her Days, short was her Race,
From womb to Grave short was the space.
Learn, parents, then to be content
When God requires what is but lent;
In youth and Childhood put no trust,
For all must die, and turn to dust.

To the Memory of Michael Eyles, who departed this life the 18 of Sept. 1798, Aged 52 years.

Weep not for me that I have lost my Breath,
My Pain were such as made me wish for death,
Christ, my Redeemer, knew which way was best
To ease my grief, and set my soul at rest.

To the Memory of Mary, the Wife of Michael Eyles, who Departed this Life the 14 of Oct. 1795, Aged 50 years.

On a Flat Stone.

To the Memory of Ann, Wife of John Brind, who Died Jan. 3, 1717, Aged 51 years.

Reader, prepare to follow me,
For as I am, so shalt thou be,
Rotting in Dark and silent Dust,
Prepare for Death, for die thou must;
Life is uncertain, Death is Sure,
Sin is the wound, Christ is the Cure.

To the Memory of Ann, Daughter of Thos. and Elizabeth Brind, who died May 19, 1808, Aged 13 months.

Also Mary, their Daughter, who Died May 25, 1808, Aged 13 months.

To the Memory of John Brind, who Died Feb. 5, 1786, Aged 55 years.

A time of Death you know full well,
But when, or how, no mortal man can tell,
Be it at night, noon, now, or then,
Death is most certain, yet uncertain when.

Head Stones.

In Memory of John Painter, who Died May 29, 1789, Aged 50 years.

In Memory of Catharine ye Wife of Isaac Brind. She died April ye 8, 1743, Aged 57.

Flat Stone.

In Memory of Margaret, ye Wife of Charles Brind. She Died Oct. ye 1, Anno Dom. 1732, Aged 75 years.

In Memory of Ann, the Wife of John Brind. She died Jan. 25, 1756, Aged 57.

Charles Brind. He Departed this life Oct. 12, Anno Dom. 1735, Aged 85.

In Memory of John Brind, who Died April 6, 1777, Aged 62 years.

Here lyeth ye Body of Abigail, ye Wife of Thos. Savory. She died August ye 26, 1721, Aged 90 years.

Mary, Daughter of Daniel and Edith Herring, was Buried Sept. 4, A. D. 1728.

In Memory of Thos. Pithouse, who died April 28, 1778, Aged 78 years.

Also Margaret, his Wife, who died Oct. 6, 1785, Aged 79 years.

Sacred to the Memory of Wm. Sainsbury, who died March 13, 1818, Aged 84 years.

This Stone is placed here to protect his Ashes, and not to record his Virtues, being registered elsewhere.

Also Ann, his Wife, who Died March 22, 1814, Aged 61 years.

In Adversity meek, and in Affliction humble,
To Death resign'd, for life Eternal.

To the Memory of Henry Avenell, who died Dec. ye 20, 1786, Aged 72 years.

To the Memory of Mary, the Wife of Henry Avenell, who Departed this life Feb. the 6, 1781, Aged 66 years.

Flat Tombs.

To the Memory of Charles Kent, who Departed this life June 25, 1814, Aged 73 years.

In Memory of John Kent, who departed this life the 29 of May, 1755, Aged 59.

Francis Merchant Buried April 5, 1748.

In Memory of Jane Merchant, second Daughter of Thos. and Dorothy Brind, of Foxbridge, Wanborough, Gent. who died March 14, 1745.

This Tomb was Erected by her Sister, Ann Brind.

Head Stone.

To the Memory of Mary, Wife of Robt. Sheppard, who died August 4, 1807, Aged 74 years.

In the North Side of the Churchyard.

Flat Stone.

In Memory of Sarah, Wife of James Howell, who died April 4, 1760, Aged 57.

In Memory of James Howell, who died Feb. 3, 1764, Aged 63 years.

Head Stones.

Here Lyeth ye Body of James, Son of James and Sarah Howell. He Departed this life August 27th, 1754, Aged 28.

Here lieth ye Body of John Blissett, who Departed this life Feb. ye 17, A. D. 1695.

Here lyeth Sabrea, ye Wife of Thos. Wells. Died July 28, 1728, Aged 49.

To the Memory of Ann, the Wife of Wm. Wells, who Departed this life the 10 of Sept. 1792, Aged 84.

In Memory of Wm. Wells, who Died Oct. 18, 1762, Aged 32 years.

In Memory of John, Son of Wm. and Ann Wells, who died July 21, 1762, Aged 20.

Flat Tomb.

To the Memory of Ann, the Wife of John Carpenter, who Departed this life the 2d of Oct. 1806, Aged 62 years.

A sudden Change on me was wrought,
By God Almighty's holy will,
When to my Grave I soon was brought,
Where I shall slumber until
The Day in which hour will come
To judge the World, and people all,
And raise the Righteous from the Dead
By his Almighty Gracious Call.

To the Memory of Elizabeth, Widow of Charles Howell, who died May 13th, 1754, Aged 92 years.

Here lyeth ye Body of John Greenhalfe, who Departed this life June ye 30, A. D. 1716.

Flat Stone.

Charles Hunt died March 26, 1772, Aged 46 years.
Mary, his Wife, Sept 2, 1785, Aged 39 years.
Charles, their Son, Nov. 6, 1770, Aged 20 years.
James, their Son, Feb. 1783, Aged 18 years.
William, their Son Jan. 3, 1786, Aged 26.
Thomas, their Son, April 23, 1798, Aged 17 years.

Head Stones.

In Memory of Ann, the Daughter of Francis and Mary Hewer, who departed this life June the 1, 1769, Aged 12 years.

Weep not for me, my parents dear,
I am not dead, but sleepeth here;
My days were short on earth, you see,
Prepare, therefore, to follow me.

In Memory of Richard Deacon, who Departed this life the 18 of Jan. 1795, Aged 52 years.

All you, my friends, who may pass by,
And on this Stone shall cast your eye,
Think on the Grave, and not on Gold,
As young must die, as well as Old;
Live like Christians while on Earth,
By doing all things that are just:
Look on my Widow, and the Fatherless,
Assist them when you see them in distress;
That friendship shewn to me out of the Grave
Continue stedfast to my little Babes,
Then at the final judgement day I trust,
To rise with you, and stand amongst the Just.

To the Memory of Lizzy, Wife of Richard Deacon, who Departed this life Dec. 3, 1815, Aged 73 years.

With Goodness Cloath'd, we may defie,
And fear not what it is to die;
Fair Virtue's paths are pleasant to be trod,
'Tis Virtue only wafts the Soul to God.
A kind good Wife, true Friend, and tender Mother,
What else, the last Day clearly will discover.

To the Memory of Richard, son of Richard and Lizzy Deacon, who Departed this life Nov. 19, 1816, Aged 34 years.

A time of death there is, you know full well,
But when, or how, no mortal man can tell;
Be it at night, noon, now, or then,
Death is most certain, but uncertain when.

In Memory of John Houlder, who Departed this life Feb. the 15, 1771, Aged 51 years.

Also Ann, the Wife of John Houlder, who Departed this life Jan. the 15, 1785, Aged 67 years.

To the Memory of Sarah, the Wife of Thos. Houlder, who died the 19th July, 1797, Aged 44 years.

A virtuous wife, in prime of life,
By Death is snatch'd away;
Her soul through Childbirth's gone to rest,
Tho' flesh is gone to clay.
She's left behind a Husband kind,
Three Daughters, and a Son,
May they prepare to meet her where
True love will ne'er be done.

To the Memory of Thos. Houlder, who Departed this life July 5, 1811, Aged 68.

In Memory of Mary, Wife of Edward Godwin. She died Oct. 29, 1769, Aged 76 years.

Grieve not, Husband, nor Children dear,
It is God's will that I am here;
I liv'd in love, and in peace dy'd,
My life desir'd, but God deny'd.

Here lyeth ye Body of John Lowder, who Departed this life Nov. ye 9, 1743, Aged 62 years.

To the Memory of Ann, Wife of Michael Tombs, who died Aug. 7, 1789, Aged 52 years.

Here lyeth ye Body of Anna Prator, Daughter of John Prator, who Departed this life Oct. 26, A. D. 1694.

Flat Tombs.

In Memory of Wm. Prator. He Departed this life June ye 5, 1744, Aged 48 years.

His Sister Elizabeth, Wife of John Haggard, Gent. She died August. 11, 1768, Aged 68.

Here lyeth ye Body of John Prator, who Departed this life July ye 4, 1723, Ætatis 84.

Also in Memory of John Prator, Jun. who died April 9, A. Dom. 1725, Aged 51.

In Memory of John, Son of John and Ann Prator, who died April 16th, 17. . Ætatis 28.

To the Memory of Ann, Wife of John Haggard, who Departed this life Jan. 30, 1809, Aged 88 years.

To the Memory of Thos. Honeybone, who died Nov. 30, 1796, Aged 52 years.

To the Memory of Ann, Wife of Thos. Honeybone, who died August 5, 1806, Aged 64 years.

Grieve not for me, my Children dear,
It is God's will that I am here,
And as I am so must you be,
Prepare, therefore, to follow me.

Also William, their Son, who died May 2d, 1807, Aged 27 years.

I was so long with pain opprest,
That wore my strength away,
It made me long for endless rest,
Which never can decay.

Here lyeth ye Body of Richard Honeybone, who died June 1, 1768, Aged 50 years.

GREAT BEDWIN.

On Monuments against North Wall of Chancel.

Here Lyeth, neer to the Body of Her Husband, ye Most Noble Lady Frances Devereux, Daughter of Robt. Earle of Essex, and Widdow of William, Duke of Somerset, who Dyed April the 24th, 1674, Aged 74 Years and Six Months.

In Gratitude to whose Memory this Monument is Erected by Thomas, Viscount Weymouth, who Married her Grand Daughter, the Lady Frances Finch, A° Dom. 1706.

Arms—Two wings conjoined: impaling, a fess, in chief three roundels.

Here lyeth Intomb'd the worthie Sr John Seymour, of Wolphall, Knight, who By Margerie His Wyfe, Daughter, of Sr Henry Wentworth, Knight, From whome the now Lord Wentworthe is Discended, had Sixe Sonnes And fower Daughters: To wete, John, who dyed unmaryed, Edward, Duke of Somerset,

Earle of Hertford, Viscount Beauchampe, and Baron Seymour, Uncle to Kinge Edwarde the Sixt, Governor of his Royall Person, protector of all his Dominions and Subjects, Lorde Treasurer and Earle Marshall of England, W. Duke, Maryed Anne, Daughter of Sr Edwarde Stanhope, Knight, By Elizabeth His Wyfe, Daughter of Sr Foulke Burgchier, Lorde Fitzwaryn, From whome the Moderne Earles of Bathe are Discended, Sr Henry Seymour, Knight, who Maryed Barbara, Daughter of Thos. Morgan, Esq. Thomas Lorde Seymour, of Sudeley, Highe Admirall of Englande, who maryed Katherine, Queene of Englande, and Wydow to Kinge Henry the Eight, One other Jhon and Anthony, who Dyed in their Infancy, Jane, Queene of Englande, Wyfe to Kinge Henry the Eight, and Mother to Kinge Edwarde the Sixt, Elizabeth, Firste Maryed to Sr Henry Vghtred, Knight, After to Gregorie, Lorde Cromwell, And last to Jhon Lorde Sainct John of Basinge, After Marquesse of Winchester, Margery, who dyed in her infancy, and Dorothe, maryed to Sr Clement Smythe, Knight. This Knight departed this lyfe at LX yeares of Age the XXI day of December Anno 1536, And was firste buryed at Eston priorie churche amongst divers of his auncestors, both Seymours and Sturmyes, Howbeit that Church being ruynd, and thereby all theire monuments either whollie spoyled, or verie much defased during the mynoritie of Edward Earle of Hertforde, Sonne to the said Duke, the said Earle after, as well for the dutyfull love he beareth to his said grandefather, as for the better contynuans of his Memory, did cause his bodie to be removed, and here to be intombed, at his owne coste and chardge, the laste daye of September, Anno 1590, in the XXXII yeare of the moste happye raigne of our gratious Soveraigne ladie Queene Elizabeth.

The statue of the Knight is lying in complete armour, the sword in the scabbard, his head resting on his helmet, and his feet upon a lion.

Arms.

Gules, two wings conjoined and inverted, argent; impaling sable, a chevron, or, between three leopards' faces caboshed of the same.

Gules, two wings conjoined and inverted, argent, a crescent of the last for difference: impaling quarterly, first sable, a fess between three martlets gules, on a chief, sable, three foxes heads argent; second, per pale azure and sable, three fleur-de-lis or; third sable, three dogs courant, in pale argent; fourth sable, on a chevron, argent, three bugle-horns, sable, between three stags' heads caboshed argent.

Per fess gules, two wings conjoined and inverted argent, in base per bend, argent and gules, in bend three double roses counter-changed.

Per fess wavy, argent and azure, in base argent, on a bend gules, three lions' faces caboshed or.

Per fess argent three demi-lions rampant gules, in base, of the last two wings conjoined and inverted.

On a brass near the above.

Bellocamp⁹ eram Graĩa genitrice Semermus
Tres habui natos, est quibus una Soror.

On Flat Stones in Nave.

Here Lyeth ye Body of Edward Durrill. He was Buried August 25, Ann. Dni 1725, Aged 57 years.

Here lyeth ye Body of Mary, the Wife of John Mills, who dyed May 1, 1728, in the 73 year of her Age.

Also Wm. Mills, Son of John and Mary Mills, who dyed Oct. 8, 1729, in the 34 year of his Age.

Also John Mills, who died Sept. ye 27, 1747, Aged 92 years.

Here Lyeth ye Body of Sarah, the Wife of Robert Hall, who Departed this life August ye 7th, 1716, Ætatis 80.

In Memory of Elizabeth, ye Wife of Edward Walter, who died Jan. 30, 1735, Aged 53 years.

In Memory of Mary, the Daughter of Joseph and Jane Wentworth, who departed this life the 7th day of Sept. 1809, Aged 12 years.

Here lyeth ye Body of Mary, ye Wife of Robert Hall, who Departed this life March ye 3, 1722, Ætatis 30.

Also Elizabeth, her Daughter, who died March ye 28th, 1724, Aged 1 year and 1 month.

In Memory of Mary, ye Wife of Thomas Walter, who died June 29, 1748, Aged 52.

Farewell, my Friends, I must away,
My Glass is run, I cannot stay;
God be your guide, and give you grace,
That Heaven may be your Resting place,
With this, our Friend, that's gone before,
To live in love for evermore.

Also Edward, their Son, Aged 1 year, and Joseph, Aged 6 years.

In Memory of Mrs. Anne Cobbe, Wife of Richard Cobbe, Cler. M. A. Daughter of Mr. John Bird. Obiit 6 March, 1732, Ætatis 26.

Here lyeth ye Body of Ambrose Smith, Sen. who dyed April 24, 1729, Aged 64.

Here lyeth ye Body of Obary, the Wife of Ambrose Smith, Sen. who dyed April 3, 1716, Aged 45.

Here lyeth the Body of Ambrose Smith, jun. who dyed March 26th, 1728, in the 52 year of his age.

North Transept.

In Memory of Isaac Bushell, of London, Apothecary, who died June the 16, 1749, Aged 41 years.

Brass taken out.

Here lyeth the Body of Robert Hall, who died April 7th, 1729, Aged 66.

South Transept.

Here lyeth the Body of Robert Savage, who Departed this life May ye 18, A. D. 1696, in the 77 year of his Age.

Here lyeth ye Body of Thomas Hawkins, of Wexcomb. He Departed this life Oct. ye 24, A. Dom. 1724, Ætatis 67.

In Memory of Mr. Richard Spencer, late of Great Bedwin, who died Feb. ye 25th, 1760, Aged 56 years.

Job xix. 25—27.

Also in Memory of Sarah, the Wife of Mr. Richard Spencer, who died Nov. ye 1st, 1764, Aged 83 years.

Here lyeth the Body of William Cannon, Son of Thomas and Lucy Cannon, who Departed this life the 22 Day of . . . . 1779, Aged 43.

Affliction sore, &c.

In Memory of Thomas Cannon, who died Sept. 12th, 1767, Aged 74.

Also here Lyeth Luci, his Wife, who died June 9th, 1741, Aged 46.

Here lyeth the Body of Francis Dunford, Son of John Dunford, by Sarah, his Wife. He died Dec. ye 30th, 1717, Aged 31 years.

Also near this place lyeth ye Bodies of ye two Sons of Francis Dunford.

Here Lyeth ye Body of John Dunford . . . . . . of West Grafton, in . . . . . . Son of John Dunford, by Sarah, his Wife. He dyed Feb. ye 21, 1719, Aged 41 years.

Also Sarah, the Wife of John Dunford, Sen. who dyed Sept. 14, 1724, Aged 64.

Under a canopy, in the south side of this transept, is a Knight Templar, carved in stone, and in good preservation: also a small piscina. In a canopy adjoining, on a grey stone, is the form of a cross. Round the edges of this stone is an inscription in an ancient character, but nearly obliterated. In the floor of the Chancel are some painted tiles, representing griffins, pheasants, fretty, gyronny, fleur-de-lis, &c. The Church consists of a chancel, nave, north and south Transepts. The Nave is supported on each side by four pointed arches, ornamented by two Saxon mouldings.

Register commenced in the year 1539.

Rev. Henry Wilson, Vicar.

The Earl of Ailesbury Lord of the Manor.

North Side of the Churchyard.

Flat Tomb.

In Memory of Joseph Balley, Sen. who died Jan. 1, 1755, Aged 70 years.

In Memory of Joseph Balley, Jun. who died May 15, 1742, Aged 25 years.

O cruel Death, that would not be deny'd,
But broke the Bonds of love so lately ty'd:
Let not man think that he repents too soon,
I found it night before I thought it noon.

In Memory of Mary, Daughter of John and Millisent Balley, who died March 30, 1776, Aged 19 years.

Weep not, dear Parents, grieve no more,
I am not lost, but gone before.

Head Stones.

In Memory of Frances, the Wife of Richard Smallbones, who died March 4, 1771, Aged 26 years.

In Memory of John, Son of Edward and Elizabeth Hawkins, who died 7 Jan. 1775, Aged 21 years.

To the Memory of Mrs. Martha Rosier, who died May 20, 1786, Aged 76 years.

Also of Mr. Thos. Rosier, Husband of the Above, who died April 10, 1796, Aged 83 years.

To the Memory of Mary Rushley, Daughter of Richard and Elizabeth Sturges, who died April 22, 1815, Aged 15 years.

Also Thomas Sturges, their Son, who died April 8th, 1814, Aged 4 years and 8 months.

Also Henry Sturges, their Son, who died April 12, 1815, Aged 15 weeks.

'Tis God that lifts our comforts high,
Or sink them in the grave;
He gives, and blessed be his name,
He takes but what he gave.

Sacred to the Memory of Hannah Lloyd, Daughter of Benjamin and Mary Lloyd, who Departed this life April 22, 1814, Aged 18 years.

Hurried from life, to dwell in Death's domain,
Silent I preach, attend ye young and vain:
Prepare to meet your God this present hour,
No state to-morrow's dawning can secure;
If youth, or health, could future prospects give,
Those flattering, flow'ry favours bid me live;
Blasted at once, learn, by this earthly date,
With awe reflect, the same may be your fate.

Sacred to the Memory of Thos. Pearson, who Departed this life 17 Sept. 1814, Aged 55 years.

Also to the Memory of Blanch Pearson, Wife of Thos. Pearson, who Departed this life August 18, 1818, Aged 54 years.

To the Memory of James Pickett, who Departed this life April 23, 1812, Aged 66 years.

In Memory of Mrs. Eliz. Reeves, late Wife of Mr. Wm. Reeves, Surgeon, who died the 15 of August, 1787, Aged 60 years.

Liv'd belov'd, and died lamented.

Be ye also ready.

In Memory of Mary Adams, who departed this life August 15, 1761, Aged 88.

Here lyeth the Body of John Adams, who died Jan. 23, 1758, Aged 50 years.

Also near this place lyeth the Body of Thos. Reeves, who died May 31, 1733, Aged 34 years.

Here Lyeth ye Body of Isaac, one of ye nineteenth Children of John and Elizabeth Bushell, who departed this life ye 19 of Jan. 1700, and in ye 17 year of his Age.

In Memory of Mrs. Anne Bird, Wife of Mr. John Bird. She died July 28, 1740, Aged 75 years.

Here lyeth ye Body of Mr. John Bird. He Departed this life April 27, A.D. 1722, Aged 66.

In Memory of John Pyke, Son of Thos. and Eliz. Pyke, who died Suddenly the 14th of Jan. 1801, Aged 26 years.

In Memory of Thos. Pyke, Son of Thos. and Eliz. Pyke, who Departed this life Oct. 31, 1788, Aged 18 years.

In Memory of Eliz. Wife of Thos. Pyke, of Netherton, Hants. who died 29 Nov. 1777, Aged 34 years.

In Memory of Eliz. the Wife of Thos. Potter, who died June 4, 1760, Aged 48 years.

Sacred to the Memory of Mr. Thos. Potter, who Departed this life April 3, 1781, Aged 72 years.

To the Memory of John Potter, who died Suddenly Feb. 28, 1790, Aged 55 years.

In the Memory of Dorothy, Wife of William Gale, who died Sept. 2, 1804, Aged 56 years.

Sacred to the Memory of Thos. Potter, who departed this life the 27 of June, 1807, Aged 69 years.

In Memory of Charles Dixon, who died July 27, 1795, Aged 58 years.

Also Elizabeth, Daughter of Charles and Mary Dixon, who died August 1, 1795, Aged 17 years.

Flat Tomb.

In Memory of Daniel Bushell, who died Sept. 22, 1772, Aged 80 years.

Also Eliz. Wife of Daniel Bushell, his Son, who died Dec. 22, 1775, Aged 52 years.

In Memory of Hannah, Wife of John Bushell, who died Feb. 4, 1819, Aged 81 years.

In Memory of Hannah, Wife of George Thatcher, who died Jan. 29, 1813, Aged 62 years.

The Grave no terror was to me,
Christ o'er it gave me victory;
Through faith in his Redemption, I
Both dy'd to live, and liv'd to die.

Also to the Memory of John, Son of George and Hannah Thatcher, who died Jan. 5, 1813, Aged 22 years.

Faith, Hope, and Resignation, fill'd his breast,
Good ground we therefore have to think he's blest.

In Memory of Charles, the fifth Son of William and Maria-Ann Pike. Obiit Dec. 15, 1810, Aged 8 years.

And Edwin, their seventh Son. Obiit Jan. 21, 1811, Aged 4 years

How happy they who thus escape while young,
Ere vice has time to stifle right with wrong,
Whose visionary life, on wings of wind,
Speeds far away, and leaves all ills behind.

Sacred to the Memory of Ann, Daughter of Thos. and Sarah Sawyer, who departed this life the 11 of April, 1810, Aged 2 years.

In Memory of Thos. Pike, who departed this life the 14 of April, 1799, Aged 65 years.

Sacred to the Memory of John Pike, Son of Thomas and Mary Pike, who Departed this life Nov. 10, 1790, Aged 24 years.

Sacred to the Memory of Martha, the Wife of Thos. Gale, who Departed this life the 2 of Nov. 1807, Aged 24 years.

This Stone was Erected June the 26th, 1803, in Memory of the undermentioned Children of James and Sarah Pike, (Viz.) Lavinia, Aged 9 years; Lucretia, 4 years; Thos.-Thelwall, 1 year; Sarah-Matilda 10 months; and Martha 10 days.

Ere sin could blight, or sorrow fade,
Death came with Friendly care,
Th' opening buds to Heav'n convey'd,
And bid them blossom there.

Flat Tomb.

Underneath are deposited the Remains of Richard Pocock, of North Bavant, in this County, who died Suddenly, Dec. 27, 1818, Aged 49 years.

Filial affection plac'd this humble Stone.

Underneath this Stone are deposited the Remains of Elvira, Daughter of James and Sarah Pike, who Departed this life March 7th, 1818, Aged 3 years.

Happy the babe who, privilege by fate
To shorten labour, and a lighter weight,
Receiv'd but yesterday the gift of breath,
Order'd to-morrow to return to death.

South Side.

Flat Tombs.

Sacred to the Memory of John Bloxham, late of this Parish, Gent. who died Feb. ye 5, 1779, Aged 78 years,
More than fifty of which he spent in the service of the late and present Earls of Ailesbury.
Diligence in inferior Stations
raised him to Offices of Superior Trust:
Approved by his Masters,
Belov'd by his Fellow Servants,
Lamented by all;
Modest and temperate, Faithful and Religious,
An Example
To all who seek to serve from the heart
Their Earthly Masters, and their Master in Heaven.

Sarah, the Wife of John Bloxham, died the 14 day of Feb. 1758, Aged 59 years.

In Memory of Catharine, the Wife of Edward Goddard, Gent. who died June the 4, 1756, Aged 81 years.

Here lyeth ye Body of Charles Becher, Jun. Gent. who died March ye 14, A. D. 1732, Aged 8 years and 6 months.

Also by him him lyeth his Brother Henry, who died in his Infancy.

Here lyeth the Body of Charles Becher, Esq. who died Oct. ye 31, Anno { Ætatis 73, Salutis 1737.

Arms—Vair, on a canton a buck's head; impaling, two bars, in chief three roundels.

Crest—A demi lion.

Head Stones.

To the Memory of John Rushley, Sen. who departed this life Feb. 19, 1787, Aged 76 years.

Also To the Memory of Thomisien Rushley, Wife of John Rushley, Sen. who departed this life July 19, 1763, Aged 52 years.

Sacred to the Memory of Ann, the Wife of Joseph Lees, who died Feb. 17, 1821, Aged 26 years.

In Memory of Wm. Winckles, who died the 18th of Dec. 1784, Aged 60 years.

Sacred to the Memory of Elizabeth Mills, who died Oct. 24, 1817, Aged 46 years.

Sacred to the Memory of Edward, Aged 4 years, and Sarah, Aged 3 years, Son and Daughter of Edward and Sarah Eaton.

In early morn of life, upon them shone
A ray of mercy, and their spirits rose,
Pure as the dew-drop that their cold sod wets,
To Him who made all, and who all sustains.
A. D. 1797.

The Lord hath sown, and the Lord will reap.
Sarah, widow of Edward Eaton, of Kelmarsh, in Northamptonshire, Gent.
A Wife most affectionate, a Parent most tender,
A Christian most exemplary,
Awaits here
the sound of the Trumpet.
On the 2 of Jan. 1798, in the 86 year of her Age,
She Departed in Sleep.
Her Sons, Wm. and Edward, in filial reverence, placed this humble Stone.

To the Memory of Edward Eaton, Second Son of Edward Eaton, of Kelmarsh, in Northamptonshire, Gent. He was several times Portreeve of this ancient Borough, beloved, respected by all. His last words were,

I never wilfully injured any one, I forgive every one.

Traveller, stop;

If thou canst not say so, go and repent.

He died on the 15 of August, 1807, in the 66th year of his Age.

Sacred to the Memory of Mary Bulling, spinster, eldest Daughter of Wm. and Susannah Bulling, late of North Creak, in the County of Norfolk, who Departed this life Jan. 3, 1817, in her 47 year.

Here lies the Body of Wm. Son of Thos. and Elizth Chouls, who died Dec. 18th, 1758, Aged 20 years.

In Memory of Mary, the Daughter of Thos. and Elizth Chouls, who died May 6, 1760, Aged 46 years.

Here lyeth the Body of Prudence, the Wife of Edward Edgerly, who died June 7th, 1757, Aged 23 years.

In Memory of Robt. Hawkins. He Departed this life Feb. 9, 1766, Aged 99 years.

In Memory of Jane Hawkins, who departed this life March 5, 1766, Aged . . years.

To the Memory of Mary, the Wife of Robert Hawkins, who Departed this life Jan. ye 29, 1779, Aged 67 years.

In Memory of Robert Hawkins, who Departed this life June ye 12, 1779, Aged 60 years.

Flat Tomb.

H. S. E.

Thomæ Shephard, Cler. uxor fidelis,
Quæ
Viva bene volentiæ, candaris, et modestiæ,
Exemplum prævuit
Mortua apud Omnes, præsertim Maritum
Triste sui desiderium reliquit.
Obiit Julii 28, 1747, Anno Ætatis 31.
In gremio matris jacet
Thomas, T. et S. Shepherd, filius,
Qui
Quinque menses natus, Obiit Feb. 6, 1746.

Head Stones.

In Memory of Frances, the Wife of Francis Mundy, who died Jan. 26, 1753, Aged 76 years.

Here lyeth the Body of Thos. Cannon, who Departed this life the 16 Day of August, 1778, Aged 50 years.

In Memory of Elizabeth, Wife of Thos. Tuthill, who died July 21, 1797, Aged 27 years.

Sacred to the Memory of Eleanor, Wife of Levi Goodman, who Departed this life the 7th of April, 1790, in the 39 year of her Age.

In Memory of Mary, Wife of Thos. Goodman. Ob. Dec. 6, 1785, Æt. 62.

Also Thos. Goodman, who Departed this life August the 9, 1796, Aged 79 years.

In Memory of Wm. Stephens, who departed this life Sept. the 26, 1751, Aged 12 years.

To the Memory of Thos. Mason, who Departed this life the 8 of August, 1805, Aged 72 years.

Also Elizabeth, who Departed this life the 11 of Jan. 1802, Aged 66 years.

In Memory of Mary, Daughter of Thomas and Elizabeth Mason, who died May 29, 1803, Aged 30 years.

Farewell, vain world, I know enough of thee,
I value not what thou canst say of me;
Thy smiles I court not, nor thy frowns I fear,
All's one to me, my Head lies quiet here;
In lingering illness Death found me long opprest,
Pitied my sighs, and kindly gave me Rest.

On a Flat Stone.

In Memory of Ann, the Wife of Alexander Newman, who died June 9th, 1731, Aged 55 years.

Here lyeth the Body of Alexander Newman, who died Sept. 21, 1763, Aged 78 years.

In Memory of Sarah, wife of William Blackmore, who died Sept. 29, 1776, Aged 48 years.

To the Memory of Frances, the wife of Alexander Newman, who died April 26, 1754, Aged 38 years.

In Memory of Edwd White, who died Oct. 25, 1754, Aged 46 years.

In Memory of Edwd White, who died Oct. 15, 1800, Aged 82 years.

Our life hangs by a slender thread,
Which soon is cut, and we are dead;
Then, Reader, boast not of thy might,
We're here at noon, and gone at night.

On a wood frame.

In Memory of Richard Batt, who Departed this life Feb. 5, 1782, Aged 39 years.

To the Memory of Mary Harding, who Departed this life Oct. 15, 1815, Aged 62 years.

To the Memory of John Harding, who died April ye 19, 1786, Aged 72 years.

To the Memory of Ruth, Wife of John Harding, who died August 17, 1809, Aged 94 years.

To the Memory of Zabulon Batt, who died Sept. 22, 1811, Aged 32 years.

Also Thos. Son of Zabulon and Eliz. who died July 25, 1807, Aged 5 weeks.

Flat Stone.

In Memory of Edward Annetts, who died August the 5, 1685, Aged 70 years.

And also Edward Annetts, who died May the 14th, 1716, Aged 37 years.

And also Susanna Annetts, who died March the 7, 1721, Aged 65 years.

And also John Dowss, who died August the 12, 1774, Aged 82 years.

And also Millisent, the Wife of John Dowss, who died July the 17, 1775, Aged 71 years.

On a wood frame.

In Memory of William, Son of Thomas and Elizabeth Davis, who died Sept. 28, 1803, Aged 1 year and 6 months.

To the Memory of Eliz. Wife of Zabulon Carter, who Departed this life the 20 of June, 1811, Aged 46 years.

To the Memory of Zabulon Carter, who Departed this life the 8 of June, 1809, Aged 87 years.

In Memory of Zabulon Carter, who died June 4, 1797, Aged 84 years.

In Memory of Zabulon, Son of Zabulon and Elizabeth Carter, who died April 30, 1794, Aged 53 years.

In Memory of Elizabeth, Wife of Zabulon Carter, who Died April 7, 1794, Aged 84 years.

In Memory of Frances, the Wife of Zabulon Carter, Jun. who died Nov. 10, 1784, Aged 49 years.

To the Memory of Ann, Daughter of Richard and Rebecca Andrews, who died Oct. 17, 1802, Aged 29 years.

In Memory of Thos. Piper, who died Dec. 3, 1754, Aged 89 years.

To the Memory of Mr. John Piper, who Departed this life the 25 of Jan. 1808, Aged 81 years.

Here lyeth the Body of Richard Dunsdon, who Departed this life Dec. 27, 1756, Aged 63 years. Also near this place lies his Mother, Mary Dunsdon.

Hic
positus est
Gulielmus Gale. Obiit 10th
of August, 1816, Ætatis 62.
An Honest man,
Deny it who can.

To the Memory of Henry Sadlier, who Departed this life the 24 of June, 1807, Aged 86 years.

To the Memory of Francis Wilmot, who died Oct. 25, 1809, Aged 41 years.

Also John, Son of Francis and Mary Wilmot, who died Nov. 25, 1806, Aged 6 years.

In Memory of Thos. Battin, who died Jan. 9, 1739, Aged 75 years.

Also Elizabeth, his Wife, Died March 19, 1748, Aged 65 years.

On wood frames.

In Memory of Joseph Paine, Son of Joseph and Mary Paine, of the City of London, who Departed this life August 12, 1792, Aged 3 years.

To the Memory of Jane, the Wife of Robert Bird, who died 21 Oct. 1798, Aged 22 years.

178

To the Memory of Ann, Daughter of John and Margaret Oram, who died 11 June, 1799, Aged 27 years.

To the Memory of Sarah, the Wife of Joseph Walters, Daughter of John and Margaret Oram, who died the 17th of Feb. 1804, Aged 29 years.

In Memory of Wm. Vivash, who died April 2nd, 1794, Aged 60 years.

Also Mary, Wife of William Vivash, who died Dec. 23, 1798, Aged 64 years.

Sacred to the Memory of John Bushell, who Departed this life August 13, 1810, Aged 69 years.

To the Memory of Mary, Wife of Thos. Bushell, who died Dec. 1, 1797, Aged 83 years.

To the Memory of Thos. Bushell, who died Jan. ye 5, 1786, Aged 91 years.

Flat Tomb.

Beneath this Stone are deposited the Remains of Elizabeth, the Wife of D. Pinckney, of Tidcomb, in this County. She died May the 18, 1800, Aged 29 years.

Whilst you, superior to a world like this,
With choirs angelic, share immortal bliss,
Accept these tears, Mortality's relief,
And till we share your joys, forgive our grief;
These humble rites, a Stone, a Verse, receive,
'Tis all a Husband, all a Friend can give.

In Memory of Mary Swait, who died May 4, 1792, Aged 44 years.

In Memory of Alexander, Son of Alexander and Sarah Swait, who died Nov. 18, 1794, Aged 10 years.

To the Memory of Alexander Swait, who died May ye 4, 1776, Aged 68 years.

Death is the painfull way that all must tread,
Joyful to them that are by virtue led;
Then grieve not, Friends, because I died so soon,
I my day's journey finished at noon.

Also Ann, his Wife, who died Nov. ye 29, 1770, Aged 52 years.

In Memory of Robert and Thomas, Sons of John and Ann Hall. Robt. died May 26, 1760, Aged 36 years, Thos. died April 20, 1747, Aged 17 years.

In Memory of Ann, ye Wife of John Hall, who died April 27, 1755, Aged 55 years.

To the Memory of James Swait, who died Oct. ye 14, 1784, Aged 79 years.

Have mercy, Lord, for I grow faint,
Unable to endure
The anguish of my aking bones,
Which thou alone canst cure.

Also Thos. Swait, his Brother, who died April ye 1, 1783, Aged 65 years.

In Memory of Ann, Wife of James Swait, who died Dec. 10, 1775, Aged 66 years.

To the Memory of Mary, Wife of Robert Long, who died Oct. 14, 1814, Aged 42 years.

To the Memory of James Long, who Departed this life the 17 of Dec. 1813, Aged 83 years.

To the Memory of Elizabeth, the Wife of John Church, who died 30 day of July, 1778, Aged 93 years.

In Memory of Martha, Wife of James Swait, who Died May 4, 1794, Aged 31 years.

A pale Consumption struck the fatal blow,
The stroke was certain, but the affect was slow;
With lingering pains Death saw me long oppres'd,
Pitied my sighs, and kindly gave me rest.

Sacred to the Memory of Elizth Kingstone, Daughter of Thos. and Catharine Kingstone, who died May 12, 1790, Aged 29 years.

Sacred to the Memory of Catharine, Wife of Thos. Kingstone, who died June 1, 1819, Aged 81 years.

To the Memory of Thomas Kingstone, who Departed this life the 30 of Oct. 1805, Aged 74 years.

Sober, tho' lib'ral, and tho' prudent, just,
Trusty, tho' cautious whom he ought to trust;
He pass'd through life, respected and admir'd,
To that blest Kingdom he so much desir'd.

In Memory of Susanna, Wife of Richard Andrews, who died May 19, 1797, Aged 32 years.

In Memory of Catharine, Daughter of Thos. and Catharine Kingstone, who died Jan. 30, 1801, Aged 24 years.

To the Memory of Ann, the Daughter of Richard and Susanna Andrews, who Departed this life the 12 of March, 1804, Aged 15 years.

Read these few lines, and mark them well:
At fifteen years of Age she fell,
In beauty bright, and splendour gay,
So blooms, so falls, the Flower of May;
In her let youth and beauty see
How short their date on earth may be.

To the Memory of Caroline, Daughter of Richard and Susanna Andrews, who Departed this life May 24, 1812, Aged 22 years.

From storms of danger, and from seas of grief,
Safe landed, now she finds a blest relief;
The grave's soft bed her sacred dust contains,
And with its God the soul in bliss remains:
Faith was her Bark, incessant Rays her Oars,
And Hope her Gale, that from these mortal shores,
Thro' Death's rough wave, to Heaven her spirit bore,
To raise redeeming love for evermore.

In Memory of Thos. Robey, who departed this life June 17, 1760, Aged 45.

Flat Tomb.

Sacred to the Memory of John Tanner, Esq. late of Tidcomb, Wilts. who departed this life March 12, 1797, Aged 46 years.

Head Stones.

In Memory of Jemima Tanner, who departed this life July the 25, 1773, Aged 52.

In Memory of Thos. Tanner, who Departed this life Feb. the 8, 1752, Aged 62.

In Memory of Mary Ball, who Departed this life Sept. the 26, 1771, Aged 63.

In Memory of Ruth Tanner, who Departed this life Jan. the 26, 1775, Aged 87 years.

In Memory of Thos. Tanner, late of . . . . . . who was here interred Sept. ye 26, 1750.

In Memory of Edward Tanner, late of Kingston Collingbourn, who Departed this life Dec. 29, 1730.

In Memory of Joseph Butt, who died Feb. 14, 1800, Aged 59 years.

Also Ann, his Wife, who died Dec. 21, 1799, Aged 59 years.

In Memory of Thos. White, who died April 13, 1741, Aged 81 years.

In Memory of Ann, Wife of Wm. Dorrell, who died May 30, 1757, Aged 63 years.

To the Memory of Thos. Edwards, who Departed this life Oct. 1, 1806, Aged 28 years.

In Memory of John Edwards, who died May 24, 1798, Aged 57 years.

In Memory of Jane, Wife of Anthony Edwards, who died May 10, 1798, Aged 82 years.

In Memory of Anthony Edwards, who died April 25, 1773, Aged 67 years.

Also near this place lieth the Body of Elizabeth, his Daughter, who died Dec. 22, 1737, Aged 2 months.

To the Memory of John Rushley, who Departed this life the 15 of Dec. 1807, Aged 62 years.

Also to the Memory of Mary, the Wife of John Rushley, who departed this life ye 23 of Feb. 1806, Aged 61 years.

Here lyeth the Body of Thomas Hawkins, who Departed this life ye 22 day of May, A. D. 1714, Aged 84.

Here lyeth the Body of Mary, Wife of Thos. Hawkins, of Wexcomb. She died Feb. ye 21, 1740, Aged 87 years.

In Memory of William, Son of William and Mary Norris, who died Sept. 9th, 1797, Aged 23 years.

Here lies a Branch, just full grown,
Which in its prime Death hath cut down,
A lovely Branch always hath been,
Who feared God, and hated sin.

In Memory of Mary, the Wife of William Norris, who Departed this life Feb. ye 20, 1782, Aged 34 years.

Flat Tombs.

Here lyeth ye Body of Francis Batt, who departed this life August 2, A. D. 1710.

Here Lyeth the Body of John Batt, who Departed this life Sept. the 13, A.D. 1765, Aged 60 years.

And also Elizabeth, Daughter of Francis Batt. She died July 27, 1720, Aged 26 years.

Sacred to the Memory of Ralph Tanner, Gent. late of Wexcombe, who Departed this life Feb. 19, 1800, Aged 72 years.

Sacred to the Memory of Martha Tanner, wife of Ralph Tanner, Gent. late of Wexcombe, who departed this life the 15 of March, 1803, Aged 66 years.

Sacred to the Memory of Jemima Tanner, second Daughter of Ralph and Martha Tanner, late of Wexcombe, who Departed this life the 11 of Dec. 1818, Aged 60 years.

Head Stones.

In Memory of Elizabeth, Daughter of John and Christian Norris, who was buried Oct. 3, 1737.

To the Memory of Thos. Hill, who died Oct. 6, 1766, Aged 69 years.

In Memory of Hannah, Wife of Thos. Hill, who died May 25, 1753, Aged 72 years.

Flat Stone.

In Memory of Mary, Wife of Wm. Dorrell, who died Sept. 9, 1750, Aged 58.

Flat Tomb.

Here lies the Body of Anne, the Wife of John Long, who died Jan. 25, 1755, Aged 78 years.

Here lyeth ye Body of John Long, who Departed this life August 4, A.D. 1731, Aged 59 years.

Head Stones.

Here Lyeth ye Body of Jemima, Wife of John Dows. She Departed this life August 21, 1772, Aged 29 years.

Sacred to the Memory of John Mannings, who died June 1, 1812, Aged 76 years.

Sacred to the Memory of Betty Mannings, the Wife of John Mannings, who Departed this life August 21, 1802, Aged 67 years.

BURBAGE.

On a Monument against North Wall of Chancel.

Near this Spot are deposited the Remains of the Rev. Henry Jenner, A.M. Rector of Rockhampton, in the County of Gloucester, Vicar of Great Bedwin, in this County, and many years Domestick Chaplain to the Right Hon[ble] the Earl of Ailesbury. He Departed this life the 4th of April, 1798, Aged 61 years.

Also in Memory of three Sons of the Rev. Henry Jenner, and Ann, his Wife; Viz. Stephen, a Lieutenant in the Army, shipwrecked on board the Catherine Transport, off Portland Island, Nov. ye 18, 1795, in the 31 year of his Age: His Body was found, and buried at Wick Regis, in the County of Dorset, together with sixteen other Officers, who were all lost in the same dreadful storm on their passage to the West Indies. Edward, who died May ye 18, 1789, in the 14 year of his Age, and rests near his Father. Decimus, who died Dec. ye 31, 1794, in the 14 year of his Age, and lies Interred at Berkeley, in the County of Glocester.

On Flat Stones in Chancel.

In Memory of Elizabeth, the Wife of Mr. James Ralfe. Obiit 9th Oct. 1749, Ætatis 48.

Elizabeth, the Wife of John Gamon. She died Jan. the 7, A. D. 1771, Aged 53 years.

Here lyeth the Body of Stephen Dore, Sen. who departed this life July ye 16, A.D. 1723, Aged 63.

On Flat Stones in Nave.

Here lyeth the Body of Francis Noyes, who Departed the 1st Day of March, Anno Dom. 1685.

Richard Baden, Son of Andrew Baden, jun. and Elizabeth, his Wife, dyed at Broad Hinton, in this County, Sept. 27, 1760, Aged 3 years and 4 months.

Elizabeth, Wife of Andrew Baden, died Jan. 5, 1770, Aged 46 years.

Memento Mori.

In Memory of Sarah, Wife of Andrew Baden, who died March ye 25, 1739, Aged 46 years.

The time that she on Earth hath spent
She Strive to Give to all Content;
And when She died she put her trust
Ever to rest amongst the just.

Here lyeth the Body of Andrew Baden, Sen. who Departed this life Feb. the 16, 1766, Aged 88.

Alice Baden, the Wife of Andrew Baden, died April the 3, 1772, Aged 84 years.

South Wall of Nave.

Mr. Philip Pearce, late of this Parish, by his Will, Dated the 18th day of August, 1803, and proved in the Consistory Court of Salisbury, Gave the Sum of Two Thousand Pounds, then in the Hands of the Right Honourable the Earl of Ailesbury, to the Minister, Churchwardens, and Overseers of the Poor of the Parish of Burbage, and their successors in Office, and to the Earl of Ailesbury, his Heirs and Executors, in Trust, for the Interest to be given about Christmas, annually, to the second Poor of the said Parish not receiving Parochial Relief, reserving Ten Pounds a Year out of the said Interest in Aid of a Charity School, for the purpose of Educating poor Children in the said Parish in Reading, the Master or Mistress of the said School, to be chosen by the Trustees.

Against the North Wall of Nave.

BENEFACTION

To Burbage. Several Sums, amounting to Seven Pounds, left by the Deacons' and Bayntons' Families, and Lodged in the Church Wardens and Overseers hands, the yearly Interest whereof is to be distributed by them to the Widows of this Parish, The Sum of Three Pounds left in the manner and form as above by John Baynton, of Burbage, 1740; also three Pounds left in the manner and form as above by Mary Baynton, 1778. The Sum of Ten Shillings, left by Mr. John Bushell, of Great Bedwin, yearly, to the Churchwardens of Burbage Six days before Christmas, and to be distributed to twenty of the honest Industrious Poor of the said Parish, which payments is to be made out of the Lands and Tenements, &c. in Burbage, lately belonging to Wm. Thomas, Esq. and John Hilliard, yeoman.

P. Pearce, } Ch.wdns.
H. Neale, }

In two of the windows in the north wall of the Chancel is some painted glass, g. o. v.

In the South wall is a piscina, on the left of which are three stone stalls.

The Church consists of Chancel, Nave, and North and South Aisles.

Register commenced in the year 1561.

Rev. — Russell, Vicar.

The Earl of Ailesbury Lord of the Manor.

EASTON.

On a Monument against North Wall of Chancel.

Sacred to the Memory of Mr. Wm. Butcher, who was Born at Rushall, in this County, on the 18th day of Jan. 1776, and Departed this life at Pamphill House, near Wimborne, in the County of Dorset, on the 22d Day of Feb. 1818, in the 43 year of his Age. He was the third Son of Mr. John Butcher, late of this Parish, to which Place, by his Particular Desire, his Remains were brought for Interment.

Also of Jane, Wife of the above-named Mr. Wm. Butcher, and only Daughter of Wm. Vale, Esq. of Portman Street, Portman Square, London, who immediately after the Decease of her Husband, incapable of sustaining her great loss, rapidly sunk into a deep decline, and Departed this life at Weymouth, in Dorsetshire, where she had retired for change of air, on the 18 Day of Jan. 1819, in the 43 year of her Age, Surviving her Husband only 11 months. Her elder Brother, Mr. John Vale, of May Fair, London, Caused this Tablet to be Erected to their Memory.

Wm. Francis, Merchant and Citizen of London, and a Native of this Place, by his last Will, Dated May 1, 1805, bequeathed the Sum of £.500 to this Parish for Ever, in manner following, Viz. I give to the Minister and Churchwardens of the Parish of Easton, in Wilts. for the time being, Five Hundred Pounds, upon trust, to invest the same in Government Securities, and to apply and distribute the Dividends, Interest, and Annual Proceeds thereof to and amongst the industrious poor of the said Parish for the time being, yearly, on Christmas Day for ever, in such way and manner as the Minister and Churchwardens for the time being, or the major part of them, shall deem most conducive to the Comfort of such Poor.

MILTON.

On a Flat Stone in Chancel.

Here Lyeth ye Body of Thos. Clerke, Esq. who departed this life April ye 13th, A.D. 1714, Aged 73 years.

Also Here lyeth Christian, his Wife, who died Dec. ye 17th, A.D. 1714.

Arms—Per chevron, three leopards' heads caboshed, in base an eagle displayed: impaling, three sinister hands.

182

Brass Plate.

Here lyeth ye Body of Ann, ye Wife of John Michell, Gent. who departed this life ye 15 Day of Oct. 1705. This Stone was desired by ye deceased never to be removed.

The Church consists of Chancel, Nave, and North Aisle.

The Rev. Thomas Hinchman Gale, Vicar.

PEWSEY.

On a Monument against the north wall of Chancel.

Beneath this Tablet rest the mortal Remains of the Rev. Joseph Townsend, M. A. Formerly of Clare Hall, in the University of Cambridge. He Departed this life on the 6 Day of Nov. 1816, in the 78 year of his Age. With what diligence he strove to improve the talents committed by his Maker to his Charge, the remembrance of his labours for fifty-three years in Christ's ministry, during which time he was Rector of this Parish, and the Fruits of his Researches after truth, as well religious as moral, economical, and physical, delivered in his writings, bear a lasting testimony. He was twice happily married, first in 1773, to Joyce, the Daughter of Thomas Nankivell, of St. Agnes, in the County of Cornwall, Gentleman, by whom he had Six Children: She died in 1783, and was buried at Croydon, in the County of Surry. In 1790, he married Lydia, the widow of Admiral Sir John Clerke, Knight, who was removed to a better world on the 3rd of June, 1814, in the 73 year of her Age, and lies buried near this place.

Against south wall of Chancel.

Near this Monument Lyes Interred ye Body of Katherine Harding, who Dyed ye 29 of Oct. 1645. She was Daughter to Sir Francis Clare, of Worcestershire, Wife to Richard Harding, Esq. one of ye Gromes of ye Bedchamber to King Charles ye 2nd, & Keeper of ye privie Purse. He dyed in Holland, in his Majsty's Service, two years before his happy Restoration, they left Behind them one Only Daugr, Honora Harding, whoe, in obedience to her Father's Comand, has set up this Small Remembrance of them both.

Arms—Argent, on a bend, gules, three martlets, argent: impaling, three chevrons, gules, within a border, engrailed, sable.

On Flat Stones in Chancel.

In Memory of Morice, Son of Peter and Elizabeth Smith, Watch Maker, in London, who died Sept. 1, 1783, Aged 75.

Here lyeth ye Body of Peter Smith. He Departed this life Nov. ye 10, A. D. 1787, Aged 93 years.

Jane, the Daughter of Richard Watson, Rector of St. Mary, Aldermary, in London, Wife first to John Bruce, Esq. of the Inner Temple; next to Dr. John Cruso, Vicar-General to the Bishop of St. David's, and prebendary of Christ's Coll. in Brecon, who there Lyeth Interred. Buried Jan. 4, 1669.

Katherine Harding, 29 Oct. 1645.

Eduardus Wood,
Chirurgorum, M. A. Wiltoniensium
Terr. Marique Sæpius,
ac
Feliciter operatus,
Hic dormit Denuo suscitandus.
Obiit Aprilis 1, A. D. 1682,
Ætatis suæ XLII.
Requiescat in pace;
Lector, o.. to memori.

Dr. Richard Watson January ye 13, 1684.

Here lyeth the Body of Thomas Deane, late of Marlborough, who died 13 July, 1776, Aged 66 years.

He was the Second Son of John Deane, of this Parish, Attorney-at-Law, who was buried here the 4 Nov. 1715, And Ann, his Wife, Daughter of Edward Nott, Esq. of Braydon, in this County. She likewise was buried here the 26 of March, 1734.

Here also lyeth the Bodies of John Deane, their third Son, who died 2d Nov. 1764, Aged 52 years.

And Elizabeth, Wife of Christopher Deavin, Daughter of the said Ann, by Wm. Munday, her second Husband. She died 27 July, 1745, Aged 26 years.

Against the North Wall of Nave.

There lies the Remains of Robert Hooper, who died August the 9th, 1782, Aged 61 years.

Also in the same Grave are deposited the Remains of Ann, his Wife, who died the 24 Sept. 1792, Aged 57 years.

There lyes the Body of Richard Hooper. He dyed March ye 31, 1776, Aged 76 years.

Death, in a good old Age,
Ended my weary Pilgrimage;
The time will come to rise, and then
I hope to be with Christ. Amen.

South Wall.

Sacred to the Memory of Richard Pye, Gent. who Departed this life Jan. the 5, 1795, Aged 83 years.

Near this place are Deposited the Remains of Wm. Hooper, who died August 3, 1791, Aged 32 years.

Also of Robert Hooper, who died April 6, 1795, Aged 32 years.

And of Richard Hooper, who died Sept. 27, 1798, Aged 37 years.

Sacred to the Memory of Henry Deacon, Esq. late of London, Wine Merchant, and of Oare, in this County. He died Jan. 27, 1757, Ætatis 57.

Also near this place lies the Body of Mrs. Elizabeth Doody, Sister to the above Mr. Deacon, who died 3 Feb. 1772, Aged 76.

Arms Azure, a cross between four lions rampant, or, on a chief of the last, three roses, gules; impaling argent, on a chevron, sable, three fountains.

On Flat Stones in Body.

Here lyeth the Body of Samuel Austin, who Departed this life Nov. the 14, 1745, Aged 63 years.

Stay awhile, and spend a tear,
Upon the Dust that slumbers here,
And while thou readest ye state of me,
Think on the glass that runs for thee.

Also here lyeth Mary, the Wife of Samuel Austin, who died Sept. 15, 1749, Aged 69 years.

I grieve to think I cannot grieve no more,
To think my dearest Friend is gone before;
But since it pleased God to part us here,
In Heaven I hope to meet my dearest Dear.

In Memory of Mary, Daughter of Thorpe and Mary Pyke. She died July ye 22, 1743, Aged 16 years.

In Memory of Mary, the Wife of Thorpe Pyke, who died Jan. 19, 1747, Aged 41 years.

Also Jane, their Daughter, lyeth near, who died March 13, 1746, Aged 18.

In Memory of Thorpe Pyke, who Departed this life March ye 25, 1753, Aged 57 years.

Against North Wall of North Aisle.

Sacred to the Memory
of Briant, the Son of
Richard and Ann Chandler,
who died 5 Feb. 1801,
Aged 15 years.

In Memory of John Winter, Gent. who died May 3, 1797, Aged 75 years.

John Winter, his Son, died Feb. ye 22, 1797, Aged 37 years.

Wm. the Son of Wm. and Mary Winter, died March 3, 1794, Aged 18 months.

Near this Pew lies the Body of Elizabeth, the Wife of James Stevens, who died March ye 25, 1764, Aged 47 years.

Under this Pew lyeth the Body of Philip Blatch, who Departed this life Nov. the 13, 1757, Aged 22 years.

On Monuments in S. Aisle.

Near this Place lyeth the Body of Mary, Wife of Christopher Allsup, who Departed this life Dec. ye 20, 1727, Aged 55 years.

Also Christopher, their Son, Aged 11 Days.

Near this place lyeth the Body of Christopher Allsup, Surgeon, who Departed this life Sept. ye 24, 1738, Aged 52 years.

Also Christian, Daughter of Christopher and Margaret Allsup, who Departed this life August, ye 19, 1762, Aged 31 years.

Sacred to the Memory of Henry Pyke, who died the 6 Nov. 1797, Aged 66 years.

Also Victoria Catharina, the Daughter of Henry and Elizabeth Pyke, who died the 5 March, 1804, Aged 22 years.

Flat Stones.

Carolus, Francisci et Mariæ Kemble Filius, 29 die Maij Natus est, Obiit 19 die Decembris, Anno Dom. 1741, Ætatis suæ 2do.

Dominus dedit, Dominus abstulit, sit nomen Domini Benedictum.

Here Lyeth the Body of Stephen Winter, who Dyed April ye 28, 1753, Aged 71 years.

Also Elizabeth, his Wife, Dyed Sept. the 2, 1742, Aged 51 years.

Also Robert and Ralph Winter, twins, Dyed April ye 26, 1724, Aged 4 Days.

Also Barnes Winter Dyed August ye 16, 1725, Aged 20 days.

Here lyeth the Body of Elizabeth, the Wife of John Winter, who dyed April ye 4, 1756, Aged 32 years. Also Victoria Catharina, Daughter of John and Elizabeth Winter, who dyed Feb. ye 9, 1756, Aged 3 months and 4 Days.

Also George and Charlotte, Son and Daughter of John and Mary Winter, Dyed young, 1765.

The Church consists of Chancel, Nave, and North and South Aisles. The Nave is supported on each side by four plain pointed arches.

Register began 1568.

The Manor belongs jointly to — Ashley, Esq. and the Trustees of St. Thomas' Hospital, London.

The Rev. Mr. Bouverie, Rector.

WOTTON.

On Monuments in Chancel.

Sacred to the Memory of the Rev. Sir Edward Ernle, Baronet, the last Male Heir of an ancient and very respectable Family. They who knew him Personally, or by Character, need no Father Inscription; for the benefit of Posterity alone here are recorded his fervent Zeal in defence of right Principles, his Simplicity of Manners, his tenderness of Heart, his social and singular engaging qualities, were intimately blended with the most awful sense of Religion, a rare and happy Union of Grace and Virtues. This Monument was erected by his Beloved Sister Mrs. Frances Ernle. He died the 26 of Dec. 1787, Aged 75 years.

Arms—Argent, on a bend, sable, three eagles displayed or, on a canton, a sinister bend, gules.

Sacred to the Memory of Henry Somerset, the Son of Thos. and Rebecca Somerset, who died at Rio de Janeiro, in South America, Dec. 7, 1808, in the 35 year of his Age.

Hatchment.

Quarterly, first and fourth argent, a chevron, sable, between three mullets, gules; second and third argent, three bugle-horns sable.

Crest—On an esquire's helmet, a squirrel, argent, holding a mullet, gules.

On the outside of the north wall.

Here lyes ye Body of John Ernle, Esq. late Fellow of New Coll. Oxon. Concerning whom truth & Friendship demands this plain Testimony. He was a faithful Servant of God, a Sincere Friend of Man, and peculiarly a Servant of ye Former by his Manner of be Friending the Latter. He Earnestly desired Eternal Happiness himself, and nobly pursued his Own by affectionately assisting That of Others, the Latter of these good purposes he endeavoured to Effect by ye kindest Advice & (where proper) by seasonable Alms. Though He was excellently Learned for his years, ye pride of knowing was his great Aversion, the pious use of it his principal care. So uncommon Goodness found an Early Reward, April 13, 1737, in ye 25 year of his Age.

Readers, Admire, Imitate, Hope.

On Flat Tombs North Side of the Church.

The Rev. Sir Edward Ernle, Bart. died Dec. 26, 1787, Aged 75 years.

Arms—On a bend, three eagles displayed, in chief a sinister hand.

Sir Michael Ernle, Bart. of Brimslade, Died Feb. 16, 1771, Aged 67.

John Ernle, Esq. died ye 13 of April, 1737, Aged 25.

Arms—On a bend three eagles displayed.

H. S.

Eduardus Ernle, De Brimslade, in Comitatu Wilts. Armiger. Obiit Feb. 27, A. D. 1753, Ætat. 65.

Arms—On a bend three eagles displayed: impaling, a chevron between three roses.

Here lies interred the Body of Mary Ernle, Relict of Micael Ernle, Esq. In hopes of a Happy Resurrection, She Departed this life Dec. 23, Anno Domini 1718, Ætatis suæ 86.

Arms—Ernle; impaling, a chevron between three crescents.

Here lies interred the Body of Mrs. Mary Ernle, Daughter of Michael Ernle, Esq. and Mary, his Wife. She Departed this life June 9, Anno Dom. 1717.

H. S. E.

Gulielmus, Madlei Samborn, Armig.
Et Mariæ uxoris suæ secundæ,
Filius natu maximus,
Ex ultraq. Stirpe fœlix majoribus,
Longe prosapia et in Regem fidelitate notissimis
Vivus
Matris et amicorum voluptas unica,
Mortuus unicus utrisq. luctus et desiderium,
Qui
Omnes ferme imo suos ipsius
Annos (breviores eheu!) virbus ac virtute vicerat,
Tandem vero ad Brimslade

Vivolarum A. g . . imbus abscissus ipse
Septimoq. die victus Pœnitentior occubit
Januarii 7°,
Anno { Ætatis suæ 24,
Salutis Nostræ 1683.
Quantam sic cecidisse cedet in gloriant.

Arms—A chevron between three mullets pierced: impaling, on a chevron between three lozenges as many fleur-de-lis.

2d Shield—Three bugle horns: impaling vair, in chief three lions rampant.

Register commenced in the year 1728.

Rev. Mr. Stone, D. D. present Rector.

The Manor belongs to St. John's College, Cambridge.

TIDCOMBE.

On Monuments in Chancel.

Sacred to the Memory of John Rendall, Late of Martin, who departed this life April 12th, 1809, Aged 46 years.

Also of Ann Rendall, his Wife, who Departed this life April 5, 1812, Aged 52 years.

Sacred to the Memory of Thomas Rendall, late of Oxenwood, who Departed this life May 14, 1815, Aged 83 years.

Also Mary Rendall, Wife of Thomas Rendall, who Departed this life Dec. 8th, 1811, Aged 73 years.

Sacred to the Memory of George Rendall, late of Hurstbourne, who Departed this life Oct. 10, 1813, Aged 42 years.

To the Memory of Caroline Webb, who died June 6, 1797, Aged 2 years.

And also of Charlotte Webb, who died Feb. 5, 1814, Aged 18 years.

This Tablet was Erected by their Mother.

The Church consists of Chancel, Nave, and North and South Aisles. In the South Wall of the Chancel is a piscina.

The Rev. Henry Elston Vicar.

Mr. Churchill, Lord of the Manor.

BUTTERMERE.

On a brass plate in Chancel.

Here lyeth Neere this Place the Body of Frances Curll, ye Daughter of Walter Curll, Esq. by Frances his Wife, who Departed this life the 15th Day of December, in the 5th year of Her Age, Anno Dom. 1669.

Her · days · though · Here · but · few · yet · happy · cause
She · knew · not · things · but · Good
But · if · there · did · appear
Ought · Blest · Christ · quitt · Her · feare · & · it · withstood
For · in · death · pangs · noe · sight · noe · groane
Without · Christ · help · Her · past · Alone.

On a Flat Stone in Chancel.

In Memory of Martha, Wife of Fráncis Charlick. She died the 25 day of Oct. 1725, in ye 44 year of her Age.

In the south wall is a piscina.

In the Churchyard.

To the Memory of Mr. Job Barrett, who died the 14 of Sept. 1781, Aged 76 years.

Under this Stone Lyeth the Body of John Alexander, Bachelor, late of Ruckley Farm, who Departed this life, in hopes of a Joyful Resurrection, almost Suddenly, at Buttermere Farm, Jan. 9th, 1764, Aged 60 years.

Register began 1799.

The Rev. Mr. Dodson Rector.

J. J. Lockhart, Esq. Lord of the Manor.

COLLINGBOURNE KINGSTON.

On Flat Stones within the Rails of the Chancel.

Sub hoc tumulo, in puluervlenta Terra,
Obdormiens vsque dum e potestate sepulchri
Redimetur, et ad vitam æternam Exper-
giscetur quiescit quicquid Terrestre,
Erat honoratissimi viri dm̄i Francisci Pile,
Baronetti, qui evivis excessit 12 die Feb.
Anno Dom. 1648, Ætatis suæ . .

Domina Jana Pile, Dni Francisci Pile, nuper de Compton Beauchamp, in Com. Berks, Baronetti, Vidua; Quæ vita summa cum pietate cum charitate peracta, Ob. Jul. 25° Anno Dni. 1692, Ætatis 80, Viduitatis 41.

Arms—On a cross, between four piles, an escutcheon charged with a sinister hand: impaling, gutte . . three roses.

M. S.

Joanæ Richards, Eduardi Richards, de Yaverland, in Insula de Victis, Armigeri, nuperrime mortui viduæ mœstissimæ, erat filia natu minima et cohæres Domini Francisci Pile, de Compton Beauchamp, in Comitatu Berks, Baronetti, evivis decessit sexto die Februarii, Anno Dom 1677, & Anno Ætatis suæ tricesimo secundo.

Arms—A chevron between four fleur-de-lis: impaling, a cross between four piles.

H. S. E.

Eduardus Richards, de Yaverland, in Insula de Victis, Armiger, Pietati literis moribusq. laude dignus, filius erat et Hæres Johannis Richards, Armigeri, cujus pater fuit Johannis Richards, Eques Aurati, Natus Vicesimo Sexto die Novembris Anno Dom. 1642, et cui tres liberi nati fuerunt, nempe, Johannes, natus vigesimo tertio die Septembris, Añ Dom 1674, Obiit undecimo die Aprilis 1675, et prope sepultus jacet; Eduardus, natus decimo octavo die Augusti, Añ Dom 1676; et Janatq. vigesimo secundo die Septembris, Añ Dom 1677, adhuc evivis, obiit decimo nono die Novembris Añ Dom 1677.

[Arms as the preceding.]

Flat Stones without the Rails.

Here lyeth the Body of Jane Richards, the Daughter of Edward Richards, of Yaverland, in the Isle of Wight, Esq. who was Buried 6 Jan. 1678, Aged 1 year, 3 months, and 14 days.

Here lyeth the Body of John Richards, the Son of Edward Richards, of Yaverland, in the Isle of Wight, Esq. who was Buried 12 April, Anno D. 1675, Aged 6 Months and 10 Days.

On a white marble monument in Chancel.

Eduardus Richards, de Compton, in agro Berceriensi, Armiger, ex antiquæ tum Paterna tum Materna Gente ortus, Uxorem duxit Rachelem, Domini Edmundi Warnford, Equitis, Filiam, ex quâ unicam suscepit prolem, paralysi tandem confectus animam Deo reddidit 26to . . . . . A. D. 1728, Ætatis suæ 53.

Vir de Rege de Rep. de Ecclesia optime moritus, In Coll. Exon 26 Annos studiis dedit non minus exemplo quam munificentia profecturus, hinc decedens summâ cum dignitate latuit, quippe publicis negotiis otium literatum, splendori innocentiam ante posuit, quam suis omnibus charus, vixerit, Uxoris Filiæ Amicorum Clientum testatur triste Desiderium.

Arms—Sable, a chevron between three fleur-de-lis argent, impaling per fess, imbattled argent and sable, on each three cross pattée counter-changed.

Sacred to the Memory of Gertrude, Wife of Gabr. Pile, Esquire, and Sister to Sir Thom. Jeay, Kt.

Behold, Heere a goodly floure soone fadinge, a beavtiful Rachell Dying in the waye of this world in Childbirth, at the Age of 22, But this Immature Death is her Greatest gaine. She being all faire within, & Having Continued Both in life and Death in faith, Holinesse, & Charity with Sobriety, is saved in Childbearing. Hir Affectionate Jacob Hath set up this Pillar to preserve His name alive Heere, But he in whom She overcame, hath made hir a living Pillar in his holy mount never to goe out more—having lived in wedlocke about 6 yeares, & Borne Gabl Gertrude, & William, of which the 2 last lye Buried Neere here about, Shee passed to an Inheritance Incorruptible, undefiled, and yt fadeth not, on the first day of March, 1630.

Stay, passenger, & with thee take a Story
Opprest with as much grief as Rich in Glory;
The worst I must Inherit, But the Bright
Embleme of virtue, Beauty, are thy Right,
With me my sorowe dyes, but thy Name
Justlie enjoyes Eternity of fame;
Your Husbands love in this faire book is shewne,
But the Brave Monument of life's your owne:
Such was your sweet example, that it must
Survive in freshnes when all this is Dust.

Arms—Argent, a cross between four piles, gules: impaling argent, on a bend, or, three roses, gules.

South Wall.

Here lyeth the Bodie of Sir Gabriell Pile, of Collingborne, Kingstone, Knight, who Departed this life the 7 day of Nov. 1626, and Dame Anne, his Wife, Dawghter to Sir Thomas Porter, of Newarke, in the County of Gloster, Knight, who Deceased the 7 of Jan. 1640.

Arms—Quarterly, first and fourth argent, a cross between four piles, gules; second or, three bugle-horns in pale, gules; third lozengy, azure and argent, over all two bars, gules.

On a Flat Stone in Nave.

In Memory of Mr. Joseph Macham, Surveyor of the King's Warehouse, in the Port of London, and Son of Cornelius Macham, of Southampton, Merchant. Born July 20th, 1684, Died Jan. 12, 1752.

Mary Macham died Sept. 7, 1776, Aged 63 years.

Wm. Macham, LL. D. Died August 25, 1789, Aged 66.

Arms—A chevron between three greyhounds courant: impaling three pears, in chief a demi-lion. *Crest*—A greyhound.

Brass taken out.

North Aisle.

Sacred to the Memory of Elizabeth Parsons, Daur of Barthol Parsons, Pastor of this Church, & Anne, his Wife, who hevinge not Ataind to the ful age of 12 at hir ende, by fervent & frequent Prayers, penitency, faith, Willingnesse to leave the worlde, Care for the Poore, disposinge of hir worldly goods, & Choise of hir funerall text, expressed such Piety, Charity, & understandinge, as is Rare to be founde in mature Age, & Hath left to hir friends Great Both joy & Sorrow, to hir selfe a good name, to the Worlde, an happy Example, this Damosel then is not dead, But Sleepeth, yea, liveth both above with the lord, & Here also in her fame & this Monument, the Dust wherein this Blessed Soul dwelt is laid up Heere Belowe in Hope of the resurrection of the Just, Feb. 26, 1627.

Posuervnt parentes mœstissimi.

Brass taken out.

M. S.
Elizabethæ, Uxoris
Henrici Jacob,
Hujus Ecclesiæ Ministri,
Quæ obiit 27 die Oct. Anno Dom. 1682,
Ætatis suæ 21,
Et prope Sepulta jacet.

The Church consists of Chancel, Nave, and North and South Aisles. The Nave is supported on each side by four pointed arches.

The Rev. D. Newbolt Vicar.

The Earl of Ailesbury Lord of the Manor.

CHUTE.

On a Monument against the north wall of Chancel.

Beneath are Deposited the Remains of Mrs. Eliz. Earle, Spinster, who died March 8th, A. D. 1780, Aged 77. She was the Eldest Daughter, and on the Death of her Brothers Charles & John, Heiress of Richard Earle, of Chute Forest, Esq.

East End.

Edward Scroggs, (Son of Wm. Scroggs, Esq.) of Chute Lodge, By Ann, 4 Daughter of Sir Edward Seymour, Bart. and Sister of Edward 8th Duke of Somerset, died August 6, 1784.

Mary, his Widow, Daughter of James Pulse, of Standen, in this County, Esq. and Constance, 2nd Daughter of Sir Philip Medows, K. M. died January 15, 1805.

To their loved memory this Marble is inscribed as a tribute of Gratitude, Respect, and filial Affection.

South Wall.

In Memory of the Lady Scroggs, Relict of Sir William Scroggs, of Chute Lodge, and Daughter of Mathew Bluck, Esq. of Hunsdon House, in Hertfordshire, who Departed this life April ye 23, 1746, Ætatis 81.

Here lyeth the Body of Samuel Collins, the Son of John Collins, Esq. & Martha, his Wife, of Chute Lodge, in ye County of Wilt̄, who died Feb. 19th, 1679.

Arms—A griffin segrant: impaling a fess cottized, in chief three lions' heads erased, bar-wise.

On Flat Stones within the Rails.

Here lyeth the Body of Humphri Norbone, Gent. who dyed the two and twentieth day of May, Anno Domini 1662, Aged 82.

Arms—Ermine, a fess nebulé, a canton charged with a ducal crown.

H. S. E.
Gulielmus Norborne, Armig.
Qui eximiam qua polluit regum peritiam,
litibus dirimendis unice adhibuit,
Frequentissimus Controversiarum arbiter
Constitutus quo in munere obcundo, laboris
extant late mercedem adeo non expetinit
ut oblatam semper respueret:
Summa erga Deum pietate, erga seipsum temperantia,
erga Clerum benevolentia,
Romæ pariter ac
Genevæ infensus,
erga vicinos hospitalitate, erga
liberos, tenero, affectu, erga omnes Charitate,
vitam præsentem ornavit futuræ providit,
Quam denique pacem ad concordiam aliis toties
restituit ipse per longum vitæ spatium
inviolatam usque coluit neminem lite,
impetens et nemine impetitus.
Obiit Maij 26, Anno Dni. 1700, Ætatis suæ 81.

Arms—Narbone: impaling a fess between three crosslets fitchy.

Hic Jacet Maria, filia
Rawlini Mallock, Armigeri, & Elizabethæ uxor. ejvs,
Elizabethæ, filiæ Johannis Collins, Armigeri,
Quæ obiit 13 Die Martii,
Anno Dni. 1679 Ætatis 1mo.
80

In Memory of Mary, the Wife of Francis Earle, Gent. She dyed the 5 day of Dec. 1724, in ye 62 year of her age.

Here lyeth ye Body of Francis Earle, Gent. who Departed this life ye 27 of Sept. A. D. 1717, in ye 75 year of his Age.

Hic jacet pars terrestris,
Richard Earle, de Chute,
in Comitatu Wilts. Generosi.
Obiit decimo sexto die Junij,
Anno { Salutis publicæ 1705,
{ Ætatis suæ 72.
Meriendum est, ut vivamus,
Vivendum ut recte meriamu . .

Here lyeth the Body of Thomas Earle, Esq. who departed this life the 21 of Nov. 1742, in the 68 year of his age.

Arms—Three escallop shells.
Crest—An escallop on an esquire's helmet.

On Flat Stones in Nave.

Sir Sidney Medows, Knight, Marshall of England, died November 15th, 1792, in the 92 year of his Age.

Arms—A chevron, ermine, between three pelicans, on a canton a shield, charged with a lion passant-guardant.
Crest—A dove.

Quæris quid pedibus calcas Sator . . .
Reliquiæ . . . . Annæ, Gulielmi
Norborn, Gen. Conjugis,
Francisci Jones de Newton Tony,
Prosapia vere Generosia orte,
Quæ cum maritum liberam amore,
Pientissimo,
Amicos, et Familiares,
Suavitate morum
Evinciret . . Stud . . . . . .
F . . . to et . . . . vmtante morbo
Div. Temtata
Morie . . . . (. . . . . dolorum medela)
. . . . . filistissimam vitam
. . . . . . tem commutavit
. . . . . næ fragilitatis
Et divinæ patia . . nitiæ
Monumentum,
Nov. 22.
An° Ætat. 47,
Salvt. 1681.

Arms—Ermine, a fess nebulé, on a canton, a crown: impaling, a fess between three crosslets fitchy.

Here lieth the Body of Body of Rachel Norborne, Daughter of William Norborne, Esq. who Deceased the 16 Day of Dec. in the 19 year of her Age, Anno Dom. 1672.

Here lyeth the Body of John Fisher, of this Parish, Gent. who dyed the 11 day of May, 1706, in the 76 year of his Age.

The Nave of the Church was rebuilt, in 1815, at the expense of Lady Medows.

The Rev. Dr. Randhof, Rector.

E. P. Medows, of Conholt Park, Esq. Lord of the Manor.

In the Churchyard.

The Tomb of General Sir Wm. Medows, K. B. he Died lamented as he lived Beloved, on the 14 of Nov. 1813, in the 75 year of his Age.

To the Memory of Emily Duke, Wife of Lieut. Colonel George Duke, and third Daughter of the late John Freeman, Esq. of Chute Lodge, who Departed this life 30 of June, 1819, Aged 59 years.

In Memory of Eliz. Freeman, Wife of John Freeman, Esq. of Chute Lodge, who died Feb. ye 7, 1764, Ætatis suæ 36.
She was the Daughter of Sir Wm. Strickland, Bart. of Boynton, in the County of York, Secretary of War To his Majesty King George the 2d.

Flat Tombs.

In Memory of John Freeman, of Chute Lodge, who Died Sept. the 7, 1794, Ætatis suæ 72.

Near this Spot are Interred the Remains of the Right Honble General Sir Wm. Medows, K. B.
Colonel of the Princess Royal's Dragoon Guards, and
Governor of Hull,
A brave and Zealous Officer,
An Affectionate Husband, a Kind Brother,
An Indulgent Master, and a Sincere Friend,
By whose munificence this Spire was Erected,
And to whose Memory it is Inscribed.

LITTLE BEDWIN.

Flat Stone in Chancel.

Hic juxta jacent Corpor tam Edmund Hungerford, de Chisbury, Armiger, Quam Elizabethæ, uxoris ejus, filiæ Johannis Wither, de Manidowne, in Com. Southn. Illa obiit 4 Die Januarii, Anno Dni. 1655, Ætatis suæ 63, Ille Decessit 18 Die Decembris, 1659, Ætatis suæ 78.

Here lyeth ye Body of Mrs. Joanna Hide, of Stichcomb, who Departed this life April ye 17, A. D. 1726.

Here lieth interred the Body of Stephen Hyde, Gent. who Died Sept. 3, A. D. 1672, Aged 33.

And also the Body of Ann Hyde, Widow of the said Stephen Hyde, who Deceased March the 7, A. D. 1705, Aged 73.

Arms—A chevron between three lozenges; impaling, barry of six, over all an eagle displayed.

Stephen Hide Departed this life Sept. the 3d Day, Anno Dom. 1672.

Here lyeth the Body of Eliz. the truly loving & truly beloved Wife of John Good, alias Freegood, of the Kingdom of Scotland. They had issue one Son, who survives. She was daughter to Nicholas Kimber, of Cheesbury, in this Parish, Yeoman, and Departed this life the 22 day of Nov. 1696, in the Forty-third year of her Age.

Her sorrowfull Husband, in testimony of his firvent love to the deare Memory of so vertuous and loving a Wife, hath dedicated this Monument to her everlasting Remembrance.

Here lyeth ye Body of Mr. Samuel Kimber, of Chisbury, who Departed this life Oct. ye 18th, Anno Dni. 1725, Ætat. 69.

Here lyeth ye Body of Wm. Farmer. He Departed this life Jan. ye 5, A. D. 1726, Aged 84 years.

On Flat Stones in North Aisle.

M. S.

Marthæ Streat,
Uxoris dulcissimæ R. Viri Richardi Streat,
C. L. A. M. Sororis et Hæredis Fratis sui Tho. Barrow,
Pharmacopolæ, Londinensis, et Paterna Stirpe ortæ
E Maternæ ex antiquâ Familia Calendrinorum in
Germania, ob Causam veræ Religionis a
Patria sua pulsa.
Si Pietas, si prisca Fides, silenes probiq. mores,
Si ingenii acumen, nitidusq. Personæ cultus
Desiderandam, merito faciunt Fœminam ovi, lector,
Et maritum luge superstitem.
Obiit 31 Dec. A. D. 1750, Ætatis 1750,
Ætatis 64.

Arms—Argent, a chevron, gules, between three water-bougets sable, over all an escutcheon, charged with three torteaux, surcharged with as many fleur-de-lis, on a chief, azure, a bugle horn, or, between two pheons, argent, on each a crescent.

Thomas Streat, Gent. died Dec. 30, 1735, Aged 71.
Mary, the Wife of Thos. Street, Gent. Died Jan. 21, 1741, Aged 83.

Arms—Azure, a fess ermine, in chief two doves close: impaling, argent, a chevron, gules, between three water-bougets, sable.

Here lyeth the Bodies of Nicholas Kimber, & Joan his Wife, with five of their Children in this Church.

In the Chancel is some painted glass, or and azure.

The Church consists of Chancel, Nave, and North and South Aisles. The Nave is supported on the north side by three plain semi arches, on the south side by three plain pointed ones.

The Rev. W. Skeyes, Rector.

The Earl of Ailesbury Lord of the Manor.

FROXFIELD.

On Flat Stones in Chancel.

Here lyeth the Body of Mr. John Stephens, who Departed this life December the 22, Anno Dom. 1668, Aged 65 years.

Arms—On a chevron three cross-crosslets between three demi lions rampant.

Here lyeth the Body of John Liddiard, Gent. Son of William Liddiard, late of Poulton, in the Parish of Mildenhall, in this County, Gent. who died June 18, 1739, in the 57 year of his Age.

Here also lieth Joanna, his Wife, Daughter of Robert Stephens, late of this place, Gent. who died April 2, 1718, in the 28 year of her Age.

Here also lyeth Joanna, their Daughter, Wife of Wm. Stirling, Gent. who died July 12, 1741, in the 24 year of her Age.

Arms—On a bend a cross patté between six mullets.

Here lieth the Body of Joane, Wife of Mr. John Stephens, who Departed this life August the 10, Anno Dom̄ 1687.

In Memory of Elizabeth Liddiard, who died ...... ye 20, Anno Dom. 1732, Aged 74 years.

She had two Husbands, ye first Robert Stephens, of this Place, Gent. ye other was Wm. Liddiard, of Poulton, in ye parish of Mildenhall.

On a Monument against the South Wall of Nave.

In Memory of Elias Ivy, Gent. who died Nov. 3rd, 1777, Aged 58 years.

Also of Elinor, his Wife, who died May 23d, 1771, Aged 54 years.

By death we rest from Care and pain,
In hope with Joy to meet again.

On Flat Stones in Nave.

Here lyeth Edward Oldfield, Esq. who died June ye 12, 1660.

Here lyeth ye Body of Elinor, the Wife of Alexander Dismore, late of Freefolk, Gent. She died at Knowle, Jan. ye 20, 1731, in the 74 year of her Age.

Arms—A chevron between three roses: impaling six lions rampant, 3 2 1.

Here lieth ye Body of Alexander Dismore, Senr, of Freefolk, Husband of Elinor Dismore, and Son of Alexander Dismore, of Rudge, who died Jan. 26, 1699, Aged 49.

Here lieth the Body of Barbary Jenkins, Relict of the Rev. Wm. Jenkins, late Ruler Dean and Vicar of Kidwelly, in Carmarthenshire, South Wales. She Died the 29 day of Nov. 1780, Aged 81 years.

Also here lieth the Body of Barbary Jenkins, Daughter of the above, who died the 4 day of March, 1777, Aged 30 years.

The Rev. Dr. Evans present Vicar.

The Earl of Ailesbury Lord of the Manor.

The
Somerset Hospital,
For Twenty Clergy
and Thirty Lay Widows,
Founded and Endowed
By the Late Most Noble
Sarah,
Duchess
Dowager of Somerset, A. D. MDCXCIV.

MANNINGFORD ABBOTS.

On Flat Stones in Chancel.

Here lyeth the Body of Mrs. Dorothy Clark, Wife of Mr. Thomas Clark, Dean Ruler of this Diacesse, and the Daughter of Francis Wroughton, of Wilcot, Esq. who dyed ye 4th of July, Anno Dom̃ 1689.

Here Lyeth the Body of the Rev. Mr. Thos. Clark, Rector of this Parish, who departed this life May the 16, 1683.

Robertus Reeks, hujus Ecclesiæ
plus 15 Annos Rector.
Ob. Octobris Anno Salutis 1708, Ætatis 38.

Flat Stones in the Body.

Here Lyeth the Body of Margreat Bankes, the Wife of Wm. Bankes. She Departed this life August the 31, 1679.

H. S. E.

The Rev. Charles Adams. Ob. Sept. 29th, 1770, Ætatis 58.

Sacrum Memoriæ Annæ Hiller. Obiit Jan. 7, 1764.

Register began in the year 1537.

The Rev. Francis B. Astley, Rector.

MANNINGFORD BRUCE.

On a Monument in Chancel.

Underneath lyeth the Body of Mary Nicholas, Daughter of Thos. Lane, of Bentley, in the County of Stafford, Esq. a family as venerable for its Antiquity, as renown'd for its loyalty, of which ye wonderfull preservation of King Charles ye Second, after ye Defeat at Worcester, is an instance never to be forgotten, in which Glorious action She her self bore a very considerable part, and that the Memory of this extraordinary service might be continued to posterity, the family was dignified with the Addition of this Signall badge of honour, the Arms of England in a Canton. She was Married to Edward Nicholas, ye Son of Sr Oliver Nicholas, Cupbearer to King James ye First, & Carver to King Charles ye first, by whom she had one only Son, who died before her, near to whose body She desir'd her own might be interred. She Died Dec. 24, Anno 1686, Aged 67 years.

Arms—Quarterly, first azure, a chevron between three owls, or; second gules, a chevron between three escallops, or; third azure, three fishes in pale, naiant, or: fourth or, on a chevron, argent, two lions, or, between three birds argent: impaling, per chevron, or and azure, a chevron, gules, between three mullets pierced, counter-changed. On a canton the arms of England.

North Wall.

Hic infra sitæ sunt Reliquiæ
Viri memoriâ dignissimi,

Eduardi Nicholas, Armigeri,
Hujus pagi Toparchæ,
Qui
Tam Ecclesiæ quam Monarchiæ Anglicanæ
Fidei inviolatæ,
Amicitiæ Fabularum exemplis non Secundæ
Patientiæ nullis dolorum cruciatibus expugnabilis,
Et Festivitatis Ingenij, qua delicias omnium,
Se reddidit
Frustra renitente Podagrâ diuturna
Exemplum posteris celebre reliquit,
Et tandem Irrequieto orbo Fractus,
Et vitæ et morum hominum pertæsus
Animam egit Jubens, Cal. Maij decimo tertio,
Anno Salutis 1706, Ætatis suæ 77.

Near this Spot are Interred the Remains of the Rev. George Wells, L. L. D. who was 52 years Rector of this Parish, and a Magistrate of this County. He Died August 26, 1815, Aged 76.

Also

The Remains of Frances, his Wife, who died April 15, 1811, Aged 69.

Beloved, Revered, Lamented.

Flat Stones.

Heare Layes the Body of Eliz. Hindley,
Buried July ye 5, 1675.

M. S.

Adolescentis optimi Edwardi Nicholas,
Filii unici Edwardi Nicholas, Armigeri,
Et Mariæ Uxoris, Antiqu . . . . . . imâ Familiâ
. . . lanorum de Bentley, in Agro Stafford oriundæ,

. . . .

. . . .

. . . .

Cœlebs Hinc ad superos Avolavit
Prid. Non. Septemb. Anno Salutis 1683,
Ætatis suæ 22.

Eduardus Nicholas, Arm. Obiit 19 die Aprilis,
Anno Ætatis 77,
Anno Dom. 1706.

Here Lyeth the Body of Ann Busfield, Daughter of Edward Nicholas Esq. who died ye 9th of August, Anno Salutis 1722, Ætatis suæ 63.

On Flat Stones in Nave.

To the Memory of Bryant Chandler, and Mary, his Wife. He Died August 3rd, 1800, Aged 65 years, She died Feb. 19, 1805, Aged 61 years.

In Memory of Richard Chandler, who died October, 1737, Aged 41.

Also of Elizabeth, his Wife, who Died August, 1755, Aged 53.

And of Thomas, their Son, who died April, 1772, Aged 43.

In Memory of Stephen Pyke. He died February 2nd, 175$\frac{0}{1}$, Aged 57.

Also of Eliz. his Wife. She died April 12, 1764, Aged 81.

In Memory of Jane Pyke, who Died October 26, 1776, Aged 63 years.

Also of Stephen Pyke, who died June 29, 1783, Aged 71 years.

Register commenced in the year 1657.
The Rev. John Wells, Rector.
— Grant, Esq. Lord of the Manor.

NEWTON.

Against south wall of Chancel.

Near this Place Lyes the Body of the Right Honble Catharine, Countess Dowager of Abingdon. She was Eldest Daughter & Coheiress of Sr Thos. Chamberlaine, of Norbrook, in the County of Oxon, Bart. had three Husbands: Her first was the Right Honble Richard, Lord Viscount Wenman, of Tuam, in the Kingdom of Ireland, by whom she had Issue one Son, Richard, who succeeded to the Title and Estate, (& was Father of the present Right Honble Phillip, Lord Viscount Wenman, & the Honble Richard Wenman, Esq.) & two Daughters, Catherine and Mary; Her second was the Right Honble James, Earl of Abingdon, Baron Norris, of Rycot, in the County of Oxon. Her third was Francis Wroughton, of Eastcot, in the County of Wilts. Esq. She departed this life Feb. 9, 1741, in the 83 year of her Age.

Arms—Three battering rams: impaling gules, an escutceeon, argent, between eight mullets, or.

Second Shield.—Quarterly, first and fourth sable, on a fess, argent, three lions' heads erased, gules, between three anchors, or; second and third per pale gules and azure, a cross-crosslet, or, over all an escutcheon, gules, charged with an inescutcheon, argent, between eight mullets, or.

Third Shield.—Argent, a chevron, gules, between three boars heads couped, sable: impaling, the same as the first shield.

North Wall.

Near this Place is Interred ye Body of Francis Wroughton, Esq. of Estcot, in this County, who Departed this Life April the 29, in the year of our Lord God 1733.

The Rev. Dr. Lewis Rector.

RUSHALL.

On Monuments in Chancel.

Near this Place lyes Interred the Body of the Rev. Mr. Thomas Giffard, Rector of this Church, who died the 15 Day of August, 1746, Aged 64 years.

Anne, Daughter to Alexander Reading, Esq. the Wife of Wm. Baxter, B. D. Rector of this Church, Dyed in Child Bed of the 9th Childe (Leaving 5 Sons & 3 Daughters Surviving) June 8th, Anno Ætatis 38, Dmq. 1670.

Deare to her Husband, Children, Neighbors, Friends,
Dearer to him in whom her life she Ends,
All Claim'd a Share in her high vertues, none
Who truly knew her, but their loss bemoane
In her, too good for this our Earth, she hastes
Therefore to Heaven, where her Soule now tastes
Pleasures above the Body, that here lies
Till the great Day, in glory to arise.

In a Vault Under the Communion Table in this Chancel, Lie Interred the Remains of Mr. Francis Giffard, of Uphaven, in this County, who died April 9, 1802, Aged 80 years.

Also of Jane, his Wife, who died Oct. 17, 1794, Aged 56 years.

Beneath are deposited the Remains of Mrs. Sarah Peck, Widow & Relict of Kenrick Peck, of Cornish, in the County of Denbigh, Esq. who died July 20, 1802, Aged 70.

Also the Remains of Beatrice Peck, their Daughter, who died Jan. 12, 1807, Aged 42 years.

North Wall of Nave.

Beneath rest the Remains of David Edmonds, Gent. who died Oct. 14, 1812, Aged 76 years, 40 of which he resided in the Parish of St. Mary le Strand, in the City of Westminster, and Justly obtained the Character of an Upright and Honest man.

On Flat Stones in Nave.

Barbarah Webb Died March 2, A. D. 1723, Ætatis 54.

Here Lyeth the Body of Lucie, the Wife of John Chandler, Yeoman, who Departed this life February the 15, A. D. 1705.

On a Monument in North Wall of Nave.

In a Vault Beneath are Deposited the Remains of Edward Poore, Esq. Lord of the Manors of Rushall and Charlton. He was the Eldest Son of Abraham Poore, Esq. of Longstreet, and Married Barbara, Daughter of Paul Methuen, Esq. of Bradford, in this County, and by her had Issue Four Sons, of whom two died in their Infancy, the other two, Edward and John-Methuen, survived him. He died April 10, 1788, Aged 73.

Arms—A fess between three mullets: impaling Methuen.

Sir Edward Poore Lord of the Manor.

UPHAVEN.

On a Monument against the south wall of Chancel.

Near this place lyes Interred the Body of Thomas Chandler, who Departed this life the 30 of Dec. 1752, Aged 52 years.

Also in the same Grave Lyeth Ann, his Wife, who departed this life the 23 Day of Sept. 1771, Aged 86 years.

Flat Stones in Chancel.

Here Lyeth ye Body of Edmund Bonner, who died April ye 18, 1733, Aged 59 years.

A Husband kind, a Father Dear,
A faithful friend, lyes Buried here;
My Days are past, my Glass is run,
My Children Dear, prepare to come.

Here Lyeth ye Body of John Gale, Junr. of Chisenbury Delafoly. He died June ye 14, Anno Dom 1729, Aged 30.

Mon. against the South Wall of Nave.

In the Aisle nearly opposite this Place are Deposited the Remains of William Howard, Gent. who Departed this life Dec. 18, 1754, Aged 76 years.

Also William Alexander, Nephew of the above Wm. Howard, who Departed this life Oct. 13, 1786, Aged 77 years.

Likewise Eleanor, Second Wife of Wm. Alexander, who Departed this life Dec. 6, 1788, Aged 75 years.

Also Mary, Daughter of Thomas and Mary Alexander, who died the 27 of March, 1795, Aged 7 years and 10 months.

Also Mary, Wife of Thomas Alexander, who died the 8 of August, 1795, Aged 40 years.

Also Ann, Wife of Thomas Alexander, who died the 22 of Feb. 1803, Aged 34 years.

Also the Above-Mentioned Thos. Alexander, who Departed this life on the 13 of July, 1811. Aged 57 years.

Sacred to the Memory of Simon Jarvis, who died May 4, 1796, Aged 45 years.

Also of Elizabeth, his Daughter. She died 2nd May, 1805, Aged 22 years.

And Elizabeth, his Wife. She died 22 Jan. 1806, Aged 55 years.

In Memory of Harriot, Daughter of Simon and Elizth Jarvis. She Died 11th Sept. 1806, Aged 22 years.

Also of Sophia, their Daughter, who Died Feb. 4, 1808, Aged 19 years.

On a Flat Stone in North Aisle.

Joseph Lampard died Sept. 24, 1796, Aged 67 years.

Sarah, Daughter of Levi and Mary Lampard, died Dec. 1st, 1800, Aged 11 months.

The Church consists of Chancel, Nave, and North Aisle. The Nave is supported by four pointed arches. The Chancel is separated from the Nave by a Gothic arch, ornamented by two Saxon mouldings.

Register commenced in the year 1687.

The Rev. Mr. White, Rector.

Wm. Wyndham, Esq. Lord of the Manor.

CHARLTON.

On a Monument against the north wall of Chancel.

Francis Giffard, of Uphaven, in this County, who died April 9th, 1802, Aged 80 years,

Bequeathed the Interest of £100, 4 per cent. Consolidated Annuities, to be Distributed in Bread to the Poor of this Parish every year on the 18 day of Jan. for ever.

Arms—Gules, three lions passant-guardant, in pale, argent.

East End.

This small Memorial of their affection and regret was Erected, by the surviving Members of the family, to Wm. Pinckney, Esq. late of Bath, and formerly of Wolfhall, in this County, who died August the 12, 1811, Aged 70.

And also to Robt. Hearne Pinckney, Son of the Above, who on the Night of the first of Oct. 1810, was accidentally drowned in the Kennet and Avon Canal, in the Thirtieth year of his Age.

Flat Stones.

Here Lyeth the Body of Wm. Pinckney, Gent. who departed this life August the 22, 1698.

Also the Body of Ann Pinckney, his Wife, who Departed this Life Feb. the 15, 1709, Aged 74 years.

Here lyeth the Body of Wm. Pinckney, Gent. who Departed this life October the 19, 1779, Aged 68 years.

Also the Body of Sarah Pinckney, his Wife, who Departed this life March 15, 1756, Aged 40 years.

Arms—In fess five lozenges.
Crest—A griffin's head, erased.

Here Lyeth the Body of Robt. Pinckney, Gent. who Died Nov. 7, 1747, Aged 83 years.

Also Martha, his Wife, who died July 24, 1752, Aged 76 years.

[Arms and Crest as the preceding.]

Here lyeth the Body of Charles Pinckney, Gent. Marshall of the Horse Guards to Queen Ann and to his present Majesty. He died Dec. ye 1st, A. D. 1716, Aged 48 years.

On Monuments in North Wall of Nave.

Near this Place lieth the Body of Mrs. Sarah Mundy, who died Jan. 18. 1763, Aged 43 years.

She was exemplary in the great lines of Duty,
Having a Constant and Pious regard
Towards God,
A tender and Affectionate love
Towards her Parents,
A kind and liberal hand
Towards the Poor and Needy.
Being endued with these singular Virtues,
We trust she has her reward with her Father
Which is in Heaven.

Near this Church are deposited the Remains of Thos. Fowle, Esq. of Durrington, in this County, who Died Feb. 3, 1783, Aged 48 years.

Also of Henry Fowle, Esq. of the same Place, who died May the 16, 1803, Aged 67 years.

And of Jane, his Wife, Daughter of Mr. Thos. Springbelt, of Wilsford, who Died Dec. the 7th, 1780, Aged 49 years.

This Monument was erected by their surviving Children
As the small and now, alas ! only Tribute
Of Gratitude, Duty, and Affection,
To the Memory of the best and kindest of Parents.

Arms—Gules, a lion passant-guardant between three cinquefoils, or : impaling gules, a chevron paly, or and azure, between three mullets, or.

On Flat Stones in Nave.

Here lyeth ye Body of Wm. Son of Henry Biggs, of Upper Woodford, Gent. who dyed ye 19 of May, 1724, Aged 2 years.

Here lyeth the Body of Ann, the Wife of Robt. Mundy, Gent. who Departed this life the 19 of April, A. D. 1727, Aged ·9 years.

Hic jacet Corpus Roberti Mundy, Gent. 1682.

Here lyeth the Body of Robert Mundy, Gent. he was buried the 7th of March, 1682.

Here lyeth the Body of Robt. Mundy, Gent. who dyed ye 2 Day of July, 1723, Aged 72 years.

On a Brass Plate.

Here lyeth ye Body of John Mundy, who Departed this life the 5 Day of June, in the year of our Lord 1674.

Here Lyeth ye Body of Bridged, ye Wife of Thomas Lavington, Sen. of Stanton-barn, Gent. who Departed this life ye 27. of April, 1716.

Also in Memory of John Mundy, Gent. who Departed this life the 5 Day of March, 1747, in the 60 year of his Age.

In the South Wall of the Chancel is a piscina and a cross. In the North Aisle are two figures, each holding a Shield of Arms: on the first shield—A chevron between three escallops, impaling a chevron between three towers; on the second—A chevron between three martlets. In this Aisle also is a piscina.

Register commenced 1695.

WILSFORD.

On a Monuments against North Wall of Chancel.

Sacred to the Memory of Thomas Chandler, Surgeon, who departed this life Feb. the 13, 1797, Aged 37 years.

Also Sarah, Wife of Thomas Chandler, who Departed this life Dec. 24, 1800, Aged 47 years.

Sacred to the Memory of Elizth Layland Layland, who Departed this life on the 28 Day of Oct. 1810, in the 32 year of her Age.

This Monument is Erected by her most Affectionate Aunt, Sarah Brathwaite.

South Wall.

Underneath are Deposited the Remains of Elizabeth, Daughter of Thos. Chandler, of Market Lavington, Surgeon, by Sarah, his Wife, who Died in her Infancy, Feb. 6, 1794.

On Flat Stones in Chancel.

In Memory of Jane, Wife of Samuel Springebelt, who died Nov. 12th, 1760, Aged 70 years.

In Memory of Eleanor, Wife of John Layland, who died Oct. 15, 1779, Aged 26 years.

Also of Ann, their Daughter, who Died Oct. 10, 1779, Aged 18 months.

Within this silent bed of Clay
My Dearest Wife and Child do lay,
Whose lives was asked, but God thought best
To take them to Eternal Rest.

Flat Stones in the Body.

To the Memory of Dorothy, Wife of Thomas Hayter, who departed this life Feb. 28th, 1808, Aged 34 years.

Also Henry, Son of Thomas and Elizabeth Hayter, who Died in his Infancy.

Underneath this Stone lyeth the Remains of Richard Hayward, of this Place, Yeoman, who Departed this life the 23. of July, 1786, Aged 61 years.

Also Sarah Hayward, his Wife, who Departed this life the 27th of March, 1792, Aged 61 years.

In the two Windows on the north side of the Nave is a little painted glass, g. or, and az. Date on the pulpit, 1629. In the south wall of chancel is a piscina.

Register began in 1588.

The Rev. Mr. Benson, of Sarum, Rector.

Sir John Astley, Bart. Lord of the Manor.

WOODBOROUGH.

On a Monument in Chancel.

Hic jacet
quod Mortale fuit Georgii Gibbes, D. D
Hujus Ecclesiæ, per XLIX Annos,
fidelis et venerandi Pastoris;
Benignus, intelligens, facundus,
Amorem omnium,
Moribus suavissimis conciliavit,
Exempli tacita suadela
ad omne Officii munus
Animos sensim Informavit;
Scientia, literis, ingenio liberali erudiit,
Bonis in Cœlo Repositam
Vitam præcipiens Beatiorem, placide quiescat anima
vitæ tranquillæ,
quoad vixit unice dedita.
Obiit xx Feb. 1813, Ætat. suæ 72.

Hoc Monumentum posuerunt
et paterno amori
Et longo Felicissimoque conjugio mœrens Vidua
lugens Filia, memorque semper felicis.

On a Flat Stone in Chancel.

Here lyeth ye Body of Dorothy Coningsby, Daughter & Coheir of John Wick, in ye County of Kent, and Wife to Wm. Coningsby, Rector of this Parish, who Departed this life ye 11 Day of Oct. 1699, Aged 73 years.

Arms—A crescent between three conies sejant: impaling a chevron charged with a crescent, in chief two martlets.

On Monuments against the South Wall of Nave.

Sacred to the Memory of Jerome Dyke, late of Woodborough, who Departed this life 19 Jan. 1782.

Five of his Daughters, Mary, Dorothy, Ann, Martha, and Charlotte,

And his Son Jonathan Waterman Dyke.
He died 6th Oct. 1791.

Likewise to the Memory of Mary, Wife of Jerome Dyke. She Departed this life the 22 April 1799.

The Lord knoweth the Days of the upright,
and their Inheritance shall be for ever.

Arms—Or, three cinquefoils sable; impaling, paly of six, or and sable, over all three crescents gules.

Sophia, Wife of Wm. Dyke, of this Parish, Died the 9 Day of Feb. 1804, Aged 28 years,
Leaving two Children, Mary and Sophia.

Wm. Dyke, of Woodborough, died the 25 Day of Feb. 1815, Aged 45 years.

Arms—Or, three cinquefoils sable: impaling argent, a fess between six fleur-de-lis (three-and-three) bar-wise, gules.

Sacred to the Memory of John, Son of Harry and Catharine Robbins, who Died 9 July, 1813.
Martha, their Daughter, died 1st Oct. 1814.
Henry, their Son, died 27 December, 1814.
Thomas, their Son, Lieut. R. N. died at Havannah, 18 August, 1816.
And also of Ann, their Danghter, who died 17 June, 1820.

East Wall of Nave.

Here lyeth ye Body of Sarah Francklyn, ye Relict and Widow of Richard Francklin, late of Woodborough, Gent. She Departed this life ye 30 of Dec. 1675.

The Rev. Mr. Wilde, Rector.

WILCOT.

On Monument in the North Wall of Chancel.

Sacred to the Memory of John Berwick, of Wilcot, Esq. who was buried here Oct. 30, 1572, as was also his Daughter Anne, Dec. 13, 1610. She Married Sir Thomas Wroughton, Knight, who died June 4, 1597, Aged 56 years, and was Buried at Broad Hinton in this County. He was the Eldest Son of Sir Wm. Wroughton, of the Same Place.

Arms—Three bears' heads, a crescent for difference.

On Flat Stones in Chancel.

Here lyeth the Body of Frances Wroughton, Daughter of Francis Wroughton, Esq. who Departed this Life the 4 Day of Jan. 17$\frac{12}{13}$, in the 81 year of her Age.

In Nave.

In Memory of Ursula Brooke. Ob. August the 10, 1697.
Jane Packer, Ob. Feb. the 9, 1687.
Jane Brooke, Daughter of Ursula Brooke, and Niece of Jane Packer, Ob. August the 3, 1744.

North Aisle.

Stephen, Son of Wm. and Ann Hazeland, died 24 Dec. 1758, Aged 24.
William, Son of William and Ann Hazeland, Clerk, M. A. died 21 June, 1763, Aged 32.
Wm. Hazeland died 7 Oct. 1784, Aged 78 years.
Ann Hazeland died 13 Oct. 1786, Aged 85.

On Flat Stones in Body.

Maurice Hiller, and Alice his beloved Wife, lie here.
Requiescant in pace.

Patience Cheyney, who deceased the thirteenth of Feb. Anno Dom̄ 1663.

In Memory of the Rev. John Mayo, LL. B. who died Jan. 6, 1779, Aged 65 years,

Having been Forty-one years Rector of Beeching Stoke, and Seventeen years Vicar of this Church. He was an Affectionate Husband and Parent, a Sincere Friend, a Chearful Companion, During his whole life, and an unremitted Attention to his Office as Clergyman, and his Duty as a Member of Society.

Here lyeth the Body of Symon ..holi.. Clerke, Rector of the Parish Church of Deane ...dash, in the County of Southampton, who died the 29 day of May, Anno Dom. 16. .

And also the Body of Patience, the Wife of the said Symon, who Died the 4 Day of April, Anno Dom̃ 1644.

Also Here lieth ye Body of Sarah, the Wife of Richard Edmonds, and Daughter of Mrs. Sarah Cheyney. She died July ye 8, 1738, Aged 59 years.

The Rev. G. Sherer, Vicar.

Lady Wroughton owns the Manor.

HEWISH.

Flat Stones in Chancel.

Here Lyeth ye Body of Mr. Simon Cheyney. He Departed this life March ye 12, 172$\frac{5}{4}$ Aged 59 years.

Here lyeth ye Body of Ann Cheyney, who Departed this life Jan. ye 4, 1741, Aged 80 years.

In the Body.

Here lyeth ye Body of Margaret Edmonds, Wid. who Dyed Sept. 7, 1709, Aged 87 years.

Also Hereby lyeth ye Body of Stephen Edmonds, Grandson of the Abovesaid Margaret, who Dyed April ye 26th, 1713, in ye 39 year of his Age.

Here lyeth ye Body of Joane, ye Wife of Richard Edmonds, who departed this life August ye 11, A. D. 1705, Aged 51 years.

Also Hereby lyeth Margaret, Daughter of ye Abovesaid, who died March 19, 1699, Aged 7 years.

Also Here lyeth ye Body of Richard Edmonds, Husband to ye Abovesaid. He Departed this life ye 18 of Dec. 1734, Aged 85 years.

Here lyeth ye Body of Alice, the Wife of Thomas Weeks, who Departed this life Dec. the 18, 1729, Aged 69 years.

Register commenced 1603.

The Rev. Mr. Moyle Rector.

MARLBOROUGH ST. MARY.

Against south wall of Chancel.

Near this place are Deposited the Remains of Margaret, Second Daughter of John Ward, Esq. and Wife to the Rev. John Joseph Goodenough, of the City of Bristol. She Died Dec. 13, 1813, in the 27 year of her Age. Also three of her Children who died in Infancy.

Arms—Or, a chevron, gules, between three gutte de sang: impaling argent, a cross patté, or.

On a Monument against the East End of Chancel.

S. E. M. I.

Reuben Bourne, Gent. Vir integer animi, et iñocenter festivus. Qui obiit sexto die Decembris, A. D. 1695. Gratitudinis ergo votivam hanc suspendit tabulam, Anna Chamberlayne, Testamenti Curatrix.

Arms—A chevron between three lions rampant: impaling a fess between three estoiles.

North Wall of Chancel.

Near this Place lyeth the Body of Jane, the Wife of Robert Sohles, of Wroughton, Gent. Eldest Daughter of Andrew Duke, of Bulford, Esq. She died Nov. 16, 1733, Anno Ætatis 41. Mors Janua Vitæ.

Arms—Gules, on a chevron, argent, three mullets, of the first, between three escallops, argent; impaling, per fess, argent and azure, three chaplets counter-changed.

Near this place lies the Remains of John Webb, of this Town, Gent. who Died 7th Feb. 1764, Aged 78. Also Elizabeth, his Wife, who died 2 June, 1762, Aged 76.

On Flat Stones in South Aisle.

Under this humble Stone rest the Remains of Elizabeth, the Daughter of William and Mary Gresley, who Died January 7, 1787, Aged 33 weeks.

Also

William, their Son, who Died September 18, 1787, Aged 18 weeks.

And also William Nigel, their Son, who Died August 23d, 1794, Aged 1 year.

Here lieth, Waiting For a Joyful Resurrection, the Body of Anna-Maria, the Wife of John Crook, Junr. And her two Sons. She Departed this life August 23, 1778, Aged 36 years.

James Died Nov. 26, 1774, Aged 1 month.

Joseph James Died April 24th, 1776, Aged 18 months.

Here Lyeth the Body of William, Son of William Gibbons, Esq. by Frances, his Wife, of Barbadoes, who Died ye 26. of Nov. 1729, Aged 15 years & 3 months.

In Memory of Mary, the Daughter of John and Jane

Coleman, who departed this life Jan. the 1, 1778, Aged 25 years.

Also in Memory of John Coleman, Gent. who Departed this Life August 28th, 1785, Aged 73 years.

Also in Memory of Jane, Wife of John Coleman, Gent. who Departed this life Sept. 14, 1791, Aged 77.

Also in Memory of William Coleman, who Departed this life Dec. 23, 1797, Aged 64 years.

On Flat Stones in Body.

Here Lyeth ye Body of Margaret, ye Wife of Thomas Hunt, who departed this life Oct. ye 11th, 1691.

& Margaret, the Daughter, who Died October ye 16th, & Also of Thomas Hunt, ye Elder, who died November ye 9th, Anno Dom. 1691.

In Memory of Joseph Gilmore, Esq. Late of This Parish, who Died on the 27th July, 1778, Aged 75 years.

Also of Mary Gilmore, his Wife, who Died 13 April, 1773, Aged 50 years.

Also of George Gilmore, their Son, who died 18 October, 1772, Aged 20 years.

Also of Carle Gilmore, their Son, Who died 24 Feb. 1768, Aged 13 years.

On a small Tablet at the West End of the Nave.

Erected to the Memory of Elizabeth, Relict of John Smith, who died April 17, 1773, Aged 61 years.

Also Elizabeth, their Daughter, who Died February 29, 1795, Aged 69 years.

And also Ann, their Daughter, who Died May 4, 1819, Aged 83 years.

On a Flat Stone within the Rails of the Chancel.

M. S.

Uxoris dilectæ Mariæ Brown,
Fœminæ siqua alia
Hoc Sacrario dignæ
Ob antiquam . . . . Fidem
flagrantem charitatem,
Quæ, Ætatis Anno 53, Salutis 1694, obiit.

Hoc inter cætera posuit Amoris
Gulielmus Grinfield, Generosus,
qui Obiit vicecimo quinto die Augusti, 1692.

Hatchment in the Chancel.

Gules, three rests, or ; impaling, gules, a chevron, vair, between three crescents, argent.

ENDOWMENTS AND BENEFACTIONS.

1615. Mr. Thomas Ray gave the Income of Several Tenements, lying in New Sarum, the one part in Trinity Street, the other in Gigant Street, to the poor Clothiers of Trowbridge, Chippenham, Westbury, and Marlbro', each Town to Receive it once in four Years, for ever.

1640. Mrs. Ann Paine, late of the Precinct of the Liberty of the Tower of London, Widdow, paid £300 to the Company of Goldsmiths of the same, for the Payment of £15 yearly during her Life, and after her decease for the payment of £15 per Annum as follows: to the poor of the said Company £5, to the Poor of the Precinct of the Tower Liberty £5, and £.5 to the poor of the Parishes of this Town.

1693. The perpetual Interest of £80, given by Doctor Cresset, to be improved for the benefit of the Minister of this Church.

1796. The Interest of £200, by Mrs. Sarah Franklyne, to be applyed for the Benefit and Increase of the Vicarage of this Parish for Ever.

John Sutton and Thomas Bailey
Churchwardens. 1812.

The Church consists of a Nave and South Aisle, but no distinct Chancel. The south side of the Nave is supported by plain round pillars and semi-arches. Under the battlements of the south side, over the entrance door, is the figure of a cat, with a rat in its mouth, carved in stone. The door-way, on the west side of the Tower, is formed by a Saxon arch.

Register commenced in 1602.

The Rev. Dr. Whinfield, V.
The Rev. Dr. Barteon late V.
The Rev. R. Hardey, present V.

The Earl of Ailesbury Lord of the Manor.

Church of St. Peter and St. Paul.

On Monuments against North Wall of Chancel.

Hic jacet, in expectatione diei supremi, Maria Coghill, alias Pearson, casta, prudens, pia. Obiit decimo septimo die mensis Octobris, Anno Domini 1733, Anno Ætatis suæ 52. Memoriæ Uxoris suæ maxime dilectæ, hoc mormor poni jussit Jacobus Coghill, de civitate Dublin, Armigeri. Hanc fastu motus, sed ut ille sciat, sciat defunctæ amici ubi deposita fuit, hæc optima Fœmina, ubi lachrymas effundant.

Arms—Quarterly, first and fourth argent, a chevron, gules, between three cocks of the same; second and third gules, on a chevron, argent, three pellets: impaling, quarterly, first and fourth gules, a chevron, ermine, between three leaves slipped, vert; second and third or, a fess imbattled . . . . in base a hurt.

To the Memory of Mr. James White, who died on the third day of April, 1787, Aged 54 years.

Also of Mrs. Elizabeth Homeward, who died on the twenty-third day of February, 1780, Aged 52 years.

Here lye the Bodies of two Sonnes and a Daughter of Sr Nicholas Hyde, Knight, Lo: Cheife Justice of ye King's Bench, & of ye Lady Marye Marye, his Wife. That is, Robert Buried 24 Jan. 1626, Francis Buried 28 Jan. 1626, Elizabeth Buried 28 February, 1626. We shall go to them, but they shall not return to us. 2 Sam. 12. 25.

Arms—Azure, a chevron argent, charged with a mullet, gules, between three lozenges, or.

Near this place lies the Body of Ann Savery, Daughter of Farewell Perry, A. M. many years Vicar of this Parish, and Wife to Servington Savery, A. M. the Son of Servington Savery, M. D. who died June 5, 1734, Aged 45 years.

Also the said Servington Savery, A. M. who died March 18, 1735, Aged 47 years.

Likewise Servington, Son of the above Servington and Ann Savery, who Died June 5th, 1753, Aged 37 years.

This Monument was Erected by Catherine Coker, in filial and affectionate remembrance of her Father, Mother, and Brother, in the year 1787.

Near this Place are also interr'd the Remains of Mary Savery, Relict of the last-mentioned Servington Savery, who died Dec. 23, 1766, Aged 51 years.

Arms—Argent, a bend, gules, charged with two leopards' heads caboshed, or, surcharged with an escutcheon, quarterly, first and fourth argent, second and third sable.

M. S.

Servingtonus Savery, Ob. 25° March, An° Dni. 1687, Ætat. 1.

Maria Savery, Ob. 4° October, An. Dni. 1692, Ætatis 30.

Catharina Savery, Ob. 30 Nov. An° Dni. 1692, Ætat. 2.

Martha Savery . . . vm Mater, Ob. 16 October, An° Dni. 1696, Ætatis 34.

Maria Savery, Ob. 16 June, An° Dni. 1697, Ætat. 2.

Servington Savery, B: Med: Et Maritus Et Pater, Hoc Monumentum, Anno Domini 1697. M. P.

Arms—Quarterly: impaling, a chevron between three crosses. [not blazoned.]

Near this Place lies Interred Mary-Anne White, Daughter of James and Catharine White, who died June 7th, 1768, Aged 25 weeks.

Also the Bodies of James, the Son, and Elizabeth, the Daughter, of James and Catharine White. James died 23 July, 1772, Aged 2 years and 3 months, Elizabeth Died 17 February, 1774, Aged 4 years and 3 months.

Against south wall of Chancel.

Sacred to the Memory of Elizabeth Clavering, only Daughter of the Rev. Thomas Burnett, D. D. Rector of West Kington, in this County, and Prebendary of Sarum, by Elizabeth, his Wife, Daughter of Philip Bathurst, Esq. She was Married to the Rev. Robt. Clavering, Rector of this Parish, Sept. 5, 1728, & Departed this life Jan. 8, 1759, in the 54 year of her age. Not from any Principle of Vanity, but out of a filial regard to the Memory of one of the best and tenderest of Mothers, and as a testimony of Gratitude for the many obligations he received from her worthy Family, Algernon Clavering, Vicar of Broad Hinton, in this County, ordered his Executor to erect this Monument, and to Lay his own Body close by the Remains of his Mother. He died of the small-pox, April 7, 1772, Aged 48 years.

In the same Grave lieth the Body of the Rev. Robt. Clavering, A. M. Formerly Student of Christ College, in Oxford, Rector of this Parish, & Vicar of Preshute. His Grandfather was Rector of Piddle Hinton, in the same County, and his Great Grandfather was the Rev. John Clavering, Fellow of Eaton College, & Rector of Gamlingue, in the County of Cambridge, who is recorded in the Baronetage of England to be the Second Son of Robt. Clavering, Esq. by Anne Daughter of Sir Thos. Grey, from whose third Son James, the present Baronet of this name, is lineally descended. He exchanged this Life for a Better, Nov. 7th, A. D. 1773, in the 80 year of his Age.

Near this Place also lie the Bodies of three of the Children of the said Robt. & Elizabeth Clavering, who Died in their Infancy; Viz. Mariamne, Elizabeth, & Rob. With whom is interr'd the Body of Dame Grace Hay, Daughter of the Rev. Thos. Clavering, Rector of Piddle Hinton, in Dorsetshire, and Relict of Sir John Hay, Baronet, of the Kingdom of Scotland. She Died Feb. 1751, Aged 96.

Arms—Quarterly; first and fourth quarterly, first and fourth or; second and third gules, over all a bend sable; second and third argent, a bugle horn, or and sable, on a chief or, three leaves, proper.

Near this Place Lyeth the Body of Ann, ye second Wife of John Hawkins, of this Town, Gent. who departed this life ye first Day of March, in ye Year of our Lord 1676, Aged 34 years.

And Peter and John, Sons of ye said John and Ann, Both Buried together ye 6th Day of July, A. D. 1677. Also Mary, third Wife of ye said John Hawkins, who Departed this life August ye 25, A. D. 1699, Aged 50 years. And Peter and Elizabeth, Son and Daughter of the said John and Mary, lyes Buried under a Tomb-Stone in this Church Yard.

Near this Place are Deposited the Remains of Susannah Halcomb, (Second Wife of Mr. John Halcomb, and Eldest Daughter of William Peck, Esq. Late of the Wiltshire Militia,) who Departed this life 25 July, 1813, in the 51st year of her Age. Amiable Affection as a Wife, Ever-anxious Solicitude, and unremitting Tenderness, as a Mother, Kindness and Sincerity as a Friend, Christian Serenity and Resignation, were virtues which, in an eminent Degree, adorned her Character, and prepared her for a Blessed Immortality Beyond the Grave.

On Monuments in N. Wall of N. Aisle.

Sacred to the Memory of that truly good-natured man, Mr. Stephen Willoughby, who, as he liv'd beloved of all, so by all was in his Death as much lamented. His Dutifull and Submissive Behaviour gained him the love and Friendship of his Superiors, His obliging and innoffensive carriage reconciled him to the love of all his equals, nor did his humanity towards his Inferiours, to whom it was ever extended to the utmost of his abilities, less gain him theirs. Thus did these, his social virtues, him endear to, and make him the delight of all his Acquaintance, But to no one more than to his very worthy friend, Mr. Henry Smith, of Bath, who has here placed this Monument to his Memory. He died the 13 Day of August, in the Year of our Lord 1746, and of his Age the 47.

Love is the Fulfilling of the Law.

James George Russell, whose Remains are Deposited in the Vault below, was born at Portsea, in the County of Southampton, and Departed this Life on the 15th Day of September, 1808, in the 30 Year of his Age.

In the Middle Aisle of this Sacred Place, and exactly opposite to this Humble Stone, rest the remains of Fanny Warner, with an infant Son. To embrace her many excellent qualities may appear ostentatious; not to mention some of them ungrateful. Suffice it therefore to say, she was one of the best of Wives, of Mothers, and of Friends. She died October 22, 1779, in the 45 year of her Age, and left behind her five Sons and two Daughters, the eldest of whom was too Young to feel its loss, the youngest only five weeks.

The ties of Humanity, the social efforts of the Mind, the Virtues of the Kindred Soul, touch'd by the cold hand of Death, may droop like an Evening Flower; But the Gloomy Night and Darkness of the Grave shall quickly pass, the Morning of the Resurrection shall arrive, then shall they re-expand their forms, beneath the Glorious Influence of the Almighty, rejoysing in a Possession of an Eternal Day.

Sacred to the Memory of Martha, Wife of Nichol. Washbourne, Surgeon of this Town, who Departed this life the 13th Jan. 1817.

On a monument against the first pillar from the east end of nave.

Hic infra jacet Corpus Humfredi Wall, Gen. in plena et certa resurrectionis spe, Ob. 29 die Jan. Anno Dom. 1719, Ætat. suæ 75.

Martha, uxor. ejus, Ob. April. 1689, Ætat. 41, Filia Wilhelmi Tarrant, Gen. Qui Ob. 19 Maij, 1681, Ætat. 63:

Et Mariæ, conjugis ejus, Ob. Feb. 1686, Ætat. 62. Quorum cineres, ut et quatuor liberorum Dict. Humfredi, et Marthæ, prope requiescunt.

Elizabeth etiam, uxor. ejus 2di, Filiæ Thomæ Chamberlayne, Armig. de Oddington, in agro Gloucestrensi, Obiit 4 Die Nov. Ano Salutis 1725, Ætatis 83°.

Arms—Party per pale, first argent, a chevron, gules, between three eagles displayed of the same; second argent, on a cross sable, five lions rampant guardant, or; impaling quarterly, first and fourth gules, eight mullets, or; second and third gules, a chevron between three escallops, or.

Monuments in the South Wall of South Aisle.

Beneath Rest the Remains of John Brathwaite, Esq. who died July 17, 1766, Aged 55 years.

Also Eliz. Wife of Francis Brathwaite, who died Jan. 3, 1767, Aged 55 years.

Also Mary, Daughter of George and Mary Brathwaite, who died March 27, 1769, Aged 28 years.

Also George, Son of Francis and Elizabeth Brathwaite, who died July 20, 1773, Aged 25 years.

Also George, Son of John Brathwaite, Esq. the Younger, by Sarah his Wife, who died August 31, 1774, Aged 16 months.

Also George, their Son, who died Sept. 20, 1774, Aged 3 weeks.

Also John Brathwait, Esq. who died Feb. 20th, 1785, Aged 42 years.

Also Sarah, the Wife of John Brathwaite, Jun. Esq. who died Oct. 30, 1804, Aged 57 years.

The Rev. John Brathwaite Died June 12th, 1812, in the 40 Year of his Age.

The East & West pinnacles were new built, the other pinnacles & Church repaired, the Bells new Cast and a treble added, Anno Dom̄ 1701. Jno Fowler and Thos. Hunt Churchwardens; towardes ye Charge of which Jno Jeffeeryes Gave £50.

Sacred to the Memory of a Beloved and Affectionate Wife and Mother, Catharine Halcombe, who Died April 1st, 1796, Aged 29 years.

Of pleasing Manners, and a gentle Mind,
She liv'd and died meek, patient, and resign'd.

Against the fourth pillar from the east end.

Sacred to the Memory of Robert Pinckney, Gent. who died 28 Jan. 1807.

On Flat Stones in Chancel.

Here lies the Body of Edward Cressett, M. A. of Oriel Coll. in Oxford, practicer of Musick, who lived a most affectionate Son .... the Church of England, and bequeathed one Hundred and Sixty Pounds to be improved to the .....uall & perpetuall benefit of the Minister ... this Church, and the Minister of St. Mary's Church in this Town, whilst continuing as ...en by Law established, but when otherwise, ...en to the Almshouse in the Marsh there. He exchanged this Life for a better, April 12, 1693, And in the year of his Age 108.

Arms—Quarterly, first and fourth a bend, in chief a demi lion; second and third a cross engrailed within a border engrailed. [Not blazoned.]

Beneath this Stone Lyeth the Body of Eliza-Mariamne Clavering, Daughter of Robt. Clavering, Rector of this Parish, and Elizabeth, his Wife. She Dyed 29 Day of August, in the year of our Lord 1734, Aged 2 years.

Flat Stone without the Rails.

Here lyeth the Body of Willm. Ragburn, who Departed this life Jan. 14, 1732, Aged 70 years.

Here also Lyeth Catharine, the Wife of Wm. Ragburn, who died Oct. 23, 1733, Aged 50 years.

Flat Stones in Body.

Ann Clarke Died August ye 20, 1725, Aged 3 years.

To the Memory of Charlotte Dansie, Daughter of Thomas and Mary Dansie. Obiit 18 Feb. 1773, Aged 10 years 10 months and 12 days.

Here Lyeth the Body of Mrs. Sarah Westmacott, the Wife of Mr. Wm. Westmacott, who died Oct. 28, 1736, Aged 42.

Also Anne Westmacott, his Second Wife, who died 1 of March, 1769, Aged 72.

Likewise Martha Spinage, Widow, who died 29 of April, 1777, Aged 73.

Hic infra reliquiæ Mariæ Lipyeatt, Viduæ, Quæ plurimi confecta annis, placidà quievit morie 8 die Augusti, Anno Dom. 1728, Ætat. 77, depositæ sunt in ipso cinei conjugis ejus charissimi, Christ. Lipyeatt, Gen. Qui ob. Sep. 1691. Spai.... in suo ipsius tumulo, præben... corpora illa quæ dum Vica... man..... communem, continu...... anima.... communi Comin ...emur urni donec Adveni Christi animam restituet, suscitabit gloriosa, et vitam æternam largitur.

Hic jacet Corpus Humfridi Wall, Gen. Obiit 29 die Jan. Ano Dom. 1719, Ætat. suæ 75.

In Memory of Eliz. Merriman, Daughter of Nath. & Eliz. Merriman, who Departed this life Oct. 17, 1773, Aged 9 years.

Benjamin, Son of Thos. & Fanny Warner, who died March 1, 1769, Aged 4 months.

Here Lyeth the Body of Mary, the Wife of Benjamin Merriman, who died May 28, 1766, Aged 45 years.

On Flat Stones in North Aisle.

Here Lyeth ye Body of Nicholas Kimber, who Died March A. D. 1721, Aged 78 years.

Here lyeth ye Body of Elizabeth, Wife of Nicholas Kimber. She Died August 16, 1723, Aged 78.

Also Timothia, their Son, Died Sept. 21, 1707, Aged 13.

Here lyeth interred the Body of Col. James Rolt. He was the Sixth Son of Henry Rolt, Esq. of Sacombe Park, Herts, and of Anne Baynton, of Spy Park, in this County. He resided 34 years at Bagden Lodge, near this Place, and was much respected as a man of good sense, sound honour and integrity. Obiit 3 March, 1793, Aged 74.

Underneath are Deposited the remains of Martha Washbourne.

Here lyeth ye Body of Amor, Son of Nichol Snow, Apothecary, of this Place. He Died April 26, A. D. 1727, Ætatis 23.

On Flat Stones in South Aisle.

Hannah Hawkes, widow, died May 2, 1768, Aged 74.

Near this Place are Interr'd the Remains of Mary Dalrymple, Widow, who died the 21 Sept. 1761, Aged 64.

 201

Under this Stone are deposited the Remains of Mrs. Sarah Bennett. Obiit 26 June, 1807, Aged 67.

On Monuments under the Gallery, at the west end.

Near this place lies the Body of Mary, the Wife of John Harding, who died June 28, 1794, Aged 44 years.

Sacred to the Memory of Mr. Willm. Parsons, Gent. late of Brompton, Middlesex, who departed this life the 16 of January, 1814, in the 84 year of his Age.

Also Mrs. Jane Parsons, Wife of the above, who departed this life the 19th of February 1814, in the 68 year of her Age.

This Monument is erected as a small Tribute of respect By Mr. David Robinson, of Kingsbridge.

South Side.

Sacred to the Memory of Elizabeth Cooper, the Wife of Thos. Cooper, who died Nov. 28, 1817, Aged 56 years.

Also Thos. Cooper, who died October 26, 1818, Aged 60 years.

Near this place lye three Children of Wm. and Frances Francis.

Richard Died April 12, 1738, Aged 14 Days.
Catharine Dy'd May 30, 1740, Aged 6 Months.
Wm. Died August 22, 1741, Aged 5 Years.

On Flat Stones under the Gallery.

In Memory of Mr. Samuel Taylor, who departed this Life the 10 of Jan. 1814, Aged 32 years.

In Memory of Mary Hill, late of Little Sodbury, in ye County of Gloucester, who died August 7, 1741, Aged 20 years.

In Memory of John Bishop. Died July ye 25, 1781, Aged 36 years.
Also here lyes two of his Sons.

Here lyeth ye Body of Ann, Daughter of Robert and Ann Jacob, of the Grange, who Departed this life Sept. ye 23, 1714.

On Flat Stones under the Tower.

Here Lyeth interred the Body of Mr. Roger Blagden, who Departed this life the 3 of May, A. D. 1674.

Here lyeth the Body of Frances, the Wife of Willm. Clarke who Departed this Life August ye 2d, A. Di. 1707, Aged 38 years.

Here lyeth ye Body of Damaris, the Wife of Willm. Bayley. She Died March 26, 1736, Aged 69.

Here also Lyeth John, Son of Wm. and Damaris Bayley. He died Nov. ye 19, 1736, Aged 49.

Here Lyeth the Body of Wm. Bayley. He Died May 2, 1729, Aged 70.

Also Mary, Daughter of George and Elizth Goldwyer, Died Jan. 5, 1729, Aged 11 Months.

Also Samuel Bayley, who died August 10, 1752, Aged 48.

A. Lipyeat, Sep. 26, 1752, Aged 68.
T. Lipyeat, Nov. 18, 1733, Aged 33.
W. Lipyeat, Jan. 11, 1737, Aged 17.

Near this Place are buried Thomas Lipyeat, & Ann, his Wife, & their Children, Jonathan, Mary, Wm. & Sarah; and Under this Stone Christopher, their Eldest Son, who died August 14, 1762, Aged 53, and Mary Phelp, his first Wife, who died March 21, 1744, Aged 36.

In Memory of Ann Lipyeatt, Second Wife of Christopher Lipyeat, who died March ye 13, 1774, Aged 61.

Brass Plate.

Here Lyeth the Body of Baylye, who dyed the 22 of Dec. 1817, Aged 50 years.

On a flat stone of black marble, with brass letters, in the Vestry.

ΔΟΞΑ

Πατρὶ, κ̀ Υιῳ, κ̀ Πνεῦ : Αγὶῳ; Ως εν αρκη, κ̀ νυι, κ̀ αεῖ.

H. S. J.

Gloriæ Immortalis,

Fran : Francis, uxoris, mart. I. D. A. D. MDCCLXVII. VIXIT ANN. LVI.	Ric : Francis, Filii, mart. kal. v. A. D. MDCCLXXIX. VIXIT ANN. XXXIX.
Gul : Francis, mariti, Dec. non. vi. A. D. MDCCLXXXIV. VIXIT ANN. LXVI.	Fran : Francis, Filiæ, kal. Jun. xvi. A. D. MDCCCXVI. ANN. LXIX.

Quiescant in Pace.

L. P.

Car. Francis, S.

A. D. MDCCCXVII.

A dove with an olive branch. | A chev. bet. 3 eag. disp.

3 F

Sacred to the Memory of John Wentworth, who departed this Life June 12, 1814, Aged 33 years.

Elizabeth Wentworth Died Jan. 4th, 1762, in the 31 Year of her Age.

John Wentworth, Father of the above Elizabeth Wentworth, Died March 31, 1762, in the 61 Year of his Age.

On a brass plate in Chancel.

Here are deposited the Remains of Servington Savery, Clerk, who departed this life June 4, 1753, Aged 37.

And Mary, his Wife, who died Dec. 23d, 1766, Aged 51.

And three of their Children, who all died young.

ENDOWMENTS AND BENEFACTIONS.

Amount of Quit Rents due and belonging to this Parish on the Monday in the Easter Week yearly, £6. 5. 2.

Amount of Do. on St. Thos. Day Yearly £1. 1*s*. 0*d*.

Which said Quit Rents, together with the Rent of three tenements situate in Silverless Street, in the Parish of St. Mary the Virgin, in this Borough, are payable without any deduction whatever, and are impropriate solely to the repairs of this Church.

1615. Mr. Thomas Ray gave the Income of Several Tenements, lying in New Sarum, the one part in Trinity Street, the other in Gigant Street, to the poor Clothiers of Trowbridge, Chippenham, Westbury, and Marlborough, each Town to receive it once in four Years for ever.

1640. Mrs. Ann Paine, late of the Precinct of the Liberty of the Tower of London, Widdow, paid £300 to the Company of Goldsmiths of the same, for the Payment of £15 yearly during her Life, and after her decease for the payment of £15 per Annum as follows: to the poor of the said Company £5, to the poor of the Precinct of the Tower Liberty £5, and £5 to the poor of the Parishes of this Town.

1693. Edward Cressett, M. A. of Oriel College, in Oxford, bequeathed the Sum of £160, to be improved to the equal and perpetual Benefit of the Minister of this Church, and the Minister of St. Mary's Church, in this Town.

1796. Mrs. Sarah Franklyn bequeathed the Sum of £200, to be applied for the Benefit and Increase of the Rectory of this Parish for Ever.

1804. Thomas Merriman Hancock, Esq. late of this Parish, bequeathed the Sum of £200, to be vested in the Publick Funds, and directed the Dividends arising from the same to be given by the Churchwardens to the Poor of this Parish, in such manner as they shall think proper and right, an the first day of January for ever.

1803. John Goldwyer, of the City of Bath, Esq. vested in four Trustees the Sum of £333. 6. 8. in the Publick Funds, producing a Dividend of £11 per Annum, and directed one Moiety to be paid to the Rector of this Parish, for the Purchase of Quartern Loaves of Wheaten Bread, to be distributed annually in the Church amongst the indigent Poor of this Parish, who shall attend Divine Service, on Christmas Day, and the four following Sundays:—the other Moiety to be paid in like manner to the Rector of Edmondesham, in the County of Dorset.

John Brisden, John White Brockway,
Churchwardens. 1817.

The Church consists of Chancel, Nave, and North and South Aisles. The Nave is supported by five shafted columns, forming as many pointed arches. The vaulting of the chancel, and the distance to the first column of the nave, is supported by stone groins. In the south wall of the chancel is the resemblance of a piscina. There are two brass plates taken out of the nave, one out of the south aisle, and one from the north.

Register commenced in 1611.

Rectors.

Arthur Herne,	24 Sept.	1630.
Nicholas Profit,	18 March,	1669.
Joshua Sacheverel,	21 January,	1684.
Farewell Perry,	5 Sept.	1723.
Robert Clavering,	12 Nov.	1773.
Thomas Meyler,	12 July,	1786.

Francis Henchman, late Rector.

Bartholomew Buckerfield, present Rector.

The Earl of Ailesbury Lord of the Manor.

PRESHUTE.

On a small Tablet against south wall of Chancel.

This Tablet, To the Memory of the Rev. Joseph Clerk, M.A. Vicar of this Parish, and many years Master of the Royal Foundation Grammar School, Marlborough, who died July 12, 1808, Aged 65 years, was erected by his Widow E. E.

" He was a Scholar, and a ripe and good one."

To the Memory of Mr. Henry B. and Sophia Edwards, the only offspring of the Rev. Joseph and Elizabeth Edwards. Sophia Died Nov. 21, 1807, in the second year of her Age; Henry died Dec. 20, 1807, in the 20 year of his Age.

Why in such haste to meet death's cold embrace,
And thus pre-occupy a Father's place?
The spirit of the Child went quickly hence,
Ascending to its blissful residence;
Nor shall the sting of Death, nor strength of Sin,
Retard thy flight, dear Youth, to enter in,
Where Virtues guard, an Host of Angels wait,
The arrival of the just at the straight gate.

On a Flat Stone in Chancel.

Here Lyeth the Body of John, Son of Stephen and Elizabeth Nalder. He died May ye 3d, 1729, Aged 5 years.

On a Monument in Body.

Here lieth the Bodyes of Jeffr Daniell, and with his Son, the Last of that antient family at Daresborough, in Cheshire, which came into Wilts, in Kg H. 8. time, Of St. Margaret's, Esq. both Members of Parlimt after K. C. ye 2. restoration, who was also of ye Convention for ye restoring of ye sd Kg. the Son of ye 1st trienniall Parlmt began ye 7th of Kg Wm. ye 3d.
Jeff. died Ap. 22, 1681,
Wm. died Ap. 25, 1697.

Arms—Quarterly, first and fourth four lozenges in pale; second and third a wolf statant regardant.

North Wall.

John Coleman of Dynton, in the County of Wilts. Yeoman, died the 28 of January, Anno Dom. 1619, who, as he lived soe he died, a good and Godly Christian, whereof he gave good Testimony by his many deeds of Charity given by his last Will, who amongst other his Charitable gifts, gave these unto the Parish of preshut, First, hee gave 45 Shillings, to be distributed presently after his decease, to ye poor of that place. He gave, moreover, a Stock of 20 Marke, To be imployed soe that the benifit might redowne to the placeing of poor Children aprentices to honest trades, and last of all he gave 20 Shillings for ye advice & councill of a learned lawyer for the imployment and preservation of this Stocke, for ye use of the poor for ever.

The baptismal font is hollowed out of black marble, and is about four feet in diameter.

The Church consists of Chancel, Nave, and South Aisle. The south side of the Nave is supported by four pointed arches.

Register commenced 1607.

The Rev. Joseph Edwards Vicar, 1807.

Bartholomew Buckerfield, present Vicar.

The Earl of Ailesbury Lord of the Manor.

OGBOURN ST. ANDREW.

On a Monument in the North Wall of Chancel.

This is ye Monument of Wm. Goddard, of Ogbourn St. Andrew, Gent. and Eliz. his Wife, and their Children, who were Wm. John, Vincent, and Thomas, Alice, these are all here interred, and died in ye same Order they were Borne, leaving no Issue behind Them, But Elizth & Lucie, Daught. to John. This Monument was erected by Thomas ye Younger Sonne Before his Death, 1655.

Arms—Quarterly, first and fourth gules, a chevron, vair, between three crescents, argent; second and third azure, a fess lozengy, between three doves' heads erased, or.

On Flat Stones in Chancel.

Here lie the Remains of Wm. Liddiard, Esq. of this Place, who Departed this Life the 4 Day of April, in the Year of our Lord 1760, Aged 48.

Here likewise are deposited the Remains of Mary, Wife of the above Wm. Liddiard, who Departed this Life the 7th of Sept. in the year of our Lord 1763, Aged 58.

Here Lyeth ye Body of Anne, ye Wife of John Liddiard, Esq. of Ruckley, & Daughter of Thomas Gegg, of Masey Hampton, Gent. who Departed this life July ye 16, 1727, Aged 40 years.

Flat Stones without the Rails.

To the Memory of Elizabeth Liddiard, who died 19 April, 1782, Aged 56 years.

Mrs. Ann Liddiard died the 18 Jan. 1784, Aged 66.

Dorothy, the Wife of Liddiard, Esq. departed this life Nov. 18, 1756, Aged 48.

On a Monument against S. E. pillar of the Tower.

Here Lyeth Ann, ye Wife of John Seymour, Jun. of this Parish, Daughter of John Goddard, of London, Gent. who (leaving Issue Thomas, John, William, Anne, Philip, Roger, Robert, Edward) died ye 3d of April, 1687, Aged 37.

Arms—Gules, two wings conjoined and inverted or; impaling Goddard.

On a Monument against the west end of south Aisle.

To the Memory of Robert Canning, who died March 23rd, 1811, Aged 65 years.

Also Jane Canning, Sister of the above Robert Canning, who died Feb. 8, 1812, Aged 64 years.

On Flat Stones in South Aisle.

Here Lyeth the Body of Mary, Wife of John Canning, who died April 23, 1799, Aged 23 years.

Here Lyeth the Body of John Liddiard, Gent. who departed this life July 6, 1703, Aged 88 years.

On a Brass Plate.

John Liddiard, Esq. Departed this life June 21, 1763, Aged 88.

Brass Plate.

Thomas Liddiard, Gent. Younger Son of William Liddiard, Esq. late of this Parish, departed this Life 24 May, 1770, Aged 28 years.

Here lyeth the Body of Mary, the Wife of John Liddiard, of Rockly, in this Parish, and Daughter of Edward Poore, of Alton, in this County, Gent. who died the 8 day of Oct. 26, 1706.

Flat Stones in Body.

Here lyeth ye Body of Thos. ye Son of Thos. Seymour, who Departed this life April the 13, A. D. 1706.

In Memory of Ann, Daughter of Thomas and Ann Seymour, of Marlbro', Woollen Draper. She died Oct. ye 26, A. D. 1732, Aged 34 years.

Here lieth ye Body of Rebecca, ye Wife of John Richens. She died Feb. ye 18, 1721, Aged 76 years.

Here Lyeth ye Body of John Richens. He died May ye 7, 1720, Aged 82 years.

Here lyeth ye Body of Robert Richens, who Deceased Oct. ye 15, 1724, Aged 43 years.

The Church consists of Chancel, Nave, and North and South Aisle. The Nave is supported by two semi-arches on each side. The vaulting of the tower is of ancient stone groins, ornamented by handsome foliage.

The Rev. Mr. Goddard, late Vicar.

The Rev. Richard Heighway, present Vicar.

John Hancock, Esq. Lord of the Manor.

Buckley House, the seat of Sir Hugh Smith, Bart. built by the Liddiard family.

OGBOURN ST. GEORGE.

On Flat Stones in Chancel.

Sacred to the Memory of William Stone, A. M. Late Vicar of this Parish. He died 11th June, 1764, Æt. 65.

Here Lye the Remains of Elizabeth, Wife of William Stone, Vicar of this Parish, Eldest Daughter of the Rev. Mr. Thomas Selfe, Late Rector of Bromham, in this County. She died April 2, in the Year of our Lord 1750, of her Age 53.

Here lyeth ye Body of William, the Son of William Greenfield, Esq. and Mary, his Wife, who Departed this life ye 19th day of Sept. A. D. 1698.

Here lyeth the Body of Mary, the Daughter of Wm. Greenfield, Esq. and Mary, his Wife, who Departed this life ye 14th Day of April, 1699.

Here Lyeth the Body of William, the Son of William Greenfield, Esq. and Mary, his Wife, who Departed this life ye 11th Day of September, A. D. 1699.

Here Lyeth the Body of Edward, Son of Edward & Martha Buckerfield. He died May ye 4, 1729, Aged 2 years.

Here Lyeth the Body of Ann Younge, the Wife of William Younge, Gent. who died in the year of our Lorde 1609.

Here Lieth the Body of Mrs. Kathrin Younge, Wife to Mr. Richard Young, Late of Ogborne Farme, who dyed the 25 of November, A. D. 1632.

In Memory of Elizabeth, the Wife of Bartholomew Buckerfield, who departed this Life April the 30th, 1774, Aged 48 years.

And of Bartholomew Buckerfield, who died Sept. 13, 1777, Aged 70 years.

Here Lyeth ye Body of Henry, Son of Henry and Eliz. Buckerfield, who died July 24, 1725, Aged 8 years.

In Memory of Mr. Robt. Clements, Vicar of this Parish, who departed this Life May ye 13, Anno Dni 1717, Ætatis 82.

West End of the Nave.

To the Memory of John Davis Cannings, Son of Thos. & Mary Cannings, who died Feb. 15, 1818, Aged 33 years.

On a small Tablet against south wall of Nave.

Memory of Martha Ann, Daughter of Thomas & Mary Canning, who Died Nov. 20, 1813, Aged 11 years.

o Charles, their Son, who died July 13, 1816, Aged 9 years.

Flat Stones in Body.

re Lieth the Body of Dixon Smith, Sonne of lm. and Sewsan Smith, deceased the Tenth of March, 1606.

1646.

Heare Lyeth the Body of Ann Dixon. Buried the 1 of June.

---

ere Lyeth the Body of Stephen, Son of Stephen l Elizabeth Nalder. He died April ye 12, 1722.

---

ere Lyeth ye Body of Mary, Wife of Thomas otter. She was Buried April ye 17th, Anno 1706, Aged 25 years.

---

ere Lyeth the Body of Mary, Daughter of Thomas and Mary Potter. She was Buried Octr. ye 2d, Anno 1719, Aged 18 years.

On a Flat Stone in North Aisle.

ere Lyeth the Body of Hannah Miles, Wife of John iles, Citizen and Haberdasher, of London, And w Resident in Reading, in the County of Barks, nd daughter of John And Elizth Pantinge, of this arish, who Departed this life the 21 day of May, nno dom̄ 1685.

lodg'd in Could Sheets of native Earth,
I, Hanna Panting, ly for Breath;
My Charmes Prefered Me to a Wife,
I dyed When love just Gave Me Life;
My Bridall fruits at Loves Command
Cropt By A Skilfull Generous Hand,
My joys, My late Enjoyments, all Are Spent
And purchase But this Braver tenment.

On Flat Stones in S. Aisle.

n spem Beatæ Resurrectioni, Infra depositi Sunt ineres Elizabethæ, uxoris ultima Isaaci Burgesse, en. Quæ obijt 20 Junij, 1726, Æt. 71.

Here Lyeth the Body of Bartholomew Buckerfield, who Departed this life May the 22, in the 60 Year of his Age, 1684.

Here Lyeth ye Body of Nathaniel Alexander, who departed this Life June 11, 1778, Aged 57 years.

Also Nathaniel, the Son of Nathaniel and Elizabeth Alexander, who departed this Life the 23 of April, 1784, Aged 28 years.

Also Elizabeth, Wife of Nathaniel Alexander, (and Eldest Daughter of Philip and Mary Buckerfield) who departed this life Oct. 29, 1767, Aged 45 years.

This inscription has been lately defaced by the Minister, the fees not continuing to be paid by the surviving friends of the deceased.

The Church consists of Chancel, Nave, and North and South Aisles. The Nave is supported on each side by round pillars, forming pointed arches. In the window of the Chancel, and in that also of the North Aisle, is a little painted glass.

Robert Clements Vicar in 1717.
Wm. Stone 1764.
John Weldon Champneys, late Vicar,
Thomas Weldon Champneys his successor.

The Manor belongs to ***** College, Cambridge.

MILDENHALL.

On a Monument against the north wall of Chancel.

Carnis Exuvias, sub certa Resurgendi spe, huic Ecclesiæ legavit, Georgius Walker, Arm. Marlburiensis.

Ob. 8 Mar. Ann. { Salutis 1724, Ætat. suæ 71.

Cape dona Extrema
Uxoris Supersitis
Longi Monumentum,
Et Pignus Amoris.

On a Monument against the East End of Chancel.

H. S. I.

Desideratissimus Juvenis Stephenus Hyde, de Stitcombe, Geñ. Corporis inclytus, animiqꝫ donis, candore morum, probitate vitæ, summâ in Deum, in amicos fide, in omnes humanitate; magum, dum vixit, viduæ matris solatium, magnum familiæ patre orbæ et ægrotantis præsidium, magnum omnium quibus ipsum scire contigit delicium; hinc scias, Lector, quanto omnium desiderio amissus sit, qui tanto omnium commodo vixerat.

Obijt Maij die 13,
Anno { Dni 1697, Ætatis suæ 32.

Anna, Mater, Margareta et Joanna, sorores, M. P.

Arms—Per fess, barry of eight, or and azure, over all an eagle displayed, gules, charged with a crescent argent, in base, azure, a chevron between three lozenges, or.

Juxta
Edoardi Pocockii, S. T. B.
In spem beatiæ resurrectionis
deponuntur Exuviæ.
Erat
Fide terrenis quæras
Ædis Xª apud Oxon.
Juvenis Alumnus,
Deinde in hujusce Parochiæ Rectorem,
(Cui per xxxv annos præfuit,)
Nec non in Ecclesiæ Cathedralis Sarum prebendarium
Adscitus,
Sui spectes Cœlestia,
Sibi vicino Deo per omnia fidelis
Primo-genitura gaudebat
Ex illo linguarum, tum Arabicæ tum Ebraicæ,
In Academia Oxoñ Prelectore celeberrimo,
Edoardo Pocockio,
Cujus sub Auspiciis
Orientis spoliis adeo onustus evasit,
Ut nisi Filii gloriam Patris fulgor Prægravasset
Ipse merito audisset
Ille Pocockius
Uxorem duxit Catharinam,
Ricardi Davi, de Novâ Saruṁ, Arṁ, Filiam;
Ex qua
Septem, ultra decem, liberos suscepit.
Obiit, octogenarius, Decembris die 27,
Anno Dni 1726.
Johannes Pocockius, A. M.
Filius, Hæres, et in isthâc Ecclesiâ, successor,
P.

Arms—Checky, or and gules, over all a lion rampant or; impaling sable, a fess, or, between three cinquefoils, argent.

South Wall.

Sacred to the Memory of the Rev. Richard Pocock, Late Rector of Mildenhall, who departed this life the 3d of Dec. 1787, Aged 67 years.

Arms—Checky, or and gules, over all a lion rampant, or; impaling sable, a lion rampant between eight crosslets, argent.

Near rest the Remains of Thomas Baskerville, Esq.
descended from an ancient Norman lineage.
In very early Life
He devoted himself to his King and Country,
Served in Germany, under the Marquis of Granby,
and afterwards in Ireland and the West Indies,
always with distinguished Honour.
He graduated in his Promotion
from the Ensign to the Lieut.-Colonel
most creditably for himself, and most respected
and esteemed by others. He was for many years in
the 50 Regt. of Infantry,
and finally promoted to the 62nd.
Born at Rickardson, Winterbourn Basset,
in this County:
He died at Poulton House, in this Parish,
4th May, 1817, Aged 85 years, leaving no Issue.
He married, first Anne, only Daughter of
the Rev. James O'Neil,
Of Ballyshannon, County of Donnegal,
in the Kingdom of Ireland.
who died in the year 1768;
and, secondly, Jane, the Youngest Daughter of
Thomas Bishop, of Kinsale, Gent.

In the Same Vault with
her Husband, Thomas Baskerville, Esq.
Rest
the Remains of his 2nd Wife,
Jane, Youngest Daughter of Thomas Bishop, Gent.
of Kinsale,
In the Kingdom of Ireland.
She Died
Jan. 22nd, 1809, Aged 60 years,
Beloved and Lamented.

Sacred to the Memory of
Anne, only Daughter of
the Rev. James O'Neil, of Ballyshannon,
County of Donnegal,
In the Kingdom of Ireland.
She was Married to
Thomas Baskerville, Esq.
and lived a Wife only 16 Months.
She died in the year 1768, and is Buried in Ireland.

Arms—O'Neil: Per fess, argent, a sinister hand, gules, in vert, a fish, naiant, proper.
Bishop: Argent, on a bend, cottized, gules, three bezants.
Baskerville: Argent, on a chevron, gules, three hurts.

On a Monument at the west end of the Church.

In Memory of William Baker, who Died Oct. ye 18, A. D. 1729, and was Interred beneath this Place, in ye 52nd year of his Age.

Shields of Arms in the Nave.

Sable, a lion rampant, argent, between eight crosslets of the same; impaling, per fess, imbattled, sable and argent, three cross-patée, counter-changed.

Checky, or and gules, over all a lion rampant, or; impaling, Long.

Sable, a lion passant, argent, on a chief of the last, three crosslets of the first.

Hatchment in the South Aisle.

Gules, a fess between two chevrons, argent: impaling argent, on two bars, sable, three fleur-de-lis, or.

The Church consists of Chancel, Nave, and North and South Aisles. The Nave is supported by three plain semi-arches on each side. It has lately been rebuilt at the expense of William Young and John Wentworth. In the Chancel Window, in painted glass, are two figures, the representations of either bishops or kings; the one on the left of the spectator hath the crosier, or sceptre, in his hand, with the letters AUGUSTIONS. The Church is handsomely decorated with oak pews.

The Rev. Richard Pocock, late Rector.

The Rev. Charles Francis present Rector.

The Earl of Ailesbury Lord of the Manor.

ALDBOURN.

On a Monument in the North Wall of Chancel.

Underneath, in a Vault, are Deposited the Remains of Rachel, the Wife of Stephen Neate, who died June the 5, 1794, Aged 59 years.

Also Ann, their Daughter, the Wife of William Browne, of Chisledon, who died July 22, 1799, Aged 32 years.

The above-named Stephen Neat, who died Dec. 15, 1816, Aged 77 years.

South Wall.

Underneath, in a Vault, are deposited the Remains of Mr. John Neate, of Devizes, who Died 21 May, 1812, Aged 67 years.

On Flat Stones in Chancel.

Here Lyeth ye Body of Mrs. Elizabeth Nicholas, near her great Grandfather, Edward Nicholas, Esq. Daughter to Edward Nicholas, Merchant, at Youghal, in Ireland, who died March ye 9th, 1712, Aged between 26 & 27 years.

Arms—A chevron between three owls.

Here Lyeth Mrs. Jane Nicholas, who Dyed April the 3d, A. D. 1707.

Arms—A chevron, engrailed, between three owls.

Here Lyeth the Body of Frances Nicholas, Widow of Oliver Nicholas, Esq. Lieutenant Governour of Portsmouth. She Departed this Life May the 2nd, Anno Domini 1697.

Arms—For Nicholas: impaling, on a bend cotiized, three lozenges, ermine.

Here lyeth the Body of Oliver Nicholas, Esq. Lieutenant Governour of his Majesties Garrison, at Portsmouth, Captain of his Royal Highness's Independant Company, and Justice of Peace for his Majesties Countye's of Wilts. and Hampshire, who Departed this life the 1 Day of December, Anno Dom. 1683, Aged 61.

To the Memory of William Shepherd, Esq. Son of Alexander and Sarah Shepherd, who Departed this Life April 7th, 1789, Aged 65 years.

Arms—Three owls in bend.

Here lie the Body of the Honble Colonel Thomas Hatton, who died 13 Jan. 1767, Aged 77.

Here Lyeth ye Body of Colonel Oliver Nicholas, of Aldborn. He Departed this Life March ye 11, 17$\frac{15}{16}$, in the 65 year of his Age.

Arms—A chevron engrailed between three owls.

Here Lyeth interred the Body of Edward Nicholas, of Alborne, Gent. who was buried the 4 of July, 1649.

On a Brass Plate.

Dorothea Reeve, vidua, mater Francisæ Nicholas, vxoris Oliver Nicholas, Armigeri. Obijt tertio die Junij, Ano Dom. 1676, Ætatis suæ Octogesimo nono.

On Monuments against the South Wall of Nave.

In Memoria Æterna erit Justus
D. Johannes Norris,
Fide juxta ac vitâ Theologus,
Hujus Ecclesiæ olim Vicarius,
16 die Martii, Anno Salutis
Humanæ 1681, Ætat. suæ 66,
Mortalis esse Desiit.
Nunc vero per Christum Fidelium servatorem
Cujus evangelium indefessus Ille
In sacris conscionibus e suggesto,
Juxta quod quicquid ei erat terrestes
Subtus inhumatur,
Per 21 et amplius annos alacri animo,
Et Studio haud mediocri illustravit.
Inter Beatos vivit Immortalis.
Ego in justitia videbo Faciem Tuã,
Satiabor cum evigilavero
ad similitudinem tuam. Psal. 17. 15.

Wood Frame, S. Wall.

In Memory of Jane, the Wife of John Hall, of Newbury, formerly Jane French, Daughter of John and Elizabeth French, late of this Parish. Early taught, and well understanding, her duty towards God and her Neighbours, as enforced in the Catechism of the Established Church, her Devotion and Gratitude became fixed and fervent, and her Charity and Kindness active and ardent during her mortal Career. She nied as she had Lived, a Zealous and faithful Christian, 14 July, 1815, Aged 51 years.

Here lyes interred ye Body of Richard Kinge, of Upham, in ye County of Wilts. Esq. Alderman and Sheriffe of the City of London, who had to Wife Martha, Daughter of Edward Goddard, Esq. of ye same County, by whome he had Issue 7 Sonnes and 3 Daughters, John died young, Richard, Nicholas, James, John, Thomas, Edward, obiit sine prole Martha and Elizabeth, . . .iscilla died Younge.

He had to his Second Wife Mary, Relict of Edward Adams, Citizen of London, and Daughter of John . . .arch, of St. Albans, in ye County of Hartford, and by whome he had Issue one Sone and 3 Daughters, Edward, now living, Rachell, Mary, and Cathorn, Obiit sine prole. He departed this life ye 22d of May, Aged 52 years, in ye year of our Lord God 1668.

Arms—Per pale, first Goddard; second a lion rampant between three crosslets fitchey; third, on a bend three lozenges, in chief a trefoil.

Here Lyeth the Body of Edne, the Son of Edne and Elizabeth Witts, who Departed this Life the 16 day of June, 1788, Aged 23 years.

Also Edne Witts, Senr. who Departed this Life the 22 of Nov. 1808, Aged 71 years.

Also Elizabeth, Wife of Edne Witts, Senr. who departed this Life the 18 of Dec. 1799, Aged 69 years.

Subtus Requiescunt Cinere,
Gulielmi Jackson, ... Ecclesiæ
per Annos quadraginta
Vicarii Dignissimi,
Qui Obijt 20 die Decem. Anno
Dom. 1723, Ætat. 75.

Arms—A chevron between three . . . . impaling, a lion rampant between three crosslets fitchy.

Here lyeth ye Body of Edward Witts, who departed this Life Oct. ye 27, A.D. 1715, Aged 66 years.

Also Richard Witts, Son of Richard and Mary Witts, who departed this Life May the 30th, 1790, Aged 38 years.

In Memory of Miriam Witts, the Daughter of Richard and Mary Witts, who died March 30, 1733, Aged 18 years.

And also Mary, the Daughter of Richard and Mary Witts, who Departed this life January ye 29th, 1771.

In Memory of Richard Witts, who Departed this life ye 17 day of August, 1747, Aged 49 years.

And also Mary Witts, the Wife of Richard Witts, who Departed this Life Jan. the 8th, 1736, Aged 55 years.

Mary, Wife of Broom Witts, who died Nov. 7th, 1816, Aged 49 years.

To the Memory of John Bacon, who died July 7, 1774, Aged 73 years.

Also Mary, his Wife, who died March 17, 1793, Aged 91 years.

And also Sarah, the Wife of Robert Church, who died March 27, 1803, Aged 63 years.

In Memory of Deborah Gould, Late of Newbury, in the County of Berks, Grocer, who departed this Life 11 June, 1790, Aged 60 years.

On a Monument against the North Wall of the Vestry.

Gulielmus Walronde, Gen. Eduardi Frater, 84 annos vita inte Gradefunctus, Anno 1614 ingressus E..viam universæ Carnis Corpore . . . tem sub hoc monumento incineres redacto, anima ejus in Cœlis secundum per Christum Iesum Resurgata carnis assumptionem expectat.

My dais are Gone like a Shadow. psal. 102.

Hic secundum Christi Adventum, in pace Expectat, Eduardus Walronde, Armiger, ex antiqua Walrondorum Familia oriundus; vir ΦΙΔΟΞΕΝΟΣ et ΠΟΛΥΞΕΝΟΣ, quem Deus in Cœlestem patriam evocavit, An. Salvtis 1615, Ætatis suæ 96.

The Righteous shall be had in ever Lasting Remembrance.

Arms—Sable, a cross gules.

On Flat Stones in South Aisle.

Here Lyeth the Body of Edward Bacon, who Departed this life July ye 5, 1684, Ætatis suæ 83.

In Memory of Alice, Wife of Anthony Javery. She died March ye 3d, Anno Dom. 1716, Aged 86 years.

Here lyeth George Gu . . . . that died ye 19 of Ap. 1709. He was a Private Soulder in King Charles the 2nd Reign, under Colonel Nicholas.

Here Lieth Mark, ye Son of Thomas and Susanna Fowler, who Departed this Life March ye 31, A. D. 1702, Aged 18 years & 7 months.

Memorandum. Anno Domini 1597.

Thomas Goddard, of Upham, Esq. gave by Will Forty Shillings a year for Ever to the poor of the Parish of Aldbourn, to be paid by the Church Wardens among the said Poor People half yearly, Viz. Twenty Shillings at Lady Day, and Twenty Shillings at Michaelmas.

At the east end of this aisle, on the top of an altar-tomb, are the figures of a family of six persons (the father, mother, three sons, and a daughter) in the attitude of prayer. Their hands are all broken off, and the head of the second son is lost. There is no inscription or date upon the tomb.

Arms—Quarterly, first and fourth Goddard; second and third vert, a fess lozengy, or, between three doves heads erased of the same, over which hangs a helmet.

Against the East Wall of North Aisle.

Memorandum. Anno Domini 1797.

Lawrence Brown, of Newbury, Gent. Gave by Will for ever the Interest of Two Hundred Pounds, in the three per cent. reduced Bank Annuities, (the Principal to continue for ever in the Bank) to be Disposed of by Mark Brown and Thomas Brown, of Aldbourn, their Executors, Administrators, and Assigns, and the survivor of them, and the Executors and administrators of such Survivor for ever, in manner following; Viz. One Moiety, or half part thereof, in purchasing three Brown Cloth Great Coats, yearly and for ever; and the other Moiety, or half part, (after deducting their reasonable expences) in purchasing five Gowns, yearly and for ever, to be given to such poor men and women of Aldbourn as they shall think most deserving the same, Provided always that Preference be for ever given to such poor men and women as are of his own kindred.

Anno Dom. 1797.

Henry Southby, Esq. gave by Will Ten Pounds to the Poor of this Parish, which was paid by S. Hayter, his Executrix, and disposed of in Bread amongst the Poor by the Minister, Churchwardens, and Overseers.

The Church consists of Chancel, Nave, North and South Aisles, and two Transepts. The Nave is supported by five pointed arches on each side, three of which, on the south, are ornamented by Saxon mouldings, the rest are plain. In the Chancel is a pointed arch.

Hatchment in the Chancel.

Argent, a chevron between three garbs, gules.

Register began in 1637.

Vicars.

The Rev. Mr. Atkinson	1637.
Mr. Norris	1662.
Mr. Jacksons	1682.
Mr. Seager	1724.
Mr. Morris	1732.
Mr. Butt	1774.

The Rev. Mr. Alderton present Vicar.

Thos. Minors Baskerville, Esq. Lord of the Manor.

The following persons were buried at Aldbourn in the year 1767.
(From the Parish Register.)

Widow Clock, aged	88 years.
Widow Reeves,	89.
Widow Gilmore,	84.
Widow Hedge,	76.
Coleman,	90.
Perkens,	85.
Knackston,	78.
Widow Dixon,	90.

AVEBURY.

On a Monument against the East End of Chancel.

Near this Place Lyeth the Body of Dame Susanna Holford, Daughter of Samuel Trotman, of Bucknell, in the County of Oxford, Esq. and Widdow of Sir Richard Holford, Late one of ye Masters in Chancery. She departed this life March the 20th, 1722, in the 68 year of her Age.

This Monument to her Memory, Samuel, her Son, hath Caused to be Erected.

Arms—Argent, in fess, a greyhound passant, sable: impaling of the field, a cross between four roses, gules.

Brass Plate.

Come nere, my frends, Behould and see,
Such as I am such shall you be,
As is my state with in this Tombe,
So must your's be Before the Doome,
For all men must, by God's Decree,
Once taste of Deth, as ye see me,
Where fore in time Remember Deth,
Before you lose your vitall Breth.
John Truslowe Here interred is, and in this grave,
Which unto me Large Benefits most Bountyfully gave,
The race he lived here on earth was threescore & seven,
Deceased in April, 93, and then was prest to Heaven.
He Havinge then no Issue Left, his Living wholy gave
To Richd Truslow of his name, for so he would it have,
Who, in remembrance of the Gyver, this Tombe hath caused to be
Within this Church of Aubury Erected as you see,
Per Richardum Truslowe, Hæredem Adoptivvm et executorum dicti Johannis, 18 Aprilis, 1593.

On Flat Stones in Chancel.

Here Lyeth the Body of Mr. John White, Vicar of Avebury, who Departed this Life October 17, Anno Domini 1712, Aged 70 years.

Here lyeth ye Body of Richard, Son of John White, Vicar of Aubury, and Mary, his Wife. He was Buried April ye 23, 1697, Aged 19 years.

Here Lyeth the Body of Mary, the Daughter of Dyer and Jane Bond, of Laycock. She was Buried July ye 22, 1708, Aged 6 Months.

Underneath Lyeth the Remains of Deborah Amore, who Departed this Life the 12th November, 1817, in the 22 year of her Age.

Also of Richard Amore, who died 10 February, 1820, Aged 31 years.

Flat Stones in Body.

To the Memory of Henry Howson, Gent. Obijt 3d of May, 1779, Æt. 73.

Also Sarah, Wife of the said Henry Howson, Gent. Obijt 7 June, 1787, Æt. 69.

Here Lyeth ye Body of Elizabeth Crips. She died Feb. the 14, A. D. 1719, Aged 40 years.

Samuel Martin, Esq. Ob. 20 Sept. 1775, Aged 55.

1662.

Here Lyeth the Body of Thomas Smith, of West Kinnet, Gent. He departed this Life the fourteenth of November.

Mors mihi lucrum.

Also ye Body of Mary, ye Wife Stawell Smith, who departed this Life ye 15th of July, 1725, in the 51 year of her Age.

Here Lyeth the Body of Richard, Son of Richard and Jane Green, of West Kenett, who Died July ye 19th, A. D. 1717, Aged 27 years.

Also Here Lyeth ye Body of Ann, ye Wife of John Beake. She died July ye 7th, with her Infant, A. D. 1723, Aged 43 years.

Here Lieth ye Body of Richard Green, of West Kennet, who departed this Life Oct. 2, 1718, Aged 68 years.

Also Here Lyeth the Body of John Beake, Sen. who Departed this life the 21 of March, 1740, Aged 59 years.

Here Lyeth the Body of Anne, ye Daughter of Richard Green, of West Kennet, who died Jan. ye 23, A. D. 1721, Aged 41 years.

Here Lyeth ye Body of Jane, ye Wife of Richard Green. She died June 12, A. D. 1723, Aged 67.

Here Lyeth the Body of Jane, the Wife of Mr. Richard Smith, of West Kennet, who Departed this Life ye 25 Day of August, Anno Dom. 1690.

Here Lieth ye Body of Elizabeth, the Wife of Edward Bayly, of Bristol, Grocer, and Daughter of Mr. Richard and Mrs. Jane Smith, of West Kennet, who Departed this Lifethe 2 Day of June, 1698.

On Flat Stones in S. Aisle.

Here Lyeth the Body of Richard Smith, of West Kennet, Gent. who Departed this Life ye 19 of December, A. D. 1765, Aged 76 years.

Here Lyeth Mary, ye Wife of Richard Smith, of West Kennett, who departed this Life May ye 5, A. D. 1720, Aged 59 years.

In Memory of Henry Smith, of West Kennet, Gent. He died March ye 16th, 1732, Ætatis 74.

Richard Smith, of Kennet, Gent. died August ye 22, 1734, Aged 78 years.

In Memory of Mary, the Wife of Mr. John Phelps, of Draycot Foliat, in this County, who Departed this life Oct. 14, 1760, in the 88 year of her Age.

H. S. E.

Johannes Phelps, de Draycot Foliat, in Com. Wilts. Gent. Obijt 30 die Novembris, Anno Dom. 1731, Ætat. 35.

Arms—A lion rampant between six crosslets fitchy, in chief a crescent for difference.

H. S. I.

Quicquid correptibus . . . . . .
Richardi Phelpes, nuper . . . .
in parochia de Chisleton . . . . .
Comitatu. Qui postquam . . . .
Septuagesimum quintum . . .
Cum Christiana Charitate,
. . . . fide speq; beatutidinis . .
Christo Domino . . . .
expiravit Undecimo, 1701.

Near underneath Lies the Body of George Stretch, who died June 7, 1748, Aged 52 years.

Here Lies the Body of Rebecca, his Wife, who died Feb. 6th, 1753, Aged 56 years.

Also Mary, the Wife of James Hitchcock, Daughter of George and Rebecca Stretch, who died Dec. 4, 1756, Aged 33.

Here Lyeth ye Body of Mary, the Wife of Walter Stretch, who Departed this Life May ye 13, A. D. 1720, Aged 61 years.

On a Flat Stone in North Aisle.

The 9 of June, 1713, died Mary Goldsmith, Eldest Daughter of Thomas Smith, of West Kennet, Gentleman, and Wife of Henry Goldsmith, Late of Bernard Inn, Gent. Aged 93.

Hatchment in the Chancel.

Quarterly, first and fourth, on a chevron, gules, three mullets, or, between three trefoils, proper; second sable, three lozenges, argent, on a chief, or, three fleur-de-lis, azure; third argent, on a fess, azure, three mullets, argent, in chief a boar's head couped, azure.

The Church consists of Chancel, Nave, and North and South Aisles. The Nave is supported on each side by two pointed arches. Over the entrance door of the south porch is a small canopy.

Register commenced 1699.

The Rev. Mr. Mayo Vicar.

OVERTON.

On a Monument against the south wall of Chancel.

Near this Places Lyes interred the Body of Mr. Mortimer Powell, Late an eminent Merchant and Citizen of London, Son of Thos. Powell, of this Parish, Esq. who Departed this Life 1 Oct. 1734, Aged 54 years.

Also the Body of his Brother, Mr. John Powell, of this Place, who dyed 3 Feb. 1735, Aged 58 years.

And Thomas Powell, of Maundits Park, in this County, Esq. who dyed 5 April, 1738, Aged 72 years.

And James Powell, of this Place, Gent. who dyed 16 May, 1738, Aged 54 years.

Arms—Party, per fess, or and gules, over all a lion rampant of the last.

On a Monument in the North Wall of Chancel.

Near this Place lie the Bodies of William Brown, Gent. who died March 8th, 1782, Aged 73 years.

Of Ann, his Wife, who died Oct. 22, 1760, Aged 54 years.

And of Mary, his Second Wife, who died Sept. 2nd, 1767, Aged 26 years.

And also of William, their Son, who died young.

Brass taken out.

Flat Stones in the Body.

Here Lyeth the Body of Mary, Wife of John Cook, Senr. who died June ye 12, 1762, Aged 51 years.

No one could think, no tongue can tell,
What I endur'd whilst I was ill;
Now Life is past, and Death is come,
The Lord was pleas'd to take me home.

Also Michael, Son of John and Ann Cook, who died Dec. 3, 1769, in the 3rd year of his Age.

Here Lyeth the Body of Sarah, Daughter of John and Mary Cook, who died August 19th, 1774, Aged 37 years.

Here Lyeth ye Body of Thomas, Son of Michael and Sarah Cook, who died Jan. 2, A. D. 1717, Aged 4 years.

Here lyeth ye Body of Michael Cook, who died Dec. ye 1, Anno Domini 1722, Ætatis 56.

In Memory of Ann, the Wife of Michael Cook, who died Sept. 8th, 1733, Aged 43 years.

Here Lyeth the Body of Michael Cook, who departed this life July ye 1, 1783, Aged 73 years.

On a Wood Frame at the East End of Body.

Robert Fowle, Gent. of Lockeridge, in 1704, Gave Twenty Pounds, and directed the Interest thereof to be distributed annually by the Churchwardens of Overton among such Poor Persons of that Parish as receive no Alms or Relief from the Rates.

The Church is but a small structure, consisting only of a Chancel and Body: in the window of the former is a little painted glass.

The Rev. Dr. Thring late Vicar.

The Rev. Dr. Hoyle, present V.

The Duke of Marlborough Lord of the Manor.

EAST KENNET.

On Monuments in Chancel.

Memoriæ Caroli Tooker, de Kennet Orientali, Qui Obiit vices. tertio die Jul. Anno Domini 1716, Ætatis suæ 39, decem nonas annuatim percipiendas hujus Ecclesiæ Ministri moriens legavit, Monumentum hoc propinqua defuncti Annæ Saunders, de Mungwel, posuit.

Car. Tooker, Armig. Car. Tooker, de Abingdon, in Agro Berks, L. L. D. Filij, qui Domi hospitalis æquus pro Tribunali, ubiq. humanus vixit, obijtq. desideratissimus Aug. 30,

Anno { Dom. 1700, Ætat. 64.

Anno, uxor superstes, generosâ Sadlerioru Familia de Elcombe orienda, Monumentum hoc Amoris nunqua morituri mœrens posuit.

Arms—Azure, on a bend engrailed, azure, three hearts, gules; impaling party, per saltier, ermine and or, in pale two shields, gules, in fess the same.

Hic jacet Anna Tooker, qui obijt vices. quinto die Feb. Anno Dom. 1707, Ætatis suæ Septuagesimo Primo. Ministro Ecclesiæ de Kennet Orientali Trecentas libras in perpetuam legavit. Vidua fuit Caroli Tooker, Arm. Filia Guliel. Sadler, Armig. Com. Wilts. Amita Annæ Saunders, de Mungwell, Viduæ, Quæ, defunctæ colens Memoriam, hoc marmor posuit.

Flat Stones in Chancel.

To the Memory of Henry, Son of Henry and Anna Maria Isherwood, who Departed this Life Dec. 15, 1782, Aged 7 years.

To the Memory of Jane, Daughter of the Reverend Mr. John and Grace Bromwich, who departed this life July 2, 1781, Aged 34 years.

Sacred to the Memory of the Rev. John Bromwich, who was Minister of this Parish upwards of 50 years. He Departed this Life Feb. 11, 1788, Aged 79 years.

Also to the Memory of Grace, his Wife, who died Dec. 4, 1792, Aged 78 years.

Register commenced 1656.

The Rev. Mr. John Gilmore Rector.

Mr. Richard Matthews Lord of the Manor, out of which £.50 is annually paid to the Rector.

WINTERBOURNE MONKTON.

On Flat Stones in Chancel.

Here Lyeth the Body of Thomas Purnell, Gent. who was Buried April ye 5, 1676.

When we have done our Parts
in this Toylsom World,
By Death wee straight way,
From the Stage are Hurl'd:
Death sends our Souls to Heaven,
Our Bodyes lay in Grave
Till the Joyful resurrection Day.

In Memory of William Hitchcock, who died August 28th, 1786, Aged 79 years.

Here also Lyeth the Body of Roger Hitchcock, who died Feb. 17, 1788, Aged 67 years.

In Memory of Tarrah, Wife of William Hitchcock, who died Sept. 7, 1733, Aged 63 years.

On a plain Stone against the North Wall of Nave.

To ye Memory of Mrs. Elizabeth Thorold, Wife to ye Rev. Mr. Thomas Thorold, Vicar of Winterbourn Monkton. She Died Suddenly ye 1 Day of June, Anno Dom. 1732, in ye 63 year of her Age.

On Flat Stones in Body.

Gulielmus Sloper, Generosus, Antiqua familiâ Monktoniæ prognatus; Sexto die Augusti, 1629, renatus, Rx Hospitio St. Clementis Attornatus, 25 die Octobris, 1712, denatus.

Hic posuit Cineres.

In Memory of Thomas Alexander, who died Dec. 12, 1775, Aged 73 years.

Death is most certain, here you see,
And Suddenly it came to me:
Prepare for Death, make no delay,
For after death come Judgment Day.

In Memory of Jane, Daughter of John and Ann Alexander, who died December ye 2d, 1779, Aged 8 months.

Also in Memory of John Alexander, who died Dec. 8, 1779, Aged 27 years.

The Rev. Dr. Mayo Rector, succeeded his father.

General Popham, of Littlecott, Lord of the Manor.

BARWICK BASSET.

On a Monument against the south Wall of Chancel.

To the Memory of Henry Webb, of this Parish, who died June 24, 1776.

By his last Will and Testament, he gave and bequeathed the sum of Three Hundred and Fifty Pounds, the Interest and dividend is to be applied for the appointment of a Schoolmaster, to teach and instruct the Children of the Poor and Indigent Parishioners residing in the Parish of Barwick Bassett, in Spelling, Reading, Writing, and Arithmetick, which said Sum of Three Hundred and Fifty Pounds, he thereby ordered to be placed out on some Government Security, likewise appointing the said Sum to be vested in the Name of John Nalder, Lord of the Manor of Bassett, or any or every future Lord or Lords, Lady or Ladies, of the said Manor, of Algernon Frampton, Minister, of the said Donative, of Barwick Bassett, or any other future Minister, and George Brown, of Avebury, Gent. whom he thereby appointed to be Trust of his said Will; with which sum of £350 was purchased the sum of £.448, in the three per cent. Consolidated Annuities, by his Sole Executrix, Mrs. Elizabeth Seymour, and by her legally conveyed, on the 7th of October, 1778, to the said John Nalder, Algernon Frampton, and George Brown.

On Flat Stones in Chancel.

Here Lyeth the Body of Frances, the Wife of Thomas Crips, who Departed this Life in prayer upon her Knees, and was Buried April the 12, 1646.

And also Fower of her Children, Beinge two Sons & two Daughters.

Here Lyeth the Body of Thomas Cripps, who disceased the 2 day of February, in the year 1677.

Beneath this Stone lie the Remains of Mrs. Elizabeth Nalder, Wife of Mr. John Nalder, Daughter of Roger and Elizabeth Spanswick, of Soby, in this County, who departed this Life Feb. 8, 1794, Aged 40 years.

This Vault has Susannah, Wife of Mr. Caleb Bailey, Daughter of J. G. Esq. and Mary, his Wife, Daughter of J. Elton, Esq.

Here lies the Body of Caleb Bailey, Esq. who departed this Life August 30, 1749, Aged 77 years.

Henry Webb died the 24th of June, 1776.

To his Memorye, Henrye Holman, and was buryed the 22 day of Oct. Anno Dom. 1599, it hath pleased god to take.

Flat Stones in Body.

In Memory of Richard Biggs, who died October 8, 1770, Aged 73 years.

Lucy, his Wife, died June 17, 1770, Aged 73 years.

Also John, their Son, died Dec. 19, 1779, Aged 50 years.

Here Lyeth the Body of Thomas Biggs, of Burderop, in this County, Yeoman, who died Oct. 13, 1788, in the 51 year of his Age.

Here Lyeth Aron Axford in ye dust,
hoping to rise among the Just,
who died April ye 14, 1733, Aged 74 years.

The ancient screen is still remaining that separates the Chancel from the Nave.

The presentation to the Living of Barwick Basset belongs to the Marquis of Lansdown.

The Rev. Mr. Greenwood Rector.

John Nalder, Esq. Lord of the Manor.

WINTERBOURNE BASSET.

On a Monument against the East End of Chancel.

Sacred to the Memory of Elizabeth, the Wife of John Tuckey, who Departed this Life June the 8th, 1809, Aged 52 years.

And of Hannah, Daughter of John and Elizabeth Tuckey, who died Nov. 28, 1818, Aged 21 years.

And Richard John Hodgson, Grandson of John and Elizabeth Tuckey, who died Jan. 14, 1819, Aged 3 years and 6 months.

Arms—Argent, a fess between three hearts, gules.

On Flat Stones in Chancel.

The Reverend William Wightwick, D. D. Rector of this Parish, who died November the 30th, 1765, in the 64 year of his Age.

Martha, Wife of William Wightwick, D. D. Daughter of the Reverend Thomas Frampton, Vicar of Broadhinton, died July the 12, 1749, in the 28 year of her Age.

William, Son of William and Martha Wightwick, died October, 1747, Aged 6 months.

On Monuments against the East Wall of the North Transept.

P. M.

Margaretæ, Uxoris Francisci Baskervill, Arm.
Filiæ Joannis Glanville, equitis, aurat. &c.
quæ postquam pietate, eleemosynis,
Et patientiâ, quantum homini datur
emicuisset
Morborum agmitic confecta,
Inter vicinorum lachrymas,
mortem diu exoptatem,
placide amplexa est,
die Mar. 28,
Ætat An. 79, Salut. 1696.
Exuvias, ipsius jussu, juxta cineres
primo-geniti filii, Gualt. Baskervill,
infra hoc mnemosynon.
Alex. Ken.cener M. P.

To the Pious Memory of the Late most Excellent and Virtuous Mrs. Mary Baskerville, Widow and Relict of Thos. Baskerville, Esq. of Richardston, in this Parish, and Lord of this Mannour, and Daughter of Richard Jones, of Hanham, in the County of Gloucester, Esq. who Lived to a good old Age, and Dy'd full of honour and merit, being blest with a plentiful Fortune, which she managed with the greatest discretion, and apply'd to the most commendable uses. She was a loving and dutiful Wife, a tender and affectionate Mother, and the very best of Grandmothers. She was a true Lover of the Church of England, and of all its true and sincere Sons: She was Religious without affectation, and without ostentation generous and free; Courteous, affable, and obliging to all She conversed with, and Compassionate and Charitable to all that were distressed and afflicted: And for a Memorial of Her and her Excellent Qualities and Virtues, George Baskerville, of this Place, Gent. Her Younger (Living) Son, in testimony of his duty and gratitude, hath erected this Monument. She changed this life for a better March 5, A. D. 1724, Aged 81 years.

O happy soul! why should we grieve or mourn for thee?
Since Thou art gone with God above to be.

Arms—Or, a chevron, gules, between three hurts; impaling argent, a lion rampant regardant, sable.

On an altar-tomb built with brick, N. Transept.

Under this Tomb Lyeth ye Body of Richard Baskerville, Esq. who departed this Life Sept. ye 14, in the year of our Lord 1739, Aged 72.

Also two Sons, Walter and Richard,
And Jane, a Grand Daughter.

Here Lyeth ye Bodie of Simon Baskerville, Esquier, ye 8 Sonne of Sir Walter Baskerville, of Earsley, in the County of Hereford, Knt. which Simon Married the Widow of William Hutchins, of Richarston, who died in 1602.

Here also Lieth ye Body of William Baskerville, of Wanborough, Sone of the Above Said Simon Baskerville, who deceased at Richarston, ye 29 day of Sept. 1604.

Also Thomas, Son of William Hutchins, of Richarston, who died May the 27, 1607.

Here Lyeth the Body of Thomas Baskerville, of Richarston, Esq. who Departed this Life Feb. 12, Anno Dom. 17$\frac{17}{18}$ Aged 76.

who had 12 Sons by his Wife, Mary, viz. John, Richard, Francis, Walter, Thomas, Thomas, Septimus, Simon, William, John, George, Walter.

Also Mary, his Wife, died May ye 3, 1724,
Aged 81 years.

Register commenced 1724.

[Children of George and Elizabeth Baskerville.]

Simon,	*born* 24 January,	1709.
Thomas,	7 June,	1711.
Mary,	30 March,	1713.
George,	27 June,	1715.
Sarah,	2 Sept.	1717.
Walter,	5 January,	1718.
John,	6 Decem.	1720.
William,	2 October,	1724.
Richard,	8 January,	1727.

[Children of Thomas and Mary Baskerville.]

Meliora,	*born* 30 April,	1733.
Thomas,	18 July,	1735.

The Church consists of Chancel, Nave, North Aisle, and North Transept. In the North Window of the Chancel and Transept is a little painted glass, g. or, and az.

The Rev. Mr. Doncaster, Rector.
Lord Holland, Lord of the Manor.

BROAD HINTON.

On a Monument in the North Wall of Chancel.

Memoriæ Sacrum Joannis Glanvilli, Militis Servientis ad lege Caroli Primi et Caroli Secundi, Filii Joannis Glanvilli, de Tavistock, in Com. Devoñ tempore Reginæ Elizabethæ, unius Justiciorum de Comūni Banco, natu secundi; Domus Commūnum in Parliamento nuper Proloquutorus, hujus Manerii Glanvillorum primi Emptoris et Proprietarii. Obiit 2 die Octoberis, Anno Doni 1661. Hoc Monumentum propriis sumptibus posuit Winifredâ Glanvill, ipsius Johannis dum vixit Uxor Amantissima, nunc Vidua Mœstissima, 29 die Septembris, A° Dom. 1673.

Arms—Azure, three crosses of St. Andrew, or: impaling, a chevron between three martlets.

In a recess, N. Wall.

Here Lyeth Syr William Wroughton, Knyght, whoe dyed in the 50 yeare of his Age, in Anno Domini 1519, and Lefte Yfsewe of his Bodie, by Dame Ellinor his Wife, doughter of Edward Leuknor, Esquier, Foure Sonnes and three Doughters, and Bylded the House of Broadhenton, An° Do. 1540.

Arms—A chevron between three boar's heads; impaling, three chevrons.

W ELISABETH BETH GRACE O GO OENE
ENGLAND TE O IERASE

East End.

In Memory of Mrs. Frances Stone, Daughter of Sr Henry Gibbs, of Middlesex, Bart. and Relict first of

Wm. Glanville, Esq. Lord of this Mannour, and afterwards of Jno Stone, Esq. of Brightwell, in Oxfordshire, who died full of years and honour, having adorned a plentiful Fortune with a bright and shining example, and distinguished herself by prudent, chearefull, and affable Behaviour, a continued course of sincere and unaffected Piety, and ye most fervent and extensive Charity. She was an ornament to the Church of England, a generous patroness of its Ministers, an Affectionate Parent to the Orphans, and a compassionate friend to the poor: And in Memory of her excellent qualities, Winifred, her only Daughter and Heir, by William Glanville, Esq. and Wife of George Bayly, Esq. of Nervington, in Oxfordshire, has given this testimony of her filial piety and gratitude. She departed this life March 6th, 171$\frac{1}{5}$, Aged 89 years.

Arms—Gules, a dexter hand, argent, holding a broken tilting spear, or, in base a spur of the last.

On a statue standing in a recess, north wall.

Memoriæ Francisci Glanville, Vice-Colonelli, filii Johannis Glanville, Comitis Aurati, Serventis Domini Regis ad Legem, et Winifridæ, Uxoris suæ, qui in Scotia, Belgia, partibus Angliæ Borealib3, et Wallia, per sexenivm fortiter militavit, sapivs et graviter vulnerat9 deinde apud Bridgwater, in Com. Somerset, cum exercitus vtrivsq3 domus Parliamentariæ, ad Locum illum munitissimum expugnandum congrasi sunt oblato pretio exempli cause necessario, et acerrima, spectator candide, se inserens ante oppidum obsidentibus redditum ad ripam fluminis mortem virilem inter pugnandum subiit 21 die Julij, Ano Ætat. suæ 28, Ano Dni. 1645. Subacam despiciens invidiam dum ipse mari et Terra resonante vindiq. fama ad nubes, &c. Sydara provect9 est herovm cœtum auctor, deniq. sub insigniis Familia Glanvillorum, de Tavisstock, in Com. Devon. unde ortum, habuit hoc Monumentum paterno hic in solo ut vides decorat9 est de illo quod conscripsit poeta elegiac, credere ne dupites Nec dedit aut Marti Juveni dabit Anglia pugnax Maiorem, sateret progenuisse parem.

Arms—Argent, three crosses of St. Andrew, or.

South Wall.

Gulielmus Glanville, Armiger, Joannis, Equitis Aurati, filius primo-genitus: Vir, si quis allus, ad antiquæ probitatis, fidei et pietatis norman factus, negotiis gerendis par, sed eorum ambitu major innocentiam honoribus prætulit, et non alio quam Eirenarchæ munere perfunctus, publicæ pacis justa et privatæ custos fidelissimus, bene latuit quo melius viveret, quietem quam in vita sequebatur. Mors æqua attulit die xi Octobris, Anno 1680, et sexaginta quinque anno natum: Cœlo maturum eidem reddidit, Uxor unanimis Francisca Claro Gibbestorum, sanguine orta, post viginti sex annos in conjugio sine querela actos, et duplicem interea partum, Francisci filii, qui in bimatu obiit, et Winifredæ filiæ, quæ Parletono Stonē, Arm. in matrimonio juncta, titulum hunc P.

Flat Stones in Chancel.

Beneath this Stone Lyeth the Body of Thomas Brown, who Departed this Life June 23, 1799, Aged 62 years.

Likewise to the Memory of Sarah, Daughter of Thomas and Mary Brown, who Departed this Life Oct. 8, 1804, Aged 27 years.

Also Mary, his Wife, who died April 26, 1817, Aged 85 years.

Beneath this Stone Lyeth the Body of Elizabeth Brown, Wife of Algernon Brown, who departed this life Sept. 1st, 1802, Aged 38 years.

On a Mouument against the North Wall of Body.

Sacred to the Memory of Ann Hughes, Wife of John Hughes, who Departed this Life March 1st, 1786, Aged 46 years.

Flat Stones in the Body.

Here Lyeth the Body of Ann Greenway, who departed this life the 20 day of Jan. Anno Dom. 1690, Aged 65 years.

Here Lyeth the Body of Thomas Norborne, Gent. who Departed this Life Feb. ye 17, A. D. 1708, Aged 82 years.

Brass Plate.

Here Lyeth the Body of Wm. Parish, of Cotemersh, within this Parish of Broad Hinton, who died in the year of our Lord 1447. Here also Lyeth the Body of Thomas Parish, Likewise of Cotemersh, who died the 20 of April, in the year of our Lord God 1610. Thos. Parish, S.T.B. Coll. Corporis Christi Oxon. Socius, et Thomæ, hic sepulti abreptus titulum avulsum restitum curavit, A. D. 1687.

Here Lyeth the Body of Mr. Thomas Alcock, Minister of this Parish from 1620, who departed this Life the 23 of November 1664.

In Memory of Thomas Vivash, who died Feb. 8th, 1728, Aged 66.

In Memory of Elizabeth, Wife of Thomas Vivash, who died March 8, 1735, Aged 68.

Elizabeth, Wife of Mr. Robert Green, Vicar of Chisleden, and Granddaughter of Mr. Henry Dudley. She died June ye 18, 1732, Ætatis 30.

H. S. E.

Basil Devenport, de Hinton Manoris Vicarius, Qui obiit 14 Augusti, Anno Dom. 1714, Ætatis 51.

Hatchment in the Body.

Quarterly, first and fourth gules, a bezant between three demi-lions argent; in chief a canton, or, charged with a cross engrailed, gules; second ermine, a bend lozenge, gules; third gules, on a cross engrailed, argent, an escutcheon, charged with a dexter hand holding a flag, gules, between eight mullets sable, over all an escutcheon of the first.

North Wall of Body.

BENEFACTION

Of Thomas Benet, of Salthrop, Esq. and his Lady, Mrs. Elizabeth Benet, to Broad Hinton. A Charity School in this place, endowed by the said Thomas Benet with £.xx per Annum, to be paid quarterly out of Quidhampton Farm. He also gave a house for the use of the School, for the Schoolmaster to reside in, and a garden for the master's use, and appointed two pounds yearly to be paid out of Quidhampton Farm, for repairing the School House and premises. Also the said Mrs. Elizabeth Benet, Anno Dom. 1741, gave certain fee farm Rents to the Amount of £.13 8*s.* 2*d.* per Annum, subject to Land Tax, to be employed for the binding and placing forth out of the Parish of Broadhinton poor Children Apprentices, who at the time of placing forth shall be of the Parish, and inhabiting within the Manor; and appointed the Vicar of Broadhinton, Wroughton, and Wotton Basset, and Liddiard Tregooze, and their Successors for ever, Trustees for the said Charity.

On an altar-tomb, in the north side of the Chancel, are the figures of a gentleman and lady, and on the side of the tomb, are eight more, four males and four females, children, perhaps, of the afore-mentioned. They are all kneeling, their hands broken off, except those of the Lady. There is no inscription, but most probably, from the Arms (a chevron between three boars' heads) some part of the Wroughton family was here interred.

In the Chancel also is a helmet, breast-plate, gauntlet, and sword, on the breast-plate is engraved the arms of Granville.

The Rev. J. Toogood present Vicar.

Lord Holland Lord of the Manor.

CHERHILL.

On a Monument in the North Wall of Body.

Mrs. Mary, Wife of John Pottow, quæ quinto decimo Julij, 1801, Obijt, Ætatis suæ 53.

Etiam Ossa et Cineres John Pottow, Qui sexto Novembris, 1810, Obijt, Ætatis suæ 73.

On Flat Stones in Body.

Here lyeth ye Body of Peter Flower, who died Dec. ye 13th, 1782, Aged 68 years.

Also Grace, his Wife, who died January 2nd, 1754, Aged 40 years.

In Memory of William Church. He died July ye 30th, 1730, Aged 81 years.

Also Mary, his Wife. She Died March ye 1st, 1733, Aged 76 years.

Here Lyeth the Body of Christopher Flower, and his two Sons, William and Edmund, dyed August 27, 1712.

William Flower, who died January ye 8th, 1747, Aged 68 years.

Also Edmund, the Son of William and Ann Flower, who died September the 25th, 1769, Aged 62 years.

Also Catharine, his Wife, who died Feb. 2nd, 1785, Aged 71 years.

On Flat Stones in S. Aisle.

Here Lyeth ye Body of William Pottow, Son of Hugh and Mary Pottow, who died November ye 27, 1774, Aged 41 years.

Also Mary, ye Wife of William Flower, who died April ye 22, 1776, Aged 33.

Here Lieth William Caswell, who Departed this Life August, A. D. 1706, Aged 58 years.

To the Memory of Uriah Pottow, who Departed this Life June the 20, 1813, Aged 73 years.

The Church consists of a Chancel, Nave, and South Aisle.

Register commenced 1754.

Thomas Greenwood Vicar, 1787.

Mr. Grubbe, of Potterne, Lord of the Manor.

CALSTONE.

On Monuments against North Wall of Chancel.

In the Vault underneath are Deposited the Remains of Henry Bailey, and of Jane his Wife.

She died April 3rd, 1765, Aged 62.

He died Sept. 13th, 1783, Aged 76.

And of Jane, their Daughter, who died in the year 1751, Aged 10 years.

Also John Baily, their Son, who died April 21st, 1801, Aged 69 years.

In the same Vault are deposited the Remains of Mary, Wife of Robert Baily, who died Oct. 14th, 1788, Aged 38 years.

Arms—Argent, on a fess engrailed azure, three fleur-de-lis, or, between three horses heads, erased, of the field.

S. J.

Spe beatæ Resurrectionis, Ossa et Cineres Mariæ Heath, Revdi Thomæ Heath, Hujus Ecclesiæ Rectoris, Conjugis Carissimæ, Cui diu et patienter gravi jecoris Morbo luctanti. Mors Requiem dedit, Kal. Martij 16, A. D. 1780, Ætat. 54. Pie vixit et Virtutis Exemplar Flebilis occidit Marito Filiabus Proximis, Pauperibus Omnibus enim placida, Ab omnibus diligebatur.

Ann, the Wife of Stephen Hale, and Daughter of the said Thomas and Mary Heath, died Dec. 16, 1815, Aged 59.

She lived an Example of Virtue, died lamented by her Husband, her Children, and the Poor; for, being kind to all, she was beloved by every one.

Etiam

Ossa et Cineres Revdi Thomæ Heath, A.M. Qui Triginta Annos Inter Ruris Otium, et Ministerii Officia, Placide et Contente cum Mariâ vixit: Qualis ipse fuit si velis scire, Lector, hoc scias, fuit homo, peccator, pœnitens, Discipulus, et Jesu Christi Servus, Cujus Meritis, non suis, confisus. Kal. Decembris 16, A. D. 1801, Ætatis 82, Obijt.

Also two of his Grand-children:
Anthony Hall, Ob. Feb. 14, 1788, Æt. 4,
Christian Hall, Ob. June 25, 1792, Æt. 15.

Here also are deposited the Remains of Elizabeth Heath, the second Wife and Relict of the above-named Rev. Thomas Heath. She was a sincere and exemplary Christian, and Died April 16th, 1818, Aged 82.

Flat Stones in the Body.

Here Lyeth the Body of Mrs. Margaret Newman, who Departed this Life Dec. 19, 1748, Aged 72.

Also ye Body of Mitchell Newman, Gent. who Departed this Life Oct. 9, 1755, Aged 70.

Also ye Body of Mrs. Elizabeth Ogden, who departed this Life Dec. 16, 1760, Aged 80.

Also the Body of Mrs. Margaret Newman, Wife of the above-named Mitchell Newman, who Departed this Life January the 5th, 1782, Aged 68 years.

Also the Body of Charlotte Jane Newman, Daughter of Mitchell and Susan Mary Newman, who departed this life Nov. the 8, 1808, Aged 20 years.

Also the Body of John Mitchell Newman, Son of Edward and Mary-Ann Newman, who died in his Infancy.

Here resteth the Body of John Michell, Esq. who was here interred on the 6 of March, 1637, Aged 29 years.

Here also Lyeth the Body of Mrs. Joanna Michell, his Widdow, who Departed this Life ye 8th of August, 1681, and in ye 72 year of her Age.

In this Vault are deposited the Remains of Mitchell Newman, Gent. Died 4 March, 1817, Aged 66 years.

Arms—A chevron between seven wolves heads erased, with as many crosslets fitchy issuing from their mouths, 4 and 3.

In the Chancel Windows are some small pieces of painted glass, or, gules, and az.

Register commenced 1760.

Rev. Thomas Heath Rector, 1760.

George Mawson Rector.

Charles Townsend present Rector.

The Marquis of Lansdowne Lord of the Manor.

YATESBURY.

On a Flat Stone in Chancel.

Here Lyeth the Body of Mr. Thomas Johnson, Rector of this Parish, who departed this Life in September, 1680.

Here also Lyeth the Body of Mrs. Elizabeth Johnson, his Wife, who Departed this Life April, 1715, Aged 75 years.

Against the East Wall of Nave.

Infra Conduntur Cineres Geo: Hungerford, L. L. D. de Studley, in hoc Agro, Arm. Ex Antiquâ Stirpe Hungerfordij, de Cadnam, licet ultimi, haud quaquam indigni, Vir summâ humanitate fide incorrupta insignis, legum Patriæ bene peritus, et fidelis dispensator, in elegantioribus Artibus multum versatus. Ob. 8 die Janij, An. 1764, Æt. 60.

Chara et fidelis Conj. Elizth, Filiæ John Pollen, Arm. Hoc Monum̃: Sac̃: Memrio Posuit.

Juxta deposuit Corpora Mariæ, Uxs primæ, quæ Ob. An. 1747°, Ætats 47.

Et Elizabethæ, unicæ filiæ ex eadem Uxre, quæ hac vita decessit An° 1748, Ætat. 11°.

Hic etiam prope cineres mariti sepulta est, Elizabetha, Geoii Hungerford, Armi: Uxor secunda et Vidua, Quæ juveniles et senescentes annos adeò pietate et benevolentiâ ornaverat, ut Obiit suis præcipuè flebilis, Die Octobris 17, A. D. 1816, Ætat. suæ 83.

Hoc functus est desiderii testimonio Nepos ætate minor, R. Pollen.

On a Monument against the South Wall of Body.

Near this Place Lyeth the Body of Sarah, the Wife of Thomas Vaisey, who Departed this life the 14 of March, 1795, Aged 51 years.

Also Near this Place Lyeth the Body of Thomas Vaisey, who Departed this Life the 24th of March, 1803, Aged 65 years.

Flat Stone in Body.

To the Memory of Daniel Ponteng, who dyed December the 28th, A. D. 1742, Aged 78 years.

In Memory of Thomas Ranger, who Departed this life April the 10th, 1794, Aged 79 years.

Also Rose, his Wife, who departed this life September the 8th, 1784, Aged 79 years.

Flat Stone in N. Aisle.

Here Lyeth the Body of John Pope, who Departed this Life March ye 12, 1709, Aged 72 years.

Here Lays my Loving Father Dear,
And all my Friends Here very Near;
Now they have Bid ye World Far Well,
I Hope in Heaven they Do Dwell,
And there For Ever to Remain,
I hope to Meet them there again.

The Church consists of Chancel, Nave, and North Aisle. The north side of the nave is supported by three pointed arches. In the south window of the Nave is a dove volant, or, in painted glass.

Register commenced 1706.

The Rev. William Money, Rector.

Mr. Tuckey, late Lord of the Manor.

COMPTON BASSET.

On a Monument in the North Wall of Chancel.

Sacred to the Memory of the Rev. James Pitcairn, LL. B. Late Prebendary of Exeter, and Twenty Years Rector of this Parish and West Kington, who died Jan. 28, 1780, Aged 64.

In Life respected, in Death Lamented.

Elizabeth, his Wife, died Oct. 4th, 1771, Aged 49 years.

Elizabeth, their Daughter, died Nov. 28, 1778, Aged 34.

Constant, another Daughter, died June 1st, 1766, Aged 3 years.

On Flat Stones in Chancel.

H. S. E.

Maria Hallifax, Thos. Hallifax, hujus Ecclesiæ Rectoris, Uxor Delectissima, quæ migravit e vitâ Feb. die 29, Anno { Ætatis 71, Salutis 1731.

Et jam Situs est in Uxorius tumulo ipse Thomas Hallifax, A. M. Qui, postquam Annos LXXXIII. Domino Jesu invigilàsset, in eodem placide Obdormivit XIII Calend. Maias, 1743.

Hic etiam sepultâ Sarah, Filiæ Thomæ et Mariæ Hallifax, quæ Obijt Die Janii vigesimo nono, Anno Domini 1752, Ætatis suæ quinquagesimo primo.

Here Lyeth the Body of Clement Burchall, Clothier, who Departed this Life ye 16 Day of July, 1709, Aged 83 years.

Here also Lyeth the Body of Elizabeth, the Wife of the above-said Clement Burchall, who departed this Life March the 21, A. D. 1707, Aged 81 years.

Flat Stones in Body.

H. S. E.

Robertus Maundrell, filius natu maximus Richardi Maundrell, Generosi, et Franciscæ Uxoris ejus, qui in Cœmeterio adjacente Requiescunt, et Priscillæ Uxor. ejus: Hæc Obijt 14 Novembris, Ille 24° Februarij, A. D. 1673.

Robertus Maundrell, filius unicus præfatorum Roberti et Priscillæ, et Margaritæ uxor. ejus, filia Henrici Hedges, de Wanborough, in hoc Comitatu, Generosi: Hæc Obijt 30 Novembris, A. D. 1676, Ille 11 Aprilis, A. D. 1705.

Robertus Maundrell, filius natu maximus præfatorum Roberti et Margaritæ, qui Obijt 15 Martij, A. D. 1731.

Robertus Maundrell, filius natu maximus Roberti modo dicti, et Hannæ uxoris ejus, qui Obijt 30 die Decembris, A. D. 1743, Ætatis . . .

Agnes Maundrell, Uxor Roberti Maundrell, Junis, quæ Obijt 7mo die Januarij, A. D. 17 . . Ætat. 42.

Hannah Maundrell, Uxor Roberti Maundrell, Senis, Mater Roberti Maundrell, Junris. Obijt 15to Die Decembris, A. D. 1741.

Here Lieth the Body of Thomas Sharp, Sen. Gent. who Departed this Life the 20 Day of December, Anno Domini 1659.

Also Richard Sharp departed ye 29 of May, 1696, Aged 7 years.

Also John Sharp departed ye 4th of June, 1696, Aged 2 years and 11 weeks:
Both Sons of Thomas and Priscilla Sharp.

Also Jane, ye Daughter of Thomas and Priscilla Sharp, Departed ye 7th of May, 1700.

Thomas Sharp, Son of ye above Thomas Sharp, Sen. Gent. Departed this Life February ye 19, 1713, Aged 61 years.

Also Priscilla Savage, Wife of Isaac Savage, Gent. and Daughter of Thomas and Priscilla Sharp, who Departed March ye 28, 1716, Aged 29 years.

Also Sharpe Savage, Son of Isaac and Priscilla Savage, who Departed April ye 4th, 1716, Aged 4 years.

Also Thomas Sharp, junr. Gent. Son of Thomas and Priscilla Sharp, who departed April ye 24, 1716, Aged 30 years.

Also Margaret, Wife of Michael Smith, Daughter of Thomas Sharp, who died Dec. 8th, 1727, Aged 36.

Also Priscilla Sharp, Wife of Thomas Sharp, Sen. who died Dec. 25, 1753, Aged 89.

Also Ann Sharp, Daughter of Thomas Sharp, who died May 9th, 1771, Aged 73.

Here Lyeth the Body of John Smith, Son of Michael and Margaret Smith, wbo died August ye 25, 1733, Aged 8 years.

Michael Smith died July 16th, 1773, Aged 80 years.

Brass Plate.

Underneath this Stone Lieth the Body of John Shacklocke, whoe Departed this Life the 19 of March, in the Year 1683.

Brass Plate.

Here Lyeth the Body of Susanna, Wife of William Piercy, who Departed this Life June 2, 1805, Aged 42 years.

On Flat Stone in N. Aisle.

Here Lyeth the Body of John Maundrell, Gent. who Departed this Life ye 23 Day of July, 1723, Aged 19 years.

Michael Long, Gent. died Dec. ye 18, 1749, Aged 75.

[The Chancel being repaired in 1812, the two following inscriptions were from thence removed, but inserted in the Reg.]

Here Lyeth ye Body of William Harding, who Deceased the 26 of Dec. 1630.

Here Lyeth the Body of Thomas Hyde, Deceased the 22 of August, 1634.

The Church consists of a Chancel, Nave, North and South Aisles: the Nave is supported by three pointed arches on each side. The ancient stone screen, ornamented by handsome foliage, is in good preservation. Most of the pews are of carved oak, the pulpit is of stone. In the Chancel the iron frame of the hour-glass, and the stone bason formerly standing in the north wall, are still preserved.

Annotatio Nomina Rectorum hujus Parochiæ, cum Ordine Successionis, ab Annos 1560, quotenus, ex Registris Parochialis, qui liceat.

1564, Richardus Read, Obijt.
1604, Laurentius Hyde, —
1618, Laurentius Wright,
1640, Gulielmus Eyre,
1649, Jacobus Nesbett, Obijt, ad finis
amp. 1652, Quinam, et ulli sequenti intervalis Rectores fuerunt incertum.
1668, Gulielmus White,
1670, Johannes Wilson,
1688, David Jenner,
1693, Michael Geddes,
1711, Thomas Hallifax,
1743, Carolus Moss,
1759, Jacobus Pitcairn,
1780, Nathaniel Hume, [*inductionem.*
1782, Jacobus Gibson, *obijt uno mense post*‸
Rev. George Hayter present Rector.

Register commenced 1563.

HEDDINGTON.

On a Monument against the south wall of Chancel.

Illic Requiescit, spe certissima Resurrectionis, Henricus Rogers, A. M. hujus Ecclesiæ Rectoris, Qui Obijt 16 Martij, An° Dom. 1669, Ætatis suæ 63.

Illic Requiescit, spe certissima Resurrectionis, Sarah Rogers, uxor Henrici Rogers prædicti, Quæ Obiit 19 Oct. Anno Dom. 1707, Ætatis suæ 88.

On Flat Stone in Chancel.

The Rev. Francis Rogers, Late Rector of this Parish, Died May ye 3, 1800, Aged 78 years.

In north transept.

1610. H. T.

If Blessed and for ever Happy Thou
wilt bee, Then See thou Dost thy Death
in Life with Care fore see.

James Rogers, present Rector.

No Lord of the Manor.

220

CALNE.

On a small Tablet S. Wall of Chancel.

Juxta conduntur Reliquiæ Gulielmi Powell Bendry, Armigeri, Civis Londinensis, nec non e cœtu Magistratuum Hujusce Comitatu, xii Nov. 1816, Ætatis suæ Anno Sexagesimo Secundo.

Arms—Two half spears, in saltier.

On a flat brass plate in Chancel.

Here Lyeth buried the Body of Roger Chevers, Clother, who had 2 Wives, Joane and Elizabeth: by Joane, his first Wife, he had Issue 2 Daughters, Elizabeth and Gillian; & by Elizabeth, his Second Wife, he had Issue 2 Sons & 5 Daughters, Henry, Jeremye, Joane, Jane, Ane, Marye, and Margery, and deceased the 3 Day of May, 1602, Ætatis suæ 56.

Here Lyeth the Body of Germanicus Shepherd, Jun. Gent. who departed this Life August ye 4th, 1747, Aged 22 years.

Also Frances, his Sister, who died in her Infancy.

Here Lyeth the Body of Mrs. Elizabeth Chiver, Wife of Henry Chiver, Gent. She Deceased the 7th of December, Anno Dni. 1630, and left behind her living 11 Children, 6 Sonnes & 5 Daughters, Ætatis suæ 39.

Arms—A chevron, engrailed, charged with a crescent.

On a Monument in east end of S. Aisle.

Beatam præstolans Resurrectionem, placide infra obdormiscit Henricus de Aranda, Benj. de Aranda, hujus Ecclesiæ Vicarii, et Eliz. ejus Uxoris, Filius Unicus Desideratissimus, Moribus candidis egregiæ indolis, et Spei optimæ Juvenis. Natus fuit Octobris 21, 1701, Denatus vero, ehu! Octob. 26 die 1716, nunquam non summo mœrore, deflendus nisi quoniam, hoc Deus voluit, cum Filio quoq. Mater, ipsa Elizabetha de Aranda, quæ Obiit 12 Kalend. Octob. 1730.

Arms—Azure, a castle, argent, within a border, or, charged with six crosses, gules; impaling, argent, a chevron, sable, between three garbs of the same.

On Monuments in the North Aisle.

Hic Situs est Johannes Ernle, Eques Auratus,
Scacrij Cancellarius, et Carolo et Jacobo Secundo
A Secretoribus consiliis,
Familiæ ac Reipublicæ Decus et Tutamen,
Ecclesiæ vere Anglicanæ filius obedientissimus,
Qui ob morum suavitatem ac candorem,
Omnibus charus, præsertim suis,
Tandem bonorum operum ac Dierum plenus,
Occubuit, Anno { Ætatis 79, Domini 1697.

Hic Etiam juxta situs est Johannis Ernle, Armiger,
Supradicti Johannes, Equitis Aurati, Pater,
Ac in utriusq. memoriam Pietatis et amoris ergo
Hoc Monumentum extruxit
Johannes Kyrle Ernle, de Whetham,
In Com. Wilts. Armiger.
Et jam hic situs est,
Avi ac Proavi Tumulo ipse Johannes Kyrle Ernle,
Armigeri,
Anno Dom. 1725, Ætatis 43.
Multis flebilis occidit
nullis flebilior quam Pauberibus
Quorum, vivens ac moriens, erat lavemen,
Et licet, non Dierum,
Bonorum operum plenus.
Thomas Johannes Ernle Hay, filius,
Thomæ, Vicecomitis de Dupplin, e Constantiâ,
Uxor. ejus Johannis Kyrle Ernle, de
Whetham, Armigeri, Filiâ unicâ, et Herede,
Natus est 12 Die Mensis Augusti, A. D. 1742,
Obijt 14 Die Mensis Octobr. A. D. 1743.

Arms—Argent, on a bend, sable, three eagles displayed, or.

H. I. S. Q.

Eleonora Stokes, uxor dilectissima Richardi Stokes,
de hoc Oppido, Generosi, Thomæ Lambert, de Boyton,
in hoc Agro Wiltoniensi, Armig.
Filia natû maxima,
Muster eximiâ virtute, moribus egregiis,
pietatem singulari,
Ingenioq. non mediocri, Mirâ constantiâ
æquanimitate, prudentia,
Nec non amicitia intergerrima
promptissimo Egenis Miserisq. Auxilio,
Rerum provida, ab avarina tamen alicissima
Deniq. corporis animiq. duobus nulli secunda,
Quam
Postquam triginta atq. octo compleverat Annos
A suis Vicinisq. omnibus quibus fuit charissima,
Eripuit Variolarum Furor in domitus
xxi Id. Octobris Anno Salutis humanæ 1705.
Cui Memoriæ gratissimæ ergo
hanc Tabulam
Mœrens Conjux
Posuit atque esse sui volut
Monumentum et Pignem Amoris.

Arms—Sable, a lion rampant argent; impaling, argent, a bend, sable, charged with three annulets, or, between two lions rampant, sable.

Richardus Stokes, Generosus, Edwardi Stokes, de Stanhawes Court, in Agro Glocester, Armigeri, Filius natu maximus, Animam Deo reddidit Jan. die 27, Ætatis suæ Anno 60, Salutis nostræ 1724.

Corpus vero quam proxime ad Uxorem Dilectissimam Eleonoram collocari ex Testamento curavit.

Arms—Sable, a lion rampant, argent.

Sacred to the Memory of Rebecca, the Wife of John Brooke, of this Parish, Gent. Ob. July, 1732, Aged 29 years.

Also the said John Brooke. Ob. Sept. 1741, Aged 42 years.

Also of Thomas Brooke, Son of the said John. Ob. 1742.

Also of John Brooke, his Eldest Son. Ob. 1753.

Also of Ann Brooke, who was Ann Earle, and Second Wife of the aforeasid John Brooke. Ob. 1754.

Also of Henry Brooke, of the Inner Temple, London, Esq. another Son of the said John and Ann. Ob. 1794.

Also of Walter Brooke, of Heddington, in this County, Esq. Ob. 25 April, 1808, Aged 67 years.

On Flat Stones in N. Aisle.

Here Lyeth the Body of Henry Chivers, Gent. who Died Dec. 28th, A. D. 1695.

Also Ann, Daughter of Henry Chevers, Jun. who died Feb. ye 11, 1718, Aged 19 weeks.

Also the said Henry Chiver, Jun. Gent. who died Jan. ye 13, 1739, Aged 45 years.

Here Lyeth the Body of Luce, the Daughter of Benedict and Luce Browne, who died Dec. ye 7, 1719.

Also Katharine, Daughter of the above, who died August ye 20, 1731.

Also Frances, ye Wife of Benedict Browne, Esq. who died Nov. ye 6, 1735.

Also Benedict Browne, Esq. who died Nov. ye 18, 1737, Aged 84 years.

Also Frances, Daughter of Benedict and Frances Browne, who Died August ye 28, 1745.

Also Benedict, Son of Benedict & Pleadwell Browne, who Died Jan. 20, 1746.

Also Frances, daughter of Benedict and Pledwell Browne, who died Feb. 9, 1746.

Also Wm. Browne, Esq. who died March ye 26, 1749.

Also Wm. Son of Benedict and Pledwell Browne, who died April 6, 1752.

Also Pledwell, Wife of Benedict Browne, Esq. who died June 27, 1752.

Also Benedict Brown, Esq. who died Feb. 19, 1766, Aged 69 years.

Also Benedict Browne Angell, Esq. died May ye 8, 1786, Aged 38 years.

Hic infra sepulti sunt Richardus Browne, Arm. Aug. 9, 1598.

Katharine, ejus Uxor, postea U . . . Tho. Moffet, M. D. filia Willi. Sadler, Arm. de Salthrope, Apl. 3, 1626.

Arms.—On a bend cottized, three lions pass. in chief a martlet.

M. S.

Benj : Mayo, Coll. Regin : Oxon. Commensalis A. B. postra de hac Oppido Pharmacopolæ. Ob. xv Kald. Nov. A. S. 1750, Ætatis 32.

Here Lyeth the Body of Elizabeth, the Daughter of Wm. and Elizabeth Hayward, Apoth. who departed this Life Oct. 16, 1703, Aged 30.

Mrs. Hayward : 1741, Æt. XC.

In ye hopes of a Joyful Resurrection, Here Lyeth ye Body of Rebecca, ye Wife of John Brooke, Jun. Gent. Daughter of Henry Groome, of Lea, Gent. who died July ye 21, A. D. 1732, Aged 29 years.

Also John Brook, Gent. who died Sept. ye 4, A. D. 1741, Aged 42 years.

Here Lyeth the Body of Susannah, Wife of John Townsend, Gent. who died May ye 28, 1752, Aged 53 years.

Also John Townsend, Gent. who died Sept. ye 30, 1757, Aged 63 years.

Here Lyeth the Body of Dorothy, ye Wife of John Norman, who died Nov. ye 19, 1706, Aged 22 years.

Here Lyeth ye Body of John Smith, who Departed this Life July ye 1st, 1771, Aged 89 years.

Also his Mother, two Wives, and three Children.

Here Lyeth the Body of John, Son of John and Frances Brooke, who died August the 22, 1719, Aged 9 years.

Also Frances, the Wife of John Brooke, who died Jan. the 18, 1734, Aged 60 years.

Also John Brooke, Husband of Frances Brooke, who died Feb. the 7, 1737, Aged 63 years.

Also Margaret, Daughter of John and Frances Brooke, who died March 16, 1766, Aged 64 years.

Also Frances, Daughter of John and Frances Brooke, who died August 15, 1777, Aged 68 years.

Also Priscilla, Daughter of John and Frances Brooke, who died Dec. ye 4, 1783, Aged 71 years.

Thomas Mathews died May 15, 1768, Aged 67 years.

Also Mary, Daughter of Thomas and Susanna Mathews, died Feb. ye 21, 1790, Aged 38 years.

Also John Flower died Sept. 8, 1804, Aged 73 years.

Susunna, his Wife died Jan. 19, 1812, Aged 81 years.

Here Lieth the Body of Joseph Simpkins, who died March ye 31, 1721.

Also Ann, his Wife, died Dec. ye 22, A. D. 1720.

John Simpkins, their Son, died August ye 16, 1723, Aged 22 years.

Here also Lyeth the Body of Joseph, the Son of Joseph and Ann Simpkins, who departed this Life March the 28, 1729, Aged 30 years.

Also ye Body of Ann, the Daughter of Joseph and Ann Simpkins, who died Dec. ye 5, 1747.

Under this Stone Lyeth the Body of John Baldwin, who died Oct. ye 24, 1745, Aged 68 years.

Also Mary, his Wife, died July 3, 1755, Aged 69 years.

Also Robert, their Son, who died June ye 3, 1791, Aged 72 years.

Also Grace, his Wife, died Oct. ye 16, 1765, Aged 43.

Here Lyeth the Body of Ann, Wife of Henry Newman, who died May ye 8, 1745, Aged 72 years.

Also Henry Newman, who died July ye 7, 1752, Aged 82 years.

Here Lieth the Body of Rebecca, Daughter of John and Mary Cale, who died June the 23, 1754, Aged 39 years.

Also John, their Son, who died June the 24, 1760, Aged 42 years.

Also Elizabeth, ye Daughter, who died Jan. the 14, 1763, Aged 54 years.

Flat Stones in the Body.

Here Lyeth the Body of Elizabeth, Wife of James Pound, who died July ye 10, 1804, Aged 59 years.

Also Frances, their Daughter, died July ye 8, 1796, Aged 21 years.

Also James Pound, who Departed this Life August 2, 1809, Aged 65 years.

Also Jane, his Second Wife, died June 28, 1814, Aged 65 years.

Here Lyeth ye Body of Elizabeth, Wife of James Pound, who died June ye 28, 1732, Aged 31 years.

Also ye Body of James Pound, who died Oct. ye 24, 1756, Aged 54 years.

Also Frances, his Daughter, who died March the 5, 1766, Aged 25 years.

Also Frances, ye Wife of James Pound, who died April ye 29, 1768, Aged 65 years.

Here Lyeth ye Body of Jonathan, Son of Jonathan Nicholas, who Departed this Life Nov. 5, 1711, Aged 16 years.

Here Lyeth ye Body of Mary, Daughter of Jonathan and Jane Nicholas, who Departed this Life Sept. 24, 1711, Aged 14 years.

Jane, Wife of Jonathan Nicholas, died May ye 28, 1725, Aged 58 years.

Here Lyeth the Body of Robert Baily, Son of John and Jane Baily, who departed this Life Aug. 28, A. D. 1720, Aged 54 years.

Here Lyeth ye Body of Betty, Daughter of Stephen and Martha Mead, who Departed this Life July ye 10, 1735, Aged 19.

Also ye Body of Martha, Wife of Stephen Mead, who Departed this Life Feb. ye 13, 1736, Aged 51.

Also Daniel Hooper died Nov. 13, 1799, Aged 13 years.

Here Lyeth the Body of Edward Carter, who departed this life March the 7, 1766, Aged 77 years.

Here Lieth the Body of William Bowman, who died May 17, 1757, Aged 27 years.

Also the Body of Peggey Bowman, who died March 21, 1758, Aged 2 years and 5 months.

Beneath Lie interred Frances, Wife of James Lowe, who died Nov. 12, 1806, Aged 79 years.

Also their 2 Children, who died Infants.

Underneath lie deposited the Remains of Edne, Jane, Edward, Thos. Wm. and Joseph Smith.

Also Mary Smith, who departed this Life 8 of Nov. 1803, Aged 76 years.

Here Lyeth the Body of Thomas Oriel, who died Feb. ye 27, 17.. Aged 65 years.

Also Ann, Wife of Thomas Oriel, who died Sept. ye 29, 1753, Aged 73 years.

Also William Oriel, who Departed April the 1st, 17.. Aged 60 years.

Also Sarah, the Wife of William Oriel, who died Dec. the 26, ... Aged 47 years.

Also William Townsend Oriel, Son of William and Katharine, who died July the 3, 178. Aged 16 years.

Also William Oriel, Son of William and Sarah Oriel, who died April the 21, 1785, Aged 36 years.

Here Lyeth the Body of Sarah Franklin, who Departed this Life Feb. 1st, 1748, Aged 47 years.

Also the Body of Mr. Jno Franklin, who Departed this Life June 10, 1752, Aged 48 years.

Subtus jacet Depositum Willi. Weeks, unica pietas Filij immatura . . . . . . præcepti, circiter annum nono decimo . . . . . Dni. 1700. Cum filio quoque simul uno quasi lecto placidi obdormivit, Gul. et Marie Weeks,

Illa } Ob. Mar. 19, A. D. 1710,
Ille } Ob. Nov. 10, A. D. 1719.

Here Lyeth the Body of George Forman, Gent. and Eleanor, his Wife.

Also Eleanor, their Daughter, who Departed this life Dec. 18, 1762.

Underneath this Stone Lieth the Body of Joseph Button, who died August 17, 1784, Aged 58 years.

Also Hannah, his Wife, died Feb. 10th, 1790, Aged 63 years.

Also Henry, their Son, died Feb. 6, 1773, Aged 3 years and 6 months.

Also Joseph and Hannah, died in their Infancy.

Here lies the Body of Sarah, Daughter of Martha and Rachel Foreman, who died Feb. 14, 1736, Aged 17 years.

Also Katharine, their Daughter, died August 10th, 1767, Aged 34 years.

Also Seven of their Children died in their Infancy.

Also Rachel Forman, who died Oct. 30th, 1783, Aged 89 years.

George Forman died Dec. 25, 1808, Aged 74 years.

Here lieth the Body of Anne, the Wife of Henry Merewether, who died 4th Dec. 1768, Aged 29 years.

Elizabeth, their Daughter, died 25th February, 1769, Aged about 4 Months.

Mary, Daughter of ye said Henry Merewether, by his Wife Mary, died 8 Jan. 1777, Aged 6 months.

Henry Merewether died 4 Sept. 1803, Aged 67 years.

Henry Alworth Merewether, Son of John and Ann Merewether, died 20 Nov. 1807, Aged 9 years.

Here Lyeth the Body of John Sadler, who died August 26, 1720, Aged 73 years.

Underneath this Stone is Interred the Remains of John Burchall, who died Sept. 4th, 1704.

Also Ann Burchall, who died March 13, 1703.

Also Clements Burchell, who died July 2nd, 1705, the above Sons and Daughter of John and Elizabeth Burchell.

Also John Bull, Esq. and Elizabeth, his first Wife.

Also Daniel Bull, Esq. their Son, who died March 29, 1791.

Also Samuel Fripp, Esq. who died Feb. 1794.

On a Monument in west end of S. Aisle.

Near this place are deposited the Remains of Daniel Bull, Esq. who died March 29, 1791, Aged 64.

Also Elizabeth Bull, who died June 19, 1729, Aged 31 years.

Also of John Bull, Esq. who died Dec. 26, 1768, Aged 75 years.

Also of Samuel Fripp, Esq. who died Feb. 4, 1794, Aged 70 years.

In Memory of Mary, the Wife of Robert Martin, who died May the 21, 1745.

Also of Mary Gill, Grandaughter of Robert and Mary Martin, who Died Feb. 25, 1745.

Also of Robert Martin, Musician, who died August the 25, 1749, in the 84 year of his Age.

Near this place are Deposited the remains of Slater Heale, Son of Ralph and Mary Heale, who, after a useful and well spent Life, in humble Reliance on the Merits of his Saviour, Calmly resigned his Spirit into the hands of him who gave it, the 15 of Nov. 1813, Aged 57.

Edmund, third Son of Slater Heale, died the 17 of June 1819, Aged 23.

Near this Monument lyeth interred the Remains of Ralph, Son of Ralph and Mary Heale, jun. who Died May 19, 1770, Aged 16 years.

Also Mary, Wife of Ralph Heale, Sen. who died May the 27, 1777, Aged 81 years.

Also Ralph Heale, Sen. who died Nov. 4, 1781, Aged 89 years.

Also Mary, Wife of Ralph Heale, Jun. who died Jan. ye 14, 1794, Aged 66 years.

Also Ralph Heale, Jun. Ob. 4th Dec. 1801, Aged 70 years.

Also of Ann Heale. Ob. 29 of May, 1805, Aged 84 years.

Near this Place Lyeth Mary, the Wife of James Cook, (with four of her Children) who Departed this Life Feb. the 17, A. D. 1705, Aged 48 years.

John died August 20, 1688, Martha died Oct. the 22, 1695, and Samuel died Feb. 2nd, 1698.

Also the Body of the said James Cook, who died Dec. ye 12, 1735, Aged 70 years.

Also George, Son of James and Mary Cook, who Died Nov. ye 14, 1737, Aged 44 years.

On Flat Stones in South Aisle.

Here lieth the Body of Jane, Wife of John Bishop, Gent. who Departed this life June ye 11, 1792, Aged 75 years.

Also John Bishop, Gent. who died May ye 17, 1800, Aged 80 years.

John Gillespy, From the City of Cumberland, died Feb. the 10, 1751, Aged 58 years.

Also John, Son of John and Mary Gillespy, who died July ye 25, 1781, Aged 61 years.

Here Lyeth the Body of Sarah, Wife of Samuel Stephens, who died Jan. 9th, 1704, and leaving 10 Children, 4 Sons and 6 Daughters, Aged 44 years.

Here Lyeth the Body of Ann, Wife of Robert Essington, Gent. who died Oct. ye 13, 1734, Aged 43 years.

Also John, Second Son of Robert Essington, who died June 15, 1732, Aged 8 years.

And Robert, fourth Son, who died Sept. 11, 1732, Aged 4 years.

Also here Lyeth the Body of Robert Essington, Gent. who departed this life Oct. 4, 1757, Aged 55 years.

William Essington, Gent. died Dec. 6, 1807, Aged 80 years.

Here Lyeth the Body of Elizabeth, ye Daughter of Stephen and Christian Hall, who died Nov. 14, 1755, Aged 7 years.

Also Christian, ye Daughter of Stephen and Christian Hall, who died July ye 3, 1768, Aged 2 years and 5 months.

Also Mathew, their Son, died July ye 8, 1782, Aged 21 years.

John Bishop died Feb. 8, 1816, Aged 55 years.

Also John Forman Bishop, Son of John and Bridget Bishop, died Jan. 19, 1806, Aged 2 years and 10 weeks.

And Jane, their Daughter, Died May 6, 1806, infant.

Here Lyeth the Body of Judith Bishop, who died Jan. ye 1st. A. D. 1708, Aged 55 years.

Also ye Body of John Bishop, the Elder, was buried July ye 31, Anno Dom. 1728, Aged 78 years.

Also Ruth, his Wife, was buried Feb. ye 14, Anno Dom. 1728, Aged 81 years.

Grace, Daughter of John Bishop, jun. was buried Feb. ye 22, Anno Dom. 1729, Aged 7 years.

Christian Kendall, died August 26, 1787, Aged 34 years.

Penelope, Wife of John Hellister, died Jan. 30, 1809, Aged 47.

Here Lyeth ye Body of Priscilla, ye Wife of John Haskins, who Departed this Life March ye 28, 1723, Aged 72.

Also the Body of Jane, Daughter of John and Priscilla Moore, who Departed this Life July ye 19, 1727, Aged 19.

Near this Place Lyeth ye Body of Richard Seager, who died August ye 13, A. D. 1714, Aged 74 years.

And also Abigail, Wife of Richard Seager. She Died August 24, 1718, Aged 78.

Bridget Hale died August ye 27, A. D. 1717, Aged 10 years.

Here Lyeth ye Body of John Hort, who died Jan. ye 21, A. D. 1718, Aged 40 years.

And also ye Body of John, Son of John Hort, who died October ye 23, 1717.

On a Flat Stone in S. Porch.

Here Lyeth the Body of Ann, Wife of George Button, who Departed this Life Jan. 2, 1765, in the 62 year of her Age.

George Button died Sept. 16, 1776, Aged 83 years.

Frances Greenland, died Feb. 14, 1806, Aged 83 years.

Arms—Ermine, a fess, gules.

Against the Gallery.

BENEFACTIONS *for the Relief of the Poor of this Parish.*

Anno Domini 1624, Dr. William Swaddon, Arch Deacon of Worcester, gave £. 4 per annum.

Anno Dom. 1626, Henry Smith, Esq. of London, gave £. 10 per annum.

A. D. 1635, Three Closes, called Bayfield, and Churchell, Lying at Baidon, in this County, were given by a Person unknown.

Anno Domini 1695, Sir John Ernly, Knight, gave

five houses, situate in this Town, for the relief and Sustenance of four Widows.

For the Honour of God, and in Gratitude to these worthy Benefactors, these Tables were Erected, Anno Domini 1731.

Ralph Hale, Thomas Barrett, Churchwardens.

BENEFACTORS

For the Education of Children.

Anno Domini .... Mr. Walker Finamore gave 40*s.* per Annum.

Anno Domini 1646, Mr. Robt. Foreman gave a Close, called Clotly, in ye Tything of Studly.

A° D. 1664, Mr. William Woodroffe gave 50*s.* per Annum.

A. D. 1660, John Bentley, of Richmond, in ye County of Surry, Esq. Founded the Free School.

Against the Gallery, on the north side of the Nave.

The Hungerford Charity, for the Sick, Wounded, or Maimed, of this Parish, having, from non-payment for 20 years, accumulated to £.400, the same was placed in the 4 per cent. A. D. 1793, and the Interest, with the original Charity, is now annually distributed agreeable to the gift of the Donor.

Rev. T. Greenwood,
Samuel Viveash,
Daniel Baily, } *Trustees.*
Richard Bleaden,
Benjamin Bowman,

BENEFACTOR.

Walter Hungerford, Esq. died in the Year 1745, of his Free Bounty gave twenty Pouuds per Annum for ever to the Poor Sick and Maimed of the Parish of Calne.

Wm. Oriel,
Robt. Baily, } *Ch. Wardens.*

BENEFACTOR.

Thomas Weeks, Gent. died in the year 1735, bequeathed a Ground in Broughton Gifford, in this County, value three Pounds per Annum, to Poor Widows of the Parish of Calne.

Hatchments.

Or, three bulls' heads caboshed, sable.

Quarterly, first and fourth sable, three spear heads imbrued proper; second or, a cross, azure; third, barry of six, gules and ermine, over an escutcheon of pretence, azure, a lion rampant, or, between eight crosslets of the last a chief of the same.

Knight of the Garter, *Crest*—Sagittarius.

Quarterly, first and fourth ermine, on a bend, azure, a or; second and third argent, a saltire, gules, a crescent for difference of the last, a chief ermine; impaling, sable, a saltire, argent, on a chief, azure, three fleur-de-lis, or.

Sable, a fess between three talbots passant, with as many arrows in their mouths, all argent: impaling argent, a fess between three lions rampant within a border, gules, charged with eight bezants.

Sable, on a bend, cottised, three lions passant, argent: impaling, or, a fess, lozengy, azure, over all a bend, gules.

Quarterly, first and fourth argent, on a bend, sable, three eagles displayed or; second and third, the arms of France: impaling, argent, on a bend, sable, three dolphins embowed argent.

Quarterly, first or, a fess lozenge, azure, over all a bend, gules; second, sable, a bend engrailed between six cinquefoils, or; third ermine, on a bend sable, three cinquefoils, argent; fourth argent, a crosslet fitchy between nine mullets, azure: impaling gules, on a chevron, argent, three tigers' heads caboshed or, between three cinquefoils, argent.

The Church consists of a Chancel, Nave, North and South Aisles. On the north and south side of the Nave are four semi and two pointed arches, supported by round massy columns, about six feet to the capital. The third and fourth arches from the west end are hid by the Organ Gallery.

Register commenced 1527.

The Rev. Dr. Bowman the late Vicar, the Rev. Thos. Greenwood the present one.

The Marquis of Lansdown Lord of the Manor.

Near Calne is '*The Retreat,*' the Seat of Henry Parry, Esq.

BLACKLAND.

On a Wood Frame against S. Wall of Chancel.

Near this Place is interred the Body of Robert Smith, of Blackland, Gent. who died the 20 of Nov. 1691, Ætatis 42.

Also to the pious Memory of Margaret Smith, his valuable Wife. Obijt August ye 31, 1725, Ætatis suæ 68.

Near this Place is Interred the Body of Robert Smith, Junior, who died the 24 of March, 1691, Æt. 9.

Arms—Azure, an escutcheon of pretence bt. six li. ramp. or.

In the S. Wall of Chancel is a piscina.

The Rev. Dr. Money Rector.

Near the Church is *Blackland House,* the Seat of John Merewether, Esq.

226

BISHOP CANNINGS.

On Monuments against North Wall of Chancel.

Near this Place Lyeth the Body of the Rev. John Shergold, A. M. who died 24 Dec. 1777, Aged 81.

Near this Place lie interred the Mortal Remains of Elizabeth Ruddle Gibbs, daughter of James and Mary Gibbs, formerly of Etchillampton, in this County, who died at Bristol, January 27th, 1816, Aged 26 years, to whose Memory this Monument is Erected by her disconsolate Mother and Affectionate Brother, as a token of their sincere and unfeigned regard.

South Wall.

Near this Place Lyes the Remains of Sarah, the Wife of John Gamble, of ye Devizes, who Dyed August ye 13th, Anno Dom̃ 1735.

In love she liv'd,
In pace She dy'd,
Her life desir'd,
But God deny'd.

On Flat Stones in Chancel.

Here Lyeth the Body of Mrs. Martha Waterman, Daughter of the Rev. Jonathan Waterman, who died July ye 1st, 1775.

Also the Body of Mrs. Ann Waterman, Daughter of the Rev. Jonathan Waterman, who died June ye 17, 1781.

Here Lyeth the Body of Mrs. Elizabeth Waterman, Dau_hter of Mr. Jonathan Waterman, Vicar of this Parish, who died August 10, 1743, Aged 19 years.

Also the Body of Mrs. Mary Waterman, Wife of the Rev. Mr. Jonathan Waterman, who died June the 7th, 1759, Aged 63 years.

Also the Body of the Rev. Mr. Jonathan Waterman, Vicar of this Parish, who died Dec. 28, 1768, Aged 80 years.

Thomas Weston, Gent. of Coate, Jun. died the 14th Day of July, 1742, Aged 53 years.

Also, Mrs. Jane Weston, his Wife, Died the 8th Day of Nov. 1757, Aged 55 years.

Here Lyeth ye Body of Thomas Weston, Sen. Gent. who Departed this Life Sept. ye 28th, A. D. 1727, Aged 68 years.

Here Lyeth ye Body of Elizabeth, ye Wife of Thomas Weston, Gent. who Departed this Life June ye 13, A. D. 1719, Aged 54 years.

And also three of their Children.

Elizabeth R. Gibbs, died 27 January, 1816, Aged 26 years.

To the Memory of George Ruddle, who Departed this life Sept. 12th, 1794, Aged 74 years.

Ask of the Good alone the Sigh sincere,
And on the new laid Sod the pitying Tear;
Of them who, piously addressing Heaven,
Hope, with their own, his Trespasses forgiven.

Here Lyeth the Body of Mary, Wife of George Ruddle, who died March 26, 1789, Aged 79 years.

Farewell, my Children dear! but know, you must,
After this life return to dust,
Faith to its Earth, as you see many,
Death and the Grave refuse not any.

Underneath this Stone are deposited the Remains of George Ruddle, Jun. who Departed this Life the 3d Day of January, 1803, Aged 53 years.

Here Lyeth ye Body of Thomas Sloper, of this Parish, Gent. who Departed this Life ye 19th of May, 1714, Aged 71 years.

Near this Stone lyeth the Body of Martha, the Wife of Mr. Thomas Sloper, Jun. She departed this Life Nov. 14, 1783, Aged 63 years.

Here Lyeth the Body of Mrs. Priscilla Sloper, who was Buried April 6th, 1734, Aged 62.

Also Mr. William Sloper, who was Buried Nov. 30th, 1763, Aged 87.

And also William Sloper, Jun. who was Buried June 19th, 1767, Aged 19.

On a Flat Stone in Nave.

Here Lyeth the Body of Robert Nash, who departed this Life the 10 Day of December, 1760, Aged 83 years.

Also Here Lyeth ye Body of Michael Nash, Son of the afore said. He died January ye 2nd, 1749, Aged 79 years.

On Monuments in a small Chapel adjoining the S. Transept.

Here Lieth the Body of Edward Ernle, of Ichilhampton, Esq. Eldest Sonne of Michael Ernle, of

Bourton, Esq. by Susan, his Wife, Eldest Daughter and Coheire of Sir Walter Hungerford, of Farley Castle, in ye County of Somerset, who Departed this Mortal Life the Last Day of November, in the yeare of or Lord God 1656.

Here Lyeth ye Body of Edward Ernle, Esq. Grandchild of ye Above said Edward Ernle, Esq. and Eldest Sonne and Heire of Sr Walter Ernle, of Ichilhampton, Baronet, by Dame Martha, his Wife, Eldest Daughter and Coheir of Edward Tooker, of the Citty of new Sarum, Esq. By Martha, his Wife, one of ye Daughters of Sr John Cooper, of ye County of Dorset, Baronet, who departed this Mortal Life the Twentye first day of June, in the yeare of or Lord God 1675.

Arms—Quarterly, first and fourth argent, on a bend sable three eagles displayed, or; second and third barry of five, argent and sable, in chief three plates: over all an escutcheon, charged with a sinister hand, gules.

John Ernele, of Bourton, Esquire Liethe Buried Underneathe this Monument, who Departed this Mortall life the firste daye of Februarie, in the Yeare of our lorde God A Thousand five Hundred threscore and Aleven.

Arms—Quarterly, first and fourth, on a bend three eagles displayed; second and third, a cross moline.

On a Flat Stone.

Here Lyeth the Body of Martha Ernle, Daughter of Walter Ernle, Esq. who Died ye 20th Day of Jany A. D. 1716, Aged 25 years.

The Church consists of Chancel, Nave, North and South Aisles, and North and South Transepts. The Nave is supported on each side by four pointed arches. In the south wall of the Chancel is a piscina.

ROWDE.

On a Monument in the North Wall of Chancel.

Sacred to the Memory of the Rev. Wm. Higginson, A.M. 51 years Vicar of this Parish, and Rector of Gretworth, in Northamptonshire, who departed this life much Lamented April 13, 1816, Aged 80 years.

South Wall.

In Memory of Robert Jeffries, Late of this Parish, who died April the 8th, 1735, in the 42 year of his Age.

Also in Memory of Ann, his Wife, and late Wife of Thomas Ladd. She died Oct. the 23, 1765, Aged 83 years.

In Memory of John Delme, Esq. of Rowdford House, near this Place, who died February the 8th, 1776.

Arms—Argent, an anchor erect, sable, charged with a lion passant, gules.

Underneath this place lyeth the Bodys of Thomas Spencer, and Elizabeth, his Wife.
He Died May ye 22, 1765, Aged 70 years.
She Died August 5, 1773, Aged 80 years.

Also in Memory of Richard Spencer Stephens, who died April the 2nd, 1769, Aged 7 Months.

Also of John Perris, who died July the 15, 1775, Aged 24 years.

Also in Memory of Sarah, Daughter of Thomas and Elizabeth Spencer, who Departed this life June the 30th, 1780, Aged 56 years.

To the Memory of Benjamin Stephens, and of Mary, his Wife.
He died the 30 of June, 1784, Aged 53 years.
She died the 5 of July, 1797,
in the 67 year of her Age.
Also of William and Benjamin, Sons of Benjamin and Mary Stephens.
Wm. died (at Prospect, in Jamaica) on the 24 of Dec. 1783, Aged 19 years,
And there lies interred.
Benjamin died Oct. the 11th, 1794, in the 30 year of his Age.

On Monuments at West End of Nave.

Underneath are deposited the Remains of Walter Post, (Son of the Rev. Walter Post, of Great Chiveral,) who died June 19, 1787, Aged 53.

Arms—Or, a fess, azure; impaling, first and fourth or, a bend azure; second and third gules.

Underneath are Deposited the Remains of Robert, (Son of Walter and Frances Post) who Departed this Life the 17th of February 1786, in his 20 year.

Hail, Spirit! disengaged from cumbrous clay,
Let not our Tears retard the blissful Flight:
The sigh dissolves in Faith; pursue thy way,
Till Heaven's full joys shall open to thy sight.

Arms—Or, a fess, azure.
Crest—A demi lion, sable, issuing out of a ducal coronet, arg.

East Wall of Nave.

Near this Place Lyeth the Body of Ann, the Wife of Samuel Webb, Jun. Clothier, and Daughter of Robert and Elizabeth Jeffers, Late of Rowdford. She Departed this Life the 30 Day of April, Ao Dom. 1703, Aged 33 years.

And also three of their Children :
Robert Departed Sept. the 6th, 1702, Aged 6 years.
Wm. Departed Jan. the 12, 1700,
Aged 1 year 9 months.
John Departed July the 21, 1707, Aged 16 weeks.

On Flat Stone in Nave.

To the Memory of Elizabeth Hiscock, of Hillwood, in the Parish of Auborne, in this County, and Daughter of Richard and Mary Witts, formerly of Rowde Farm, in this Parish, who died Nov. 28, 1806, Aged 82 years.

On Monuments in the North Aisle.

In the Alley Near this Place Lyeth the Body of Samuel, Son of Samuel Webb, Jun. who died Sept. ye 21, Añ Dom̃ 1726, Aged 33 years.

Also to the Memory of Ann, Ann, Daughters of Eleazar and Elizabeth Webb :

Ann Died Nov. ye 23, An. Dom̃ 1726,
Aged 14 weeks.

Ann Died Dec. ye 4, An. Dom̃ 1729,
Aged 11 months.

To the Memory of Mr. Samuel Webb, Sen. of this Parish, Clothier, who Departed this Life the 18th Day of May, and in the 75 year of his Age, 1707.

As also of his two wifes, Sarah, who Departed this life the 18th day of August, 1689;

Elizabeth, who departed this life the 29 day of Sept. 1699.

Near this Place lyeth Interred the Body of Edgar Webb, Clothier, who Departed this life the 10 of Oct. 1674, Aged 49.

Near this Place lyeth also the Body of Elizabeth Webb, the Wife of Edgar Webb. She Departed this life the 21 of Dec. 1694, Aged 70.

In the Alley neere this Place Resteth the Body of Eleazar Webb, late of this Parish, Clothier, who left this world the 29 of Sept. 1647.

Nemo ante obitum felix.

Near this Place lyeth the Body of Samuel Webb, Son of Samuel Webb, Sen. He dyed 9th Feb. 1739, Aged 77 years.

In Vestry Room.

Over Against this Place Lyeth the Body of Abigail, the Wife of Timothy Richards, Vicar of this Parish, and Daughter of Samuel White, of Polshot, Gent. Shee Departed the 19th of May, 1643.

Dormit, non est Mortua ; Quiescit, non Periit.

Monuments in the East Wall of South Aisle.

Near this Place lieth the Body of Richard Webb, late of this Parish, Gent. Deceased, who departed the 16th Day of August, Anno Domini 1715, Aged 82 years.

He gave by his last Will, in writing, Dated the 27 Day of May, 1715, ye Clear yearly Rent of certain Houses, and a Ground called Stovy Croft, with the Appurtenances lying in this Parish, to be Distributed Amongst the Poor of this Parish, not receiving Alms of the Parish, on every 21 Day of December Yearly for ever ; at the Direction of the Trustees therein named, for their lives ; And after the Decease of the Survivours of them, at the Discretion of the Overseers of the Poor of the said Parish likewise to fulfil the same ; as by the said Will more at large appears.

1730.

Eleazar Webb, Wm. Stephens, Churchwardens.

An ACCOUNT of the BENEFACTIONS to the Poor of the Parish of Rowde.

The Rent of an House, Orchard, Garden, and a ground, commonly called Stovy Croft, to be paid Annually, on St. Thos. Day, was Given by Richard Webb, late of this Parish, Gent. to such as are not Chargeable to the Parish.

The rent of some House, and a ground commonly called Barrows Close, to be paid Annually on the 27 day of March, was given by Mr. John Wicks, and also a Cloth and Cushion for the Pulpit, Twelve Shillings per annum was given out of the rent of a ground commonly called Hawkin's Grove.

The Interest of Ten Pounds Per Annum, to be paid once in every two years, was given by Francis Ellyott, late of this Parish, Gent.

In Memory of Jane, Wife of Wm. Jordan. She Departed this life April 16, 1772, Aged 66 years.

Farewell, vain world, I have seen enough of thee,
Nor value not what thou canst say of me ;
Thy smiles I court not, nor thy frowns I fear,
For now my head lies quiet here ;
What faults you see in me take care to shun,
And look at home, there's something to be done.

Hatchment in the Chancel.

Or, an anchor, sable, between two lions passant guardant, gules, a crescent of the last for difference.

Rowdeford House, the Seat of Wadham Lock, Esq.

The Church consists of a Chancel, Nave, North and South Aisles. The Nave is supported by seven pointed arches, four on the north side, and three on the south.

Register commenced 1606.

The Rev. Edward Vincent Vicar.

Wadham Lock, Esq. Lord of the Manor.

BROMHAM.

On Monuments against North Wall of Chancel.

Deo immortali Sacrum.
Hic jacet,
In spem beatæ immortalitatis,
Johannes Collinson,
Baccalaureus Sacerdos,
Hujus Templi quondam Vicarius.
Objit 4 Septembris,
Anno Christi 1764,
Ætatis ineunte 50.

Hugo Webbe,
Hujus Ecclesiæ quondam
Rector.
Qui objit
Novemb. 12, Anno Dom.
1597.

Anna Webbe,
Uxor Georgij Webbe,
filij Hugonis Webbe.
Quæ Objit Novemb. 17,
1617.
Ille parens conjux fuit hæc monumenta maritus,
hæc posuit sponsæ fillius Illa patri
Georgius Webbe,
S : Theol : Bach : Pastor. Ecclesiæ
de Steepleashton.

Above this inscription are two small statues, one of which, a male figure, hath its hands broken off at the wrist.

H. S. E.
Gulielmus Norris, Armiger,
Hospitij Lincolniensis Socius,
Legum Municipalium peritus,
Patronus, et Assertor
Rebus adversis major, par Secundis
Gummis et animi, et corporis facultatibus
spartam quam nactus est ornavit,
Qui invidet minor est,
Dum prolis numerosæ,
Fœliciter inserviret commodis,
Laboribus et Ætati confectus,
Placide obdormivit 7mo Sept. A. D. 1730,
Postquam annos Septuaginta et quatuor
impleverat.
Ne Patris optimi de Familia suâ amplissime
De pauperibus Clientibus quam maxime
Promeriti,
Pereat Memoria.
Hoc exiguum immensi amoris,
Pietatis,
Et Gratitudinis Monumentum. F. F.
Johannes Norris, Armiger,
Hæres et Executor Testamentarius.

Quarterly, first and fourth argent; second and third gules, a fretty, or, a fess, azure; impaling, ermine, three chevronells, gules.

Elizabeth Richardes
Departed this life June 22.
Blessed are the Dead which die
in the Lord.
Revel. 14.
The Righteous
Shall be had in Everlasting Remembrance.

Henry Season, M. D.
who Dyed Nov. ye 10th, 1775,
Aged 82 years.
Tis not the Tomb, in Marble polished high,
The sculptur'd Urn, or glittering Trophies nigh,
The Classic Learning on an impious Stone,
Where Latin tells what English blush'd to own,
Can shroud the guilty from the Eye of God,
Incline his Balance, or avert his Rod;
That hand can raise the Cripple and the Poor
Spread on the Way, or gathered at the Door,
And blast the Villain, though to altars fled,
Who robs us living, and insults us dead.*

Against the north wall under the Tower.

Neare this lieth the Bodye of
Fardinando Hughes. Departed
this Life 11th of April, Anno
Domini 1640.
As i was so are yee,
as i am so shall you bee.

Mary, the Daughter of Mr. Ferdinando Hughes,
Departed this life June the 28th,
And Elizabeth the other Daughter
of the said Ferdinando, Deceased March
the 18th, Both in the year 1647.
Over against this Place two Sisters Lye,
Who were Translated in their Infancy;

---

* Written by the Rev. John Rolte.

Mary, the Eldest, led the way, and Death
Soone after seized sweet Elizabeth :
But be it knowne, Death did it for the best,
That they the sooner might Lye down to rest,
And let them rest within that bed of clay,
Untill their Joyful Resurrection Day.

Tempora mutantur, nos mutamur in . . tis

Mon. against the North Wall of Nave.

Margery Seagar, Wife of Robert Seagar, Departed this life Jan. 18, 1618.

Blessed are the Dead which dy in the Lord,
they rest from thayr
Labours, and thayer
workes follow them.
Rev. 14. 13.

Arms—Quarterly, first and fourth a chevron, ermine, guttée d'or; second, a fess, in chief a lion passant guardant; third, a bend raguly.

Here Lyeth ye Body of Mrs. Mary, Wife of ye late Samuel Hicks, dece'sd. She died March ye 23rd, 1741, in ye 90 year of her Age.

Alco here Lyeth ye Body of Mr. Henry Hicks, Son of ye said Samuel and Mary Hicks, who died June ye 25, 1751, Aged 67.

Also here Lyeth ye Body of Mr. Joseph Hicks, Brother to the said Henry, and Son of Samuel and Mary Hicks, who died March ye 13, 1760, Aged 71.

S. Wall of S. Aisle.

Near this Place lies Interred the Body of Mrs. Mary Gregory, Relict of the late John Gregory, Esq. of London, who departed this life July 20, 1796, Aged 65.

Near this Place lyeth the Body of Mr. Francis Leigh, Clothier, who Departed this life the 13th day of September, 1669, in the 77 year of his Age.

And also the Body of Mr. John Leigh, his Onely Son, who Departed this Life unmarried, the 2 day of April, 1672, in the 47 year of his Age.

In Memory of Mr. John Andrews, Late Merchant of the City of London, who fell by ye hand of ye Enemy near Pama, in the East Indies, October, 1763, in the 34 year of his Age, sincerely and justly regretted by his relations and friends.

Sacred to the Memory of Mr. Richard Fennell, of Highgate, in the County of Middlesex, who Departed this Life 24 April, 1818, Aged 60 years.

"The Lord knoweth the days of the upright,
and their inheritance shall be for ever."

To the Memory of Mrs. Cope, Relict of Berkely Cope, Esq. who died at Bromham, Sept. the ninth, 1791, Aged 52 years.

With manners formed to shine in polish'd Life,
A Duteous Daughter, and attentive Wife ;
Tir'd of the World, she sought this peaceful Seat,
To hear the word, and sit at Jesus feet,
That one thing needful, which whoe'er shall chuse,
Nor Heaven can forfeit, nor his Soul can lose.

To the Memory of James Banks, late Officer of the Royal Navy, Son of John and Ann Banks, and Grandson of Mr. John Rogers, late of Wyats, Departed this life April the 25th, 1772, Aged 21 years.

Safe in the Haven now my Vessel lies,
The Pilot's wafted to his native skies ;
Through Life's rough Ocean I in safety past,
And Hope's firm Anchor in my Saviour Cast.

Also to the Memory of John Banks, Sen. who Departed this Life April the 13, 1785, in the 66 year of his Age.

Also to the Memory of Ann, Wife of John Banks, who died July the 5, 1796, Aged 72 years.

On Flat Stones in South Aisle.

Here lyeth ye Body of Mrs. Barbara Webb, Wife of Mr. William Webb, of Nethersucet, who departed this life ye 5 Day of April, 1718.

Here lyeth the Body of Mr. William Webb, of Nethersucet, who Departed this life Oct. 1722.

Brass Plate.

Elizabeth Eyre, the Wife of Thomas Eyre, Gent. and Daughter of John Yerbury, Gent. Departed this life the 29 of August, 1637.

Heere lyes an Heire, who to an Heire was joynd,
And dyinge lefte a little Heire Behind,
Hard Hearted Death heerein was somewhat mild,
Hee tooke the Mother, But Hee spar'd the Child,
Yet the one's more happy farre than is the other,
The Child's an Heire on Earth, in Heaven the Mother,
Where with triumphant Saints and Angells bright,
Shee now enjoyes her blessed Saviour's sight.

Here Lyeth ye Body of John Tuck, Gent. Sen. who died May ye 14th, A. D. 1732.

Also Here Lyeth ye Body of Mary, the Wife of John Tuck, who died April ye 8th, A. D. 1720, Aged 81 years.

Also Here Lyeth ye Body of John Tuck, Jun. who died Oct. the 3d, A. D. 1731, Aged 21 years.

At the East End of the Baynton Chapel.

Sir Edward Bayntun, Knight of the Bath, Son and heir of Sir Edward Bayntun, Knight. Obijt 2 Sept. 1679, Ætat. 61.

Henry Bayntun, Esq. Son and Heir of Sir Edward Bayntun, Knight of the Bath. Obijt 11 July, 1691, Ætat. 27.

John Bayntun, Esq. only Son and Heir of Henry Bayntun, Esq. by Lady Ann Wilmot. He was the Nineteenth in Lineal Descent from Sir Henry Bayntun, Knight Marshall of the Houshold to Henry 2nd. Obijt 24 April, 1716, Ætat. 22.

South Wall.

Lady Ann Wilmot, Eldest Daughter and Coheiress of John, Earl of Rochester. She was the Wife of Henry Bayntun, Esq. and after his decease of the Honble Francis Grevill. Obijt August 8, 1703.

Arms—A bend of seven lozenges; impaling a fess charged with three escallops between as many griffins' heads, erased.

North side of the Chapel.

Here rest the remains of Sir Edward Bayntun Rolt, Bart. Second Son of Thomas Rolt, of Sacombe Park, in the County of Herts. Esq. and Nephew and Heir of John Bayntun, of Spye Park, in the County of Wilts. Esq. who died Jan. 3rd, 1800, Aged 89.

Also of Dame Mary, his Wife, who died March 26, 1799, Aged 81.

On a Flat Stone.

Sir Edward Bayntun, Knight, Son and Heir of Sir Henry Bayntun, Kt. Obijt 8 Dec. 1657.

On a brass plate by a large figure.

Orate pro aĩa Johis Baynton, Armigeri, filij et hered. Roberti Baynton, Militis, Consanguinum et hered. Ricardi Beauchamp, domino de Sc̃o Amando, qui obijt ultimo die mensis Octoberis, Anno dñi Millmo VD XVI. cujus aĩe propicietur Deus. Amen.

Round the edge of a Tomb.

Hic jacet Elizabeth, dña de Sco. Amando, filia, ... nerico dño de Sco. Amando. Obijt

---

On an altar-tomb of grey marble, about 17ft. 6in. long, and 3ft. 3in. broad, is a figure of alabaster, in armour, with his hands meeting on his breast, his head lying on a pillow, and his feet resting on a dog. In this Chapel are two helmets and a pair of gauntlets in good preservation.

Shields of Arms in the south Window of the Chapel.

1. Azure, three salmons, naiant, argent.
2. [As the preceding.] Impaling, gules, two li. pass. guard. or.
3. Argent, on a bend, gules, a lion rampant, azure.
4. Or, a chevron, gules, between three wreaths, azure, each charged with five roses, gules, seeded or.

In the Vaulting, beginning at the east end.

1. Azure, a cross flory, between four martlets, or.
2. Quarterly, first and fourth, fretty or and sable, on a chief of the last three bezants; second and third or, seven mascles, gules, 3 3 1.
3. Or, seven mascles, gules, 331.
4. Argent, over a bend, gules, a lion rampant, azure.
5. Quarterly, first and fourth argent, over a bend, gules, a lion rampant, azure; second, or, a chevron, gules, between three wreaths, azure, each charged with five roses, gules, seeded or; third, or, a chevron between three bucks' heads (without horns) erased, gules.
6. Fretty, or and sable, on a chief, sable, three bezants.
7. Azure, three salmons naiant, argent.
8. Or, a chevron, gules, between three wreaths, azure, each charged with five roses, gules, seeded or.
9. Azure, a fess between six martlets, or.
10. Quarterly, first and fourth or, seven mascles, gules, 331; second and third, fretty, or and sable, on a chief, sable, three bezants.
11. Or, over a bend, gules, a lion rampant, azure.
12. Argent, a cross, gules.
13. Or, over a bend, gules, a lion rampant, azure; impaling or, on a wreath, azure, five roses, gules, seeded, or.
14. Or, seven mascles, gules, 331; impaling fretty or and sable, on a chief, sable, three bezants.
15. Gules, a fess between six martlets, or.

The Church consists of Chancel, Nave, and South Aisle: with the addition of the Baynton Chapel.

Register commenced 1560.

The Rev. H. Baynton, M.A. Rector.

The Rev. Dr. Starkey, Lord of the Manor.

ETCHELHAMPTON.

On a Monument against the north Wall of Chancel.

H. S. E.

Gertruda Ernle, nata Johannis St. Loe, de Knighton, in Agro Wiltoniensi, Generosi, conjux fidelis et Relicta mœrens Ed. Ernle, Armigeri, Domino hujus Manerij, cuj. sanctitas in sacris, philostorgiâ in liberos, urbanitas in proximos, largitas in egenos, comitas in singulos conspicue tanquam lucerna ardens emituit, omnium planctu et desiderio. Objit 21mo Aprilis, Anno Domini 1662.

South Wall.

In Memory of James Gibbs, who died Dec. 3, 1792, Aged 44.

On Flat Stones in Chancel.

Here lyeth the Body of Michael, Sone of Michael Ernly, Borne Decem. the 7th, and dyed the 1st of Feb. All in 1659.

Here Lyeth ye Body of Guy, elder Son of Robert Bayly, Elder, of this Parish, Born Jan. 23, Anº Dom. . . . . . Deceased Annº Dom. 1672.

Here Lyeth the Body of Sir Walter Ernle, Baronet, who Departed this Life July ye 16th, Anº Dom. 1732, Ætatis 56.

Arms—Quarterly, first and fourth azure, on a bend three eagles displayed; second and third, barry of six, gules and . . . in chief three roundels.

On Monuments in North Wall of Nave.

Margaret Bailey, Spinster, died 26, Dec. 1788, Aged 71.

Richad Bayley, Gent. died 10th of January, 1790, Aged 70.

This Monument was Erected by their Nephew, Edward Bayly, of London, Wine Merchant.

H. S. E.

Honoria Lettisima, Conjux Henrici Eyre, Gent.
Unica Filia Hæresque superstes Roberti
Baily, Gent. ex Mariâ Uxore suscepta,
Charissima Mater Johannis Eyre, filij, et
Filiæ Susannæ, quam vix enixa est
puerpera, quin morbido languore Correpta,
unde 10 die post editum partim,
vie placide que obdormivit
Ultimo mensis Januarij, Anno Ætatis suæ 31,
Dominique 1685.
Hoc Memoriæ Sacrum
Mœstissimus posuit
H. E.

Arms—On a chevron three quatrefoils, surtout an escutcheon charged with a fess engrailed bt. three horses' heads erased.

On an altar tomb by the north wall of the nave, are two statues of a male and female lying: the former is in armour, with his feet resting on a lion. On one side of the tomb are ten small figures, on the opposite side two.

Register commenced 1630.

The Rev. Thomas Anthony Methuen Rector.

Lady Grosvenor Drake Lady of the Manor.

ALL CANNINGS.

On Monuments against the north wall of Chancel.

Near this Place is Interred the Body of Gartrude, the Daughter of the Rev. Mr. John Ernle, and Elizabeth, his Wife, who Departed this Life the 8th Day of February, 1715, Aged 9 months.

In Memory of Mrs. Elizabeth Ernle, the Wife of the Rev. Mr. John Ernle (afterwards Sir John, by the Death of his Brother Sir Walter), and Daughter of John Smith, of Alton Priors, in this County, Esq. who Departed this Life the 9th day of March, 1729, Aged 39 years.

She was a person that was endued with all the accomplishments, both in Body and Mind, as rendered her an ornament to her Sex. An Affectionate Wife, a Tender Mother, an Indulgent Mistress, a Charitable Neighbour, and Sincere Friend. As She was universally beloved whilst Living, so her Death (by all those who had the Happiness of her acquaintance) is looked upon as a publick loss.

In Memory of Walter Ernle, Esq. Son of Sir John Ernle, Bart. and Elizabeth, his Wife, who Departed this Life the 28th Day of November, 1733, Aged 20 years.

Also in Memory of Sir John Ernle, Bart. Rector of this Parish. He was Son of Walter Ernle, Esq. and Brother to the late Sir Walter Ernle, Bart. both of Conock, and Grandson of Sir Walter Ernle, of Echillhampton, Bart. both in this County, who departed this Life the 30th Day of March, 1734, Aged 53 years.

To the Memory of Charlotte Georgiana Methuen, who Departed this Life Nov. 10th. 1820, Aged 4 years and 6 months.

South Wall.

Sacred to the Memory of William Fowle, Esq. who departed this life at Wiltshire Estate, in the Island of Jamaica, on July 8th, 1796, in the 61 year of his Age. Though a Native of this County, he passed greater part of his time in the West Indies, where he was an eminent and successful Practitioner of Physic, and where, by his integrity and beneficence, he raised himself to the highest esteem. As a small tribute of Gratitude and Affection to so worthy an Uncle, this Monument was Erected by William Fowle, Esq. of Durrington, in this County.

Arms—Gules, a lion passant guardant between three roses, or.

Sacred to the Memory of Mr. John Fowle, of Oxford, who Departed this life March 22, 1772, Aged 40.

To the Memory of the Rev. Wm. Fowle, M. A. who was a Native of this Parish, his Father of a Respectable Family here, his Mother the Eldest Daughter of John Smith, Esq. of Alton Prior. He was Educated at Marlborough School, and Oriel College, in the University of Oxford. In the year 1734, he became Rector of this Parish, in the Room of his Uncle the Rev. Sir John Ernle, Baronet. He constantly resided and discharged all the Duties of his Office with Diligence and Regularity till within a few Days of his Death. He was of a Friendly benevolent Temper, and remarkable inoffensive. He lived and died unmarried, but he discharged the duties of a Father by his paternal care of a numerous family of Nephews and Nieces, as well in his Life time as at his Death. His Executors have Erected this Monument to his Memory as a lasting Testimony of their Esteem, Regard, and Gratitude, to their great and good Benefactor. He died 21 May, 1770, Aged 62.

On Flat Stones in Chancel.

Jane, Wife of Wm. Fowle, Sen. died Dec. 5th, 1749, Aged 71.

Wm. Fowle, Sen. Died March 2nd, 1735, Aged 56.

Under this Stone were Interred the Remains of the Rev. Mr. Wm. Fowle, M. A. 1770.

Under this Stone were Interred the Remains of Mrs. Jane Andrews, Wife of Mr. Thomas Andrews, of this Parish, and Niece of the Rev. William Fowle, M. A. who died 26 April, 1790, Aged 52 years.

Under this Stone were Interred, in a leaden Coffin, the Remains of Mr. John Fowle, of Oxford, 1772.

Thomas Andrews, Gent. died 22 March, 1816, Aged 81 years.

Ann Kinninmond, the Wife of Henry Kinninmond, Rector of Alcanings, was Buried here Easter Munday, the 24th of April, Anno Domini 1671.

Here Lyeth the Body of Elizabeth, the Wife of George Stoodley, Rector of this Parish. She Departed this life the 20th Day, and was Buried the 24 Day of December, Anno Domini 1694, Aged 49 years.

Here Lyeth the Body of Martha, the Daughter of Mrs. Ann Lunn, of Rochester, in Kent, who Dyed in the 20th year of her Age, and was buried the 28 day of Sept. 1707.

Against the first Pillar, north side of the Nave from the E. end.

Near this Place Lieth the Bodys of John Beake, and Mary, his Wife.

He died August 7th, 1781, Aged 73 years.

She died May 17, 1789, Aged 77 years.

And John Beake, their Son died 30 March, 1807, Aged 70 years.

Against the second Pillar.

Near this Place Lyeth ye Body of Daniel Chandler, who died Dec. 17 . . . . Aged 65.

On Flat Stones in Nave.

In Memory of Simon, Son of Wm. and Hester Miells, who died July 20th, 1796, Aged 32 years.

Also in Memory of Emma, Wife of William Weston, and Daughter of William and Hester Miells, who died May 5th, 1797, Aged 34 years.

And of Hester, Wife of Wm. Miells, who died May 7th, 1797, Aged 71 years.

Also of William Miells, who died Oct. 11, 1808, Aged 86 years.

And of William Miells, Jun. who Died Dec. 30, 1805, Aged 39 years.

Here Lyeth the Body of Andrew Cozens, who died ye . . . day of March, Anno Dom 1709, Aged 27.

Here Lyeth the Body of Mary, the Wife of Andrew Cozens, who Died the 20th of April, A. D. 1711.

Andrew Cozens, 1732, Aged 77 years.

On Monument in N. Wall of N. Aisle.

Near this Place lyeth the Body of Daniel Cosens, who died Oct. ye 2nd, A. D. 1730, Aged 38 years.

Arms—Azure, two bars imbattled, argent.

S. Wall of S. Aisle.

To ye Memory of Thomas Ferris, jun. Carpenter, of this Parish, who dy'd Jan. ye 9th, $172\frac{8}{7}$ Aged 53 years.

Here lyes our Brother, who was well belov'd,
From us too soon, Alass! too soon remov'd;
Sweet was his temper, honest was his mind,
His Act's were harmless, and his thoughts refin'd.
A famous artist, in his business past,
But, ha! his genius was too fine to last.
God's will be done, his Virtuous Soul is blest,
Crown'd with ye bliss of everlasting rest.

Also in Memory of Thomas Ferris, Sen.
He dy'd Feb. ye 14, $172\frac{9}{30}$
Aged 91 years.

He and his Son were Carpenters of ys Parish 70 years.

1581. Anno . Dñi.
Oneli : Honore : and
Preise : be : Geven : to : God
Where : so : ever : a Dead
Carkas : is : even : thither
Will : the e : gles : restore.
I : Beleve : that : mi : Redemer : liveth : and :
That : I : shall : rise : owte : of : thee : earth
in : the : last : dai : and : shall : be : coverede :
againe : wite : mi : skinne : and : shall : se
God : in : mi : flese : ica : and : I : mi : selfe : shall
beholde : him : not : withe : other's
but : with : these : same : eies.
Deathe : in : Iesus : Christe : onli
is : eternall : Salvacion.
William Ernle,
And Jone, his Wife.

Arms—Quarterly, first and fourth on a bend three eagles displayed; second and third a cross moline.

On Flat Stones in S. Aisle.

In Memory of John Manning, who died July ye 6, 1755, Aged 69 years.
He was a tender Father, And a good Master,
A good Neighbour, And a sincere Friend.
Also in Memory of Mary, Daughter of John Manning, who died the 25 of November, 1762,
Aged 39 years.

Under this Stone lyeth Sabra, Wife of William Maslen, who Died Oct. 15, 1763, Aged 45 years.
Also under this Stone lyeth William Maslen, who Died July the 17th, 1790, Aged 72 years.

In the south Transept.

Here Lieth the Body of John Nicholas, Esq. Son of Edward Nicholas, of Hitcham, in the County of Bucks. Esq. and Grandson of Sir Edward Nicholas, Knight, who was Principal Secretary of State to their Majestys King Charles ye first and second. He Departed this life on the 25 of February, 1737, Aged 64 years.

Arms—Quarterly, first and fourth argent, on a cross, gules, a regal crown, or, in first quarter a crescent for difference, gules; a fess between three choughs, proper.

Sacred to the Memory of ..... Riggs, Esq.
of Wichbury, in the County of Wilts.
who Departed this Life April 5, 1774,
Aged 67.
And Also to Penelope, his Wife,
Daughter and Coheiress
Of the late John Nicholas, Esq.
Of West Horseley, in the County
of Surry.
She died September 2nd, 1772,
Aged 72.

Arms—Gules, a fess ermine between three talbots, holding in their mouths an arrow, argent, over all an escutcheon, quarterly, first and fourth argent, on a cross, gules, the regal crown, or; second and third argent, a fess between three choughs, proper.

The Church consists of Chancel, Nave, North and South Aisle, and North and South Transepts. The nave is supported on each side by three pointed arches, resting upon round pillars.

Register commenced 1578.

The Rev. Thomas Anthony Methuen, Rector.

The Earl of Pembroke Lord of the Manor.

STANTON BARNARD.

On a Monument against North Wall of Chancel.

H. S. J.
Michael Smith, Generosus,
Pietatis, Virtutis, Charitatis,
Exemplum, haud vulgare.
Obijt Maij 5to An. Ætatis 74,
Dñi 1720.
Unicâ Prole eademq; Femineâ superstite
A Barbara conjuge Secundâ
Thomæ Powel, Generosi, filiâ
Procreata,
Quæ ut Marito Dilectissimo,
justa perageret,
Hoc condidit Monumentum,
Ob Utriusq; Memoriam,
Quos Tumulo tandem Sociandos.
Mors sola potuit sejungere.

Arms—Argent, on a fess, gules, three fleur-de-lis, argent, between three saltires, couped, sable: impaling, per fess, or and argent, a lion rampant, gules.

On a Flat Stone.

Here lyeth the Body of Thomas, Son of Thomas & Bridget Lavington. He Died May the 29, 1751, Aged 66 years.
Also Ann Lavington, his Wife. She died July the 28, 1756, Aged 67 years.
Also in Memory of Thomas Lavington, Son of Thomas and Ann Lavington, who died Feb. ye 10th, 1777, Aged 57 years.
And of Jane Walter, Widow of Thomas Walter, and Daughter of Thomas and Ann Lavington, who died 25 May, 1808, Aged 87 years.

Brass Plate.

Beneath this Place Lies Mr. John Shortnost, Vicar, and Priscilia, his Wife.

She died 4 Feb. 1712.
He 18 Jan. 1731.

Mon. East Wall of Nave.

John Booth, sonne of Thos. Booth, of Gossop, in Chefshire, descended from Sir Thos. Booth, of Barton, in Lankash. Kt. So improved is Ancient Stock by his wisdome & Piety, that he served in matters of High trust Lodow, Duke of Lenox & Richmond, & after that Frances, Dowager of the same, with approoved faith & Integrity untill his Death. He Maryed Christian, Coheire to Wm. Unwing, Descended from Robt. Unw̃ of Horton, Esq. by whome he had 8 Children, of which 7 Deceased young, & Barbara Maryed to George Vaughan, Esq. He dyed July 15, 1635.

Arms—Argent, three boars' heads erased, and erect sable, in chief a mullet of the last: impaling azure, a crescent, argent, between three fleur-de-lis, or; in chief three tusks, proper.

Arms—Argent, three boars' heads erased and erect, sable, in chief a mullet, of the last, charged with a crescent, of the field.

On Flat Stones in Nave.

1659. Here lyeth the Bodie of Jefferie Burtdon, of this Parish, Gent. in Libris Doctus, Amor° Pietatis, who Departed the thirteenth Day of January, in the Eightie second year of his Age.

Under this Stone Lyeth the Body of Thos. Church, Gent. who Departed this Life July 11, 1762, Aged 68. He was warm and constant in his Devotions to God, Kind to his Wife, Affectionate to his Relations, Charitable to the Poor, Honest and Beneficent to all men. Reader, if thou desirest happiness here and hereafter, go and do Likewise.

Here Lyeth ye Body of Daniel Dyke, Sen. who Departed this life Nov. ye 26, A. D. 1707, Aged 83 years.

Here Lyeth also Margery, his Wife, who died Jan. 13, 1727.

They had Six Children, whereof two only Survived them, (Viz.) Daniel and Mary.

Here Lyeth ye Body of Jane, late Wife of Emanuel Mugge, M. A. Rector of Stockton, in Warwickshire, and Vicar of Inckborough, in Worcestershire, the only Daughter of Henry Reeks, Apothecary, in Oxford. She died June 11, 1736.

In Memory of Wm. Lyddall, who died May 26, 1750, Aged 56.

Also in Memory of Barbara Lyddall, who Departed this Life March 11th, 1780, Aged 77 years.

In Memory of Mary, the Wife of Joseph Stroud, who died Jan. 26, 1795, Aged 63 years.

The Rev. Walter Birch, Vicar.

STURT.

On a Monument by the North Wall of Chancel.

Here ly ye Remains of
Eliz. Ellis.
Ob. 28 Apr. 1701.

She kept ye faith, She ran her race,
She not in vain received God's grace,
And heaven is now her resting Place.

Whoere this monument doest see,
Prepare himself to follow me.

URCHFONT.

On Monuments against the south wall of Chancel.

Underneath are Deposited the Remains of Olive, Wife of Robert Tothill, Esq. late Senior Clark of the Privy Seal to his Majesty King George the Second, one of his Justices of the Peace for the Counties of Wilts. Middlesex, and Kent, and one of the Governors of the Hospital of Christ, St. Thomas, and St. Bartholomew, who dyed Nov. 14th, 1731, Aged 53 years.

And of the said Robert Tothill, who dyed Feb. 13th, 1753, Aged 78 years.

Sir Wm. Pynsent, Bart. his Kinsman and Executor, erected this Monument pursuant to his Will.

Arms—Azure, on a bend, argent, cottized or, a lion rampant, sable: impaling, or, on a fess, sable, three mullets, argent, between as many lions rampant, sable.
Crest—A dove with an olive branch, proper.

Near this Place are deposited the Remains of Daniel Compton, Esq. who died the 25 of January, 1817, Aged 52.

Mon. against the North Wall of Nave.

Sacred to the Memory of Jacob Giddings, Late of Etchelhampton, who died March 28, 1808, Aged 70 years.

Also of Sarah, Wife of the above Jacob Giddings, who died July 14th, 1778, Aged 50 years.

And of their Daughter Elizabeth, who died May 26, 1801, Aged 35 years.

Sacred to the Memory of Ann, Daughter of Richard and Sarah Hallilay, of Wedhampton, who died 6 March, 1819, (of the Dropsy) Aged 33 years.

Under the severest pains she would ever praise God for all his Mercies; and, with Pious resignation, say, "Not my will, but thine be done."

236

In Memory of Wm. Pierce, of Crookwood, who died Nov. 20th, 1733, Aged 42 years.

Also in Memory of Jane, Wife of Seymour Pierce, who died Dec. the 26th, 1776, Aged 59 years.

Belov'd while she lived,
Her life was much desir'd,
Her death was much lamented,
But God her Soul requir'd.

Also of Seymour Pierce, who died Feb. the 11th, 1783, Aged 80 years.

Sacred to the Memory of William Keetch, Gent. who Departed this Life May 21, 1806, Aged 50 years.

In Memory of John, ye Son of Solomon & Mary Giddings. He died Dec. 29th, 175 .

Death in my Prime, cropt me betime,
And eas'd me of my pain;
And you must dye, and with me lye,
Till Christ rise us again.

On Monuments in South Wall of Nave.

Sacred to the Memory of Joseph Mundy, who Departed this Life 16th Sept. 1817, Aged 58 years.

Mr. Wm. Pierce, of Wedhampton, was Buried ye 7 of August, 1730.

Also Mary, his Wife, was buried ye 10th of April, 1742.

Near this Place lyeth ye Body of Thomas Snooke, who died the 12 day of Dec. 1758, Aged 55 years.

In Memory of Wm. & Vincent, sons of William and Elizabeth Pierce.

William Died May the 18th, 1742, Aged 24 years.
Vincent died August the 25th, 1746, Aged 24 years.

In Memory of the Rev. Mr. John Swallow, who was 42 years Vicar of this Parish, and died Oct. the 18th, 1728, Aged 67 years.

In Memory of Vincent Snook, who died Feb. 7th, 1800, Aged 61 years.

Also of Sarah, Daughter of Vincent and Mary Snook, who died Nov. 28th, 1784, Aged 17 years.

On a flat brass plate in nave.

Here lyeth the Bodey of John Giddings, of Erchefont, who dyed the 21st daye of Sepr Anno Dom 1615.

Flat Stones.

William Pierce, Sen. Dyed August 4, 1730, Aged 73 years.

Mary, his Wife, Dyed April 7th, 1743, Aged 82 years.

Also William Pierce, their Son, Dyed Jan. 25, 1760, Aged 73 years.

Also Elizabeth, his Wife, Dyed May 16, 1774, Aged 82 years.

And also in Memory of Elizabeth, Wife of Edward Pierce, Sen. who Departed this Life Sept. 3, 1787, Aged 56 years.

In Memory of Sarah, Wife of John Baily, who died ye 14th March, 1773, Aged 41 years.

Also in Memory of Sarah, Wife of Joseph Munday, who died ye 8th March, 1792, Aged 28 years.

In Memory of Martha, Wife of Josiah Giddings, who died the 27th June, 1778, Aged 42.

And of Sarah, his Second Wife, who died the 15th July, 1792, Aged 58.

Also of Josiah Giddings, who died the 23 Feb. 1813, Aged 83 years.

On a Monument in the North Aisle.

Near this Place Lyeth ye Body of Mrs. Jane Snooke. She Died Jan. ye 8th, 1774, Aged 75 years.

Also Robert, the Son of James and Sarah Giddings. He died May 19th, 1779, Aged 30 years.

My blooming youth is past and gone,
My friends, lament no more;
Prepare yourselves to follow me,
I am but just before.

Here rest the Body of James Giddings, who was Father of the above Robert Giddings, who departed this life Feb. ye 7th, 1786, Aged 84.

Also in Memory of Sarah, Wife of the above James Giddings, who died Feb. 24, 1800, Aged 88 years.

On Monuments in N. Transept.

Near this Place are deposited the Remains of Wm. Wroughton, of Eastcott, in the County of Wilts. Esq. who Departed this life Oct. the 3rd, Anno Dom 1750, Ætat. 52 years.

And also of Mrs. Sarah Wroughton, Wife of the above Wm. Wroughton, Esq. who departed this life the 22 of August, 1777, Ætat. 77.

Arms—Argent, a chevron, gules, between three boars' heads, couped, sable: impaling, Long.

Sacred to the Memory of Seymour Wroughton, Esq. of Eastcott, who Departed this life May 31, 1789, Aged 53.

Arms—Argent, a chevron, gules, between three boars' heads, couped, sable.

Underneath are Deposited the Remains of the Rev. George Jaques, L. L. B. 44 years resident Vicar of this Parish, and Prebendary of the Cathedral Church of Wells, whom his tender affection, his cheerful cordial disposition, and his benevolent heart, deservedly endeared to all. Ob. Dec. 2nd, Anno Dom̄ 1772, Æt. 77.

Mon. West End of S. Aisle.

Near this Place lyeth the Body of William Crook, Sen. who died 17th May, 1770, Aged 77 years.

Also of Elizabeth Crook, Wife of the above William Crook, Sen. who died the 7th of April, 1777, Aged 83 years.

To the Memory of Joseph Crook, who died 20th March, 1731, Aged 84 years.

Monuments in S. Transept.

Near this Place lieth interred the Body of James Long, of Wedhampton, in the Parish of Urchfont, Gentleman, who was of the Chiveral Branch of the ancient Family of the Longs, of Wiltshire, being the Great Grandson of Thomas Long, Esq. heretofore of little Chiveral, in the said County of Wilts. He Departed this Life the 21st day of October, in the year of our Lord 1768, Aged 74.

Arms—Sable, a lion rampant between eight cross crosslets arg.

Near this Place are deposited the Remains of Daniel Compton, Gent. who Departed this life Nov. 26th, 1780, Aged 60.

Also of Judith, Wife of Daniel Compton, Gent. who departed this life June 4th, 1789, Aged 55.

Near this Place lyes Hannah, Daughter of Robert and Joyce Noyes. She died Feb. 19th, 1759, Aged 24 years.

My life was nothing else but pain,
While here on earth I did remain;
Therefore, dear friends, don't grieve for me,
But trust in Christ, who set me free.

Also Mary, their Daughter, died 12 August, 1763, Aged 32 years.

Sacred to the Memory of John Compton, Gent. Youngest Son of the late Daniel and Judith Compton. He departed this life Jan. the 19th, 1801, Aged 32.

Near this Place lyeth the Body of Thomas Ernle, Gent. of Wedhampton, Son of Walter Ernle, Esq. of Conock, who departed this life the 7th of July, Anno Dom. 1725, Aged 29 years.

Arms—Quarterly, first and fourth argent; second and third barry of four, argent and sable, in chief three plates: over all, on a bend, sable, three eagles displayed, or.

On Flat Stones in South Aisle.

In Memory of Edward, Mary, and Elizabeth, Son and Daughters of William and Mary Pierce, of Wedhampton. 1765.

In Memory of William Keetch, who died March the 7th, 1769, Aged 51 years.

Also Mary, Daughter of Wm. & Betty Keetch, died in 1757, Aged 9 months.

And also in Memory of Betty K. wife of Wm. Keetch, who Departed this life Oct. the 16th, 1787, Aged 70 years.

Mr. Vincent Snook was buried 22 of August, 1693.

Elizabeth, his Wife was buried 9th of May, 1721.

Also Mr. Vincent Snooke, their Grandson, was buried 25 of Sept. 1751.

On a Flat Stone in Nave.

In Memory of Richard Amor, of Crookwood, who died April ye 25, 1706, Aged 54 years.

Also Ann, Wife of Richard Amor. She died Dec. ye 6, 1731, Aged 81 years.

Near this lies Francis, Son of Richard and Ann Amor. He died July ye 25, 1712, Aged 25.

Hatchment in the Chancel.

Quarterly, first and fourth gules, a chevron engrailed between three estoiles, argent; second and third ermine, a lion rampant, sable, armed gules.

Hatchment.

Quarterly, first and fourth gules, a chevron engrailed between three estoiles, argent; second and third ermine, a lion rampant, sable, armed gules. On an escutcheon, argent, a sinister hand, gules. Impaling argent, a bend cottized sable, in chief a cross crosslet, sable.

The Church consists of Chancel, Nave, North and South Aisles, and North and South Transepts. The nave is supported on each side by three pointed arches.

In two windows on the north side of the chancel, and also in one on the south side, is some painted glass.

William Salmon, Esq. Lord of the Manor.

CHERRINGTON.

On Monuments against the north Wall of Chancel.

H. S. E.

Isaacus Warriner, de Conock, in hâc Parochiâ, Arm̃ et 1738, hujusce Comitatu Vicecomes. In Spe Resurrectionis beatæ, ob. vi Jul : A. D. 1752, Ætat. 84.

Etiam Giffordus Warriner, Arm̃. Obiit 2° Maij, 1787, Ætat. 77.

Arms—A lion rampant : impaling quarterly, first and fourth . . . second and third, two bars, in chief three roundels.

Mr. John White, Vicar of Chitton, was buried ye 8th day of December, 1671.

South Wall.

Near this Place lyeth the Body of Mr. William Hayward, who died Dec. 9th, 1765, Aged 74 years.

And of Susanna, his Wife, who died August 20th, 1723, Aged 19 years.

And of Sarah, his Second Wife, who died July 23rd, 1752, Aged 57 years.

And also the Body of Mr. Richard Holloway, who who died Feb. 7th, 1770, Aged 45 years.

And of Elizabeth-Susanna, his Widow, who was the Daughter and only Child of the above William Hayward, and Susanna, his Wife, who died Nov. 22, 1794, Aged 71 years.

On Flat Stones in Chancel.

Hic subtus conditæ jacent Reliquiæ Venerabilis Viri, Gualteri Ernle, Armigeri, nuper de Conock, intra parochiam de Cherington, Filij celsissimi Domini Gualteri Ernle, Baronetti, de Ichilhampton pridem incolæ, qui Vicecomitis officio functus est, hujusce Comitatus ad Añ Dom̃ 1710, Mortalitatem et explevit 27 die Feb. Anno { Dni 1720, Ætatis suæ 67.

H. S. I.

Spe certissima Resurrectionis, Gertrudis, Marita Isaaci Warriner, Geñ. Filia Gualteri Ernle, Arm̃. Ob. 21 Decembris, An° Dom̃ 1709, Ætat. 27.

Etiam Ernle et Eduardus Warriner, Geñ Fil : Giff. Warriner, Arm̃ et Eliza. ux.

Ernle ob. 16 Maij, Ætat. 12 Ann.

Eduardus ob. 4 Augusti, Ætat. 9 meñ.

1754.

Etiam Elizabetha, Marita Giff. Warriner, pdict. Obiit 17 Nov. 1757, Ætat. 39.

Etiam Gualterus Gulielmus Warriner, Geñ. Obiit 15 Nov. 1780, Ætat. 30.

Here Lyeth ye Body of Susanna, ye Wife of Mr. William Hayward, and Daughter of Mr. Samuel and Elizabeth Dyke, who Departed this Life August ye 20th, A. D. 1723, Aged 19 years.

On Monuments against the South Wall of Nave.

Thomas Biggs. Sen. was buried June ye 9th, 1708.

And also Martha, his Wife, was buried Decem. ye 10th, And Martha, their Daughter, was buried Dec. ye 5, Both in 1693.

Near this Place was Interred ye Body of Richard Amor, jun. who Departed this Life ye 15th of March, 1767, Aged 23 years.

On Flat Stones in Nave.

In Memory of the Reverend Mr. John Pierce, who was 40 years Vicar of this Parish. He died May the 22, 1768, Aged 74 years.

Also of Priscila, his Wife.

She died July the 10th, 1759, Aged 77 years.

Also of Elizabeth Lucey Shorthose, who died July the 19th, A. D. 177 . Aged 85 years.

In Memory of Ann, Wife of John Pierce, who died March 19th, 1780, Aged 57 years.

Also in Memory of John Pierce, who died January 2nd, 1788, Aged 53 years.

A faithful Friend, a Father Dear,
A tender Husband lyeth here ;
The loss is great as we sustain,
In Heaven we hope to meet again.

Here Lies the Body of Richard Amor, who Departed this Life April the 28th, 1750, Aged 38 years.

Also of Elizabeth, his Wife, who died April 9th, 1762, Aged 44 years.

Affliction sore, etc.

Also of Jane, their Daughter, and Wife of Daniel Mathews, who died Sept. 23, 1761, Aged 24 years.

On Monument in N. Wall of N. Aisle.

Near this Place lies Interred the Body of Richard Yerbury, Gent. who died April ye 4, 1740, Aged 86 years.

S. Wall of S. Aisle.

Near this Place
Lyeth the Body of
Wm. Mannings,
who departed ys
Life ye 28 Day of
Feb. Anno Dom.
172 4/5 Aged 37 years

Hatchments in the Chancel.

Quarterly, first and fourth gules, a fess checky, or and ermine, between two antelopes, courant, argent; second and third arg. on a bend, sable, three eagles displayed, or: impaling or.

Per fess or and argent, on a lion rampant, azure an escutcheon of Ernle: impaling, Long.

Per fess or and argent, a lion rampant, sable: impaling quarterly, first and fourth argent; second and third sable, two bars, argent, in chief three plates; over all, on a bend, sable, three eagles displayed, or.

The Church consists of a Chancel, Nave, North and South Aisles. The Nave is supported on each side by three pointed arches. In the Chancel window is some painted glass, g. az. and or. and part of two figures in the east window of south aisle.

Register commenced 1585.

The Rev. S. Clarke, Vicar.

The Manor belongs to the Alms-house of Heytesbury.

Conock House, the Seat of Henry Ernle Warriner, Esq.

MARDEN.

On Monuments against North Wall of Chancel.

Underneath lyeth ye Body of Mr. John Hayward, who Departed this life the 9th Day of Jan. 1770, Aged 79 years.

In Memory of Philip Hayward, late of Orcheston St. Mary, in this County, who died the 9th day of April, in the year of our Lord, 1760, Aged 54 years.

Near this place is Intered the Remains of Mrs. Jane Hayward, who, in her long and tedious illness, was calm and resigned, and her death attended with a blessed prospect of future felicity, through the merits of her dear Redeemer. She obtained her release from this troublesome world May the 31, 1761, Aged 62 years.

South Wall.

Sacred to the Memory of Mr. William Hayward, who died Dec. 2nd, 1806, Aged 31 years.

In Memory of Mr. Wm. Hayward, late of Marden, who deceased April the 21st, in the Year of our Lord 1729, Aged 63 years.

Each minute wears this life away,
Labour for that time can't decay.

Beneath also lieth Interr'd the Body of Mary, his Wife, who Departed this Life Jan. the 9th, in the Year of our Lord, 1734, Aged 67 years.

And also the Body of Philip, their Son, who Died Nov. 26, A.D. 1703, Aged about 2 years.

On a Flat Stone.

In Memory of Wm. Hayward, who died Oct. 4th, 1774, Aged 41 years.

All-conquering Death Life's union Breaks,
Which sets our spirits free,
And gives them rapid wings to fly
Beyond Mortality.

Also in Memory of Jenny Hayward, Relict of Wm. Hayward, who died 17th March, 1819, Aged 75 years.

On a Flat Stone in Nave.

Underneath Lyeth the Body of Richard Hayward, who died April ye 12, 1772, Aged 76 years.

Also of Ann, his Wife, who died April ye 9, 1768, Aged 60 years.

Tho' greedy worms destroy our skin,
And gnaw our wasting flesh,
'Tis God shall raise our Souls again,
And Clothes them all afresh:
'Tis God that lifts our comforts high,
Or sinks them in the grave;
He gives, and Blessed be His name,
He takes but that he gave.

Register commenced 1685.

The Rev. Mr. Parsons, Vicar.

BEECHING STOKE.

On Monuments against the south wall of Chancel.

Sacred to the Memory of Mrs. Barbara Mayo,
Widow of the Rev. John Mayo,
Late Rector of this Parish, and Vicar of Wilcot,
who died Feb. 11th, 1796,
Aged 77 years.
Also of
Mrs. Lucy Mayo, their Daughter,
who died Feb. 4th, 1812,
Aged 67 years.

Sacred to the Memory of
Mrs. Ann Saunders,
Widow of Mr. Samuel Saunders, of Ilminster,
who died Dec. 26, 1798,
Aged 83 years.
Also
of Mr. James Mayo,
Son of the Rev. John Mayo,
Late Rector of this Parish,
And Vicar of Wilcot,
who died Nov. 15th, 1802,
Aged 55 years.

On Flat Stones in Chancel.

Here Lyeth ye Body of Mathew Raymond, Son of ye said George Raymond, who dyed Nov. 2, A. D. 1690, Ætatis 81.

Here Lyeth the Body of Mary, the Wife of Mathew Raymond, of this Parish, Gent. who Departed this life August ye 8, Anno Domini 1683, Ætatis 65.

Hatchment.

Sable, three bars, argent: impaling, per pale, argent, a chevron engrailed, gules and sable, in chief, 1st, a torteaux, 2d, a pellet.

The Rev. Charles Mayo, Rector.

The Manor belongs to the Dean and Chapter of Winchester.

POTTERN.

On Monuments by the North Wall of Chancel.

Dum vitæ Probitas honesta
Morum deamata Comitas,
Et Pietate minimè fucata,
Humani generis sunt Deliciæ,
Sacra sit Memoriæ
Francescæ, Uxoris delectissimæ
T. Hunt Grubbe, Arm̄.
Quæ filiolâ unâ filijsq,
Bimus spe optimâ, superstitibus,
Ad auras recessit superas
Oct: 18, 1767,
Annos nata 30.

Hoc bene merenti Mnemosynon
Conjux mœstissimus.
D. D. D.

Arms—Vert, on a chevron, argent, three cross-crosslets, gules, between three demi-lions, rampant, or: impaling, ermine, three crescents, gules.

Juxta Recondita sunt Ossa Ricardi Rooke, Gen: qui Animam Efflavit tricessimo primo die Decembris, Anno Dom: 1723, Æt. 48.

Hic etiam Jacet R. R. hujusce R: et Mariannæ Rooke, Fil: ob: Nov. 8, 1736, Æt. 24.

Reliquiæ Etiam Mariannæ Rooke, quæ Ob: die Mar: 15, 1765, Æt. 72.
Non Male Nota.

H. R. E.

Daniel Tanner, de Bedwin Magna natus.
Ob. 13 Feb: Ann: Dom. 1803, Æt. 77.

Arms—Argent, three Moors' heads, in profile, proper.

Infra Requiescunt Cineres Marthæ Tanner, Filiæ natu Maximæ Danielis Tanner, Arm̄: de Erchfont, Agro Wiltoniensis. Ob: Apl: 27: An. Dom. 1789, Ætat. 33.

Etiamque Janæ, prædictæ Marthæ Sororis. Ob. 28 Apri: Ann. Dom. 1794, Ætat. 21.

Arms—As the preceding.

South Wall.

Juxta requiescit, certâ spe resurrectionis,
Walterus Grubbe, Arm.
Vir eximiis animi imbutus,
Conjugalis amoris ingens exemplar,
Ob Fidem, Probitatem, Prudentiam, Amicitiam, et Benevolentiam, notissimus;
Constans Factonis impugnator acerrimus,
ob veramin Deum Pietatem spectabilis,
(Ah! quid dicam)
Vir profecto unde quaque desideratissimus.
Obijt sexto die Septembris,
Anno { Dom. 1715,
Ætat. 60.

Prope etiam conduntur ossa
Rebeccæ Grubbe,
Conjugis suæ dilectissimæ,
E generosâ Breretonorum Familiâ, in Agro Lincolniensi, oriundæ.
Quæ Obijt xxiv die Maij,
Anno { Dom. 1713,
Ætat. 57.

Arms—Vert, on a chevron, argent, three cross crosslets sable, surcharged with an escutcheon, argent, two bars, sable, between three demi lions rampant, or.

In Memory of Mrs. Thomazin Grubbe, who died Oct. 18th, 1723, Aged 65.

Also of Mrs. Thomazin Brooke, who died April 25, 1744, Aged 47.

And of Mrs. Margaret Grubbe, who died Dec. 10th, 1749, Aged 83.

Against S. E. Pillar of the Tower.

Underneath this Inscription are the Remains of Mr. Richard Bowman, late Vicar of this Church, and only Son of Francis Bowman, Esq. Gentleman Usher to King Charles ye 2d. Obijt 12 die Januarij, MDCXCII. Ætat. suæ 52.

And Likewise Those of his Wife, Mrs. Susanna Bowman. Obijt 8 die Aprilis, Ann. Dom. 1711, Ætat. suæ 74.

They had 5 Sons, and 2 Daughters, the only surviving one (Mr. Richard Bowman) hath, as a sincere testimony of his great respect, Dedicated this Monument to their Memories.

 241

Near this Place, in hopes of a blessed Resurrection, lyeth the Body of Capt. John Gaishford, of Worton, who died July 31, 1724, Aged 56 years.

And that of his Wife Mrs. Ann Gaishford, Daughter of Mr. Richard, and Mrs. Susanna Bowman.

Mr. Richard Gaishford, and Mrs. Anne Rendal, their Son and Daughter.

Where also Stephen, ye Eldest Son of Mr. Stephen Gaishford, of Westbury, in the County of Wilts. and Grandson to the late Captain Gaishford, is deposited. He dyed August 24, 1724, at 3 years of Age.

Hatchments in the Chancel.

Azure, on a chevron, argent, three cross-crosslets, sable, between three demi lions rampant, or: impaling azure, on a chevron, argent, three mill rinds, sable, in chief, on a canton, or, a trefoil, sable. Impal. also for Grubbe and Long.

Arms—Grubbe: impaling, argent, a chevron, gules, between three bucks' heads, caboshed, sable.

Monument in N. Transept.

Near this Place lyeth the Body of John Parsons, who Departed this Life Decem. ye 2d, 1761, Aged 68 years.

Also in the same Grave with his Father, lyeth the Body of Thos. Parsons, who Departed this life the 20 of Sept. 1768, in the 33 year of his Age.

And also in ye same Grave lyeth ye Remains of Sarah, Wife of John Parsons, who departed this life July ye 11th, 1782, Aged 78 years.

Now here together we do rest,
In hopes to raise again,
Hoping we shall happy be,
With Christ for to remain.

Mon. against N. Wall over the N. entrance.

To the Memory of Mr. Charles Wray, formerly of Fleet Street, London, but late of Bath, who died 27 of Jan. 1791, Aged 72 years, Son of the Rev. Wm Wray, M. A. many years Rector of Broad Chalk, Stour-Provest, and Todber, Grandson of Thomas Byng, some years Major of the Wiltshire Militia, and Great Grandson of the Rev. Robert Byng, D. D. formerly Rector of Allcanings, in this County, of which he was deprived by his adherence to King Charles 2d, died before his Restoration, and was buried in St. John's Church, Devizes.

Near the same Place lie the Remains of
Thomas and Ann Byng,
his Grandfather and Grandmother,
Charles and Edward Byng, his Uncles,
Elizabeth Wray, his Mother, and
Elizabeth Wray, his Sister.
Erected in gratefull Remembrance by his Nephew,
Robt. Bateman Wray.

Arms—Azure, on a chief, or, three martlets, gules.

South Wall.

To the Memory of William Long, Sen. Gent. and Bathsheba, his Wife.

He	died	Oct. 31,	1706,	Aged	81	years.
She		May 14,	1696,		45	

Also to the Memory of Wm. Long, Jun. Gent. & of Sarah, Ann, & Bathsheba, His Daughters, by Elizabeth, his Wife.

He	died	July 23,	1721	aged	33	
Sarah		Jun. 22,			10	years.
Ann		Jul. 12,	1719		4	
Bath.		Jan. 9,			3	weeks.

Also Near this Place lyeth
the
Bodies of Elizabeth, Wife of
Wm. Long, Jun. Gent. and
Also of Richard, their Son.
She Died March ye 2, 17.. Aged 74.
He died Nov. 22, 1753, Aged 40.

Arms—Long: impaling, azure, a chevron, ermine, between three crosslets, fitchy, or.

To the Memory of Henry Kent, Esq. who died 14th Jan. 1759, Aged 77 years.

Christian Kent, Wife of the said Henry Kent, who died 4 Sept. 1763, Aged 74.

Joanna Kent, Daughter of the said Henry and Christian Kent, who died 13th Sept. 1743, Aged 23.

Christian, another Daughter of the said Henry and Christian, who died 4 Feb. 1774, Aged 59.

And of Henry Kent, D. D. late of Whistley House, in this Parish, who died 27 Dec. 1799, Aged 81, At whose special direction this Monument was Erected.

After a long Life, passed in literary Pursuits, his End was accompanied with Acts of Benevolence, of which his Relations and Friends were the Partakers; Nor were the Poor omitted in his Bequests: as the divers Sums given by his last Will to the Hospitals of Sarum and Bath, the Society for the Benefit of Clergymen's Widows and Orphans in this Diocese, the Needy in this and Neighbouring Parishes, besides other Charitable Donations, form Testimony.

He left, also, to Merton College, in Oxford, of which he was formerly Fellow, all his valuable and extensive Library, together with an handsome Sum for its Augmentation.

Mrs. Frances Ferris, and Mrs. Mary Norris, the Administratrixes to his Will, have directed this Inscription to be engraved, as a Mark of their Gratitude and Esteem for the Deceased.

Arms—Azure, a lion passant guardant, or, in chief ermine.

On brass plates within the rails.

Heare Lyeth ye Body of William Rook, Gent. who Departed this life ye 23 day of June, Anno Dom 1701, Aged 43 years.

Here also lyeth the Body of Hester, his late Deceased Wife, who Departed this life ye 7 day of Oct. Ann. Dom̃ 1737, Aged 76 years.

Sacred to the Memory of Elizabeth Palmer, Wife of John Palmer, who died Oct. 25, 1800, Aged 54 years.

Also of James Rooke, who died May 8, 1813, Aged 65 years.

And also of James Palmer, who died April 7, 1815, Aged 54 years.

Here lieth Interred the Body of Mrs. Elizabeth Rooke, the O . . . Daughter of Mr. Richard Rooke. This Damsell Departed in the Faith of Christ the 13 of April, Ann. Dom. 1685, Ætatis suæ 21.

She was her Father's joy, her Virgin . . . . .
is nowe asleep amonge the blessed dead
Shees gone before, hir Father follow after
to rest with her is welbeloved daugh . . .
Her life was innocent and vertuous, til .
with greiuous paines at last & Soo . . . .
When Christ her lord appears sheel rise again
To life that's full of Joy, and free from . . . .

Here lieth the Body of Elizabeth, Wife of Mr. John Gray, of Stratton, and Daughter of William Rook, Gent. and of Hester, his Wife. She Departed this Life the 7th of July, 1717, Aged 23 years.

M. S.

Anna, Giffordi Yerbury Uxoris, de Conock, in parochia de Cherington, Generosi. Obiit magno (suo et nimium fatali) Climacterico, Calend. Januarij, Anno post partum Salutem, 1687.

And also here lieth the Body of Philip Smith, Seniour, Gent. who Departed this life the 8 Day of March, Anno Domini 1715, Aged 69 years.

And also the Body of Jane, his Wife, who Departed this life the 5th day of May, Anno Dom. 1721, Aged 67 years.

On a Brass Plate.

Here Lyeth the Body of Hugh Rook, Gentleman, who departed this life the 25 day of Oct. Anno Domini 1686.

Here Lyeth ye Body of Thomas Grubbe, who departed this life the 25 Day of October, in the year 1791, Aged 68 years..

Brass Plate.

Depositum Susanna Grubbe, Filia Thomæ Grubbe, Armigeri, et Thomazin, Ux. ejus. Obiit Vicesimo Septimo Die Septembris, Anno Dom̃ 1684.

Underneath are Interred the Remains of Frances, Wife of Thomas Hunt Grubbe, Esq. of Eastwell, in this Parish, who died October 18, 1767, Aged 30 years.

Also two of their Sons, who died in their Infancy.

Also of Thomas Hunt Grubbe, Esq. who died August 13th, 1772, Aged 39.

On Flat Stones in Nave.

Here Lyeth the Body of William Pitt, Gent. who Departed this life the 12 Day of April, 1761, Aged 75 years.

George Pitt died Feb. the 7, 1782, Aged 78 years.

In Memory of Richard Pitt, who Departed this Life the 19th Day of January, 176·8

Also in Memory of Robert Pitt, who departed this life the 27th day of March, 1784, Aged 79 years.

Underneath this Stone are Deposited the mortal Remains of Edward May, Gent. who Departed this Life on the 11th day of January, 1770, Aged 35 years.

Also Mary, Wife of the above Edward May, Gent. who Departed this Life on the 9th Day of September, 1775, Aged . . years.

Also Mary, their Daughter, who died May the 1st, 1769, Aged 2 years.

Underneath this Stone, in a Vault, are deposited the Mortal Remains of William Drewett, Gent. late of the Parish of Colerne, (in this County) who Departed this Life the 10 day of Nov. 1813, Aged 52 years.

Also

In the same Vault are deposited the mortal Remains of Philip May, Gent. (of Marston, in this Parish,) who departed this Life on the 5th day of Feb. 1815, Aged 51 years.

H. S. E.

John Flower, Esq. of West Grimsteed, Son of John Flower, Gent. of Worton, Dyed June the 24, 1723, Aged 73.

George Flower, Esq. Ob. June 3d, A. D. 1746, Æt. 63.

Joseph Spearing, Gent. Ob. April 10, 1774, Æt. 64.
Jenevera, his Wife, Ob. April 16th 1775, Æt. 52.
Also George, their Son, died in his infancy.

Arms—A unicorn passant, in chief three fleur-de-lis.

Johannes Merewether, de Worton, in hac Parochia, Generosi, hic conduntur Exuviæ.

Pthsi suæ (eheu) Prosapiæ nimium Fatali
Præmatura morit occubuit
Cal. Martii Anº Domi. 1688, Ætat. suæ 34.

Against S. W. Pillar of the Tower.

The Inhabitants of the Parish of Potterne, in grateful Commemoration of their Pious Benefactors, Set up this Tablet in their Church the 31 May, 1731.

David Scurlock, Vicar.
Henry Kent, } Ch.-wardens.
Wm. Read, }

The Sum of Sixty Pounds was Given by several unknown hands, about the year 1670, the interest of it to be applied to the use of the Poor of Potterne for ever.

Walter Grubbe, Esq. of this Parish, Bequeathed by his last Will and Testament, in the Month of Sept. 1715, the Interest of Ten Pounds to the Poor of Potterne for ever.

Mrs. Thomazin Grubbe, Likewise of this Parish, Bequeathed by her last Will and Testament, the Sum of Fifty Pounds, to buy a Carpet for the Communion Table, and a Pulpit Cloth, both of Crimson Velvet; and also the Interest of another and further Sum of Fifty Pounds to the Poor of Potterne, for Ever.

Mr. Thomas Flower, a Native of this Parish, Bequeathed, by his last Will and Testament, in the year 1723, the Sum of Five Hundred Pounds, Viz. Three Hundred Pounds, part thereof to provide Plate for the Communion Service, and to Erect an Organ in the Church, and the Interest of the Remaining two Hundred Pounds for the Perpetual Maintenance of an Organist in the Parish of Potterne.

William Grubbe, Esq. of the Parish of Laurence Jewry, London, In his life time, Ceiled the Church, Erected a Beautiful New Altar Piece in the Chancel, and set up the King's Arms, handsomely Carved and Gilded, at his own proper Cost and Charge; And also bequeathed by his last Will and Testament, in the month of August, 1729, the Interest of One Hundred Pounds to the Poor of this Parish for ever.

Robert Pitt, Gent. of this Parish, Bequeathed by last Will and Testament, in March, 1784, the Interest of Five Hundred Pounds to the Poor for Ever.

Against north-west Pillar of the Tower.

The Inhabitants of the Parish of Potterne, in grateful Commemoration of their Pious Benefactors, Set up this Tablet in their Church, the 9th of May, 1812.

George Edmondstone, Vicar.
John Tanner, Esq. } Ch.-wardens.
James White, }

John Shorter, Gent. of the Tything of Worton, Died 22 April, 1797, and by his last Will Gave the Interest of One Hundred Pounds to be laid out in Bread, and Given to the Poor of the same Tything of Worton, Yearly, for Ever

Henry Kent, D. D. of Whistley House, in this Parish, who Died 27 Decem. 1799, Gave by Will to the Vicar and Churchwardens of Potterne two Hundred Pounds, to be by them placed out at Interest, such Interest to be applied by them in the purchase of Cloth for outer Garments, for the use of such Five of the Oldest and Poorest Men, and of such Five of the Oldest and Poorest Women of the said Parish of Pottern, who should not actually reside in any Work-House, Poor-House, or Alms-House within the said Parish.

The Church consists of Chancel, Nave, North and South Transepts.

WEST LAVINGTON.

On Monuments by the South Wall of Chancel.

In Memoriam
Margaritæ, quæ nupta Gulielmo Hunt,
Armigero, de Lavington Episcopi, tertio Iduum
Augusti, Anno Dom̄ MDCCXXIX.
Morte obijt repentinâ quarto Iduum Septembris,
Anno Dom̄ MDCCXXXI, ejusq; Ætatis 34.
Matrona hæcce perdigna, ita animum
instituit, ut decorum sinceræ Pietatis exemplum,
Virtutis, Charitatis, & Conjugalis in Verum,
affectus, fui vicissim quam amantissimum, juxta
exhibuerit, ac proinde morum venustate, ita
enituit, ut in Superiores Loco et Dignitate
Obsequium et Reverentiam in Equales summam
Benignitatem et Candorem in Inferiores,
deniq. cujuscunq. sortis Misericordiam et
Urbanitatem usq. præbuerit.
Hisce Virtutibus insignita in propinquo
jacet inhumata sub lapide sepulchrali, plurimum
quidem lugenda, non solum marito,
admodum luctuoso verum etiam omnibus
quorum consuetudine uti contigit.
Qui legis hæc operæ pretium erit,
tam illustre pietatis exemplum æmulari;
cum Vita hæc sit adeo caduca et incerta,
Mors autem Omnibus inevitabilis,
Ne quosquam leteat quâ stirpe exemplar,
hoc spectabile esset oriundum.
En! perquam erat amabilis Filia Thomæ
Smith, de Shaw, Armigeri,
Suscepta, ex Elizebetha, dilecta sua uxore,
utrisq. Vitâ defunctis, qui dum viverent
præluxerunt Vitâ cunctis imitandâ, et sepulti
jaceut in Ecclesia parochiali de Melksham,

ubi nitidum Monimentum in Piam eorum Memoriam Erectum extat.

Hoc Monimentum, ut gratum animum expleret, positum est Impensis Mariti, Anno Salutis Humanæ 1732.

Arms—Quarterly, first and fourth azure, on a bend, or, two water bougets of the same between three leopards' heads caboshed, gules; second and third vert, on a chevron, argent, three cross-crosslets, sable, between three demi-lions rampant: impaling, gules, on a chevron, argent, three leopards' heads caboshed, sable, between three cinquefoils of the second.

In Memoriam
Thomæ Hunt, de Lavington Episcopi, Armigeri,
Necnon Mariæ, dilectissimæ conjugis,
Quorum alter inter alias quam plurimus
et eximias Animi, dotes quibus innotuit,
ad sublevandas Miserorum calamitates,
præ Cæteris summopere se constulit.
Altera in hoc unum penè incubuit, ut
esset virtutum quarumcunq. quæ Vitam
Christianam maxime exornavit, tum cultrix,
tum Exemplar vere spectabile.

Uterq. in eodem sepulchro conduntur in hoc Sacrario

Exuviæ etiam Gratiæ Hunt, Matris
prædicti Thomæ, una cum Thoma Hunt,
ejusdem Thomæ Filio infantulo,
in eodem Sacrario separatim conquiescunt,
in spem Beatæ Resuscitationis.

Monimentum hoc pio, studio, et impensis,
Filii Gulielmi Hunt, Armigeri,
Susanna, Sorore, ad idem conserente,
Erectum est, Anno Dom. MDCCXXXII.

Ossa etiam eodemq. Sacrario Annæ Mariæ
Filiæ infantulæ Gulielmi et Annæ
Hunt, de Lavington Episcopi, sepulti sunt.

Etiamq. Reliquiæ Gualteri Grubbe
Hunt, Filii Infantuli ejusdem Gulielmi et
Annæ Hunt, in eodem Sacrario requiescunt.

Reliquiæ Deniq. Gulielmi Hunt, de
Lavington Episcopi, Armigeri, eodem Sacrario
eodemq. sepulchro, una cum Margarita,
Charissima prima sua Uxore, in spe beatæ
Resuscitationis, requiescunt.

Arms—Azure, on a bend or, three leopards' heads caboshed, gules, between two water-bougets, or: impaling vert, on a chevron, argent, three cross-crosslets, sable, between three demi-lions rampant, or.

On Flat Stones in Chancel.

Here lyeth the Body of Grace, the Wife of Wm. Hunt, Gent. who was buried Oct. ye 15, 1670.

Here lyeth the Body of the Rev. Robt. Burnett, LL. B. late Vicar of this Parish, who died Nov. ye 25, 1769, in the 63 year of his Age.

Mrs. Margarita Hunt died the 10th day of Sept. in ye year of our Lord, 1731, and in the 31 year of her Age. She was an exemplary Pattern of Religion, Virtue, Charity, and Conjugal Affection; and as to her Behaviour she was Remarkable; Intreating her superiors with ye greatest Respect, her Equals wth Courtesy, good-nature & Affability, and her meanest Inferiors wth ye utmost Compassion and Civility: for these real virtues, and Personal qualifications, she lies under this Stone interred, much lamented, not only by her mournfull Husband, William Hunt, of this Parish, Esq. but by all that knew her.

Reader, endeavour to follow her Pious Example; this life at best is most uncertain, but Death is sure. This much-lamented Gentlewoman was marryed to her afflicted Husband, ye 11th Day of August, in ye year of our Lord 1729, and Died a Sudden death the 10th Day of September, 1731.

Here lye the Remains of Anna-Maria and Walter-Grubbe Hunt, infant Children of William and Ann Hunt, of Lavington Epi.

Anna-Maria Died the 23rd day of March, 1737, Aged 14 weeks.

Walter died the 20th day of Oct. 1740, Aged 6 months.

Also the Remains of William Hunt, Esq. who, together with his beloved first Wife Margaret, is Interred in the same grave, in hopes of a blessed Resurrection. He died the 10th day of May, 1763, Aged 56 years.

In Memory of Thomas Hunt, of Lavington Episcopi, Esq. and also his beloved Wife, both interred in the same Grave. He died the 16th day of May, 1726, Aged 60 years.

She died the 21 Day of July, 1726, Aged 65 years.

Brass Plates in the Floor of the Chancel.

Here lyeth the Body of Thomas White, Gent. late of this Parish, who departed this life the 2d day of December, 1675, And in the 46th year of his Age.

Arms—A fess between three garbs.

Here Lyeth the Body of John White, Gent. late of this Parish, who Departed this life the 25th day of November, 1693, and in the 25 year of his Age.

Arms—As before.

Mr. Norreys Street, Surgeon, died April 3rd, 1760, Aged 33.

Mrs. Anne Street, Widow, died Dec. 31, 1762, Aged 53.

Here lyeth the Body of Bartholomew Shorthose, Vicar, who deceased the 27th of Jan. Ano 1664.

On brass plates against the S. side of a low altar-tomb of free-stone, N. side of the Nave.

Depositum Johannis Marten, nuper Vicarii hujus Ecclesiæ, qui Obijt Sept. 16, Anno Dom̄ 1718, et hic requiescit, in spem beatæ Resurrectionis.

Hic unacum conjuge jacet Maria, Uxor Johannis Marten, hujus Ecclesiæ nuper Pastoris; Piam efflavit animam Die Maij 26, Anno { Dom. 1722, Ætatis 72.

Against South side of the Nave.

To the Memory of Jane,
2d Wife of the Rev. J. Williams.
She died August 26, 1790,
Aged 24 years.

Ah, Jana! Uxorem optima,
Mulierum amantissima,
Vale!

On a Flat Stone in Nave.

Underneath are laid the Remains of Jane, 2d Wife of the Rev. J. Williams, with her two Infant Sons. She died August 26, 1790, Aged 24 years.

In the same Vault is deposited Elizabeth, Wife of William Sainsbury, Surgeon. She died Dec. 7th, 1791, Aged 30.

Also John Sainsbury, Sen. who died April 16th, 1793, Aged 66.

Also Jane, Relict of the above John Sainsbury. She died August 19th, 1808, Aged.77.

On a Brass Plate.

In certain hope and expectation of a Blessed Resurrection, Resteth here the Body of Christopher Merewether, who Departed this Life the ninth day of Feb. in the year of our Lord One Thousand Six Hundred and Sixty.

Monuments in N. Transept.

To the Memory of John Smith, Gent. who died April 9th, 1786, Aged 71 years.

Also Allen, his Wife, Died 30th Sept. 1803, Aged 80 years.

Near this Spot
are deposited the Remains of
Miss Sarah Hewett,
late of Windsor, in the County of Berks.
who Departed this life at Clifton,
January the 9th, 1821, Aged 50 years.

The gentle Heart, entombed beneath,
E'er it was chill'd by Icy Death,
Glow'd with the warmth to Virtue dear,
Was open, generous, and sincere,
Griev'd at the tear on Misery's cheek,
In sympathy devoutly meek,
Which ne'er the timid sufferer task'd
By coldly waiting to be ask'd,
In silence the Relief was given,
And chronicled alone in Heav'n,
Whose watchful Angels set apart
The hallow'd Incense of the Heart.

To perpetuate the Memorial
of an unbroken Friendship
of Forty years duration,
This Tablet is erected
by her affectionate and grateful Relative,
Thomas Smith.

East Wall N. Transept.

In Memory of Sarah Amor, (Daughter of John Amor, late of Patney, in the County of Wilts. Gent. deceased, by Mary, his Wife, also Deceased) who died the 18th July, 1753, Aged 29 years.

Jane, (Wife of Wm. Amor, of Littleton Pannell, within this Parish, Gent.) who died the 20th 1772, Aged 60 years.

The Above Named William Amor, who Died the 28 Feb. 1777, Aged 55 years.

Robert Amor, Gent. (Nephew of the Above Named Wm. Amor) who died the 12 May, 1781, Aged 22 years.

And of William Amor, Gent. (another Nephew of the Above Named William Amor) who died the 8 Jan. 1783, Aged 20 years.

Brass Plate in the Floor of N. Transept.

Here lyeth the Body of
Peter Anderton, Gent.
late of this Parish, who
departed this life April
the 23,
Anno { Dom. 1699, Ætat. 67.

Flat Stones.

William Smith, of Fidington, in the Parish of West Lavington. He died Sept. the ... 17.. Aged 45 years.

And of John Smith, his Son, who died April the 9, 1756, Aged 71.

Here Lyeth ye Body of Mary, Wife of Thomas Newman, who died the 18 Day of Jan. 1773, Aged 60 years.

In Memory of Mary, Wife of William Smith, who died June ye 8th, 1756, Aged 70 years.

On a Mon. S. Wall of S. Chancel

Beneath are Deposited the Remains of Thomas à Becket, Esq. Lineal Descendant from the Ancient Family of the Beckets, of Littleton Pannell, in the County of Wilts. and also of Phillippa, his Wife, Youngest Daughter of George Tanner, Esq. of Penleigh, in the same County. She died 18 December, 1791. He died 1st of Feb. 1792.

Arms—Or, a chevron between three lions' heads, erased.

On Flat Stones in Chancel.

Here lyeth the Body of William Beckett, Gent. who departed this life the 9th day of Feb. 1677, Aged 3 years 8 months.

Here lyeth the Body of Margaret Beckett, Wife of William Beckett, of Littleton Pannell, in this Parish, Gent. She was one of the Daughters of John Trowe, of the City of Oxford, Gent. and dyed the 3rd day of June, 1738, Aged 43 years, leaving two Sons, Thos. & William.

Also here lie the Remains of William Beckett, of Littleton Pannell, aforesaid, Gent. who, together with his beloved Wife Margaret, is Interred in the same Grave, who died Nov. ye 17th, 1754, Aged 59.

Sub hoc marmore jacet Sepultus
Johannes Harvest, filius et hæres
Johannis Harvest, de Potterne,
in Comitatu Wilton. Generos.
qui dum vixit pietate in Deum,
honore in Regem, obsequio in parentes,
Charitate in omnes, aliisq. virtutibus
laudandis cæteros juvenis superavit,
et a Christo divinitus instinctus,
predijs terrenis posthabitis imo et
fastiditis præmia celœtia præoptavit,
quibus ut maturnis frueretur, e
vita migravit Dec. 3° Anno Ætat.
22 ineunte, Anno Domini 1671.

Exhaustis oculis omne extendatur in ævum,
Ut Luctus Lachrymas Marmora mœsta dabuerit.

On Flat Stones in S. Aisle.

Hic situs est illibatus cinis
Saræ Harvest, filiæ natu
minoris Johannes Harvest,
de Potterne, in Comitatu
Wiltoñ Generosi, quæ
cum annis viginti-tribus virgineà
egerit vitam, et jam matura viro
nulli nisi Christo suo sponso,
nupsit et in thalamum ejus cœlestem,
accepta thecam hanc corpoream
hic reconditam ad consummationem
hujus sæculi reliquit, ut tempore
messis.
Hos cineros niveos Christo mandante recondat
Horrea messores in sua grana tua,
Animam expiravit
Anno Domini 1672.

Wiłłus Yorke hic situs est.

Arms—A saltire, in chief a crescent and label, over all, on an escutcheon, a cross pattée.

Anna Yorke hic sita est.

Arms—A saltire, in chief a crescent: impaling a fess ermine, between three horses passant.

Here lyeth the Body of Francis Meriweather, Gent. who dyed the 22 day of March, 1669.

On a Brass Plate.

Heare Lyeth ye Body of Mrs. Katharine Poulgraine, Wife of Roger Poulgraine, Gent. who departed this life the 16 day of July, Anno Dom̄ 1712, Aged 45 years.

Here Lyeth the Body of Praxey Meriweather, who died the 16th Day of July, 1677.

Mon. West End of Nave.

In Memory of the Rev. Mr. John Buchanan, Minister of this Parish, who died March ye 2d, A.D. 1769.

Mon. N. side of S. Aisle.

Huic Juxta sita sunt corpora
Annæ Yorke, relictæ Wiłłi Yorke,
nuper de Bassetts Downe,
generosi, filiæ Simonis Stampe,
Armigeri, quæ quidem Anna peperit
eidem Wiłło quatuor filios, Viz.
Wiłłum, Edwardum, Carolum, et Carolum,
totidemq. filias, Viz.
Annam, Janam, Mariam, et Susannam,
et cum viro suo felicem prolongavit
vitam per annos 51 et amplius, ac
tandem, ætatis 79 annorum, in
gloriam cœlestis regni translata
est sexto die Septembris, An°
Dni 1661.

Wiłłi Yorke, generosi, filij
unigeniti Wiłłi Yorke, Armigeri,
et Elizabethæ Uxoris, ejus filiæ,
et Cohæredis Wiłłi Bower, nup.
de Lavington Epi. Armigeri:
Juvenis admodum serenæ
indolis ac præter æquæ vos suos

multum literati qui in prima
juventute sua nondum duodecem
annorum, duodecimo die Augusti,
Anno Dom. 1659, ex hac luce
migravit.
Hunc tantus superis ostendunt fata necvstra
esse sinunt
Resurgemus.

Arms— . . . . A saltire . . . . crescent, gules; impaling, a fess, ermine, between three horses passant.

2d— . . . a saltire . . . charged with an escutcheon, surcharged with a cross-pattée, in chief a crescent and label, gules.

On a white marble Monument in Danvers' Chapel.

Here lyeth the Body of Henry Danvers, Esq. Son and Heire apparant of Sir John Danvers, Knt. by Dame Elizabeth, Grandchild and heire of Sir John Dauntesey, Kt. & Lord of this Place, and he was Nephew & heire of Henry Danvers, Baron of Dauntesey, Earle of Danby, one of his Maties privie Councell, & Knight of the Most noble order of the Garter. As he was of an auncient & noble Family, so of a Personage comely and beautifull, but of a singular Piety, Understanding, Sobriety, and Sweetness of Disposition, Whereby he was growne up to be the great Expectation of his Country, the hope & support of his Family, & the Comfort & delight of all his Relations and friendes, but was snatched from them all, to their inexpressible griefe, and irreparable losse, Dying Novemb. 19th: 1654, in the 21 yeare of his Age, & on the 2d of Decemb. following, (the day of his birth) was here (at the feet of his Deare Mother) buryed. He gave all of his great estate in his power unto his Sister Ann Danvers, afterwards married to Sir Henry Lee, of Ditchley, in the County of Oxford, Baronet, by whom she had two Daughters, Eleanora and Ann. The Lady Eleanora, now Wife of James Lord Norreys, Baron of Rycott, & the Lady Ann Lee, having in their Infancy lost both their Parents, their Father dying before the birth of the Younger, & their Mother in Childbed of her, no sooner understood that they were Heires, not only of their Mother's estate, but also thereby of his their Uncle's great Kindnesse, in a thankefull acknowledgmt thereof, & to his memory and honor have at their joynt Charge erected this Monument.

Lector, quisquis es, paucis accipe quod
Multis potuit tentari, nullis eloqui
Domina Elizabetha,
Johannis Dantesey, Equitis,
hujus latifundij quondam possessioris,
neptis, et ex asse hæres Johannis Danvers,
Equitis (cui filium unicum filias tres,
Charissima amoris pignora Reliquit)
Conjux Lætissima fœmina,
Summa in cœleste nume pietate,
in Conjugem affectu maximo et reverentia,
in suavissimos liberos,
Etopth. incredibili,
in omnes singulari comitate, et candore prædita;
Constantiæ simul et modestiæ
Exemplar unicum; virtutum omnium archivum,
et ærarivm; cui nobile genus conjugium
progenies, et reliqua
Fortunæ bona inter ultima numeranda,
nono Julij, Ano Æræ Christianæ 1636,
Ætatis suo (hev nimis contractæ!) 31,
inter bonorum omnium (qui norunt)
preces et vota, inter acerbos suorum planctus,
et eiulatus
infantaria, piisimam animam deo suo efflavit,
Digna longiori fato, nisi quod cœlo dignior.
Cujus fœlicissimæ memoriæ
maritus charissimus cenotaphium hoc, licet longe
vertuit impar, affectus tamen sui et mœroris
æternum monumentum
Extruxit, posuit, sacravit.

Junij, 1..3, diuturna et .... trienni ... egritudine Fract9 invicto Tame ani ... E vivis decessit, Maria ac Dulcia fil: Amantissima pietatis ergo Monumentum hoc posuere ... es tu viator hoc tristi exemplo comotus Fata etiam Animo perpendens Quam nihil hic firmum ac stabile discas Rerv. omn. fore aliquando vicessitudinem spiritis rebus mortalim deu .. immorta .. Timere vale, et pijs tuis precibus, defunctam Deo Commenda.

Lord Churchill Lord of the Manor.

MARKET LAVINGTON.

On a Flat Stone in Chancel.

John Sainsbury, Gent. died the 6th of April, 1735,
Aged 47.
Mary, his Wife, died the 13th of June, 1731,
Aged 47.
John, their Son, died December the 5, 1736,
Aged 20.
To whose Memory this is dedicated by Samuel Sainsbury, Jun.

Arms—Within a border ingrailed, three lozenges, in bend.

On Monuments against North Wall of Chancel.

Near this Place are deposited the Remains of Wm. Merewether, Jun. Gent. (late of Easterton) who died
Dec. 31, 1783, Aged 35 years.
Also Jane, Wife of Wm. Merewether, Sen. Gent. who died March 4th, 1784, Aged 57 years.
Also Wm. Merewether, Gent. who died June 3, 1785,
Aged 66 years.

Also Francis Merewether, Gent. Son of William and Jane Merewether, who died Feb. 19, 1792, in the 35 year of his Age.

Near this Place lye the Bodies of 4 Children, Sons & Daughters of John and Jane Axford, Viz.
John Died 22 Nov. 1750, Aged 1 year & 9 months.
Jane died 17 Jan. 1752, Aged 3 Days.
Francis died 16 July, 1757, Aged 4 years.
Ann Died Nov. the 1st, 1758, Aged 2 years.
Also Jane, Wife of John Axford, Died 3 Nov. 1758, Aged 43 years.
And also near this Place lyeth the Body of John Axford, of Eastcott, Gent. who Departed this life Feb. 8, 1784, Aged 62 years.
Also Mrs. Trickey, Wife of the Rev. Mr. Trickey, who died Sept. the 27, 1798, Aged 52 years.

Thomas Sainsbury, Esq. Son of Samuel and Elizabeth Sainsbury, Born the 25 of Decemb. 1730, died 16 May, 1795. Chosen Alderman of the Ward of Billingsgate in the year 1778, Sheriff of London and Middlesex, September, 1780, and Lord Mayor of London, 1786.

To this shrine, traveller, attentive turn,
And pause awhile o'er Sainsbury's urn,
Of him who's now an inmate of the skies,
Beneath this tomb all that was mortal lies:
In honour firm, and faithful to his trust,
In every station moral, wise, and just;
A Magistrate observant of the laws;
A Briton, ardent in his Country's cause;
A tender Husband, Father, Brother, Friend,
Esteem'd through life, Lamented in his end:
Such Sainsbury was; now, 'midst angelic lays,
He wants no tribute of vain mortal praise,
Yet from oblivion such rare worth to claim
This honest marble here records his name:
Here shall his RELATIVES their visits pay,
And with their tears embalm his honoured clay,
And his example shall instruct our youth
To walk the paths of Virtue and of truth.

Near this Place Lieth the Body of Samuel Sainsbury, of this Town, Gent. who Departed this Life 14 Oct. 1748, Aged 56 years.
Elizabeth, his Wife, who Departed this life 12 July, 1765, Aged 66 years.
And Samuel Sainsbury, Gent. their Eldest Son, who Departed this life 29 August, 1768, Aged 50 years.

Arms—Azure, a bend of loz. within a border ingrailed or; impaling argent, on a pale, sable, three crescents argent.

Here lieth the Body of William Sainsbury, Gent. who Departed this life March ye 14, 1704, Aged 49.
Also here lies the Body of Grace, his Wife, who Departed this Life Jan. 23, 1726, Aged 66.

Ano Dni	In this Chancel are Interred
1665, Dec. 25,	John Merewether, Son of John, de Cheverel Magna, buried there Jan. 2d, 1620.
1665 May 22,	And Mary his Wife & Several of their Children, Viz.
1677, Feb. 26,	John their eldest Son,
1645, Oct. 26,	Thomas, their Younger Son.
1653, Feb. 9,	Grace, } wife of { Wm. Shergoll, / Ann, } wife of { Edmond Felkes.
1672, Mar. 8.	Jenevera, successively Wife of
1656, Oct 3,	Christopher Merewether, de Wotton, John Yerbury, of Trowbridge, Gent. Eliz. their Youngest Daughter.
1688, Nov. 14,	Eliz. Wife of Francis, yr second Son, and Grand Children, viz.
1693, Mar. 12,	John, the Eldest Son of Francis.
1689, Oct. 29,	Joan, his Sister, wife of Phil. Planck. Christopher, eldest son of Christopher.
1663, Aug. 8,	Ann, 2d Dau. of John Yerbury.
1679, Dec. 12,	Mary, Wife of Wm. Suter.

To whose Memory this is dedicated by Francis Merewether, yr only Surviving Son, Año Salutis 1694, Ætat. suæ 6.

Arms—Or, three martlets, sable, on a chief azure, a sun in full glory, proper.

On Flat Stones in Chancel.

Here Lyeth the Body of Peter Noys, Gent. who was buried Feb. ye 10th, 1737, Aged 88.
Also of Samuel, Son of Samuel Sainsbury, Gent. was Buried August 21, 1742, Aged 34.
And also Mary, Daughter of Henry Chivers Vince, Esq. by Mary, his Wife, who died Oct. ye 7, 1745, Aged 9 Days.
Likewise Mary-Ann, Dau. of Henry Chivers, Vince, Esq. by Ann, his Wife, who died May ye 18, 1764, Aged 10 weeks.

Here lyeth ye Body of Wm. Sainsbury, Gent. who dyed ye 20th of January, Anno 1680.

Remember this, oh! man, that slightly passeth by,
That death will lay thee once
noe doubt as low as I:
It will divide twixt thee
& thy relacions deare,
and twill disjoyne where
union is so neare:
But wouldst thou dye & live,
and live & dye no more,
Then live & dye to Christ,
and live for evermore.

Here
Also lyeth the Body of Mary, his Wife, who died July 28, Anno Dom. 1719, Aged 94.

Thomas Sainsbury, Esq. died May 16, 1795, Aged 63.
Eliza Maria Sainsbury, Relict of the above Thomas Sainsbury, Esq. died Dec. 14th, 1800, Aged 48 years.

Mon. East End of Nave.

Under this Marble are deposited the Remains of Richard Legg, Gent. who died Jan. 14th, 1778, Aged 81 years.

Also of Jane, his Wife, who died April 28th, 1777, Aged 57 years.

Likewise of Nathaniel, their Son, who died March 21, 1773, Aged 26 years.

Also Richard Legg, Eldest Son of the above Richard Legg, and Jane, his Wife, who died August 7, 1800, Aged 57 years.

And Bridget, his Wife, who died Feb. 21, 1810, Aged 57 years.

Arms—Azure, a buck's head caboshed, or.

Here Lyeth ye Body of John Smith, of this Town, Gent. who departed this life ye 16 of May, Anno Dom. 1713, Ætatis suæ 64.

Arms—On a fess between three saltires couped, three fleur-de-lis: impaling, a bend lozengy.

Under the Pew below lie interred the Bodies of the Rev. Thomas Tanner, Clerk, 46 years the diligent, pious, resident Minister of this Parish, who died Decem. 18, A. D. 1718, Aged 78 years.

And of that excellent woman, Mrs. Sarah Tanner, his Wife, Daughter of Joseph Willoughby, of this Town, Gent. who died June 16, A. D. 1711, Aged 63 years.

To the Memory of these his Honor'd Parents, their Eldest Son, Thomas, Bishop of St. Asaph, P. P.

Sacred to the Memory of John Shergold, Gent. who departed this life May 19, 1788, Aged 52.

And Catharine, his Wife, who died July 10th, 1810, Aged 59 years.

Also Eliza Ford died March 22, 1797, Aged 76.

Likewise Joseph Barwell, died January 24, 1792, Aged 46.

Eliza, Wife of Joseph Barwell, died Feb. 2d, 1793, Aged 48.

Arms—Checky, argent and gules, a lion rampant-guardant, or. Impaling argent, on a chevron, gules, three lozenges of the field between three lions' heads erased, gules.

South Wall.

Underneath Rest the Remains of Amram Edwards, who died June the 28th, 1783, Aged 59 years.

Also Ann, his Wife, died August the 2, 1782, Aged 60 years.

Also John, the Son of John and Mary Garratt, who died Sept. 27th, 1785, Aged 2 months.

On Monument at West End of Nave.

Near this Place lieth the Body of Robert Hayward, of this Town, Gent. who Departed this Life the 20th of January, 1726, Aged 78 years.

And also of Sarah, his Wife, who Departed this Life the 6th of July, 1745, Aged 85 years.

Also of Alice, their Daughter, who Departed this Life the 5th of Nov. 1769, Aged 82 years.

Arms—Argent, on a pale, sable, three crescents argent: impaling fretty, or and azure.

Mon. against the North Wall of Nave.

M. S.

Samuelis Coleman, E Coll. Reg. Oxon. Medici, Filij Pauli Coleman, ex hoc agro, unici; Juvenis siquis alius ad medicinã nati adeò annos et operam superavit, a.. sed provectioris virtutis spem optima, Variolarum labes præcidit viii idus Aprilis, Æræ Xtianæ 1683, Ætat. 22.

On Flat Stones in Nave.

Here lye interred John Samwell, Gent. who died Oct. 12, 1715, Aged 58 years;

And Sarah, his Wife, who died April 6, 1716, Aged 64 years;

Also their Children, the Reverend John Samwell, Clerk, who died Sept. 18, 1734, Aged 58 years,

And Thomas Samwell, Gent. who died July 9th, 1751, Aged 69 years,

And Sarah Samwell, who died Jan. 19, 1698, Aged 25 years,

And Lucy, the Wife of John Samwell, Clerk, who died Jan. 30, 174¾, Aged 56 years.

In Memory of John Legg, Son of Richard and Jane Legg, late resident in this town, who departed this Life the 5th of April, 1802.

Also Jane, Sister of the above John Legg, who departed this life the 14th of Nov. 1816.

Here lyeth the Body of Andrew Hill, who Departed this Life ye 26 of Jan. 1726, Aged 75 years.

In Memory of John Fowle, Gent. late of Easterton, who died Sept. 29th, 1781, Aged 70.

And Jane Fowle, his Sister, who died Oct. 20th, Aged 64.

South Wall of South Aisle.

Near this Place are deposited the Remains of John Barter, who died February 2d, 1783, Aged 63 years.

Sacred to the Memory of Francis Draper. Obijt Sep. 26, 1802, Aged 71 years.

Sacred to the Memory of Ann, Wife of the Rev. Joseph Legg, who died June 15, 1796, Aged 33 years.

Also their Daughter Elizabeth, Aged 7 years.

Jos Legg, Jun. died June 3, 1807, Aged 24 years.

Donation Table against the north side of the Nave.

To the Memory
Of the Right Reverend
Thomas Tanner, D. D.
Lord Bishop of St. Asaph,
Who,
From a testimony of Regard
To this his Native Place,
Bequeathed,
In his last Will and Testament,
A Donation of Two Hundred Pounds,
which was applied
In the purchase of an Estate
Situate at Patney, in Wilts.
the Rent of which
to be applied annually on St. Paul's Day
In manner following, (i. e.)

	£.	s.	d.
To the Minister for a Discourse	0	13	4
To buy four Bibles for the use of the Poor	1	0	0
Towards the Education of three poor Child.	1	0	0
To be spent at a Friendly Meeting of the Principal Inhabitants	1	0	0
To the Ringers for two short Peals	0	6	0
To the Sexton and Clerk	0	3	0

The Residue to be given to the Poor by the Vicar, or his Curate.

The Minister,
H. C. Vince, Esq.
J. B. Vince, Esq.
Rev. J. Williams,
J. Roberts, Gent.
Wm. Smith, Gent.
T. K. Willoughby, Gent.
Jas. Slade, Gent.
Wm. Merewether, Gent.
Nov. 22, 1733.

} Surviving Trustees of the above Charity.

Hatchment.

Or, three martlets, sable, on a chief, azure, the sun in full glory, proper. Impaling .... a chevron, ermine, between three escallops, argent.

The Church consists of a Chancel, Nave, North and South Aisles. The Nave is supported on each side by three pointed arches.

The Rev. George Rogers, Vicar.

The Earl of Radnor, Lord of the Manor.

This Tablet
Records the Names and Contributions
Of those well-disposed Individuals
At whose Expence this Church was ceiled, A. D. 1797.

	£.	s.	d.
Rt. Hon. the Earl of Radnor	20	0	0
Rev. John Dobson, Vicar	5	5	0
Rev. J. Williams, Curate	5	5	0
H. C. Vince, Sen. Esq.	5	5	0
W. H. Grubb, Esq.	5	5	0
W. Sainsbury, Esq.	5	5	0
Richard Legg, Gent.	10	10	0
Rev. Joseph Legg	1	1	0
Mr. Shorter	5	5	0
Mr. Woodman, } Churchwardens	5	5	0
Mr. John Garrett, } Churchwardens	5	5	0
Mr. Smith, of Elston	2	2	0
Mr. Edwards	3	3	0
Mr. Lacy	3	3	0
Mr. Jacob Giddings	2	2	0
Mr. Shergold	1	1	0
Mr. Grant	1	1	0
Mr. Gully	1	1	0
	87	4	0

GREAT CHEVERELL.

On Monuments against North Wall of Chancel.

Underneath Lyeth the Body of the Rev. Walter Post, A.M. Late Rector of this Parish, who died May ye 25, 1772, Aged 78 years.

Also the Bodies of Anna Dorothea, and Elizabeth, Wives of the Rev. Walter Post.

Anna Dorothea } died { May 14, 1774, Aged 32 years
Elizabeth } died { Dec. 11, 1761, Aged 112.

Also the Body of Jemima, his Daughter, Wife of John Shergold, Gent. who died Feb. ye 1st, 1771, Aged 36 years.

Also the Bodies of Jemima, Mary, Sarah, & Jemima, Daughters of the said John Shergold, Gent.

Jemima died Decem. ye 24, 1759, Aged 9 months.
Mary Died July ye 12th, 1761, Aged 3 months.
Sarah died Feb. ye 10th, 1771, Aged 7 years.
Jemima died May ye 4th, 1771, Aged 5 weeks.

Sub sedile proxime jacet
Corpus Mariæ, Uxoris
Johan: Hayes, S. T. P.
Hujus Ecclesiæ Rectoris,
Quæ hoc seculo decessit,
(Mœstum sinquens maritum,
Et modo natam lachrymantem)

Conjux Mater pientissima,
Cal. Jun. an. { Redemptionis 1720, Ætat. suæ XL Connubij }
Heu nimium cito nisi spe
Resurrectionis et Ævi
Quo neq; Nubunt neq; Moriuntur,
Pares sint Angelis.

Hic, in sinu Matris suæ reposita, dormit Elizabetha,
Johannis et Mariæ Hayes
Nata Unica,
Obijt 4 Noñ Julij, Anno { Dom. 1726, Ætat. suæ 7. }

In eodem etiam tumulo
repositum est
Quod Mortale fuit
Prædicti Johannis Hayes,
S. T. P. hujus Ecclesiæ nonodecim
Annos Rectoris:
Viri Pietatis eximiæ, probitatis integerrimæ,
et Pastoris Vigilantissimus.
Ob. Cal. Maij,
Anno Redemptionis 1731,
Ætatis 60.

On Flat Stones in Chancel.

Here lyeth the Body of the Rev. Mr. Thomas Aylmer, B. D. formerly Fellow of Corpus Xti College, in Cambridge, late Vicar of Lavington, who died August 23, 1734, Aged 37.

P. M. S.

Revdi Nathanielus Shute, S. T. B. hujus Ecclesiæ Rectoris, Sarisburiensis Præbendarij, Pater, Avus, Proavus, ordini sacerdotali decora alumnis equestri nomine Christophorus patria, Eboracensis provinciam ille suam per annos 31 summa, fide gessit, pietate ornavit, mercedem dein. accepturus. Obijt Feb. 29, A. D. 1711, Æt. 64.

Here alsoe lyeth ye Body of Mrs. Joan Shute, ye Relict of Mr. Nathaniel Shute, who departed this life ye 14th of July, A° Dni 1715, Ætat. suæ 55.

Here lyes the Body of Martha, the only Daughter of N. Shute, Rector, and Joan, his Wife, whose towardly disposition to Piety and vertue rendred her very dear to her Parents. Ob. Apr. 12th, A. D. 1709, & Æt. 12.
Non refert quam diu vixeris, sed quam bene.

On a Monument at the East End of Nave.

In a Vault near this Place are Deposited the Remains of Ann Long, Relict of the late Lewis Long, of Wotton Basset, in this County, Esq. who Departed this life April 13th, 1792, Aged 79.

This Stone is erected as a Tribute of filial Regard to her Memory, which will ever live in the tenderest Affections of her surviving Family.

South Wall.

In Memory of
of Sir James Stonehouse, Bart.
Doctor of Physick,
nearly Sixteen Years Rector of this Parish,
and more than thirty of Little Cheverel.
His principal Rule of Action was,
" All things whatsoever ye would that Men
" Should do to you, do ye also to them."
Mat. vii. 12.

His Heart's desire and Prayer was,
to " grow in Grace, and in the knowledge
" of our Lord and Saviour Jesus Christ."
2 Peter iii. 18.
Reader,
Go, and do Thou Likewise.
He died December the 8th, 1795,
in the 80th year of his Age.

On a Flat Stone in Nave.

Elizabeth, Daughter of William and Margaret Coles, dyed August the 14, 1766, Aged 22 years.

On a Monument in the North Aisle.

Here under lies James Townsend, of this Parish, Gent. who Departed this Life the 12th of July, 1730, in the 76 year of his Age.

He was a Man of great Patience, Stedfast faith, sincere intentions, strictly just to the utmost of his Power, free from vice, a loving Husband, a kind and indulgent Father, a sure Friend, a loss to the Oppressed, and greatly lamented by all that truly knew him.

Also here under lies
Mrs. Katherine Townsend, Relict of James Townsend, Gent. and Daughter of Mr. John Hunt. of Ham, Gent. who Departed this life August ye 30th, 1737, Aged 84.

She was an affectionate Wife, a kind and tender Mother, and much esteemed for her great Piety and Extensive Charity, and whose death is Greatly Lamented by all that knew her, and more especially by the Poor of this Parish.

We grieve, indeed, but grieve for them in vain,
Their death's our loss, to them Immortall gain.

Arms—Azure, a chevron, ermine, between three escallops, argent: impaling azure, a chevron voided between three martlets, argent.

The Church consists of Chancel, Nave, and N. Aisle.

Register commenced 1653.

The Rev. Robert Morris, Rector.

The Manor belongs to the Almshouse of Heytesbury.

LITTLE CHEVERELL.

On Monuments against the North Wall of Nave.

Sacred to the Memory of Mary Alexander, who Departed this life with a truly pious resignation, on the 15 Day of July, 1790, Aged 74 years.

Kind Angels watch this sleeping dust
Till Jesus comes to raise the Just;
Then may she wake with sweet surprise,
And in her Saviour's image rise.

Also to the Memory of Mary Alexander, who Departed this life Jan. 22, 1797, Aged 60 years.

Also to the Memory of John Alexander, who Departed this Life June 25, 1815, Aged 77 years.

Near this Place lyeth the Body of Edward Alexander, who departed this life Jan. ye 25, 1742, Aged 39 years.

Farewell, dear Wife, my life is past,
My love to you so long did last;
But as for me no sorrow take,
But love my Chlldren for my sake.

Also in the same Grave lyeth the Remains of Edward, Son of Edward and Mary Alexander, who Departed this Life May the 25, 1782, Aged 41.

Now here together we doth rest, in hopes to
rise again, Hoping that we shall happy be
With Christ for to remain.

The Lord gave, and the Lord hath taken away,
Blessed be the name of the Lord.

Also 4 Children, 1 Son and 3 Daughters, of Edward & Ann Alexander, died Young.

Flat Stones.

Underneath are deposited the remains of Joshua Taylor, Gent. late of Beckington, Somerset, who died 21st March, 1799, Aged 80 years.

Underneath this Stone lyeth the Body of Thomas Axford, and of Mary, his Wife.

She died 10 June, 1777, Aged 66 years.
He died 3 Jany, 1778, Aged 66.

Also of Thomas, their Son, who died 11th August, 1782, Aged 31.

In Memory of Mary, Daughter of Thomas and Mary Axford, who Departed this life 7 April, 1803, Aged 58 years.

On a Flat Stone in Chancel.

Underneath are Interred the Bodies of Mary, Wife of John Shergold, M. A. Rector of this Church, who died Sept. 6, 1741, Aged 30 years.

And of Mary & Mary, two of their Children, who died Infants.

The Rev. W. Edwards, Rector.

SEEND.

On a Monument against the north Wall of Chancel.

Near this Marble are Interred the Remains of George Husey, B. D. Formerly Fellow of St. John's College, in Cambridge, Chaplain to his Grace the Duke of Somerset, & Rector of Trowbridge, in Wilts, where he died ye 14th of July, 1741, in ye 41 year of his age. Also of George Husey, his only Son, who, having attained to the Age of 19, Died June 6th, 1748, having merited the Esteem of all that knew him by a temper and deportment truly affable and humane. He died unacquainted with a foe, and much lamented by all his Friends.

Mary Husey, the inconsolable Widow, caused this Monument to be erected in the year 1759, to preserve, amongst others, the Memory of a most affectionate Husband, and a very dutiful Son.

Near this Place lyeth the Body of Mary, Wife of the Rev. George Husey, only Daughter of John Houlton, Esq. and Mary, his Wife.

Arms—Ermine, three bars, gules.

On a Monument against the East End of Chancel.

Near this Place lyeth ye Body of John Houlton, of this Parish, Esq. who Departed this life August, 1st. A. D. 1704, Æt. 36:

Whose excellent Nature, and obliging Demeanour, have left him a monument in the hearts of his Friends more durable than this of Marble.

Near this Place also lieth the Body of Mary, the Wife of John Houlton, who Departed this Life the 30th of June, 1730, Æt. 51.

Arms—On a fess wavy, three roundels between three talbots heads erased: impaling, on a fess a lion passant-guardant between three roundels.

South Wall.

Here rest the remains of Vincent John Briscoe, Esq. an eminent West India Merchant, who departed this life April 29th, 1770, Aged 49.

He first married Lady Mary Seymour, only Daughter of Edward, late Duke of Somerset, by whom he left a Son and a Daughter, and by his 2d Wife, Daughter of Mattw Shiffner, Esq. 3 Sons and 1 Daughter.

Indued with a good Understanding, and most amiable Disposition, he exercised the former in discovering, the latter in rewarding, merit.

Uniformly exemplary in all the Duties and Relations

of Life, and particularly eminent in those of his profession, uniting the Christian, the Man of Business, and the Gentleman, he gained general Esteem and Affection.

The Manner of his Death exalted his Character: Patient, and submitting to the Divine Will, He died much lamented as he lived most beloved.

Those nearly connected with him are best able to illustrate his Virtues, but the heart-feeling Sigh, the drooping Tear, and generous Emulations, are the most grateful Tributes to his Memory.

Arms—Argent, three greyhounds, in pale, courant, sable: impaling, azure, a bend sinister between three estoiles in chief, in base an anchor, or.

To the Memory of the Right Honourable Lady Mary Briscoe, only Daughter of Edward, late Duke of Somerset, and Wife of Vincent Briscoe, Esq. of London, who dyed July 21st, 1762, Aged 33 years, leaving two Children; Mary, born the 13th August, 1760, and Joseph Seymour born the 5th Sept. 1761.

This Monument was Erected by her affectionate and afflicted Husband.

Within this sacred Tomb, the last retreat,
The Peaceful Haven of the good and great,
Lyes one, who, rich in every Female Grace,
And Bless'd with ev'ry Honest Art to please,
Through Life's deceitfull path with prudence mov'd,
And found the way to be esteem'd and lov'd.
Oh! had Exalted Virtue a longer Date,
Longer for us to Love and Imitate:
But cease that Wish, taught by this silent urn,
That all is vain, but to admire and Mourn.

Arms—Argent, three greyhounds courant in pale, sable: impaling, gules, two wings conjoined and inverted, or.

On Flat Stones in Chancel.

Here lyeth the Body of John Houlton, Esq. Son of John Houlton, Esq. who died Nov. the 10, 1764, Aged 66 years.

Hoc sub Lapide requiescunt cineres Johannis Houlton, Armigeri, Qui obijt 1 Augusti, Anno Dom. 1704, Ætatis 36.

Hic jacet Corpus Mariæ, Uxoris Johannis Houlton. Quæ Obijt 30 Junij, 1730, Ætatis 51.

Here lieth the Body of Amelia Jane Shomberg, who died Feb. the 9th, 1798, Aged 3 years and 7 months.

Prosper Dugdale, Wife of Thomas Dugdale, of this Parish, Gent. was underneath interred March the 17, 1676, Ætatis LXIIII.

Against South side of the Nave.

Near this Place lie the Bodies of William Tipper, of this Parish, Gent. and of Elizabeth, his Wife.

He dy'd May 28, 1651.
She dyed Oct. 7th, 1660.

Near this Place lie also the Bodies of John Somner, Son of Edward Somner, of this Parish, Gent. and of Mary, his Wife, Daughter of William and Elizabeth Tipper. He dyed December 26th, 1670. She dy'd May 30th, 1666. To them were born 7 Children, Viz. Mary, Jane, Elizabeth, Joan, Edward, Joan, Ann.

Joan	Dy'd	Sept. 5, 1665,	Aged	10 months.
Jane		July 25, 1672,		20 years.
Ann		Nov. 20, 1683,		20 years.
Joan		April 17, 1684,		23 years.
Mary		July 4, 1696,		46 years.

Also near this Place lyeth the Body of Edward Somner, of this Parish, Esq. who Departed this life the 9th day of August, in the year of our { Lord 1710, his Age 53.

Arms—Vert, a fess dancette, ermine.

Near this Place, in a Vault, lie interred the Remains of Robert Usher, who died 4th Jan. 1774, Aged 30 years.

To whose Memory this Monument is Erected.

Also in the same Vault lie interred the Remains of James Usher, who died the 5th of March, 1773, Aged 23 years.

Near this Place lieth the Body of Mary, Wife of Laurence Baker, who Departed this life ye 31 of Jan. 1692.

Also near this Place lieth the Body of Laurence Baker, who died ye 26th of May, 1736.

On Flat Stones in Nave.

Thomas Dugdale, de Seend hesid. Gent. Qui primus ex antiqua ejusdem cognominis familia de Clethero, apud Lancastriensis, in hac Parochia sedem fixit; filius erat Revrendi Christopheri Dugdale, olim de Polshot, et Ecclesiæ ibidem Rectoris.

Cui Christophero, ex fratre, nepos fuit Gulielmus Dugdale, Eques Auratus, de Blythe Hall, in Comitatu Warwicensi, Rei antiquaria peritia, Illustris A quo ortus est Johannes Dugdale, Eques, de Coventry, in dict: com.

Thomas Dugdale Uxorem habuit Elizabetham, Johannis Trimnel, de Earlstoak, in hoc Comitatu Wiltoniensi, Filiam, unde natus est Thomas Dugdale, Gen. Qui pater fuit Thomæ Dugdale, Civis Londinensis.

Thomas Dugdale, senior, sepulchro conditus est Aprilis 3, Anno Dom̄ 1669, Ætatis 85.

Elizabetha, Uxor, Aprilis 26, 1664, Ætat. 70.

Ann, the first Wife of Thomas Dugdale, of the City of London, Sole Daughter of Mr. Jacob Selby, of Bradford, was Underneath interred Dec. 5, 1682, Æt. 23. Also the Son of the said Thomas and Ann Dugdale, was interred Dec. 1682, Æt. 30 Days.

Arms—A cross moline, in chief a roundel.

Here lyeth the Body of Ann Somner, Daughter of John Somner, Gent. and Mary, his Wife, who Departed this Life the 20th of Nov. Añ Dom̃ 1683, Ætatis suæ 20.

Also the Body of Joan Somner, her Sister, who departed this life the 17th of April, Añ 1684, Ætatis suæ 23.

Beneath this Marble Stone are lodged here
Two Virgin Sisters, to each other dear;
Whose race was short, whose glase was quickly run,
Death cropt those flowers by the Morning Sun,
That was the time by Heaven judged best
To send for them from trouble unto rest:
Weep not overmuch, let this abate your sorrow,
When th: bridegroome came their oyle was not to borrow
Their lamps were trim'd, themselves were ready drest,
When they were called to the Nuptiall feast.
Why fear wee death, which cureth each disease,
And of much grief and trouble doth us ease?
Other misfortunes often comes to grieve us,
Death strikes but once, & that stroke doth relieve us.

Here lye the Remains of her Grace, Mary, Dutchess Dowager of Somerset, Daughter and Sole Heiress of Daniel Webb, of Monkton Farley, in the County of Wilts. Esq. and likewise sole Heiress to her Uncle Edward Somner, of this place, Esq. who Departed this Life Feb. 1st, 1768, Aged 70.

Here also lyeth Elizabeth Webb, her Grace's Mother, who Departed this life Oct. 2nd, 1725, Aged 72.

Arms—Quarterly, first and fourth, on a pile three lions passant guardant between six fleur-de-lis; second and third, two wings conjoined and inverted: over all, on an escutcheon, a fess, dancette.

Here lyeth the Body of John Somner, Gent. who Departed this life the 26 Day of Decem. An° 1670, Ætatis 48.

Also Here lyeth the Body of Joane Somner, (Daughter of the said John Somner, and Mary, his Wife,) who Departed this Life the 5th Day of Septtember, An° 1656, Aged 10 months.

Arms—A fess dancette, ermine.

On a Brass Plate.

The Right Honble Lady Mary Briscoe, Ob. July 21, 1762, Aged 33.

Here lyeth the Body of Jane Somner, (Daughter of John Somner, Gent. and Mary, his Wife.) She Departed this life the 25th Day of July, 1672, Ætatis suæ 20.

Virgins, when you your purest beauties see,
Thinke them but tennants to Mortalitie;
Thers noe content on earth, joyes soon are fled,
Healthfull to day we live, to-morrow dead;
I was as you are now, young, faire, and cleare,
And you shall once be as you see me here.

Underneath lyeth Interred the Body of Mrs. Philippa Jervis, of this Place, Widow. She was Baptized March ye 11, 1659, and died March ye 11, 1735.

On a Monument in the North Aisle.

Near this Place lie Interred the Remains of Catharine Price, Wife of the Rev. Robert Price, L. L. D. Prebendary of Durham, Canon Residentiary of Sarum, and Vicar of this Parish, who Departed this Life the 11th Day of Feb. 1795, in the 31 year of her Age.

Arms—Gules, a lion rampant, argent, a crescent of the same for difference: impaling argent, a chevron, gules, between three boars' heads, couped, sable.

On Monuments by N. Wall of N. Aisle.

Near this Place is Interred the Body of Wm. Somner, of this Parish, Senior, who Departed this Life the 15th of April, in the year of our Lord God 1654.

Also the Body of Elinor, his Wife, who Departed this Life the 22 of Dec. in ye yere of our Lord 1653.

Ann, (the Wife of Henry Gowin,) their Daughter. Shee Departed this life the 12 of Feb. Anno Dom. 1650.

Near this Place also lyeth the Body of Wm. Somner, (Groser) their 3rd Son, who departed this life the 10th Day of March, Anno Dom. 1681.

Also the Body of Elizabeth, his Wife, who departed this life the 13th day of July, in the Year of our Lord 1687.

To the Memory of Thomas Dugdale, second of that name, in this Parish of Seend, Gentleman, who lyeth underneath interred.

And of Prosper, his Virtuous, only, & Beloved Wife, Daughter and Heire of the Learned and Pious Mr. John Audry, of Melksham, Minister of the Gospel, & Katharine, his Wife, Daughter of Wm. Tipper, of this Parish, Gentleman. The said Thomas and Prosper had Issue five sons and five Daughters. Thomas Dugdale was Interred the 16th of Feb. 1684, Ætat. 54. Prosper Dugdale was Interred (Entering into the Chancel) the 17 of March, 1676, Ætat. 44.

The Memory of the Just is Blessed,
But the name of the wicked shall rott. Prov. chap. 10th, v.7.

Arms—Argent, a cross moline, gules, in chief a torteaux: impaling argent, on a bend, azure, three cinquefoils, or.

Brass Plate in N. Wall of N. Aisle.

Here ly the Bodys of Mrs. Florence Deverell, wife of Richard Deverell, Gent. who Departed this life the 2d Day of January, Anno Dom. 1699.

And Mrs. Frances Cross, who departed this life the 1st day of February, Anno Domini 1701.

Near this Place lyeth the Body of Richard Deverell, Son of Mr. Richard Deverell, and Florence his Wife. He Departed this Life the 13th of September, 1690, Æt. 11 weeks.

Also the Body of John, their Son, who Departed this life ye 29 day of March, 1694, Æt. 2 years and 18 weeks.

On a Monument in S. Aisle.

Near this Place are deposited the Remains of Wadham Locke, late of Devizes, in this County, who departed this life 28 of June, 1799, Aged 53 years.

This Stone was Erected with filial Respect
by his only Son, to perpetuate the Memory
of an Affectionate Husband,
a good Father, and a sincere Friend.

Arms—1st, 3d, and 5th, azure, a dove rising . . . ; 2d, or, a crescent argent; 4th and 6th, or: impaling, arg. a canton sable.
Crest—A dove, close, holding a padlock in its beak.

On a brass plate east end of S. Aisle.

Here lie interred Ambrose Awdry. Ob. the 14 of May, 1766, Æt. 73;

And Jane Awdry, his Wife. Ob. the 22 of August, 1769, Æt. 78.

Also Elizabeth Awdry, their Grand Daughter. Ob. the 7 of April, 1778, Æt. 8.

Flat Stones.

Under this Stone lyeth the Body of Mr. Phineas James Brown, who Departed this life June the 6, 1781, Aged 54 years.

Also of Lydia, the Wife of Phineas James Brown, who died Dec. 20th, 1791, Aged 67 years.

Underneath lieth interred Mrs. Jane Hicks, who died Jan. 10th, 1787, Aged 66.

Also Mr. Jeffry Hicks, her Husband, and 3 of their Children, namely, Jane, John, and Thomas.

Against the Gallery.

BENEFACTIONS.

Given by William Tipper, Esq. by Will, dated 1651, bequeathed to the Poor of this Parish (not receiving Alms) for ever, the clear yearly Rent and Profits of a Close of Pasture Land, situate in this Parish, Commonly called West field, containing by Estimation five acres (more or less) to be distributed in Coats or Waistcoats, on the 21 Day of December, yearly, at the discretion of the Chapelwardens and Overseers of the Poor of this Parish.

Mr. Daniel Jones (Gent.) of this Parish, Gave by his last Will the Sum of Five Pounds Yearly, Chargeable for ever on his Freehold Estate, situated at Poulshot, in this County. The Sum of two Pounds to be equally divided on Christmas Day between Four Singers who constantly attend the Chapel, and are the most deserving. The Sum of two Pounds to be applied towards the Education of the Children at the Sunday School in Seend: And the Sum of one Pound to be also given amongst Eight of the Children attending such School, at the direction of the Minister and Chapelwardens. Dated the 2d Day of March, 1808.

This Gallery and Side Aisle were
erected in the year 1726.
Bohun Fox, Vicar,
Wm. Rawlings, & Daniel Somner,
Chapelwardens.

Hatchments in the Nave.

1.

Quarterly, first and fourth or, on a pile, gules, three lions passant guardant or, between six fleur-de-lis, azure; second and third gules, two wings conjoined and inverted, or.

2.

First, per fess, or and argent, on a pile, gules, three lions passant guardant, or, between six fleur-de-lis, azure, in base, argent, three demi-lions, rampant, gules; second, per fess, gules, two wings conjoined and inverted or, in base per bend, argent and gules, in bend three roses counter-changed; third, per fess, vair, argent, and azure, in base argent, on a bend, gules, three leopards' heads caboshed, or. In the fess point an escutcheon azure *or* sable, charged with a fretty, or.

3.

Argent, a bend cottized azure, three cinquefoils, or: impaling, the same.

4.

First, argent, a chevron between three garbs, sable, in chief a crescent for difference, gules; second sable, two bars ermine, in chief three cross-pattée, or; third, argent, the sun in full glory, gules, in chief a crescent, sable.

On the left side of this shield is an escutcheon, bearing on the sinister side the third quartering of the above, with the impaling of the second; on the dexter side the first quartering, impaling of the second.

On a Free Tomb Stone.

Sacred to the Memory of the Hon[ble] and Rev. Edward Seymour, M. A. Rector of Upton Lovell, in this County, and only Surviving Son of the Right Hon[ble] Lord Wm. Seymour. He Departed this life April 22d, 1820, Aged 52 years, Greatly Respected and Deeply Lamented by his numerous Friends, and by all Ranks in this Parish, to which he manifested the warmest attachment.

Arms—Somerset.

The Chapel consists of a Chancel, Nave, North and South Aisles. The Nave is supported on each side by four pointed arches, over which are as many Gothic windows.

The Rev. J. Smith, Vicar.

Wm. Long, Esq. Lord of the Manor.

POULSHOT.

On a small Monument against North Wall of Chancel.

Near this Place lyeth the Body of Mr. Daniel Bolwell, who died the 23rd Day of December, in the year of our Lord 1763, Aged 72 years.

On a wood tablet.

An Extract
from the Will of the Rev. Benjamin
Blayney, D. D late Rector of this Parish,
and Regius Professor of Hebrew in the
University of Oxford, bearing Date
the 22nd Day of November, 1800 :

"I also give, will, and desire, that my Executors do settle, and secure out of the Produce of my personal Estate, in such manner as they legally may, unto the Rector of Poulshot, in the County of Wilts, who shall succeed me in the said Living, and to the Vicars of the Parishes of Pottern and Melksham, in the said County, who shall be incumbents at the time of my Decease, and to their Successors, the Rector and Vicars of the said Parishes for the time being, for ever, One Annuity, or yearly Sum of Twelve Pounds, to be paid yearly towards the Support of the Charity School in the said Parish of Poulshot (hitherto maintained by voluntary annual Subscriptions of my Self and others, who, I trust, will not discontinue their benevolent aid) and to be applied at the Direction of the Rector of the said Parish of Poulshot, to whom I earnestly recommend the Patronage of the said School, and entreat him to superintend further, and promote the same, as I have endeavoured to do, for the Glory of God and the Benefit of the Parish."

On a Flat Stone.

Beneath are Deposited the Remains of the Rev. Richard Sanderson, A. B. Rector of this Parish, who died 28th Dec. 1782, Aged 43 years.

Here also are interred the Remains of Mary, Wife of the Rev. Richard Sanderson, who Died 23d March, 1795, Aged 61 years.

On Brass Plates.

To the Memory of Edward Palmer, Gent. who died 4th Nov. 1739, Aged 70 years.

And of Barbara, his Wife, who died 3 Octor, 1743, Aged 71 years.

Samuel White, the Younger, Gent. Departed this Life January 24th, Anno Domini 1632, Ætatis suæ 24.

Who so reflects his eye upon this Stone,
May here behold the Monument of One
Whose life to Mortalls was a great delight,
And his Death precious in his Maker's Sight;
For bee this spoken to his endlesse Fame,
Hee was as white in vertues as in Name;
His Actions was so just, so square, so even,
That hee was not so fit for Earth as Heaven:
Then for his Death let us noe more bee sorry,
Since now hee raigneth in immortall Glory,

On a Flat Stone in Nave.

Underneath this Stone lyeth the
Bodys hereafter mentioned :
John May, Sen. who Dyed
Sept. ye 19th, 1719, Aged 68 years.
Also Ann, his Wife, who Dyed
April ye 23d, 1724, Aged 67 years.
Also William, Son of William
May, of Worton, who Dyed
May ye 11th, 1726, Aged 2 years.
Also John May, Jun. who Dyed
Sept. ye 11th, 1727, Aged 33 years.
Ann, Wife of Mr. John Sloper,
Sen. Dyed Oct. ye 3d, 1742,
Aged 46 years.

On a wood tablet in the N. Wall of Nave.

1733. Given by Mr. Daniel Mayo,
the Sum of Twenty Pounds,
to be Disposed of
by the Minister, Churchwardens,
and Overseers, the yearly Interest of
which to teach such Poor Children
of Poulshott,
as they shall think proper.

Monuments in the Churchyard.

South Side.

Near this Place lyeth the Body of Henry Mayo, who Departed this life the 16 day of July, A. Di. 1712.

East End.

Near this Place lyeth the Body of John Stephens, who dyed ye 28th of Oct. 1667.

And of Sarah, his Wife, who dyed the 3d of June, 1686.

Also of James Palmer, who died the .. of May, 1668.

And of Sarah, his Wife, Daughter of ...... who .... the 7th of May, 1698.

North Side.

Nere this Place lyeth ye Body of John Godwin. He Dyed 25 Feb. 1740, Aged 89.

Also Frances, Wife of Mr. John Palmer. She Dyed 18th Nov. 1740, Aged 36.

Near this Place lyeth the Body of Ann, Wife of John Godwin, who died Oct. ye 20, A. D. 1731, Aged 71 years.

Also in Memory of Ann, Daughter of John and Ann Godwin, who died March ye 17, Anno Dom. 1728, Aged 40 years.

Joseph Godwin Ob. August 20, 1744, Æt. 46.

Near this Place lyeth the Body of Hester Townsend, who Departed this life on the 20th Day of December, Anno Domine 1733, Aged 70 years.

Register commenced 1627.

The Rev. Dr. Skinner, Rector.

EARL STOKE.

On Flat Stones in Chancel.

Here Lyeth ye Body of Catharine, ye Wife of William Brouncker, Esq. who Deceased January ye 3d, Anno Domini 1679, Aged 53.

Arms—Two bars engrailed between nine martlets, 3 3 3.

Here lyeth ye Body of William Brouncker, Esq. who Departed this life ye 6th Day of March, An. Domini 1679, Aged 61.

Arms—Imbattled, six roundels, in chief, on a lozenge, a cross pattée : impaling, two bars engrailed between 9 martlets.

Here lyeth ye Body of John, the Youngest Soñe of Williã Brūncker, Esq. & Katharine, his Wife, who deceased ye 13 day of August, Año Dom̃ 1681, Aged 21 years.

Arms—Imbattled, six roundels, 3 & 3, a martlet for difference, in chief, on a lozenge, a cross pattée.

White marble.

Here lyeth ye Body of Anne, Eldest Daughter of William Brouncker, Esq. and Katharine, his Wife, who dyed ye 25 of September, Anno Dni. 1684.

Arms—As before.

On a brass plate under the arch.

Memento Morio.

Here lyeth the Body of Eleanor, the Wife of Isaac Axford, Gent. who Departed this life the 16 Day of October, 1726, in the 83 year of her Age.

Here also Lyeth the Body of Isaac Axford, Gent. who Departed this life 17 of Nov. 1729, in the 83 year of his Age.

On Flat Stone in Nave.

John, Sonne of Richard Brounck, Gent. Departed April 17, 1681.

Here lieth ye Body . . . . ne, the Wife . . . . iam Baylie . . . . Departed . . . . . . fe the 27 . f Mearch, 1682.

Mon. against the North Wall of Nave.

Near this Place lyeth ye Body of Elizabeth, Wife of the Reverend Mr. Thomas, who Departed this life on the 29th of April, 1730, Aged 55 years.

She lives, tho' dead, in Memory of those who knew her life, and saw its holy Close.

Underneath lie Interred ye Body of Jane, wife of Hugh Tilly, Sen. who Died Dec. ye 31, 1750, Aged 70 years.

South Wall.

Beneath lies interred the Body of Anna Maria, the much-lamented Daughter of Abraham Bincks, Apothecary in this Town. She Departed this life July the 31st, 1737, Aged 32 years. In Memory of whom her loving Father hath erected this Monument.

COULSTON.

On a Monument in Chancel.

Infra juxta Cineres Paternos Corpus suum sepeliri voluit, Jacobus Meredith, A. M. Floruit aliquando in Collegio Wadhami, apud Oxonienses, alumnus et Socius, postea hujusce Ecclesiæ per annos septem Rector. Obiit Septembris 29, 1746, Ætatis 38. Uxor mœrens hoc marmor sacrum Memoriæ Conjugis amantissimi Posuit.

Arms—Argent, a lion rampant, sable, gorged or.

On a Brass Plate.

Near this Place lyeth the Body of the Rev. Mr. James Meredith, late Rector of this Parish, who Departed this life the third Day of June, in the 48 year of his Age, Anno Domini 1712.

On Flat Stones in Chancel.

Here lyeth the Body of Ruth Tipper, Wife of Jeffery Tipper, who Deceased October . . . . An. Dom. 1641.

Here lyeth the Body of William and Jeams, Sones of Richard Pinock. William Died April the 26, 1672.

In Memory of Mary, Wife of William Flower, Clerk, Rector of ye Parish, Daughter of Sarah Stileman, of Steeple Ashton, Widow, by her first Husband, John Paradice, of Keevil, Clothier. Ob. May ye 11th, 1750, Aged 38.

Also Sarah, Wife of John Elliott, Officer of Excise, Daughter of ye said Sarah, by her second Husband, Thomas Stileman, of Steeple Ashton, Gent. Ob. May ye 3, 1748, Aged 22 years.

Here lyeth, with her Husband, the Body of Mrs. Ann F.... Relict of the Rev. James Meredith, formerly Rector of this Parish, who ..... 16, 1730.

On Flat Stones in Nave.

Here lyeth the Body of Jane Coward, Widow, who Died April the second, 1737, Aged 73 years.

Here lyeth the Body of Margaret, the Daughter of John Pinnock, and Margaret, his Wife, who departed this life the 28 Day of Nov. A. D. 1729, Aged 6 weeks.

Hatchments.

Long: impaling sable, a fess between three fleur-de-lis, argent.

In a lozenge, quarterly, first and fourth argent, a canton, sable; second and third sable, two bars, argent, in chief three plates.

In a lozenge, gules, a spread eagle between three fleur-de-lis, argent: impaling, the same.

The Rev. John Selwyn, Rector.

G. W. Taylor, Lord of the Manor.

Near the Church is the Seat of Lady Mary Long.

MELKSHAM.

On Monuments against the north Wall of Chancel.

Near this Place are Deposited the Remains of Jeremiah Awdry, Esq. who Departed this Life Oct. 11th, A. D. 1754, Aged 60 years.

Also of Mrs. Martha Awdry, Sister of the above Jeremiah Awdry, who Departed this Life June 30th, A. D. 1769.

Arms—Argent, on a bend cottized, gules, three cinquefoils, arg.

To the Memory of Mrs. Dyonisia Thresher, Second Daughter and Coheiress of John Thresher, Esq. of Bradford, in this County, who Departed this Life, Jan. 18th, 1806, in the 70th year of her Age.

In her various social relations, mild, gentle, and benevolent, She exhibited a pleasing Example of the salutary influence of sincere Christianity, and had the happiness to unite an unremitting anxiety to discover, with an extensive power to relieve, the Sufferings of the Unfortunate. Many have experienced her Charities, may all imitate her Virtues.

This Monument was Erected by her nearest Relatives, as a token of their affectionate regard for her memory, and their heart-felt sorrow for her loss.

To the Memory of Elizabeth, Wife of John Crosdill, Esq. and formerly of Robert Colebrooke, Esq. of Chilham Castle, in the County of Kent. She was third Daughter of John Thresher, Esq. of Bradford, in this County, and Departed this life the 26th of May, 1807, Aged 70 years, humbly trusting in the all-sufficient merits of her Blessed Saviour for a joyful Resurrection.

To the Memory of Mrs. Mary Thresher, of the Parish of Melksham, youngest Daughter and Coheiress of John Thresher, Esq. of Bradford, in this County, who departed this life 12 Decem. 1816, Aged 77 years, after 20 years of severe suffering, borne with exemplary resignation to the Will of her Almighty Father, with Faith sincere and Humility unfeigned. Her benevolence was unbounded, and her Memory is endeared to the hearts of many who experienced her kindness. She lived beloved, and died lamented. This humble Tribute of Gratitude and Esteem is erected by her surviving Relatives as a testimony of her worth, and their affection.

West Wall of Chancel.

Near this Place Lyeth Interred the Body of John Awdry, of this Parish, Gent. who Departed this Life the 6 Day of May, Anno Dom. 1698, Ætat. 41.

Near this Place lie also the Bodies of John, Son of John Awdry, by Judith, his Wife, and of Unity, their Daughter. He died Oct. 10, 1703, in the 16 year of his Age. She died Feb. 24th, 1708, in the 18 year of her Age.

Arms—Argent, on a bend cottized, azure, three cinquefoils, or: impaling, argent, a fess between three mascles, or.

Near this Place also lyeth the Body of Ambrose Awdry, Gent. Son of the above-mentioned John and Judith Awdry, who died March ye 10th, 1728, Ætat. 36.

Near this Place lieth interred the Body of Henry, Coulthurst, of Beanacre, in the County of Wilts. Gent. who Departed this Life the 17th of August, 1743, Aged 65.

Also one Daughter and two Sons of the aforesaid Henry Coulthurst, (by Mary his Wife, Eldest Daughter of Richard Osborne, of Wotton Underedge, in the County of Gloucester, Esq.) Viz. Mary dyed Jan. 30th, 1715, Aged 7 months 13 days; Osborne died May 25th, 1729, Aged 6 years 9 months; Osborne dyed Oct. 5th, 1738, Aged 10 years 9 months.

Here lies also interred the remains of the abovesaid Mary Coulthurst, who died the 13th of Nov. 1768.

And also the remains of Jane Maria, Daughter of the late John Wood, Esq. of Bath, and Wife to Henry, Son of the abovesaid Henry and Mary Coulthurst, who died at Boulogne, in France, May 11th, 1770, Aged 40 years and 7 months.

Near this Stone are interred the Remains of Henry Coulthurst, Esq. who died at Uxbridge, in Middlesex, August ye 14th, 1786, Aged 65 years.

Arms—Argent, a fess between two horses passant, sable: impaling arg. a bend ermines between two lions ramp. sable.

East End.

Here lie the Remains of Priscilla, the Wife of John Awdry, of Notton, Esq. and Daughter of Ambrose Goddard, of Swindon, in this County Esq. who Departed this Life Dec. 2d, 1768, Aged 68 years.

Also of Elizabeth, their Daughter, who died April 9th, 1769, Aged 1 year and 8 months.

Likewise of Mary Magdalen Masse, second Wife of the above John Awdry, and Daughter of James Masse, Merchant, of the City of Lohdon, who Departed this life Feb. 22, 1771, Aged 30 years.

In the above Vault rests the Body of John Awdry, Esq. who died on the 11th of May, 1802, Aged 70 years.

Also of Sarah Susanna, his Widow, who died Jan. 1st, 1816, Aged 75 years.

Arms—Argent, on a bend, cottized, azure, three cinquefoils, or, a crescent, sable, for difference.

South Wall.

In Memoriam Isaaci Selfe, et Margaret, parentum Jacobus Self, filius hoc posuit, Qui postquam nonegessiam secundum Ætatis compleverit annum, numerosa sobole fœlix, viz. quatuor filijs cum tredecim filiabus, unacum nepotibus nepotumq; prole adnumerum 83, mandatâ Creatori animâ lubens devita migravit, Feb. 10, A° Dom̄ 1656.

Here lie the Remains of the Rev. Mr. Bohun Fox, Vicar of this Parish for fifty-three years. He discharged the duties of his Pastoral Office with Fidelity and Zeal, Defended ye Doctrine and Discipline of ye Church of England by his Excellent Discourses and Writings, asserted the Right and Revenues of his Station with Resolution and Success.

The Instruction of the Poor was his Peculiar Care: To this end he established, and constantly superintended, a Charity School, for ye Virtuous Education and half Clothing of poor Children, and endowed it by his last Will with the perpetual Interest of One Hundred and Thirty-five Pounds.

His Learning, his Integrity, and great Abilities, recommended him to the unanimous Suffrage of the Clergy of the Diocese to represent them in Convocation in the most interesting times, when the late Pious and Glorious Queen Anne cordially proposed the Advancement of the Dignity, Purity, and Discipline of the Church.

As he owed ye Principles of his distinguished Endowments to his happy Education in Winchester College, his Gratitude was expressed to that celebrated Foundation, by settling on poor Scholars of Merit, educated there, an ample Provision for Ever.

He dyed April 3d, 1750,
In the 78 year of his Age.

Near him lyes Interred the Body of Ann, his Wife, Daughter of the Rev. Francis Horton, Canon of the Cathedral Church of Sarum, and Vicar of this Parish. She Departed this Life January ye 9th, 1740, Aged 78 years.

This Monument was Erected to their Memory by Robert Fox, of Birmingham, in the County of Warwick, his sole Heir and Executor.

Arms—Or, a chevron between three foxes heads erased, gules: impaling, azure, a buck's head caboshed, argent.

Sacred to the Memory of Sarah, the beloved Wife of Thomas Bruges, Esq. who Departed this life in the Hope of a Happy Immortality, on the 23 Day of Feb. 1801, in the 51 year of her Age.

Likewise to the Memory of Sarah, Daughter of the said Thomas and Sarah Bruges, who Departed this Life on the 11th Day of Sept. 1784, Aged 2 years and 3 Months.

Also to the Memory of Mary, their Second Daughter, who Departed this life on the 1st day of April, 1799, Aged 15 years and 10 months.

Likewise to the Memory of Sarah Bruges, their youngest Daughter, and, alas! the only surviving Child, of her disconsolate Father. She Departed this life on the 26th Day of April, 1804, Aged 17 years and 10 months.

Arms—Argent, on a cross, ermines, a leopard's head caboshed: impaling argent, on a fess . . . three saltires . . .

This Tablet is meant to record the Memory of John Awdry, Clerk, instituted to the Vicarage of Melksham on the Presentation of Gertrude, Widow and Relict of Henry Bronker, Esq. on the 21 day of Sept. 1601, and died in the year 1639.

Arms—Argent, on a bend cottized, gules, 3 cinquefoils, argent.

On Flat Stones in Chancel.

Underneath lieth Mrs. Margaret Webb, who departed this life the 4th of June, 1783, in the 78th year of her Age.

She was Daughter of Isaac Selfe, of Beanacre, Esq. by his Wife Ruth, Daughter of John Boman, Esq. and Widow of Mr. Daniel Webb, heretofore of this Place, by whom she had only one Daughter, named Elizabeth, who, marrying Thomas Smith, late of Shaw, in this Parish, Esq. had four Sons and three Daughters, whereof Elizabeth, the second Daughter, Wife of Robert Neale, of Corsham, Esq. the only Survivor, and who, in grateful Remembrance of her worthy ancestor, has caused this Stone to be Placed here the 6 Day of June, 1766.

Arms—Azure, a cross . . . between four swallows: impaling, ermine, three chevrons . . . .

Here lyeth the Body of Thomas Taylor, of this Parish, Clothier, who Departed this life Feb. ye 23d, 1749, in ye 39 year of his Age.

Also near this Place lyeth two of his Children, by Mary, his Wife, who died Dec. ye 17 & 24, 1743.

In Memory of Mary, Wife of John Taylor, who died April ye 29, 1763, Aged 52 years.

Here also lies the Body of Mrs. Ann Awdry, Relict of the above Mr. Ambrose Awdry, and Daughter of the Rev. Mr. John Tayler, Rector of Charlinch, in ye County of Somerset, who departed this life Jan. 4th, A. D. 1719, Aged 52 years.

Near this Place also lies the Body of John Awdry, eldest Son of the abovesaid Ambrose and Anne Awdry, who died Oct. 28, A. D. 1734, Aged 10 years.

Arms—On a bend, cottized, three cinquefoils; impaling ermine, on a chief dancetté three escallops.

On Monuments in East End of S. Aisle.

Juxta Reconditum quod reliquum est viri integerrimi Jacob Selfe, De Place House, in hac Parochia, Armigeri, E Familia de Selfe, de Beanacre, oriundi, Qui Diem extremum clausit,

Anno { Salutis 1730,
Ætatis suæ 58.

Jacob Selfe, de Beanacre, Arm̄ Consanguineus et Hæres, hoc Marmor Memoriæ Sacrum Ponendum curavit.

Arms—Three chevrons, gules.

Sacred to those Virtues which adorn the Christian System, this Marble perpetuates the Memory of many true Believers, who now rest in full assurance of a Blessed Resurrection at the last Day.

Thomas Selfe, Rector of the adjoining Parish of Bromham, (who married first Elizabeth, Daughter of Henry Smith, of this Parish, Gent: Secondly, Sarah, Relict of Eleazar Webb, Gent. who, leaving no Issue, lies buried at Bromham,) died 17 Nov. 1741, Æt. 67. Elizabeth, his first Wife died July 24, 1728, Æt. 56. Their male issue were Thomas and Isaac, who both died without Children, and lie buried in St. Mildred's Church, in London: Thomas 10 Jan. 1726, Æt. 27, and Isaac 12 Jan. 1738, Æt. 32. Their Daughters were, Elizabeth, Ann, Margaretta, and Mary. Elizabeth was married to the Rev. Wm. Stone: She placidly resigned her soul to him that gave it the 2d of April, 175. Æt. 53, and was buried at Ogborne St. George, in this County, leaving only one Child, named William. Ann, the 2d Daughter was Married to the Rev. Richard Jenkyns. He died 9th March, 1748, Æt. 43, and She, weary of this Life, Chearfully received her Call to a better the 7th of June following, Æt. 48: they left two Children, Mary and Richard, Mary was born the 20th of August, 1735, and after an exemplary life of Sweetness, Innocence, and well-doing, (having never made one foe) died a Virgin, an ill-spared Victim to Inoculation, the 13th Nov. 1757. Margaretta, the 3d Daughter, was married to James Yorke, of the City of Wells, Gent. The shock she received at the Death of her justly-beloved Niece, hastened her own; as a Christian, she nobly struggled with grief, but it was too mighty for her: she made a good end of a well-spent life May 23d, 1759, Æt. 56. Mary, the 4th and last Daughter, died an Infant. Reader, you see what they once were, you know, too, what they now are; be you, therefore, wise in time.

Arms—In a lozenge quarterly, first and fourth azure, a saltire or, second and third azure, a chevron between three pheons, or.

Ermine, three chevrons, gules: impaling per pale, azure and gules, a chevron between three lions pass. guardant, or.

Flat Stones within the Rails of Chancel.

Here lyeth the Body of Mrs. Bridget Greenfield, who Departed this life the 18th of March, A. D. 1687.

Here lie the Remains of Martha Awdry, who departed this life June the 30th, 1769.

Arms—On a bend, cottized, three cinquefoils: impaling, a fess between three mascles.

Here lieth the Body of Elizabeth Rutty, wife of Thos. Rutty, died April ye 14th, 1775. Aged 86 years.

Also Mary Agatha Lanham, Daughter of Joseph and Elizabeth Lanham, who died August the 18th 1780, Aged 24 years.

Mon. in S. Aisle.

M. S. Jacob Selfe, de Beanacre, in Agro Wiltoniensi, Et Maria Uxoris, Johannis Ashe, de Freshford, in Com. Som̄ Filiæ:

Obierunt { Ille Jan. 15, 1702, Æt. 82.
Illa Junij 8, 1701, Æt. 64.

Arms—Erm. 3 chevrons gules: impaling, arg. 2 chevrons sable.

On an Altar Tomb.

To the Memory of Ambrose Awdry, of Seend, Gentleman, and Mary, his Wife, who are underneath interred. He dyed January the 9th, 1738, Æt. 75. She dyed June the 29th, 1719, Æt. 48.

The Memory of the Just is Blessed,
But the name of the Wicked shall Rot.
Prov. x. v. 7.

Arms—Argent, on a bend cottized, azure, three cinquefoils, or: impaling, ermine, three chevrons, gules.

Juxta reconduntur exuvia Isaaci Selfe, Generosi, Amicis vicinis, et notis omĩbus per chari. Qui Obijt die 14 Mensis Martij, Anno Domini 1682, Ætatis suæ 48.

Inhumantur quoque propè Corporâ liberorum ejus,

Elizabethæ & Gul. } defunct. { Anno 1671. Anno 1673.

Monumentum hoc posuit amoris ergo Anna Selfe, uxor et mater superstes mœrens. Hanc ne depereas, lector, vitam perituram æternum, ut possis vivere vive Deo.

Arms—Ermine, three chevrons, gules, on the middle one a crescent, argent: impaling, argent, a bend, sable, on a chief of the last three woolpacks . . . .

On brass plates in S. Aisle.

Here lyeth Buried the Body of Ambrose Dauntesey, Esq. ye Eldest Sonne of Sir John Dauntesey, Knight, who had to Wife Gartrude, the Widdowe of Henry Brouncker, Esq. wch lieth Buried Here by him, & Died Both wthin a Yeare, & Had by Her 4 Sonnes And 2 Daughters. He Deceased the 29th of November, 1612. A Zealous Christian, and Welbeloved by All Men.

Here Lieth Buried the Bodie of Gertrude Dauntesey, First the Wife of Henry Bruncker, Esq. by whom She had one Sonne and one Daughter. She Died the Wife of Ambrose Dauntesey, Esquir by whom She had 4 Sonnes and 2 Daughters, And Deceased the 18 of February, 1611, in the Faith of Christ, and Favor of his People.

Separated awhile from that pure Spirit which once animated the now lifeless remains of faded Beauty, the Vault below contains all that was Mortal of Anna Maria Jenkyns, the beloved only Daughter of Richard & Anne Jenkyns. Having lived 14 years and upwards the Delight of all, and the Constant Source of inexpressible Happiness to her fond Parents, She left them, loaded with Grief, yet filled with Hope, on the 6th of December, 1778.

Christian Moralist, if the loss of a lovely Innocent, conspicuous for early Piety and filial love, for friendly Affection and Goodness of Heart, for Purity of Mind and Chastity of Manners, with an Elegant Person, and a Strength of Genius and Understanding, which yielded the Most promising Hopes, be the object of rational sorrow, let the Tear drop, and hence take the unfinished Design of Female Excellence.

In the same Vault are deposited, in full Assurance of a glorious Resurrection to Life eternal, the Remains of Richard Jenkyns, Esq. the once happy Father of the above-named Anna-Maria, who closed his sorrows the 31 Day of July, 1806.

Near this Place lies the Body of Isaac Selfe, Esquire, of Beanacre, in this Parish, whose amiable Disposition and great Integrity, Recommended him to the Esteem of all who knew him. Nor was he less exemplary for Piety, Charity, and Hospitality. By his Second Wife Penelope, the Daughter and Coheir of Charles Lord Lucas (by Penelope, Daughter of Francis, Earl of Scarsdale,) he had three sons and three Daughters. By his Third Marriage he left no issue. He Departed this Life Anno Domini 1733, Aged 70 years.

In the same Grave Lie also the Remains of Jacob Selfe, of Beanacre, Esq. his youngest and last surviving Son, who, in regard to the Memory of the best of Fathers, Directed this Monument to be Erected. He died July 24th, 1757, Aged 62 years.

To the Memory of Mrs. Elizabeth Smith, who lies Buried near this Place, in the same Grave with her Father Daniel Webb, of this Parish, Gent. She was Wife of Thomas Smith, of Shaw, Esq. and Died January 12, 1719, in the 42 year of her Age. Also near the same Place lie Buried two Sons and a Daughter of the above-named Thomas and Elizabeth Smith. Thomas, their Eldest Son, who died July 3d, 1698, being but 10 weeks three days old; Thomas, their next born, who died March 14th, 1699, at the Age of 16 weeks five days; Ann, who Died Dec. 24, 1714, at the Age of nine years, six months, 24 days.

Also the Body of the above-named Thomas Smith, Esq. by whose death the Church of England hath lost a Son truly exemplary and conformable, the State a Member always ready for its Support, his Neighbours a Gentleman of strict justice and fidelity, his Friends a pattern of true goodness, joined with a sound judgement and discretion.

So long then as an hearty zeal for the best religion and form of government, an unblemished uprightness and integrity, a pious and prudent œconomy, shall continue to be esteemed and admired, so long must remain precious the Memory of Mr. Smith. Ob. 21° Julij, A.D. 1723, Æt. 50.

Arms—Gules, on a chevron, argent, three lions' heads erased, sable, between three cinquefoils, argent: impaling, argent, a cross, gules, between four doves, proper.

H. S.

Quod Mortale Fuit Thomæ Fudge, B.A. Obiit 3 Nov. 1782, Æt. 74.

Necnon Janæ, Conjugis ejus amantissimæ. Obijt 23tio Feb. A.D. 1801, Æt. 74.

Near this Place Lyeth Interred the Body of John May, of Shaw, in this Parish, who Departed this life the 27 of January, Anno Dni. 1684, Aged 90 years.

Mors tua, Mors Christi, fraus Mundi, Gloria Cœli, Et dolor Inferni, sint meditanda tibi.

On Flat Stones in S. Aisle.

Beneath this Stone lyeth the Body of Mrs. Sarah Tayler, Wife of Mr. Thomas Tayler, of this Parish, Clothier, and Youngest Daughter of Robert Smith, of this Parish, Gent. She died June ye 6, 1736, Aged 35 years, much regretted and lamented by all that knew her.

Beneath this Stone lyeth the Body of Robert Smith, Gent. of this Parish, who Departed this life Oct. 24, Anno { Æt. 76. Salut. 1729.

Here lieth the Body of Mary, the Wife of Henry Smith, of this Parish, Gent. She Departed this life May the 3d, 1755, Aged 52.

Here lyeth the Body of Penelope Selfe, Eldest Daughter of Isaac Selfe, of Beanacre, in the County of Wilts. Esq. by Penelope, his Wife, One of the Daughters, and Coheiress, of Charles Lord Lucas, Baron of Shenfield, in the County of Essex, who Departed this life the 26 Day of May, in the year of our Lord, 1718, her Age 25.

Arms—Ermine, three chevrons.

Here lyeth ye Body of Mrs. Anne Selfe, Daughter of Thomas Smith, of Froomzellwood, in ye County of Somerset, Gent. and Wife of Isaac Selfe, of ye Middle Temple, London, Gent. Son and Heire of Jacob Selfe, of Beanacre, in ye County of Wilts. Gent. who departed this life ye 13 Day of Oct. Anno Dom. 1681, Æt. suæ 21.

Also Here Lyeth ye Body of Jacob Selfe, Son of Isaac Selfe, by Ann, his Wife, who Departed this life the 8 day of Feb. Anno Dom. 1686.

Arms—Ermine, three chevrons: impaling, on a chevron, three lions' heads erazed between three cinquefoils.

Underneath this Stone lieth Margaret, eldest Daughter of Richard Guppey, of Sandridg Hill, in the Parish of Melksham, Gent. and third Wife of Isaac Selfe, of Beanacre, in the County of Wilts. Esq. She dyed 1st of August, 1734, Aged 73.

Arms—Ermine, three chevrons: impaling on a chevron three fleur-de-lis between as many roses, slipped.

Here lyeth the Body of Richard Guppey, of Sandridg hill Park, in this Parish, Gent. who departed this life the 27th Day of September, 1723, Ætat. 67.

Also the Body of Margaret, his Wife, who departed this life August ye 29, 1757, Aged 86 years.

Arms—On a chevron, three fleur-de-lis between as many roses. Impaling, on a fess wavy, three roundels between as many lions' heads erased.

Here lies the Body of Ellin Owen, Spinster, who died the 2d of April, 1728.

She was a Lady of Exemplary Piety, strictest Vertue, and great Humanity and Charity. Her Soul, thus adorned with Divine graces, She Chearfully resigned to Heaven, whither her whole life aspired.

Arms—A lion rampant, in chief a canton.

Here lieth the Body of John Smith, of Shaw, Esq. who departed this life the 21 of August, A.D. 1757, Aged 54.

Arms—Gules, on a chevron, argent, three lions' heads caboshed between as many cinquefoils... Impaling, argent, on a chevron, gules, three trefoils ... between as many lions' heads caboshed.

On a Brass Plate.

Here lyeth the Body of Mrs. Rebecca Guppey, late of this Parish, who Departed this life Nov. 22, 1735, Aged 60.

Her desire was, that her Grave might never be opened.

Here lieth the Body of Thomas Kington, of Wotton, in this County, Gent. who Departed this Life July ye 9th, 1757, Aged 57 years.

Here lieth the Body of Jane, Relict of the above Thomas Kington, Gent. died Oct. ye 9th, 1768, Aged 69 years.

Arms—On a chevron, three fleur-de-lis between as many roses; impaling guttée, in chief three chess-rooks.

N. Side of the Nave, against 2d Pillar from the east End.

Near this Pillar lyes Interred ye Body of Mr. John Rutty, late of this Parish, Clothier, who Departed this life the 13th of Nov. 1707, in the 79th year of his Age.

As also the Body of Mrs. Margery Rutty, his Widow, (Daughter of Mr. Henry Webb, of Payswick, in the County of Gloucester, Clothier,) who Departed this life the 12 of August, 1714, in the 83 year of her Age. They lived together 45 years, and had issue 2 Sons and 3 Daughrs, which all survived them, Viz. Henry, John, Ann, Sarah, and Mary.

On Flat Stones in Nave.

And also in Memory of Sarah, Wife of Thomas Wilshire, who Departed this Life the 26 Day of Feb. in 175- Aged 50 years.

Here lyeth the Body of Mr. Peter de Jersey, of Guernsey, Esq. who Departed this Life May 3rd, 1781, Aged Twenty Years, two Months, and fifteen Days.

Short was my life,
The longer is my rest,
God took me hence
Because he thought it best.

Brass Plate.

Mrs. Ann Osgood Died 21 Dec. 1769,
Aged 79 years.

Here lyeth ye Body of Jane Flower, Wife of Thos. Flower, of Beanacre, Gent. deceased, who Departed this life the 22d day of March, Añ Dom̃ 1704/5 Aged 59 years.

Here Lyes the Body of Thomas Flower, of this Parish, Gent. who Departed this Life May the 1, 1758, Aged 58 years.

Also of John Flower, Brother of the said Thomas, who Departed this life May ye 6th, 1753, Aged 55 years.

On a small Monument in the south side under the Tower.

To the Memory of John Edwards Freemantle, Esq. Lieut. Col. of the Royal Bucks Militia, and formerly of the Coldstream Regiment of Foot Guards. He Departed this Life at Bath, on the 21 Day of March, 1805, Aged 43 years. He married Catharine, second Daughter of the Rt. Hon. Lord Ongley, who has caused this Tablet to be Erected to his Memory.

On Flat Stones.

H. S. E.
Wm. Jeffreys Wood
died 5 May, 1795, Aged 29 years.

Here lieth an infant Son of John and Hester Jones, of this Parish, who died Nov. ye 17, 1761, Aged one Month.

On Flat Stones in N. Aisle.

Here lieth the Body of Esther Robins, second Wife of Richard Buntur Robins, who died July the 6th, 1780, Aged 80 years.

To the Memory of Joseph Howgate, Esq. of this Parish. He died 5th April, 1820, Aged 81.

Underneath are interred the Remains of Susanna Webb, Spinster, Sister to Benjamin Webb, Esq. many years an Inhabitant of this Place. She Departed this life the 21 of Feb. 1814.

Brass Plate.

Here lyeth the Body of Henry Robins, Gent. who Departed this life the 31 of January, in the year 1778, Aged 38 years.

Hatchments.

Quarterly, first and fourth ermine, a chevron gules; second and third gules, a fretty or: impaling ermine, two bars vert: supporters, two wyverns, sable.
Crest—A baron's coronet.

In a lozenge, argent, a chevron, gules, between three boars' heads, couped and erect, azure, issuing out of each a crosslet, fitchy, gules.

Quarterly, first and fourth Long; second and third per pale, first argent, three indorse sable, second azure.

Sable, a lion, rampant, between eight cross-crosslets, argent, over all an escutcheon, azure: impaling argent, two indorse, sable.

Argent, a chevron, gules, between three boars' heads erased, a crosslet fitchy, gules, issuing from each.

Quarterly, first and fourth ermine, a chevron, gules; second and third gules, a fretty or: impaling per fess, ermine, two bars vert, two chevrons argent, in base a fleur-de-lis, or.

Against the Gallery.

Benefactions to this Parish.

A. D. 1750. The Rev. Bohun Fox, Vicar of this Parish, Gave by Will, the Interest of One Hundred and thirty-five Pounds, then on Mortgage, But now on Security of the Melksham Turnpike Trust, the said Interest to be appropriated by the Vicar of this Parish for the time being annually in the Educating and Part Cloathing of Poor Children, inhabitants of this Parish, as far as the said Interest will admit of.

A. D. 1757. Jacob Selfe, of Bradford, in this County, Gave by Will, the Interest of One Hundred Pounds, to be distributed annually at Christmas in Bread or Meat to Twenty-four Poor Housekeepers of this Parish, not receiving alms, under the direction of the Owner of the Estate of the said Jacob Selfe, in this Parish, for the time being, one-third part of the same to be distributed as aforesaid to Housekeepers within the Tything of Beanacre in this Parish.

The Church consists of Chancel, Nave, North and South Aisles, and North and South Transepts. The nave is supported by four pointed arches, resting on round pillars.

The Rev. Joseph Smith Vicar.

John and Daniel Jones Long, Esqrs. Lords of the Manor.

SEMINGTON.

On a Monument against the north Wall of Chancel.

In this Chancel lie the Remains of Wm. Blagden, Gent. of Littleton. He died Feb. the 2d, 1697, Ann : Æt. 38.

Robert Bisse, Gent. He died July the 31st, 1723, Aged 55.

Mary, Daughter of Robert & Eleanor Bisse. She died May 15, 1717, Aged 16 years.

Mrs. Eleanor Bisse, Relict of Robert Bisse, Gent. late of Littleton. She died April the 13th, 1743, Aged 81.

Edward Blagden, Esq. of Keevil, Son of the late Edward Blagden, Esq. of Keevil, by Ann, his Wife. He died Oct. 7th, 1748, Ann. Æt. 37.

Mrs. Joan Bisse, Daughter of Robert Bisse, Gent. by Eleanor, his Wife. She died Decem. the 31st, 1770, Aged 68 years.

In compliance with the last Will, and at the Expense of the said Mrs. Joan Bisse, this Monument was erected to the Memory of her Ancestors, by the Care of her affectionate Executrix Anne Blagden.

Arms—Sable, three escallops in pale, argent: impaling argent, indented, three trefoils vert, on a chief azure, three annulets argent.

On Flat Stones in Chancel.

Here lyeth ye Body of Mrs. Joane Richmond, of Littletõ, who Departed this life ye 2d of February, Añ Dm̃ 1697, Ætatis suæ ..

Here lyeth ye Body of Mary Bisse, Daughter of Robert and Elianor Bisse, who Departed this life ye 15th of May, Ano Dni. 1717, Aged 16 years.

Here Lyeth the Body of Edward Blagden, Esq. Son of the late Edward Blagden, Esq. of Keevil, by Ann, his Wife, who died the 7th day of October, Ann. Dom. 1748.

Here lieth the Body of Christopher Somner, Gent. who Departed this life at Littleton, the 27th Day of October, 1688, Anno Ætatis suæ 26.

Here lyeth the Body of Thomas Somner, Esq. who Liv'd at Wellow, in Sumerset, was Buryed April ye 28, MDCXCII. Ætatis suæ 42.

On a Monument against the North Wall of Nave.

To the Memory of James Matravers, of this Place, Gent. who died 16th March, 1799, Aged 66 years.

And Grace, his Wife, who died 25 Decem. 1793, Aged 62 years.

Also Sarah, Daughter of James and Grace Matravers, who died 27th Oct. 1770, Aged 3 years and 5 months.

Also Mary, Wife of James Hippisly, Daughter of James Matravers, by Elizabeth his first Wife, who died 6th July, 1788, Aged 27 years.

Also James Matravers Hippisly, Son of James and Mary Hippisly, who died 15th May, 1789, Aged 2 years and Six Months.

Life how short, Eternity how Long.

On Flat Stones in Nave.

Underneath lie the Remains of Betty, the Wife of Wm. Bruges, Gent. who Departed this life June 22d, 1803, Aged 56 years.

Underneath lie the Remains of Edmund Lewis, Surgeon, who departed this life June 28th, 1804, in the 37 year of his Age.

Brass Plates.

Here Lyeth the Body of Thomas Gerrish, of this Place, Yeoman, who, after a long, well-spent Life, to the age of 78, dyed ye 29th of October, 1738, having lived a loving Husband, a tender Parent, a good Neighbour, and a stedfast Friend.

Here lyeth the Body of Ann Somner, (Wife of Thomas Somner, Gent, Decd, Daughter of William Blagdon, Gent. and Elianer His wife) whoe Departed this life the Seaventh day of January, 1683, Anno Ætatis 48.

In the Chancel window is a little painted glass, or, g. and az. The are also some remains of the Dantesey Arms, having DANTESEY written upon it.

Register commenced 1686.

The Rev. Mr. Hay, Vicar.

The Duke of Somerset Lord of the Manor.

KEEVIL.

On Monuments against the North wall of Chancel.

Near this Place lyeth the Body of Roger Gaisford, of Bulkington, Gent. who Departed this life the 8th Day of January, 1757, Aged 58 years.

Also near this Place lyeth ye Body of Betty, Wife of the above Roger Gaisford, Gent. who Departed this life the 30th day of August, 1757, Aged 60.

Also near this Place lyeth the Body of Stephen, Son of the above Roger and Betty Gaisford, who Departed this life Decem. ye 8th, 1763, in the 20th year of his Age.

Sacred to the Memory of Sarah, Wife of John Lewis, who died Sept. 16th, 1810, Aged 39 years.

South Wall.

John Harris, Esq.
Citizen and Alderman of London.

Dead and Alive! How so? tis true:
'Tis false, both first & last,
Like never hearde: yet nothing new,
'Tis present and tis past.
He was with us, yet now with God,
In life was dead, now lives
The burning bush and Aaron's Rod;
The God who takes, & gives:
And faith and reason doe agree,
Though repugnant were,
That, in their several senses, we
May see them very cleare.

He died at Bathe, the 25 day
of May, 1657, and neare to this
Place lyeth Interred.
Also Hester, his Pious Relict, who Died
Near London, the 10th of June, 1673,
Now in the same Grave lyeth
buried with him.

Arms—Sable, a trefoil, or, between three crescents, argent: impaling, gules, on a bend, or, three li. pass. gules.

Flat Stones.

Here lyeth ye Body of John, ye Son of Mr. Richard White, Gent. who was Buryed January the 3d, 1703.

Here also Lyeth the Body of Mrs. Jone White, Daughter of Richard White, Gent. of Bulkington, who Departed this life May ye 14th, An. Dom. 1724, Aged 70 years. Mors Janua Vitæ.

Here lyeth ye Body of William Blagden, Gent. who Deceased Nov. ye 2, 167-

---

Here Lyeth ye Body of Stephen Gaysford, the Elder, of Marston, in the County of Wilts, Gent. who Departed this life ye 22 Day of March, Anno Dom. 1687.

Here lyeth ye Body of Richard, ye Son of Mr. John White, Gent. who was Buryed August the 19th, 1694.

Mon. against the North Wall of Nave.

Near this Place are Interred the Remains of Tuck Gaisford, who died April 4th, 1789, Aged 65 years.

Also of Mary, Daughter of Tuck and Mary Gaisford, who died July the 11th, 1774, Aged 19 years.

Also in Memory of Ann, Mary, Robert, George, and Sarah, Sons and Daughters of Tuck and Ann Gaisford. Ann died June the 17th, 1774, Aged 10 years and 6 months; Mary died March the 10th, 1775, Aged 6 months; Robert Tuck died May the 27th, 1776, Aged 6 years and 3 months; George died July the 21st, 1779, Aged 3 years and 4 months; Sarah died Nov. the 14, 1784, in the 20 year of her Age.

Also in Memory of Ann, the 2d Wife of Tuck Gaisford, who died June the 6th, 1819, in the 84 year of her Age.

Near this Place lyeth the Body of Mr. Wm. Gaisford, of Bulckington, who died July ye 11th, 1754, Aged 62 years.

In Memory of Mary, Wife of Edward Gardner, who died Jan. 15, 1760, Aged 63.

In Memory of Mrs. Jane Talbot, Relict of the Rev. Mr. Thomas Talbot, of Margam, in Glamorganshire, and only Daughter of Thomas Beach, Esq. of this Place, who Departed this life Jan. 22, 1768, Aged 42 years. This Monument was Erected by her youngest Son and Executor, Christopher Talbot, Esq.

Thine be this Tribute, O lamented Shade!
This duteous Tribute to thy Mem'ry paid,
These tender sorrows, thine, for ever dear;
'Tis Nature claims this sympathetick Tear,
Or were her Voice too weak to bid it flow,
Yet see—our Kindred is one Scene of Woe!
Doubtful where most with Justice to commend,
The Wife, the Widow, Parent, or the Friend.

Arms—Gules, a lion rampant within a border ingrailed, or: impaling, vair, argent, and gules, on a canton, or, a buck's head caboshed, sable.

South Wall.

Near this Pillar, in the South Isle, are interred the Remains of the Rev. James Richardson, Late Vicar of Keevil, who died August the 29th, 1782, in the 70th year of his Age.

Also in the same Grave are interred the Remains of Mrs. Ann Richardson, Wife of the Rev. James Richardson, and Daughter of John Beach, Gent. Citizen of London. She Died April the 10, 1774, Aged 53 years.

Arms—Or, on a chevron, sable, three lions' heads erased, arg.

East End.

Near this Place are Interred the Remains of George Gilbert, who Died March the 15, 1788, in the 35 year of his Age.

Also near this Place are Interred the Remains of Jane

Gilbert, Wife of George Gilbert, who died Nov. the 15, 1794, Aged 39 years.
Also of Sarah Gilbert, Daughter of George and Jane Gilbert, who died May the 19th, 1799, in the 21 year of her Age.

In Memory of Thomas Gilbert, Gent. who died March ye 5th, 1761, Aged ....
Also Elizabeth, his Beloved Wife, died September ye 15th, 1720, Aged 34.
Also of Sarah, Wife of George Gilbert, Gent. who died May ye 1st, 1769, Aged 53.
Also Elizabeth Gilbert, who died April the 9th, 1781, Aged 60.
Also to the Memory of George Gilbert Gent. who Died Dec. 17, 1791, Aged 76 years.
Also of Thomas Gilbert, Son of the Above, who died Dec. the 31st, 1792, Aged 35 years.

Near this Place lie interred the Remains of Elizth Watts, Wife of James Watts, Daughter of George and Sarah Gilbert, who Departed this life Feb the 20th, 1796, Aged 41 years.

Sacred to the Memory of Mrs. Dorothy Beach, who died Feb. 18, 1772, Aged 82 years.
As also Mrs. Sophia Beach, who died July 31, 1787, Aged 81 years.
They were Daughters of Wm. Beach, Esq. And Ann his Wife.

Beneath this Place lies interred the Remains of William Beach, Esq. of Keevill, who Departed this life August 1st, 1741, Aged 85.
Near him lies his truly affectionate Wife, Ann Beach, who survived him but eight months. She was Daughter to the Rev. Gilbert Wither, of Hall-Place, in Hampshire, and Departed this life April 6th, 1742, Aged 80.
Also the Remains of Joan Beach, their well-beloved & dutiful Daughter, who died June 29th, 1765, Aged 62.

Arms—Vair, argent, and gules, on a canton, or, a buck's head caboshed, sable: impaling, argent, a chevron, gules, between three crescents, sable.

On a Flat Stone in Nave.

Here lyeth the Body of Daniel Usher, who Departed this life Feb. the 18th, 1753, Aged 82 years.

Brass Plates in N. Transept.

Here lyeth ye Body of Elizabeth Gaisford, Wife of Thos. Gilbert, who Departed this life Sept. ye 15, in ye Year of our Lord, 1720, Aged 34 years.

Here lyeth the Body of Jane Flower, Wife of Robert Flower, who Departed this life ye 25 of Sept. Ano Dom. 1662.

Here lyeth ye Body of John Haskens, of this Parish, who Departed this life ye 14th Day of April, Anno Dom. 1689, Aged 51 years.
Memento Mori.
Also here lyeth ye Body of John, ye Son of John Haskens, who Departed this life ye 5th Day of March, A. D. 172$\frac{3}{4}$, Aged 47 years.

In Memory of Stephen Cox, of the City of Bristol, who Departed this Life June the 18, 1761, Aged 50 years.
Also Susanna, his Wife, who Departed this life the 4th of Dec. 1761, Aged 55 years.

On Monuments in West End of S. Aisle.

Sacred to the Memory of Edward Blagden, Esq. who died Oct. 20th, 1730, Aged 43 years.
Also of Ann, his Wife, who died April 4th, 1769, Aged 79 years.
Also of Ann Blagden, their Daughter, who died August 10th, 1773, Aged 60 years.
And of Eleanor Blagden, their Daughter, who died February 23d, 1785, Aged 62 years.
Also of Ann Dare, Cousin to the Above, who died April 17th, 1807, Aged 83 years.
Also of Betty Roberts, her Sister, and Widow of General John Roberts, of Taunton, M. P. who died July 4th, 1808, Aged 72 years.

Arms—Argent, indented, three trefoils proper, on a chief, sable, three annulets, or.

South Wall.

Sacred to the Memory of John Chamberlaine, Esq. F. S. A. Keeper of His Majesty's Drawings and Medals. Pure and undeviating in his Conduct, he was honoured with the confidence and esteem of the best of Sovereigns during a period of nearly fifty years. His disconsolate Widow and Family have placed this Marble to commemorate the best of Husbands and the best of Fathers, whose gentleness of Nature, and urbanity of manners, gained him the friendship and affection of all who knew him. Obijt Jan. 12th, 1812, Ætatis suæ 67.
Also of Fredrick Chamberlain, his Youngest Son, late of Trin. Coll. Cambridge. He served as a Lieut. in the 16th Light Dragoons, under the Duke of Wellington, and died most sincerely and deservedly Lamented of a Consumption from fatigue, on the 24th Jan. 1815, Aged 28 years.

Arms—An escutcheon between eight mullets: impaling, a fess between six annulets, 3 & 3.

Near this Place Lyeth the Body of Job Ellis, who Departed this Life March the 9th, 1800, Aged 34 years.

His years on earth they was but few,
And wasted like the Morning dew;
When he could stay no longer here
He left his tender Mother dear
To the kind providence of Heaven,
And dy'd in hopes to be forgiven.

On Flat Brass Plates.

Here lyeth ye Body of Roger Blagden, the Eldest, Gent. And of Roger, his Sonn, And Ann, his Wife. And Alsoe Martha, the Wife of Edward Blagden, Gent. who departed this life the 11 Day of Julie, 1683.

Underneath lie interred the Remains of Ann, the Wife of the Rev. Mr. Richardson, Vicar of Keevil. She died April 10, 1774, Aged 53 years.

On a Tablet in S. Aisle.

BENEFACTION

Given by Mrs. Joan White, of Bulkington, in the Parish of Keevil, by Will, dated the 16th Day of October, 1724. Assigned to John Gaisford, Gent. Henry Marjeram, Yeo: Thomas Wilkins, Weaver, Wm. Gibbs, John Burbidge, Yeo: and Thomas Nash, Yeo: all of Bulkington aforesaid, an Annuity of Forty Shillings, to be paid out of her all and singular Messuages, Tenemts, Lands, and Hereditaments, lying in the Tything of Bulkington, in the Parish of Keevil, aforesaid, to be by them distributed on the Feast of St. Thomas the Apostle, or within twelve Days next after the said Feast, amongst such poor Inhabitants of Bulkington as they, or the greater number of them, shall think fit. By the same Will, it is also ordered, that the two Survivors of the above-mentioned Assignees, shall assign over to six others of the principal Inhabitants of Bulkington, the said Annuity to be by them distributed at the time and manner above-mentioned, and that the like assignment be made by the two surviving Assignees from time to time for ever, in order that the aforesaid Annuity be disposed of for the purpose above-mentioned.

The Church consists of Chancel, Nave, South Aisle, and North Transept. The south side is supported by three pointed arches. The Nave has been handsomely re-pewed, by the direction of the Rev. Thomas Spencer.

At the East End of the Chancel, outside.

Near this Place lyeth the Body of the Rev. Nathaniel Brewer, Late Vicar of Keevil, who Departed this Life March ye 17, 1734, in the 67 year of his Age. Also near this Place lyeth the Body of Mrs. Elizth Brewer, who died May the 18, 1759, Aged 63 years.

STEEPLE ASHTON.

On a Monument against the north Wall of Chancel.

H. S. E.

Anna, Uxor dilecta Avery Thompson, A. M. et Barth: Martyn, hujus Ecclæ Vicarij, Filia. Obijt 11mo Die Augu... A. D. 1734, Æt. 43. Amoris Conjugalis, en! Exemplar.

Arms—A lion passant guardant: impaling, an eagle with two heads, displayed.

Near this, in the South Isle lie interred the Remains of Henry Long, Esq. of Rood Ashton, who was Buried March 26th, 1672.

Also of Richard Long, of Rood Ashton, Nephew and adopted Heir of Henry, Second Son of Richard Long, of Collingburn Kingston, by Elizabeth, Sister of the said Henry, and Grandson of Thomas Long, of Little Chiverel, of the ancient Family of the Longs of Wraxall, Wilts. The first named Richard Long, of Rood Ashton, married Elizabeth, Daughter of Thos. Long, of Rowden, Esq. by whom he had a Son, named Richard. who married Ann, the Sole Daughter and Heiress of John Martyn, of Hinton, in this Parish, Gent. who died in 1701, Aged 49, and Grace, his Wife, who died in 1746, Aged 78, both Interred in this Church. The said Richard, by Ann, his Wife, had two Sons and three Daughters. He died May 6th, 1760, Aged 70, to whose Memory in particularly, as also to the Memory of the said several deceased Persons, the said Ann, his sorrowful Widow, hath Caused this Monument to be Erected.

The above-mentioned Ann Long died Jan. 19th, 1768, Æ. 71.

Richard, her Eldest Son, died Sept. 3d, 1787, Æ. 39, and was buried in the Parish Church of Whaddon, in this County.

Ellen, her Youngest Daughter, died May 19th, 1794, Ætat. 62.

Her Youngest Son, John Long, D. D. Fellow of All-Souls College, Oxford, and Rector of Chelsfield, in Kent, died October 17th, 1797, Aged 65 years.

On Flat Stones in Chancel.

Here lyeth the Body of John, Son of John Martyn, of Hinton, Gentleman, and Grace, his Wife, who departed this life on October ye 12th, An. Dom̃ 1708, Ætatis 17mo.

Here Lieth the Body of Elizabeth, Daughter of Mr. Samuel Martyn, of Chippenham, who died August the 4, A. D. 1732, Aged 1 year.

Here lyeth the Body of Mr. Samuel Martyn, of East Town, who died Feb. the 19th, 1687, Aged 30.

Here lyeth ye Body of Mr. John Martyn, Son of Mr. Samuel Martyn, who Departed this life Nov. 19th, 1714, Aged 28.

Arms—An eagle with two heads displayed.

M. S.

Una Vixerunt, Una Resurgunt, Qui hic una Tumulantur, Robertus Beach, Generosus, Qui Obijt Jan. 22, 1672, et Gratia Beach, Uxor Ejus, Quæ Obijt Apr. 28, 1685. Quos jus & Charitas olim adornavant, eorum cineros jam dissocians vetant, par est nimirum, ut unicum conjungeret monumentum, Quos fideli conjugio univerat Deus, Veni et Avi, Viator, mortalitatis et unitatis memor.

Arms—Vair: impaling, a fleur-de-lis within a border.

Brass Plate.

Anna, Uxor Rogeri Markes, Geñ. et filia Walteri Hungerford, Armigeri, obijt 21° Die Augusti, 1662.

Mon. against the first pillar from the W. end in S. side of Nave.

Near this Place lie the Remains of Wm. Long, of the City of Bath, who Departed this life July 9th, 1783, Aged 52 years.

Also of Ann and Jane, two Infant Daughters.

This Monument is erected to preserve the Memory of a kind Husband and tender Parent, by his sorrowful Widow, Ann Long.

Arms—Sable, a lion rampant between eight crosslets, argent.

First Pillar N. Side.

Anna, Uxor Johannis Brown, Annos Nata, 62, Obiit 11° die Decembris, 1761.

Johannes Brown, Annos Natus 87, Obijt 5° Julij, 1768.

Anna, filia J. & Annæ Brown, Annos nata 72, Obijt 5° Decembris, MDCCXCV.

Maria, Filia J. et Annæ Brown, Annos Nata 67, Obijt 12° Septembris, MDCCXCVII.

T. Owen, A. M. posuit.

West End.

Underneath lyeth Enterr'd the Body of Elizth Silverthorn, Spinster, of East Town, who died March ye 20, 1756, Aged 72 years.

On Flat Stones in Nave.

[Brass Plate.]

Here lyeth the Body of Thomas Flower, Gent. who Departed this life the 17 day of March, Ann. Doñ 1671.

Here lyeth the Body of Betty, Wife of Robert Rogers, Daughter of John and Betty Long, who Departed this life August 27th, 1791, Aged 56 years.

Also Here lyeth the Body of Mrs. Sarah Long, Spinster, Daughter of John and Sarah Long. Died Nov. ye 1, 1757, Aged 62 years.

Also Here lyeth the Body of George, Son of George and Sarah Ball, who died August ye 19, A. D. 1756, Aged 3 years.

Tho. D'Arcy died the 7th Dec. 1819, Aged 70 years.

Here lie the Remains of Henry Flower, of West Ashton, who died July ye 7th, 1789, Aged 63 years.

Also of Henry, Son of Henry and Mary Flower, who died July ye 17th, 1761, Aged 3 years.

John Brown died July 5th, 1768, Aged 87 years.

Ann Brown, Wife of John Brown, died Dec. 11th, 1761, Aged 62 years.

Ann Brown, Daughter of John and Ann Brown, died Dec. 5, 1795, Aged 72 years.

Mary Brown, Second Daughter of John and Ann Brown, died Sept. 11th, 1797, in the 68 year of her Age.

Betty, Wife of John Long, died May 24th, 1748.

Wm. Long died July 9th, 1783.

Ann and Jane, Daughters of Wm. Long.

Jane Long, grand Daughter of the above Wm. Long, died March 10, 1812, Aged 1 year and 6 months.

On monuments in the north aisle, beginning at the east end.

To the Memory of Thomas Bennett, Esq. of this Place, who died ye 23d of Feb. 1728, Aged 66 years. And of Thomas Bennet, Esq. of Comb-hay, in the County of Somerset, his Second Son, who died the 4th of March, 1728, Aged 32.

As also of Thomas Bennett Smith, Son of Robert Smith, Esq. of Comb-hay, and Mary, his Wife, the only surviving Daughter and Heiress of Thos. Bennett, Sen. who died the 23 of Sept. 1729, Aged 7 months.

Arms—Per fess, imbattled, gules and argent, in chief a pale between two demi-lions rampant, argent, crowned or, in base, on a pale, gules, a demi-lion rampant, argent: impaling per fess or and argent, a lion rampant azure.

Sacred to the Memory of Anne Cary, the Wife of Robert Cary, of Hampstead, in the County of Middlesex, Esq. She was the Daughter of Robert Smith, Esq. of Comb-hay, in the County of Somerset. She died the 15th Sept. 1772, Leaving Issue Anne and Mary.

Arms—Argent, on a bend, sable, three roses argent: impaling gules, on a chevron, or, three leopards' heads caboshed, sable, between three cinquefoils, argent.

To the Memory of John Smith Esq. of Comb-hay, in the County of Somerset, Son of Robert Smith, Esq. by Mary, Daughter of Thomas Bennett, Esq. of this Place. He married Ann, Daughter of Lord Viscount Tracy: She died on the 12 Day of April, 1765, and He on the 12th Day of Nov. 1775; She in the forty-first, and He in the forty-ninth year of their respective ages. He had the honour to represent the City of Bath in the first, second, and third Parliaments of George the Third, and discharged the Duties of the Appointment to the satisfaction of his Constituents. They left one Son, and had no other Issue but a Daughter, who died in her Infancy.

Arms—Quarterly, first and fourth gules, on a chevron or, three leopards' heads caboshed, sable, between three cinquefoils, arg. second and third, per fess imbattled, gules and argent, in chief a pale argent between two demi-lions rampant argent, crowned or, in base, on a pale, gules, a demi-lion rampant, argent, crowned, or: impaling or, an escallop in bend, sable, between two plain cottises, gules.

On flat stones near the above.

To the Memory of Christopher, Son of Thomas Bennett, Esq. who died the 5 of Feb. A. D. 1707.

Also in Memory of Ann Hudson, Widdow, who died the 20th of Nov. A. D. 1732, Aged 76.

Here lyeth the Body of Rebecca, the Wife of Chr. Bennett, who deceased .... of Feb. 1654.

Here lyeth the Body of Jeane, the Daughter of Thomas Bennett, Gent. who Departed this life .... 13, Anno Domini ....

Here lyeth the Body of John Bennett, Gent. who Deceased the 4th Day of January, An° Dom. 1661.

Thomas Bennett, Jun. Esq. Dyed March the 4th, 1728, Aged 33 years.

Brass Plate.

John Stileman, of this Parish, Gent. was buried Nov. 19, 1641.

John Stileman, Gent. Son of the above-mentioned John Stileman, buried Dec. 21, 1691.

John Stileman, Gent. Son of the above-mentioned John Stileman, buried Sept. 25, 1713.

John Stileman, Gent. Son of the above John Stileman and Christian his Wife, Buried August 2d, 1725, Aged 16.

Arms—An unicorn, in chief three billets: impaling a cross between four swords inverted.

Over the north door.

John Sharp died July the first, 1814, Aged 17 years.

On Monuments in West End of N. Aisle.

On the North Side of this Church Yard lie the Remains of Dorothy, third Daughter of Thos. Browne, of Camfield Place, near Hatfield, Hertfordshire, Esq. by Martha, his Wife, Daughter of George Nedham, of Wymondley Priory, Hertfordshire, Esq. She died at Bath, unmarried, March 7th, 1807, Aged 59 years.

John Hicks, Gent. died Dec. 14, 1782, in the 82 year of his Age.

John Lewis Hicks, Esq. his Son, M. A. of Queen's College, in the University of Oxford, Captain in the Wiltshire Militia, eminent for his Knowledge in Modern Languages, as well as in Greek and Roman Literature, died in the 42 year of his Age, Jan. 19th, 1788.

Arms—Gules, a fess, wavy, between three fleur-de-lis, or.

Here lyeth the Body of Margery, Daughter of Stephen Wilkins, and of Elizabeth, his Wife, who Departed this life the 21 Day of January, Anno Dom. 1712, Aged 10 months and 25 days.

In Memory of Stephen Wilkins. He Dy'd the 25 of Oct. 1730, Aged 47 years.

Also in Memory of Elizabeth, his Wife. She Dy'd the 21 of Feb. 1729, Aged 43 years.

Also in Memory of Thomas and Thomas, Sons of Joseph and Ann Wilkins: One Dy'd the 7th of Oct. 1739, in his Infancy, the Other Dy'd ye 20th of March, 1747, Aged 1 year & 3 months.

On an Altar-Tomb.

Here lyeth the Body of Elizth Lewis, Widow of George Lewis, Rector of Quarly, in Hants. and Daughter of Samuel Pitman, Esq. Lord of the Manor of Quarly, who Departed this life Ap. 23, 1762, In hopes of a joyful Resurrection through the Merits of our Lord and Saviour Jesus Christ.

Also Here lyeth the Body of Maria Susanna, only Daughter of the Rev. Mr. George Lewis, and Elizth his Wife. She Departed this life April 13, 1780, in the Seventy Second year of her Age.

On Flat Stones.

To the Memory of Mary, the Daughter of Daniel Pryor, who died the 8th Day of July, A. D. 1733, Aged 41.

Here lyeth the Body of Daniel Pryor, the Elder, who Departed this life the 25 Day of Feb. in the year of our Lord 1727/8.

Also Here lyeth the Body of Daniel Pryor, who Departed this life Jan. .. 1769.

Here lieth the Body of Henry Browne, who Departed this Life the 25 Day of Feb. Anno Domini 1710, Aged 52 years.

Here Lyeth the Body of Maurice Jarvice, who died Septem. the 8, A. D. 1722, Aged 32 years.
As also of George, his Son, who died March the 27, A. D. 1736, Aged 15 yea[illegible]

Here lyeth ye Body of Thos. Hickes. He Departed this life ye 16 day of April, 1687.

Here lies ye Body of George Hancock, who Departed this life January ye 28, A. D. 1733, Aged 65 years.

To the Memory of Jean, the Daughter of Mr. Matthew Burges, and of Mary, His Wife, who Departed this life Jan. the 4th, A. D. 173 . Aged 27 years.
Here Lyeth the Body of Elizabeth Burges, the Daughter of Matthew Burges, and of Mary, his Wife, who Departed this life the 13 Day . . . . 1717, Aged 18 years.

Here lyeth the Body of Mrs. Jean Tipper. Departed in 1725.

Here lyeth the Body of Henry Martyn, Junior, who Departed this life the 5th Day of April, Anno Domini 1690.

Here lyeth the Body of Mrs. Anne Tipper. Departed in 1723.

On Monuments at the West End of South Aisle.

In Memory of Lieut. Col. Thomas De la Beche, Son of Thomas and Henry Beach, who died at Bath, in Jamaica, on the 1st June, 1801, Aged 45 years.

To the Memory of the Honourable Thomas Beach, Esq. Son of Thos. Beach, Esq. of West Ashton and Wolley, in the County of Wilts. Formerly his Majesty's Attorney General, a Member of the Honble House of Assembly, and lastly, Chief Justice of the Island of Jamaica, who died in Spanish Town the 29th June, 1774, Aged 58 years.
Also of Helen Beach, his Wife, one of the Daughters and Coheiresses of John Hynes, Esq. of Westmorland, in the said Island, who was also a Member of the House of Assembly. She died in Spanish Town the 24th June, 1771, Aged 38 years.
This Monument is erected by their affectionate Son, Thomas Beach, Esq. a Captain in his Majesty's 81st, or Gordon's Highlanders.

Arms—Quarterly, first and fourth vair, argent and gules, on a canton, azure, a pile, or; second and third vair, or and azure, a pale, ermine, on a chief, argent, two chaplets, azure: over all, on an escutcheon, quarterly, first snd fourth azure, a tower argent between two lions combatant or; second and third or, a lion rampant-regardant, or, on a canton, sable, a horse's head erased, argent.
Crest—A demi-lion rampant argent, gorged or, holding a shield, azure, charged with a pile, or.

To the Memory of Mrs. Jannet Gowland, Wife of Thomas Gowland, Esq. and Daughter of the above Thomas and Helen Beach, who died December 30th, 1809, Aged 50 years.

In Memory of John Hynes De la Beche, Son of Thomas and Helen Beach, who died at Frankfort on the Maine, on the 26 April, 1803, Aged 58 years.

Flat Stones.

H. S. E.

Eliztha Turner, Vidua Georgii Turner, de Lin...d, in Com. Surrey, Armigeri, quæ Obiit vicesimo septimo Die Decembris, Anno Dom̄ 172- Ætat. 66.
Arms—Vair, on a pale three trefoils, crescent for difference: impaling, per fess indented, three chaplets.

Here lies ye Body of Mrs. Grace Beach, Daughter of Mr. Thomas Beach, of West Ashton, who died Feb. ye 7, 1732. *Arms*—Vair.

H. S. E.

Thomas Beach, de West Ashton, Gent. Vir Probitatis, Amicitiæ, Charitatis, plenus; qui Obijt Decimo die Nov. Anno Dom̄ 1729, Ætat. 92.

Here lyeth the Body of Mr. Robert Beach, Son of Mr. Thomas Beach, of West Ashton, Gent. who Departed this life June the 16th, Anno Dni. 1710.

In Memory of Mrs. Elizabeth Beach, Daughter of Thomas and Elizth Beach, Esq. of West Ashton, who Departed this life Nov. 8th, 1785, Aged 74.
Also in Memory of Mrs. Ann Catharine Beach, Sister of the above-mentioned Mrs. Elizabeth Beach, who Departed this life Feb. the 3d, 1804, Aged 84.

Brass Plate.

Francis Long, Son of Francis and Sarah Long, Died Dec. 10, 1815, Aged 92 years.

Also Here lyeth the Body of Francis Long, Son of John and Sarah Long, who departed this life Ma.. . . . . in the year of our Lord . . . 1762.

Underneath lie the Remains of Anne, Wife of the Rev. Wm. Wainhouse, Daughter of Wm. Beach, Esq. of Keevil. She died Feb. the 10th, 1771, in the 22 year of her Age.

Blessed are the meek.

On a Brass Plate.

To the Memory of Ann Wilkins, who dyed Dec. 26, 1685, Aged 42 years.

Also to the Memory of Jane Rogers, Widow of Francis Rogers. She Dy'd Dec. ye 12, 1747, Aged 79 years.

Here lyeth the Body of Wm. Clift, who Departed this life . . . . July, 1744, Aged 76 years.

Also here lieth the Body of Catherine Clift, the Wife of Wm. Clift, who Departed this Life March ye 20, A. D. 1768, Aged 68 years.

Also in Memory of Ann, Daughter of Wm. and Catherine Clift. She died Nov. ye 26, 17 . 3, Aged 51 years.

Also in Memory of Elizabeth Clift, their Daughter. She Died May ye 15, 1787, Aged 50 years.

Brass Plates.

Underneath are Interred the Remains of Mr. William Clift, of Keevil Wick, who died Feb. 2d, 1799, Aged 58 years.

Here lieth ye Body of Peter Crook, who deceased ye 8 of April, 1633, who gave to this Church 20s. and to ye poore of this towne 11s. a year for ever.

Roger Crooke, Gent. was buried Feb. the 20th, 1655.
Roger Crooke, Gent. was buried Aug. the first, 1675.

Brass Plate against S. side of S. Aisle.

In Spe B. Resur. I. S. D. Exuviæ Roberti Foulkes, A. D. 1771, Ætat. 77.

Flat Stone.

H. S. E.

Robertus Foulkes, A. M. hujusce Ecclesiæ per annos 23 Vicarius fidelis, et Christinæ Religionis Ornamentum. Ob. Augusti 24, A. D. 1771, Ætat. 77.

Underneath are interred Richard Long, Esq, who died May 6, 1760, Aged 71, And Ann, his Widow, who Died Jan. 19th, 1768, Aged 71.

Against S. E. Pillar of the Nave.

To the Dear Memory of Anne, Wife of the Rev. Wm. Wainhouse, Daughter of William Beach, Esq. of Keevil. She died Feb. 10th, 1771, in the 22 year of her age. In Temper meek and humble, in Manners gentle and engaging; to her Lot, in Life & Death, resigned.

Rest, virtuous spirit! to the latent grief
Death, on thy slumbers stealing, brought Relief;
Thy youthful Days, in silent sufferings past,
Kind Heaven repaid with smiles & peace at last.

Arms—Indented, or, a fess indented, azure, in base an escallop, azure, on a chief of the last two escallops, or: impaling, vair, argent and gules, on a canton, or, a buck's head caboshed, sable.

Against N. Side of the Nave.

This Church was Founded unto the Honour of Almighty God, between the years of our Lord 1480 and 1500. The North Ile was Built at the Cost and Charge of Robert Long and Edith his Wife. The South Ile, for the most part, was built at the Cost and Charge of Walter Leucas and Maud his Wife. The rest of the Church with the Steeple was built at the Cost and Charge of the Parishioners then Living.

West End of Nave.

Upon this Tower was a famous and lofty Spire, containing in height above the Tower ninety three feet, which a violent storm of thunder and lightning rent, and made a great breach therein, July 25, 1670. The Parish, willing to preserve such a noble and Complete Spire, endeavoured to repair the same by employing able workmen for that purpose, but such was the uncontrollable Providence of Almighty God, that, when the Spire was almost finished, and the workmen labouring thereon, another terrible Storm of Thunder and Lightning happened on the 15th Oct. in the same year, which threw down the Spire, killed the two workmen labouring thereon, and beat down the Top of the Tower, great part of the Body of the Church, and part of the Iles thereof. The Reparation whereof cost the Parishioners, and some well-disposed Neighbours, the Sum of 420 pounds, and was finished in the year 1675. John Stileman and John Tucker Ch.-Wardens.

S. Wall of S. Aisle.

For Encouragement of Industrious Poor, John Brown, late of this Parish of Steeple Ashton, Joyner, did, by his last Will, Charitably give ye Rents & Profits of one piece of Ground, lying in Windmill field, in this Parish, containing 4 Acres (and let for £.5 10*s*. a year) for ever. And also did order ye sum of two Hundred Pounds to be laid out in other Lands within 5 miles of this Parish, and ye Rents & Profits thereof likewise to be Given for Ever unto four Poor Men of this Parish, having Families, to be equally divided amongst them, who must be of good repute, dwelling within 3 furlongs of the Crosse here, and must be Members of ye Church of England, and such as have not at any time received Alms of ye Parish, but have bred up their Families by their own Industry, and are above ye Age of 45 years: and by his said Will did order Laurence Howell, Wm. Chapman,

Daniel Symbs ye Elder, & John Oatley, from & after ye 25 Day of March, 1722, to have ye Benefit of this Charity during their respective Lives; and that ye said Laurence Howell should collect and receive ye rents of ye said Lands during his life, and distribute them accordingly, the other 3 persons each allowing him two shillings a year for his Trouble of Collecting. Pursuant to ye above, ye said Sum of two Hundred Pounds hath been laid out in ye purchase of Certain Lands, being at Bower-hill, situate in ye Parish of Melksham, Containing 8 Acres, & let for 8 Pounds a Year. Within one Month after ye decease of either of the said persons above-named, or of any other Person who hereafter shall be admitted to share of this Charity, the Minister of this Parish for ye time being may present unto two of the next Justices of ye Peace (who have no Estate real or personal in ye Parish) any other Poor man dwelling, & so to be qualified as aforesaid; and if, by his Examination upon oath, such poor man shall appear so to be dwelling & so to be qualified, and ye said Justices shall so Certifie him to be, then such poor man so presented, paying to ye said Justices Clarkes 5 Shillings a piece for such Certificate, and allowing two Shillings a Year to ye receiver of ye Rents, shall be entitled to an equal share of this Charity: or if ye said Justices ever after such Examination, shall find that ye person so presented is not dwelling & qualified to be admitted & entitled to such share in his stead; But ye said Will provides that no more than four persons at one time shall be admitted to this Charity, and that after ye Death of ye said Laurence Howell, such person as hath longest been entitled to a share, shall be Collector of ye Rents, and that on ye Death of either of ye persons at any time entitled to a share of this Charity, his Widow, Children, or Child, shall be entitled to his Share untill the 25 day of March next after such his decease: and that this Table from time to time be maintained in repair out of ye Profits of ye said Lands, to prevent ye Misapplying of ye said Charity, and to encourage others to ye like. This Table was erected at ye Expence of his Widow and Executrix, and an attested Copy of his Will Given in ye hands of ye Churchwardens of ye Parish, to be by them laid up in ye Church Chest amongst other parish Writings. Anno Dom. 1726.

Brass Plate.

Sepulchrum Sam. Martyn, Gen. Nov. 12, 1643.

Hic spiritus ablentis exvuiæ jacent mox induendæ cum (iuberite Judice) latus tremendæ postulat clangor tubæ tumulis resurgum dormientes undique plerique coram Judicis vultu cadent At Ipse Stabit (rectus in foro poli) Tensa Patroni nempe suffultus manu Spe præmij repletus haud pœnæ metu terris opera dicavit ac cœlis fidem Dat terra laudem præmium cœli dabunt Homines manu loquantur haud linguâ bonos Laudare recta qui volunt faciant edem.

Memento Mori.

To the Memory of Deborah Marks, who Departed this life the 8th day of March, 1730, Aged 99.

Hatchments.

Long: impaling sable, on a fess, or, two mullets sable between three cinquefoils, argent.

Quarterly, first and fourth argent, a spread eagle, gules; second and third gules, on a chevron argent, three leopards' heads caboshed, sable, between three cinquefoils, argent.

Gules, a chevron, or, three leopards' heads caboshed, sable, between three cinquefoils, argent: impaling or, on a bend cottized gules, an escallop, sable.

This Church is a very large and beautiful structure, having, from its external form and interior decorations, more the resemblance of a Cathedral. It has a Chancel, Nave, and North and South Aisles. The Nave is supported on each side by four lofty pointed arches, resting on massy columns. The vaulting of the aisles is of stone, ornamented with handsome foliage; that of the nave and chancel is of wood, it appears to have been formerly of stone, but the falling of the Tower in 1670, probably occasioned its ruin.

Register commenced 1558.

The Rev. Mr. Hay, Vicar.

ATWORTH.

On a Monument against the north Wall of Chancel.

Near this Place Lyeth ye Body of Elizabeth, Wife of Thomas Godwin, of Ford Farm, Gent. who died August ye 18th, A. D. 1718, Aged 73 years.

Also the Body of Mrs. Rebecca Martyn, Sister of ye Said Thomas Godwyn, who Died ye same day, Aged 82 years.

As also the Body of Mrs. Abigail Godwyn, Widow, who died Nov. ye 8th, A. D. 1719, Aged 73 years.

Neare this Place Lyeth the Body of Edward tydcomb, Gent. late of atworth, Sirgan, who dyed the 11th day of december, 1689, Aged 38 years.

Underneath is Interred ye Remains of Mrs. Mary, daughter of Thomas Godwin, Gent. of Ford farm, in the Parish of Bradford, by Elizth his Wife, and Wife of John Lucker, Gent. of the City of Bristol, who Departed this life the 24 day of Oct. 1764, Aged 82 years.

South Wall.

Nere under this Place Lye buried ye Body of Mrs. Mary Abbott, ye vertueous and loving Wife of Mr. John Abbott, Citizen of London, who Departed this life ye 26 day of Decem. Ann. Dom. 1693.

Here lyeth the Body of Mrs. Elizabeth Yerbury, of Cottles, Wid. Relict of Mr. John Yerbury, who Departed this life the 2d day of March, Anno Dom̄. 1698.

Let no person remove this Stone.

Sacred to ye Memory of Mrs. Jane Brown, Widow,
Daughter of William Powlet, of Cottles, Esq.
who, out of her Estate in Cottles,
gave the perpetual Anūal Rents
of 31 pounds, Viz.

To ye Curate of Atford for weekly Catechizing xl.
To a person for teaching poor Children xl.
For buying books for those Children vl.
For Clothing poor Children vl.
For a Scholar in the University from Marlburgh Schoole vl.
And out of her lands in Warwickshire to the Minister of Maxstock for weekly Catechizing xxl.

She died July ye 26, A. Dni .... Aged 87.

Hatchment—In a lozenge, sable, on a bend cottized argent, three lions passant of the same: impaling sable, three swords argent, points meeting in base, hilted or.

Shusanna Sheapheard, Wife of John Sheapherd, who Departed this life .... June 1678.

Brass Plate.

Here lyeth the Body of Mary, the Wife of Michael Tidcombe, of Atford, Daughter of John and Elizth Yerbury. Deceased the 17th of June, Anno Dom. 1657.

Mon. against the North Wall of Nave.

Sacred to the Memory of Mary, Wife of Guilliam Webb, Gent. The best of Wives, a tender Mother, Lamented by all who knew her. She died July 16th, 1800, Aged 57.

Also Guilliam Webb, Gent. who Departed this life the 16th Day of May 1811, Aged 72 years.

In my full age here do I lie:
If thou art old prepare to die;
If thou art young prepare also,
When death do call we all must go.

Also Hester Gunning, Daughter of the above, who Departed this life the 31 Day of Oct. 1805, Aged 39 years.

Also Joan, the Wife of Guilliam Webb, Jun. who Departed this life the 21 Day of Sept. 1805, Aged 30 years.

Lament no more, ye pious Friends,
For our return to dust,
Since God have made you all amends,
And plac'd us with the Just.

Hatchment in the Nave.

Quarterly, first and fourth argent, a fess sable, in chief three cinquefoils of the last: second and third sable, a fess engrailed between six crosslets fitchy or: impaling azure, an unicorn passant argent, on a chief, gules, three fleur-de-lis, or.

Crest—A stork's head erased, argent, on an esquire's helmet.

Register commenced 1653.

In the Chancel and north window of the Nave is a little painted glass, g. or, & az.

The Rev. Mr. Blomberg Rector.

Mr. Hales Lord of the Manor.

CHALDFIELD.

On Flat Stones.

Here Lyeth the Body of Margaret Horton, late Wife of Edward Horton, of Great Chaldfield, in the County of Wilts, Gent. And Eldest Daughter of Sir William Dodington, Late of Breamore, in the County of Southampton, Knight, who Departed this life the 30th Day of November, 1670.

In Memory of Mary, the Wife of Henry Miles, who Departed this life the 12 day of July, Anno Dom. 1738, Aged 29 years.

To the Memory of Caterine, the Wife of Thomas Miles, who Departed this life the 18 Day of October, A.D. 1730, Aged 54.

Also near this Place lyeth ye Body of Thos Miles, who Departed this life ye 13 day of June, A.D. 1733, Aged 62 years.

Shields of Arms carved in the ancient Stone Screen:

1. Gules, a fess engrailed ermine between three griffins' heads erazed, argent: impaling azure, a fess of five fusils, gules.
2. Gules, a fess engrailed ermine between three griffins' heads erazed, argent: impaling azure, three lions rampant arg. armed gules.
3. Gules, a fess engrailed ermine, between three griffins' heads erazed argent.
4. Gules, a fess engrailed ermine between three griffins' heads erazed argent: impaling azure, a chevron between three dogs' heads erazed, sable.
5. Gules, a fess engrailed ermine between three griffins' heads, erazed, argent: impaling azure, three fishes naiant, arg. within a border, or.

In the west window of the Nave, and south window of the south aisle, is some painted glass, G. O. & V. In the south aisle is a small piscina.

Near the Church is an ancient house, built in the Gothic style, having several statues holding shields of arms blazoned as those mentioned above.

WHADDON.

On a white marble monument in Long's Chapel.

Sacred to the Memory of Walter Long, of this Place of South Wraxhall, and of the City of Bath, Esq. only Son of Thomas Long, of South Wraxhall, Esq. by Mary his Wife.

Nature and Education combined to qualify him for gaining that esteem which the suavity of his Manners and an excellent understanding confirmed; while early habits of application, and a memory rendered powerful by judicious employment, gave accuracy to his judgment, and energy to his language. He was an elegant Scholar, a cheerful companion, and a worthy man. To his numerous tenantry he was conspicuously munificent; and when the dangers of the Country called for extraordinary aid, he nobly devoted the produce of their labours to the defence of their Liberty. He departed this life on the 18th day of January, 1807 in the 95th year of his Age, when his remains were deposited in this Mausoleum, with those of his sisters, Ellen Long, who died 26th of February, 1787, Aged 70, and Ann Long, who died 29th December, 1802, Aged 89. His Sister Mary Long died 20th August, 1776, Aged 66, and was born at Wraxhall: with these, and the surviving Sister Katherine Long, he shared the blessings of reciprocal and deserved affection.

Arms—Sable, a lion rampant between eight cross-crosslets argent.

Crest—a lion's head erased, or, holding in its mouth a sinister hand, gules.

West Wall.

Thou shalt come to thy Grave in a full Age, Like as a Shock of Corn cometh in his season. Job. ch. v. ver. 26.

Sacred to the Memory of Catherine Long, Spinster, (the Youngest Daughter of Thomas Long, of South Wraxhall, in the County of Wilts. Esquire) whose earthly remains are Deposited in the mausoleum underneath. She died on the 15th of January, 1814, in the 97th year of her Age.

Endowed with a sound Understanding and active disposition, this worthy person exercised through a length of days those useful duties and Christian virtues which adorn both human nature and religion; for she was pious and devout towards God, abounding in works of Charity to her fellow-creatures under poverty or distress, and generous to her friends, acquaintance, and domesticks. Unaccustomed to scenes of public life, she sought for, and enjoyed in rural retirement, those Comforts, which not Riches, but a good Conscience only could administer, when joined to a stedfast faith in the gracious promises of the Gospel.

This Monument is Erected in testimony of the very grateful and especial regard which was justly due and borne to Mrs. Catherine Long by the Rev. Charles Coxwell, Clerk, and Thomas Bruges, Esq. on whom she was pleased to constitute her Executors and Residuary Legatees.

Flat Stones.

Here lies the Body of Sir Walter Long, of Whaddon, in ye County of Wilts. Baronet, who Departed this Life the 21st of May, Anno 1710, Aged 84 years.

Arms—Two flanches ermine, a lion rampant between six cross-crosslets.

Here lyes the Body of Calthrop Long, Esq. . . . . Parker, of Arwarton, in the County of Suffolk, Baronett, by Dame Rebecka, his Wife, Daughter of Sir Walter Long, the Elder, of Whaddon, Baronett. He Changed his Name according to his Grandfather's Will, who left him the Estate. He dyed the 10th of May, 1729, Aged 72 years.

Brass Plate.

. . . .

. . . .

Bailie, Gent, which said Henrie Long
died the first day of Maie, 1612, and
in the tenth year of the Raigne of
King James.

On Flat Stones in Nave.

In Memory of the Reverend Mr. John Lewis, Rector of ys Church, who died Nov. 23d, A. D. 1744, in the .2d year of his Age.

In Memory of the Reverend Mr. Anthony Drewett, 25 years Rector of this Parish, who died July 19, ...

White Marble.

Here lie the Remains of Jane Cooper (wife of the Rev. Dr. Cooper, Rector of this Parish) who departed this life Oct. 25th, 1783, Aged 47 years.

Her form the Beauties of her mind express'd,
Her mind was Virtue by the Graces dress'd.

Here lie the Remains of the Rev. Edward Cooper, L. L. D. Vicar of Sunning, in the County of Berks. and formerly Rector of this Parish, who Departed this life August 27th, 1792, in the sixty-fifth year of his Age.

In the Chancel are hanging two helmets, gauntlets, dagger, and spur, in good preservation.

The Rev. Mr. Edey, Rector.

Mr. Long Lord of the Manor.

BROUGHTON GIFFORD.

On a small Monument against the north Wall of Chancel.

Sacred to the Memory of William Curtis, Esq. of this Parish, who died the 19th of Sept. 1806, in the sixty-seventh year of his Age.

South Wall.

Sacred to the Memory of Joseph Smith, Esq. of Bradford, Wilts. who Departed this Mortal State July 8th, 1804, Aged 77 years.

Also of his Wife, Penolope Smith, Eldest Daughter and Coheiress of Mr. John Golding, Deceased. She died the 12th of Nov. 1779, Aged 45 years.

Also their Infant Daughter Penelope, who died the 4th of Nov. 1760, in the 3d year of her Age.

Also their only Son Joseph Smith, who Departed this Life the 28 of May, 1781, in the 21 Year of his Age, then Student of Oriel College, Oxford.

Flat Stone.

Spe certa Resurgendi in Christo, sub hoc Marmore depositæ sunt Exuviæ Reverendissimi Edmundi Proby, S. T. P. filij natu tertij Petri Proby, de Elton, in Comitatu Huntington, Equitis Aurati, qui per annos quinquaginta et ultra fere duos hujus Ecclesiæ Rector; tandem, A° Dni 1684, Ætatis suæ 86, moriens abdormiit. *Arms*—Ermine, on a fess a lion passant.

On a Flat Stone in Nave.

Here lieth the Body of Wm. Gore, Gentleman, late of Broughton, deacesed, And was buried the Eight and twenty day of April, in the Year of our Lord 1616.

On a Monument in the South Aisle.

Metam properamus ad unam.

Sacred to the Memory of Henry Harding, of this Parish, Gent. who died June 3d, 1774, Æt. 67.

Also of his two Sisters, Mrs. Ann Harding, & Mrs. Betty Paradice: Mrs. Harding died May 3d, 1781, Æt. 75, Mrs. Paradice died July 11th, 1786, Æt. 70. The latter, in compliance with the Deed, and to fulfil the Intention of her Sister, in the year 1782, vested in Government Securities £900 Stock, which, producing an Annual Interest of £27, is to be applied for ever under the direction of three Trustees, appointed for that purpose, as also the Rector and Churchwardens for the Time being, to the following Charities; Viz. £20 per annum to a master for the Education of 20 Poor Boys or Girls; £7 per Ann. to be distributed at Christmas amongst such 10 poor Persons as have not been entered on the Parish book, or received Relief of any kind from the Parish for one Twelvemonth, previous to their making such application.

May the Deeds of the Righteous and their Alms be had in Everlasting Remembrance.

Sacred to the Memory of Isaac Dark, who died Sept. 26, 1818, Aged 63 years.

Shew us thy mercy, O Lord, and grant us thy salvation.

Sacred to the Memory of Stephen Dark, of Maiden Bradley, who Departed this life Feb. 3d, 1815, Aged 23 years.

North Aisle.

Near this Place lyeth ye Body of Thomas Hunt, who died Feb. the 10th, 17 18/19, Aged 45 years.

Dear Wife & Children do not weep,
For in Christ, my Lord, I am fallen asleep.
Memento Morio.

On a brass plate against south side of the Nave.

Robert Longe, second Soñe of Heñ Longe, of Whaddon, in the County of Wilts. Esq. married Millesaint, Daughter of Thos. Witsey, Preacher of God's Word, by whom he had IIII soñes, Robert, Edward, Henry, Posthumus. He died An° Dñi 1620, Nov. XIII. Æta. suæ XLVI. in Pioufe Memory of whome, His Mornfull Wife erected this more loving than costly Representation.

The Life of Man is a trewe Lotterie,
Where venterous Death draws forth lotts Short & Longe
Yet free from fraude, and partiall Flatterie,
He Shufled Sheilds of severall size amonge,
Drewe Longe, and soe drewe longer his short daies,
Th' ancient daies beyonde all time to praise.

Arms—Two flanches azure, a lion rampant, charged with a crescent between eight cross crosslets.

In two windows of the North Aisle is a little painted glass, O. G. Az.

Register began 1667.

Rev. Charles Strong, Rector.

Benjamin Hobhouse Lord of the Manor.

HOLT.

On a Monument against the North wall of Chancel.

Here Lyeth the Body of Anne Blanchard, Wife of Wm. Blanchard, of Katherine, Esq. and daughter of Francis Baber, of Chece-magna, in the County of Sumerset, Esq. who Departed this life the first of July, Anno Dom̄ 1674.

On Monuments at the East End of Nave.

Near this Place lieth the Remains of Mrs. Unity Godwin, Second Wife of Mr. Jeremiah Godwin, who died April 28th, 1789, Aged 76 years.

Also Thomas Holder, who Departed this life August 27, 1790, Aged 50 years.

Underneath the second Stone from the .... are deposited the Mortal Remains of Mr. Paul Harvey, who Died Jan. 13th, 1807, in the 53 year of his Age.

He was an Affectionate Husband, a Sincere Friend, a Worthy Christian, who lived and died Beloved by all who knew him.

Here Under lyeth ye Body of Elizth Wife of John Baily, ye Elder, of Hoult, Gent. Dyed April the 11th, 1703.

Also lyeth the Body of John Baily, ye Elder. Dyed April ye 25th, Anō Dom̄ 1712, Aged 82 years.

Here also lyeth the Body of John Bailey, who Departed this life April ye 25th, Anō Dom̄ 1720, Aged 52 years.

Memento mori.

Also James Baily, Gent. Died Nov. ye 16, 1730, Aged 54.

And also in Memory of Morues Matravers. He died May ye 3, 1741, Aged 31 years.

Arms—Argent, on a fess.... three fleur-de-lis .... between three horses' heads erased, sable.

On Monuments at the West End of South Aisle.

Near this Place lye the Bodies of Richard Earle, late of this Parish, Gent. who Departed this life the 18th Day of Nov. 1718, in the 78th year of his Age,

And also of Ann, his Wife, Daughter of John Shepherd, of Lansdown, in the County of Somerset.

Likewise of Ann, their Daughter, who Departed this life April 28th, 1724, in the 48th year of her Age.

Also of Several of their Children, And of the Family of the Earles, are here interred.

This Stone was Erected by John Earle (Second Son of Richard and Ann Earle abovesaid) to the Memory of his Family, 1728.

Likewise in Memory of John Earle, Sen. who died January 23, 1741, Aged 61 years.

Also in Memory of Elizabeth, Wife of John Earle, who died May 26, 1744, Aged 55 years.

And also in Memory of Frances Earle, who died May 6, 1753, Aged 71 years.

Arms—Three escallops.

Near this Place lie the Remains of James Burton, Esq. Lord of the Manor of Holt, who died March 19th, 1812, Aged 81 years.

And also of Maria Susanna, his beloved Wife, who died July 2d, 1786, Aged 46 years.

Near this Place lie the Remains of Mary, Wife of James Chapman, who Departed this life May the 16, 1819, Aged 47 years.

Seek ye the Lord while he may be found,
call ye upon him while he is near.
55th Chapter of Isaiah, and the 6th Verse.

South Wall.

Near this Place lieth ye Body of John Earl Godwin, who Departed this life Sept. 23d, 1790, Aged 59 years. Not lost, but gone before.

Also Ann, Wife of John Hunt Godwin, who Departed this life August 27th, 1810, Aged 40 years.

Also Elizabeth, Wife of John Earle Godwin, who Departed this life Feb. 11th, 1817, Aged 81 years.

I am the Resurrection and the life, saith the Lord; he that believeth in me, though he were dead, yet shall he live; And whosoever liveth and believeth in me shall never die. St. John 11. 25, 26.

Near this Place lieth the Remains of Mary, the Wife of Richard Tayler, Jun. who Departed this life Nov. 12, 1802, in the 20th year of her Age.

Also Joanna, the Wife of Richard Tayler, Sen. who Departed this life Nov. 29th, 1806, in the 78 year of her Age.

Our trust is in the tender mercy of God
for ever and ever.

Also to the Memory of Richard Tayler, who died Feb. 24th, 1820, Aged 49 years.

East End.

Near this Place lyeth the Body of Jonathan, Son of Jeremiah and Priscilla Godwin, who died Nov. ye 28, 1761, Aged 28 years.

Also near this Place lieth the Body of Priscilla Godwin, who Departed this Life November ye 8th, 1765, Aged 67 years.

Underneath this Place lie the Remains of Jeremiah Godwin, Sen. who Departed this life September the 9th, 1777, Aged 72 years.

Also near this Place lieth the Body of Jeremiah Godwin, Jun. who Departed this Life May ye 7th, 1795, Aged 59 years.

Blessed are the Dead which die in the Lord.

Could youth or strength keep off ye stroke of Death,
Then I had been as you are now on earth;
But, lo! I'm gone before to silent rest,
And in ye grave am equall'd with ye best;
Yea, free from toil, and care, and wörldly Griefe,
Which load poor mortalls still without releife;
From those I'm free, all tears are wiped away,
Glory attends mee now, and endlesse joy.

Erected in Memory of John Shewring, late of this Parish, who Deceased April ye 28, 1691, buried near this Place.

277

Near this Place lyeth ye Body of Elizabeth, Wife of Morues Matravers, who Departed this life July ye 15, 1767, Aged 62 years.

Nobis vivere Christo, et mori Lucrum.

Underneath rest the Remains of Annis, Wife of John Bailey, the Elder, of this Parish, who had issue five Sons and Seven Daughters. She Departed this life November 21, 1646.

This Stony Register is for her Bones,
Her fame is more perpet'al than the Stones;
And Still her Goodness, though herself be gone,
Shall live when earthly Monumnts are none:
Who, reading this, can choose but drop a tear
For such a loving Wife and Mother dear.

Joan, Daughter of John and Annis Bailey, Died July 23d, 1642.
Edward, their third Son, died November 27th, 1643.
Mary, their Daughter, Died August 14th, 1650.
Ann, their Daughter, died February 7, 1651.
Giles, their fourth Son, Died December 14th, 1658.
John their second Son, late of Batheaston, in the County of Somerset, Died January 14th, 1662.

If for to live be but a Misery,
If by Death good men gain Eternity;
If out of trouble Death doth Mortals raise,
If that by Death a happy change displays;
True Honour matchless lives Eternally.
Here rest their Corps, their souls are fled on high
Of those whose Dust doth here engaged remain,
That when the World dissolve, will come again.

Also the Above Said John Bailey, the Elder, who Departed this life January 15, 1667, Aged 87 years.
Ann, Wife of John Bailey (Son of Edward, Deceased) Died 1667.
Ann, their Daughter, died 1674.
Edward, their Son died 1691.
Sarah, his Daughter, by Sarah, his Second Wife, Died 1698.
Joshua, their Son, died 1699.

In this Isle rest the Remains of Gooditha, third Wife of John Baily, Died 1711.
Also the Said John Baily Died 1712.

Hatchment in the Nave.

Azure, a fess engrailed, ermine, between three talbots' heads erased, or.

Crest—On an esquire's helmet, a fire-brand, proper.

The Chapel, which is connected to Bradford, consists of Chancel, Nave, and South Aisle.

The Rev. Mr. Blomberg Vicar.

— Watkins, Esq. Lord of the Manor.

BRADFORD.

On Monuments against the North wall of Chancel.

Near this Place, in the Family Vault, are interred the Remains of Mr. Mawbey Tugwell, Youngest Son of the late Mr. William Tugwell. He married Penelope, fourth Daughter of Daniel Clutterbuck, Esq. of Bradford Leigh, and Departed this life 13th of May, 1815, Aged 41 years,
Leaving Issue by her 5 Infant Children.

Arms—Azure, three garbs proper, on a chief, argent, a boar's head couped, sable: impaling, azure, a lion rampant, argent, in chief three escallops of the last.

To the Memory of Mr. Humphry Tugwell.
In Religion, he was Zealous and Sincere:
He was Generous, Just, and Benevolent;
A warm and Steady Friend,
An Indulgent Husband, A fond Parent,
A Kind and Humane Master.
He carried on an extensive Manufactory in this Town upwards of Fifty Years with unblemished integrity,
And Departed this life the 22d Day of August, 1775, Aged 71 years.
He had Issue, by Elizabeth, his Wife,
Fitz-Daniel Tugwell, who died Dec. 3d, 1747, Aged 10 years,
Thomas Tugwell, May 24, 1769, Aged 24 years.
Wm. Tugwell, Dec. 25, 1774, Aged 32 years.
Also three other Children, who Died in their Infancy.

Also to the Memory of the above Mrs. Elizth Tugwell, who was exemplary in the performance of every religious and paternal duty;
and died on the 7th of June, 1801, Aged 90 years.

Arms—Quarterly, first argent, a boar's head couped, sable; second, sable, a ducal crown, or; third azure, three garbs, pp.; fourth argent, a lion passant sable.

Daniel Clutterbuck, of this Place, Gent. died the 16th of April, 1769, Aged 56 years.

Mark the perfect man, and behold the upright,
For the end of that man is peace. Psal. 37, v. 37.

Arms—Azure, a lion rampant argent, in chief three escallops of the last.

Juxta Hoc Marmor Depositum jacet quicquid mortale fuit Johannis Thresher, Armig. Eduardi Thresher Filij unici, qui vividos aliquot juventæ annos Londini, inter juris peritos exegit, legum studijs enixe incumbens in his miro ingenii acumine, et viribus ditatus, tam feliciter, et mature claruit, ut plerisq; fui temporis usq; celeberrimis, hisce studijs famam sectantibus, multum præcelluisse merito diceretur, fori decus grande in ipso honorum aditu Famæq. crescentis flore nitentem, cum jam Filium fœtus videret Obijt Pater huic dum viveret, ingenium insigne, et præclarum integritas inviolabilis, Aliæq. optimæ indolis Dotes, Gratiæ et Honoris apud omnes, Plurimum conciliarunt commercium, ad Parochiam de Bradford, et villas circumjacentes, peculiariter respiciens: (Heu! priscam Angliæ Gentis gloriam Vellus aureum) Prosperis et honestis artibus excoluit, et sibi et Patriæ mortuo patre Johannes, Filius (jam sepulchri ut peritus ingenij particeps) privata publicis anteponens, ad sedes paternas solum natale, huc jubens secessit, hic otio indulgebat, sibi gratissimo honesto tamen ac utili amicis, quippe patriæq. strenue consulens, hic liberalitate benevolentia ac candore, pariter notabilis apud omnes multum desideratus supremum naturæ debitum solvit De Ellen uxore ejus, Filia Henrici Long, de Melksham, Armig. de Ellen, Soror et Cohærede Johannis Trenchard, nuper de Cutteridge, Com. Wilts. Armig. Sex suscepit Filias, quarum solum quatuor huic superesse vivebant, Viz. Ellen, Dyonisia, Elizabetha, et Maria.

Obijt { Pater die 18 Feb. 1725, Ætat. 65.
{ Filius die 17 Aug. 1741, Ætat. 52.

Filij Conjugis dilecti Vidua, hoc Marmor utriusq. Pientissime posuit.

Arms—Argent, a chevron, gules, between three crosslets fitchy, gules, issuing out of as many boars' heads, couped and erect, sable: impaling Long, between two flanches.

Triste Monumentum intueare, Lector, et postquam Epitaphium tacitè, perlegisti nigrum, sub pedibus aspice marmor, tunc si possis supprime luctus. Ab annos a prosapia, ac honestis parentibus ortus, nunc fato correptus (Carolus Steward) multorum lachrimis inibi sepultur, dum superstes nurâ integritate innocuus, dulcique indole conus, et affabilis bonis moribus ornatus, ac virtutibus tam eximie decoratus ut æquando, haud parem reperies, proh, dolor! quam plurima vitæ pensum absolvunt, et supremum inducunt diem, hic casu infausto, ex equo labente delapsus, mox graviter pectore contusus, tandem apostematâ intumuit, languit, et occubuit, xi Julij, Anno Dñi MDCXCVIII. Amice Valeto, summum nec metuas Diem, nec optes justa hæ piæ Memoriæ Chari Mariti, uxor lagubris Maria Steward, Dicavit, et marmora parentavit, 1701.

Arms—Or, a fess checky argent and azure, within a border ermine: impaling sable, a li. pass. guard. between 3 helmets, or.

[South Wall.

Ad Ædis hujusce latus boreale viri præstantissimi Antonij Methuen, Arm̄ Conduntur Exuviæ, Pauli Methuen, de Bradford, Arm̄ Filij natu secundi, antiquissimo stemmate de Methuen, in Regno Scotiæ, oriundi, et Gertrudæ, Conjugis Pientissimæ, Thomæ Moore, de Spargrove, in Com. Somerset. Arm̄ (Ex Elizabetha Uxore, Filia primogenita Dni Johannis Bampfylde, de Poltimore, in Agro Devon. Baronetti) Filiæ et Cohæredis. Obierunt,

Ille, Maij 10, 1717, Annos Natus 67.
Illa, Jul. 20, 1699, Annos Nata 40.

Juxta Proavorum Cineres Thomæ Methuen, Arm̄ Antonij et Gertrudæ, Filij unici, requiescit depositum: Qui nihil non æquum et liberale, Et fecit semper et cogitavit tranquilus, patient, clemens, benignus, ingenio minime vulgari, singulari prorsus humanitate, et Annæ uxoris, Filiæ Isaaci Selfe, Arm. de Beanacre, in Agro Wiltoniensi (Ex uxore Penelope, præhonorabilis Caroli Lucas, Baronis de Shenfield, in Com. Essex, Filiâ et Cohærede) cujus formam inter Primas venustam, et commendabant et superabant ineffabilis morum suavitas, Animiq. cunctis virtutibus ornati Parentiores Illiciæ. Obierunt,

Ille, Jan. 2, 1737, Æt. 53,
Illa, Maij 15, 1733, Æt. 37.

Parentibus bene meritis, Paulus Methuen," Arm̄: Here et Filius unicus, P.

Arms—Quarterly, first and fourth argent, three tigers' heads erazed, proper; second and third argent, two bars engrailed sable between nine martlets, gules, 3 3 3: impaling quarterly, first and fourth ermine, three chevronells, gules: second and third argent, a fess between six annulets, gules.

Under the Tomb, opposite the door beneath, Lye the Bodies of John Rogers, A. M. His dear Wife Elizabeth, and Several of his Family. He was Forty-three years Vicar of this Parish, and Died April 20, 1754, in the 76 year of his Age.

Remember them which have the rule over you, for they watch for your souls as they that must give Account, that they may do it with joy, and not with Grief, for that is unprofitable for you.

Arms—Az. a mullet, argent, on a chief, or, a fleur-de-lis, gules.

To Perpetuate the Memory of a truly Pious, Virtuous, Affectionate, Good Wife, Susannah Rogers, who Died May the 1st, 1775, Aged 22 years,

This Monument was Erected Anº Dom̄ 1756.

Arms—As before.

Flat Stones.

Here lyeth the Body of John Thresher, Esq. who died 17 of August, 1741, Aged 52 years.

Also the Body of Ellin, Wife of the said John Thresher, Esq. who Died April the 17th, 1753, Aged 42 years.

Here lieth the Body of Dionysia Thresher, Wife of Edward Thresher, of this Parish, Esq. who Departed this life Nov. 10, 1692, Aged 32 years.

Also the Body of the said Edward Thresher, who died the 18 of Feb. 1725, Aged 65.

Arms—Argent, a chevron between three crosslets fitchy issuing out of as many boars' heads couped and erect: impaling, Long, between two flanches.

In co Wilts. —BRADFORD. 279

Here lyeth ye Body of Dennis Compton Jun. Son of Walter Compton, Esq. of Hartpury, who Departed this life ye 16th of May, 1714. He was Dame Mary Stuard Brother.

Arms—Three helmets, a crescent for difference.

Rev. Robt. Taunton, L. L. D. July 17th, 1797, Aged 54 years.

Frances Taunton, May 24, 1803, Aged 16 years.

Elizabeth Weeks Taunton, March 11th, 1815, Aged 33 years.

Frances Taunton, Nov. 25, 1819, Aged 67 years.

Plurimus summa probitate notus omnibus in vita Charitis, cunctis in morte flendus.
Hic jacet Carolus Steward, Armiger, de Cummerwell, Parochiæ hujus appendiæ, Fragili vale dicens mundo xi Julij Anno MDCLXXXXIII.
Mœstissimam relinquens conjugem Mariam, ex Antiqua Comptonorum Familia in Agro Gloucesterensi.
Æterna pace Quiescat.

Arms—A fess checky within a border, ermine: impaling a lion passant-guardant between three helmets.

Here Lyeth the Body of John Peirce, Gent. who Departed this life the 20 Day of November, Anno Dom. 1697, Aged 24 years.

Here Lyeth the Body of Quærina Curll, the Wife of John Curll, of this Parish, Clothiere. She Departed this life the 28 Day of April, Anº Dom̄ 1678, Aged 31 years.

Alsoe Here lyeth the Body of Walter Curll, the Son of John Curll, and Quærina, his Wife. Hee Departed this life the 30th Day of April, Anº Dom̄ 1677, Aged one year and 7 months.

Underneath is Interred Elizabeth, Daughter of George and Sarah Bethell, who died January the 2d, 1770, Aged nine months.

Also Sarah, the Wife of George Bethell, who died January the 7th, 1777, Aged 54 years.

George Bethell, Esq. died March the 26th, 1795, Aged 65 years.

On Monuments at East End of Nave.

Sacred to ye Memory of Mr. John Renison, Clothier of this Town, and Ann, his Wife. She departed this life, in humble hopes of a Blessed Immortality, the 18th of November, 1793, Æt. 48: He also Departed this life the 4th of February, 1816, Æt. 71. In every Relation of life he was a strictly upright conscientious and honest man, beloved and respected by all who knew him. Filial Gratitude and affection hath raised this Monument to perpetuate the Remembrance of such worthy Parents.

Near this Place are deposited the Remains of Samuel Cam, one of his Majesty's Justices of the Peace for the County of Wilts. He Departed this life Nov. 7th, 1792, Aged 78 years.

By his first Wife, Elizabeth Cam, he had ten Children. They and their Mother, together with Elizth Cam, one of his three Daughters by his last Wife Mary Cam, are buried with him in the same Grave. Mary Cam, and his other two by her, Charlotte and Harriet Cam, are buried in the Sepulchral Ground belonging to Lewins Mead Chapel, Bristol. Maria Teresa Cam, one of his Daughters by Elizabeth, his first Wife, married Mr. Isaac Hillier, by whom he had a Family; Charlotte Cam, one of his three Daughters, by Mary, his last Wife, Married Benjamin Hobhouse, Barrister at Law, by whom she had several Children. By him this Monument was Erected A. D. 1794.

Near this Place are deposited the Remains of Mr. Walter Browne, who Departed this life August 1st, 1796, in the 52 year of his Age.

On a Monument against the North Wall of Nave.

Underneath are Deposited the Remains of Francis Smith, Lieut.-General of his Majesty's Forces, and Colonel of the 11th Regiment of foot, who Died November 7th, 1791, Aged 68.

Arms—Azure, two bars, or, between three broad arrows argent.

On Monuments against south side of the Nave.

Near this Place lieth the Body of Edward Cottle, of Bradford Leigh, who Departed this Life Feb. 14, 1718, Aged about 52 years.

Also the Body of Edward Cottle, Jun. Son of the Above Named Edward Cottle, & Ann his Wife, who Died Feb. 15th, 1727, Aged 27 years.

Also the Body of Ann, Wife of Edward Cottle, Sen. who died March 13, 1728, Aged 62 years.

Richard, Son of Edward & Ann Cottle, died Feb. 16th, 1736, Aged 31 years.

Edward, Son of Richard & Mary Cottle, died March 25th, 1758, Aged 26 years.

Also in Memory of Mary, Wife of Richard Cottle, who died May the 30th, 1773, Aged 69 years.

Arms—Or, a bend, gules.

In Memory of John Ferrett, Esq. Born in this Town March the 15th, 1702, and died May the 12th, 1770, Aged 68 years.

On whose Soul, O Blessed Lord God, have mercy.

There needs no epitaph this good man's worth to raise,
Name him but only and you record his Praise.

In the family Vault, in the adjoining Church Yard, are deposited the Remains of Thomas Timbrell, Esq.

who Departed this life on the 23d day of April, 1815, Aged 83 years.

Likewise Elizth, Wife of the above Thomas Timbrell, who died on the 8th day of March, 1805, Aged 77 years.

Arms—Quarterly, first and fourth gules, an escallop argent: second and third argent.

Crest—A lion's head couped, quarterly, first and fourth gules, second and third argent.

Near this Place are deposited the Remains of John Baskerville, Esq. many years a Deputy Lieutenant for this County, who died March 15, 1800, Aged 54 years. He was a just and honest man, and a sincere Friend.

Also the Body of Joseph Baskerville, Esq. Second and Youngest Son of the above John Baskerville, who died Oct. 7th, 1812.

Also the Body of Hester, Wife of the above John Baskerville. She Departed this life Decem. 16, 1809.

Arms—A chevron between three roundels: impaling argent, a cross, in chief an eagle displayed.

In a Vault near this Monument are interred the Remains of Thomas Bush, Esq. who, after leading a Virtuous and exemplary life died Novem. 21, 1809, Aged 68, beloved and Respected by all who knew him. He was a good Christian, an affectionate Husband, an indulgent Father, a sincere Friend, an active Magistrate, and a valuable Member of Society.

The Memory of the just is Blessed.

Arms—A dog erect, gorged, in chief three crosslets fitchy.

In Memory of George Bethell, Esq. who died March 26th, Anno Dom. 1795, Aged 63.

This Marble, in filial affection, is raised by his three surviving Daughters. He was uniformly respected as a Man of strict integrity, an upright Magistrate, and the poor Man's Friend.

Sacred also to the Memory of Sarah, his Wife, who Departed this life January 7th, 1777, Aged 32.

And of Elizth their Daughter, who died an Infant.

West End of Nave.

Memoriæ Ricardi Whatly, hujus Parochiæ Armigeri, Eleanor Uxoris ejus, et Progenici subnumeratæ, quorum Reliquiæ prope deponuntur: Hoc Marmor sola deplorante Filia erectum sacrum est:

Ricardus, Pater, Obijt 4to Nov. 1782, Ætat 73.
Eleanor, Obijt 10mo Decem. 1786, Ætat. 61.
Et Progenies, Viz.
Anna, 9no Decem. 1756, Mense Ætat. 9.
Maria, 30mo Janij, 1765, Ann. Ætat. 11.
Ricardus, 7mo Oct. 1774, Ætat. 14.
Johannes, 23o Maij, 1769, Ætat. 25.
Gulielmus, 28o Nov. 1781, Ætat. 16.
Eleanora, 16o Nov. 1787, Ætat. 29.

In Memory of Caroline, Wife of Mr. William Gaisford, of Seend, in this County, who died July 1st, 1813, Aged 33 years.

Likewise of their Infant Daughter Caroline, who died August 23, 1813, Aged 6 months.

On Flat Stones in Nave.

[Brass Plate.

Here Lyeth Buryed the Body of Anne, lately sole Daughter and Heire of John Yewe, of Bradforde, in the County of Wiltes. Gent. and Wife of Gyford Longe, Gent. who had Issue by her Anne and Catheryn their Daughters. She dyed the 26th of March, 1601, whose knowne good lyfe sheweth that God hath taken her sowle to his Mercye.

Walter Burcombe died Nov. 17th, 1814, Aged 33 years.
Richard Burcombe.
Elizabeth, Wife of Wm. Goodall Burcombe, died Sept. 25, 1797, Aged 56 years.
Wm. Goodall Burcombe died August 8th, 1816, Aged 75 years.

Underneath this Stone are Deposited the Bodies of John Lea, and Susanna, his Wife.
He died 20 December, ...
She 2 Feb. 1730, Aged 67.

Also near this place are Deposited the Bodies of David Lea and Willm Lea, Sons of the abovesaid John and Susanna Lea. David Departed this life the .... Nov. 1772, Aged 67 years, Wm. Nov. 15, 1776.

Here Lyeth the Body of Esther Cooper, Widw, who Departed this life December the 31, Anno Dom 1707, Aged 96 years.

Also Here Lyeth the Body of Richard Cooper, of Bradford, Clothier, Son of the said Esther Cooper, who Departed this life February ye 6th Day, Anno Dom. 1723, Aged 74 years.

Here Lyeth the Body of Robert Cooper, who departed this Life the 29 Day of Feb. 1631, Ætatis suæ 55.

Here lyeth the Body of Martha, Daughter of Richard and Mary Edwards. She Departed this life May the 10, A.D. 1740, Aged 22.

Here lyeth the Body of John Whatly, of this Parish, who died Aug. 8, Anno Dom. 1717, Aged 46 years.

West End of N. Aisle.

Near this Monument are interred the Remains of Ann Bailward, Late of this Place, Widow, who Departed this life the 25th day of July, 1788, Aged 75 years.

Also of Samuel Bailward, late of Horsington, in the County of Somerset, Esq. her Son, who died the 9th Day of April, 1800, Aged 53 years.

Henry Methuen Bailward, Esq. (of the Royal Navy) Son of the above Samuel Bailward, died July 1st, 1812, Aged 24 years.

On Monuments by N. Wall of N. Aisle.

Near this Tablet are Deposited the Remains of the Rev. Edward Bowles, late Vicar of this Parish. He Departed this life the first day of February, 1808, in the 48 year of his Age.

Mors omnia sternit.

Sacred to the Memory of Edward Baily, of Ashly, Gent. He died Oct. ye 18, 1760, Æt. 80.

Also Ann, his Wife, Eldest of Wm. Harding, of Broughton Giffard, Gent. (in this County.) She died Decem. ye 29th, 1759, Æt. 75.

Also Edward Fisher, Second Son of Wm. and Margaret Fisher. He died April ye 5th, 1761, Æt. 4.

Also Ann Lewis, Relict of the Rev. John Lewis, of Whaddon, in this County. She died November ye 8th, 1758, Æt. 40.

Also to the Memory of Mrs. Margaret Fisher, Wife of Mr. William Fisher, and Daughter of the abovesaid Edward and Ann Baily. She died May 30th, 1796, Aged 71 years.

This Buryall ...ce and Tombe was Erected by Willm Baily, of this Towne, Mercer, Ann. Di 1695.

* * * * [Illegible.] * * *
* * * * * * * * * *

Also

Here lyeth ye Body of Wm Baily, of this Towne, Mercer, who Departed this life ye 25 Day of March, Anno Domini 1712, Aged 68 years.

Near this Place lyeth the Body of Michaell Tidcombe, who deceased ye 26 day of July, Anno Dom. 1662.

Tidcombus tumulo jacet hoc Michaelis in alto sospes dum clangit buccina surge maner.

Also neare this Place lieth ye Body of Sarah, ye Daughter of ye said Michaell Tidcombe, who Deceased ye 11th Day of July, Ano Dom 1661.

East End of North Aisle.

Frances Taunton, 2d Daughter and 6th Child, of the Rev. Robert Taunton, L. L. D. and Frances, his Wife, deluding the fond hopes of Relatives, who anticipated in her opening graces the loveliness of personal charms, and a still more captivating loveliness of mind, fell an early victim to Consumption on the 24th of May, 1803, Aged 16 years.

Elizabeth Weeks Taunton, eldest Daughter and 3d Child of the Rev. Robert Taunton, L. L. D. and Frances, his Wife, having, through a long and severe trial of debilitated health, evinced a pious resignation to the decrees of Providence only exceeded by the warm benevolence with which she ever interested herself to assuage the cares and sufferings of others, Departed this life on the 11th of March, 1815, Aged 33 years.

Richard Hobbs Taunton, fifth Son and seventh Child of the Rev. Robert Taunton, L. L. D. and Frances, his Wife, Lieut. in H. M. 22d Light Dragoons, fell a Victim to the Cholera Morbus, which so fatally ravaged the British Camps in India in the Pendaree War, on the 19th of May, 1819, Aged 30 years. On the 17th of the same Month, this young Officer, in high health and spirits, wrote to his friends that the fatal disorder had disappeared from the Camp—About 7 o'clock in the Morning of the 19th, he was himself seized with it, and before Noon he lay a Corpse.

Rev. Robert Taunton, L. L. D. having adorned a strong and comprehensive mind with useful and extensive knowledge, having conscientiously discharged the Duties of Husband, Father, Friend, Citizen, and Christian, Departed to seek his Reward, July 17th, 1797, Aged 57 years.

The afflicted Mother of his eight helpless orphans, Erected this Monument to his Memory.

Their departure is taken from Misery, and their going from us to be utter destruction, but they are in peace.

Frances Taunton, Relict of the Rev. Robert Taunton, L. L. D. and Daughter and Coheiress of Leonard Cropp, Esq. of the County of Hampshire, having, with a rare and happy union of masculine good sense, religiously fulfilled the sacred trust of Education which devolved on her by the decease of her Husband, and further bequeathing to her Children a faithful pattern of that warm benevolence in action, and that pious resignation in affliction, which Christianity enjoins, Departed this life on the 25th of Nov. 1819, Aged 67 years.

On Flat Stones in N. Aisle.

Hic jacet Johannes Jones, Filius Johannis Jones, de Bradford, Pharmacopolæ, Qui Obijt Primo die Aprilis, Anno Dom. 1703, Ætatis suæ 9.

Hic sepultus est Johannes Jones, de Bradford, nuper Pharmacopolæ, Qui Obijt Sexto die Februarij, Anno Dom. 1709, Ætatis suæ 44.

Here lies the Body of Daniel Jones, who died Dec. 1732, Aged 57.

And that of Elizabeth, his wife, who died April 28th, MDCCL. Aged 75.

Likewise the Body of Daniel Jones, their Son, who died June 9th, MDCCLXX. Aged XLVIII.

Here Lyeth the Body of Daniel Jones, who Departed this life December ye 2d, A. D. 1732, Aged 58 years.

Joseph Wood, died March the 29, 1725.

Mary, Wife of Simon Wood, died Feb. 21, 1763.

William, Son of Simon and Sarah Wood, Died May the 24, 1765.

Wm. Wood, Son of the said Joseph Wood, died December, 1767.

Thomas Baskerville, Departed this life September ye 4th, 1779.

Brass Plate, west end.

Here lyeth the Body of Rosewell Smithfield, Son of Rosewell Smithfield, of this Parish, Clothier. He Departed this life July 22d, 1726, Aged 17 years.

Also here Lyeth the Body of Elizabeth Smithfield, Mother of the said Rosewell Smithfield, who died ye 17th Feb. Aged 70, 1742.

Benefactions

Against the Gallery at the East End of the Nave.

Samuel Cam, Esq. by his Will, dated the 23 October, 1792, gave £100 Stock in the 3 per Cent. Consol Bank Annuities, to Benjamin Hobhouse, Daniel Clutterbuck, Isaac Hillier, and Thomas Bush, Esq. in trust, to distribute the Dividends thereof yearly in Bread to such poor persons of the Parish of Bradford as they deem proper objects, and who do not receive Alms.

Mrs. Elizabeth Tugwell, by Codicil to her Will, dated dated July 12, 1799, gave £100 Stock in the 5 per Cent. New Navy Annuities, in trust, that her Grandson, Mawbey Tugwell, should distribute the Dividends thereof Yearly among 40 old and infirm Persons, on the 15th day of January, in such manner as She had in her lifetime directed, and after his decease that his Executors should transfer the same Stock to the Churchwardens of the Parish, to apply the Dividends as before.

Donum
Thomæ Lewis, hujus Ecclesiæ Vicarij,
Anno Ætatis suæ Octogesimo secund°,
Annoq. Domini 1707,
Exempli gratia, non ob ostentationem,
Sed in Honorem Sanctæ et Individuæ
Trinitatis ac usum Ecclesiæ,
Gratis Datum.

John Ferrett, Esq. of London, gave, in ye Year of our Lord 1754, from sincere regard and Esteem to this his Native Town, the Painted Glass which adorns the South and East Windows of this Church. He also gave, for the use of the Church, an elegant and complete Service of Communion Plate; and in the year 1747, gave to the Society for promoting Christian Knowledge, of which he was a Member, £50, on condition that Bibles, Common Prayer, and other Religious Books and Tracts, on the same terms the Society supplies their own Members, and free of all Expences whatsoever, to the value of 50 Shillings, should be for ever Annually sent to the resident Minister for distributing on, or about the Festival of our Lord's Nativity: But the same, having been in arrear, it was finally agreed, on the 6th of June, 1821, betwen the Rev. Howell Jones, resident Minister, Mr. T. H. Saunders, & Mr. J. P. Renison, Churchwardens, of this Parish, and the Rev. Dr. Gaskin, Secretary to the said Society, that the Amount of arrears should be added to the original Sum given by Mr. Ferrett, and that Books to the Value of £4. 4s. be for ever Annually sent. Application to be made to the Society by the Minister or Churchwardens in each year.

Against the Gallery at West End of Nave.

The Charity School, with the Schoolmaster's House, were given by Mr. Anthony Methuen, and the fee thereof by the Honourable Lady Paulet and the Rev. Mr. Wright, to put them in repair. The Rev. Mr. Rogers applied £35, part of £50 were given by Edward Dike, Clerk, and about £20 more subscribed by different persons.

The Charity School is endowed with an Estate at Holt, purchased with £250 given by Mr. Francis Smith, and now Rented by Mr. John Godwin, and the Dividends of £237 .. 12 .. 6 in the 4 per Cent. Bank Annuities, the dividends of £400 3 per Cent. Consol Bank Annuities, given by the Will of John Strawbridge, late of this Place, Gent. dated the 12th March, 1805. These Funds are now vested in the names of Daniel Clutterbuck, and Thomas Bush, Esqrs. as Trustees for the said School.

The same John Strawbridge Also gave £400 3 per Cent. Consol Bank Annuities to Mawbey Tugwell and John Renison, the then Churchwardens of this Parish, in trust, to distribute the dividends yearly in Crowns or half Crowns to such persons of the said Parish as do not receive Alms, at the same time as Mr. Curl's Charity is paid and distributed.

John Curl, Esq. of Turleigh, by his Will, dated the 28th Day of December, 1703, gave the Sum of £30 per Annum, to be paid out of the Rents of his Estate at Chirton, in Wilts. and to be distributed on the Feast of St. Thomas the Apostle, between 120 of such poor persons of the Borough of Bradford and the Tything of Winsley Leigh and Woolley, who live by their honest labour, and as the Vicar of Bradford shall nominate and appoint, in five Shillings each, and directed the Churchwardens and Overseers to take an Account thereof, and see the same Distributed.

Mr. Edward Thresher, by Will, Gave £100 to the Poor of this Parish, which is now increased to £120 3 per Cent. Consol Bank Annuities, and is invested in the names of Richard Atwood and Thomas Bush, Esqrs. who divide the Dividends thereof Yearly at Christmas, in Crowns and half Crowns among the Poor of the said Parish.

West End of Nave.

John Ferrett, Esq. by Will, gave to his Nephew, Richard Wiltshire, and the Minister and Churchwardens of this Parish, £250 three per cent. Old South Sea Annuities, in trust, to apply the Dividends for purchasing for 20 poor Men and Women of the Town of Bradford only, who do not receive Alms of the Parish, of sober and religious lives and conversation, and who constantly attend Divine Service in the Parish Church when able, one 6d. loaf each, to be delivered to them the first Sunday in the Month, and at Christmas, Easter, and Whitsuntide, in each year immediately after Morning Service.

Hatchment in the North Aisle.

Argent, a li. passant sable; on a chief, sable, a ducal crown or: impaling, Long.

The Church consists of a Chancel, Nave, and North Aisle. The north side of the Nave is supported by five pointed arches.—— Under a canopy in the south wall of Chancel, is the figure of a Knight Templar, carved in stone, his right arm is broken off. In the opposite wall is another statue, also much mutilated.

Register commenced 1569.

Earl of Pembroke Lord of the Manor.

Frederick William Blomberg Vicar.

SOUTH WRAXALL.

On Monuments by the South Wall of Chancel.

Near this Place are deposited the Remains of James Finch, Esq. of Bradford Leigh, who died Feb. 14, 1815, Aged 53 years.

Under here lyeth ye Body of Anne Bennett, Relict of John Bennet, of Steeplaishton, and late of Tilshead, Gent. who deceased the 17th of February, 1708, Aged 78 years.

Also Here Lyeth ye Body of Ann Harris, Second Daughter of Ann Bennett, who Departed this life March 25, A. D. 1728.

Near this Place lyeth ye Body of Ann, ye only Daughter of James and Dorcas May, of ye Devizes. She Departed this life August ye 13, A. D. 1700, Aged 25 years.

Also near this lyeth ye Body of Dorcas, Mother of ye Above Said Ann May, who Departed this life ye 16 of March, 1725, Ætatis suæ 75.

East End of Chancel.

Heare Lyeth the Body of William Jones, who Departed this life the 18th of August, 1660.

Laugh not, Fanatickes, though he be gone,
He have Fought his fight, and hath woone a Crowne;
Though from we he is gone, in Heaven he takes his rest,
Singing Allelujah, and is for ever blest:
In life he taught to dye, and he did give
In Death a greate example how to live:
If wisdom, learning, and knowledge, cannot dwell
Secure from change, vain bubble Earth, Farewell.

On Monuments against the North Wall of Nave.

In Memory of Stephen Iles, Esq. formerly of Piddle Hinton, Dorset, lately of this Place, who died on the 7 July, 1816, Aged 68 years.

This Tablet was erected by Mrs. Jane Iles, his Widow and Relict.

Qualis vita, finis ita.

Memoriæ Sacrum of Stephen, Son of Stephen and Ann Bowyer, of Ford Farm, who died Nov. 16, 1780, Aged 19 years.

Also near this Place rest the Remains of Stephen Bowyer. He was one of the best of Husbands, of Fathers, and of Friends. He died December the 25, 1784, Aged 53 years.

Also near this Place rest the Remains of Ann, Wife of Stephen Bowyer, who died October the 5th, 1795, Aged 63 years.

Preserve, O Vault! inviolate thy trust
Till Heaven's high Mandate claims the sacred dust:
When the last trump the awak'ning sound shall give,
Rise ye that sleep, your Saviour bids you live.

Near this Place lieth the Body of Edmund Grant, of this Parish, who Departed this life the 8th of Sept. 1771, Aged 85 years.

Death in a very good Old Age
Ended my weary pilgrem Stage,
It was to me a end of pain,
Hoping to enter life again.

Near this Place lieth the Body of Richard Grant, who Departed this life the 6th Day of April, Anno Domini 1715.

Also near this Place Lyeth the Body of Margaret, the Wife of Richard Grant, who Departed this life the 10th Day of October, Anno Domini 1715.

In love they liv'd, in peace they dy'd,
Their lives desir'd, but God deny'd.

And also near this Place lyeth the Body of John, Son of Richard and Margaret Grant, who departed this life November the 29th, Anno Domini 1744, Aged 65 years.

A ling'ring grief laid me asleep,
And Christ my soul doth safely keep.

And also near this Place Lyeth the Body of Joseph Webb, who Departed this life in January, 1750, Aged 75.

And also near this place Lyeth the Body of Ann, Wife of Joseph Webb. She died July the 18th, 1751, Aged 68 years.

Arms—Sable, a chevron argent.

South Wall.

Metam properamus ad unam.

Near this place underneath lies Interred the Body of Sarah Nevell, Spinster, who departed this life July ye 23d, 1755, Aged 66.

Also near this Place lieth the Body of John Bath, who Departed this life Feb. ye 11th, 1764, Aged 54 years.

And also Elizabeth, Wife of John Bath. She Departed this life December the 26th, 1760, Aged 37 years.

And also John, their Son, died in his Infancy.

Likewise John, Son of John and Mary Bath (and Grandson of the above John and Eliz^th^ Bath) who Departed this life Sept. 15th, 1789, Aged 1 year & 6 Months.

On Monuments in the South Aisle.

In this Isle are interred the Remains of Thomas Long, Esq. who died the 28th day of January, 1759, Aged 80 years and ten Months.

As also the Remains of Mary, Wife of the said Thomas Long, who died the 18th day of July, 1733, Aged 48 years and three Months.

In sincere Duty and Respect to whose paternal Virtues and goodness, this Monument was erected.

Arms—Long: impaling ermine, on a pale, gules, three pears, or.

Near this Place Lyeth ye Body of Henry Long, of Melksham, Esq. He Departed this life 31 of March, 1686, Aged 28 years.

Near this Place lyeth also ye Body of Ann, ye Wife of Henry Long, Esq. She Departed this life ye 4th of Oct. 1705, Aged 48 years.

Also near this place lyeth the Body of John Long, Second Son of Henry Long, Jun. of Melksham, and Grandson to ye two deceased persons above written. He Departed this life ye 31 of Oct. A. D. 1712, Aged 9 months.

Arms—Sable, a lion rampant, argent, between eight cross crosslets, or; impaling sable, a lion rampant argent.

Upon an altar-tomb, under an arch in the south wall, is a statue lying: on a shield is borne the arms of Long.——Date in the South Aisle 1566.

Register commenced 1695.

Frederick-William Blomberg Vicar.

— Long, Esq. Lord of the Manor.

MONKTON FARLEY.

On Monuments against the North wall of Chancel.

Here under lyeth ye Body of **Wm. Watson, Esq.** who Departed this life ye 4th of March, 1695, he was aged 79.

Here Lyeth also the Body of Elizabeth Watson, Wife of William Watson, Esq. who Deceased the 23d of February, Anno Dom. 1701, Aged 85 years.

Arms— . . . . in chief three martlets: impaling, ten billets, 4 3 2 1, in chief a demi lion rampant.

Crest—A fox passant.

Here Lieth Buried the Bodye of William Bromfeld, Late of Lewisham, in the County of Kent, Esquyre, deceased the twentie day of November, 1582.

Arms—On a chevron three flowers, in chief a canton charged with the head of a spear.

Here Lyeth ye Body of Mary, the Daughter of Thomas Sartain, Rector of Monkton Farleigh, who departed this life Sept. ye 22, 1712, Aged 25 years.

Here also Lyeth ye Body of Mr. Thomas Sartain, late Rector of this place, who Deceased April ye 10th, 1713.

Mori Lucrum.

East End.

Near this Place resteth the Body of Richard White, Rector of this Parish, who Departed this life December ye 18th, 1735, Aged 49.

We brought nothing into this World, and it is certain can carry nothing out. The Lord gave, and the Lord hath taken away.

Near this Place lye Interred the Bodies of Richard, John, James, and Sarah, Children of ye Rev. Richard Ford, A. M. by Sarah, his Wife, who all died in their Infancy.

He was Rector of this Parish, Vicar of South Stoke, and Chaplain to ye Right Honble ye Earl of Cardigan.

Also the Body of the aforesaid Richard Ford, who died Jan. the 7th, 1756, Aged 49.

Blessed are ye dead which die in the Lord.

Mors Janua Vitæ. 1750.

Here lyeth Buried the Body of Sara Grant, deceased 27° die Novembris, Anno Dom. 1602.

Five Pounds She gave unto the poore,
Wm. King gave so much more:
Imploy th' increase, keepe Stocke in Store.

On Flat Stones within the rails of the Chancel.

To the Deare Memory of .... King, Gent. who died Feb. .... 1665.

Here lyeth the Body .....nold King, deceased the 30th day of ...cember, 1697.

Here lyeth ye Body of Mr. James Pearce, of London, Merchant. He died Jan. ye 16th, 1744, Aged 51.

Also Ann, his Wife, died April ye 4th, 1754, Aged 52.

Also the Body of Henrietta Martin Pearce, Daughter of the above James and Ann Pearce, who died Dec. 10, 1772, Aged 49.

Here lyeth ye Body of James Basset, who died ye 19 Day of August, 1691.

Here lyeth ye Body of Sarah Basset, who died ye 11 Day of September, 1691.

Here Lyeth the Body of William King, Gent. He deceased the 26th Day of July, Anno Dom. 1697.

On Monuments against the North Wall of Nave.

Here lyeth ye Body of Mary, ye Wife of James Bassett, who was buried Oct. ye 4th, 1695.

In Memory of Mary Hayward, who departed this life Oct. ye 10th, A. D. 1717, Aged 74.

Also Peter Deverell, who Departed this life July ye 10, A. D. 1727, Aged 65.

Also Mary, Wife of Peter Deverell, who Departed this life Feb. ye 27, A. D. 1727, Aged 61.

In Memory of Mary, Wife of Thomas Tailer, who departed this life Sept. ye 12, 1727, Aged 26 years.

Also in Memory of William Harper, Jun. who Departed this life the 8 of Jan. 1759, Aged 29 years.

Near this Place lyeth the Body of Patiance, Wife of William Harper, Sen. who Departed this life July ye 30, 1769, Aged 76 years.

Of worldly cares I had my share,
When I was living as you are,
But God from it hath set me free,
In a good Old Age hath taken me.
Remember, all are borne to dye,
Then think upon eternity,
For as we are, so must you be,
Prepare for death, and follow me.

North Wall.

Near this Place lieth the Bodies of Jane, Elizabeth, and Susanna, Daughters of Jeremiah Cottle, Gent. of this Parish, by Sarah, his Wife.

Jane,	died	April 5, 1754,	Aged	1 year.
Elizth,		Jany 8, 1765,		34 years.
Susna,		July 24, 1769,		22 years.

Forbear, dear friends, to mourn and weep,
Since in this grave we sweetly sleep,
And leave this troublesome world behind,
A Glorious Crown we hope to find.

Near under this Place lyeth ye Body of Thomas Butler, Yeoman, who Departed this life ye 3 Day of December, A. D. 1713, Aged 75 years.

Also near under this Place lyeth ye Body of Margaret, ye Daughter of Thomas & Elizabeth Butler, who Departed this life ye 11th day of August, A. D. 1709, Aged 3 Wickes.

Also near under this Place lyeth ye Body of John, ye Son of Thomas and Elizabeth Butler, who Departed this life ye 15 Day of January, A. D. 17$\frac{10}{11}$, Aged 3 Wickes and 2 Days.

In love they liv'd, in peace they died,
Their lives desir'd, but God denied.

In Memory of Richard Grant, of Bradford Leigh. Ob. ... April, 1763, Æt. 77.

Ann Pitman, Wife of James Pitman, of Bradford, Daughter of Wm. and Mary Grant, Objit 23 Aprilis, A. D. 1775, Ætat. 54.

Sacred to the Memory of Mary, Widow of John Cottle, Gent. who Departed this life April 23, 1788, Aged 73.

Many are the troubles of the Righteous,
But the Lord delivereth them out of all.

In Memory of William Cottle, Gent. He died March the 2d, 1733, Aged 74 years.

Also in Memory of Mary, his Wife. She died Nov. 21, 1738, Aged 76.

And also in Memory of William, their Son. He Died Jan. 23, 1722, Aged 21.

And also in Memory of John, their Son. He Died July 16, 1751, Aged 46.

A lingering grief laid me asleep,
And Christ my soul doth safely keep.

Also John Cottle, Gent. Son of the above John Cottle, who Departed this life Jan. the 20th, 1814, Aged 76 years.

On a Flat Stone.

In Memory of Benjamin Elderton, who Departed this life February the 17, 1771.

Also o. . . . . Elderton, his Mother, li. . here.

Also Ann, her daughter,
And Wife of Edmond Biggs,
Also lies here.

The Rev. Dr. Robinson, Rector.

Register commenced 1570.

SOUTH WILTSHIRE

SOUTH WILTS.

AMESBURY HUNDRED.

AMESBURY.

On Monuments against the North Wall of the Chancel.

Near this Place lies Interred
Mary Keene, Relict of William Keene, Esq.
of Whitehall, London,
Daughter of Thomas Hayward, Esq.
of Little Amesbury,
who died Dec. the 8th, 1764, Aged 67 years.

Near this Place lies in a Vault Her only
Sister, with the rest of her Friends.

How lov'd, how valu'd once avails Thee not,
To whom related, or by whom begot;
A heap of Dust alone remains of thee,
'Tis all thou art, and all the Proud shall be.

Arms—A fess between 3 mullets, impaling, a bull's head erased between three mullets.

Here lys Interred ye Body of
John Thurloe,
late of Lincoln's Inn,
Son of John Thurloe, of Lincoln's Inn, Esq.
and Ann, his Wife, who was ye 3d Daughter,
of Sr John Litcott,
of East Moulsy, in the County of Surry, Knight.
This, their Eldest Son in the Town of Amesbury,
Departed this Life in
The Faith & fear of Jesus Christ,
March ye 29th, 1682,
For whom his Mother erected this Monument. 1683.

Arms—A chevron, ermine, between 3 cinquefoils.

On Monuments against South Wall of Chancel.

Near this Place lieth the Body of Mr. James Bloxham, who died April 26, 1781, Aged 85 years.
Also Sarah, his Widow,
who died Dec. 14, 1796, Aged 81 years.

Underneath this Place are buryed the Body of William Cousins, Son of Thos. Cousins, who dyed the 4th of Dec. 1709, as Also of John, Wm. and Thos. Cousins, sons of William and Mary Cousins. John dyed the 10 of May, 1711, Aged 17 years, Wm. dyed May the 4, 1713, Aged 32 years, and Thos. dyed July the 10th, 1718, Aged 30 years. And also Mary, ye Daughter of William and Mary Cousins, ye Wife of William Lewis, of Noock, Gent, who dyed Nov. ye 19, 1722, Aged 37 years. And also Mary ye Wife of William Cousins, who dyed Feb. 8, 1727, Aged 68.

In a Vault beneath this Tablet are deposited the Remains of Thos. Mist, of Long Acre, in the County of Middx. Obiit 9th May, 1767, Ætat. 56 years.

On Flat Stones in Chancel.

M. S.

Georgii Cuthbert, cujus innocentia ipso, hoc marmore clarior Dei gratias illi adeo conciliavit, ut amalo venturo eum eripuit, Nat. Jan. 16, 1712, Denat. Maii 8, 1725.

In Memory of the Rev. Thos. Holland, who for half a century was Minister of this Parish, a small Living, yet he never solicited for a Greater, nor improved to his owne Advantage His marvellous Talents in applying the Powers of Nature To the useful Purposes of Life, the most curious and complete Engine which the world now enjoys for raising water being invented by him. He died the 11th of May, in the year of our Lord 1730, Aged 84 years.

By him Lyeth Susanna Frances, his eldest Daughter, who truly resembled him in his friendly and disinterested spirit. She died July the 10th, in the year 1741, Aged 61 years.

Arms—A lion rampant guardant, between 9 fleur-de lis.

Here lyeth the Body of William Rigdon, Gent. ye Son of Edmund and Elizabeth Rigdon, ... ham, in ye County of Kent, who departed this Life ye 24th of Nov. Anno Dom. 1717, Æt. 30.

Arms—On a chevron, 3 griffins' heads erased.

Here rest the Remains of the late Rev. Thomas Neale, Vicar of Berwick St. James, and P. C. of Amesbury, Wilts. Aged 62 years, Universally esteemed for true Christian Piety, Learning, and Benevolence.

Henry Cox, Gent. Son of Henry and Catherine Cox, died March 11, 1802, Aged 45 years.

Catherine Cox, Wife of Henry Cox, Gent. and Daughter of the Rev. Henry Head, and Ann his Wife, died 23d of June, 1763, Aged 31 years.

Henry Cox, Gent. died 17th Feb. 1798, Aged 69 years.

The Rev. Henry Head, Vicar of Compton Chamberlaine, died 2d March, 1747, Aged 58 years.

Anne Head, widow of the Rev. Henry Head, died 26 Nov. 1763, Aged 72 years.

Here Lyeth the Body of Giles Sadler, Gent. Grandson to Sr Ralph Sadler, Kt, of Standwin House, in Herefordshire, sometime privy Counceller to King Henry 8th and Queene Elizabeth of Famous Memory, and Son to Henry Sadler, of Everly, in the County of Wilts. Gent. who, at Ambrosbury, the third of January, Anno Domini 1680, died in hope of a happy Resurrection, being of age 83 years.

Here Also lyes all that was Mortal of Whitfeild Boorn, Gent. of this Towne, Nephew to Mr. Giles Sadler, who Resigned this Uncertain life the 13th of Dec. Anno Dom. 1733, in the 65th year of his age.

Altho' his body here doth Lye
Till the last Trump doth it raise,
His Soul is now in Heaven high,
And sings Jehovah's praise.

Here lyeth also Anne, his Wife. She dyed ye 27th of Dec. 1774, Aged 78 years.

In the South Transept.

Near this Place lies interred
John Bundy,
of Long Acre, London,
who Departed this life the 30th May, 1794,
Aged 52 years.

In Memory of Jane Pinckney, Daughter of Phillip and Jane Pinckney, of this Place, who Departed this life the 18th Day of December, 1812, in the 40th Year of her Age.

Sacred to the Memory of Phillip Pinkney, who died 14th January, 1812, Aged 80 years.

In Memory of Charles Pinckney, Gent.
Younger Son of
Philip and Jane Pinckney,
of this Place,
who departed this life
the 16th Day of October, 1806,
in the 25th year of his Age.

On Flat Stones in S. Aisle.

Here lieth the Body of William Stallord, Sen. who died January the 22d, 1720, Aged 80 years.

Here lieth the Body of Elinor the Wife of William Stallord, Sen. who died . . . . . . 1725.

Hatchment in the Chancel.

Quarterly, first and fourth argent, a heart gules, on a chief azure, 3 mullets; second and third azure, a bend between 6 trefoils or, impaling azure, a chevron between 3 lozenges, or.

This Church consists of a Chancel, Nave, South Aisle, and North and South Transepts.

The Right Honble Lord Douglas Lord of the Manor.

BULFORD.

On a Monument against E. Wall of Chancel.

Underneath lyes the Body of Anthony Southby, third Son of Richard Southby, Esq. and Ann, his Wife. He died the 18th of May, 1773, in the 13th year of his Age.

Good, Gentle, Sprightly, Tender, and Sincere,
Loving to all, to all who knew him Dear:
Wise Heaven, whilst in opening fragrance bloom'd
It's choicest Gifts, his kindred Soul resum'd.
Blest youth! yet must thy weeping friends deplore,
So early cropt fair Virtue's budding Flow'r.

X

On a Monument in South Wall of Chancel.

Sacred to the Memory of
Richard Southby, Esq.
heretofore of Southmarston, in this County,
And late of this Place,
who departed this life March 18th, 1791,
Aged 71.

And also of
Richard Duke Southby, Esq.
his Eldest Son, who survived him only to Dec. 16th,
in the same Year,
Aged 33.

This Monument is designed
as the most expressive and effectual Testimony
now, alas! in their power,
of a truly Conjugal, Filial, and Fraternal
Regard and Affection,
So justly due to them in their respective Characters,
and never to be recollected
but with the most tender and lasting Regret
by an inconsolable Widow, and her three Daughters,
their mournful survivors.

Arms—Quarterly, first and fourth or, a chevron between three roses, gules; second and third, per fess, argent and azure, three chaplets counterchanged, impaling, gules, a saltire, or, on a chief of the same, three lions rampant, gules, bar-ways.

On Flat Stones in Chancel.

Here lieth the Body of Richard Duke, Esq.
who died Nov. 3, 1757, Aged 68 years.

Arms—Per fess, three chaplets.

Here lyeth ye Body of Catherine, wife of Andr. Duke, Jun. Esq. who departed this life ye 15th day of Dec. Anno Domini 1719.

Arms—Per fess, 3 chaplets, over all, on an escutcheon, 3 escallop shells between 7 crosslets, fitchy.

Here lyeth the Body of Andrew Duke, Esq. who
died Feb. ye 23, Annoq. Dñi 1729.
Aged about 69 years.

And in or near the same place
were Interr'd Dorothy and Salina,
two Sisters of the said
Andrew Duke:
to witt, ye said Dorothy, the 14th Day of Dec. 1662,
And ye said Salina the 20th day of Apr. 1666.

Its requested that this Stone
Might not be removed.

Arms—Three chaplets, impaling, a fess, imbattled, between three doves.

Here lieth the Body
of George Turberville, younger Sone
of Thos. Turberville, of Beare Reages,
in the County of Dorset, Esquire,
who deceased the 9th Day of January, 1671.

Nave.

Sacred to the Memory of Mathew Devenish, who died 25th April, 1811, Aged 40 years.

On Flat Stones in Nave.

Here lieth the Body of Mary Beer, Single Woman.
She Departed this life Dec. 4, 1766, Aged 84 years.

Here lieth the Body of Martha, the wife of Thos. Pain,
who died Oct. 26, 1785,
Aged 94 years.

Here lies Sarah, the Wife of Henry Axford, and Daughter of William and Ann Reeves, Late of this Parish. She died Feb. 19, 1733, Aged 29 years.

Arms—On a bend, cottised, 3 lozenges.

On a Brass Plate.

Here lyeth buried the bodye of Thomas . . onell, Gent. who dyed the 26 daye of December, Anno Domini 1589.
Beati qui moriuntur in Domino.

Register commenced 1766.

Lady Charity Ann Pollen owns the Manor, and also has the right of presentation to the Living.

DURRINGTON.

On a Monument in Chancel.

To the Memory of that worthy Matrone, Mrs. Hester Conham, Widdow, Indeed Grand Daughter to Mr. Thomas Higbed, Martyr, and Wife of the Wor: Abraham Conham, Batchelour in Divinity, and Channon Resident Sometimes in the Cathedrall of Sarum, who Deceased the 3d of April, 1647, Aged 79.

If Righteous Age a Gowne of Glory bee,
Therfore this Gowne was doubly due to thee,
Who wert lesse old than Righteous, yet tis told
Thou liv'dst unto the Prophets Wondrous old.

Arms—Gules, a dove perched, argent, on a snake, or, impaling azure, a chevron, ermine, between 3 swans, argent.

On Flat Stones.

In Memory of Alice, Wife of the Reverend Mr. Thos. Moore, A.M. Rector of Steepleton, Dorsetshire, who died the second of September, 1750, in the 47th year of her age.

Memento mori.

Arms—A chevron, engrailed, between 3 moor cocks.

Under this Marble lie the Remains of the Rev. Mr. Thomas Moore, A. M. Rector of Steepleton, Dorset. He died August the 3d, 1753, in the 57th year of his Age.

Arms—As before.
Crest—A moor's head.

Here lyeth the Body of Mrs. Phenicia Poore, who departed this life May the 28th, 1741, Aged 66 years.

Arms—A fess between three mullets.

Under this Marble lie the Remains of Thomas Moore, Esq. He died June 23, 1783, in the 57th year of his age.

Arms—The same as the preceding.

Edward Lawes, Gent. died Dec. 21, 1743, Aged 27 years.

Thomas Lawes, Gent. died May 10, 1766, Aged 52 years.

Here lyeth the Body of Philip Poore, Èsq. who Departed this Life August the 5th, 1693.

Arms—A fess between 3 mullets, ... [defaced.]

Arms against the North Wall of the Nave.

1634. Sable, 5 lozenges or, 131.

On a Brass Plate in Chancel.

An Epitaph on the immature Death of His Deare Brother, John Poore, who Departed this life the 24 of August, An° Dñi 1633, Ætatis suæ 3 years.

Fraternall Love commaunds me to bestow
A Superscription on thee, though I know
Thou needest not my verse, nor can it give
Thee Life, by whome it onely hopes to live;
Yet suffer it to informe the Reader's eye
Of what a Stock this Graft was, here doth ly;
A Bude that promised fruite, but fore twas blowne,
Death nipt it blooming, ere the fruit was growne.

In the Vaulting of the South Aisle are the following Arms, *cut in Wood.*

Quarterly, first and fourth argent, a fess azure, between three mullets gules; second or, on a bend, engrailed, gules, three crosslets, fitchy, argent; third azure, a chevron, ermine, between three swans, per pale.

On the Pulpit and many of the pews is some ancient carved work in oak.

In the north window of the Nave is some painted glass.

The Rev. Dr. Owen Rector, or Vicar.

Register commenced 1591.

MILSTON.

On a Monument in Chancel.

Near this Place are Deposited the Remains of Beata, Relict of the late Harcourt Powell, Esq. Member of Parliament for Newtown, Hants. She died Feb. 14, 1797, Aged 59 years.

On Flat Stones in Chancel.

In Memory of
the Rev. Mr. Will. Mundy,
Rector of this Parish 53 years,
who Departed this life Jan. 23, 1757,
Aged 77.
Also Elizabeth, his Wife, who Departed this
life August the 29th, 1766,
Aged 82 years.

Here lyeth the Body of Robt. Harris, Rector of this Place, who died the 4th of November, 1662.

Against North Wall of Nave.

In Memory of
Charles Penruddocke, Esq. Second Son of
the late Charles Penruddocke, Esq.
one of the representatives for this County,
who died Nov. the 6th, 1799,
in the 26th year of his age.

In the East Window is some painted glass.

Orate pro nom Roberti Herrys
Statu Magistri Idectis natalis
Sci . Johes . Mathew . Sci Mar . cus

In the bottom part of the Window is the following Arms, inverted:

Gules, a chevron, ermine, between nine cross pattee, six in chief, three in base, argent.

The Rev. Dr. Toogood, Rector.

Thomas Rendall, Esq. Lord of the Manor.

BOSCOMBE.

In Chancel.

Sacred to the Memory of the Rev. John Jennings, A. M. Rector of this Parish, and Vicar of Idmiston, who died August 5th, 1768, Aged 47.

And of Deborah, his Wife, Daughter of the Rev. Thos. Frampton, of Broad Hinton, in this County, who died Oct. 3, 1783, Aged 56 years.

H. S. E.
Johannis Kent, Armigeri,
Obiit xi die Aprilis,
Anno { Dom. 1710. / Ætat. 84. }

Arms—A lion statant guardant, a chief ermine.

The Rev. Henry Donne [*or* Dun], Rector.

Lady Ayres owns the Manor.

ALLINGTON.

[*No Monuments or Inscriptions in this Church.*]

In the North Window of the Nave is a little painted glass.

The Rev. F. W. Fowle, Rector.

Wm. Wyndham, of Sarum, Esq. Lord of the Manor.

NEWTON TONEY.

On a Monument in Chancel.

Adventum Jesu Christi Præstolatur,
Ann Jones, uxor Franc : Jones : necnon Filia
Joh : et Ann Reyves, de Ranson, in Comitatu Dorset,
quæ dũm in terris peregrinata est, Cœlicolam
præ setulit, et virtuti fuit admodum similis
Humilis, modesta, mitis, liberalis, et castitas pectoris, quam casta,
Corpore formosa, attamen mente formosior,
Sanctitate erga Deum, amore erga maritum, pietate erga liberos eximia
Nota pluribus non injuriâ, sed beneficio,
cujus præciosa memoria omni epitaphio duribilior,
superstes erit, etiam cum ipsa sepulchra fuerint sepulta
Undecim liberos peperit fœcunda mater,
Octo filios, tres filias filiorum tres,
Joh : Franc : Guliel : etiam num supersunt,
pariter et singulæ filiæ, Elijai, Ann,
Milicent, materna probitatis, atq. Sept. 13, et Ætatis suæ 50.
Vitâ Mortali exutâ, induit immortalitatem.

On Flat Stones in Chancel.

Here lyeth ye Body of Elizabeth
Fiennes, 2nd Daughter of Nathaniel
Fiennes, Esq. by Frances,
Eldest daughter of Richard
Whithed, Esq. who dyed the 4
day of October, in the yeare 1668,
And of her age the 12 Allmoste.

Arms—Three lions rampant.

Here lieth ye Body of Mrs. Honour
Harper, daughter of Sr Henry Whithed,
of Tuderleigh, who
Departed this life Feb. 24,
in ye Yeare of our Lord 1674.

Arms—A fess between 3 fleur-de-lis.

Against North Wall of Nave.

To the much-honoured Memory of
Harry Earle, Esq.
who died Jan. 31, 1774, Aged 61 years.

And of Ann Earle,
who died March 3rd, 1791, Aged 79 years.

To one of the most amiable of Husbands and of Wives,
To one of the dearest the best of Fathers & of Mothers,
in just Reverence
For the many excellent Virtues
Which eminently adorned their Lives,
This Marble, a small but sincere Tribute
of Filial Duty and Affection,
is mournfully inscribed by their
only surviving Son. A. D. 1791.

Arms—Gules, within a border engrailed, or, three escallop shells, argent. Impaling argent, on a chief azure, three crescents, of the first.

Sacred to the Memory of
Harriett, the wife of James Wapshare, Esq.
And Daughter of the late
William Leigh Symes, Esq.
She died April 6th, 1814,
Aged 24 years.

Hope deluded asks a tear;
Stranger, pause and sigh,
Youth and Beauty moulder here!
Go, and learn to die.

R. C. T.

Brass Plate.

Within this Church lie interred the following Persons of the Family of William Benson, Esq. one of the Auditors of the Imprest, and formerly of Wilbury House, in this Parish. He died in London A. D. 1754, & was buried at Bromley, in the County of Middlesex.

Eleanor, first Wife of William Benson	Feb. 5,	1721.
Agnes Benson, his Daughter	May 1,	1724.
Benjamin Benson, his Son	Jan. 12,	1727.
Earle Benson, his Son	Sept. 3,	1737.
Eleanor Benson, his Daughter	June 25,	1742.
William Earle Benson, his Son	Feb. 5,	1762.
Martha Benson, his Daughter	May 24,	1764.
Eleanor, Daughter of Wm. Earle Benson	Dec. 5,	1767.
Harry Earle, (late Benson) Son of Wm. Benson	Feb. 10,	1774.
Ann Earle, Wife of Harry Earle	March 10,	1791.
Wm. Benson Earle, Son of Harry and Ann Earle	March 31,	1796.

Arms—1. Argent, on a bend cottised, gules, 3 trefoils, vert.
2. Argent, on a chevron, sable, 3 cross flory, of the first.
3. Or, on a chevron dancette, sable, 3 bezants.
4. Sable, fretty, argent.
5. Sable, 11 bezants, 32123 between two flanches argent.
6. Gules, a chief ermine.
7. Azure, a chevron, or, between 3 leopards' heads cabossed, of the same.
8. Azure, vair, ancient argent, a chief, checky, or and gules.
9. Gules, two wings conjoined and inverted . . . within a border engrailed, or.
10. Quarterly, first and fourth sable, a cross pattee, or; second and third gules, dancette, on a chief or, a lion passant guardant, sable.
11. [The same as the preceding.]
12. Azure, 3 sturgeons naiant, in pale, debruised by a fretty, argent.

Crest—A bear's head erased and gorged.

South Wall.

Underneath are deposited the Remains of
Wm. Benson Earle, Esq.
of the Close of Salisbury,
who died March 21, 1796,
Aged 55.

East End of Nave.

In Memory of the Honourable
Nathaniell Fiennes, Second
Sonne of William Lord Viscount
Say and Seale, who Departed
this life the 16th Day of December,
1669, in the 62 Year of his Age.
And
of his Two Eldest Daughters,
Frances and Elizabeth, by Frances
his Wife, Daughter of Richard
Whithed, of Tuderly, in ye County of
Southton, Esq. who both died in
the Flower of their Age.
Here lyes also the Honble Frances
Fiennes, who died the 7th of Oct. 1691,
in the 70th year of her Age, Leaving
Only two Daughters,
Mary and Cecilia. Cecilia
Born June ye 7th, 1662, Died 10th April, 1741,
At Hackney.

Arms—Three lions rampant, impaling, a fess between three fleur-de-lis.

On a Mon. in N. Aisle.

To the Memory of
Sir Charles Warre Malet, Baronet,
(of Wilbury House,)
Whose merits and talents shed an additional lustre
on the ancient and respectable family
from which he sprung.
He died on the 23d of January, A. D. 1815, Aged 62.
His mortal remains are deposited in a vault
near this tablet.
At an early age he was appointed
to the civil service of the Honble East India Company
in which he filled several very important Offices:
He was for many years Resident Minister
at the Court of Poona,
And for some time acted as Governor of Bombay.
By his liberal attention
to the opinions, customs, and institutions,
of the various tribes and casts of Hindostan,
by his firmness, zeal, talents, and integrity,
he not only advanced the interests of his employers
in the Mahratta empire,
But upheld the honour and character of his Country
throughout the extensive Regions of the East.
Relieved from public cares,
his active and patriotic spirit
accompanied him in his domestic retirement:
when his country was menaced with invasion by France,
He distinguished himself
in animating the loyal yeomanry
and peasantry of the district,
and was intrusted with the command
of the first battalion of the local-Militia of this County.

He was conspicuous for his domestic virtues,
Affectionate to his family, sincere in his friendships,
Charitable to the poor, and Benevolent to all.
As it was his avowed ambition
to emulate the virtues of his Ancestors,
So has he left a bright example
for the imitation of his Descendants.

Arms—Quarterly, first and fourth azure, 3 escallop shells . . . second and third gules, two demi lions passant guardant . . . . . impaling ermine, on a chief, gules, 3 billets, or, in fess point an escutcheon, charged with a dexter hand.

[A small brass plate taken from the Nave.]

The Rev. Hugh Price, Rector.

WEST CHOLDERTON.

North Wall.

Devoted to God,
Anno Dom. 1753,
A Charity of £.12 a Year
for ever,
by Anthony Cracherode,
late of this Parish, Esq.
The Minister, Churchwardens,
Parish Clerk, Trustees.
The Deed of trust
in the Chest below.
1763.

To the Memory of Anthony Cracherode, formerly of the Inner Temple, and late of this Parish, Esq. He was bred up to the law, which he practised in the Temple, from the year 1702, to the year 1730. In the year 1714, his late Majesty, King George the First, granted him for life the Offices of Chief Clerk, Register, and sole Examiner, in the Chancery of the Island of Barbadoes, and Clerk of the Crown, and Clerk of the Peace there to be executed by his deputies. In the year 1715, he was appointed Sollicitor for the affairs of his Majesty's Treasury, which Office He executed with distinguished zeal and uprightness for the Crown Interest till the year 1730, when he voluntarily resigned it, serving his King and Country afterwards as a Member of Parliament: lastly, well considering the brevity of human life, he chose to retire from all Publick business, and settled in this Parish, devoting the remainder of his days in Religious attention to the only and most important business, that of a future and happy immortality. He died in the 72d year of his Age, in the year of our Lord 1752.

On a Brass Plate.

Cuthbert Rives, of the Age of 56 Yeares.
He deceased the 3d Day of August, Anno 1594.

Come nere, my frends, behould and see,
Suche as I am, suche shall you be;
As is my State within This tombe,
So must thou be before the dome;
For all men must, by god's decree,
Once taste of deth, as you se me:
Wherfore in time Remember deth,
Before you lose your vitall breth.

On a Flat Stone. Chancel

Mr. Edward Beckham,
Formerly Fellow of Oriel College, Oxon,
And Rector of this Place,
Son of Edward Beckham, D. D.
of Sparle, in Norfolk.
He died the 16th of Feb.
Anno { Domini 1746.
Ætatis 30.

In the Chancel are three perfect squares of Roman pavement, on two of which are griffins passant, on the other a greyhound courant, or.

Register commenced 1651.

NORTH TIDWORTH.

On Flat Stones in Chancel.

In Memory of Thomas Humphreys, Esq. who died Nov, 9th, 1783, Aged 76.

Frances, his Wife, (a Daughter of Lieut. Gen. John Richmond, alias Webb, of Biddesden) died in London, Feb. 9th, 1777, and was buried at St. Giles's, Cripplegate, by whom she had Issue two Sons and four Daughters.

Here lyeth the Body of Mary Warton, ye Daughter of Mr. Anthony Warton, L. B. and Mary his Wife, who was Born 28th day of September, 1678, and dyed ye 27th Day of June, 1681.

Here lyeth the Body of Elizabeth Pierce, Daughter of Mr. Robert and Elizabeth Pierce, who departed this life the 5th of May, 1703.

Here lyeth the Body of Mrs. Jane Pierce, Daughter of Mr. Robert Pierce, late Rector of this Parish, who Departed this life the 8th of May, 1757.

On Brass Plate in North Wall of the Nave.

The Widdowes Mite in Memory of
Elizabeth Willis, Widdow, who
died the 7 day of January, 1636, and
Gave to the Poore of this Parish
Five Pounds, the Income of it to
be paid to the Poore every Good
Friday, placed Heere by her
Executor, Ben : Smith.

Hatchment.

Quarterly, first and fourth sable, a bend nebule, or, between two unicorns' heads erased, or; second and third azure, a chevron, ermine, between 3 leopards' heads cabossed, or.

The Rev. John Hughes, Rector.

Mr. Poore, or Thos. Ashton Smith, Lord of the Manor.

FIGHELDEAN.

North Wall.

Edward Poore,
Lord of this Manor,
And that of Tidworth Zouch,
in this County,
died at the latter, Sept. 1, A. D. 1787,
in the 78th year of his age,
And lies buried here.

Arms—A fess, azure, between 3 mullets, gules.

Near this Place
is interred Hester,
Wife of Smart Poore, Gent.
of this Parish,
who Departed this life March 1, 1770,
Aged 43.

Also Smart Poore, Gent.
Ob. Sept. 20, 1773, Æt. 62.

Also, in Memory of Amelia Martha Cox,
Ob. 31 August, 1794, Aged 7 weeks,
Grand Daughter of Mr. Smart Poore.

Arms—The same as the preceding.

Near this Place lies Edward Poore, Gent. descended from the Antient Family of the Poores of this County, who departed this life May ye 24th, 1716, Aged 65: Who left behind him Ann his Wife, and three Sons by her, Edward, Smart, and Abram Poore.

Arms—The same as before.

South Wall.

Near this Place is interred Smart Poore, Gent. of this Parish, who Departed this life the 22d of May, 1747, Aged 63.

Also Elizabeth, his Wife, who Departed this life the 18th of July, 1751, Aged 62.

In this Chancell Lies the Body of John Yorke, Clerk, M. A. late Vicar of this Parish, who died Feb. 4th, A. D. 1740, Æt. 45, Justly lamented by all that knew him for his remarkable sweetness of temper, and affability of Manners, which rendered him a most agreeable Friend and Neighbour, as well as a most kind and indulgent Husband; and these his amiable Qualities received Stability, Ornament, and Merit, from their happy Connexion with all Christian Graces requisite to the Character of a Good Man and an exemplary Minister of the Gospel.

Also, in the same grave lies the Body of William Yorke, of New College, Oxon, Son of the said John and Elizabeth his Wife, who died March 23, 1753, Æt. 21. In whose Praise nothing greater need be said, than this just Eulogium, That he inherited, and as far as Age and opportunity allowed, Represented his Father's Virtues.

A good life hath but a few days; but a good name endureth for ever. Eccles. 41. 13.

This Monument was erected out of an affectionate Regard to the Memories of her beloved Husband And Son by their Mournful Survivor Eliz.th Yorke.

Elizabeth York died Jan. 23, 1771, Aged 82.

Arms—Argent, a saltire azure, impaling sable, a battle-axe between three plates.

Near this spot is interred Michael Hicks Beach, Esq. who died Sept. the 27th, 1815, Aged 34 years. He was the eldest Son of Michael Hicks Beach, Esq. and of Henrietta Maria, his Wife.

In Affectionate Remembrance of his Memory,
This Monument was Erected by his Widow,
Caroline Jane Hicks Beach.

Arms—Vair, a canton charged with a mullet, surcharged with a crescent.

South Aisle.

Near this Place lyeth the Body of
Henry Clarke, late
of this Parish, Esq.
who dyed on the 21st day of
April, 1712, in the 44th year of his Age.
Besides Large and Publick Charityes to the
Hospitalls of St. Thomas, Christchurch,
& Bethleem in London, & for propagating
the Gospell in foreigne Parts, He left twelve
Pounds per Annum to this Parish for ever;
Viz.
£.5 per Annum for teaching 10 poor
Children of Hackleston & Fittleton,
10*s*. per Annum to buy them books;
40*s*. Yearly for relief of the Poor of this Parish,
£.4 for putting out a boy every year of
Hackleston and of Fittleton,
and 10*s*. to the
Minister for preaching a Sermon in this Church
on the 8th Day of Dec. Yearly.
The Memory of the Just is Blessed. Prov. 10. 7.

Arms—Azure, a chevron between three swans, argent, impaling per pale; first ermine, in chief, a lion's head erased, gules; second . . . .

The Rev. John Perkinson, Rector.

Michael Hicks Beach, Lord of the Manor.

LUDGERSHALL.

By the South Wall of the Nave.

S. Side.] Heare lyeth the Body of Sir Rychard Brydges Knyght whose Soule Jehu take to his Mercy he decessed the fyrst daye of August Anno . .

N. Side.] Heare Lyeth the Lady Jane wife to Sir Rychard Brydges Knyght & dowghter to Sir Wylyam Spencer Knyght.

[The above is a handsome tomb of free-stone, on which are placed the statues of Sir Richard Brydges and his Lady: the Knight is in armour, with his sword in the scabbard, his head resting on a helmet, and his feet upon a lion.]

On Flat Stones in Chancel.

In Memory of Ann, the Daughter of the Rev. Mr. Richard Yaldwyn, Jun. and Ann, his Wife, who died Feb. y^e 15, 1754, Aged 16 years.

Walter Clarges, Esq. Son of Sir Walter Clarges, of Westminster, Baronet, who dyed Jan. 26, 172$\frac{3}{2}$
Aged 26 years.

In Memory of the Rev. Mr. Richard Yaldwyn, M. A. who was Rector of this Parish 56 years, died May y^e 10th, 1763, Aged 85 years.

Also of Jane, his Wife, died August 14th, 1775, Aged 92 years.

In Memory of William Yaldwyn, of Blackdown, in Sussex, Gent. Son of the Rev. Mr. Richard Yaldwyn, and Jane, his Wife, who died Oct. the 1st, 1751, Aged 40 years.

Also Mr. Thomas Yaldwin, their Son, who died Dec. ye 13th, 1726, Aged 13 years.

On a Monument in N. Wall of the Nave.

In Memory of Thomas Gale, Gent. who died Nov. 27, 1723, Aged 28 years.

Also of Alice, his Wife, who died Dec. 1, 1777, Aged 81 years.

Also of Thomas, their Son, who died March 20, 1723, Aged 7 years.

And of John, their Son, who died Sept. 23, 1771, Aged 50 years.

This Monument was Erected by William Everett, of Heytesbury, in this County, who married the Daughter of Thomas and Alice Gale.

On a Flat Stone in N. Aisle.

Here lyeth ye Body of Elizabeth, Daughter of Mr. George Tarrant, who died July . . 1734, Aged 10 weeks.

Inscription on the south side of the Tower.

FE PM CN TM
1675

In the Churchyard.

Head Stones.

In Memory of Robt. Horne, who died Jan. 9th, 1787, Aged 69 years.

Afflictions sore long time I bore,
Physicians were in vain;
Till Death did seize, and God did please,
And Ease me of my Pain,

In Memory of Ann Horne, who died June 5th, 1802, Aged 80 years.

In patience Great She bore the Cross,
Of stern Affliction's frown,
And counted all things here but Lost,
To wear in Heaven a Crown.

In Memory of Mr. James Horne, who departed this life October the 9th, 1791, Aged 44 years.

In Memory of Sarah, the Wife of Thomas Smith, who died Nov. 10th, 1747, Aged 44 years.

In Memory of Mary, Wife of Richard Hutchens, only Daughter of John Gale, Gent. She died Feb. ye 18th, 1761, Aged 35 years.

Also two of their Children, Richard and Elizabeth, both died young.

In Memory of James Hutchens, who died Nov. 2, 1766, Aged 45 years.

Flat Tomb.

In Memory of Elizabeth, wife of Roger Hutchens, who died April ye 11th, 1761, Aged 71 years.

Here by my Friends now do I lay,
Whom God before me took away;
I follow them, as you must me,
To live with Christ Eternally.

In Memory of Roger Hitchens, who died March ye 23, 1765, Aged 76 years.

Head Stones.

Here Lyeth ye Body of Eleanor, ye Wife of Nicholas Drury. She died March 30th, 1744, Aged 46 years.

In Memory of Nicholas Drury, who died Jan. 3rd, 1740, Aged 74 years.

In Memory of Dinah, ye Daughter of Daniel and Mary Dobss, who died Feb. the 10th, 1743, Aged 6 years.

In Memory of John Beale, who Departed this life January 20, 1789, Aged 70 years.

Certain and uncertain is the life of Man,
Certain to die, but yet uncertain when;
An instance here we have before our eyes
How soon the strongest man grow sick & dies.

In Memory of Elizabeth, Wife of John Beale, who died March 1st, 1761, Aged 80 years.

A faithful Friend, a Mother dear,
A loving wife, now buried here:
In love She lived, in pace She died,
Her life desired, but God denied.

In Memory of Mary, the Wife of William Crouch, who died Oct. ye 31, 1741, Aged 57 years.

William Lansley died Sept. 19th, 1768, Aged 81 years.

Sacred to the Memory of Sarah, Wife of Jonas Lansley, who died Oct. 28, 1771, Aged 40 years.

Also Sarah, the second Wife of Jonas Lansley, who died June 17th, 1810, Aged 80 years.

Sacred to the Memory of Emma Sturges, Daughter of James and Ann Sturges, who departed this life February 20th, 1816, Aged 10 years.

My warning was but a day,
When Jehovah call'd I did obey;
But prepare to die, for that is good,
A rose may wither in its Bud.

Sacred to the Memory of James Sturges, a Faithful Son of James and Ann Sturges, who departed this life March 20th, 1818, Aged 25 years,

Worn out with Pain and long desease,
All human help was in vain;
When God did please, then he gave ease,
And cur'd me of my Pain.

On a Flat Tomb.

Here lyeth the Body of William Sturges, and of Elizabeth, his Wife. He died August ye 1st, 1734, Aged 79 years. She died Nov. ye 16, 1717, Aged 60 years.

This Tomb was set up by Order of Mary Sturges, their Daughter, never to be removed.

Under this Stone are Deposited the Remains of Selwyn Sturgess, who died Sept. 16, 1813, Aged 80 years.

Also of Elizabeth, his wife, who died 13th, 1813, Aged 72.

They were Antient and Respectable Inhabitants of this Place, and Brought up, by Constant Example of honest Industry and Uprightness a numerous family of Children. As a Tribute of Respect to their Memory, this Stone was Erected by a Friend to the Family.

Head Stones.

In Memory of Sarah, the Wife of Ephraim Sturgess, who died Dec. 17th, 1784, Aged 49 years.

My Husband dear my life is past,
My love to you so long did last;
And now for me no sorrow take,
But love my Child still for my sake.

In Memory of Ephraim Sturgess, who died April 27, 1794, Aged 56 years.

How Strangly fond of life poor Mortals be,
Now few who see my bed would change with me;
But, serious reader, tell me which is Best,
The Toilsom Journey, Or the Traveler's Rest.

Here lyeth the Body of Anne, the Wife of John Hutchens, who Dyed March ye 16, 1715, Aged 28 years.

Flat Tomb.

In Memory of John Newman, who Departed this life March the 14th, 1736, Aged 77 years.

Also Margaret, his Wife, who departed this life May the 1st, 1764, Aged 99 years.

Head Stones.

Sacred to the Memory of Ann, Wife of Thomas Smith, who Departed this life the 12th of July, 1801, Aged 44 years.

Pain was my portion, Physic was my food,
Groans my Devotion, Drugs did me no good;
Christ my Physician known what was best,
To Ease me of my pain, my Soul he took to Rest.

Sacred to the Memory of Sarah Blake, Daughter of Thomas and Mary Blake, who Departed this Life July 4th, 1800, Aged 19 years.

Now in the Bloom of my Years,
I left my Friends in floods of tears;
I soon sprung up, soon was gone,
So frail's the life of Every one.

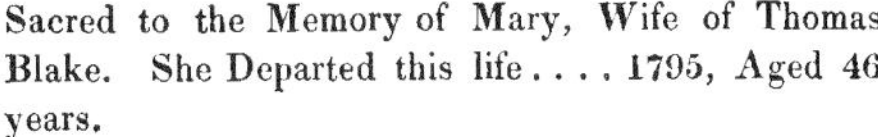

Sacred to the Memory of Mary, Wife of Thomas Blake. She Departed this life . . . . 1795, Aged 46 years.

Farewell to you my Husband Dear,
My Children and my Friends,
I hope in Heaven to see you all,
When all things have an end.

Memento Mori.

Here lieth the Body of Mr. John Capps, many years a worthy Resident of This Borough, departed this Life in full hopes of a Blessed Immortality, Dec. 31st, 1778, Ætatis 70 years.

Register commenced 1609.

The Rev. John Selwyn, Rector.

Sir James Graham, Bart. Lord of the Manor.

SALISBURY.

St. Edmund's Church.

On a small Monument in the North Wall of Chancel.

James Stirling Samber, D. D.
The Resident Rector of this Parish thirty-nine Years,
died 15th March, 1801, Aged 79.

Jane Samber, the Wife of J. S. Samber, D. D.
and Daughter of John Eyre, Esq. of Putney, Surry,
died 3rd May, 1793, Aged 72.

This Tablet is Inscribed to the Memory
of her beloved Parents, by their only
Child, Jane Catherine Samber.

On a Monument in South Wall of Chancel.

The windows of this chancel
were presented by the munificence
of Samuel Whitchurch, Esq.
An Inhabitant of this Parish,
In the Year 1818.

The Members of the Vestry
unanimously resolved
To perpetuate their sense of the Donor's Liberality,
By the erection of
This Tablet.

Arms—Gules, on a fess ermine, 3 estoils, or,

On Flat Stones in Chancel.

Betty,
Wife of
Mr. John Gast,
Died Dec. 2nd, 1774,
Aged 58 years.

H. S. E.
Maria Naish,
Uxor Thomæ Naish, Cler.
Obiit
18 die Feb.
Anno { Ætat. 83.
Dñi 1718. }

Etiam
Dictus Thomas Naish,
Qui obiit
xxvi die Decembris,
Anno { Dñi MDCCXXVII.
Ætat. LXXX. }

H. S. E.
Johannes Naish, Arm.
Naupagis in Navali Regio,
juxta Portsmouth;
Operam navantibus Præsectus ipse
Naupergorum peritissimus.
Obiit v^to^ die Decembris,
Anno { Dñi MDCCXXVII.
Ætat. LXI. }

Item Martha, Uxor
Johannes Naish,
Heu! paucis modo Mensibus
suo desideratissimo superstes Conjugi,
obiit xxvii die Augusti,
Anno { Dom MDCCXXVII.
Ætat. LIX. }

In Memory of
Mr. John Naish,
of this City, Innholder,
who dyed the 20th of August, 1731,
Aged 66 years.

And also of Mary, this third Wife,
Who dyed the 12th of June, 1732,
Aged 51 years.

Here rest the Remains
of Mary Bucknall,
Wife of Thomas Bucknall, Esq.
who departed this Life
the 28th June, 1766,
Aged 65.

Also of
Thomas Bucknall, Esq.
who died the 30th Oct. 1783,
Aged 89.

Arms—Party per pale, sinister, on a chevron a mullet between three greyhounds, two in chief, one in base; on the dexter side 6 martlets, 3
2
1

On a White Marble Monument against the N. Wall of Body.

In Memory
Of Sir Wadham Wyndham, Knight, 9th Son of Sir John Wyndham, of Orchard Wyndham, in the County of Somerset, who died in the College of this Church Dec. 25th, 1668, Aged 58.

Of Barbara, Widow of Sir Wad^m^ Wyndham, and Daughter of Sir George Clerke, of Walford, in the County of Northampton, Knight, who died Dec. 26th, 1704, Aged 77.

Of Wadham Wyndham, 4th Son of Sir Wadham Wyndham, who died Feb. 19th, 1736, Aged 74.

Of Sarah, Widow of Wadham Wyndam, and Daughter of William Hearst, Esq. of the Close of this City, who died April 15th, 1758, Aged 81.

Of Wadham 1st Son of Wad^m^ and Sarah Wyndham, who died May 7th, 1729, Aged 26.

Of Barbara, Daughter of Wadham and Sarah Wyndham, who died Dec. 29th, 1774, Aged 73.

Of Arundell, Wife of Henry Wyndham, and Daughter of Thomas Penruddocke, Esq. of Compton Chamberlayne, in this County, who died Sept. 3d, 1780, Aged 66.

Of Henry Wyndham, 2nd Son of Wadham and Sarah Wyndham, who died Oct. 6th, 1788, Aged 79.

Of Caroline, Wife of Henry Penruddocke Wyndham, Daughter and Heiress of Edward Hearst, Esq. of the Close, of this City, who died Aug. 3d, 1817, Aged 80.

On a Monument of White Marble in the S. Side of the Body.

H. S. E.
Marshall Hill, Armiger,
Ortus Parentibus Francisco et Elizabetha, Genere & Virtute præclaris
Iis tamen Dotibus instructus, ut Prosapiæ gloriâ minus indigerit
In Collegio Lincolniensi, inter Causidicos Legum Municipalium
Studio sedulò et feliciter incubit:
In utroq. Gymnasio Virtutis et Pietatis Cultor indefessus,
Utriusq. loci Ornamentum et Delicia
Formæ Elegantiâ, admodum Spectabilis
Animi tamen Virtutibus multo Excellentior
Fuit enim
Parentum monitis promptè et lubenter Obsequens,
Amicorum commodis inservire Paratissimus,
Erga Pauperes sine Gloriolæ aucupio Liberalis,
Ab omni contentione ita penitus abhorrens,
Ut Pacem Semper coleret, etiam in Damnum sibi cessuram,
Ita Justitiæ tenax,
Ut eam unice sequeretur ducem,
In humanis Negotiis ita Assiduus, ut Otium sibi raro indulgeret,
Divinis interim officiis ita intentus, ut iisdem nunquam non vacaret,
Quarum Virtutum Exemplar
Etsi diutius inter nos superesse vetuerit, Deus
Illarum tamen ut vigeret Memoriâ
Monumentum hoc fieri curavit
Mœrens et Pientissima mater.
Natus Londini 13° die Julii, A. D. 1682;
Valetudinis causa ad aquas Calidas Bathoniæ profectus
a Variolis correptus, Occubuit primo die Julii,
A. D. 1707.

Arms—Gules, two bars, ermine, in chief, a lion passant, or.

On Flat Stones in Body.

Here Lyeth the Body of Edmund Pitman, Esq. Son of Edmund Pitman, Esq. Recorder of this City. He died Dec. 18th, 1743, Aged 52.

In the same Vault Lye the Remains of Elizabeth, Widow of Edmund Pitman, Esq. and Daughter of James Hunt, Esq. of Popham, in the County of Southton. She deceased Nov. 2d, 1751.

Here Lyeth the Body
of Cary Hunt,
Son of Cary Hunt, Esq.
of Upton Greys, in the County of Hants.
He died Jan. 4th, 1742, Aged 17 years.

In Memory of John Long, of this City, Gent. who dyed Nov. ye 23rd, 1732, Aged 41.

Arms—A lion rampant between eight crosslets, in chief a mullet.

In Memory of Mrs. Eleanor Clare, Relict of Thomas Clare, of Hatesbury, Gent. Dyed the 9th May, 1748, Aged 67.

In Memory of Mr. Richard Long, Alderman, of this City, Born 1st August, 1655, Baptised ye last day of that Month, and dyed 12th July, 1724.

Under the Mayor's Seat also Lieth Mrs. Mary Long, his Daughter, who Died the 7th May, 1751.

Arms—Party, per pale, sinister; quarterly, first and fourth gules, a lion rampant, or; second and third argent, a fess reguly, azure, between three pellets, two in chief, one in base, dexter, sable, a lion rampant, argent, between eight crosslets, or.

Crest—A demi-lion, argent.

In Memory of Mrs. Alice Long, Relict of Richard Long, of this City, who died Feb. ye 21st, 1734, Aged 76.

E

Here Lyeth the Body of Mr. Thomas Breun, Coll. of Excise, Born in Suffolk, who dyed April ye 6th, 1758, Aged 56.

Arms—Three crescents in pale.

Joannæ Mariæ Stirling, ob. Dec. 21st, 1726.

Frances Samber, Ob. 13 Ap : 1730, Ætat. 10.

In Memory of Mrs. Sarah Long, who departed this Life the 27th day of October, 1748.

And also of Mrs. Lucy Long, who died 14th Sept. 1787, Aged 85.

Hic Jacet Maria Hippisley, Johannis et Luciæ Gore Filia unica, et Roberti Hippisley Uxor charissima. Obiit vicesimo sexto die Aprilis, A. D. 1755, Ætatis suæ 36.

Here Lyeth the Body of Rebecca, the Wife of Edward Kirmar, Gent. and Daughter of Herbert Saladin, Esq. and Anne, his Wife, who departed this Life ye 22d of February, 1708, in the 52d year of her age.

Here lyeth the Body of Herbert Salladin, Esq. who departed this Life the 1st Day of July, 1716, Aged 83 years.

Here Lyeth the Body of Lucy, the Wife of Mr. John Gore, who died the 22 August, 1750.

Here Lyeth the Body of . . . . . Salladin, the Wife of Mr. Herbert, Salladin, who died the 1st of March, 1765, Aged 86 years.

H. S. E.

Lucy Salladin Gore, Daughter of John and Lucy Gore, Obiit . . . . May, 1725, Ætat. 6 months.

H. S. E.

Also the Body of John William Hippisley, who dyed 15th September, 1740.

And also Lucy Ellen Hippisley, who died 23d July, 1742.

Quod tuos infra pedes neglectum nunc latet et conculcatum, aliquando fuit Lucia Hippisley, omnium quotquot uspiam sunt . . . . ditissimus thesaurus, quam venustam, innocentem, et valde amabilem obisse, siquidem homo sis lugebis, siu supra humanitatem sapis, lætabere mortalia reliquit A. D. 1755, annum ætatis agens septimum.

Also the Body of John William Hippisley Trenchard, Esq. Son of the above Mary Hippisley, and Brother of the said Lucy, who died December ye 8th, 1801, Aged 61 years.

On Monuments against N. Wall of the N. Aisle.

Here Lyeth Interred Anne, the Wife of Mr. John Baskerville, who Departed this Life the 21st of February, 1749.

Here also Lies interred John Baskerville, Gent. who Departed this life the 13th of February, 1761, Aged 81 years.

In Memory of Thomas Baskerville, Gent. and Mary his Wife. He died 16th April, 1781, Aged 69 years. She died 5th Dec. 1768, Aged 57.

Juxta sub communi marmore depositæ sunt exuviæ Samuelis Legg Samber, M. D. et Katherinæ uxoris ejus, qui senectutis maturitate, sensim collapsi, et resurrectionem felicem unà expectantes tranquille, uti vixerant obierunt Ille } An. Et. { 81, } Salutis { 1761.
Illa } { 86, } { 1772.

Patri optimo, Matri dulcissimæ, Monumentum hoc munus extremum consecravit Jacobus Stirling Samber, D. D.

On a Flat Stone in N. Aisle.

Hannah, Wife of William Stephens, born July 6th, 1747, died Nov. 3d, 1779.

William Stephens, late an Alderman of the City, and Mayor in the Year 1782, Born Dec. 25th, 1744, Died August 8th, 1799.

Ann Higginson died 15th June, 1801, Aged 79.

H. S. E.

Franciscus Kenton, Arm. Natus vicesimo tertio die Janrij 1634, Denatus vicesimo secundo die Janrij 1720.

Arms—Azure, a fess ermine, in chief 3 fleur-de-lis, or.

Here lieth the Body of Francis Kenton, Esq. who died March 3, 1755, Aged 67 years.

Near this Place
are interred the Remains of Henrietta, Wife of Francis Kenton, Esq. who died April 12th 1777,
In the 77th Year of her age.

Arms—Party, per pale, sinister, argent, on a chevron, sable, three qu tre oils, or, dexter; quarterly, first and fourth azure, a fess, ermine, in chief three fleur-de-lis, or; second and third gules, a lion ramp nt, argent.

H. S. E.

Mary Duport, deceased 23d May, 1785, Aged 58.
Daughter of Isaac Duport, Esq.

H. S· E.

Susan de Convenent, Daughter of the Rev. John Paul de Convenent, Aged 22 years, Died 1st Dec. 1782.

On Monuments in South wall of S. aisle.

Sacred to the Memory of Joseph Everett, Esq.
An Inhabitant of this Parish Forty years.
He died on the 24 of July, 1818.

Qualis fuit, læta dies Resurrectionis demonstravit.

Sacred to the Memory of John Wyche, Esq. Captain in the Honble East India Company's Service,
And late a Magistrate of this City,
who died the 7th of April, 1805, Aged 74 years.

Also of Elizabeth, his Wife, second Daughter of Edmund Abbott, of Winterbourn Dantsey, Esq. who died the 11th of March, 1798, Aged 60 years.

And of
Elizabeth-Ann, their Daughter,
Wife of the Rev. W. Slade, of Warminster,
who died the 30th of March, 1814,
Aged 48 years.

Hic prope serventur,
Diuque serventur Inviolabiles
Exuviæ
Luciæ Hippisley,
Roberti et Mariæ Hippisley, Filiæ,
Obiit 23° die Jan'ȷ 7mo.

Oh! Born to Bless & Dye, in Temper Mild,
In sense a Woman, tho' in Age a Child;
In whom Love, Innocence, & Beauty shin'd
Clear from those Clouds of Vice yt shade ye mind:
Beheld, Admir'd, & Lost, Thy Parent's Pride,
Who never gav'st them grief, but when you dy'd;
Justly Bewail'd by Earth, Preserv'd by Heaven,
Wherein a Better, Happier State is giv'n.
This last sad mark of Love I now can give,
Who to thy Memory consecrate this Stone,
And spake thy Mother's Sorrows in my Own.

Juxta Filiæ cineres, volunt et suas jacere Mariæ Hippisley, Joh. et Luciæ Gore Filiæ unica, et Rob. Hippisley Uxor charissima Fœmina, jam raris virtutibus, et suavitate morum facili insignis, ut nullum suis, et imprimus marito, vel amandi viva, vel lugendi mortua statuerit, modum. Obiit vicmo sexto die Aprilis, A. D. 1754, suæq. ætatis 36.

On Flat Stones in S. Aisle.

In Memory of Mrs. Pen. Church, third Daughter of the Rev. Mr. Thos. Church, Rector of Steventon, Hants.

Here Lyeth ye Body of Mrs. Alice Hower, Daughter of George Hower, Gent. who died Oct. 18

Underneath this Stone is interred the remains of Mrs. Elizabeth Whatmore, Wife of Edward Whatmore, Esq. late of Marshwood, in this County. Born March 25th, 1730, Died March 15th, 1797.

Here lieth the Body of Mr. John Hower, Son of George Hower, Gent. who died January ye 5th, 1715.

On a Brass Plate.

Elizabeth, second Daughter of Edmund Abbott, Esq. of Winterbourn Dantsey, and Wife of John Wyche, Esq. of this City, Died 11th March, 1798, Aged 60 years.

Here lieth the Body of George Henry Everett, who died April 8th, 1790, Aged 8 months.

Also of Charles Kellow, who died April 11th, 1808, Aged 86.

Also of Joseph Everett, who died July 24, 1818.

Also of Maria, second Daughter of Joseph and T. M. Everett, who died the 18th of January, 1820.

In Memory of Mary, Wife of Thomas Smith, who died Jan. 22d, 1772, Aged 68 years.

Thomas Smith died 8th June, 1784, Aged 76 years.

By his Will he Bequeathed Two Thousand Pounds, the Interest thereof to be paid Weekly to four poor Men and four Poor Women of this Parish.

Donations.

Mr. THOMAS SMITH, in the Year One Thousand Seven Hundred and eighty-four, left TWO THOUSAND POUNDS, in Trust, to the Minister and Churchwardens of this Parish, to be vested in the Public Funds, and the Interest thereof to be weekly and equally distributed to four poor Men, and four poor Women, who are Inhabitants of this Parish, and have lived in it Ten Years.

EDWARD FROUD, Esquire, in the Year One thousand Seven hundred and fifty, Endowed an Hospital in this Parish for Six Men and Six Women, with an Allowance of Three Shillings and Sixpence each, Weekly.

Thomas Thresher,
Thomas Goddard, Church Wardens, 1790.

On Flat Stones under the Tower.

Here lyeth the Body of Mrs. Elizabeth Hill, who dyed ye 3d of August, 1719, Aged 57 years.

In Memory of Robert Bateman Wray, Esq. who died the 12th of March, 1779, Aged 64 years.

Also of Margaret, his Wife, who died the 12th of November, 1794, Aged 79 years.

And also of Robert Bateman Wray, Esq. their Son, who died the 27th of August, 1814, Aged 71 years.

And of Jane, his Wife, who died the 31 of August, 1818, Aged 65 years.

GOD'S Deliverance;
or a Memorative of the
FALL of the TOWER.

AMONGST

The many Eminent Mercies that the Inhabitants of St. EDMUND'S Parish have received, We may reckon the special Providence of God, whereby We the Parishioners and our Families were saved from remarkable and imminent dangers on the Sabbath Day, being June the 26th, 1653, when the Mayor, and many other Principal Inhabitants of the City, with a great multitude of Godly Christians, were met at St. Edmund's Church, for the Publick Worship of God, The Walls of the Tower thereof were become ruinous and broken, and (by the unwary attempts of some who, in order to the reparation, had uncovered the Roof, and undermined some Pillars) only . . . fallen, the main Pillars did bulge out, and sensibly shake, the Clefts in the Walls were seen to open and shut with ringing the Sermon Bell that Day, neither were there any considerable props set to support it, so that Nothing but the very Hand of God did keep the Stones and Timber from falling until the next Day, That his own People were all secure at Home, neither Man, Woman, or Child, receiving any Hurt thereby. St. Luke, chap. 13. v. 4. When We consider what God hath formerly permitted when the Tower of Siloam fell,* and when the Church of Black-friars, in London, fell upon a People, met as We were, for Worship, but in another Religion, when we apprehend what Danger We were in, Though not sensible of it at that Time, how sad an Outcry would have been made, not in our Parish only, but in our City, Exodus, chap. 12. v. 30, like the Great Cry in Egypt, where almost every House would have suffered in the Death of so many, if God had mingled our blood with our Sacrifice that Day, and when We seriously recollect and set before Us all the Circumstances of this our Salvation; We cannot but break forth into Praise, and say, Revelations, chap. v. Salvation, and Glory, and Honour, and Power, unto the Lord our GOD; and in a lively Sense of the Mercy, desiring to perpetuate the Memory of it unto Posterity, that so the Generations to come may praise God as We the Living do this Day—We do Order and Appoint that the 26th Day of June Yearly shall be unto the People of St. Edmund's Parish a Day of solemn and publick Thanksgiving unto GOD for the same, And we beseech our Brethren of this and the following generations, Rom. chap. 12. v. 1st. by the Mercies of God, to present themselves living Sacrifices wholly acceptable unto God, in their reasonable Service of him that Day, as long as there shall be one stone upon another in St. Edmund's Church, and an inhabitant left in St. Edmund's Parish. And We do further Order, that either in the Windows, or the Walls, or the Gates, of our New Builded Church (if not in all of them) there be made, as shall be thought fit, some MONUMENTS of this late Deliverance, Isaiah chap. 60. v. 18, That our WALLS may mention the Salvation, and our GATES the Praises of the LORD.

St. Thomas' Church.

On a monument in the north side of the middle chancel.

Elizabeth Eyre was ye Wife of ye Thos. Eyre, Esq. Mother of these xv Childrẽ A virtuous Matrõ A Good Neighbour Charitable & an Enemie To Idolatry in ye Year of God She Departed this Life ye 24th of December 1612 Aged 65.

On a monument in the south side of the middle chancel.

In ye Parish Church of St Stevens, in Colemâ Street, Londō lieth Buried ye Body of Mr. Christopher Eyre, 4th Sonne of ye Worth Thos. Eyre, Esq. Aldeim̄ of this Cittie, who Attained Prosperously to be an East India Merchant Adventurer, and Committee of ye Honble company of ye East India Merchants, & Upper Warden of ye worth Company of Leathersellers, & one of ye common Councell of ye Honbl: Cittie of London. Who Lived vertuously, & gave Liberaily & Charitably to ye Cittie of London, & Also to this Cittie for ye erecting of an Almeshouse in this Cittie, and Maintenance Thereof for ever, & for A weekly Lecture in this Parishe for ever. & being of ye Age of 47 Years, Departed this Life in ye Year of God Hating Idolatry. His late Loving Wife, Daughter of George Smithes, Aldermâ of ye Honble Cittie of Londō erected this & ye Opposite Monument according to his Will.

On a Monument against the North Wall of the Chancel.

H. S. E.
JOHANNES GOUGH,
Johannis Gough, de hac Civitate, gen. &
Catharinæ uxoris Filius unicus,
Ingenio, Probitate, & modesta,
Niteus Juvenis,
qui in Coll Reg. in Oxoñ
Ad Divitis Animi nativas dotes
Ampliori apparatu excolendus,
Literarum studijs sedulus, incumbens
Variolis
iniquo Juvenib. morbo correpte,
Quarum sub Tyrannide luctatus diu,
Sed tand fatiscens Animan efflavit
Martii die 13°, Anno { Dom. 17 09/10, Ætat. 19.

Posuit hoc Catharina Gough, Vidua,
Accumulatæ in Matre Calamitatis,
Pientissimi in Filio Obsequii,
Æmuliq. exutraq. parte Amoris
Monumentum.

Arms—Sable, on a fess or, a lion-passant gules, between three boars' heads, couped, argent, two in chief, one in base.

St. Martin's Church.

On a Marble Monument against N. Wall of Chancel.

To the Memory of
Bennett Swayne, Esq. of Milford, near this City, who departed this Life at Epsom, in the County of Surry, after a Lingering illness, and was interred amongst his Ancestors near this place. He dyed a Batchelor, on the 10th day of July, 1748, Aged 52 years, And by his Will directed this Monument to be erected for himself and family.

Thomas Swayne, Esq. younger Brother of the said Bennet Swayne, died, in London, a Batchelor, on the 29th of Feb. 1747, Aged 51 years, and lies buried in the same grave with his Brother. The said Bennet Swayne and Thomas Swayne were Children of Bennet Swayne, Esq. of Milford, aforesaid, by Elizabeth, his Wife, one of the Daughters of Nicholas Skinner, formerly of London, Merchant, by Katherine, his Wife, who was of the Family of the Hoopers, of Bearedge, in the County of Dorset.

Also to the Memory of Bennet Swayne, Esq. formerly of Milford, aforesaid, Grandfather of the said Bennet Swayne, Esq. and Thomas Swayne, who lyes also buried near this place.

On a Brass Plate against North Wall of Chancel.

Johannes Sebastianus,
Carpe t̃erus utoriu Devoĩensis
Linguarum italicæ, gallicæ, hispanicæ,
im̄o latinæ, græcæ, hebraicæ, non ignarus,
qui decennali peregrinatione
ΠΟΛΛΩΝ ΑΝΘΡΩΠΩΝ ΙΔΕΝ
Ασεα και NOON ΕΤΝΩ,
tandem in patriam,
Suam post varios casus, et multa pericula rerum,
Sanus deo propitio reversus,
et quinque fere lustra
Ministerio verbi divini functus, hic demum,
in quiescit nature, debitum persoluit satis longavo,
Anno Ætatis climacterico magno 1632.
Avi viator plura tecum nore libet.
he gave the Hospitall of this Citie a
Hundred pounds for ever;
To the Trenitie forty lb.
To the Carpenters XXIIII.

North Wall.

Nemo ante obitum beatus.
In Memoriam ornati juvenis Danelis
Hales, necnon fratris sui Eduardi
Hales, filiorum Danielis Hales,
ex domo altæ ccclesianensi in
Comitatu Somerset, quorum ambo
dum vixerunt
pij et morigeri,
ambo tabidi, et Laserilli,
jam vero morte personati pacem ingressi,
sunt et in cubilibus suis,
beatam resurrectionem expectantes,
requiescunt,
Augusti 23, 1645,
Ætat. D. H. 28. Æt. E. H. 8.

On a Monument against S. Wall of Chancel.

Juxta conduntur Reliquiæ
Gulielmi Ludlow, de Clarendon,
Generosi,
Amore maritali usus est,
Non nisi supremo die
Soluto
Humani, nihila se alienum putans,
Pauperes amicos Deum
Sibi conciliavit.

Hic etiam jacet quicq . . . . mortale Annæ Ludlow,
Qua obiit 7° April, 1749, Ætat 20.
Filia fuit Gul. et Eliz. Ludlow unica,
Filia . . . . digna parentibus.

Arms—Party, per pale, sinister argent, on a chevron, azure, three bezants or, between three bulls' heads caboshed, gules; dexter, argent, a chevron, sable, between three dogs' heads erased, of the last, over the chevron a shield of the first.

Crest—A demi dog, sable.

Mon. of White Marble S. Wall.

Near this Spot are interred the Remains of
Mrs. Mary Thomas, of this City,
Who died the 18th of May, 1781,
in the 86th Year of her Age.

This Monument was erected to her Memory
by the Rev. Alex. Thistlethwayte, of
Queen's College, Oxford,
As a small token of his Gratitude
for her great Liberality.

On Flat Stones within the Rails.

Thomas Frome, Gent. died Feb. 5th, 1771,
Aged 64 years.

Dorothy, Wife of the above Thomas Frome, died
July 31, 1777, Aged 70 years.

Arms—A fess between three griffins segrant, two in chief, one one in base.

Georgius Frome, De Sarum, Gen. Obiit 30° Julii,
Anno { Dom. 1725,
Ætat. 48.

Dorothea, Relicia Geo. Frome, Obiit 27 Aprilis,
Anno { Dom. 1749,
Ætat. 74.

Arms—Party per pale, sinister, three boars' heads couped, two in chief, one in base; dexter, a fess between three griffins, segrant, two in chief, one in base.

Here lieth the Body of John, ye Son of Thomas
Clarke, who dyed Sept. 29, 1685.

Alsoe Edworth, ye Daughter of Thomas Clarke,
who dyed October ye 9th, 1685.

H. S. E.

John Hill, Esq. Son of Francis Hill, Esq. of the
Close, in this City, Dyed Xmas Day, 1726,
Aged 62 years.

His Widow caused this Stone
to be laid on 8 ult.
Here made in Memory
Of her dear Husband.

On Flat Stones without the Rails of the Chancel.

H. S. E.

Edmund Ludlow, ye 2d Son
of Edmund Ludlow, Gent.
and Catherine, his Wife,
late of Clarendon Park,
{ Obiit 4th Apr. 1719,
Ætat. 29.

Katharine Castle, who died 8th June, 1793, Aged 52.

Here Lyeth Mrs. Catharine Egerton,
Daughter of the Honble Charles Egerton, Esq.
Son of the Right Honourable
The Earl of Bridgwater,
And youngest Brother of his Grace,
the Late Duke of Bridgewater,
Who Dyed the 25th of Nov. 1743,
in ye One and Twentieth Year of her Age.

Arms—A lion rampant between three pheons, two in chief, one in base.

Here Also Lyeth
Mrs. Elizabeth Grenville,
Daughter of the Honourable
Francis Grenville, Esq.
Eldest Son of ye Right Honble Foulk Lord Brooke,
who Died the 7th of January, 1745.

Arms—On a cross five roundlets, within a border invecked.

Mrs. Elizabeth Ludlow
Died Dec. 16th, 1764,
Aged 70.

Here lies the Body of Ann Reaves, the Daughter of Henry Goddard, Esq. of Birchin Wood, in ye County of Hants. She Dyed August ye 2d, 1754, Aged 83, Leaving two Daughters, Frances, ye Eldest, marryed to Richard Scrope, Esq. of Castlecombe, and Elizabeth, ye youngest, married to the Rev. John Lumley, Rector of this Parish.

Also of the Body of the said Elizabeth Lumley, who dyed June 22d, 1763.

And near it the Body of the said Rev. Mr. John Lumley.

Arms—A chevron, vair, between three crescents, two in chief, one in base.

In Memory of Sarah Slater, who died 6th April, 1797, Daughter of Thomas Slater, Gent. and Edith, his Wife.

Arms—A cross.

H. S. E.

Catharine, Widow of Edmund Ludlow, of Clarendon, Gent. and Daughter of the Rev. John Newham, M. A. Late Rector of West Deane, in the County of Wilts. Obiit Junii 4°, An° Dñi. 1715, Ætat. 62.

H. S. E.

Mr. William Ludlow, of Clarendon, Eldest Son of Edmund and Catherine Ludlow, who dyed Anno 1729, Aged 42 years.

And also of Henry Ludlow, who died May ye 19th, 1760, Aged 46 years.

Here Lyeth the Body of John King, of Clarendon, who departed this life, ye 18th Day of March, 1714, Aged 78 years.

In Memory of Thomas Cooksey, Gent. who died 29th Sept. 1793, Aged 75 years.

Also of Sarah, his Wife, who died 6th May, 1809, Aged 78 years.

In Memory of Mrs. Jane Prince, who Departed this life, November the 23rd, 1754.

Here lyeth ye Body of John Greenville, Gent. who dyed ye 24th of June, 1674.

Arms—Party, per pale, sinister, a lion rampant, dexter, vert, two bars, or, in chief a leopard passant, of the same.

H. S. E.

William Jay, Gent. was born the 3d of July, 1684, and died the 16th of May, 1754.

Also

Edith Slater, Widow, his Sister, was born the 1st of August, 1694, died the 4th of March, 1777.

Arms—On a bend three roses.

Samuel Lindsay, Esq. Late Captain in the 14th Regiment of foot, died 17th Sept. 1801, in the 74th year of his age.

Arms—Gules, in fess, checky, azure and argent.

Here lyes the Body of Bennet Swayne, Late of Hackney, in ye County of Middlesex, Esquire, who Departed this Life the first day of April, 1798, Aged 62 years.

Here Lyeth the Body of Bennet Swayne, Gentleman, Late of Milford, in this Parish, who Departed this Life the 21st Day of August, 1697, Aged 83 years.

H. S. E.

Rev. Petrus Terry, A. M. Ecclesiæ Cathedralis Sarum Succentor et Prebendarius, de St. Martin's et Clatford, in Comitatu Hants. Rector. Obiit Septimo die Junii,

Anno { Domini 1727,
Ætatis 74.

Here also Lyeth the Body of Mrs. Mary Terry, Widow of the Rev. Mr. Terry, who departed this Life Sept. 22d, 1739, Aged 64.

On a small Monument in the E. end of the Body of the Church.

In Memory of Mary, Widow of the Rev. Mr. Lindsay, Rector of Penshurst, Kent, and Daughter of William Taunton, Esq. Gov. of Portland Castle, who died 21st Dec. 1775, in her 80th year.

Also of

Charles Lindsay Egerton, Son of Scroop Egerton, Esq. and Anna Maria, his Wife, Aged 5 years.

And of Captain Samuel Lindsay, Son of the above Samuel and Mary Lindsay, who died 17th Sept. 1801, in his 74th year.

Arms—Party per pale, sinister; quarterly, first and fourth argent, a crescent, gules; second and third gules, a crescent argent; dexter, gules, in fesse, checky, azure and argent.

On a Monument against the first Pillar from the E. end of Nave.

Henry Chester, Esq. Obiit 28th of October, 1786, Æt. 48.

Hetty Chester, his Wife, Ob. 13th July 1812, Æt. 75.

Against the third Pillar from E. End.

Near the Outward West End of the South Aisle of this Church lie the Remains of Lætitia Lee, Widow, who died Feb. 22d, 1800, Aged 78.

This tribute of departed worth was erected to the Memory of one of the best of Mothers, by her Dutiful and Affectionate Daughter, Frances Henrietta Elderton.

Arms—Arms, party per pale, sinister, argent, a cross ingrailed, sable, between four mullets of the same; dexter, gules, in fess checky, azure and or, between ten billets argent, four in chief, 321 in base.

On the Fourth Pillar.

Near this Place are deposited the Remains of Martha, Wife of Mr. Ambrose Burch, and Daughter of Mr. William Elderton, who died 7th of April, 1778, Aged 60.

A good Christian, a sincere Friend, and kind Relation.

Against the third Pillar on the north side from the east end.

Near this Place are deposited the Remains of the Rev. H. P. Baker, B. A. Late of Queen's College, Oxford. He was the Eldest Son of Edward Baker, Esq. of this City, by Jane, Daughter of Thomas Phipps, Esq. of Westbury Leigh, in this County. This excellent young Man, whose goodness of Heart and Mildness of Manners deservedly endeared Him to all his Relations and Friends, exchanged this Life for a Better at the early age of twenty-two, on the eighteenth Day of October, in the Year of our Lord 1794.

M. S.

Johannis Baker, Armigeri,
Hac vita defunctus est
Vicesimo primo Die Martii,
Anno { Salutis 1768,
Ætatis 68.

Hic etiam depositum
est quod mortale suit
Elizabethæ, Uxoris
Supra dicti Joannis Baker,
quæ placide obdormivit
15 Die Domini 1777,
Ætatis 71.

H. S. E.

Mr. John Baker, Alderman of this City, who died April the 20th, 1743, Aged 66.

Here Lyeth the Body of Jane, Wife of William Bowles, of this City, Clothier, and Daughter of John Baker, of the said City, and Anne, his Wife, who Dyed June 21st, 1735, Aged 36 years.

Also in Memory of . . ncey, Daughter of the said John and Ann Baker, who dyed January ye 1st, 1742.

Also in Memory of Anne, Wife of the above Mr. John Baker, who dyed 30th Oct. 1750, Aged 77.

H. S. E.

Johannes Rolfe, Armiger,
Qui Obiit 17 die Octobris,
Anno { Dom. 1735,
Ætat. 73.

Arms—Party per pale, sinister, a fess between three griffins' heads erased, two in chief, one in base; dexter argent, three doves conjoined, sable.

H. S. E.

Whit Bourn Biggs, Gent. Obiit September 17, 1768, Ætat. 34.

Also

Ann, his Wife, who departed this Life March 1st, 1770, Aged 16 years.

H. S. E.

Mr. Samuel Rolfe, of This City who Departed this Life March ye 26th, 1755, Aged 67.

Also Mrs. Katharine Rolfe, Wife to Mr. Sam. Rolfe, who Departed this Life August ye 16, 1717, Aged 61.

And also Sarah, their Daughter, who Departed This Life Jan. the 25, 1753, Aged 36 years.

In Memory of Mr. John Rolfe, who Departed this Life April 10th, 1783, Aged 66 years.

Also in Memory of Mrs. Mary Rolfe, Wife of Mr. John Rolfe, who Departed this Life, Nov. 4th, 1800, Aged 66 years.

Here Resteth ye Body of Edward Windover, Gent. Once Citizen and Alderman of Sarum, Died Dec. 7, 1618, Aged 80.

Abr: Harris Departed this Life June ye 3d, 1704, Aged 55.

Henricus et Joannes,
Gulielmi Goldwyer,
de Clauso Novæ Sarum, Gent.
Filii. Quorum Ille
A. M. et Col. Exon Socius.
Obiit 22 Octobris, 1731,
Anno Ætatis 33.
Hen. 1 Feb. 1731, Anno Ætat. 26.

Maria, Uxor. Gul. Goldwyer,
Obiit 3 Maij, 1738,
Ætatis 71.

Hic prope Cineres Suorum Sepultus jacet
Gulielmus Goldwyer,
Qui Obiit 29 die Junii,
Anno { Dñi 1748. Ætat. 83.

Carissimam Conjugem
Elizabetham, inter Suorum Cineres dormientem
Richardus Payne, A. R. brevi ipse
hic ponendus posuit A. D. 1734.

Arms—A fess between three lions' heads caboshed, on an escutcheon, over the fess, a chevron between three roundels.

Brass Plate taken away.

Here lyeth the Body of Mrs. Rebecca Stoddart, who departed this life ye 10th day of August, 1715, Aged 32 years.

In Memory of Mrs. Elizabeth Maton, who died Jan. ye 5th, 1766, Aged 71 years.

Also in Memory of James Bartlett, Esq. who died July ye 22d, 1768, Aged 66 years.

And of Unity, his Relict,
who died Oct. 19th, 1772, Aged 52 years.

Here Lyeth the Body of Mrs. Sarah Inglish, Wife of Mr. . . . . Inglish, of London, Apothecary, and Daughter of Mr. Edward . . . . of this City, who Departed this Life Dec. 172 . Aged 32 years 8 months.

Here Lyeth ye Body of Elizabeth Bath, who dyed March 23, 1700, Aged 21 years.

Here Lyeth the Body of Sarah, the Wife of Ed . . . . . . .but, Daughter of William Windsor, of this Parish, who dyed August ye 20th, 1708, Aged 34 years.

Brass Plate taken out.

Mary, ye Daughter of William Windsor, of this Parish, Obiit Augst ye 10th, Anno Dom. 1703, Aged 22 years.

Here Lieth the Body
of Ann, Daughter of
Daniel and Ann Floyd,
who Died May the 25th, 1722,
Aged 14 years.

Here Also Lieth her Sister Sarah Westley,
who Died March the 2d, 1761,
Aged 44 years.

Here Lyeth the Body of Daniel, Son
of Mr. Daniel and Ann
Floyd, who Dyed the 26th of October, 1728,
Aged 25 years.

Also
Here Lieth the Body of
Richard, Son of Richard and Elizabeth Floyd,
who died 22d Feb. 1777,
Aged 28.

Here lyeth ye Body of Sarah, ye Daughter of Daniel and Ann Floyd, who dyed April ye 5th, 1716, Aged 2 years.

Here Also Lyeth the Body of Daniel, Son of Richard and Elizabeth Floyd, who dyed March ye 14, 1746, Aged Eleven months.

In Memory of Mr. Daniel Floyd, Late Alderman of this City, who died Dec. the 27th, 1755,
Aged 73 years.

Here Also Lieth
Ann, his Wife,
who died March the 8th, 1772,
Aged 95 years.

Here lieth the Body of
Elizabeth, Wife of Robert Woods,
who died July 10th, 1787, Aged 35 years.

Also three of their Children, who died in their infancy.

Here Lyeth the Body of Elizabeth, the Wife of Richard Fry, who dyed Nov. ye 2d, 1700, Aged 61.

Here lieth the Body of Richard Fry, who Dyed September the 10th, 1707, Aged 64.

Here lieth ye Body of Joseph Jennings, of this City, Tanner, who Departed this Life January ye 23rd, 17$\frac{10}{11}$, Aged 64 years.

In Memory of Rebecca, Wife of Edward Baker, Esq. Alderman of this City, who died May ye 9th, 1771, Age d65.

She was a .... Christian, and excell'd
in all those Virtues which adorn human Nature:
Her Piety was Exemplary, Her Charity universal.
As She lived Esteemed and beloved,
So She died Regretted by all her Relations,
Friends, and acquaintances.

Also in Memory of the said Edward Baker, who died October 5th, 1772, Aged 60.

In Memory of Edward Smith, Gent. who died 25th Oct. 1771, Aged 80 years.

On Monuments against N. Wall of the N. Aisle.

Sacred to the Memory of Ann Blake, Daughter of John Blake, Esq. who Departed this Life 4th Jan. 1812, Aged 47 years.

Sacred to the Memory of John Blake, Esq. who Departed this Life the 20th of Jan. 1803, Aged 69.

Also of Margaret, Wife of the above John Blake, Esq. who died June 10th, 1812, Aged 78 years.

In the South Isle of this Church are interred the remains of Mr. Josiah Rolfe, late of this City, Clothier, who departed this life ye 17th of Feb. 1796, Aged 73 years.

And Also Mr. Samuel Rolfe, Son of the abovesaid Mr. Josiah Rolfe, and Mrs. Joan Rolfe, who departed this Life ye 2d of Nov. 1797, Aged 25 years.

From this short scene of Grief & Pain,
Their Souls have taken Flight,
Hoping a safe retreat to gain
In Realms of endless Light.

Arms—Argent, three doves sable, two in chief, one in base.
Crest—A dove, argent, with an olive branch.

In Memory of Mr. Joseph Willis, late Mayor of this City, who Died April 23d, 1772, Aged 34 years.

Also of Mrs. Jane Willis, Relict of Mr. Joseph Willis, who died Nov. 14, 1777.

In the Middle Isle of this Church are deposited the Remains of William Goldwyer, of the Close, in this City.
Buried July 2d, 1748, Aged 82 years.
Mary, his Wife, Buried May 8th, 1738.

Their Children.

Henry, an Infant, Buried May 18th, 1696.
William, an Infant, Buried August 5th, 1696.
Prudence, an Infant, Buried Sept. 2d, 1697.
The Rev. Henry, Buried Oct. 24, 1731.
John, Buried Feb. 4, 1732.
Edward, who Died Nov. 16, 1774, Aged 68.
Jane, his Wife, Buried August 11th, 1746.
George, late of Marlborough, who Died Jan. 10th, 1774, Aged 71.
Elizabeth, his Wife, Died June 6th, 1798, Aged 92.

Likewise, of their Children,
Thomas, who Died Nov. 27th, 1773, Aged 23.
Henry, who Died Dec. 25th, 1801, Aged 69.
Also Jane, a Spinster, of this City,
Grand Daughter of the above William and Mary,
and Daughter of
William Goldwyer, Late of Blandford.
She Died 12th Jan. 1800, Aged 72.

Arms—On a bend three stirrups.
Crest—A stag's head, erased.

On Flat Stones in N. Aisle.

H. S. E.

Edmund White, of Laverstock, near this City, Gent. who Died June 7th, 1744, Aged 55.
Here Lyeth the Body of Mrs. Mary Penny, who departed this life ye 25th of December, 1712, Aged 83.

Here Lyeth the Body of John White, Son of Edmund and Elizabeth White, of Stockbridge, who dyed the 20th of January, 172$\frac{1}{2}$, Aged 24 years.

Here lieth the Body of Edmund Heath, who died April 1st, 1744, Aged 38.

Also Ann Heath, who died April 17th, 1751, Aged 41.

Here Lieth the Body of Thomas Cooper, of this City, Esq. who died 6th Jan. 1773, Aged 79.

And Likewise Sarah, his Wife, who died 5 April, 1754, Aged 68.

Here Lyeth ye Body of Martha, Wife of Thomas Goodbee, who died July the 11th, 1723, Aged 48.

Here Lyeth the Body of Mr. Thomas Atwood. He was the Eldest Son of Mr. Thomas Atwood, of Ashford, in ye County . . . . . He Dyed ye 21st of June, ... Aged 54 years.

Here Lyeth the Body of Mrs. Elizabeth Goodfellow, Wife of Mr. Mat. Goodfellow, of this City. She was third Daughter of Mr. Edward Johnson, of Patingham, in the County of Stafford. She Departed this Life the 25th Day of March, 1751, Aged 43.

Here also
Lieth the Body of the said Mathew Goodfellow,
who died the 21 day of February, 1776,
Aged 85 years.

H. S. E.

Gulielmus Newman,
Qui Obiit 19
Die Jul. Anno { Dom 1755,
Ætat. 52.

Also
Rosannah, his Wife,
who Died December 23, 1760,
Aged 75 years.

Hic conditæ jacent Reliqu . .
Mariæ Ernll . . . .
Viduæ
Guil. Jeri. Ernll . . . .
. . . de Conock, infra paro . . .
de Carington, in hoc Comi . . .
Et Filiæ
Angonii Hunger . . .
. . . de Lea, in Comitatu pre . .
Illa . . ccedit hanc vitan . . .
. . die Sep. Anno Dom. . . . .
Ætat. suæ 76.

Arms—Quarterly, second and third two bars in chief, three roundels, on a bend, over all six eagles displayed.

Here Lyeth the Body of Mr. James Thring, who Departed this Life June the 30th, 1740, Aged 26 years.

Also Ann, Wife of Mr. William White, jun. Tallow Chandler, in this City, who Died Feb. 16, 1775, Aged 37 years.

Here Lyeth the Body of John, Son of Mr. John and Sarah Waters, who Departed this Life October the 26th, 1731, in the 21 year of his Age.

Here Lyeth the Body of Mr. John Waters, sen. Who Departed this Life January the 3d, 1750, Aged 76 years.

Here also Lieth the Body of Penelope, Wife of Mr. John Waters, who Departed this Life Sept. the 7th, 1759, Aged 73 years.

In Memory of Mr. John Blake, Late Alderman of this City, who died Dec. 31, 1774, Aged 73 years.

Here lieth the Body of Margaret Blake, Widow of John Blake, who died October 26th, 1796, in the 87 year of her Age.

Also of
Mrs. Margaret Blake, their Daughter, who Departed this Life 19th March, 1811.

In Memory of Mr. John Sanger, who Died April 9th, 1773, Aged 70 years.

On Monuments against S. Wall of S. aisle.

Joannes Feltham
obiit Vigesimo et tertio die Sept.
Anno 1784,
Ætatis suæ 50.

Ejus Memoriæ
Hoc testimonium doloris,
Filii studiose tribuunt.

H. S. E.

Mary, Wife of John Edgar, Ob. Nov. 13, 1770, Æt. 18.

The Virtues of Piety, Patience, and Benevolence,
Shed a Lustre on the Short Circle
of her Life.

Sacred to the Memory of Thomas Snow, Late of this City. He died Nov. the 18th, A. D. 1776, Aged 57 years.

Also in Memory of Mrs. Elizabeth Tatum, who Died Sept. 12th, 1798, Aged 76 years.

Near this Place lie interred the Remains of Edmund Baker, Esq. late of this City, who departed this Life the first Day of November, 1796, in the fifty fourth year of his Age.

Also the Remains of Mrs. Jane Baker, his Wife, who died 10th Feb. 1800, in the fifty-third year of her Age.

Arms—Party per pale, sinister, sable, a trefoil argent, between eight mullets of the same, dexter argent, a tower imbattled, sable, between three keys of the same, pale-wise, two in chief, one in base.

Near this Place lieth the Body of James Bartlett, Esq. who died July 22d, 1768, Aged 66.
To whose Memory this Monument is erected by Unity, his Relict,
As a Testimony of her Respect and Affection.

Likewise near this Place are interred
The Bodies of Mrs. Elizabeth Maton, Widow,
Sister of the said James Bartlett,
who died Jan. 5th, 1766, Aged 71.

And of James and Elizabeth, his Son and Daughter,
who both died in the fifteenth year
of their Age.

The above Unity,
Relict of the said James Bartlett, Esq.
and Daughter of Ambrose Awdry, Gent.
of Chippenham, in this County,
died Oct. 19, 1772, Aged 52,
and is buried in the same Grave with him.

On Flat Stones in S. Aisle.

Here Lyes the Body of Richard Goodridge, of this Parish, who Dyed 18 Day of October, 1640.

Here Lyeth the Body of Amnah, the Wife of Mr. John Clayton, who Departed this Life ye 17th of May, 1714, in ye 28th year of her age.

Here Lyes Buried the Body of Edward Windover, Gent. who died the first Day of April, 1645.

Arms—A mullet between two bars, in chief three demi-lions rampant.

Mrs. Mary Ruddle, died Nov. 5th, 1776,
Aged 76 years.

H. S. E.
Gulielmus Wastfelde, Armiger,
Qui Obiit
24 die Octobris, Anno { Dom. 1735. Ætat. suæ 85.

Here also Lyeth the Body of Mr. Samuel Rolfe, Son of Mr. Josiah Rolfe, and Joan, his Wife, who died the 2d of Nov. 1797, Aged 25 years.

Arms—On a fess, three catherine wheels between six billets.

Here lieth the Body of Mr. John Rolfe, Late Citizen and Skinner of London, who Departed this Life the 18th Day of October, 1733, Aged 91 years.

Also near this Place Lieth the Body of his Late Brother, Mr. Josiah Rolfe, Late of this City, Clothier, who departed this Life the 12th Day of Oct. 1728, Aged 88 years.

And here also Lieth the Body of Mr. Josiah Rolfe, late of this City, Clothier, and Grandson of the above Mr. Josiah Rolfe, who Departed this Life the 17th Day of February, 1796, Aged 73 years.

Here Lieth the Body of Elizabeth, Wife of Mr. John Snow, who Departed this Life Feb. the 2, 1749.

Here also Lieth the Body of Mr. John Snow, who Departed this Life the 30th of Dec. 1764.

Here Lyeth the Body of Dorothy Haytery.
And also the Body of Mary Harvey, her Niece, who dyed February the 20th, 173¾.

Here Lyeth the Body of Christopher Willmott,
Of this Parish,
who Departed this Life Nov. ye 27th, A. D. 1726,
Aged 81 years.

On a small Brass in S. Aisle.

Mr. Godwin Died 2d October, 1785.

Beneath this Stone are Interred the Remains of Jane Marsh, Spinster, who died the 6th of April, 1794, Aged 75 years.

H. S. E.
John Fuller, Esq.
Youngest Son of Major-General Fuller,
of Gregory's,
in Buckinghamshire.
He died March 27th, 1777,
Aged 48 years.
Also Ann, his Wife,
who died February 19, 1817,
Aged 89 years.

Here Lyeth ye Body of John Wilmot, who dyed ye 13th day of Feb. 1716, Aged 66 years.

Here also Lyeth the Body of John Wilmot, jun. who dyed December ye 23d, 1738, Aged 51 years.

Here lyeth the Body of John, ye Son of John and Elizabeth Case, who dyed ye 24th of December, 1715, in ye 5th year of his Age.

Here Lyeth ye Body of John Case, who departed this Life ye 15th of June, 1723, Aged 38 years.

Near this Place Lyeth four of his Children.

Hatchments.

Party per pale, sinister gules, three lions passant guardant or, on the chief a label, argent; dexter argent, a cross engrailed sable, between four eagles displayed, of the same

On S. Wall of S. Aisle.

Quarterly, first and fourth argent, a fess, gules, between six lion's heads erased, of the same: second quarterly—1st, or, a bend, gules—2d argent, two bars sable, in chief a griffin segrejant, of the same—3d, or, a chevron, gules, between three leaves vert—4th, argent, a griffin segrejant, sable: third, same as the second.

Party per pale, sinister, argent, a chevron, gules, between three water bougets, sable; dexter, argent, a fess, sable, between three griffins' heads erased, of the same.

Party, per pale, sinister, azure, two bars, or, between three pheons of the same, two in chief, one in base; dexter, azure, three crescents, or, two in chief, one in base.

Crest—A griffin's head, argent.

In Chancel.

Argent, on a cross, sable, five crescents, or.

St. Thomas' Church.

On Flat Stones in Chancel.

H. S. E.
Rich. Eyre,
Obijt Feb. 16, Anº Dñi 85,
Ætatis suæ 50.

H. S. E.

Dorothy G. a child of Mr. William Green, Aged 7 years, dyed June ye 15th, 1714.

H. S. E.

Mary, the Wife of Mr. Charles Viner, dyed the 1st of October, 1682.

And of Mr. Charles Viner, her Husband, who died Nov. 16th, 1702, Aº Æt. 57.

Mr. James Green dyed August ye 1st, 1700.

Mr. Maurice Green dyed March ye 29th, 1677.

Here Lyeth Mary, the Wife of Mr. William Green, who dyed the 14th of March, $170\frac{0}{1}$, Aged 26.

H. S. E.

Lyeth the Body of Mrs. Su. Green, who dyed ye 24th of Dec. 1725, Aged 67.

Tho. Ward, LL. D. Dr. Obiit Martii 20, Anno 1695.

Dora Uxor. Thoæ Ward, Obiit Xbris 24º, Anº 1695.

On a Brass Plate.

Depositum Samuelis Prigg, De Bristol, Gen. Qui Obiit Primo Septembris, 1722.

On a Border of Brass.

Of John Webbe, late Maior of this Cittie, who Ended this Lyife the firste daye of February, in the yere of oure Lorde God one Thousand fyve Hundred LXX. he Maryed with Anne Wylforde, Daughter to Nicholas Wylforde, Citizen and Marchaunt Taylor of London.

Underneath lie the Earthly remains of Mrs. Mary Hodgson, who departed this Life 23 March, 1802, Aged 66 years.

Here lies Jane, ye Daughter of
Herbert and Ann Saladine,
who died ye 30th September,
Anno Domini 1692.

Arms—A lion rampant guardant.

Brass Plate.

Happie Elizabeth, Late Wife of
The Wo[rll] Thomas Eyre.
She is not Heere, but gone to Blisse,
Heere is her Happie dust,
She is not heere, for Gods Shee is,
An Heire with all the juste :
Tis needlesse Heere to Blaze her fame,
For well was knowne her Life,
Her Wisedome, good report, and name,
Her true Love as a Wife :
Yea, her true love, as freinde to all,
Her Harte no Pride did Love,
But Lov'd and helpte the poore & Thral,
Yea, Lov'd the Lord A Bove.
Who hath her Crowne wth peace and joye,
With happines and Reste,
And theare shall be without Annoye,
With blessed Saints still Bleste.

Died 24th Decembris, A° Dni 1612.
The said Thomas and Elizabeth
had 9 Sonnes and 5 Daughters.

Heere was Laid on the
Eight of August, 1638,
The Body of Robert Eyre, Esquire, Counsellour att
Law, in this City, the Eldest Sonn of the
Above Named Thomas and Elizabeth.

Here Lyeth
the Body of John Gough, Gent.
who departed this Life the 22
Day of December, 1695,
in the 44th year of his Age.

Arms—Party per pale, sinister, gules, a lion rampant argent, dexter sable, on a fess, or, a lion passant gules, between three boar's heads couped, argent.

Here Lyeth the Body of John Gough, son of John and Catherine Gough, Gent. who departed this Life the 13th of March, 170$\frac{9}{10}$ in ye Nineteenth year of his Age.

Here Lyeth the Body of Catherine Gough, Wife of John Gough, Sen. Some time since dec[d] and Mother of John Gough, Jun. also dec[d] who was the best of Sons, for whom She greatly Lamented, & died ye 2d Day of Dec. Anno Dom. 1718, Aged 55.

Exuviæ Nicolai Hobart, filii Gulielmi Hobart, de Ravenshal, in agro Suffolciensi, Armigeri. Obiit Maii XXII. 1652.

Arms—An estoil between two flanches, ermine.

The Rev. Brock Rund, M. A. Minister of this Parish, died Dec. 26, 1773, Aged 36.

Arms—Quarterly, first and fourth a lion rampant; second and third, on a bend a robe, in fess a crescent.

John Conant Bin[d] Born at Budley, in Devon, Somtyme fellow of Exeter Colledge, in Oxford, afterward Rector of Lyminaton, in Somersetshire, and the Late Learned orthodox & Faitheull Minister of this Parish, fell on Sleep Ap. 13, in the 65 year of his Age, & was Buried Here Ap. 15, 1653.

He was a Burning & a Shineing light.

Here Lyeth the Body of Mary, Wife of Timothie Sacheverell, Pastor of Tarrant Hinton, in the County of Dorcet, who died March 14, 1652, Anno Ætatis suæ 26.

Here Rests the Corpse of a Dear Wife
that Did to God Devote Her Life ;
who at the first travaile At ye Birth
expiring traveld to this Earth.
Here lyes her Sonne, yt from ye Wombe
immediately went to the tombe.
There's hopes yt life in Death is Gaine,
To both secur'd from future Paine :
Then rest, sweet babe, with thy Dear Mother,
In life & Death each joynd together.

Ambo Reviviscint.

On Flat Stones in Body.

Here Lyeth the Body of David Coldwell, Son of Robert and Mary Coldwell, Born the 22d Day of Oct. in the year of Our Lord, 1705, and Departed this Life the 31st day of January, 1736.

Here Lyeth the Body of Elizabeth, ye Wife of Mr. John Gore, who dyed the 24 day of November 1701.

Here Lyeth ye Body of John Gore, Gent. who dyed ye 15th of March, 1715, Aged 66.

Arms—Party, per pale, sinister, party per fess, in chief a lion rampant, in base two bends; dexter, three bulls' heads caboshed, two in chief, one in base.

In Memory of Thomas Chubb, Esq. who died 12th March, 1815, Aged 67 years.

Champeny Rocke, Died 20th May, 1809,
Aged 27 years.

Underneath are interred three Daughters of Joseph Tanner, Esq. and Catherine, his Wife; viz. Mary, who died 3rd Nov. 1794, Aged 6 weeks, Catherine, who died 25th July, 1799, Aged 7 weeks,
And
Catherine, who died 14th March, 1806, Aged 6 months.
Also Catherine Mahon,
Mother of the above-named Catherine Tanner,
who died 12 July, 1808, Aged 68 years.
And
William Mahon, her Son,
who died 3rd May, 1816, Aged 63 years.

Here Lieth the Body of Mrs. Tanner, Wife of Mr. Tanner, Alderman of this City. She died 17th Nov. 1794, Aged 64 years.

In Memory of Charles Curtoys, Late of this City, Surgeon, who died Sept. 1st, 1786, Aged 36.

H. S. E.
John Tanner, Esq.
Son of the Late Mr. Alderman Tanner,
who died the 10th day of Nov. 1800,
Aged 49 years.

Richard Halsey, Esq. Alderman and Justice of the peace for the City of Chichester, died ye 31 of July, 1792, Aged 68 years.

In Memory of Mr. Joseph Legas,
Late of this City, Surgeon,
who died 18th May, 1793, Aged 41.

Brass taken away.

John Cooper, Esq. died the 7th of August, 1779, Aged 52 years.

Elizabeth Editha Mille....
Relict of Mr. Henry Mille....
Late of Philadelphia,
and Sister of Mr. Charles Curtoys,
whose Remains are
deposited in this Isle,
Died 27 May, 1812,
Aged 51 years.

Ann Davis, Relict of the Rev. John Davis, Late Rector of Padworth, Berks, Died Sept. 25th, 1717, Aged 77 years.

Rachel, the Wife of John Cooper, Esq. and Daughter of Edward Poore, Esq. died the 6th of March, 1770, Aged 37 years.
Also her Infant Daughter.

Buried Here, John, Son of Robert and Mary Cooper, Died 30th September, 1745, Aged 3 months.

Catherine Elizabeth Rider died the 5th of February, 1819, Aged 23 years.

Here Lyeth the Body of Elizabeth, ye Wife of Giles Freem.. who Departed this Life the 11th of June, Anno Dom. 1668.

Brass taken out

Charles Joseph Targett
died the 23d April 1802, Aged 2 months.
John Targett died the 27th of March, 1807,
Aged 2 years.
William Grigg Targett died the first of Sept. 1812,
Aged 4 years and a half.

H. S. E.
Charles Joseph, Son of Mathew and Elizabeth Targett, died 26th April, 1796, Aged one Year and ten Months.
Also Sarah Sophia, Died 6th March, 1820,
Aged 6 years.

Mary Serrell, the Daughter of
Samuel Serrell, Esq. of the Isle of Purbeck,
Dyed Dec. ye 21st, 1746, Aged 24.

In Memory of Mrs. Phillippa Long, Relict of the Late Walter Long, Esq. of this City. She died March 14th, 1798, Aged 90 years.

Samuel Long, Esq. third Son of the Late Walter Long, Esq. of this City, Died 5th January, 1812, Aged 76 years.

Arms—A lion rampant between eight crosslets.
Crest—A demi lion rampant.

In Memory of Lucy Long, Daughter of Walter Long, Esq. who Departed this Life the 17 Nov. 1762.

In Memory of Walter Long, Esq. of this City, who Died Jan. the 15th, 1760, Aged 78.

Arms—Party, per pale, sinister, party per fess indented, argent and sable, in chief three bezants, in base a greyhound courant, sable; dexter sable, a lion rampant, argent, between eight crosslets of the same.

In Memory of Mary, ye Wife of Mr. Walter Long, of this City, who dyed ye 12th of April, 1723, Aged 23 years.

And also his three Daughters,
Anne dyed ye 11th of Dec. 1721, Aged 5 months.
Elizabeth dyed ye 4th of May, 1723, Aged 2 years.
Mary dyed ye 5th of May, 1723, Aged 4 years.

Arms—Party per pale, sinister, a lion rampant crowned; dexter, a lion rampant between eight crosslets.

Edward Couey Departed this Life ye 11th of December, 1718, in ye 21st year of his Age.

Here Lyeth the Body of Mrs. Lucy Long, who Departed this Life the 20th of Feb. 1743.

And also of Mrs. Mary Long, who dyed ye 4th February, 1764.

In Memory of Henry Long, of this City, Gent. who dyed ye 7th of Feb. 1727, Aged 69.

Martha, his Wife, dyed ye 17th of March, 1731, Aged 71.

H. S. E.

Martha, Uxor Henrici Biggs,
Filia Henrici et Martha Long,
Obiit die Aprilis, Anno { Dom. 1709. / Ætat. 23. }

Here also Lieth Henry, Son of Henry and Martha Biggs, who died the 2d Day of May, A.D. 1709, Aged 2 years and 4 months.

Here also Lieth Martha, the Daughter of Henry and Martha Biggs, who died Oct. 13, 171. Aged three Years and 10 months.

On Flat Stones in S. Aisle.

Here Lyeth the Body of Mr. Tristram Walton, who Departed this Life Feb. the 13th, 1750, Aged 71 years.

Here Also Lyeth the Body of Lucy, his Wife, who Departed this Life July 19th, 1745.

In Memory of Ann, the Wife of Mr. James Burch, who died July the 11th, 1764, Aged 75 years.

Also of James, Son of Mr. James and Ann Burch, who died August the 25th, 1739, Aged 19 years.

Here lies the Earthly Remains of Mary Rowell, Youngest Daughter of Francis and Lucy Sambroke, of the Inner Temple, London, Gent. and Relict of the Rev. Thomas Rowell, Rector of Horsehenin, in Cambridgeshire, who departed this Life the 14th of October, 1757, Aged 53.

Here Lieth the Body of Mr. George Smith, who Died December 25, 1776, Aged 75 years.

Brass taken out.

H. S. E.

William Son of Tristram and Lucy Walton, dyed ye 27th of Jan. 1721, Aged six weeks.

Also Praxead, their Daughter, dyed ye 20th Apr. 1722, Aged 3 years and 9 months.

And Lucy Walton, their Daughter, dyed ye 17th of May, 1723, Aged 2 years and 9 months.

Here Lieth the Body of Mr. Richard Smith, who died 28th Oct. 1783, Aged 64 years.

Also Alice Rebecca, his Wife, who died 23 March, 1793, Aged 75 years.

Here Lieth the Body of John Smith, Son of Richard and Alice Rebecca Smith, who died 2d Oct. 1793, Aged 45 years.

H. S. E.

William Cockey, Gent. who Died ye 29th of September, 1705, Aged 67 years.

Here Lyeth ye Body of Mrs. Mary Cockey, the Wife of William Cockey, Gent. who Departed this Life the 2d of June 1721.

H. S. E.

Amy, Wife of John Parsons, Obiit June 27, 1636, Aged 38 years.

Here Lyeth the Body of Margaret, the Wife of James Bennett, who Departed this Life 10th of March, 166$\frac{7}{8}$.

On a Brass Plate.

Here Lyeth Buried the Body of Anthonye, the Sonne of Charles Wootton, of this Citie, who Deceased the 26 of Januarie, in the Year 1589.

Here Lyeth Lieut. Colonel John Doyne, Son of Philip Doyne, of Wells, in the County of Wexford, in the Kingdom of Ireland, he died July . . . 1765.

Here Lyeth the Body of Mr. Robert Loring, who departed this Life ye 19th of August, 1724, Aged 77 years.

Elizabeth Prowse, Wife of Mr. George Prowse, died the 24 March, 1728.

Elizabeth Prowse, Daughter of Mr. George and Elizabeth Prowse, died the 22 October, 1757.

Here Lyeth the Body of Sarah, the Wife of Mr. Robert Loring, who Departed this Life the 15th day of May, 1724, Aged 73 years.

Here Lyeth ye Body of George, the son of Mr. George Prowse, and Elizabeth, his Wife, who Dyed ye 6th Day of June, Anno Domini 1703, Aged 6 years & 10 months.

Ann, Wife of Richard Minifie, Died August 29th, 1683, Aged 40.

Richard Minifie Died August 28, 1706, Aged 74.

Ann, Wife of Richard Knight, Esq. Daughter of Richard and Ann Minifie, Died August 1st, 1709, Aged 45.

Arms—Quarterly, first and fourth argent, on a fess sable, between three stags' heads erased, of the same, horns, or, a fretty argent between two martlets of the same; second and third gules, on a chevron argent three pheons sable, between three doves, or, two in chief, one in base. On an inescutcheon, quarterly, first and fourth sable, on a chevron, or, between three annulets, of the same, three eagles displayed, sable; second and third argent, on a chevron, gules, three doves volant, argent, between three pellets, sable, on them as many fleur-de-lis, or.

Crest—A stag's head sable, horns or.

Here Lyeth the Body of William Smith, Gent. Citizen and Alderman of this City, who departed this Life ye 19th day of Dec. Anno Domini 1714, Aged 93.

Near this Place also Lieth ye Bodyes of Jane and Elizabeth, his two Wives.

H. S. E.

Thomas Haskett, Gener. Obijt

28 die Octob. Anno { Dñi 1722, Ætat. 80. }

H. J.

Maria Haskett, Uxor

Thomas Haskett. Obijt 7 die Jan.

Anno { Dñi 1683. Ætat. 44. }

Arms—Argent, on a bend, sable, three garbs, or, in chief a mullet, gules, on an escutcheon, azure, a gauntlet, argent, on a chief, or, two roses, gules.

S. Chapel.

Here Lieth the Body of Mary Shaw, Wife of the Late John Shaw, D. D. who dyed the 11th of Jan. 1778.

Here Lieth the Body of Martha Clifton, Wife of the Late Thomas Clifton, D. D. who died 13th Dec. 1781.

H. S. E.

Thomas Clifton, D. D. Rector of Boyton, he died June 27th, 1768.

Here Lyeth the Body of Mr. Charles Clifton, Son of Mr. Thomas Clifton, and Mary, his Wife, who died August ye 27, 1726, Aged 23 years.

Here also Lyeth the Body of Thomas Clifton, Late Alderman of this City, who Departed this Life Dec. 24th, 1733, Aged 62.

Here Lyes the Body of Mrs. Grace Nicholls, Wife of Mr. Richard Nicholls, who dyed June the 30, 1711.

Under this Stone are deposited the Remains of John Stanhope, Esq. of Wickham, in the County of Southampton, Rear Admiral of the Red in his Majesty's Navy, in which Service he had been honorably engaged for more than 45 years. He came to this City in his Way to Bath, for the Recovery of his declining health, the 30th Day of November, 1800, when his Illness, rapidly increasing, he here departed this Life on the Day following, in the 56 Year of his Age.

Elizabeth, the Wife of Mr. William Clemens, Alderman, dyed ye 14th of December, 1698, Aged 59 years.

Here Lyeth the Body of Jane Viner, Daughter of Mr. William Viner, who dyed the 1st of May, 1681, Aged 37 years.

Brass taken out.

Here Lyeth the Body of Mr. Nicholas Parsons, sen. who was Some time Maior of this Citty, And Dyed the 4th of August, 1695.

Here Lieth the Body of Mr. John Parsons, senior, who dyed the 7th of October. 1715, Aged 66.

And Amy, the Wife of John Parsons, ob. June 27th, 1686, Æt. 38 years.

H. S. E.

Mr. John Bernard, late an eminent Apothecary in this City, who died Octor. 2d, 1754, Aged 47 years.

Mary, Wife of John Bernard, died June the 4th, 1763, Aged 50 years.

Also Mary Bernard, their Daughter, died Oct. the 1st, 1798, Aged 64 years.

Also William and Mary, Son and Daughter of John Bernard, and Mary, his Wife, who died very young.

Here Lyeth ye Body of Catherine ye Wife of John Nicholls, of London, Vintner, who departed this Life ye 8th of November, 1715, Aged 22 years.

Nothing but Death, & his non Sparing Dart,
Could part ye Love Residing in each heart.

H. S. E.

William Green, Gent. Senior Alderman of this City, Dyed Feb. 13th, 1742, Aged 83.

Mary, Wife of William Green, dyed Feb. 8th, 1743, Aged 69.

Here Lyeth here Mary, the Daughter of Mr. Jonathan Newman, of this City, who Departed this Life ye 6 of January, 1723, in ye 20th year of her Age.

And near this Place are more of his Children.

H. S. E.

Thomas Light, Gent. Alderman of this City, who died Octor. 23, 1745, Aged 60 years.

Margaret, his Wife, Died 21st March, 1768, Aged 76.

Arms—Party per pale, three bulls' heads erased, two in chief, one in base; dexter, a chevron between three swans, two in chief, one in base.

H. S. E.

Sarah Hayter, Obiit 7 February, 1722.

Arms—Three bulls' heads erased.

Here Lyeth the Body of James Hayter, Gent. and Alderman of this City, who died the 13 of Nov. 1713, Aged 62.

Arms—Party, per pale, sinister, a lion rampant between twelve crosslets; dexter, three bulls' heads erased.

Underneath lie the Remains of William Hayter, Esq. of Newtontoney, in the County of Wilts. who departed this Life the 23d Day of July, 1805, Aged 65 years.

Also of Elizabeth, his Wife, who was Daughter of Scroop Egerton, Esq. She died April 27th, 1810, Aged 63 years.

Arms—Party, per pale, sinister, argent, a lion rampant, gules, between three pheons, sable; dexter, azure, three bulls' heads erased, or.

Crest—A bull's head erased, or, pierced through the neck with a spear.

Here Lyeth ye Body of Joanna Wife of Mr. James Hayter, Gent. who dyed Jan. 27th, 171· Aged 56 years.

Jacobus Hayter, Gent.
Qui Obiit 28
die Feb. Anno { Dom. 1741. / Ætat. suæ 46.

Here Lyeth Mrs. Rachel Powell, Daughter of Thomas Powell, Gent. of Overton, in this County, And Sister to Mr. John Hayter, of this City, who dyed ye 30 day of December, 1729.

H. S. E.

James Light, who died July ye 28th, 1720,
& Johanna Light, who Died Feb. ye 4th, 1703.

Here Lieth Mrs. Mary Powell, Daughter of Thomas Powell, Gent. of Overton, in this County, and Sister to Mrs. Johanna Hayter, of this City, who died ye 3 day of April, 1719.

Sophia Hayter died August 14th, 1793, Aged 19. Also of Harriot, Wife of I. F. Patherick. She died Nov. 14, 1803, Aged 33 years.

Both Daughters of William Hayter, Esq. and Elizabeth his Wife.

Here Lyeth the Body of Thomas Greene, Gent. who departed this Life April 10th, 1715.

Here also Lyeth the Body of John Bennett, the Son of Mr. Francis Bennett, and Sarah, his Wife, who Departed this Life January the 22d, 172¾, Aged 4 years and 3 months.

Rev. Henry Bennett, Died December 1st, 1796, Aged 69 years.

Here lyeth the Body of Mrs. Anne Bennett, Widow of Francis Bennett, of Dorsetshire, Gent. Sister to Mr. Thomas Greene, and Grandmother to John Bennett, both buried Close by her. She Departed this Life December the 22d, 1724.

Here Lyeth Buried the Body of Mary, the third Daughter of Mr. Jonnathan and Mrs. Elizabeth Hill, who Departed this Life the 28th Day of April, 1673.

[. .] Brass taken out.

Here Lieth the Body of Elizabeth Brooke, Youngest Daughter of Henry Brooke, Esq. of Christchurch, Hants. who Departed this Life Oct. the 3rd, 1797, Aged 2 years and 10 months.

Here Lieth the Body of Thomas Hayter, Esq. who died July the 12th, 1762, Aged 28 years.

H. S. E.

Ann King, the Daughter of Mr. Benjamin King, and of Ann, his Wife, who died ye 7th of March, 1705, Aged 29 years.

Here Lyeth ye Body of Isaac Blake, who dyed the 7th of January, 1707, Aged 54 years.

Also the Body of Ann, his Wife, who dyed April 14, 1740, Aged 77 years.

Here Lyeth ye Body of Mrs. Ann King, Widow, who departed this Life ye 15th of March, 1724, Aged 74 years.

H. S. E.

Edvardus Garrard, Arm. obiit v° die February,

Anno { Ætat. XLIJ. / Do^ni MDCCXXXIJ. }

Nec Non

Vidua ejusdem

Anna, Quæ Obijt 14° Junii,

Anno { Ætatis LVIJ. / Salutis MDCCXLVIIJ. }

Arms—Party per pale, sinister, argent, a chevron, sable, between three garbs of the same; dexter, argent, on a fess, sable, a lion passant, argent.

H. S. E.

Anna, Edwardi et Annæ Garrard, Gent.

Filia natu maxima,

Quæ obiit 3° die Maij,

Anno { Domini 1733. / Ætatis 21. }

Dorothea, Hen. Brown, Uxoris Dorothea, Filia unica, Quam

Mensis Maij die 14, A. D. 1743.

Febris abripuit violenta octo septimanarum tridui Infantulam.

Nec Non

Filius eorum Thomas Garrard Brown,

Qui vixit menses v. dies 9,

Obiit Aprilis XII^mo A.D. 1755.

In Memory of Ann, the Wife of Mr. Amb. Froud, who Died Nov. 11th, 1762.

Here Lyeth the Body of Mr. Edward Mason, who Died the 4th Day of August, Anno Dom. 1671.

Here also Lieth the Body of Edith, the Wife of Mr. Edward Mason, who dyed the 29th of November, 1701.

Here Lyeth ye Body of Susanna, Daughter of Edward Garrard, Esq. And of Ann, his Wife, who Departed this Life February the 18, 1727, Aged 3 months.

Here Lyeth the Body of Robert Blanford, who dyed the 23 of June, 1691, in ye 22d year of his Age.

Here Lyeth the Body of Ann Blanford, the Wife of Robert Blanford, who Departed this Life the 24th of January, 1713, Aged 78.

H. S. E.

Edwardus Garrard, Edwardi Garrard, Arm[ri] et Annæ Uxoris, Filius; qui puerili admodum ætate, prompti ingenij, morumq. plurima dedit specimina.

Natus { 16 die Jan[rij] } Anno 1728,
Obijt { 30 die Sept. } Domini 1738.

All joy, all joy in Heaven.

Ibidem deposita est Anna,
Henrici Dorothea Brown
Filia dilectissima, quæ obiit
Die Nativitatis X[ti]
Anno 1750, Ætatis suæ 5.

Here Lyeth the Body of Mrs. Elizabeth King, Daughter of Mr. Benjamin, and Ann King, who departed this Life March ye 28, 1732, Aged 50 years.

Here also Lyeth Buried her Sister, Mrs. Mary Baker, the Widow of the Rev. Mr. John Baker, Late Vicar of Rowde, in this County, who dyed the 2d of February, 1752, Aged 50 years.

Here Lyeth the Body of Mrs. Ann Foyle, Wife of the Rev. Mr. Edward Foyle, Rector of Kimpton, in Hants. She died August 4, 1764, Aged 28 years.

Also the Body of Ann Foyle, their Daughter, who dyed July 6th, 1765, Aged 5 years 9 months.

The Rev. Henry Rigby, M. A. died 15th May, 1819, Aged 77 years.

H. S. E.

Thomas, filius Johannis Strong, & Catherinæ, uxoris, Natus quartus,
Obiit 26 die November,
Anno { Æ v. c. MDCXIX.
Ætat. suæ 18.

Mr. Joseph Gibbs died 29th Jan, 1761, Aged 65 years.

Also Dulcibella, his Wife, died 17th Oct. 1768, Aged 72 years.

Here Lieth the Body of Mr. Joseph West, Son-in-law to Alderman Waterman, who Departed this Life Dec. 23, 1748.

Here Lieth ye Body of Elizabeth, Wife of Mr. Joseph West, who died the 15th of Oct. 1745.

Here Lieth the Body of Mrs. Martha Waterman, ye Wife of Mr. William Waterman, sen. who died April ye 8th, 1726, Aged 72 years.

H. S. E.

Elizabeth Smith, Daughter of Caleb and Elizabeth Smith, who died Oct. 17, 1777, Aged 41 years.

Also Mary Smith, another of their Daughters, who died May 1st, 1794, Aged 31 years.

H. S. E.

Betty, the Wife of Charles Brander, Esq. and Daughter of Mr. William Waterman, jun. late of this City. She Departed this Life May the 24th, 1768.

Here Lyeth the Body of Mr. William Waterman, who departed this Life the 19th of February, 1719, Aged 31 years.

Here Lieth the Body of Mr. William Waterman, Alderman of this City, who departed this Life the 30th of December, 1715, Aged 63, Father of Mrs. Martha Hillman, who Lyeth here by.

H. S. E.

Martha, Uxor Gulielmi Hillman, Pharmacopola, Qui Obiit 25th Februarii, Anno Domini 1787, Æt. 28.

Also Mrs. Martha Hillman, Daughter of William and Martha Hillman, who died 3rd September, 1768, Aged 69 years.

Likewise Rawlins Hillman, who died 24th Jan. 1794, Aged 60 years.

Also William Henry, and Godfrey, two of his Children, died in their Infancy.

Likewise William Henry, Son of William Hillman, who died 22d June, 1795, Aged 10 years.

H. S. E.

Johannes Strong, Gen. hujus .... Ci..tatis Statulo uni per annos triginta Clericus: in negotiis publicis procurandis, dum cinerent vires, vigilans & sagax, in conservandis quantum officii, ratio postularet privilegijs, constans et fidelis. Obiit 10 Apr. Testo Resurrect. Dom. Æ. v.c. 1704, Ætat. suæ 62.

C. U. & E. F. M. M. P. P.

On Flat Stones in the North Chapel.

Here Lyeth the Body
of Mr. Joseph Gifforde,
one of the Justices of the Peace
for this City,
who Departed this Life June ye 2d, Anno Dom. 1729,
Aged 63 years.
Also Thomasin, his Wife,
who dyed the 1st of March, 1730.

Jane, Relick of William Washer, Esq. June 3d, 1805.

H. S. E.

Robertus Heath, M. D. Robt Heath, Armigero, natus,
R. Heath, Esquite, Aurato
Utriusq. Banco
sub Carolijmi Auspiciis,
Judice Primario prognatus,
Avi hisce titulis insigniti,
Nepos dignissimus,
Obijt 14° Martii, 1724,
Ætat. 67.

Arms—A cross engrailed between twelve billets.

Here Lieth the Body of
Captain Cornelius Mitchell,
Son of Thomas Mitchell, Gent.
and Barbara, his Wife,
who died March ye 16th, 1761,
Aged 41 years.

Arms—A chevron between seven crosslets fitchy, issuing out of as many boars' heads, couped close, four in chief, three in base.

Crest—Dexter hand holding a sword.

M. S.

Elizabeth Eyre,
Daughter of the
Honorable Sir Anthony Chester,
of Chichley, in the County of Bucks, Baronet,
And Wife of
Charles Nicholas Eyre, Esquire,
By whom She had
Charles Chester Eyre.
She was Born the XI of Feb. MDCLIX.
dyed the XI of Mar. MDCCV.

C. A. P. D.

Arms—On a chevron, three quarterfoils, in chief a crescent; impaling, a chevron engrailed between three rams' heads horned, two in chief, one in base.

Under this Marble
Lyes Interred the Body of Jane Eyre,
Who dyed of an Apoplexy,
on the 7th day of Nov.
Anno Salutis Humanæ 1695,
Aged 69 Years and one Month.
She was the second Wife to Nicholas Eyre,
who dyed the 3d day of August, Anno Dom. 1677,
in the 74th year of his Age,
by whom She had Issue
three Sons and two Daughters;
Viz.
Charles-Nicholas, William, and John, now Living,
Mary and Martha Deceased.
C. A. P. D. 1695.

Arms—On a chevron three quarterfoils, impaling, three lions heads erased, bar-wise.

To the Memory of
Richard John Gough,
Late of Warminster, Wilts.
Attorney at Law,
who died the 29th of June, 1811,
Aged 44 years.

R. S. W.
Oct. 22, 1803.

Here Lyeth ye Body of
Gabriel Barnaby, M. A.
Rector of Wolverton and Wyke, in Hants.
Fellow of Winchester Coll.
Son of Gabriel Barnaby, Gent.
and Mary his Wife,
Daughter of William Ray, a Magistrate in this City,
Obiit March 2d, Anno Domini 1718,
Ætatis 60.

Here lieth the Body of Mary, the Relick of Gabriel Barnaby, an Attorney at Law of this City. She was Daughter of Mr. Thomas Ray, a Clothier, upon the Ditch, in this Parish, by Margaret, his Wife. She was Submissive to her Husband, and after his Decease continued in a Widowhood truely Honourable. She had a rare and surprising understanding, and an uncommon quickness and strength of parts, which were not sensibly impaired by ye decay of old Age, but were daily improved by ye experience of many years. As She was blessed with an extraordinary length of days, so she made the true and best use of that Blessing; for, by a regular Devotion, and constant Piety towards God, by Charity, Good Will, and Beneficence towards her Neighbour, She endeavoured to work out her Salvation here, that She might obtain Life and Immortality hereafter. She died the 20th Day of August,

In the year { of her Age 96.
of Our Lord 1724.

This toombe Stone was Laide here by the Appoyntment & at the cost of Thomas Raye, the Elder Alderman of this Citty, in Memory of, and to cover the interred Corps of his Beloved and Eldest Sonn Thomas, who, while Hee lived, was a Dutievil & Obidient Child unto his Parents, a Tender Loving Husband to his Deare Wife Barbarah, the Daughter of Francis Swanton, Esq. a neate, ingenious, Civill, free, Loving Person to all his Relacions, Frinds, & Acquaintance. Hee Departed this life, a Penitent, faithfull, Cheareful Christian, and a Zealous Sonn of the Church of England, one the 26th Day of September, in the yeare of our Lord God 1661, of the Age of 24 years, 7 months, and 15 Dayes.

There Rest, Deare Child, in Peaceful Bliss,
In this thy sleeping toome,
That time, by Mouldring thy Cropt budd
To dust, may make a Roome,
That my dead Corps, when down it drops,
May once Againe embrace
Thy blessed Dust, that in mine eyes,
Was once a Lovelie face.

Here Lieth the Body of Mrs. Sarah Goddard, Daughter of Mr. Thomas Goddard, of this City, who dyed Feb. the 5th, 1756, Aged 77.

Arms—A fess between three battle-axes, two in chief, one in base, in chief a crescent.

Here Lyeth the Body of William Ray, Esq. Late Consull at Smirna, who dyed ye 2d of February, 1704, in ye 64th year of his Age.

H. S. E.

Abigail, Ux: Johannis Vince, Quæ ob: 10 die Junii, 1705, Æt: 22.
Ac etiam Alicia Wyche, Uxor Benj: Wyche, Gent. et Mater præd: Abig: Vince,
Quæ ob: 30 die Nov. 1728.
Denique, præd: Benj: Wyche,
Qui Obijt 25 die Aprilis,
Anno { Dom. 1734. Ætat. 77. }
Juxta etiam jacet Rob: Nepos
Benj. Wyche, ob. Feb. 2, 1729,
Ætat. suæ 4.
Nec non
Ben. Wyche, A. M. Rector de Lockston,
Nepos prædicti Ben. Wyche,
Ob. 6 Apr. A. D. 1752, Æt. 32.

To the Memory of Richard Samuel Wyche, Gent. who died July ye 31st, 1736, Aged 44 years.

And to the Memory of Ann, his Wife, daughter of Mr. Robt. Coope, Late of this City. She died Jan. ye 27th, 1762, Aged 66 years.

Also Alice Wyche Gough, their Daughter, Wife of Lieut. Richard Gough, died March 5th 1785, Aged 59 years.

Richard Gough, Lieut. in his Majesty's Late 85 Regiment, died 29th May, 1794, Aged 71 years.

Here Lyeth the Body of
Mrs. Mary Barnaby, Daughter
of Gabriel Barnaby, Gent.
by Mary his Wife,
Daughter of William Ray,
A Magistrate in this City,
Obijt April 2d, Anno { Ætat. 72. Dom. 1728. }

Here Lieth the Body of
Barbara Mitchell, Relict of
Mr. Thomas Mitchell, and Daughter
of Mr. Richard Eyre, Alderman of
this City, who died Dec. 10, 1751, Aged 82.

Here also lieth the Body of
the Rev. Mr. James Foster,
who died Sept. 23, 1772,
Aged 67.

Also the Body of
Melior Foster, Relict of the
Rev. Mr. James Foster,
and Daughter of
Mr. Thomas and Barbara Mitchell,
who died 28th Oct. 1787,
Aged 85.

Here Lyeth the Body of Elizabeth, the Daughter of Thomas Bennett, Gent. and Winiefred, his Wife, who Departed this Life 15 July, A. D. 1681, Ætatis suæ iij.

H. S. E.

Samuel & Robertus, Filii ..cardi-Samuelis Wyche, Gen. Samuel obiit xxxj° die Decembris, Ætat. a° j°. ....rt. obiit iv die Januarij, æt. a° 2°, A° Dom. 1712.
Oh Dolor!
... etiam S. E. Benjamin Wyche, Filius natu maximus, præd. Ric. Sam. Wyche, Obiit vi die Feb. A° Dñi 1719, Æt. a° 3°. . . . . filii erepti vi° Hebdomadas. Oh maxime Dolor, Avi lector et luge.

Here lieth buried Katherine, ye sole Daughter of Mr. Daniell Hales, first married to Mr. Edward Edmonds, merchant, of this City, & afterwards to Mr. John Thistlethwayte. Shee died May ye 26, Anº Dom. 1676.

To the Memory of Miss Catharine Powell, Eldest Daughter of Sir Alexander Powell, Knight, and Dame Catherine, his late Wife. She dyed the 8th of Jan. 1777, Aged 19.

Also of Alexander Powell, Esq. their youngest Son, who died 29 Sep. 1779, in the 17th year of his Age.

H. S. E.

Dorothy Clarke, Daughter of Richard Stanly, Esq. of Crundal, in Hampshire, Relict of Benjamin Clarke, Gent. of Stanley, near Wakefield, in Yorkshire, who dyed June ye 9th, 1729, in the 49th year of her Age.

Arms—In pale, three escallops between two flanches ermine, impaling, per fess indented, in chief three stags' heads caboshed bar-wise, in base three eagles' legs erased.

Sacred to the Memory of William Michael Burrough, Son of Michael Burrough, Esq. Alderman of this City, who died the 12th of June, 1805, in the 10th year of his age.

Underneath is Interred the Body of Rebecca the second Wife of Mr. Alexander Powell. She was the Daughter of Mathew Pitts, Esq. late of this City, and dyed the 11th of March, 1753, Aged 29 years.

Sir Alexander Powell, Kt is also interred under this Stone.

Arms—A chevron between three lions paws, two in chief, one in base, in chief a crescent, on an escutcheon, quarterly, first and fourth, a fess checky between three roundels, two in chief, one in base: second and third a crosslet.

Underneath is interred the Body of Dame Catherine Powell, the third Wife of Sir Alexander Powell, of this City, Knight, and one of the Daughters of the Right Rev. Dr. Edw. Willes, Lord Bishop of Bath and Wells, who Departed this Life the 21st Feb. 1772, Aged 49.

Alex. their eldest child, died the 26th Jan. 1760, in the 4th year of his Age, and is buried near this place. Ann, his first Wife, is also buried here. She was the eldest Daughter of Thos. Gatehouse, Esq. of Lower Wallop, in Hampshire, and died the 26th Apr. 1747, Aged 29.

Arms—A chevron between three lions' paws, two in chief, one in base; impaling, a chevron between three mullets, two in chief one in base.

Here Lyeth the Body of John Powell, late of this City, Gent. who Departed this Life Jan. ye 2d, 1737, Aged 63.

And under this Stone is interred his Daughter, Mrs. Catherine Powell, who died 6th Jan. 1757, Aged 50 years.

Here Lyeth the Body of Anne Powell, Late the Wife of John Powell, of this City, Gent. who dyed ye 20 day of August, 1727, Aged 50 years.

Here Lyeth ye Body of Anne Powell, Daughter of John Powell, ye younger, Gent. & Ann his Wife, who Departed this Life the 3d Day of May, 1709, Aged 5 years.

Here Lyeth ye Body of Martha, Late Wife of Nathanael Webb, Gent. who Departed this Life ye 27 day of December, Anno Domini 1718, Aged 65.

Arms—A cross between four doves, conjoined, impaling, a griffin segrejant.

H. S. E.

Gulielmus Webb, de Hospitis Lincolniensis, in Comitatu Middlesexiæ, Generosus, filius dum vixit unicus Nathanielis Webb, Generosi, et Marthæ, uxoris ejus. Obiit 14º Decembris, A. D. 1708, et Ætatis suæ 25.

Arms—A cross between four doves conjoined.

Elizabetha, Filia Johannis Ballard, M.D. et Dorothæ, Uxoris Ejus, Obijt Septembris xxmo

Anno { Dom. 1734.
Ætatis 28.

Here lieth the Body of Sarah, the Wife of Scroope Egerton, Esq. who died Nov. 13th, 1759.

Also of Scroope Egerton, Esq. who died April 6th, 1767, Aged 45 years.

And of

Anna Maria, his Widow, who died 20th Jan. 1797, in the 74th year of her Age.

Here Lyeth the Body of
Edward Edmonds, Alderman of this Citty, who died the 7th day of July, 17..
Aged about 76 years.

Henrietta, only Daughter of Joseph and Henrietta Maberly, of Bedford Row, London, died 13th Nov. 1818, Aged 5 years and 9 months.

Here Lyeth ye Body of James Markes, Esq. Deceased ye 19 of November, 1679, who marryed ye Daughter and heire of Thomas Chafin, Esq. of ye Close, in Sarum.

Here Lyeth the Body of Lady Markes, Relict of James Markes, Esq. who dyed the 22d of November, Anno Dom. 1692.

Arms—On a lion rampant, a crescent between eight fleur-de-lis, a canton, ermine, impaling, a talbot passant, in chief ermine.

In Memory of Harriot Tatum, Daughter of John and Catherine Tatum, of this City, who died Nov. the 17, 1758, aged ten weeks.

H. S. E.

Quod unicum mori potuit
Piæ beneficæ que mulieris,
Temperantiæ Philips,
Quæ Obiit Dec^bri^ 1mo
A. D. 1742, Ætatis suæ 68.

Ibidem deposita est,
Soror haud absimilis
Margaret Philips,
Quæ obiit Dec. X^mo^, A. D. 1756,
Ætatis suæ 81.

Arms—On a chevron engrailed, three doves' heads erased.

Here Lyeth the Body of Lady Chafin, Relict of Thomas Chafin, of the Close of Sarum, Esq. Daughter and one of the Coheiresses of Thomas Hawker, of Heightsbury, in the County of Wilts. Esq. who Departed this life the 4th Day of January, Anno Dom. 169½.

Arms—A talbot passant, in chief ermine, impaling, a falcon perched.

Here lieth the Body of Elizabeth Michell, Daughter of the Rev. Mr. Thomas Michell, and Eleanor, his Wife, who, died Jan. 2, 1757, Aged 7 months.

Here Lyeth ye Body of Katherine, Daughter of Scroope Egerton, Esq. and Sarah his Wife. She died August 6th, 174. aged one year.

Here Lyeth the Body of Henrietta, ye Daughter of John Gore, Gent. who dyed February the 2d, 1683, Aged 2 years and 2 weeks.

Here Lyeth Ann, the Daughter of John Gore, Gent. who dyed ye 20 day of October, 1686.

Here lyeth Elizabeth ye Daughter of John Gore, Gent. who dyed the 8th of January, 1687.

Here Lyeth the Body of Mr. Francis Stevens, Son of Mr. John Stevens, of the Close of Sarum, and Margaret, his Wife, Born May the 18th, 1657, Deceased March ye 18th, 1686.

Also ye Body of Mary, third Daughter of Herbert Saladin, Esq. and Anne, his Wife, first married to the said Francis Stevens, afterwards to Mr. John Gauntlett, of Netherhampton, who departed this life the 30th of March, 1714, in the 54th year of her Age.

Here Lyeth ye Body of Mr. Samuell Brachar, who died September ye 5th, 1674, Aged 35.

Brass from a stone taken away.

Johannis Ballard, M. D.
Qui post praxin in hac civitate
per XL annos, perite feliciter pie
exercitam,
obiit Nov^ris^ 9,
Anno { Domini 1725,
Ætatis 71.

Thomas Tatum, Esq. Died 14th January, 1819, Aged 52 years.

In Memory of Catherine, Daughter of John and Catherine Tatum, who died September 20, 1760, Aged five years four months.

In Memory also of John, Son of John and Catherine Tatum, who died September 23, 1760, Aged three years ten months.
They were lovely in their Lives,
And in Death they were not divided.

Thomas Shuckburgh Tatum,
Born March 13th, 1798,
Died July 2d, 1800.

Here Lyeth the Body of Mary Pike, who died April the 9th, 1766, Aged 49 years.

Here Lieth Mrs. Ann Cracherode, widow of Mr. Thomas Cracherode, and Sister to Mrs. Temperance and Margaret Phillips, who died December ye 10th, 1759, in the 81 year of her Age.

Arms—A saltire, ermine, between four leopards' heads erased; impaling, on a chevron, ingrailed, three doves' heads erased.

H. S. E.

Nov[r] 25th 1739. Elizabeth Edmonds, wife of Edward Edmonds, who was buried Sept. 23, 1709.

H. S. E.

Rob[tus] Edmonds, Filius Henrici Edmonds, hujus Civitatis nuper Alderman, Qui Obiit quinto die Maij, 1714.

In North Aisle.

Here Lieth the Body of John Thomas Tatum, Son of John and Catherine Tatum, who departed this life Nov. 23d, 1781, Aged 20 years.

Here Lyeth the Body of Dr. John Tatum, who Departed this Life December 27th, 1783, Aged 59 years.
Also
of Catherine, his Wife, who died August 14th, 1793, Aged 67 years.

H. S. E.

Catharina Maria Tatum, Joannis Tatum, M. D. & Catharinæ, filia. Nata Oct. 12, 1762, Obiit Jan. 1, 1794.

Here Lyeth the Body of Judeth Wansborough, the Daughter of Thomas Wansborough, and Judeth, his Wife, who Departed this Life May, 1678.

In Memory of Francis Le Breton, second Son of the Dean of the Island of Jersey, and Lieutenant in the Royal Navy, who Departed this Life Nov. 17th, A. D. 1798, Aged 28 years.

Jane, Wife of Samuel Hawes, born 15 April, 1742, died 9 Dec. 1783.

Samuel, Son of Samuel and Jane Hawes, born 4 June, 1769, died 16 April, 1770.

Also of Samuel Hawes, Gent. who died August 6th, 1800, Aged 55 years.

Here Lyeth the Body of Mr. Richard Tounsen, who died Octor. ye 23, 1763, Aged 61 years.

Here Lyeth ye Body of Mr. Roger Bedbury, who departed July ye 13th, 1676.

Here Lyeth ye Body of Thomas, ye Son of Mr. Roger Bedbury, who dyed August 17th, 1675.

Robert Alexander, Gent. died July ye 16th, 1644.

In Memory of Mr. Francis Hamwood, Late Steward to the Hon[ble] Lieut. Gen. Cholmondle. He died Jan. ye 30th, 1762, Aged 57 years.

Here lieth the Body of Margaret, the Sister of Mr. Arthur Helme, juniour, who Departed this Life the 25th of Aprill, 1672.

H. S. E.

Rich[us] Eyre, Pharmacopola, Filius Gulielmi et Gratia Eyre, Obiit 13 die Januarii,

Anno { Dom. 1727, Ætat. 25.

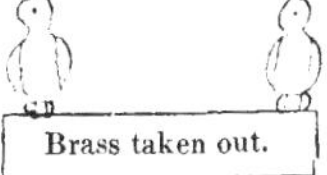

M. W. died April 1st, 1764.

Beneath this Stone Rest the Remains of
Mr. Thomas Robert Guest,
Many Years an Inhabitant of this City.
He was Born on the 3d of June, 1755,
And died the 16th of December, 1818.
A Man, in his intercourse with the world, of
a most excellent and upright mind.
His domestic virtues
are more deeply engraven in the hearts of his
afflicted Family, to whom his loss is irreparable.

Here Lyeth ye Body of James, Son of William and Mary Millett, who departed this life Sept. ye 7th, 1737, Aged one year and seven weeks.

Here Lyeth the Body of William, Son of William and Mary Millett, who departed this Life June ye 12, 1734, Aged one year and 8 months.

Also Here Lieth ye Body of Thomas, Son of William and Mary Millett, who Departed this Life August ye 25th, 1736, Aged one year.

Here Lyeth ye Body of Sarah, Wife of William Millett, and Daughter of Thomas and Mary Morgan, of Upwood, in the Parish of Hanley, in the County of Dorsett, who departed this life December ye 13th, 1730, Aged 55 years.

H. S. E.

Ann Haskett, Obijt Nov. 11th, 1726.

In the North Porch.

Underneath this Stone are deposited
the Remains of Mr. John Noble,
Painter and Glazier,
and one of the Common Council
of the Corporation of this City.
He died September 12, 1817,
in the 66 year of his Age.
He was a truly humble and sincere
Christian, Possessing the ornament
of a meek and quiet Spirit, and making
the word of God the guide of his Conduct.
He passed through life universally respected,
and in Death was not less lamented.

Reader, go and do thou likewise.

Amelia Corbin
Died Nov. 24th, 1774,
Aged 2 years and 5 months.

ELSTUB AND EVERLEY HUNDRED.

WESTWOOD.

On Flat Stones in Chancel.

Here Lieth interred the Body of Mr. George Houghton, who Departed this life December 6, 1759, Aged 58.

Also, here lieth interred the Body of Mrs. Ann, the Wife of the above, who Departed this life Feb. 7th, 1782, Aged 82 years.

Here Lieth the Body of Daniel Bendy, who Departed this Life March 5th, 1772, Aged . . years.

In Memory of Thomas Sumpsion, who died April ye 14, 1739, Aged 26 years.

Samuel, his Son, died May 19, 1739, Aged 13 months.

Also in Memory of Jane, Relict of Thomas Sumpsion, and Wife of Robert Witcombe. She died July the 6, 1770, Aged 64 years.

Also in Memory of Robert Witcombe, who Died May 24, 1774, Aged 64 years.

On a Monument against South Wall of Nave.

This Monument is inscribed
to the Memory of
Richard Cox, Esq.
who died the 2d day of January, 1789,
Aged 60 years.

O'er this exalted Artist's hallow'd Urn,
Genius shall droop, and pensive Friendship mourn:
Bold plastic Skill with Honour mark'd his name,
Brought Independence, and a well-earn'd Fame.
Amidst these shades, in life's calm eve, retir'd,
He died lamented, as he liv'd admir'd.

Arms—Argent, three cocks, gules; on a chief, azure, a pale, of the first, charged with a rose, gules, between two ostrich feathers, or.

This Monument adjoining,
was Erected by Mary,
the Widow of Richard Cox, Esq.
in Conformity to his Will.
She died June 17, 1789,
Aged 41 years,
And is buried in the same Vault.

Against North Wall of Nave.

To the Memory of John Painter, late of Hilmarton, in this County, who died Feb. ye 17th, 1728, Aged 73 years.

On a Flat Stone in Nave.

This Erected by her Executor Oliver Cromwell.
Anthony Millett.

Here lyethe ye Body of
Thomas Garland, who departed
Jan. ye 5th, 1719,
Ætatis suæ 78.

Also here lyeth the Body of Grace,
the Wife of Tobi Garland,
who Departed this Life the 14th day of Nov. 1709.

North Aisle.

Here resteth, expecting the second coming of our Saviour Christ unto judgement, the Bodie of John Farewell, late of Westwood, in the Countie of Wilts. Esquire, Justice of Peace and quorum of the several Counties of Somerset and Wilts. who left this life the nineteenth day of Sept. Anno Dom. 1642, Ætatis suæ 63.

Farewell, that Gentleman who in his life
Liv'd died beloved of his most loyall Wife;
His constancie to such as did him knowe,
Leaves him lamented in his urne belowe;
His courteous name his stocke, his kin can tell,
How fast a friend they found in this Farewell.

Mortuorum vita in memoria
vivorum posita est
Finis legis est Christus.

Arms—Quarterly, first and fourth gules, on a chevron, argent, a mullet, of the first, between three escallops, sable; second and third sable, a saltire argent, in fess point a crescent of the same: impaling, or, on a bend, gules, three mullets, sable; in chief a crescent for difference, sable.

EPITAPH.

C lose in the bosome of this Mournful Tomb,
H urry'd from Earth to his Eternal home,
A n early Trophy of Death's Conquering Power,
R eposing, waits for Nature's last great hour.
L ife, like a Morning Vision fled away,
E re we could perfectly perceive the day,
S o soon we lose what long we'd have to stay.

F ate tooke no pity on his tender years,
R egarded not his parents pious tears,
A ll their vain grief the victim could not save,
N or keep their boy from the devouring Grave;
C rown'd with his native Innocence he fell,
K ings Crown'd with Lawrel seldom dye so well.
L et age and youth from hence this maxim know,
I f Heaven commands, the best are forc'd to go,
N othing that's good is permanent below.

Charles Francklin
Departed this Life March 6, 170$\frac{4}{5}$
...... years.

On Flat Stones in N. Aisle.

Here lyeth the Body of Margreat, the Daughter of William Power, and of Margreat his Wife, who Departed this life Nov. 7, 1721, Aged 9 weekes.

Here lyeth the Body of Mistress Elizabeth Savage, wife of Charles Savage, of Westwood, in the County of Wilts. Esq. who Departed this life the 16th Day of February, 1713-14.

Here Lyeth the Body of Charles Savage, Esq. who departed this life the one ..... Day of Feb. Anno Dom. 1714.

The Church consists of Chancel, Nave, and N. Aisle.

COLLINGBOURNE DUCIS.

On a Monument in Chancel.

Near Rest the Remains of the Rev. William Tomlins, M. A. Many years Rector of this Parish, beloved and revered for his exemplary Discharge of every pastoral and Christian Duty. His Death was an inexpressible loss and grief to all with whom he stood connected by the Functions of his Sacred Office or the Ties of social intercourse.

On a flat stone near the above.

Here rest the Remains of the Rev. William Tomlins, late Rector of this Parish, Obiit 17mo Nov. 1787, Ætatis 78.

Also Sophia his Wife, Obiit 3d April, 1786, Æt. 74.

Arms in Chancel—On a chevron three roundels between three leopards' heads caboshed.

On a Monument against N. Wall of Nave.

Near this Place lies Interred the Body of John Vincent, Gent. who departed this life June 5th, 1756, in the 70th year of his Age.

Also near this Place is interred Dorothy, Wife of John Vincent, Gent. who Departed this life February the 21st, 1753, in the 63d year of her age.

Arms—Azure, three cinquefoils or.

The Church consists of Chancel, Nave, North and South Aisles.

The Earl of Aylesbury Lord of the Manor.

EVERLEY.

Upon the North Wall of the Nave.

In Memory of Francis Dugdale Astley, Esquire, the munificent Founder, Builder, and Donor of this Church, and of all the Ecclesiastical buildings appertaining to it, of the Patteshull branch, He was lineally descended from the very ancient and honorable house of Astley Castle, in the County of Warwick, distinguished by King Henry VI. with the most Noble Order of the Garter. In the year 1776, he married Mary, second daughter and co-heiress (with Dorothea Lady Lethbridge) of William Buckler, of Boreham, in this County, Esquire, by whom he has left three sons, survivors. He married, secondly, in 1805, Anne, daughter of Henry Geast, Esquire, and Niece of Richard Dugdale, Esquire, of Blythe Hall, Warwickshire, who was descended from Sir William Dugdale, Knight: by Her he had no Issue. Reader, reflect, that disregard of truth is, in places like this, the most unhallowed, and the plain detail of character is all that the best of men can or would approve or allow, the name on this marble lives, and will long live, in the memorials of his actions: the good deeds of the encourager of planting and husbandry: of the resident and considerate land-owner: of the active and upright magistrate: the public-spirited friend of the British King and Constitution. Go deeper, reader, and thou mayest learn that he was loved and revered for his exemplary discharge of the duties of Husband, Father, Friend, and Christian.

He died the 26th of April, and was deposited in the Vault beneath, May the 4th, 1818, Aged 76 years.

Shields of Arms:

1. Azure, a cinquefoil ermine.
2. Sable, on a bend cottized argent, three lions passant of the last.
3. Argent, three lozenges in fess, gules.
4. Argent, a chevron counter-imbattled sable, between three griffins' heads erased, or.
5. As the first.
6. Azure, three stirrup-irons and strap, or.
7. Azure, a chevron between three swans' heads erased argent.
8. Argent, a cross-moline, gules, in chief a crescent of the last, for difference.

In East Window of the Chancel, in stained Glass: Azure, a cinquefoil, ermine. *Crest*—On a wreath, azure and ermine, a plume of ostrich feathers, argent, issuing out of a ducal coronet, or.

'Fide sed cui vide.'

Hatchments in the Chancel.

Azure, a cinquefoil, ermine, impaling per fess; quarterly, first and fourth sable, on a fess, or, three mullets of the first between three griffins' heads erased of the second; second and third azure, three stirrup-irons, or, within a border argent, charged with ten pellets, in base quarterly, first and fourth azure, a chevron between three swans' heads erased, argent; second and third argent, on a cross-moline, gules, a celestial crown, or, in chief a crescent, gules, for difference.

Quarterly, first and fourth azure, a cinquefoil ermine, on an escutcheon argent, a sinister hand gules; second and third ermine, on a bend sable, two hands per pale holding a horse-shoe ermine, over all, on an escutcheon, gules, a saltire, or, charged with a cross engrailed argent.

Azure, a cinquefoil argent, within a border ingrailed or, impaling, quarterly, first and fourth sable, on a fess, or, three estoiles, gules, between three griffins' heads erased or; second and third, three stirrup-irons per pale, straps or, within a border sable, charged with ten plates.

NETHERAVON.

On Monuments in Chancel.

Dedicated to the Memory of Daniel Herne, Esq. of West Amesbury, in this County, who Departed this life the 22d of January, 1814, Aged 80 years. And is interred near his Brother Thomas.

Arms—Sable, a chevron, ermine, between three storks' heads erased, argent.

Near the Wall, on the East side of this Chancel, are deposited the Remains of Thomas Herne, of Bloomsbury, in the County of Middlesex, Esq. descended from a Family long resident in this Parish. He married Mary, Daughter of Richard Marriott, Esq. of the Exchequer Office, but died without Issue, June 25, 1790, Aged 63 years.

This Monument was erected by Daniel Herne, Esq. To the Memory of a Brother much loved and esteemed.

Arms—Sable, a chevron ermine, between three storks argent.

In Memory of Dorothy, Wife of Richard Chandler Hale, Esq. who died Sept. 12, 1776, Aged 56 years.

Also the Body of Richard Chandler Hale, Esq. who died Jan. 1777, Aged 50 years.

On Flat Stones.

In Memory of Richard Compton, who died July 29, 1779, Aged 66 years.

Here resteth the Body of Anne Gape, the Widd. of Thomas Gape, Esq. and Daughter of William Backhouse, of London, Esq. who Departed this life the 29 of April, 1686.

On a Brass Plate.

In Certain Hope and expectation
of a Blessed Resurrection, Resteth
Here the Body of John Samwell, who
Departed this life the 17th Day of May,
A. Dom. 1669.

The Church consists of Chancel, Nave, North and South Aisles. The Nave is supported by four plain arches on each side, and round pillars.

Michael Hicks Beach, Esq. Lord of the Manor.

ENFORD.

North Aisle.

Here lyeth Buryed ye Bodye of Mrs. Jenever Baskervile, Widowe, ye late wife of William Baskerville, of Wanbrough, Esquire, by whome She had Issue Elizabeth ye Wife of Thomas Petre, Sonn of John Lord Petre, and Marye, ye wife of Thomas Foster, Esq. Her Vertuous life, Bountyfull Hospitalyte, & Charitable Rellevince of ye Poore, Have left Her Name Gracious on Earth, & Founde a Rewarde Glorious in Heaven, whether she Departed ye 2 daye of Jan. 1615.

Arms—Azure, a chevron, gules, between three hurts; impaling or, three eagles displayed, issuing out of as many crescents, azure.

Gules, a bend or, between three escallops, argent; impaling azure, a chevron, gules, between three hurts.

Quarterly, first and fourth argent, a chevron, vert, between three bugle-horns, sable; second and third argent, on a bend, sable, three birds, or; impaling, argent, a chevron, gules, between three hurts.

South Wall of the Chancel.

Beneath are Deposited the Remains of Abraham Poore, of Longstreet, in this Parish, Esq. who died November 26, 1767, Aged 80. He was the third Son of Edward Poore, of Figheldean, Esq. and Married Ann, Daughter of John Herne, of Netheravon, Gent. She died February 18, 1759, Aged 70, and is Interred beneath. He had Issue three Sons and five Daughters, of which Children four died in their Infancy; of the other four Edward died April 10, 1788, Aged 73, and is Interred at Rushall. He married Barbara, the Daughter of Paul Methuen, of Bradford, Esq. by whom he left Issue two Sons, John, died Unmarried Feb. 27, 1797, Aged 79, and is Interred beneath, Ann died Unmarried Oct. 15, 1757, Aged 37, and is Interred beneath. Hester married her Cousin, Smart Poore, of Alton, Esq. She died March 1, 1770, Aged 43, and is interred at Figheldean, leaving Issue one Daughter.

Arms—A chevron between three mullets, impaling, a chevron ermine, between three storks.

In Memory of Henry Hunt, and of Mary his Wife.
She died 12 May, 1740, Aged 32.
He died 26 July, 1773, Aged 65.
Also Henry, their Son, Died 18th March, 1776, Aged 44.
And Mary, their Daughter, Wife of John Marshall, died the 22d Oct. 1786, Aged 55.

In Memory of Elizabeth, Wife of Thomas Hunt. She was an affectionate Wife, a tender and discreet Mother. Her Memory will be Justly dear to the good and wise, who know that Piety and true happiness generally accompany the faithful performance of the duties of domestick Life. She died the 15th of Jan. 1789, Aged 37.

As a Testimony of filial and fraternal Respect and Affection, and of the deep regret he feels for the loss of the best of Wives, Thomas Hunt hath caused this Monument to be erected.

The Rev. John Prince Vicar.

John Bennet, Esq. Lord of the Manor.

FITTLETON.

On Flat Stones in Chancel.

Jane, Wife of Robert Merchant, died 4 of January, 1769, Aged 64.

Rev. Robert Merchant, B. D. Rector of Fittleton Forty years, died 7 of April, 1773, Aged 91.

Judith, Uxor. Rogeri Key,
Deo efflavit Animam
Jan. 28, 1701.

Hic requiescit,
Spe Resurrectionis
Dominus, Johannes Buckenham,
hujus Ecclesiæ Rector dignissimus.
Omnigena virtute sane exumus,
Septem per annos Officium fideliter,
postquam præstitisset,
fato proh dolor
functus est,
14 Junij, Anno Dom.
1693.

Close by his Right Side lies Elizabeth, his Wife, who lived with her Husband 5 years from her Virginity, and was a Widow 24, who departed not from the Temple, but served God with Fasting and Praying, Luke ye 2d. A Woman full of Good Works and Alms deeds, which She did (Acts ye 9.) till her death, Oct. ye 28, 1717, Ætat. 55.

Arms—A lion rampant, impaling, a unicorn's head erased, in chief three lozenges, bar-wise.

On a Brass Plate S. Wall of Chancel.

Thomas Jay, uppon ye death of Thomas Jay, His Father, one of his Majtis Justices for this County of Wiltes, & sometime parson of this Place, who died April 28, 1623.

Courteous Beholder, if you long to know
Who Tis yt dwells in Sacred peace below,
Lift up your eyes, Read, and but use his name,
Each Toung will tell Large Stories of his fame.
T'was an admired oricle yt did teach
All by a Pious life which hee did preach;
Twas one yt in ye common wealth did beare
As great a stroake of worthiness as heare;
Twas one yt being Rich, made all the poore
Neighbouringe near to him, Sharers in his Store;
Twas one soe innocent, yt he durst trust
Those whom his owne experience knew unjust;
Twas one yt joy'd to dy when few could live,
A Better Reason to desire to live:
Boldly hee look'd on death, and smil'd, yet wept,
Showers of Repentant Teares for sin so slept.
Memento Mori.

Thomas Jeaye, upon the death of Ann, his Wife, who dyed the 11 day of Sept. A. D. 1612, Leaving beehinde her XI Children, 5 Sonnes VI Daughters.

The joy of Jeaye is gonne from world's woe
To heavenly Joy and happie rest,
But left some Joyes, her deerest Joy to cheere,
Amidst his cares in sad and pensive brest.

Arms—Argent, on a chevron, sable, a sun in full glory between three lions' heads erased, gules; impaling, quarterly, first and fourth a bend, ermine, between two eagles displayed, sable; second and third sable, on a chevron argent, three fleur-de-lis, gules, between three towers argent.

Argent, on a chevron, sable, a sun in full glory between three lions' heads erased, gules; impaling quarterly, first and fourth gules, two bars ermine; second and third . . . . . a lion rampant, gules.

On a Flat Stone in Nave.

Rev. Robt. Merchant, B. D. Fellow of Magdalen College, Oxford, Son of Jane and Rev. Robt. Merchant, late Rector of Fittleton, died 6 May, 1779, Aged 40.

In the North Aisle.

Near this Spot is Interred William Beach, Esq. of Neatheravon House, who departed this life on the 9th of June, 1790, Aged 70.

The remains of Ann, his Wife, who died at Oakley Hall, on the 4th of Jan. 1788, Aged 69, and are deposited in the parish Church of Dean, in the County of Southampton.

In affectionate Reverence of their Memory, Michael Hicks Beach, their Son-in-Law, and Henrietta Maria Hicks Beach, their Daughter, Erected this Monument.

This Marble is dedicated to the Memory of Henrietta Maria, the eldest Daughter of Michael Hicks Beach, Esq. and Henrietta Maria his Wife. She died June the 22, 1808, Aged 23 years.

Also of Ann, their second Daughter, who died Oct. the 15, 1802, Aged 17 years, and was buried in the Church of Witcombe, in Gloucestershire.

Also of Jane, their third Daughter, who Died Jan. the 1st, 1796, Aged 9 years, and was Interred at Low Layton, in the County of Essex.

And Likewise of William and Charles, who died Infants.

Register began 1623.

ALTON PRIOR.

On a Brass Plate in Chancel.

This was but One, though taking Room for three,
Religion, Wisdom, Hospitalitie:
But since Heave̅ Gate to Enter by is straight,
His Fleashes Burdẽ Heere he left to wait,
Til ye last Trum̃pe blow opẽ ye wide Gate,
To give it entrac̃e To ye Soule its mate.

Williã Button, Esq. Dying A. Dñi, 1590, Æt. 64, left by his Wife Mary, Daugh. to Sir Wm. Kallwey, Knt. VI Sons, Ambrose, Knt. Wm. who Married Jane, Daughter to John Lambe, of Coulstõ, John, Francis, Edward, and Henry, 2 Daughters, Dorothea, married to John Drake, of moñt Drake, in the County of Devõ, Esq. & Cecilie, Married to Sir Sir Tho. Mewys, of Kingstõ, in the Isle of Wight, Knight.

Erected by Sir William Button, Knight, Grand Child to the first William, and Sonne and heire to the latter, in pious Memory.

On a Flat Stone in Chancel.

Here Lyeth the Body of John Smith, Esq. who died August the 8th, 1742, Aged 31 years.

Also near this Place lyeth the Body of Dela River Smith, Wife of the above-named, who died Nov. the 23d, 1728, Aged 34.

Arms—On a fess three fleur-de-lis between as many saltires, annulets for difference, over all an escutcheon; quarterly, first and fourth manche; second and third three quarterfoils.
Crest—An ostrich holding a horse-shoe.

On Flat Stones in Nave.

Underneath are laid the remains of Wm. Hitchcock, who departed this life March 3, 1812, Aged 66 years.

In Memory of Elizabeth Hitchcock, who died Nov. 4, 1786, Aged 76 years.

In Memory of Sarah Hitchcock, who Died Dec. 14, 1769, Aged 54 years.

Here lyeth ye Body of William Hitchcock. He died Sept. 20, 1730, Aged 60.

ALTON BARNES.

In Chancel Window.

William Lamplugh, Grandson to Archbishop, Lam̄ Prebendary of Lincoln, and Rector of this Parish, &c. Ob. 2 Nov. 1737, Æt. 37. He Rebuilt the Parsonage House, and upon which account this Memorial was put by Anne, his Wife, Daughter of J. Smith, D. D. Provost of Qu. Coll. Oxon.

Arms—Or, a cross fleury sable, impaling, azure, a tower argent, on a chief or, three storks' heads erased, gules.
Crest—A goat's head erased, argent, horns, or.

Flat Stones.

Of Sarah, Wife of George William Crowe, Esq. who died 14 June, 1814, Aged 43 years.

Here Lyeth ye Body of Francis Skull, Gent. late of this Parish. He was a person of great Probity, strict justice, and universal Charity. In all exercises of Devotion, he was uniform and regular, and in doing every act of Kindness and Benevolence, Constant and Persevering. As these amiable Qualities made him beloved by Every one that knew him, so his Death could not but cause much grief in them for the loss of so good a Christian and Neighbour. He Died April 27, 1735, In the 66 year of his Age.

Arms—A fess charged with a chaplet, between three billetts; a crescent, for difference.

On Flat Stones in Body.

Here lies the Body of Robert Reeks, Gent. who died August 29, 1743, Aged 75 years.

At the foot of this Stone lies the Body of Jane, the Wife of Robert Reeks, Obiit the 20 Day of August, 1761, Aged 87.

In Memory of William Stone, sen. who Died August ye 20th, 1716, Aged 75.

Also Elizabeth, his Wife, Died March ye 1, 1748-9, Aged 95.

Also William Stone, Son of William and Elizabeth Stone, died July the 27th, 1751, Aged 65 years.

Elizabeth Stone, Wife of William Stone, Jun. died April the 12, 1785, Aged 79.

On a Monument in Nave.

H. S. E.

Elizabeth, Daughter of Thomas and Mary Chandler, who died Sept. 27th, 1785.

Thomas Chandler, who died June 12, 1790, Aged 62.

Mary Chandler, who died Sept. 15th, 1800, Aged 82.

Warner South, Rector Altonensis, non incelebris, Ecclesiæ Cathedralis Wellensis Prebend. Novi Coll. Socius, Hic juxta situs est. Natus . . . .

Denatus est { A° X^{ti} 1652. / Ætatis suæ 66.

Morbo Correptus et senectute, sed jam dat. lapis quam noller lectus quietem; spe Resurgendi.

Etiam hic provoto suo jacet Elizabetha, conjux pia, Obiit A° X^{ti} 1677.

Libros habuere { Elizabetham et Warnerum, } qui ut utriq. justa facere

Marcus, hæc Parentavit, A° Dom. 1677.

H. S. E.

Gulielmus Budd, L. L. B. Quondam Novi Coll. Oxon Socius, et hujus Eccl. Rector. Qui obiit . . Die Sept. Anno Dom. 1685, Ætatis 56.

Against the West End of the Church.

Underneath are Deposited the Remains of the Rev. Nicholas Preston, A. M. 40 years Rector of this Parish, who Departed this life Dec. 16, 1777, Aged 77.

The Warden of New College, Oxford, is the Lord of the Manor.

The Rev. William Crowe, LL. B. Rector.

Register commenced 1593.

There were no persons interred either in the Church or Churchyard from the year 1592 to 1602.

PATNEY.

On a Monument in the North Wall of the Chancel.

Sacred to the Memory
of
Thomas Noyes Lewis,
late of Wedhampton, Gent.
who Departed this Life 5th April, 1811,
Aged 51 years.

John Lewis, late of Devizes, Gent. who Departed this Life 8th May, 1814, Aged 46 years.

South Wall.

To the Memory of
Mrs. Eliza Cookson,
Wife of the Rev. Mr. Cookson,
and Daughter of Mr. Richard Bull, Druggist,
of Ludgate Hill, London.
She Died Sept. 21, 1755.
Her Faith was Humble, her Piety Sincere,
her Charity Universal.

On a Flat Stone in Chancel.

Underneath
lyeth the Body of
George Lewis,
And of Mary, his Wife.
She died April 7th, 1779,
Aged 53 years.
He died Jan. 9th, 1786,
Aged 78 years.

Also of
George Lewis, Jun.
who Departed this Life
ye 3rd of July, 1799,
Aged 35 years.

And of Sophia Ford Lewis,
Daughter of George Lewis,
Jun. and Ann, his Wife,
who Departed this Life 10 April, 1807,
In the 16 year of her Age.

On a small Monument against S. Wall of Nave.

Near this Place Lyeth ye Body of
Robert, ye Son of William and Mary
Hayward,
of Marden,
who departed this life the 9th of Sept. 1722,
Aged 28 years.

Opposite the Gallery, in the South Wall.

Near this Place
lies interred ye Body
of Mr. Robert Amor,
who died July the 4th,
1740,
In the 66 year of his Age.

In the East Window of Chancel is a little painted glass, V. O. and G. In the South Wall is a piscina.

The Rev. Richard Cutler, Rector.

LAVERSTOKE.

On a white marble monument against the north wall of Chancel.

Near this Place lieth the Body of Peter Bathurst, late of Clarendon Park, in this County, Esq. a man well worthy of imitation both in public and in private life. In private life a lover of letters and liberal knowledge, affectionate and affable to a numerous Family, by all of whom he was respected and beloved, a master of that economy, which, while it kept him free, enabled him at once to be both generous and just. In public life a lover of his Country, which he long and faithfully served in Parliament, under different reigns and different administrations, without seeking, or even expecting, any other reward, than the honest consciousness of having acted as became him. He was twice married: first to Leonora Maria, sole Daughter and Heiress of Charles How, of Grytworth, in the County of Northampton, Esq. by whom he left two Daughters; and, secondly, to the Lady Selina Shirley, one of the Daughters of Robert Earl of Ferrars, by whom he left five Sons, and ten Daughters. He died the 25th Day of April, 1748, Aged Sixty-two years.

His Widow, the Lady Selina, hath erected this Monument, being desirous, as far as possible, to perpetuate his memory when the living witnesses of his virtues are no more.

Arms—Sable, two bars, ermine, in chief three cross pattee or, a crescent above, of the same, on an escutcheon or, a fess sable, between three wolves' heads, couped, of the same; impaling, quarterly, first and fourth, paley of six, or and sable, a canton, ermine; second and third quarterly, France and England.

On Flat Stones in Chancel.

Here Lyeth Buried the Body of Nathaniell Marshall, Gent. who deceased ye 7th Day of August, Anno Dom. 1698, in the 78 year of his Age.

.... Lyeth Jane, ye Wife of Thos. Safe, who dyed August ye 20th, 1706, Aged 33.

Against North Wall of the Body.

Here Lyeth the Body of William Fawkoner, of Westbury, Esquire, in the County of South. Deceased xx March, Anno Dom. 1644, Ætatis suæ 82.

On a Brass Plate.

Off Yor charite p^y^ for the Soul of Antony Ernley, esquier, and Margarett, his Wyfe, which Antony Decessid the 17 Day of November, An. Dom. 1530, on who^s^ Soule Jhu have mrc̃y.

Against South Wall of the Body.

Sacred to the Memory of Catherine Burrough, Late of Andover, Spinster, who died the 22d Day of February, 1813, Aged 58 years. She was the Daughter of Thomas Burrough, Gent. and Catherine his Wife, formerly of this Parish.

On Flat Stones in Body.

Here Lieth the Body of James Dyer, of London, who departed this Life Dec. 1st, 1786.

Sacred to the Memory of Mary Duval, who died May 30th 1813, Aged 70 years.

Hatchment in the Chancel.

Sable, two bars ermine, in chief three cross pattee or, on an escutcheon, azure, a chevron, or, between three two-headed eagles displayed, of the same, two in chief, one in base.

Extracts from the Parish Register.

[Marriages.]

1729, April 20th. *John Burrough = Ann Martyn of Sarum.

1777, Oct. 20. Thos. Carey, y^e^ younger, of the Island of Guernsey = Elizabeth Burrough, by Licence.

[Burials.]

1734, *John Burrough, Jan. Ann Burrough Aug. 17.
1748, April 30, Peter Bathurst, Esq.
1748, Jan. 18, Catherine Burrough.
1750, Feb. 13, Thos. son of Mr. Thomas Burrough.
1759, April 9, Thomas Burrough.
1762, Sept. 7, Mrs. Mary Burrough.
1762, Dec. 14, Elizabeth Burrough.
1770, April 4, Catharine, wife of Mr. Thos. Burrough.
1770, Dec. 21, The Lady Selina Bathurst.
1779, Nov. 1, The Lady Bathurst Cooper.
1781, Jan. 17, Mr. James Burrough.
1784, Sept. 25, Mr. Thomas Burrough.

[Baptisms.]

1754, Sept. 22, Catherine d. of Mr. Thomas and Catherine Burrough.

1757, March 12, Thos. s. of Mr. Thos. and Catherine Burrough.

Thos. Burrough, Gent of Laverstoke, Wilts. = Catherine.
- Thomas, a Judge of the Court of .... b. at Laverstock, 1757.
- Catherine. b. 1754.

2d. Selina Shirley d. of Robert, Earl Ferrars, died 1770. = Pet. Bathurst, Esq. of Clarendon Park, b. 1686, d. 1748. = 1. Leonora Maria, d. & sole h. of Ch. How, of Grytworth, co. Northampton, Esq.
- Five Sons, Ten Daughters.
- Daug. Daug.

WEST HARNHAM.

On small Tablets by the north wall of Chancel.

In Memory of Maria Kirkman, Widow of John Kirkman, Esq. late Alderman, and one of the Representatives in Parliament for the City of London. Died 8th Dec. 1805, Aged 63 years.

To the Memory of Maria and Ann Kirkman, whose short Lives exhibited the true loveliness of the Female Character under the influence of Virtue and Religion. Maria died Dec. 4th, 1791, Aged 22 years. Ann Died June 28th, 1799, Aged 28 years.

On Flat Stones in Chancel.

Here Lyeth the Body of Mr. Charles Riley, who dyed the 5th Day of May, An° Dom. 1688.

Flat Stones in Chancel.

Heare Lyeth Buried Mary, the Wife of Stephen Bowman, Gent. who Departed this Life the sixteenth Day of December, 1644.

Here Lieth the Body of Mr. John Chappel, Prebend of Coumb and Harnham. He died the 17th of August, 1672.

Here Lyeth ye Body of Robert Chappell, Gent. ye Son of John Chappell, who departed this Life ye 11th of Dec. 1709, Aged 72 years.

M. S.

Isabell Langley, Wife of John Langley, Departed This Life in Hope of A Better, August 2d, 1662. And also of John Langley, who Departed this Life ye 26 of October, 1709, in ye 90 year of his age.

James Hussey Died Dec. 18, 1805, Aged 5 months.

On Flat Stones in Body.

Here Lyeth the Body of Mr. William Turner, who departed this Life ye 28th Day of May, Anno Dom. 1699, Ætat. suæ 61.

On the Right hand Lyeth the Body of Mary, ye Wife of the said William Turner, who Departed this Life the 11th of March, A° Dom. 1700, Aged 73.

H. S. E.

Here Lyeth ye Body of Mr. Charles Turner, Youngest Sonne of Mr. William Turner, and Mary, his Wife, who Departed this Life ye 9th Day of Nov. Anno Dom. 1691, Ætat. suæ 20.

Elizabeth Bates Buried January ye 17 Day, 1684.

On Flat Stones in S. Aisle.

Here Lyeth Buried the Body of Edward Blacker, Esq. Eldest Sonne and Heir of William Blacker, Late of the Close, of Sarum, Esq. Obiit nono Die Augusti, 1658.

Here Lieth the Body of Wil. Blacker, the younger Sonne of Will. Blacker, Esq. Deceased, who was Buried the 22d day of August, in the year of our Lord 1645.

On a Hatchment against N. Wall of Chancel.

In Memoriam laudabilis viri Stephani Bowman, Generosi, humaniter mortui divinitus Coronatt, Anno Domini 1659, Martij die 23, Ætat. 78.

Arms—Or, a chevron, gules, between three bows of the same, impaling gules, a bend of the limb of a tree, raguly and trunked, argent.

On a Hatchment by the south wall of Nave.

Here under Lieth Buried the Body of John Younge, Esquire, Ætatis suæ 55, Died the second Day of September, 1659.

Arms—Or, a chevron, ermine, between three profile heads, sable; impaling, gules, a fess, ermine, between two wolves passant, argent.

Register commenced 1568.

Rev. Francis Baker, Vicar.

NETHERHAMPTON.

Margaret, the Wife of John Gauntlett, Esq. Dyed May ye 22d, 1674.

Margaret, Daughter of John Gauntlett, Esq. Dyed August ye 17, 1678.

John Gauntlett, Esq. eldest Son of William Gauntlett, Dyed April ye 14th, 1719, Aged 75.

William Gauntlett, Gent. Dyed May ye 11th, 1690.

Margery, Late Wife of William Gauntlett, Gent. Dyed August ye 31st, 1687.

Gauntlett Fry, Esq. Youngest Son of Robert Fry, of Bruton, in the County of Somerset, Gent. Dyed May ye 7th, 1746.

Margaret, the Wife of Gauntlett Fry, Esq. died March ye 10th, 1744.

Susannah, the Widow and Relict of Robert Fry, of Bruton, in Somersetshire, Gent. second Daughter of William Gauntlett, Gent. Dyed March ye 21, 1715, Aged 69.

Catharine, eldest Daughter of William Gauntlett, Gent. Dyed June ye 10th, 1713, Aged 70.

Sarah Sharp, the Widow and Relict of the Rev. Mr. Thos. Sharp, and Eldest Daughter of Robert Fry, of Bruton, in the County of Somerset, Gent. Died Feb. ye 8th, 1740.

Mrs. Susannah Sharp, Daughter of the Rev. Mr. Thos, Sharp, Died April 1st, 1708, Aged 62.

On flat stones in the Body.

Here Lyeth the Body of Elizabeth, Widdow of James Cobham, Rector of Patney, in this County, and third Daughter of William Gauntlett, Gent. who departed this Life the 3d of May, 1718, in the 70th Year of her Age.

Catharina, Filia Johannis Gauntlett . . . Margaretæ uxoris . . . . quæ Maij 15 23 Die, Anno Dom. 1672.

Here Lyeth ye Body of Mrs. Susanna Bayley, who Dyed December ye 9th, 1716.

Hatchments in the Chancel.

Quarterly, first and fourth gules, three horses in pale, argent, second and third gules, a chevron, argent, between three gauntlets on an escutcheon of the same.

Crest—A dexter hand holding a sword pierced through a profile head.

N. Wall of Chancel.

Gules, a chevron, argent, between three gauntlets of the same.

ON A SHIELD.

Gules, a chevron between three gauntlets, argent, an escutcheon of pretence of the same, on a chief, sable, two mullets of the first; impaling argent, on a chief, sable, two mullets argent.

SHIELD.

Gules, a chevron between three gauntlets, argent, an escutcheon of pretence, gules, a lion rampant, argent; impaling gules, a lion rampant, argent.

Register began 1767.

Henry Hetley, Vicar.

BRITFORD.

On Flat Stones in Chancel.

In Memory of Richard Jervoise, Esq. who Departed this Life March 17th, 1762, Ætat. 58.

Also, in Memory of Ann, his Wife, who Departed this Life Sept. 25, 1756, Ætat. 47.

In Memory of Master Richard Jervoise, who Departed this Life May ye 11th, 1745, Aged 7 years, Fourth Son of Richard Jervoise, Esq. and Ann, his Wife. Also of Mr. Thomas Jervoise, who Departed this Life April 3d, 1755, Aged 18 years, their Eldest Son.

H. S. E.

Gulielmus Powell, A. M. Ecclesiæ hujus per An. 39 Vicarius, nec non paroch: de Langford Parva Rector. Obiit 5to Julii, A. D. 1719, Ætatis suæ 72.

Here Lyeth the Body of Rebecca, Wife of William Powell, and Daughter of John Newham, Rector of West Dean, who dyed of the Small pox, Nov. the 25th, 1742, in the 87 year of her Age.

In Memory of Mrs. Elizabeth Cocker, who Departed this Life October the 1st, 1737, Aged 65 years.

Arms—Within a border ingrailed, on a bend, three tigers' heads caboshed.

Here Lyeth the Body of the Rev. Mr. Francis Powell, Late Rector of Stanton St. Quintin, and Prebendary of the Cathedral Church of Sarum, Son of the Rev. Mr. William Powell, and Rebeccah his Wife. He Dyed ye 6 of Dec. 1758, Aged 61 years.

Here Lyeth the Body of Mrs. Ely Cooe, who Departed this Life April 13, 1710, Aged 44 years.

Here also Lyeth the Body of Thomas Cooe, the Son of John, and Ely Cooe his Wife, who Departed this Life Feb. ye 6th, 1706.

Here also Lyeth the Body of Mr. John Cooe, who Departed this Life October the 9th, A. D. 1719, Aged 52 years.

Here also Lyeth Elizabeth, Wife of John Cooe, who Died Jan. ye 20th, 1760, Aged 74 years.

Here Lyeth ye Body of Ann, the Wife of Mr. John Venables, who died ye 1st of April, 1702.

Here Lyeth the Body of Mr. John Venables, who Departed this Life the 10th Day of March, 1694, Aged 88 years.

In Memory of Mr. Robt. Powell, Late Alderman of ye City of New Sarum. Ob. Mar. 29th, 1765, Ætat. 73.

Also of Mrs. Ann Powell. Ob. Feb. 21st, 1766, Ætat. 65.

On a Flat Stone under the Tower.

Under this Stone are Deposited the Remains of James Neave, Esq. of Nunton, near this Parish. He died September 18th, 1794, Aged 63 years..

Here also Lie the Remains of Mrs. Hannah Neave, Relict of James Neave, Esq. She died March 3d, 1819, Aged 86 years.

In the North Transept.

In Memory of Mary, Relict of the Rev. James Foster, whose whole Life exhibited a laudable example of Charity, Piety, and every other Christian Virtue. She Died Jan. 16, 1809, in the 87 Year of her Age.

In Memory of the Rev. James Foster, Clerk, Vicar of this Parish 15 years, who died Oct. 2d, 1787, Aged 49 years.

On Flat Stones in Body.

Here Lyeth ye Body of Mr. Robert Edmonds, who Dyed ye 24 Day of Feb. 1689, Aged 77 years.

H. S. E.

Henricus Edmonds, Civ. Novi Sarum Aldermannus,
Obijt undecmo die Dec. Anno { Ætat. suæ 63. Dom. 1795.

Henricus Edmonds, Clericus,
filius Hen. Edmonds,
Obijt Decmo quinto die Decbris
Anno { Ætat. sua . . Dom. 1708.

Mary Edmonds, Wife of Alderman Edmonds, dyed ye 13 of Dec. 1714, Aged 70 years.

In Memory of William and Mary Ann Randell, Son and Daughter of William Randell, Late of Longford Farm, who both Died in their Infancy.

Rowland, Son of John and Ann Newman, died Feb. 7th, 1788, Aged 17 months.

Likewise, Rowland their Son, who died Jan. 30th, 1791, Aged 17 months.

In the West Porch.

. .

. . .

On a small Monument by the north wall of Body.

Sacred to the Memory of John Newman, Gent. who Died 2d July, 1806, Aged 63 years.

Also of Ann, his Wife, who died 24 August, 1793, Aged 40 years.

On a Monument in the North Aisle.

Deo optimo Maximo Munificentissimo,
hoc grati animi sui, et suorum, qualecunque sit, testimonium, prope cellas cineribus accipiendas destinatas, poni curavit Jacob, Comes Radnoriæ, eò quod familiæ suæ, præter quæ universo hominum generi libenter præstitit, peculiaria insuper indulsit beneficia, quam fidei reformatæ causâ patriâ exulantem, fortunis carentem, contumeliis objectam, in hac terra libertatis, tum in rebus sacris, tum civicis domicilio, providè locaverit, et divitiis continuò, non ex fraude, non ex peculatu, non cum mentis integræ, aut famæ injuriâ, sed e commercio felici, ex nuptiis uberibus, atque testamenta facientum liberalitate conquisitis, necnon honoribus postremò, atque sede magnates inter Britannicos hæreditariâ ditaverit, foverit, adauxerit, quam denique, sic extrinsecus curantem divino auxilio nec permiserit carare, nec tamen abuti voluerit absit, ut favor numinis, tam propitius abstrahatur, sed præsertim absit, ut beneficiorum, quæ tanta jamjam percepta fuerint, animo grata excidat memoria. Radnor, 1777.

Hatc ments against the North Wall of Chancel.

No I. Quarterly, first and fourth sable, a chevron, argent, between three eagles displayed, of the same; second and third argent, on a fess, sable, between three falcons azure, a tigers' head caboshed, or, between two mullets of the same.

Crest—A wolf's head erased sable, tongue gules.

II. Quarterly: first and fourth sable, a chevron, argent, between three eagles' displayed, of the same; second quarterly, first and fourth azure, three stirrup-irons, or; second and third sable, three argent, over all an escutcheon, azure, on a chevron, or, three cinquefoils, gules, a canton, ermine.

III. Quarterly, first and fourth sable, a chevron, argent, between three eagles displayed, of the same; second and third gules, fretty of argent.

IV. Quarterly, first and fourth sable, a chevron, argent, between three eagles displayed, of the same: second and third, sable, three swords pointing in base, argent; on an escutcheon, quarterly, first and fourth argent, on a fess, sable, between three falcons, azure, a tiger's head caboshed, or, between two mullets of the same; second and third or, a chevron, sable, between three eagles, displayed, of the same; impaling, the same as the escutcheon.

Register began 1589.

William Crane Vicar in the year 1662.
William Richards, late Vicar.
Rev. Mr. Morris present oue.

ALDERBURY.

On a Monument against the north wall of Chancel.

In Memory of Thos. Stringer, Esq. of Ivy Church, who Departed this life May 6th, Anno Dom. 1702, Aged 63 years.

Also in Memory of Jane, first Wife to Thomas Stringer, Esq. Late Wife of Jon. Hill, of Cholderton, who Dyed July ye 17th, 1740, Aged 89 years.

She opened her mouth with wisdom, and in her tongue was the law of kindness.

Mark the perfect man, and behold the uprighht, for ye end of yt man is peace.

Against the North Wall of Chancel.

ANNO DOMI · 1612.

On the outside, opposite, in 1814, a stone coffin was found, deposited perhaps at that time, and to which the above date may refer.

Arms—Barry of eight, or and gules, on a chief azure, three escallops, or; impaling, argent, on a bend, gules, cottised, three lozenges, ermine. [R. G. M.

On Flat Stones in Chancel.

Here Lyeth the Body of Robert Pinckney, Gent. who dyed Sept. 20th, 1721, Aged 84.

Here the wicked cease from troubling,
Here the weary be at rest.

Arms—A fess loz.

Here Lyeth the Body of Elizabeth, Wife of Stepʰ Bungey, who Departed this Life Nov. the 9th, 1756, Aged 38.

Here Lyeth the Body of Stephen Bungey, who died May 14, 1758, Aged 43 years.

Against North Wall of Body.

In Memory of Mr. Robert Moody, who died Feb. 16th, 1754, Aged 51 years.

Also, of Susannah, his Wife, who died October 16th, 1764, Aged 56 years.

On a flat stone in the Body.

Sacred to the Memory of Mr. John Best,
who died 18th Nov. 1805, Aged 46.

Hugh Stephens, present Vicar.

Earl of Radnor Lord of the Manor.

WEST GRIMSTEAD.

H. S. E.

Gulielmus Hyde, Gent. obiit 7mo die Junii, Anno Dom. 1691.

Here Lyeth the Body of Christopher Ew...d, of Clarendon Park, who died Sept. 7th, 1700, Aged 59 years.

Also Mary, the Wife of Christopher..... who Died June ye 11th, 1685, Aged 46 years.

Against ye North wall, Underneath this Monument, Lyeth the Body of William Hebbard, who Departed this Life October 15th, 1792, Aged 40 years.

Kind angels guard his sleeping Dust,
Till Christ doth come to call the Just,
Then may he wake with sweet surprise,
And in our Saviour's Image rise.

Underneath, near this Monument, lieth the Body of Hannah, Wife of William Hebbard, who Departed this Life January 10th, 1809, Aged 66 years.

Against west end of North Aisle.

In Memory of John Hayter, who Dyed March ye 15, 1755, Aged 76 years.

On a Flat Stone in North Aisle.

The Eternal Memory of Walter Hayter, of Witherington Farm, Gent. who, to his owne everlasting Gaine, tho' to Great Loss of ye Poore, & All Good Men, by Impartial Death was taken hence the 24th of April, Anno Dom. 1681, Aged 63.

On a Flat Stone in Body.

Here Lyeth ye Body of Henery Hayter, of Claringdon Parke, who Departed this Life ye 2d of Feb. Anno Dom. 1666, Aged 45.

Hatchment in the Chancel.

Azure, on a chevron, or, a crest, sable, between three loz. or.

In 1798, the Rev. Mr. Wells, Rector.

Rev. Joseph Griffith Late Rector.

Rev. Mr. Stranway present Rector.

WEST DEAN.

Against the North Wall of Chancel.

M. S.

Johannis Evelin, A.R. patris merito colendi, ac Elizabetha, uxoris suæ, matris pariter venerandæ Georgius Evelin, filius natu maximus, dedicavit: Hæc obiit Septimo Die Maii, Aõ: 1625, Ætat. suæ Sexagesimo: ille decimo secundo.

I heard a voyce from Heaven, saying, write From Henceforth Blessed are the Dead which Dye in the Lord, even so sayth the Spirit, that they rest from their Labours, and their workes Followeth them. Apoca. chap. 14, v. 13.

Arms—Quarterly, first and fourth azure, a griffin passant, argent, a chief of the same: impaling argent, two bars azure, between six martlets of the same 3 2 1.

South Wall.

Hic jacet Elizabetha Tirell, filia Georgii Evelyn, Armig. uxor. Johannis Tirell, de Heron, militis, comitatu Essexiæ, ivnioris, qui propter pietatem erga Devm, et fidelem amorem erga maritum, hoc erexit monumentum, ad perpetuam memoriam unicam reliquit filiolam Elizabetham, colin puerperio mœrens tamquam rara Phœnix vitam dedit, A. D. 1629.

Arms—Two chevrons, argent, within a border ingrailed gules, impaling, a chief or, in fess argent, a griffin passant, or, in base azure, on three bars, argent, as many martlets on each, azure.

On Flat Stones in Chancel.

H. S. E.

Abrahamus Francke, S.T.P. hujusce Ecclesiæ Rector, nec non in Ecclesiâ Sarisburiensi Præbendarius, Serenissimis Princibus Georgio 1mo et 2do Capellanus, et SStæ Trinitatis Collegij apud Cantabrigienses olim Socius. Obijt 1o die Sept. 1733, Ætat. suæ 48.

Nathaniel Francke, A. M. frater Abri Francke, non longius abhinc jacet sepultus. Obijt 16o Martii, 1727, Ætat. suæ 30.

Arms—A saltire ingrailed, on an escutcheon, a chevron; in chief two fleur-de- is, in base a tower imbattled.

Here Lyeth the Body of Mrs. Anne Sloper, Daughter of ye Reverend Mr. Walter Sloper, who Departed this Life March the 7th, 1722.

Here Lyeth the Body of Mrs. Elizabeth Sloper, the Daughter of Mr. Walter Sloper, Rector of this Place, and Anne his wife, who Dyed Jan. 24th, 1698, in the 12th year of her Age.

Also near this Place Lyeth ye Body of Mrs. Anne Sloper, wife of Walter Sloper, Rector of this Parish, who Dyed Oct. ye 12th, 1700.

Walter, ye Son of Walter Sloper, Rector, and Anne, his wife, who Dyed August ye 24th, 1702, Aged 17.

Walter Sloper, M.A. Rector of this Parish, who Dyed June the 1st, 1714, Aged 61.

On Flat Stones in Body.

Here Lyeth the Body of Mary Emmott, who died June 23d, 1790, Aged 48 years.

Here is Buried Dorothy, Wife of Mr. Phillip Emmott, who died Nov. 20th, 1779, Aged 74 years.

Also Richard, their Son, who died Sept. 16, 1765, Aged 26 years.

In Memory of Rachel Emmott, who Departed this Life April the 21st, 1794, Aged 47 years.

Here Lyeth the Body of Phillip Emmott, who died Feb. 26, 1786, Aged 45 years.

Here Lyeth the Body of Richard Emmott, who died August 14, 1735, Aged 56 years.

Here also Lieth Phillip Emmott, his Son, who Died May 2nd 1779, Aged 61 years.

Against South Wall of S. Aisle.

In Memory of William Brooke, who died Jan. 7th, 1799, Aged 57 years.

Also of Ann, his Wife, who died Nov. 29th, 1802, Aged 43 years.

And also of William Brooke, Son of the above William Brooke, who died Feb. 8th, 1813, Aged 37 years.

Arms—Or, a cross ingrailed, gules and sable.

Mon. of White Marble.

P. M.

Of Sir John Evelyn, of West Deane, in ye County of Wilts.

Here Lyes {what, Reader, thou shalt seek in vaine
In other tombs,} a Long liv'd happy man ;
Whose mind and Body kept so just a pace
Thro' all ye various turnings of his Race,
That neither fail'd : till ye Soul went away,
His sence remain'd, and Death out run decay.
To him ye Great, To him ye meane repair'd,
Th' one's Adviser, and the other's Guard:
Peace by him dwelt, 'twas his delightfull toyl
To make New Friends, and Foes to reconcile,
And what he taught he did himselfe commende,
Kind to his Foes, and Faithfull to his Friends ;
In publick and in Private Acts of Love,
Such as He now a Saint exerts above,
His Life was spent, And when Late Death
Sent welcom summons for his breath,
Zeal bore him upward, and his Active minde,
Broke out in Prayer, and Left his Dust behind,
26th Day of June, in ye yeare 1685, & of his Age 84.

This being erected by his Beloved Daughter, ye Honorable Mrs. Elizabeth Pierrpont.

Arms—A griffin passant.

Mon. of White Marble. 

For this Then (quitting other Tendernesses)
Darte a Prayer,—Drop a Teare,
You yt Read, & you yt Heare,
And never think yt Long Life Here is All,
Shrubs stand Contemn'd when Cedars for us fall.
Deceas'd April ye 26, in ye year of Our Lord 1669, His Age 35.

Nec vilius ipsum,
Lugeri voluit Conjux mœstissima, E. P.

Of Robert Pierrpont,
Eldest Son of the Hon. William, Esq.
And Heire to the whole Family.

The Bodie,

Which yet as one of her worst Enemies the
Soule yt dwelt int, did as twere despise, At
Thirty Five, when grown full Ripe for Action,
Then She Forsooke It, if not unkindly, saye
Untimely, too Readily, too Soon ;
So some Suns are over cast at Noone.
Yet twas Deriv'd frome High and Noble Stocke,
Crown'd wth an Earledome on Eyther side,
There of Shrewsbury, of Kingston here stood
Heire Apparent unto. This had in its Veines,
Beside ye Blood of Both, their Seminal,
Their Bullion Vertues, too readie Coynable
Into Exploits as Greate as Eyther Ancestor's
Had, but Occasion Call'd, wch was (and was
The only thing yt was) Here wanting—

Healthie and sound, It Pass'd thro' Italie, & France,
& Spaine, Un-mutilated, Un-Diseased,
Without ye Marks of Sin, or Chance,
Return'd Match'd wth a Ladye
Of whom, Though all Good might,
Nothing must here be said,
Se Vaults spake not ye Living, but ye Dead,
Yet This, To parte with Her alone,
I Over heard, was that expiring Grone ;
Both Great Examples, never to Refuse
In Matches what wise Parents chuse.
Blest with Five Hopefull Childeren, Eache enough
To Enrich ye Future Age, & To Invite
A body's Longer Staye in this, if ought
Might doet :

But

Thus It was, Too big For It
The Soule was grown, & Soules once fit
To Mount at Heaven's Call,
Soone Let ye Mantle of ye Bodies fall :
So was, & so did, This.

A Soule

That had Great Parts, & many very Singular,
Of a Nature in All most sweete & Obliging,
Of a very Generous & Cleare Temper,
Perfectly Loyal to 's Prince in all Sub & Supra ....
euer Pre-Judging for Authoritie :
Of Great Reverence & Pietie to 's Parents,
Of a most entire Affection to 's Wife,
Of Great Indulgence unto his Children,
Of Unmovable Constancy to his Friend,
Learned, much beyond ye Gentlemen of his Age,
in Language & Arts, chiefly Mathematical,
Spake Little, but to Purpose, Could not Chide,
Suffered in its Displeasure more than did,
Observ'd Things well, Not to Find Fault but Praise,
Look'd through Men, yea Nations, quickly spi'd
The Talent uppermost in Eache, Got That. [having
Religion It had Plac'd in highest Top o'th Spirit, &^
[ances
Many seene, The Best reserving, yet Inferior observ-^
[so prizing
for any Person, Thing, or Rite, yt shew'd like sacred,^
All about Devotion, as not to slight Its shaddow.

A most Candid Interpreter of all Men's Actions, hardly
Speaking Ill of Any, Though Ill deserving;
Infirmities It had, (Who not?) of Malice None,
Of Frailtie Some, wch still It selfe did own wthout Disguise,
Without Defense, but never wthout Revenge upon It selfe
in Penances of greate retirmts prayer, study, & spare dyet,
Whom nothing could prevaile with to speake an untruth, nor
any Advantag engage in an Unhandsome Actione,
Would doe no Wrong, nor if foreseen Suffer, being
guarded wth a prudence often to Prevent it, ever wth
a Courage yt dar'd to be Honest agt all Terrors, [Death
Above Feares, Greifes, or any Cowing Passion, Fac'd‸
familiarly, & Unconcern'd Discours'd of It, Shew'd
Such Patience & Passive Valoe ith Cutting off
his Legg, as was to Admiration.

A Soule (in fine)
Of Qualities, as well as Make, Divine,
Wch soaring Thus up to these skirts of Glory
Was quickly caught up Higher, & Left Here
The yet Unperfect Flesh, to be Matur'd
For Glory too, gainst a (Hop'd) Joint-Glorious
Resurrection.

Arms—Argent, a lion rampant, sable, between eight cinquefoils, gules, in chief, on a crescent, sable, a label, or,

Benefactions

To the Parishes of West Dean and East Grimstead.

Sir John Evelyn, by Will, Dated March 5th, 1684, bequeathed the sum of Twenty Pounds, charged on the Dean Estate for ever, payable annually on St. Thomas' Day, and to be distributed in Money, Food, Clothing, or other Provisions, at the Discretion of the Lord of the Manor, as follows: To the Poor of the Parish of West Dean the Sum of £.8, of East Grinstead £.4, of White Parish £.4, of Broughton £.4.

Edward Thistlethwayte, Gentleman, by Will, Dated October 27th, 1730, bequeathed a Cottage and Lands, situate at East Grimstead, the Clear Rent of which to be equally Divided between the two united Parishes, and to be distributed amongst the Poor of each, who are not Relieved by their Parish, at the discretion of the Minister, Church Warden, and Overseer of West Dean.

The Rent of the above, subject to Taxes and Repairs, is now, in the present year, 1791, the sum of £.10 9*s.* 0*d.*

Register commenced 1678.

RECTORS.

Rev. Mr. Sterne, succeeded by
— Mr. Yaldon,
— Mr. Wray,
— Mr. Gum,
— Mr. Dawkins, the late R.
— Mr. Glossop, the present one.

WINTERBOURNE EARLS.

On Monuments in Chancel.

Underneath are deposited the Remains of Nicholas Elliott, Esq. who died 8th March, 1776, Aged 54 years.

He was one of his Majesty's Justices of the Peace, and deputy Lieutenant for the County of Wilts.

Likewise, of Jane Elliott, his Widow, who died 4th March, 1786, Aged 58.

Arms—Azure, a fess or, impaling gules, three escallops argent.

Sacred to the Memory of Ann Elliott, who was Born 2nd Dec. A. D. 1760, Daughter of Sir Alexander Powell, Kt. married to Nicholas Elliott, Esq. A. D. 1785, departed this Life 1st March, A. D. 1787. She was mild and Amiable, her Soul and Countenance were always serene.

Quæq. tibi Virtus et Gratia amabilis Uxor, vita imitanda vale, morte imitanda vale.

Siste, Viator,
Et tuam paulisper contemplare humanitatem,
nempe, vicini pulveris inquilini
Johannes Nicholas, Armiger, de Winterborn, comitis
in Agro Wiltoniensi.
Et Susanna, Uxor Eivs,
Hic Mortalitatis tuæ monent,
qui postquam virtutibus innumeris,
Et numerosâ prole,
{ filiis 3 / filiabus 8 } orbem ditarant
Annosque 55 Conivgali nexu feliciter complucrant,
Eorvm consortio adscripti sunt,
qui nec nubunt, nec nubuntur,
{ Hic / illa } absoluto æt. anno { 78 / 84 } { præivit / seq. est } { Dec. 9no 1644, / Martii 6to 1657 }

filii { Edwardus, / Matthæus, / Johannes, } { Aulâ / Eccl / Castris } Inclaruerunt.

Johannes, natu minor, sed fato prior, sæviente bello
civili inter armorum strepitus, in pace requiescit.
Matthæus, purpurâ academicâ insignitus,
{ primo, Ecclæ Bristolensis, / Deinde, divini Pavli Londini, } Decanus,
Et Ecclæ Sarum canonicus,
multa, ab Catharorum Tyrannide passus ut intemerata
Deo regi, et Ecclæ præstaret fidem,
Rebus tandem favente Cœlo,
in melius mutatis
sub bono principe, et florente Eccla
quod maximum morienti solatium, vitam mutavit
apud Sarum { 13 Aug. 1661.

Eduardus, nascendi prærogativa, et honore primus, iu ordinem . . . equestrem relatus, et utrique Carolo a secretis, post longum cum Carolo 2do exilium, qui semper fidus adhæsit achates omnibus adversæ fortunæ procellis superstes, hoc minime mendaci monumento piæ defunctorum memoriæ prentavit, Anno 1662, Avi viator æternitatem cogita.

Arms—Argent, a fess wavy between three ravens, proper, impaling sable, a chevron, ermine, between three talbots, argent.

Flat Stones in Chancel.

Hic jacet Elizabetha Nicholas, Filia Gulielmi Fowkes, De Bulwick, in Agro Northton Matthæi Nicholas, ... depost. Ecctiæ D: Pauli Londini Decani, conjux et Relicta: quem prole quinta auxerat, e quibus quatuor supersunt, Fœmina pietate ubique notâ, in ultimis spectatâ prudentiâ, vitæ suæ muniis pari, quæ cum per Annos quinquaginta minus uxoris pariter, ac matris piæ, sepræstitisset exemplar mamillæ tandem morbo, quo per triennium summâ cum patientiâ, Laboravit Aprilis VIto cessit Anno { Ætat. suæ 73. Sal. 1673.

Arms—A fess between three ravens; impaling, a fleur-de-lis.

Siste, Viator,

H. S. E.

Joannes Elliott, L. L. Doctor Div . . . . s Sarisburiensis Cancellarius, Ecclesiæ Filius; Vir honestioris Famæ, Et qu . . m Judicibus vel optimis Lub . . . um, est et con . . gens, Amittis diminutæ Consolentiæ . . . omnia integræ, et vel in . . . . is . . . ideo dutares calluisse leges, ut ne violaret. Obiit 18 die Augusti, Anno Æra Christariæ 1670. Vale.

Arms—A fess.

H. S. E.

Elizab. uxor. Nicholai Elliott, Gen. et Filius ejus Nicholaus. Hic obiit ii. die 9bris Ætatis suæ 4 et ½, An° Dom 1680, illa obiit 5° die Xbris Ætatis suæ 30, Annoque Dom. 1680.

H. S. E.

Nicholas Elliott, Generosus, De Winterbourn Gunner, Obiit 8 die Julii, A° { Dom. 1720, Ætatis suæ xc.

Cum tot annos sancte ac tranquille, Egisset Vitamq. quam elegerat privatam suavissimæ morum comitate Æcclesiam, quam amabat pietate sincera Religionem quam cosuit, incorrupta fide adonasset, bonis omnibus sui desiderii reliquit.

Here Lyeth the Body of Susanna Nicholas, Relict of John Nicholas, who died March 6, Anno Dom. 1657.

On a Brass Plate.

Here Lieth, in the Grave of his Father, Edward Elliot, Gent. who Departed this Life 28 March, 1727, in the 93 year of his Age.

Brass Plate.

Hic jacet Mattheivs Nicholas, L. L. Dr. Di Pauli Londini Decanus, B. Mariæ Sarum Canon Residentiarius. Beatam in Christo Resurrectionem prætolans. Obijt Augusti 14, 1661.

Si noris hominem satis est in nomine honoris
Ni noris superant cætera vera fidem.

On Flat Stones in Body.

Here Lyeth the Body of Henry White, Gent. who dyed Jan. ye 10th, 171 8/9, Aged 89 years.

And also Susannah, his Wife, who died Dec. ye 21st, 1717, Aged 84 years.

And also John Gauntlet, their Grand son, who dyed November 14, 1713, Aged 25 years.

On a Brass Plate.

Here Lyeth the Body of John Elliott, Esq. who Died 19th Feb. 1733, Aged 60.

Body.	Chancel.

Hatchment.

Azure, a fess or; impaling, or, a chevron, gules, between three lion's paws, erased, of the same..

George Fort, Esq. Lord of the Manor.

Rev. Peter Harrison, Curate.

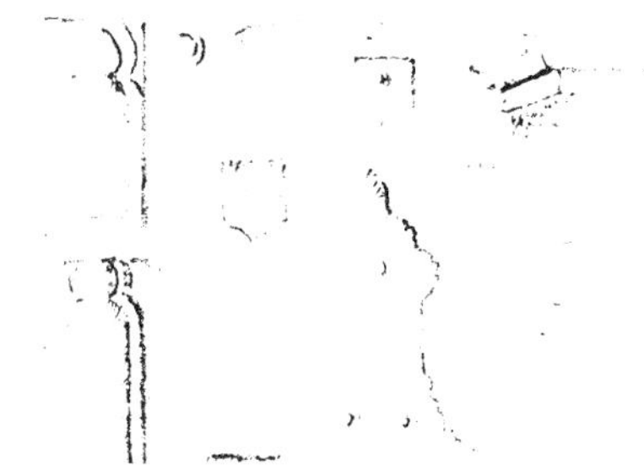

WINTERBOURNE DANTSEY.

Against the North Wall of Chancel.

This Marble is Erected by a grateful Husband, to perpetuate the Memory of Susanna Skinner, Daughter of Thomas Dyke, Lately of the City of New Sarum, Esq. the most kind, affectionate, and justly Lamented Wife of the Rev. John Skinner, D. D. Rector of Poulshot, in this County. She died Feb. 5, 1805, Aged 58.

On Flat Stones in Chancel.

Beneath lie the Remains of Mary, Wife of Thos. Dyke, Gent. of the City of New Sarum. She died Sept. 25, 1787, Aged 70.

Also the Remains of Thomas Dyke, Gent. who died Jan. 3, 1792, Aged 82.

Here Lyeth the Body of Daniel Dyke, of Woodborough, Gent. who Departed this Life March 21st, 1749, Aged 80 years.

Here Lyeth the Body of Elizabeth, wife of Daniel Dyke, of Woodborough, Gent. who departed this Life Decem. the 25, 1745, Aged 78 years.

Also the Body of William Dyke, of Sissingcut, Gent. Son of Danl & Elizth Dyke, who departed this Life April 1st, 1776, Aged 79 years.

Dl Dyke, Gent. Obiit 7th May 1791, Aged 37 years.

The Parsonage belongs to Thomas Webb Dyke.

Wadham Wyndham, Esq. Lord of the Manor.

Register commenced 1561.

WINTERBOURNE GUNNER.

Beneath the Adjoining seat repose the Ashes of Elizth, ye Wife of William Powell, of this Parish, who Expired suddenly, May the 1st, 1753.

Mens habitat Cœlum, cineres conduntur in Urnâ, Pectore sed sponsi vivit imago tui; qui rursus tandem mortali lege peractâ, hic tecum conjux optat habere locum.

At her Feet lie buried five of their Children.

On Flat Stones in Chancel.

Here Lieth the Body of Mr. Amphilles Dampny, who dyed April ye 3rd, 1733.

Here Lyeth ye Body of Mrs. Frances Clark, who died October ye 30th, 1714, Aged 87 years.

Here Lyeth ye Body of Ann, ye Wife of Henry Dampney, who died July ye 10th, Anno Dom. 1700.

Against North Wall of Body.

Sacred to the Memory of William Cusse, who died October 19th, 1814, Aged 39 years.

I fear'd not death, mark well the reason why,
He that believes in Christ shall never die.

On Flat Stones in Body.

Here Lieth the Body of Mary, ye Wife of Mathew Bee, of Winterburn Gunur, Gent. who departed this Life May ye 8th, Anno Dom. 1667.

Here Lyeth the Body of Mary, the Daughter of Mathew Bee, of Winterburn Gunner, Gentleman, who Departed this Life the 7th Day of September, in the Year of our Lord God 1661.

Here Lyeth the Body of Mr. Samuel Cusse, of Ford, in ye Parish of Winterbourn Gunner, who Died Nov. the 7th, 1734, Aged 56 years.

The Rev. Charles Coleman Late Rector.

The Rev. Mr. Coleman present Rector.

Mr. Templeman, of Whichbury, lately purchased the Lordship of the Manor of Mr. Elliott.

FARLEY.

Against North Wall of the Body.

To the Memory of Henry Thomas, Earl of Ilchester, who Died Sept. 5th, 1802, in the 56th year of his Age: and of Mary Theresa, his first Wife, Daughter of Standish Grady, Esq. of the County of Limerick, in the Kingdom of Ireland, to whom he was Married in 1772, and by which Marriage he had Eight Children, two of whom Died in Infancy, and are buried here.

By his second Marriage with Maria, third Daughter of William Digby, Dean of Durham, he had three Sons, who with their Brother Henry Stephen, the Present Earl, and their five Sisters, survive to lament the loss of a most Affectionate Father.

The purest Christian Humility was his peculiar Characteristic, from the Contemplation of which, and his many other virtues, his Widow, who thus records the Period of her severe Affliction, derives the utmost Consolation, convinced that he for whom She mourns is happy.

Against West End of Body.

To the Memory of the best of Husbands,
And the most excellent of Men,
CHARLES JAMES FOX,
who died September 13th, 1806, Aged 57,
And is buried in Westminster Abbey.
His most affectionate Wife Places this Tablet.

A Patriot's even Course he Steer'd,
Mid Faction's wildest Storms unmoved,
By all who mark'd his Mind, revered,
By all who knew his Heart, beloved.

R. Fitz-Patrick.

Hatchment.

Arms—Ermine, on a chevron, azure, three foxes heads erased, or, in chief a canton azure, charged with a fleur-de-lis, or; impaling, barry of six, or and azure, over all, on a bend sable, cottized gules, three escallops, or.

On Monuments in north Transept.

Here lies the Body of Charles Fox, Esq. second Son of the Rt Honble Sr Stephen Fox, by his first wife, which Charles was paymaster of the forces to King James, King William, and Queen Anne. He died Aged 53.

Representative in Parliament for the City of Salisbury, September 9th, 1713. He married Elizabeth Carr Trollop, sole Daughter and heire of Sir William Trollop, Baronet, of Caswick, in the County of Lincoln, which Elizabeth died March 15th, 1704, Aged 42 years, and is interred near this place.

Hic jacet Honorab Dna Dna Elizabetha Fox, Honobilis viri Stephani Fox, Eqtis aur. F. Regiis, qui Fisco nunc præsunt Curatoribus Conjux per quadraginta & quinque annos conjunctissima, quem bene multis auxit fœcunda Liberis, sed cunctis præter, qui adhuc bini supersunt immaturâ morte dudum præreptis vixit, Illa quidem, dum vixit, bene, nec vero potuit latere, sanctis in mediâ nimirum aulâ moribus, largâ erga egenos manu, et rei familiaris, tam laute provida ut, vix maritus superstes majori cum laude, aut minori cum imidia publice providerit. Decessit uno minor Septuagenariâ, Augusti II. MDCXCVI.

Arms—Ermine, on a chevron, azure, three foxes heads erased, or; in chief, on a canton, azure, a fleur-de-lis, or: impaling gules, a chevron ermine, between three talbots' heads erased, or.

Cy Gist Le Tres Honorable et Le Tres Ancien Chevalier, Sr Stephen Fox, Fondateur de Ceans, Qui Trespassa age de 90 ans, Le Vingt troisieme de Septembre, 1716.

Cy Gist La Tres Hon. Dame Christine Hope, espouse en econ de noces du tres Honorable Chevalier Etienne Fox, Fille trespassa age de 39 Ans, le dix septieme de Fevrier, 1718. Dieu Aye Merci de Leu . s ames.

Arms—Ermine, on a chevron azure, three foxes heads erased or; in chief, on a canton, azure, a fleur-de-lis or; impaling, azure, on a chevron, or, between three bezants, a stag courant, sable.

Underneath are deposited the Remains of the Honourable Charlotte Elizabeth Fox, the dearly beloved Daughter of Lord and Lady Ilchester. This most amiable Child Died at Melbury, in Dorsetshire, aged exactly eleven years, on the 16th of March, 1755. May the Almighty God have Mercy on her Soul.

Near this Place lies buried the Honourable Miss Juliana Judith Fox, third Daughter to the Right Honourable Stephen Lord Ilchester and Stavordale, by Elizabeth, his Wife. She Died the 24 of April, 1749, in the fourth year of her age.

Hatchments.

Ermine, on a chevron azure, three foxes heads erased, or, on a canton, azure, a fleur-de-lis, or, in chief a crescent, gules; impaling, quarterly, the arms of England.

Per pale gules and sable, three lions passant guardant in pale argent: impaling 1st, quarterly, first and fourth sable, two lions passant argent; second and third ermine, on a chevron, azure, three foxes tails erased, or, on a canton, azure, a fleur-de-lis or: 2d impalement, quarterly—first and fourth azure, a fleur-de-lis argent; second and third argent, a saltire, gules.

Inscription on the Alms House.

Deo opt. max. bonorum omnium largitori, isthoc quantulumcunque grati Animi monumentum acceptum refert Scolæ hujus et Ptochtrophii Fundator, humilis gratabundus, Anno Salutis reparatæ 1681.
Quid tibi Divitiæ prosunt quas congeris Hospes, solas quas dederis semper habebis opes.

Rev. Hugh Stephens Vicar.

The Earl of Ilchester Lord of the Manor.

PITTON.

On Flat Stones in Chancel.

Here Lyeth the Body of the Reverend Mr. John Rea . . ling, who Departed this Life December the 25, Anno Domini 1730, Aged 67.

Here Lyeth the Body of the Rev. Mr. Thomas Read . . . Warden of Farley Hospital, and Rector of West Grimstead, who Departed this Life Feb. the 6th, 1701, Aged 81.

On Flat Stones in Body.

Sacred to the Memory of Mrs. Letitia Hayter, who died 17 Dec. 1796, Aged 82 years.

Arms—Two lions passant guardant.

H. S. E.

Martha, the Wife of William Slater, of New Sarum, Gent. and Daughter of William Hayter, Gent. and Martha, his Wife, died the ninth of May, 1785.

Also

the said William Slater, who died the 30th Day of January, 1791, Aged 68 years.

Arms—Two lions passant guardant, a saltire.

Here Lyeth the Body of William Hayter, of Laverstock, Gent. who Died Sept. ye 6th, 1718, Aged 27 years.

Earl of Ilchester Lord of the Manor.

WINTERSLOW.

Mon. against south wall of Body.

Dorothea, Johannis Thistlethwayte, de Middleton, Et Collegii prope Winton socius, Uxor Charissima, Gabrielis Thistlethwayte, hujus Ecclesiæ Rectoris, Filia; Cui vita fuit morum suavitate Condita, Pietate et Charitate, feliciter ornata, his et aliis virtutibus enisa sedes Cœlestes, affectavit et hujusce vitæ tentatibus terrenis Maior tandem attigit.

Nata } erat { April 23rd, 1667,
Denata } erat { Octor. 2, 1715.

Arms—On a bend three pheons, impaling the same.

On a Monument against the north wall of Chancel.

Under this Marble Lieth Buried the Body of Gabriell Pile, Esq. The Fourth Sonne of Sir Gabriell Pile, Knight, who Departed this Life the xxiii day of August, 1639.

Arms—Argent, on a cross, gules, a martlet, argent, between four passion nails, gules: impaling or, on a bend, azure, three pheons, or.

Brass Plate E. End of Chancel.

In obitum Dorotheæ Stanisby, Epitaphium hoc pia Marmoreo tegeris Dorothæa sepulcho Maxima cujus erat cura placere Deo vita, voluptatem mors, luctum fecit amicis, tristior, hæc presens, legitor illa vigens, Te vivam coluere omnes, prolesq. sepultam, te matrem referet, non sine laude suam. Obijt 19° die Junij, 1587.

On Flat Stones in Chancel.

H. S. E.

Alexander Thistlethwayte, the only Son of Gabriel Thistlethwayte, Rector of this Church, who departed this Life the fourth Day of July, in the Year 1708, Aged 37.

Arms—On a bend, three pheons, in chief a crescent for diff.

Here Lyeth the Body of Catherine Thistlethwayte, Daughter of the Reverend Mr. Gabriel Thistlethwayte, Late Rector of this Parish, who died March 31st, 177 .

Here Lyeth ye Body of Katherine, the Daughter and Heire of Andrew Chaldecot, of the Isle of Purbeck, in the County of Dorset, Esq. and wife of Alexander Thistlethwayte, Esq. the Fifth of that name, who dyed the 26 day of February, Anno Dom. 167$\frac{3}{4}$.
Here Lieth the Body of Mrs. Catherine Thistlethwayte, Daughter of the above-said Alexander Thistlethwayte, Esq. and Catherine, his Wife, who died Sept. the 16, 1746, Aged 80 years.

Here Lyeth the Body of Francis Thistlethwayte, 2d Son to Francis Thistlethwayte, Esq. who dyed ye 6th of July, 1714, Aged 25.

Against the South Wall of Chancel.

Hic jacet corpus Ceciliæ Thistlethwaite, uxoris Alexandri Thistlethwaite, et Filiæ Anthonii Hungerford, Militis, quæ ex hac vita migravit Decimo die Julij, Annoq. Dom. 1637.

Arms—Or, on a bend, azure, three pheons, or: impaling sable, two bars argent, in chief three plates.

On monuments against north wall of north aisle.

Sacrum Memoriæ hoc ipso Marmore Perenniori Peregrini Thistlethwayte, A. M. Collegij Btæ Mriæ Winton, prope Winton, et Socij, et ornamenti, Peregrini Thistlethwayte, de Winterslow, Generosi, Filii natu Maximi; Vir erat in dictis facetus, in moribus probus, in literis, tum sacris tum profanis, haud vulgariter eruditus, in Amicitijs excolendis utile, cum dulci fœliciter admiscuit, qui et jucunde prodesse, potuit et serio Delectare, proh! fluxas humani generis delicias, proh! brevem perspicacis ingenij dieculam, Obijt Jan. 17, Anno Dom. 1694, Ætatis suæ 44.

Here Lieth the Body of John Thistlethwayt, Esq. Brother & Heyre to Giles, who was Buried May ye 7th, 1599, about ye Age of 67, wthout Issue male, Leaving this Manor to Alex. His Nephew, ye 3d, who was Son to Alexander, ye Brother of the forsd Robert Giles, & John, who was Here Buried ye 20th of January, 1647, Aged 63.

Arms—Quarterly, first and fourth or, on a chevron, azure, three pheons, or; second sable, two bars argent, in chief three plates—third or, three sable.

Here Lyeth the Body of Alexander Thistlethwayte, ye 4th of yt Name, Son and Heyre to ye 3d, who died Dec. ye 18th, 1670, Æta: 59 the 14th of July Before.

Here Lieth ye Body of Alex. Thistlethwayte, Esq. ye 5th of yt Name, Son & Heyre to ye 4, who Died ye 20th of Jan. 1715, Ætat. 79, 11th of April before.

Here Lyeth ye Body of Giles, 2d Son of Alex. Thistlethwayte, Esq. & Heyre to his Brother Robert, Both Died Batchelours, Giles Died ye 9 of July, 1584, A Bout 60 years of Age. As Also Dorothy, Daughter of Sr Edw. Penrudock, & Wife to Alex. ye 3d of That Name, who Died Nov. ye 1st, 1657, Ætat. 70.

Near this Place lie the Bodies of Mr. John Cooper, & Mary his Wife. He Dyed September 3d, 1732, Aged 59, She died the Thursday following, being the 7th Day of the same Month, Aged 53.

Also Edward, their Son, who dyed the same day his Mother did, Aged 27.

Near this Place lieth Mr. John Cooper, Jun. who dyed Septem. ye 29th, 1747, Aged 50.

Also Mary, his Wife, dyed March the 15th, 1785, Aged 83 years.

Also William, ye Son of John and Mary Cooper, who dyed Sept. the 2d, 1762, Aged 18 years.

Near this Place lie the Body of Margaret, Wife of Mr. Edward Cooper, who dyed July 10th, 1771, Aged 27 years.

And Margaret their Daughter, who Died Dec. 21st, 1771, Aged 7 Months.

Also the said Edward Cooper, who died 20th June, 1789, Aged 48 years.

And Mary, their Daughter, Wife of Mr. James Batt, died 26 January, 1804, Aged 35 years.

On Flat Stone in Body.

Here Lyeth the Body of Henry Edmonds, Gent. who departed this Life the 28th of January, 1692, Aged 85 years.

Arms—A fess, vair, in chief three martlets.

Brass taken out.

On a Flat Stone in S. Aisle.

Here Lyeth Dorothy Thistlethwayte, Daughter of Peregrine Thistlethwayte, who died ye 14th Day of October, 1670.

Hatchment in N. Aisle.

Arms—Or, on a chevron, azure, three pheons, or, impaling azure, a fess, or, between three fleur-de-lis, of the same.

Rev. Mr. Peter Bellangie Brodie late Rector, succeeded the Rev. Dr. Robert Thistlethwayte.

Present Rector, Rev. Matthew Marsh.

Lord Holland Lord of the Manor, having purchased it of Alexander Thistlethwayte, Esq.

IDMISTON.

On a Monument against the north wall of Chancel.

H. S. E.

Rev^dus Johannes Bowle, A. M. E. S. A. Qui Elizabetham uxorem duxit filiam Johannis Elliott, Arm. Literis Græcis et Latinis, Linguarum Gallicæ, Hispanicæ, et Italicæ peritiam adjunxit, in omni fere Literatum genere versatus, præsertim studio Antiquitatis trahebatur, post vitam probe et honeste actam, Animam Deo reddidit, gloriosæ resurrectionis spei plenus, Die 26 Octobris, Anno Dom. 1788, Ætatis suæ 63.

Against the South Wall.

S. M.

Elizabethæ, Rev^di Johannis Bowle, A. M. conjugis carissimæ; Fœminæ piæ, probæ, castæ, inculpabilis, Quæ lubenter animam Deo reddidit decimo Calendas Maij, Anno Salutis Humanæ, 1759.

Gratitudinis ergo et amoris, Monumentum hoc maritus F. F. Ipse jubet mortis te meminisse Deus.

Arms—Argent, a chevron, sable, between three eagles heads erased of the same; impaling azure, a fess or.

H. S. E.

Elisabetha, Rev^di Johannis Bowle, et Elisabethæ uxoris ejus, filia natu major. Heu Flebilis Obijt Quarto die Martii, Anno Salutis 1669, Ætatis XIV.

H. S. E.

Richardus Bowle, Armiger, filius Johannis Bowle, Episcopi Roffensis, et Chiliarchus in Exercitu, Regis Charoli Primi, qui obiit 8vo die Novem. Anno Dom. 1678.

On Flat Stones in Chancel.

Mistress Elizabeth Bowle Died April the 22nd, 1759.

Rev. John Bowle died Oct. ye 26th, 1788, Aged 63 years.

Beneath this Stone are deposited the Remains of John Bowle, Esq. who Departed this Life March 2d, 1743, Aged 40 years.

And of Sarah, his Wife, Daughter of the Rev. Thomas Westley, Rector of Berkley, Somersetshire, who Departed this Life July 3rd, 1785, Aged 85 years.

Mr. Thos. Pile Bowle Died June 22d, 1782, Aged 24.

In Memory of Bridget Ann Courtney, who died Feb. the 19th, 1801, Aged 42 years.

On a Monument in Body.

Ægidii Rowbach, Armigeri, Qui postquam per septuaginta et quinque annos inservivit Dei volutati suaviter, in Christo abdormivit Decemb. 2°, Anno Dom. 1633. Ric. Chaundler, ex sorore nepos et hæres, in assem totum institutus hoc mnemosvnon, quale quale est mœrens posuit.

Arms—Azure, a bend checky, or and gules.

On a Monument in the North Aisle.

In Memoriam Georgiæ D^næ Mariæ Chaundler, uxoris Ric. Chaundler, de Idmerston, com. Wilt. arm. Joh. Palmer, Med. D^ris Filiæ, Formæ Venustate ornatissimæ virtutibus impensius decoratæ, quam obfirmata in Deum pietas, affectus in suos profusus, erga omnes mens benigna, consuetudo placida, mores integerrimi Cœlo maturam sæculo desideratissimam fecerant, post septem liberos susceptos, et cum Cœlo divisos, octavo demum puerperio extincta est, ita nobilissimo sexus sui fato, tanquam pro patriâ fortiter occumbens, aliis vitam præstitura, suam, amisit maritus luctu pene obrutus, et ingrate superstes, amoris nunquam intermorituri pie memor dulces charissimæ conjugis exuvias hic deposuit. Obiit April 26, 1680, Ætat. suæ A° 30.

Arms—Quarterly, first and fourth party per pale, chevron azure and sable, three cherub heads or; second and third azure, a bend checky or and gules; impaling sable, with a bend as before.

In North Aisle.

In Memory of Christian, Wife of the Rev. Mr. Thomas Clemens, who died Nov. 21st, 1754, Aged 88 years.

Near this Place Lyeth the Body of the Rev. Mr. Thomas Clemens, who Dyed March ye 25th, 1747.

Under the Tower.

Near this Place lie the Remains of John Andrews, of Porton, who, by Integrity of Mind and useful Abilities duely exerted, has left an Example worthy of Imitation. He departed this Life the 17th Day of January, 1766, Aged 77 years.

Wm. Beach of Nether Haven, Esq. Lord of the Manor. The Rev. Mr. Davis, present Vicar.

NUNTON.

On Flat Stones in Chancel.

Here Rest the Remains of Martha, Wife of William Batt, Esq. Daughter and Heiress of Jonathan Clark, Esq. and Martha, his Wife, late of this Parish, who died Sept. 17th, 1764, Aged 70.

And also of William Batt, Esq. who died July 28th, 1772, Aged 84.

To the pious Memory of his Honoured and Worthy Parents, their only surviving Son, William Batt, dedicates this Stone.

Arms—A fess, ermine, between three dexter hands, over all an escutcheon of pretence, on a bend, between three roundels, as many swans.

Here Lyeth the Body of the Reverend Mr. George Gifford, Minister of Downton, and this Place, who dyed ye 2d of April, 1721, Aged 39. An unworthy Minister of Jesus Christ.

Here Lyeth ye Body of Mary Taunton, the Relict of Richard Taunton, late Merchant in Southampton, and Sister of Jasper Bampton, of this Parish, Gent. who departed this Life the 23d Day of November, 1729, in the 67th year of her Age.

Mon. against south wall of Body.

This Marble was placed here by William Batt, the Younger, of New Hall, in this Parish, Esq. as the Last Testimony of his Love, and a small Tribute due to the Memory of Martha, his beloved Wife, who was one of the Daughters of John Cray, Late of Ibsley, in the County of Southampton, Esq. and Departed this Life, Dec. 12th, 1755, Aged 34.

And also of

Martha, his only Sister, Relict of Richard Bingham, of Bingham Melcombe, in the County of Dorset, Esq. and Wife of Pery Buckley, of Winkfield Place, in the County of Berks. Esq. who died at New Hall, Feb. 23, 1765, Aged 43 years.

With the Remains of these Dear and truly Valuable Friends, which rest Underneath, he intends his own shall be deposited.

Arms—Sable, a fess, ermine, between three dexter hands, argent; impaling, argent, on a bend three greyhounds, courant, gules, between two eagles, displayed, sable.

On Flat Stones in Body.

Here Lyeth ye Body of John Clark, who Died Septem. 1669.

H. S. E.

Elizabeth Bampton, Uxor. Jasperi Bampton, Gent. Obijt 5° die February,

Anno { Ætatis { 61.
Domini { 1718.

Here Lieth ye Body of Elizabeth, the Wife of Sam. Fishlock. Dyed Aug. ye 18, 1691.

On a Tablet in South Aisle.

Here under Lyeth Buried Charles Hartshorne, Gent. He was Servant and Steward to the Right Honble Edward Lord Gorges, of Langford, where he obtained Love and Favour of all men, and dyed in The faith of Christ, the 14th of April, Anno Dom. 1644.

South Aisle.

In Memory of Mrs. Margaret Wheeler, who died March 31, 1779, Aged 68 years.

In South Wall of Chancel is a small piscina.

Rev. Mr. Webb late Vicar, Rev. Thos. Leer present Vicar.

Nunton House belongs to Thomas John Batt, Esq.

ODSTOCK.

On Monuments in Chancel.

Near this Place are deposited the Remains of Robert Secundus Bedwell, Esq. Son of the Rev. John Bedwell, Rector of Hatherop, in Gloucestershire, and great Nephew of the Rev. John Bedwell, Rector of this Parish, who departed this Life Dec. 4th, 1794, Aged 22 years.

In the Vault near this Monument lies the Body of Anna Maria Webb, Daughter of Sir John Webb, Bart. of this Place, and Mary his Wife. She died April 30th, 1765, Aged 16 months, 11 days.

In the Vault near this Monument Lies the Body of Frances Maria Webb, Daughter of Sir John Webb, Bart. of this Place, and Mary his Wife. She died June 28, 1763, Aged 3 years and 11 Days.

In the vault near this Monument lies the Body of Thomas Webb, Son of Sir John Webb, Bart. of this Place, and Mary, his Wife. He died Aug. 15th, 1768, Aged 1 year, 2 months, and 11 Days.

In the Vault near this Monument lies the Body of Julia Webb, Daughter of Sir John Webb, Bart. of this Place, and Mary, his Wife. She died Jan. 3rd, 1769, Aged 3 months and 3 Days.

On Flat Stones in Body.

Here Lyeth the Body of Sarah, the Daughter of William Chub, who Died Jan. the 18th, 1679.

William, the Son of Anthony Chub, of this Parish, died June the 20th, 1670, Aged 63.

William, the second Son of William Smith, of New Sarum, and Grand Son of the said William Chub, was here Buryed September the third, 1678, Aged 16 Months.

Here Lyeth ye Body of Mary, ye Daughter of William and Mary Chubb, who dyed ye 6th of March, $07\frac{11}{12}$ Aged one year and 6 months.

On the Pulpit.

1580.

God bless and save our Royal Queen,
The Lyke on earth was never seen.

From the information of the Parish Clerk, the Rev. John Bedwell, formerly Rector of this Parish, died in April, 1814, Aged 103 years, but there is no monument or inscription to his Memory.

The Rev. Mr. May, late Rector.

Rev. Charles Grove, present Rector.

The Earl of Radnor Lord of the Manor, who purchased it, about the year 1790, of Sir John Webb, Bart.

HOMINGTON.

On a Flat Stone in Chancel.

Here Lyeth the Body of George Stanley, Gent. who dyed Oct. the 19th, 1719 . . . . 51st year of his Age.

Arms—Indented at honour point, in base three eagles' legs erased, in chief three stags' heads caboshed, a crescent for difference: impaling, a fess between three mill rinds.

On Flat Stones in Body.

Hic jacet David Humphreys, hujus parochiæ Minister, Qui Obiit 17 die Maij,

Anno { Dom. 1731, Ætat. 86.

Here Lyeth ye Body of William Gray, who Departed this Life April ye 28th, 1724, Aged 81 years.

Here also Lyeth the Body of Elizabeth, Wife of William Gray, who Departed this Life Nov. 8th, 1703, Aged 56 years.

Here Lyeth the Body of Mary Mitchell, Widdow of Samuel Mitchell, sen. who Departed this Life June the 21st, 1730, Aged 52 years.

Here Lyeth ye Body of Samuel Mitchell, who died May 2d, 1790, Aged 82 years.

Here Lyeth the Body of Grace, ye Wife of Thomas Phetyplace, who departed this Life Feb. 1778.

Against North Wall of North Aisle.

In Memory of Edward Wyndham, Esq. son of Thomas Wyndham, Esq. of this Place, and Grandson of Sir Edmund Wyndham, Knight Marshal of Cathanger, in the County of Somerset. He died in the year 1723, in the 64 year of his Age.

Of Penelope, Wife of Edmund Wyndham, and Daughter of George Dodington, Esq. of Dodington, in the County of Somerset. She Died in the year 1715, in the 56 year of her Age.

And of Thomas Wyndham, Esq. Son of Edmund and Penelope Wyndham, who died September the 5th, 1777, in the 85th year of his age, by whose death this Branch of the Family is become extinct.

This Monument was erected in grateful remembrance of Benefits received from Thomas Wyndham, Esq. by his Kinsman Lieutenant-Colonel Wadham Wyndham, of the City of New Sarum.

Arms—Azure, a chevron or, between three lions' heads erased, of the same.

In North Aisle.

Here Lyeth ye Body of Christopher Baylie, who Died Dec. ye 22, 1729, in ye 24 year of his Age.

Register commenced 1605.

Rev. Mr. Benson Rector.

Lord Radnor Lord of the Manor.

COMBE BISSET.

On a Flat Stone in Chancel.

Here Lyeth the Bodys of Elizabeth and Charles, the Wife and Son of Edward Combe, who died Dec. 30, 1680.

In North Aisle.

Sacred to the Memory of Mrs. Elizabeth Fleetwood, who died Dec. 3rd, 1813, Aged 80 years.

Also of
Miss Elizabeth Fleetwood, who died Nov. 5th, 1812, Aged 44 years.

Hatchments.

[In North Aisle.]

Sable, a sinister hand closed, argent, a canton, gules; impaling, gules, on a chevron sable, between three lions' heads, erased, of the same, a fleur-de-lis, argent, between two annulets of the same.

[In Body of the Church.]

Quarterly, first and fourth or, two bars argent, in chief three tigers' heads caboshed, gules; second and third argent, a chevon, sable, between three towers imbattled, gules: impaling, argent, three blackbirds proper.

[In Chancel.]

Vair, argent and gules, on a canton or, a stag's head caboshed sable.

In the Chancel Window, and in three windows of the North Aisle, are a few pieces of painted glass.

Rev. Joseph Gilbanks late Vicar, Rev. Francis Baker the present one.—Register commenced 1630.

The Manor belongs to the Earl of Radnor.

STRATFORD TONEY.

Flat Stones in Chancel.

Johannes Reeks, D. D. hujus Ecclesiæ Rector.
Obiit die Junii 29,
Anno { Salutis 1770, Ætatis 57.

Susanna Reeks, Vidua Johannis Reeks, D. D.
Obiit Die Dec. 18th,
Anno { Salutis 1787, Ætatis 67.

Hic situs est Franciscus Ketelbæus, Reverendus, sacræ Theologiæ Doctor, et hujus Ecclesiæ pius Rector. Obiit vi. sepultus fuit die Nobris 11,
Anno { Salutis 1656, Ætatis suæ 68.

Arms—Two chevrons.

In Memory of the Rev. Charles Reeks, who Died 27th July, 1783, Aged 54.

Sacred to the Memory of Lloyd Williams, second Son of the Rev. Lloyd Williams, Vicar of Whitchurch, Hants. who died 22nd August, 1810, Aged 20 years.

Against west end of Body.

In Memory of Elizabeth, second Wife of Richard Hill, Alderman of Sarum, Daughter of John Huntley, of Chiltern, who died March 4th, 1715, Aged 49.

Sett up by her Husband, Son of Mr. Mathew Hill, of Sarum, Apothecary, who was born in this Parish, and Buried in this Church in November, 1666, Aged 38.

On Flat Stone in Body.

Margaret Dench, Wife of Henry Dench, of Cowesfield, who was the only Daughter of Rowland Hill, of Sarum, by Margaret Hill, his first Wife, died 28th Oct. 1790, Aged 61 years, and was buried under this Stone.

Margaret Hill died 23rd August, 1734, Aged 40 years.

Richard Hill, Son of Rowland and Margaret, died July, 1745, Aged 18 years.

Rowland Hill died 25th March, 1767.

Margaret Hill, Richard, and Rowland, were all Buried in this Church.

Register commenced in the year 1552.

Rev. Mr. Brown, late Rector.

Rev. Thomas Stockwell, present Rector.

G. P. Jervoise, Esq. Lord of the Manor.

BISHOPSTON.

On a Monument in Chancel.

Near this Place are deposited the Remains of the Rev. William Barford, Clerk, upwards of 30 years Rector of this Parish, who Died 1st June, 1780, in in the 83d year of his Age.

Also Susanna, his Wife, who died 11th Oct. 1767, Aged 67 years, by whom he had 15 Children, 2 of whom are buried near them, William Barford, who Died 11th Dec. 1747, and the Rev. Thomas Barford, who died 20th Nov. 1764.

As a grateful Tribute to their Memory, their surviving Children have erected this Monument.

On Flat Stones in Chancel.

H. S. E.

Reverendus Nathanael Trotman, Clericus; Qui certa fœlicis resurrectionis spe mortalitatem suam exuit vicesimo secundo die Februarij,

Anno { Ætatis 41, Salutis 1719.

Arms—A cross between four cinquefoils; impaling, on a bend between two water-bougets, three tigers' heads caboshed.

H. S. E.

EXUVIUM

Rev. Richardi Roots, A. M. Ecclesiæ hujus Viginti prope Annos Rectoris, perquam fidelis. Necnon

Winæfridæ, uxoris ejus dilectissima, quæ variolis correpta mortem. Obiit 5to 7bris, 1731, Annos 56 Nata Ille diu superstes ad Annum 1747, tandem Xto quem sincere prædicavit piam efflavit Animam 30mo scilicet 7to Annos 73 Natus.

Here Lyeth Mary, ye Wife of Captain Edwd Moyle. She was one of the Daughters of Mr. Anthony Trotman, Late of this Place. Ob. 25 Junij, Anno Dom. 1724, Ætatis 64.

Here Lyeth ye Body of Richard Cooper, Clerk, who Departed this Life February ye 14th, in 1713, Aged 65 years.

Hic jacet Thomas Hill, Cler. Rector de Bishopston, et Ecclesiæ Stæ Mariæ Virginis, Sarum Canonicus Residentiarius. Obijt 28 Novembris 1671, Ætatis suæ 59.

Against the South Wall of Body.

H. S. E.

Michal, Relicta Geo: Button, de Throop, Gent. Mater Septem Filiorum et Filiæ unicæ, inter quos nonnullos fere ab incunabulis, et omnes prudenter educavit, et elocavit, quorum gratiâ ad mortem permansit vidua. Obiit Jun. 14, Anno Dom. 1737, Ætatis suæ 85.

H. S. E.

Maria, Filia ejus unica, et Uxor secunda Rev. Richardi Roots, A. M. hujus Ecclesiæ Rectoris. Obiit Sept. 3°, Anno Domini 1745, Ætatis suæ 53.

North Wall of Body.

Sacred to the Memory of Mr. William Rowden, who died 1st Sept. 1770, Aged 34 years.

Also of

Mrs. Catherine Rowden, his Wife, Daughter of the Rev. William Barford, Rector of this Parish, who died 21 July, 1780, Aged 40 years.

And of

John, Son of the above William and Catherine Rowden, who died 31 Dec. 1782, Aged 15.

On Flat Stones in Body.

In Memory of Michael Button, late Druggist of the City of New Sarum, who died Jan. ye 9th, 1751, Aged 66 years.

Arms—Ermine, a fess.

Here Lyeth ye Body of William Whithart, who died June, 1735, in the 17th year of his Age.

On Monument in N. Transept.

Beneath this Stone are deposited the Remains of John Rooke, Esq. of Throope, who died the 23d of April, 1813, in the 83 year of his Age.

Also of Elizabeth, his Wife, Daughter of the Rev. William Barford, A. M. who died the 8th of March, 1800, in the 70th year of her Age.

Here Lyeth Buried the Body of Charles Vaughan, of Fallerisdoune, Esquire, Son of Sur Rychard Vaughan, of Brodwardin.

On a Flat Stone in North Transept.

H. S. E.

Cœcilia, Uxor secunda Geo: Button de Throope, Gent. Obiit Aug. 7, Anno Dom. 1749, Ætat. suæ 30.

In the Chancel, and in the north and south transepts, is a little painted glass.

Register commenced 1653.

RECTORS.

1669, Rev. Thomas Hill.
1673, R. Caldecot.
1688, John Younger.
1710, Richard Cooper.
1716, Nathaniel Trotman.
1730, Richard Roots.
1780, William Barford.

The Honble Wm. Neville, late Rector.
The Rev. Thomas Bramley, present Rector.
The Earl of Pembroke Lord of the Manor.

DOWNTON.

On a Monument against the north wall of Chancel.

To the deservedly beloved and respected Memory of Anthony Lord Feversham, Baron of Downton, who died at Barford, in this Parish, where he had principally resided, June 18th, 1763, Aged 68 years, and was interred in this Chancel.

He was the only surviving Son of Anthony Duncombe, Esq. by Jane, Eldest Daughter and Coheir of the Honble Frederick Cornwallis, 2d Son of Frederick Lord Cornwallis, of Eye, and Nephew and Heir of Sir Charles Duncombe, Lord Mayor of London. On his Return from his Travels into foreign Parts in 1721, He was Elected to Parliament for the City of New Sarum, as he was also in the years 1722, and 1727; to the two succeeding Parliaments, he was returned for the adjacent Borough, which he continually represented, till raised in 1747, to the House of Peers. By his first Marriage with the Honble Margaret Verney, Daughter of George Lord Willoughby de Brooke, he had several Children, who died without Issue, particularly a Son George, whose premature Death is Lamented by his Parents on a Monument near adjoining. He intermarried, secondly, with Frances, Daughter of Peter Bathurst, of Clarendon Park, in this County, Esq. and, thirdly, with Ann, Daughter of Sir Thomas Hales, of Howletts and Beaksbourne, in the County of Kent, Bart. (who wedded, secondly, William, Earl of Radnor,) and by each of these latter Marriages, left a Daughter surviving, named after their respective Mothers; the younger of whom, Anne, the Wife of Jacob Earl of Radnor, consecrates, with the highest filial affection, this Monument.

Against the South Wall of Chancel.

To the Right Honble Margaret Lady Feversham, only Daughter to the Right Honble George Verney Lord Willoughby de Broke, died October 9th, 1755, in the 59th year of her Age.

LADY FEVERSHAM'S CHARACTER.

She had all the advantages of Birth and Fortune, improved by an Education suitable to her Rank and Quality. In her Youth, she was remarkable for the Beauty of her Person, and the sweetness of her Manners; and her Virtues, throughout the whole extent of her Life, gained her the esteem and admiration of all who knew her. Her conjugal and maternal affection, the ease and Dignity with which she administred the affairs of her Family, the courtesy and affability with which she received the very lowest of those who had access to her, and her compassionate tenderness to all who wanted, and were within the reach of her good offices, conspired to form one complete evidence of an excellent understanding, conducted by a mind naturally good, and thoroughly influenced by religious principles, which she received from her Father. Her Behaviour under her Afflictions gave the full lustre to this assemblage of good qualities. Bereaved of all her Children (the last of which, and the sole remaining hope of the family, was just upon the verge of Manhood), She bare it with the most perfect resignation to the will of God, and under a constant state of ill health for thirty years, she never lost the natural chearfulness of her Temper, and hardly seemed to feel her own pains, though she was most sensibly touched with the trouble and concern which she gave to those about her, especially to her Husband, who loved her with the most sincere Affection, and was her constant unwearied Companion in all her sufferings. After the most happy union between them for near forty years, when the time was come that was to put an end to their mutual happiness, she met Death, not with impatience of Life, nor with perturbation, but with a fortitude of mind which could only be inspired by her blessed Redeemer, in whom she trusted, and in whose arms we will leave her pious Soul to rest.

Arms—Quarterly, first and fourth per chevron ingrailed three talbots heads erased; second and third guttee, on a fess three doves conjoined: impaling, three cross in chief vair ermine.

Against North Wall of Chancel.

To the Memory of the Right Honourable Frances Lady Feversham, Fifth Daughter of Peter Bathurst, of Clarendon Park, in the County of Wilts. Esquire, and second Wife to the Right Honourable Anthony Lord Feversham.

Her conduct and behaviour, both before she married and after, were discreet, sensible, and prudent: Her conversation was, at times, easy and cheerful; yet, in this, as in every thing else, she took care to preserve a Dignity which made her equally respected, honoured, and beloved. She died in the flower of her youth, before the vices or follies of the world had taken any hold of her; and so little was she captivated with outward pomp and grandeur, or altered in the native Innocency of her Heart by the great addition of all wordly enjoyments which her Marriage had brought along with it, that, to her honour, let this favourite saying, (which is here set down almost in her own words) ever be remembered of her: "The vanities generally attendant on wealth and titles, will, too soon, I fear, overtake and overrun me, in spite of all my endeavours to keep them back; but I will remain what I was, and what I am, as long as I can." This good and valuable young Lady, with a perfect Resignation to the will of God, and in full and stedfast Faith in Jesus Christ for the pardon and remission of her sins, Died the 21st day of November, 1757, in the 26th year of her age, leaving a sad and sorrowful Husband behind Her, and an infant Daughter by him but ten days old.

Arms—Quarterly, as the preceding: impaling two bars ermine, in chief three cross pattee.

Against south wall of Chancel.

To the Memory of George, the Son of Anthony Duncombe, Esq. of Barford, and the Hon. Margaret Verney, his wife. He dyed in the flower of Youth, regretted by all who knew him, having, by a tender and affectionate respect, endeared himself to his Parents, and by an obliging and courteous behaviour, which was natural to him, gained the love and esteem of all his acquaintance; and if Modesty and sweetness of temper, joyned with good sense, are signs of a Generous Mind, and when found in Youth will prognosticate what the Man will be, he had given great hopes that he would one day prove a valuable friend both to rich and poor, and an Ornament to his Family and Country.

He was born to the Expectation of a great Fortune, but that was not to be discovered by any part of his behaviour, which was untainted by ye prospect of affluence before him; a great indication that, had it pleased God to prolong his Life, he would have enjoyed Riches with the same moderation of mind with which, in his younger Days, he viewed them at a Distance.

As aggravating as these Circumstances are to those most nearly concerned in the loss, yet they afford them this Comfort, that he lived long enough to give proofs of a mind furnished with principles of Honour and Virtue. He dyed with a perfect resignation to the Will of God, and a firm trust in his blessed Redeemer, and is (as they confidently hope and trust) far Happier than they could make him.

This Monument was erected by his Mournful Parents; the only thing they ever did unwillingly for for their Son, but it was the last and only Gift they could bestow. He was born the 7th Day of March, 1722, He dyed the 9th Day of August, 1741.

Arms—Quarterly, first and fourth per chevron ingrailed, three talbots' heads erased; second and third guttee, on a fess, three doves conjoined.

In North Transept.

Sacred to the Memory of Diana Webb, Daughter of Sir Charles Shuckburgh, Bart. who died the 9th 1753, Aged 50 years.

Also of Nicholas Webb, her Husband, Vicar of this Parish upwards of 50 years, who died 15 Jan. 1775, Aged 83 years.

Also of John Shuckburgh, Esq. Son-in-law of the said Nicholas Webb, who died Dec. 14, 1782, Aged 38 years.

And of Diana, his Wife, Daughter of the above Nicholas and Diana Webb, who died June 27, 1788.

South Transept.

Here Lyeth Sir Charles Duncombe, Knight, who dyed the 9th of April, 1711, in ye 63d year of his Age.

Arms—Party, per chevron ingrailed, gules and argent, three talbots heads erased, counter-changed.

Near this Place are deposited the Remains of George Spence, who died 3 Jan. 1794, Aged 10 years.

Sacred to the Memory of Thomas Barclay, Esq. formerly of London, Merchant, who Departed this Life the 12th of December, 1784, in the 69 year of his Age.

Near this Place lie the Remains of Bartholomew Lynch, Gent. who, till his Death, which happened 30 August, 1759, at the age of 60 years, was a faithfull and respected Domestick of Anthony, Late Lord Feversham. The Parish of Downton, in consequence of an Annuity of £100 given by his Will for apprenticeing poor Children thereto belonging, which, at the time of its expiration in 1786, had actually apprenticed 202 poor Children, erects this Memorial of him as its grateful acknowledgment of his Charity and Beneficence, and as an Incentive to the Imitation of so worthy an Example.

In Memory of Susannah, Wife of Mr. John Sheffield, Surgeon. She Died December 27, 1779, Aged 31 years.

Also three of their Children, who died in their Infancy.

In Memory of Henry Noyes, Gent. who died Jan. 20, 1762, Aged 82.

Also of Emma, his Wife, who died October 3, 1757, Aged 75.

Also of Henry, their Son, who Died Jan. 20th, 1773, Aged 62.

Also of Emma, their Daughter, who died July 16, 1784, Aged 73.

On Flat Stones in S. Transept.

Here Lyeth the Body of Francis, the Son of Richard and Margaret Jencks, who departed this Life the 7 day of February, 1714, in the 10 Year of his Age.

Here Lyeth the Body of John Bampton, of Lower Woodfield, of this Parish, who dyed the 9th of February, 1688.

Here also Lyeth ye Body of his Son John Bampton, who died the 29th of Dec. 1733, Aged 70 years.

Here Lyeth ye Body of John Lynche, Gent. who departed this Life ye 10th Day of Jan. in ye Year of our Lord, 1662, being in ye 20th year of his Age.

Here Lyeth ye Body of Mathew Shepherd, who Dyed April ye 5th, 1716, Aged 62 years.

Here Lyeth the Body of Barnabas, Son of Barnabas and Alice Rumsey, of Downton. He dyed April 20, 1605.

Here Lieth the Body of Ann, ye Daughter of Ambres Lam, and Ann his Wife, who Died ye 15th Day of December, 1683.

Here Lyeth Elizabeth, 2d Wife of John Fanstone. She was buried July 30, 1681.

Here Lyeth Sarah, the Wife of Mathew Shepard, who departed this Life the 1st Day of May, 1720, Aged 71 years.

Hatchments.

Quarterly, first and fourth per chevron gules and argent, in chief three talbots heads, erased, counter-changed; second and third sable, guttee d'eau, on a fess, argent, three doves, sable; impaling, gules, three arrows, argent.

Per chevron, gules and argent, three talbots' heads erased, counter-changed; impaling, gules, three crosses, or, in chief vair ermine, and erminois.

Per chevron, gules and argent, three talbots' heads erased, counter-changed; impaling, gules, on a bend argent, between six crosslets fitchy of the same, on an escutcheon of pretence or, a demi-lion, gules, a crescent for difference.

Talbot; impaling, sable, two bars ermine, in chief three cross pattee, or.

Quarterly, first and fourth gules, on a bend, argent, three mullets, sable; second and third quarterly—first and fourth argent, second and third gules; on an escutcheon of pretence, a talbot, argent.

Benefactions

In one Thousand seven Hundred and Eighty-four, Mrs. Emma Noyle gave Two Hundred Pounds to the Vicar and Churchwardens of Downton, which Sum is placed in the public Funds, and the Interest of this Money She wills shall be employed to pay a School-mistress at Charleton to teach Six or Eight Children of that place to read and work, and also a School-mistress in the Tything of East Downton for the same purpose; further directing, that the scholars shall be nominated and chosen by the said Vicar and Churchwardens for the time being, provided that there be never more than one Child out of one Family at either of the said Schools at the same time.

The Charity School in Downton was founded in 1679 by Sir Joseph Ashe, for the Instruction of twelve poor Boys, Sons of Freeholders, in the said Borough; if none such to be found, any Children of the Inhabitants in the said Borough, the Children to remain only three years in the School. This School is endowed with a School House, the Rent of the ground of the two Fairs of Downton, and with the Interest of one Hundred and Thirty Pounds in the Publick Funds.

Legacy to the Parish of Downton.

In 1626, Mr. William Stockman, of Downton, gave Chadwell Farm, in White Parish; and directed that the Rents should be distributed yearly among such poor Persons as should be surcharged by Children within the said Parish, according to the choice of the Feoffees, with the Consent of the Vicar or Curate of the said Parish, and not to go to the Increase of the Church-box of the said Parish.

Register commenced 1602.

The Rev. Mr. Gifford Vicar in 1720.
The Rev. Nicholas Webb late Vicar.
The Rev. Thomas Lear present Vicar.

Earl of Radnor Lord of the Manor.

STANDLINCH.

Against the South Wall of Chancel.

To the Memory of his Beloved Wife Joane, the 3d Daughter of Coll. John Penrodock, of Compton, Esq. (who was beheaded for the King's Cause) who brought forth 3 sons, & 6 Daughters, and one Son abortive, of wch, and the Collic, She Dyed the 10th of Jan. 168 8/9, in a deep sense of her Virtue, & Pious zeal for Re-building this Little Church, Founded in the year 1147, wth a gratefull, but sad heart, this Monument was Erected by Her Ever Loving M. B.

Arms—Two lions rampant, on a canton a fretty; impaling, a bend of the limb of a tree, reguly and trunked.

WHITE PARISH.

On a Monument against the north wall of Chancel.

Here Lyeth the Body of Mary, the Late Wife of Anthony Hungerford, of Blackbourton, in the County of Oxon, Esq. the Relict of Anthony St. Barbe, late of Whiteparish, Esq. deceased, and daughter of Robt. Mason, Esq. late of Lincolnes Inne, and Recorder of London, also Deceased. Shee was buried the Second day of December, 1692.

Arms—Two bars, in chief three roundels; impaling, a lion rampant, with two heads.

Against south wall of Chancel.

R. H. P.
Illas quondam Malorum
Edouardus St. Barbe, Armiger,
Ab alto Sanguine Genus ducens inclytum,
Sanctus nomine nec minus Animi
Sanctioris.
A planta pedis, usq. ad Cœlum capitis,
Ab juvente pene ætate Valetudinarius,
Nihilo Saluatori minus suo,
Etiam in acerbissimis gratiarum,
Fœcundus,
Æque Injuriarum, ac Ærumnarum patiens,
Inimicis benevolus,
Ultimi Scripturæ Testamenti prudentissime
et ex Animi sui
Sententiâ.
Depositus inter precandum xv Calendarum Aprilis.
Multâ luce Gloriaq. cœlesti,
Fretus in sacro-sanctum Christi gremium,
Certamine illo præclaro decertato,
Cursu peracto servata Fide,
Et vitam, et Animam, placidissime reposuit
Ætatis } Anno { 51,
Salutis } Anno { 1671.
Plus satis tribularer, si nescirem misericordias Domini.

On a Monument in Nave.

Near this Marble are interred the Remains of Francis Tregagle, of Melshet Park, Esq. who Departed this Life Jan. 13th, 1759, in the 54th year of his Age. And also of Mary, his Wife, Died Nov. 1st, 1759, Aged 50 years.

He was the second Son of John Tregagle, of Treverdour, in Cornwall, Esq. by Jane, his Wife, eldest Daughter of Sir Paul, and Sister of Sir Francis Whichcot, of Aswarby, in the County of Lincoln, Bart. And, by a very close application to the study of the Law, in the Society of New Inn, London, he became an eminent Man in his Profession, and did, with the highest Character for his Honesty, Diligence, and Abilities, acquire a moderate Fortune, which he left, by Will, to his Younger Brother Nath. Tregagle, Esq. who at that time was a Merchant residing at George Town, Winyaw, in South Carolina, but now lives at Melshet Park aforesaid, and has, out of Gratitude and the most affectionate Love and Respect for his said dear Brother Francis Tregagle, erected this Monument to his Memory. 1763.

Arms—Azure, three stags tripping or; impaling argent, a saltire sable, on a chief gules three woolpacks argent.

On Flat Stones in Nave.

Here Lieth the Body of Barbara, the Wife of James Lynche, Gent. who dyed the 21 Day of June, 1690.

Here Lyeth the Body of William Hitchcock, Gent. who Departed this Life Jan. the 21, 1733, Aged 63 years.

Arms—On a cross five fleur-de-lis, in chief a lion rampant.

Here Lyeth ye Body of Mary, ye Wife of William Hitchcock, Gent. who dyed Jan. ye 27, 1679.

Also Here Lyeth ye Body of William Hitchcock, Esq. who Departed this Life May ye 12, 1729, Aged 82 years.

Underneath lye the Body of Gyles Eyre, Esq. eldest Son of Sir Giles Eyre, Knight, and of Mabel, his Wife. She dyed ye 6 March, 1728, Aged 74. He ye 28 Nov. 1734, Aged 70.

Arms—Quarterly, first and fourth, on a chevron, three quatrefoils; second and third three oaks trees: impaling three crescents, charged with as many escallops.

In west end of south aisle.

Here Lyeth Dorothy Eyre, Eldest Daughter of John Ryves of Ranston, in the County of Dorset, Esq. Wife of Gyles Eyre, of Brickworth, Esq. who dyed Jan. 15th, 1667, Ætatis suæ 23.

Hic flosculus evanciit.

Here Lyeth Gyles Eyre, Esq. one of ye outer Barresters of Lincolnes Inne, Husband of Dorothy, who dyed

Deuided & united by one Grave,
Husband & wife intomb'd here yu have,
Who living lov'd, & dying did desier
In Chaster brestes to Cherish still love's Fier;
Beauty is but skin deep, and skin is Dust,
Our scene is ended, and to earth we must,
Till, Phenix-like, our Ashes live above,
Wth Saints and Angells God to Praise & Love.

Monuments in S. Aisle.

Buried here Gyles Eyre, Esq. and Jane, his Wife. A man much oppressed by publick power for his laudable opposition to the measures taken in the Reigns of James and Charles the first. In the year 1640, for then well-known court reasons, he was .... was afterwards plundered at Brickworth by the King's Soldiers of £2000 value, and imprisoned for refusing to pay the sum of £400 illegally demanded of him by two instruments under the privy seal, bearing date at Oxford, 14th Feb. 1643.* He was Baptized Feb. 1572, dyed Jan. 1655, haveing Issue 7 sons (3 of whom were likewise members of Parliament) and 4 Daughters.

Arms—A man's leg couped at the midst of the thigh.

Here Lyeth Henry Eyre, one of ye Outter Barristers of Lincolnes Inne, who Died July 18th, 1678, Ætatis suæ 53.

Arms—Argent, on a chevron, sable, three quatrefoils, or; impaling argent, manche gules.

Near this Place Lieth the Remains of Samuel Orr,* Esq. of Brickworth House, who Departed this Life the 13th of May, 1812, Aged 58 years.

H. S. E.

Henricus Eyre, de Medio Templo Londini, Armiger, Filius Ægidii Eyre, Militis, Uñ Justic̃ de Banco, nuper Regis, natu tertius, Scholæ publicæ huic Parochiæ Benefactor munificus, qui obiit anno ætatis suæ 38, Salutis 1704.

In Memoriam Johannes Eyre, de Brickworth, Armiger, frater natu major H. E.

Arms—Argent, on a chevron, sable, three quatrefoils, or; in chief a mullet.

Near this Place lie the Bodies of Henry and Harriet Eyre, Late of Brickworth House, who Departed this Life on the following Dates:
Harriot, 5th January, 1799, Aged 74,
Henry, 28th September, 1799, Aged 75.
This Monument was Erected
By their Nephew and Nieces,
Children of their Brother John Eyre, Esq.
of Landford, in this County.

Arms—Per pale, argent, on a chevron, sable, three quatrefoils, or; impaling the same, a crescent, gules, for difference.

---

* Lord Clarendon, in his History, vol. ii. p. 67, after noticing the difficulty Charles the First met with to pay his army, adds, "By letters, and all other gentle ways, he invited those who were able to consider how much their own security and property were concerned and depended upon the preservation of his rights; and offered to sell any of his lands, or to give any personal security, for whatsoever money would be lent to him at interest," &c.

The following letter, bearing the autograph of Charles, and sealed with his own seal, I met with among some family papers at Eastwell, where it is at present:

'To our Trusty and well-beloved John Grubb, Esq.

'CHARLES, R.

'Trusty and well-beloved, Wee greete you well. Though Wee are unwilling in the least degree to press upon our good subjects, yet we must obey that necessity which compels us, in this publique distraction, when our Owne Money and Revenue is seized and deteyned from us, to lay hold on any thing which, with God's blessing, may be a meanes to preserve this Kingdome. Wee must, therefore, desire you forthwith to lend us the sum of two hundred pounds, in Money or Plate, for our necessary support, and the maintenance of our army, which we are compelled to raise for the defence of our Person, the Protestant Religion, and ye Lawes of ye Land. Wee have trusted this Bearer to receive it of you, and Wee doe promise you, in ye word of a king, to repay it with Interest. And of this Service we cannot doubt, well knowing you are too much concerned in the safety of our Person, and the preservation of the publique Peace, to neglect this opportunity of expressing your care of both.

'Given at our Court, at Oxford, this 17th Day of February, 1642.'

* He married a Miss Eyre.

In Memory of Mr. Henry Dench, who died the 26th of June, 1803, in the 77 year of his Age.

Under are interred the Bodies of those Religious and Just Persons, Ferdinando Younge, and Susan, his Virtuous and Beloved Wife, who was one of the Daughters and Coheiresses of Edward Wayte, of Farleigh Castle, in the County of Somerset. Also the Bodies of Elizabeth and Susan Young, their ever Dutiful and affectionate Daughters. Ferdinando was the third Son of Edward Younge, who Lived in this Parish, by Joane, Daughter of Bower, of Ewerne, in the County of Dorset. The said Edward was second Son of John Younge, of Little Durnford, descended from Joanne, Daughter of Hyde, of Hatch. There likewise is buried Edward Younge, Son of the fore-named Edward, who married Amphillis, Daughter of Chafin, of Chettle, but had no Issue. This is Erected by the Direction of Edward Younge, of Little Durnford, in Reverence to the Memory of his Indulgent Parents and Sisters, with whose Remains he Desires his Body may be Deposited, when it shall please Providence to call him out of this Mortal Life.

Arms—Vair, azure and argent, in chief, gules, three lions rampant or, over all an escutcheon of pretence, argent, a chevron sable, between three bugle horns of the same.

On Flat Stones in south aisle.

Buried here Gyles Eyre, Esq. Eldest Son of Gyles Eyre, and Ann, Daughter of Sir Richard Norton, of Rotherfield, in the County of Southton Kt. and Bart. his Wife, Sir Gyles Eyre, Kt. his Eldest Son, Dorothy, Daughter of John Ryves, of Ranston, in the County of Dorset, Esq. his first Wife, the Right Honble Christabella, Baroness Glasford, in Scotland, his Second Wife, & Divers Children.

Here Lyeth ye Body of John Eyre, Esq. Second Son of Sir Gyles Eyre, Knight, and one of the Benchers of Lincolnes Inn, A person of natural abilities, and acquired knowledge, in the Law of the Country inferior to few. Elected a Member of Seven Parliaments, and therein shewed himself (like many of his Ancestors) a lover of liberty and independency, Served his Country at his own expence, not served himself at the expence of his Country. Dyed at Lincolnes Inn, the 2d day of Nov. 1715, Aged 50 years.

On Flat Stone in North Aisle.

Here Lyeth ye Body of Morgan Jones, of this Parish, Vicar, who dyed August ye 4th, 1688.

On a Flat Stone in Chancel.

In Memory of the Rev. Mr. Richard Budde, Rector of Sherfield, and Vicar of this Place, who died Sept. ye 16, 1769, Aged 66 years.

Hatchments.

Argent, on a cross, azure, five fleur-de-lis, or, in chief a lion rampant, gules; impaling argent, three bust-profile heads, sable.

Azure, three stags tripping, or; impaling argent, a saltire sable, in chief, gules, three woolpacks, or.

Argent, on a cross, azure, five fleur-de-lis or, in chief a lion rampant gules; impaling argent, in chief, on a chevron sable, three quatrefoils, or, in base three bust-profile heads sable.

Quarterly, first and fourth, argent, on a chevron, sable, three quatrefoils or; second and third or, three trees proper: impaling azure, on three crescents, argent, as many escallops, gules.

Quarterly, first and fourth argent, on a chevron, sable, three quatrefoils or; second or, three oaks proper; third azure, on a bend cottized, sable, three lozenges, ermine, an escutcheon of pretence, azure, on three crescents argent, as many escallops, gules.

Argent, a chevron, gules, in chief, three turtles, between two roses in base, two cross pattee, a mullet and crescent, gules; impaling argent, on a chevron, sable, three quatrefoils, or.

In 1651, The Rev. Richard Page Vicar.
1668, The Rev. Morgan Jones.
1703, The Rev. William Clarkson.
1720, The Rev. Francis Wallice.
1730, The Rev. Mr. Budden.
The Rev. Mr. Gibson late Vicar.
The Rev. John Wayne present Vicar.

The Manor belongs to Miss Eyre.

Extract from the Register, which began in 1559.

[Births.]

1559, April 21, Edward Pickernell, son of William Pickernell, Esq.
1585, Dec. 28, [baptized] John St. Barbe and Robert St. Barbe, twins of Edward St. Barbe, Esq.
1620, June 22, Edward, Son of Edw. St. Barbe, Esq.
1623, Dec. 28, Mary, d. of Edward St. Barbe, Esq.
1623, Feb. 22, John, son of Giles Eyre, Gent.
1624, Jan. 19, Wm. son of Edw. St. Barbe, Esq.
1625, June 9, Thos. Son of Giles Eyre, Gent.
1626, July 7, Anna, daughter of Edward St. Barbe.
1626, Jan. 21, Edward, son of Gyles Eyre, Gent.
1628, Oct. 23, Henry, son of Gyles Eyre, Gent.
1629, July 28, Nathaniel, son of Edward St. Barbe.
1631, April 28, Catherine d. of Gyles Eyre, Gent.
1633, Sept. 18, Samuel, the son of Ed. St. Barbe.

1640, Jan. 28, John, son of Giles Eyre, Jun.
1642, July 2, Francis, son of Giles Eyre, Jun.
1657, Jan. 25, Joseph Eyre, son of Robert Eyre.
1667, March 28, Henry, son of Giles Eyre.
1749, Jane, daughter of John Eyre Esq. of Landford.

[Between the years 1642 and 1646, there were many people married by one Fox of Harnham, without leave of licence.]

[Burials.

1655, Feb. 16, Giles Eyre, Esq.
1667, Jan. 16, Dorothy, Wife of Giles Eyre.
1681, May 7, Mary daughter of Giles Eyre, Esq.
1686, August 2, Christabella, daughter of Giles Eyre.
1704, June 13, Henry Eyre, Esq.

FYFIELD.

On a Monument against the north wall of Chancel.

Here lye the Bodyes of George Fitz-James, Esq. Lord of the Manor of Clatford, who exchanged this Life for a better May 9, Anno Dom. 1693, Ætat. 42.

And of his only son George Fitz-James, who died the 6th of August, 1698, Ætat. 7, and was Buried in his Father's grave.

And also of Mrs. Ann Percivall, Wife of George Fitz-James, Esq. and afterwards of Edmund Percivall, Esq. of Heybridge Hall, in the County of Essex, who died September the 9th, 1746, Aged 86.

Arms—Azure, a dolphin embowed argent; impaling, gules, on a bend, argent, two lions passant gules, with as many cinquefoils of the same.

Against the South Wall of Chancel.

Sacred to the Memory of John Wheeler, Gent. who Departed this Life the 9th of June, 1779, Aged 56 years.

Also of Emma, Wife of John Wheeler, Gent. who departed this Life 26 Sept. 1761, Aged 36 years.

Also of Blanch, Daughter of John and Emma Wheeler, who departed this Life 3d Dec. 1772, Aged 29 years.

Also of Christian, Daughter of John and Emma Wheeler, who departed this Life 13 May, 1775, Aged 25 years.

Arms—A fess indented between three doves.

On Flat Stones in Chancel.

Elias Delme, of Lockeridge, Esq. Died 28 Jan. 1763, Aged 84 years.

Here Lyeth the Body of John Doubleday, Gent. who departed this Life at Lockeridge, May 6, 1753, in the 67 year of his Age.

On a Monument in Body.

Here rest, released from a Sea of Troubles, the Mortal Remains of Mr. James Shipton, who, after a long and painfull Illness, resigned himself with Fortitude to his Creator, the 6th of August, 1793, Æt. 69. To say much would be superfluous, "His Conduct is a Legacy for all." This Stone also perpetuates the Memory of Elizabeth, Daughter of John and Elizabeth Shipton, who died Feb. 18th, 1789, Aged 2 years. And of Mrs. Elizabeth Shipton, Relict of Mr. James Shipton, who Died March 24th, 1804, Æt. 76.

Against south Wall.

Nicholas Dymore, Gent. to whom this Marble is Sacred, was a Native of this Village, and Departed this Life the 14th Day of February, 1805, Aged 68 years. He supported through Life a Character truly respectable, and died sincerely and generally lamented by a numerous acquaintance.

Near this Spot are deposited the Remains of John Dymore, of the Tything of Lockeridge, in the County of Wilts. Gentleman, who died the 29 day of July, 1806, Aged 66 years.

The Rev. Mr. Thring, late Vicar.
The Rev. Charles Hoyle, present Vicar.

Mr. Fowle, of Kinbury, the late, Mr. Goodman the present, Lord of the Manor.

DEVIZES.
St. John's.

On Monuments in North Chancel.

Josiah Eyles Heathcote, Esq.

To whose Memory this Monument has been Erected, was the only Son of George Heathcote, Esq. of London, by Maria Eyles, the Eldest Daughter of John Eyles, Esq. of Southbroom House, near Devizes. He was a Gentleman whose Courtesy, Hospitality, Polite manners, and animated conversation, united with the highest Principles of Honour and Probity, made him pleasing to, and esteemed by, his Equals, While his unbounded Benevolence and Extensive Charities, made him Equally beloved and revered by his Domestics, and drew down on him the best Blessings on this side of the Grave, those of the Poor and Destitute. A fit of apoplexy terminated his exemplary Life, on the 22d Day of August, 1811, in the 63 year of his Age. Nor was his sudden Death, though appalling, justly to be lamented, saving him, as it did, from the languors and sufferings of lingering disease, and prepared, as he happily was, by firm faith, lively, though humble, hope, and truly Christian piety, to appear before the awful tribunal of his Saviour and his God.

Arms—Quarterly, first and fourth ermine, three roundels charged with a cross, surcharged with nine roundels; second and third, a fess ingrailed, in chief three fleur-de-lis.

Near this Stone are deposited the Remains of Edward Eyles, Esq. fourth and only surviving Son of John Eyles, Esq. and Mary, his Wife, who having spent the earlier part of his Life abroad in places of public Trust, in which he acquitted himself with honor and reputation, passed the remainder of it in that retirement which was necessary to a constitution impaired by business and injured by a foreign climate, and in that peace of mind which ever attends on the religious discharge of all the Duties of Life. When abroad, he married Mary, Widow of the Honble Governor Gumley, and Daughter of Sir John Wittewrong, Baronet; but she dying six months after their Marriage, he continued a Widower till his Death, which happened on the 13th of March, 1792, in the 79th year of his Age. His only Nephew and Niece, in gratitude for the regard expressed towards them in his last Will, have jointly caused this Monument to be erected to his Memory.

East End.

Hic exuvias sui deposuit
Johannes Pierce, generosus,
Singulare,
Pietatis, ac Probitatis,
Hodie et Seris Posteris
Exemplum,
Inter primores hujus oppidi jam olim
Primus,
Inter Patronos ejusdem, proh dolor! ultimus,
Ita suis prospexit, ut etiam proficeret alienis,
Ita singulis profecit, ut una proficeret universis,
Ita prosuit ad tempus, ut et prodesset in æternum,
Testor ea quæ erogavit,
Inter alia non pauca,
In templum Dei reparandum,
In Clerum Domini sub levandum,
In Pædagogum hujus oppidi
Præmus excitandum,
In collapsas vias regias,
In sarta tecta præstanda,
In ptochotrophiâ hujus paræciæ,
Plenius dehinc alendâ.
Avi, viator, et imitare;
Quem superare necis
Tandem omnibus tum pietatis,
Tum charitatis muneribus,
Unice perfunctis
In terrâ, in cœlum demigravit
iv idus Februarius, 1641.

Near this Place
are Deposited all that was Mortal
of Edward Pierce, Gent.
three times Mayor of this Town,
to whom he was a constant
and generous Benefactor.
He departed this Life Nov. 12, 1684,
in hopes of a joyfull resurrection through
Jesus Christ.

Robert Pierce, Gent.
died May 1, 1692, Aged 69.

Richard Hope, Gent.
died Dec. 31, 1731, Aged 80.

Frances Hope,
died Jan. 8, 1770, Aged 68.

Arms—Sable, a bend nebule between two unicorns' heads erased, or.

Beneath this Place is interred the Body of Robert Byng, Doctor in Divinity, who deceased the 8th Day of February, Anno Dom. 1658.

On a Brass Plate near the above.

Underneath are the Remains of Edward Byng Wilkins, Late organist of this Church. He died the 13 of July, 1768, in the 20 year of his age.

Flat Stones in Chancel.

In Memory of the Rev. John Walton, who departed this life the 7th of August, 1745, Aged 39.

And Eleanor, his Daughter, Died 13 Jan. 1756, Aged 20.

And Mary, Wife of T. R. Humphreys, Esq. died 23rd March, 1777, Aged 40.

And Anne, Widow of the Rev. John Walton, died 3d March, 1779, Aged 73.

Also F. Richmond Humphreys, Esq. died June 6th, 1797, Aged 62 years.

M. S.

Reverendi Jacobi Dyer, Rectoris olim hujus Ecclesiæ,
Qui decimo octavo calendarum Septembris MDCXC.

Diem Obiit supremum. Prope cujus cineres sepulta subtus jacet Maria, dilecta conjux Georgii Gibbes, Qui prædictum Jacobum Dyer Maternum, habuit avum, Filia fuit Johannis Clarke, de Knightsbridge, in Agro Middlesexiæ, Generosi, Septimo nonarum Martii decessit, 1764, annos nata quadraginta duos. Hoc saxum tam annoris quam pietatis, voluit esse pignus. G. C.

On Flat Stones in Middle Chancel.

In Memory of Sarah, Wife of William Webb, who died Nov. 19th, 1749, Aged 45 years.

Also in Memory of William Webb, who died April 24th, 1777, Aged 72 years.

Also in Memory of Jane, his Wife, who Died June 2d, 1778, Aged 59 years.

In Memory of Susanna Barrie, Daughter of Robert Thresher, jun. who died March the 3rd, 1772, Aged 43 years.

In Memory of Mr. Thomas Saddler, who died ye 17 of August, Aged 64 years.

Also of Frances, his Wife, who died March ye 23d, 1767.

On Monuments in south Chancel.

Sacred to the Memory of George Heathcote, Esq. a man of strict honour, integrity, and Christian piety, in private life, a warm friend and diligent magistrate, an able and strenuous assertor of the liberty of his Country, which he manifested in his Conduct when Lord Mayor of the City of London, and as a Member of the British Senate, to which he was chosen in three successive Parliaments; but, observing the torrent of corruption too powerful to be opposed by the utmost efforts and examples of a few steady patriots, he chose to retire from all public employments, and to dedicate the remainder of his Life to the cultivating those Virtues in the rising generation which he had the mortification to see neglected and despised in the present, and in promoting the arts and sciences, of which he was an admirer and patron. Thus employed, he ended his days on the 7th of June, 1768, Aged 68 years, in that peace and tranquillity ever attendant on conscious virtue, to whose memory his affectionate Wife, Maria Heathcote, caused this Monument to be erected.

Arms—Ermine, on three pomme as many crosses or; impaling argent, a fess ingrailed sable, in chief three fleur-de-lis of the last.

Sacred to the Memory of Mrs. Maria Heathcote, Widow of George Heathcote, Esq. and Daughter of John Eyles, Esq. and Mary his Wife, of Southbroom House, near this Borough. She was born on the 12th day of June, 1707, and Died on the 5th Day of Jan. 1792. Reader, this Marble is placed here to remind thee, if thou knewest her, to inform thee if thou didst not, that the Christian piety of this excellent woman shone conspicuous in all the relative duties of life. Her Son pays this tribute to the Memory of his beloved Mother, hoping that her example may not be forgotten by some, nor lost to others.

Arms—Ermine, on three pomme as many crosses, or; impaling argent, a fess ingrailed sable, in chief three fleur-de-lis of the last.

Sacred to the Memory of Thomas Middleton Trollope, Esq. (eldest son of Sir Thomas Trollope, of Casewick, in the County of Lincoln, Bart.) In the year 1759, he married Isabella, one of the Daughters of Sir John Thorold, Bart. of Cranwell, and had Issue five Sons and three Daughters, who were living at the time of his Decease, the 27th Day of April, Anno 1779, Ætatis 59. He was a Christian from conviction, and his conduct through life was, in every respect exemplary, so that not only his Family and Relations, but all who knew him, revere his Memory, and Deplore his Death. An impartial magistrate, to the Poor a Friend; in his own sufferings (which were many) resigned and patient, yet ever ready to alleviate the sorrows of others, and zealous to promote, as far as in his power, the welfare and happiness of all mankind. In testimony of esteem and affection, and to perpetuate a character so worthy of imitation, his afflicted Widow caused this Stone to be inscribed, Anno 1779.

To the Memory of Elizabeth and John, Wife and Son of John Shergold, M. A. Rector of this Church. She having lived greatly beloved, dyed greatly lamented, on Jan. 13, Anno { Dom. 172 5/6, Ætat. 29. }

He dyed in his Infancy, four days before his said Mother.

The Lord gave, and the Lord hath taken away, Blessed be the name of the Lord.

Arms—Argent, on a chevron ..... gules, between three bears' heads erased of the last; impaling sable, a unicorn or, on a chief or, three roses slipped proper.

Near this Place lye the Remains of John, the Son of George Flower, of West Grimstead, Esq. and Kathrine, his Wife, who dyed on the 20th of May, 1725, Aged four months. Happy Child, of such is the Kingdom of God.

Where also lye the Remains of the said Katherine, a Daughter of John Eyles, Esq. of Chalford, in Gloucestershire, most dutiful, a Wife most loving and most beloved, a Mother most tender, a Neighbour most benevolent and charitable, possest of every domestick virtue, of great prudence and uniform good nature, of steady piety and true Devotion, of most exemplary patience and resignation under a continued indisposition and stubborn infirmity of body, with a courage and easyness of temper, a chearfulness and peace of mind scarce to be expected, ever to be admired, a preparative to and a pledge of that more complete happiness she now enjoys. She dyed on the 11th of August, 1727, Aged 31 years. Learn, Reader, bless her Memory, and follow her example.
G. F. M. M. P. C. I.

Arms—Sable, a unicorn or, on a chief of the same three roses slipped proper; impaling argent: a fess engrailed, sable, in chief three fleur-de-lis sable.

Near this Place lye interred the Remains of John Eyles, Esq. who departed this life the 6th of July, 1752, Ætat. 75.

Also of Mary Eyles, his Wife, who resigned this Life the 29th of April, 1744, Ætatis 62.

Also of Francis Eyles, Esq. their Son, who died the 4th of September, 1750, Ætatis 45.

Also of Joseph Eyles, Gent. another Son, who died the 20th of Feb. 1738, Æt. 27.

Also of Elizabeth Eyles, their Daughter, who died young.

Also of Francis Eyles, Esq. Brother to John Eyles, Esq. who departed this Life the 10th of Dec. 1735, Ætat. 56.

Also of Maria Heathcote, Daughter of George Heathcote, Esq. who Died the 4th of November, 1747, Ætat. 2 years and 4 months.

Also of John Turner, Esq. who died the 6th of May, 1761, Ætat. 50.

And his Widow, Eleonora Turner, Daughter of John Eyles, Esq. She Departed this Life the 13 of Jan. 1762, Ætat. 45.

In respect to, and out of an affectionate love of whose Memories, Edward Eyles, Esq. ordered this Monument to be erected, A. D. 1757.

Arms—Argent, a fess sable.

To the Memory of the Rev. Edward Innes, Rector of Devizes, who, in the Publick duties of his sacred Office, was diligent, pious, and unaffectedly devout. In private life was upright, just, meek, modest, and humane. Trusting his failings to the mercy of his God, and confident in the hope of a resurrection to a blessed immortality, he departed this Mortal life on the 18 Day of Nov. 1788, Aged 67 years.

On Flat Stones in S. Chancel.

Here Lyeth the Remains of Robert Sloper, jun. who Died April 24th, 1773, Aged 62 years.

To the Memory of Charles ~~Fowler~~, late of this Burrough, Gent. who Departed this life ye 25th of June, Anno Dom. 1719, Aged sixty years.

With him also lies Interred the Body of Ann his Wife, who Died Feb. 27th, 1728, Aged 71 years.

Arms—A unicorn, in chief three roses slipt.

G. F. } Ob. { May 20, 1725, } Ætat. { 20.
K. F. } Ob. { August 11, 1727, } Ætat. { 31.

To the Memory of George Flower, late of West Grimstead, Esq. who Departed this Life the 25th Day of June, Anno Dom. 1729, Aged 35 years.

On a Brass Plate.

Here Lieth the Body of Joseph Eyles, Gent. Son of John Eyles, of Southbroome, and Grandson of Sir John Eyles, Knight. Ob. Feb. 20, 1739, æt. 27.

And also the Body of Elizabeth Eyles, his Sister. Ob. Jan. 21, 1715, æt. 1 year.

Here lyeth the Body of Mary Eyles, wife of John Eyles, of South Broome, Esq. and Daughter of John Eyles, of Chalford, in Gloucestershire, Esq. Ob. 29 April, 1744, æt. 63.

Arms—A fess ingrailed, in chief three fleur-de lis.

On Flat Stones in Nave.

Underneath are Deposited the Remains of William Neate, who died Oct. 17, 1769, Aged 74 years.

Also underneath are Deposited the Remains of Robert, Son of William and Katharine Neate, who died July ye 22d, 1777, Aged 51 years.

Underneath also are Deposited the Remains of Katherine, the Wife of William Neate. She died August 2, 1778, Aged . . years.

And also of Thomas Neate, who died the 3d Jan. 1804, Aged 74 years.

Underneath Lies interred the Body of Wm. Powell, Gent. Sometime one of ye Masters of this Burgh, who died Feb. 3, Anno Dom. 1730, ætatis suæ 54.

Mrs. Mary Webb dyed August 30, 1753, Aged 76 years.

Underneath lye interred the Body of Mr. John Allen, Apothecary, who died the 20th of Oct. 1742, and of Mary, his beloved Wife, who Dyed ye 30th of Jan. 1743.

Here lyeth Anne, the Wife of Charles Innes, Citizen of London. Ob. 19 Sept. 1796, Ætat. 32.

Anne, Wife of Thomas Neate, Died 6 March, 1790, Aged 58.

Also Jane, their Daughter, died March, 1790, Aged 20.

Also Martha Neate, Daughter of William and Katharine Neate, died the 18th of April, 1803, Aged 80 years.

Ann Neate died 3 Oct. 1809.

To the Memory of Mary, Wife of Edward Bayly, Gent. who died 12th April, 1755, Aged 33 years.

And of Katherine, Daughter of Edward and Mary Bayly, who died 27th April, 1768, Aged 16 years.

Also Rebecca, Second Wife of Edward Bayly, Gent. who died 3d Feb. 1770, Aged 50 years.

Edward Bayly, Gent. died 10th April, 1786, Aged 60 years.

Also to the Memory of Frances, Daughter of Edward Bayly, Gent. by Fanny, his third Wife, who died 12 May, 1789, Aged 12 years.

Also to the Memory of Ann, Daughter of Edward Bayly, Gent. by Fanny his Wife, who died 10 April, 1798, Aged 18 years.

Underneath this Stone are deposited the Remains of John Powell, Gent. and Mary, his 1st Wife, and also Sarah his last Wife. He was buried the 26th of August, 1718, Aged 77. Sarah, his widow, survived him till the 9th of Nov. 1741, Aged . . . .

Also John Powell, Gent. Son of the aforesaid John Powell, and Jane his Wife. She was buried the 13th of Sept. 1719. He the 3rd of March, 1757, Aged 85.

Also Jane, Daughter of the aforesaid John and Jane Powell, who died Nov. ye 28, 1768.

Under this Stone is interred the Remains of John Powell, Esq. of Marlbrough, and also Ann, his Wife. She died May 22, 1765, He died Sept. 24, 1770.

In Memory of Mr. William Flewell, surgeon, who Departed this Life the 26 of Oct. 1742, Aged 42.

Also, in Memory of Mrs. Ann Flewell, Wife of Mr. William Flewell, who Departed this Life March 6, 1743, Aged 36.

In Memory of Stephen Powell, Sen. Gent. who departed this life the 16th of April, 1756, Aged 63 years.

Also of his Son, Stephen Powell, Gent. who departed this life the 1st of June, 1771, Aged 50 years.

In Memory also of John Powell, Gent. Son of Stephen Powell, jun. who departed this life the 19 of June, 1774, Aged 26 years.

Here lyeth Interred the Body of Thomas Cooper, Esquire, Cittizen and Merchant of London, who departed this life the 23d day of August, Anno Dom. 1670, in the 55 year of his Age.

Also here Lyeth the Body of Samuel Wright Webb, Mercer, and of Benjamin Webb, Gent. Both Sons of Benjamin Webb, Gent. Benjamin Died in ye year 1755.

Here Lyeth ye Body of Mary, ye Wife of John Anstie, of this Burrough. She Died ye 3d of June, 1731, Ætat. 28.

And also John, ye Son of the said John and Mary Anstie. He died ye 9 of Dec. 1727, Ætat. 9 weeks.

Here Lyeth the Body of Edward Eyles, Esquire, who dyed the First of April, 1672.

Here Lyeth ye Body of Mary Eyles, of this Burrow, Widdow, who departed this life ye 6th of Dec. 1671.

On monuments against north wall of north aisle.

Beatis Manibus Thomæ Long, Comitatu
Wiltoniensi, Generosi,
Qui obijt 7° die Aprilis,
Anno Domini 1671,
Ætatis suæ 54.

Quos calcas cineres, viator, ille
Sperans deposuit resuscitandos
Qui proli, pariter suæq. charus
Uxori, lachrimis dolenda liquit
Viris funera: Quem benignior sors,
Indignum minimi labore morbi,
Vita surripuit molestiori.

Arms—Sable, a lion rampant, argent, charged with an estoil, gules, between eight cross-crosslets of the second; impaling sable, a unicorn, or, on a chief of the same, three roses slipt pp.

Sacred to the Memory of George Willy, of New Park, Esq. who died unmarried Dec. 25, 1770, Aged 73.

Also of his Brother, William Willy, of London, Esq. who represented this Borough in Parliament several years, during which he uniformly evinced a faithful and zealous attention to the interest of his Country. He died unmarried, in the exercise of that honourable trust, May 23, 1765, Aged 61.

Arms—Ermine, on two bars, vert, three martlets proper.

Sacred to the Memory of James Sutton, who died Dec. 29, 1784, Aged one year and eight months.

George William Sutton, who died also in his infancy.

Mary Sutton, who Died April 18, 1791, Aged 14 years and 8 months.

Sons and Daughter of James Sutton, Esq. and Eleanor his Wife, of New Park, near this Town.

Of such is the Kingdom of Heaven.

Arms—Argent, a canton sable; impaling, ermine, on a chevron four lozenges between three fleur-de-lis.

Sacred to the Memory of Prince Sutton, Esq. who died justly esteemed and respected for his strict integrity, particularly displayed in the discharge of his duty as Justice of this Borough, Sept. 13, 1779, Aged 78.

Also of Mary, his Wife, Sister of George and William Willey, Esq. who died Jan. 23, 1768, Aged 66.

Also of their several children, Willy Sutton, of New Park, Esq. who died unmarried, Sept. 12, 1775, Aged 43, Mary Sutton, who died March 24, 1767, Aged 31, Sarah Sutton, who died Dec. 22, 1754, Aged 15, Ann Sutton, who died in her infancy.

Arms—Argent, a canton sable; impaling for Willy.

Near this Place are deposited the Remains of James Sutton, who departed this life Oct. 24th, 1788, Aged 63.

Also, in the same Grave are the Remains of Anne, his Widow, who died Nov. 23, 1788, Aged 55.

Sacred to the Memory of John Dick, M. D. who, on his way from Bath to London, departed this Life on the 3rd day of Feb. 1817, in the 29th year of his Age.

On Monuments in North Transept.

In Memory of Eleanor Holdsworth, Wife of Winch Holdsworth, D. D. of Chalfont, Bucks. and Daughter of John Merewether, M. B. of this Place. Ob. Jan. 4th, 1758, Ætat. 62.

Sacred to the Memory of Solomon Hughes, who died on the 15th of April, 1791, in the 79 year of his Age,

Also in Memory of Elizabeth, his Widow, who died Jan. 28th, 1813, in the 77 year of her Age.

Sub tumulo marmores jacet corpus Johannis Drew, Arm. defuncti juxta duos liberos ejus natam et natum Ætatis suæ 26 annorum, qui obiit 23 die Septembris, 1660, annoque 1mo R. Caroli S. pia Resurreccionis Expectaciones.

Near this Place Lyeth the Body of John Merewether, M. B. Eminent for Learning and Goodness, diligent and Charitable in his Profession, excelling in every relation of Life. Ob. May 18th, 1724, An. Ætat. 69.

Under him Lyeth Francis, his youngest Son, Ob. July 25, 1716, An. Ætat. 22.

Over her Husband lieth Jane Merewether, his beloved Wife. Ob. Jan. 4th, 1725, An. Ætat. 69.

Anna Merewether. Obiit 23 Sept. Anno Dom. 1690.

Arms—Or, on an escutcheon, between three martlets sable, a saltire ingrailed between twelve billets of the same, on a chief argent, the sun in full glory or; impaling, the escutcheon on the first.

On Flat Stones in North Transept.

M. S.

Sarah, uxoris Gulielmi Hughes, et Filiæ Joannis et Maria Bevan, nuper defunctor. Obiit 13mo die Julii, Anno Dom. 1786, Ætatis suæ 29.

In Memory of John Drewe, Esq. who died the 23 Sept. 1660, Aged 26 years.

Also of Thomas Marsh, Late of Warminster, who died the 8 April, 1764, Aged 59 years.

And of Solomon Hughes, of this Town, who died the 15th April, 1791, Aged 78 years.

Also Four of his Children, by Elizabeth, his Wife, who died in their Infancy.

And of Elizabeth, his Widow, who died Jan. 28, 1813, in the 77 year of her Age.

On a Brass Plate.

Richard, Son of Jeffery and Martha Everett, died Oct. ye 21, 1776, Aged 33 years.

Also 2 of his Sons who Died in their infancy.

Also Mary Giffard Everett, Daughter of William and Leonora Everett, who died Nov. ye 18, 1808.

Here Lyeth ye Body of Edward Watton, of this Borough, Gent. Ob. 23 Oct. Anno 1727, Ætatis 64.

Also the Body of Eliz. Watton, Daughter of Edward and Eliz. Watton, Ob. 21 Feb. Anno 1730, Ætat. 27.

Thomas, Son of Richard and Mary Everett, who Died at Maidstone, in Kent, Jan. ye 20, 1802, Aged 25 years and 4 months.

Also Mary, Wife of Richard Everett, who Died April ye 15, 1807, Aged 63 years.

Hic Jacent
John Merewether, M. B.
Francis Merewether, Ann Merewether
Memoriæ patris optimi . . . .
Qui felicissime cum ægris versatus erat,
Cujus indefessa in medicina diligentia,
et seria commiseratio
Omni populo arridebam,
Qui q . id unice in vita studebat,
ut prodesset omnibus nemini nocere,
Hunc Lapidem . . . . Filius ejus primo-genitus
Johannes Merewether, M. B.
Subiter quem suum etiam corpus,
Sepeliendum vellei

To the Memory of Martha Sutton, who Died 11th August, 1797.

On Monuments in S. Aisle, West End.

M. S.

Thomæ Payne, Medici, qui obiit July 23°, 1674.

Necnon Willoughby, conjugis ejus dilectissimæ, Quæ obiit 13 Aug. 1664.

Samuel Willoughby, ambobus gener. P.

South wall, over the south entrance.

Near this Place are deposited the Remains of James Sutton, Esq. Late of New Park, in the County of Wilts, a Magistrate of this County, and the Justice of this Borough, which he represented in four succeeding Parliaments. He was Born 6 July, 1733, and Died July 6, 1801. He married Eleanor, second Daughter of Anthony Addington, M. D. by whom he had issue two Sons, and three Daughters. His private Life was distinguished by an ardent and unaffected piety, and by an active benevolence. His Public conduct invariably displayed an honourable spirit of independence, and a firm attachment to the constitution of his Country. The inhabitants of this Town and neighbourhood attended the interment of their Benefactor and Friend with the feelings of true sorrow; nor will the remembrance of his amiable and useful virtues ever cease to be cherished with affection and respect by themselves and their descendants. To his honoured memory, this monument is erected by his afflicted Widow, in grateful recollection of that happiness which was terminated by his death, and in the humble hope of sharing with him and their beloved children a blessed immortality.

In Memory of Thomas Thurman, Gent. who died March 28, 1777, aged 86. In his Life-time he gave to buy Linen Cloth for the Poor of this Town for ever the Interest of £200; To the Rector for Reading Prayers Mondays and Tuesdays the Interest of £200; To the Infirmary at Salisbury £200; To the Society for the Propagating of the Gospel in Foreign Parts £200; To the Society for Promoting Christian Knowledge £200. He likewise contributed largely towards erecting an Altar Piece and ornamenting the Chancel. By his Will he gave, To the Poor Inhabitants of this Town, to be distributed within three months after his Decease £1000, To the Poor receiving Alms £50, To the Poor of 2 Alms Houses £8 : 8*s*. For Clothing, Educating, and Apprenticing Thirty poor Boys £732, For Clothing, Educating, and Apprenticing Fifteen poor Girls £294 : 15*s*. To the Poor of the Parish of Potterne £100, To the Trustees appointed for erecting a Charity School, for instructing Indians in the Protestant Religion £200: The Residue of his Estate to be distributed amongst the poor Tradesmen and Women of this Town, Amounting to £1978 : 8 : 7.

Also, in Memory of Susannah his first Wife, Anne, his second Wife,

And of his Son John Thurman, Gent. who Died Nov. 3rd, 1764, Aged 43.

Arms—Argent, on a pale, azure, a tilting-spear of the first between two lions rampants, gules.

In Memory of Mary, Wife of Joseph Needham, jun. Ob. 1 August 1732, Æt. 19.

And also Penelope, wife of Joseph Needham, Ob. 19 May, 1738, Ætat. 22.

In Memory of Joseph Needham, who Died April 7, 1778, Aged 75.

Arms—Argent, a bend ingrailed between two bucks' heads caboshed, azure; impaling azure, a unicorn or, on a chief of the last three roses proper.

On a monument in S. Transept.

In Memory of Thomas Wilde, Gent. and Elizabeth, his Wife. Also John Wilde and Ann, their beloved Son and Daughter. This Stone is Erected by Mrs. Imber, of Winchester, their only surviving Daughter. 1773.

On Flat Stones in S. Transept.

H. S. E.

Thomas and Ann, Son and Daughter of Thomas and Elizabeth Wilde. Ann died Oct. 14th, 1696, Aged 10 years, Thomss died June 22, 1697, Aged 8 months.

Hic Jacent Reliquiæ Johannis Wild. Obiit Sept. 10, 1727, Ætat. 24.

Elizabeth Wild Dyed December 17, 1751, Aged 89.

Anna Wild, Filiæ Tho. & Eliz. Wild, Gent. Obiit 24 April 1722, Ætat. 22.

Thomas Wild, Gent. Obiit 20 Jan. 1731, Ætat. 78.

Ann, Wife of William Ludlow, Departed this Life Feb. 9th, 1784, Aged 31.

Two of their Children died in their Infancy.

On Flat Stones in south aisle.

Underneath are Deposited the Remains of Eleanor Baily, Relict of the Reverend John Baily, Rector of South Cadbury, and of Sparkford, in the County of Somerset, and Daughter of Francis Hollesnewman, Esq. of the same County. She Died the 12th Feb. 1782, Aged 79 years.

And of Caroline Florence Carpenter, Daughter of Richard and Sarah Carpenter, who Departed this Life March 10th, 1792, Aged 18 years.

Also of Richard Carpenter, who Died April 20, 1803, Aged 83 years.

In Memory of Ann Cambridge, who Departed this Life March 22, 1806, Aged 60 years.

Underneath Lyeth the Remains of Barbara, Wife of John Herne, and Daughter of the Rev. Mr. George Bradford, Vicar of Marden. She departed this life the 6th Day of August, 1733, Aged 44.

Also Underneath Lyeth the Remains of Mr. John Herne, who Departed this Life the 10th day of Oct. 1770, Aged 78 years.

Mrs. Mary White died Nov. 4th, 1767, Aged 78 years.

Thomas Thurman, Gent. 1777.

M. S. 1796.

A List of Benefactors

To this Town and Parish.

N. B. Benefactions extending to the Town are marked * Confined to the Parish thus ¶.

A. D.

1572 Given by Mr. Henry Morris to ye Poor per Annum for ever £.1 0 0.

* Given by Mr. John Archard to ye Poor £.10.

*1587 Given by the Rev. Mr. Keymes, to be lent gratis £.20 0 0

*1595 Given by ye Lady Sherrington, to be lent gratis £.40 0 0.

*1603 Given by ye Rev. Mr. Atwell, to ye poor per Ann. £.1 6 8.

*1616 Given by Sir Henry Baynton, Kt. to ye Poor £10 0 0

*1616 Given by ye said Sir Henry Baynton, to be lent gratis £.20 0 0

*1620 Given by ye Virginia Company, to be lent gratis £.40 0 0.

*1622 Given by Mr. Thomas Shepherd, to be lent gratis £.10 0 0.

*1623 Given by Mr. Ralph Pierce to ye Poor £5 0.

*1624 Given by Mr. William Barret, to be lent gratis £.5 0 0.

*1631 Given by Robert Hyde, Esq. to be lent gratis £.10 0 0.

* Given by Mr. Anthony Hort to ye New Alms House per Ann. £.1 0 0.

* Given by Mr. William Boke to ye two Alms Houses, per Ann. £.1 6 0.

On Tablets inside the Tower.

Given by Elizabeth Imber
Sixteen Pounds a year, to be paid by the Dean
and Chapter of the Cathedral
Church in Winchester for ever.
This Money is to put Seven Girls to School, to learn
To read and work, and go to Church on Sundays,
and towards Clothing them, as is mentioned in
the Declaration of Trust, a Copy of which is left
with the Minister for the time being, and his
Successors for ever.

A. D. 1704. Given by Mary Eyles, Widow of . . . . . The Rents and Profits of the Messuage, formerly called the Salutation, now the Elm Tree, to be applyed for buying Coals for Six Alms House Men, putting six poor Natives to School, and buying linen Shifts for poor Women; being in all per An. £.8 0.

1750 Given by Thomas Sutton, Gent. to the poor of the New Alms House the Interest of £.20.

A. D.

¶ 1728. Given by Mrs. Kent, the Interest thereof to to be laid out in Bread, and given to ye Poor every Christmas Day, for ever, £.20 0 0.

¶ 1731. Given by Mr. Thomas Wild, the Interest thereof to be applyed yearly towards teaching and Clothing five poor Children, £.100 0 0.

¶ 1739. Given by Mr. Thomas Giffard, Ironmonger, the Interest thereof to be laid out in Bread, and given to the Poor, every St. Thomas Day for ever, £.10 0 0.

¶ Given by John Drew, Esq. to ye Poor per Ann. £.6 9 0.

* Given by Mr. Coventry, to be disposed of in Bread, per Ann. £.6 10 0.

¶ Given by . . . . to ye Poor an Annuity, payable out of a tenement lately ye Angel Inn, of £.1 19 6.

¶ Given by Mr. Griffin Nicholas to ye Poor £.50 0 0.

* Given by Eliz. Strangeways to ye Minister and Poor £.40 0 0.

¶ 1638. Given by Mr. Michael Nicholas to ye Poor £.5 0 0.

* Given by Mr. Samuel Martin to ye Poor £.10.

* 1641. Given by Mr. John Pierce, for Charitable and other good uses £.270 0 0.

---

* 1647. Given by Mr. Edward Northey, to be lent gratis £.24 0 0.

¶ Given by Robert Nicholas, Esq. to ye Poor £.10 0 0.

* 1664. Given by William Woodroffe, for ye Instruction of ten Poor Boys, per Ann. £.5.

¶ 1670. Given by Mary Collier to ye Minister and Poor £.20 0 0.

* Given by Mr. Richard Hillet to ye Poor, £.20 0 0.

¶ Given by Mr. John Rogers to ye Poor £.10.

¶ Given by Sir John Eyles, Kt. to ye Poor a House and £.60 0 0

* Given by John Smith, Esq. to erect a School and School House withal £.300 0 0.

Mr. Wm. Neate, & } *Churchwardens.*
Mr. Thos. Maslen, }

East end of North Aisle.

A. D.

1759. Given by Mr. James Milns, late Officer of Excise, the Interest of One Hundred Pounds for ever, to be distributed every Sunday in three-penny Loaves to such indigent Persons of this Parish who do not receive Alms, attend Divine Service, and are of the Communion of the Church of England.

Given by Mrs. Joan Bisse, by Will, to ye Poor of St. John's Parish £.100: the Interest of which to be laid out Weekly in Bread. Which Legacy is confirmed by the Will of her Executrix, Mrs. Ann Blagdon, who bequeathed to the Rector and Churchwardens for the time being, in lieu of the above £.100, the sum of Four Pounds per Annum, settled on her Estate at Littleton.

The Church consists of a Chancel, Nave, north and south Aisles, and north and south Transepts. The Nave is supported on each side by five pointed arches. The Tower is an oblong structure, measuring from north to south 29 ft. 6 in. and from east to west 21 ft.

The Rev. James Liddiard Rector.

St. Mary's.

On a Monument against the north wall of Chancel.

H. S.
Jacobus Harris, Generosus,
Qui
Recentoribus Generosi indicus
repudiatis,
Fidem vere apostolicum, cultu inconcussu
cohonestavit
Pietatem utut languentem
Illustri exemplo
Restauravit;
Inter Domesticos Patris familiâs,
Munus feliciter adimplevit,
In omnes deniq. affabilem,
sed in seipsum scrupolose severum;
se præstitit quoad siceret;
Ea autem instabilitas rerum,
Ut qui florenti ætate vigebat
Variolarum vi. ereptus,
vergeret inopinato in occasum
En integrum,
Et ecce sincerum,
Nam hic requiescit in pace.
Obiit v° Calend. Augusti, MDCXCV.

Arms—Sable, a chevron between three bears or; impaling argent, a lion passant sable, between three fleur-de-lis, or.

X

East End.

In Memory of Mrs. Rebecca Garth, who died Feb. 9th, 1785, Widow of John Garth, Esq. Daughter and Coheiress of John Brompton, Esq. Distinguished by her exemplary Piety, endowed with every Christian Virtue, beloved, respected, and regretted.

This Monument is Erected by her Dutiful and Affections Sons and Daughters, as a just tribute to the best of Mothers.

Blessed are the Righteous, they shall be had in everlasting Remembrance, and their works shall follow them.

Arms—Or, two lions passant between three crosslets, fitchy sable, crescent for difference; impaling, or, two lions passant, gules.

M. S.

Post tantos Labores
Totidemq. sermones,
Hic demum quiete silet
Dignissime Reverendus
Henricus Johnson, A. M.
Hujus Ecclesiæ Rector,
Pulpitiq. dominator,
Cocionator strenuus frequensq.
Præpoteus ac desiderabilis,
Dictis factisq. primævus,
Verè et omninode Theologus
Sacris Paginis
Literis infuetis
Versatissimus,
Rara tamen Modestia
Præstabas,
Vir sobrietate vitæ gravis,
Suavitate morum placidus,
Nulliq. molestus,
Quem in sylvis vivarium solitudini vacantem,
Dolorosa heu! tandem fistula,
Sibi fœliciter gravitaq. aliis
In sanctorum turbam,
Fideliumq. Salutem,
Erogavit.
Oct. 31, 1681.

Sacred to the Memory of Miss Frances Garth, Youngest Daughter of John and Rebecca Garth. She Died in London March 6th, 1768, Aged 24, and lies underneath, near her Father.

Under the three Stones Beneath lye the Bodies of Sara, the Pious and faithfull Wife of John Tayler, of this Parish, Gent. who died 16 July, 1674, Ætatis suæ 62, And of their three Sons and two Daughters: Isaac, Mr of Arts, and Rector of Almer, in cō Dorset, A constant and faithfull Preacher of the word, died 18th April, 1673, A° Ætatis suæ 28; James died 9th July, 1650, A° Ætatis suæ 3; Timothy died 25 May, 1656, A° Ætatis suæ 7; Sarah died 20 August 1651, An° Ætatis suæ 15; Mary died 8th June, 1647, A° Ætatis suæ 7.

North Wall.

In Memory of Richard Griffiths, Apothecary, Died the 31 July, 1758, Aged 32 years.

Robertus, Filius Roberti Townsend, A. M. hujus Ecclesiæ Rectoris. Obiit 23 Sept. An. 1700, Ætatis suæ 3.

Here Lyeth ye Body of Simon . . . . .
Citizen and Grocer of London, ...
Sonne of Walter Ashton, of . . . . .
in ye County of Staff: Gent. . . . . . .
Had by Elizabeth, Daughter . . . . .
Wheler, Esq. 5 Children, wh . . . .
This Life ye 4 of August, 1638,
Aged Forty years.

Arms—On a fess, a crescent charged with a crescent, in chief three lozenges.

Flat Stones in Chancel.

Henry Wilcocks, Batchelor of Arts, Son of James Wilcocks, Batchelor of Divinity, Departed this Life ye 3d Day of Oct. 1681, Aged 19 years.

Here Lyeth ye Body of the Rev. Mr. John Gordon, Rector of Little Cheverell, who died July ye 31, 1735, Aged 70.

Here Lyeth the Body of Mary Gurnell, Wife of Thomas Gurnell, Esq. of the Parish of Great Ealing, in the County of Middlesex, who died April 22, 1782, Aged 52.

Sacred to the Memory of Ellen, Wife of Duncan Macfarlane, Esq. of Maidenhead Bridge, in the County of Berks, who departed this Life March the 2nd, 1808, Aged 63.

In Hopes of a Joyfull Resurrection unto Eternal Bliss, hereunder lieth what is Mortal of Mary, first the Wife of James Harris, Gent. Deceased, and afterwards of John Locke, of this Borough, Gent. A Wife, Parent, and Friend, most virtuous, tender, loving, and sincere, most cautious of the true religion, under the most severe affliction most truly meek, patient, and resigned; who, amidst the painful tears of her Husband, Children, and Relations most beloved, Departed this life the 25 of June, 1739, Ætatis 67.

On Flat Stones in Nave.

Charles Lowe, Gent. Departed this life the 11th of Nov. 1785, Aged 46.

Sarah Lowe, Wife of Charles Lowe, Gent. died 15th Jan. 1808, Aged 71 years.

Sarah Lowe, Wife of Henry Swann Lowe, died 9th March, 1801, Aged 27 years.

Also Thomas Wright Lowe, Son of the above-named Charles and Sarah Lowe, died 25 Oct. 1816, Aged 52 years.

In Memory of Mr. Edward Phillips, Clothier, of this Borough, who died Nov. 10, 1751, Aged 69 years.

Also of Jane, his Wife, who died August 15, 1751, Aged 70 years.

Also of Timothy, their Son, who died June 11, 1745, Aged 22 years.

Also of Edward Poore, their Grandson, who died in his Infancy, Dec. 17, 1743.

Also of Jane, their Daughter, the Wife of George Webb Poore, Gent. who died the 5th Day of Dec. 17 . . .

Also of Mary Ann Poore, their Daughter, who died the next Day, Aged 15 weeks and two Days.

And of George Webb Poore, Gent. who died Nov. 9, 1766, Aged 51 years.

Underneath are deposited the Remains of Edward Phillips, Clothier, who died April 17th, 1767, Aged 34 years.

And of Hannah, his Wife, who died April 26, 1757, Aged 35 years.

Sacred to the Memory of Sally Wilkinson, Daughter of William and Sibella Wilkinson, of Streatham, in Surrey, who Departed this Life May the 12th, 1797, Aged 15 years.

Underneath are Deposited the Remains of Mrs. Jane Hardyman, who died 12th January, 1802.

In Memory of Elizabeth, Wife of Benjamin Fuller. She Departed this Life Sept. 9th, 1741, Aged 32.

Also of Ann, their Daughter, who died in her Infancy, March 27, 1739.

Ann Fuller, Daughter of Benj. and Eliz. Fuller, died Feb. 5 : 174$\frac{8}{9}$, Aged 8 years.

Also in Memory of Elizabeth, the second Wife of Benjamin Fuller. She departed this life the 15th day of December, 1774, Aged 76 years.

On a Monument in the North Aisle.

Near this Place are deposited the Remains of Abel Filkes, Esq. many years a medical practitioner in this Town. He was an ornament to his profession, and much esteemed and respected by all his Friends and Relations, by whom his loss will be long regretted. He died Dec. 20th, 1815, Aged 65.

Also James Filkes, Son of the above, who died Sept. 20th, 1796, Aged 8 years.

On Flat Stones in North Aisle.

Infra hoc Saxum jacet corpus Johannis Overton, hujus Municipii incolæ, qui obiit primo die Maij, Anno Dom. 1730, et Ætatis suæ 61.

Hic etiam . . . . Hannah Overton, prædicti Johannis Overton neptis, quæ in infantia . . ia vitam cum morte Anno futura . . . commutavit, Disce quid esq. . . . . . . monitis parento virator, vita et mort . . . . . . sequiro ipse ducem.

Here Lyeth the Body of Robert Forman, Gent. who departed this Life February the 12, Anno Dom. 1692.

Here lyeth the Body of Margaret Hope, Wife of Edward Hope, ye younger, Gent. of this Borough, who Departed this Life December ye 1st, Anno Dom. 1689.

Here Lyeth the Body of Robert Hulbert, jun. who Departed this Life the 11th Day of Oct. 1742, Aged 42 years.

Here Lieth the Body of Edward Hope, Gent. who departed this Life the 3 Day of Feb. 1706, Aged 66 years.

On a Monument in S. Aisle.

In the Chancel of this Church lie Interred the Remains of John Garth, Esq. Son of Colonel Thomas Garth, of Harold, in the County of Bedford, by Elizabeth, Daughter of Thomas Colleton, Esq. April 27th, 1732, he was chosen the Recorder, and Feb. 26, 1739, elected Representative in Parliament for this Borough of Devizes. Zealous in its Service, and attentive to its Prosperity, this honour was repeatedly conferred upon him for the remainder of his Life, ever esteeming it a real honour to represent a Borough Distinguished for its Loyalty, Freedom, and Integrity. To the sedentary way of living (which he fell into from an early and continued love for the pleasures of literature), the illness was chiefly owing that occasioned his Death, which happened on the 26th of December, 1764, Aged 63. With his Cotemporaries his Virtues are in Remembrance: to Posterity the Example of his Life may be Recommended; his Wife losing by his Death the tenderest Husband, his Children an affectionate Father, his Constituents a faithful Servant, and his Country an useful Citizen, and truly virtuous Man. In testimony of her sincerest and most dutiful respect, this Monument is erected to his Memory by his afflicted widow Rebecca Garth.

Arms—Or, two lions passant armed gules, between three crosslets fitchy, sable; impaling or, two lions passant gules.

On Flat Stones under the Tower.

Here Lyeth the Body of Mary, ye Wife of John Smith, who Departed this life Jan. the 16, A. D. 172½, Aged 25 years.

Here also Lyeth ye Body of Grace, the Wife of John Smith, who Departed this Life August 17 . . Aged 36 years.

James Filks died
Nov. 23, 1745, Aged 57.
Mrs. Ann Filks, Wife of the above,
dyed June 6, 1761, Aged 75.

Children of the above here interred:
Elizabeth Filks died Dec. 9, 1754, Aged 24.
Mary Filks died Aug. 12, 1759, Aged 34.
John Filks died April 27, 1760, Aged 39.
Ann, Wife of the Rev. Mr. John Needham, of Bristol, died August 26, 1775, Aged 58.
Also Four children died in their Infancy.

Here lyeth the Body of Sarah, the Daughter of Mr. John Filkes, who Departed this life Oct. 1719, Aged 26 years.

Here lyeth also the Body of John Filkes, Gent. who Departed this Life 1st Day of August, 1728, Aged 66 years.

Here Lyeth the Body of Dionisia, Wife of John Cooke, jun. Glover, who dyed Nov. ye 18, A. D. 1733, Aged 27 years.

On a wood frame in south aisle.

Anno Dom. 1750. To the sacred Memory of Eleanor his Wife, Late Mrs. Eleanor Powell, who also gave Six two-penny Loaves of Bread to Six poor Widows of this Parish weekly for ever, not receiving Alms, as the Churchwarden shall think fit.

On a wooden frame in north aisle.

Anno Dom. 1718. To the sacred Memory of Mr. Philip Phillips, Late of this Borough, who gave Six two-penny Loaves of Bread to six such poor persons of this Parish weekly for ever not receiving Alms, as the Churchwarden shall think fit.

Against the vaulting of the Nave.

Orate pro: aĩa Willi Smyth, qui ista eccliãm fieri fecit, qui obiit primo die mensis Junij, Anno Dñi Mill CCCC XXXVI.

The Church consists of a Chancel, Nave, North and South Aisles: the Nave is supported by five pointed arches on each side.

The Rev. James Liddiard Rector.

The Chapelry of St. James.

On Flat Stones in Chancel.

Robert Nicholas Esq. Dyed ye 20 Day of December, A. D. 1667.

Here Lyeth also ye Body of Griffin Nicholas, Gent. ob. December ye 11th, 1717, Anno Ætat. suæ 71.

In Memory of William Coward, who died Dec. 23rd, 1766, Aged 34 years.

Mary-Ann, his Daughter, died October 7th, 1766, Aged 4 years.

Under this Stone lyes the Remains of Mrs. Hannah Barnes, late Wife of Charles Barnes, of Essendon, in the County of Herts. Esq. who Departed this life Nov. the 26th, 1779, Aged 71 years.

Also underneath lieth the remains of Charles Barnes, Esq. who died 27 Feb. 1801, Aged 84 years.

In Memory of Jane, Wife of Thomas Coward, who departed this life 20th October, 1796, Aged 34 years.

Also of Thomas Coward, who died 7th Oct. 1812, Aged 51 years.

And also of Mary, Daughter of Thomas and Jane Coward, who died 6th June, 1818, Aged 31 years.

On Flat Stones in Nave.

In Memory of Mary, the Wife of James Filkes, who Departed this life the 31 day of August, Anno Dom. 1735, Aged 78 years.

Underneath lie the Remains of Joseph Alexander, who departed this Life the 3rd of January, 1795, in the 36 year of his Age.

On Monuments in the North Aisle.

In Memory of John Paradice, and Jane his Wife.

John	Died	10th September	1731	Ætat.	72
Jane		2nd March	1706		46

William	Died	22nd July	1712	Ætat.	24
Richard		29th April	1725		31
Mary		2nd February	1726		29
Francis		22nd September	1728		29
Edward		11th November	1738		35

Susannah, Wife of Richard Read, died 6th Jan. 1766, Aged 64.

Mary, Wife of William Read, died 13th Jan. 1778, Aged 38.

William Read died 8th Feb. 1779, Aged 43.

Richard Read died 24th December, 1790, Aged 88.

And Richard Read, jun. died 2d Feb. 1792, Aged 52.

Also of Ann, Wife of Richard Read, jun. who died 12 August, 1809, Aged 68 years.

Against North Wall of North Aisle.

M. S.

Roberti Nicholas, Armri, olim in Burgo de Devizes Justiciarii, cujus Æquitas oppressorum grates, liberalitas pauperum preces, integritas bonorum favorem, facile conciliavit, et retinuit facillime, omnibus multum flebilis occidit quotquot virtutis et pacis amantes 7mo die Januarii,

Anno { Domini 1725,
Ætatis suæ 65.

Primis ille nuptiis duxit Martham, Henrici Bright filiam, ex Aulâ Novâ, prope Pakerstain, in co. Suffolcia, juxta maritum, illa etiam jacet sepulta, quæ mortua est, Aug. 26, 1692. Feliet prius enixa partu, Robertum, natum 7 Maii, 1686, mortuum 27 Aprilis, 1722; Annam, natum 5 Junii, 1688, mortuum 7 Sep. 1690; Johannem, natum 1 Jul. 1691, mortuum 31 Aug. 1746. Secundis deinde nuptiis duxit Janam, Johannis Child, apud Devizes, filiam unicam, quæ mortua est, 21 Sept. 1725. Illius cum natis, quos marito peperit, Johanne Child, nato 7 Sept. mortuo 28 Oct. 1694; Eduardo, nato 6 Jan. 1695, mortuo 28 Feb. 173$\frac{0}{1}$; Thoma, nato 19 Jan. 1696, mortuo 9 March, 1702; Janâ, natâ 24 Feb. 1701, mortuâ 2 Sept. 1765.

Lector, quicunque sis, pro certo habeas quod morti nos debemur omnes, nec incertior mortuorum est resuscitatio, ita vivas ut nunquam te vixisse pudeat, sic neque moriturus unquam mortum perlimebis.

Near this place are deposited the Remains of Bridget Nicholas, Wife of Edward Nicholas, Daughter of Oliffe and Joan Richmond, of Ashton Keynes, in this County. She died Jan. 12, 175$\frac{1}{2}$, and her reward is with her, for she was distinguished in every relation of life, a dutiful Daughter, a prudent Wife, and a tender Parent, ever a sincere and pious Member of the Church of England. Though left a Widow in the bloom of life, when youth and pleasure are too strong incentives, these she subjected to the interest of her only Child: the culture of his Mind and improvement of his Fortune engrossed her Cares; yet of such exemplary justice, that, though left in circumstances which would little more than supply the decent accommodations of life, she generously gave up the greatest part of her income to dischaige Family Debts she had no share in contracting, disdaining to be exposed to the piercing taunts of undischarged creditors, nobly rescuing from infamy succeeding generations, and preferring fair Fame and Virtue, the Flower of Honour, to the vain glare and false charms of Wealth and Luxury. Thus provident without parsimony, charitable without ostentation, cheerful without levity, and hospitable with œconomy, she united those graces which rendered her esteemed by all: It were an injury to the Publick to deprive it of so fair an example, an injury to her Memory not to give this just Character of her, and not to attempt it unpardonable in him who has derived such inestimable benefits from it. Her only surviving Son, E. R. Nicholas, M. B. erected this Marble as a sincere testimony of the regard and esteem he bears to the Memory of his ever-honoured Parent.

Underneath her lie interred her two other Children, John and Jane, who died in their Infancy.

In Memory of Jenny Nicholas, Wife of E. R. Nicholas, M. B. Daughter of W. and K. Neate, of Devizes. She died Oct. 12, A. D. 1766, Aged 38.

Her life, though short, in every station was a most fair pattern of excellence and perfection, for it was her utmost endeavour to be, as she had every requisite to make her, as good a Daughter and as good a Wife, as good a Parent and as good a Christian, as Woman possibly could be. She was to her Husband the best of Wives; her affectionate assiduity in his illness appeared to be as much her pleasure as her Duty: such was her painful cares, such her anxious concern for his health, that she daily impaired her own, and proved, by her too early end, that innate gentleness of temper, enlarged benevolence, unaffected modesty, and spotless purity of heart, exempt none from the power of the grave; yet constant and devout attention to the sacred purposes of religious worship had so prepared her, that in her last hour of trial, strengthened by prayer, by faith supported, she with such ease and serenity of mind, superior to all the terrors of Death, resigned her affections towards this world, as if well assured of the perfect enjoyment of endless peace and everlasting happiness in the Life of the world to Come.

Arms—Azure, a chevron engrailed between three owls, or.
Crest—An owl, or, on a cap of dignity.

On a Monument opposite the preceding.

Blush not, Marble,
To rescue from oblivion
The Memory of Oliffe Richmond Nicholas,
Eldest Son
Of Edward-Richmond and Jenny Nicholas.
He died March 3d, 1767,
In the 14th year of his Age.

1.

Why do thy pensive kindred join
In vain, Dear Boy, to mourn thy fate?
The fleeting joys of thee and thine,
And pleasure of too short a date?
Why cruel Death's untimely haste upbraid,
And weep the wound its savage stroke has made?

2.

How frail, alas, thy fairest bloom!
Henceforth be every tear suppress;
Or shed for joy, that from the tomb,
Thou soar'st to mansions of the blest,
From vice, from pain, from earth to heaven remov'd,
Thy memory honour'd, as thy life belov'd.

3.

Thy morals pure in opening youth,
For learning thy unfoil'd desire,
Thy gentlest manners, strictest truth,
Shall future times to virtue sire;
While here the letter'd marble speaks thy name,
And pays this last just tribute to thy fame.

North Wall of North Aisle.

Near this place lyeth the Body of Thomas, the Son of Robert Hayward, of Rowndway, who died the 9th Day of May, 1738, Aged 21 years.

Beneath this Stone lyeth the Remains of Robert Hayward and Elizabeth his Wife. He dyed Oct. ye 5th, 1763, Aged 55 years. She dyed Sept. 25, 1765, Aged 63 years.

In Memory of Mary, Wife of Robert Hayward, Jun. She died Oct. 31, 1775, Aged 30 years.

Also of Robert Hayward, Jun. who died 11th Dec. 1814, Aged 79 years.

M. S.

Roberti Nicholas, A. B. Roberti Nicholas, de Burgo de Devizes, Armigeri, et Marthæ uxoris ejus, natu maximi Filij, Rectoris de Manningford Bruce, qui obiit 27 die Aprilis, Anno Dni CIƆDCCXXVII.

On Flat Stones in North Aisle.

In Memory of Robert Hayward, and Mary his Wife. She Died 31 Oct. 1775, Aged 30 years. He died 11th Dec. 1814, Aged 79 years.

Joseph Wight, late Grocer in Devizes, died Feb. 4, 1756, Aged 65 years.

Against East End of South Aisle.

Beneath this Place is Interred the Bodyes of Robert Drewe, Gentleman, and Jane his Daughter, who Departed this life ye 29 and 30 of March, 1671.

Ann, Daughter of Robert Drewe, junior, dyed January ye 20, 1693.

Also here lyeth ye Body of Robert Drewe, Gent. who dyed ye 10th of December, 1695.

West End.

Beneath this is interred the Bodys of Thomas and Elinor, Son and Daughter of Mr. Henry Flower, by Mary his Second Wife. Elinor Died Nov. 12, 1705, Aged 18 months, Thomas Died April 10th, 1706, Aged 10 months.

Here also is Interred the Body of Elinor the Daughter of Mr. Henry Flower. She Died the 5th of May, 1712, Aged 3 years and 6 weeks.

Near this Place is Interred the Body of Mrs. Sarah Jones, Daughter of Thomas Jones, Esq. of the Priory of Uske, in the County of Monmouth. Ob. Jan. 22, 1743, Æt. 56.

Also here is Interred the Body of Mrs. Mary Flower, Wife of Henry Flower, Gent. (and Sister to the above-said Mrs. Sarah Jones.) Ob. April 12, 1748, Ætat. 70.

Also the Body of the said Henry Flower, Gent. Ob. August 29, 1750, Ætat. 85.

Also Mr. Edward Flower, Son of the aforesaid. Ob. 14 July, 1769, Æt. 51.

Sacred to the Memory of John Flower, Gent. who Departed this Life the 11th of Feb. 1788, Aged 75.

On Flat Stones in south aisle.

In Memory of Mary, the Wife of Richard Smith, who Departed this life the 12th of December, 1765, Aged 79.

In Memory of Ann, Wife of William Smith. Obiit ye 27th of March, 1707, Aged 56.

In Memory of Thomas, Son of William Smith. Ob. ye 18 of Oct. 1720.

In Memory of Richard Smith, who departed this life 14th of May, 1766, Aged 80.

The Chapel consists of a Chancel, Nave, North and South Aisles.

The Rev. Mr. Macdonald Minister.

BRADLEY.

On Monuments in S. Aisle.

In Memory of William Long, Esq. of Melksham, who Departed this Life June the 15th, 1773, in the 64 year of his Age.

Like as a father pitieth his own children, even so is the Lord merciful unto them that fear him; for he knoweth whereof we are made, he remembereth that we are but dust. The days of man are but as grass: he flourisheth as a flower of the field; as soon as the wind goeth over it, it is gone, and the place thereof shall know it no more; but the merciful goodness of the Lord endureth for ever and ever upon them that fear him. Part of the 103 Psalm.

Arms—Quarterly, first and fourth Long; second and third perpale, first argent, second azure.

Near this Place is Deposited the Body of William Trenchard, Esq. of Cutteridge, in the County of Wilts. (by ye Body of Ellen, his beloved Wife.) He died the 22d of August, in the year of our Lord 1713, and in the 76th year of his Age.

His Wife was the Daughter of Sir George Norton, of Abbot's Leigh, in the County of Somerset, by whom he had ten Children, whereof four lye buryed in this Church, and only four survived him; viz. John, Anna, Frances, and Ellen, which three Daughters he made joint Executrixes, who in performance of his Will, and in grateful Memory of their indulgent Parent, erected this Monument.

Arms—Quarterly, first and fourth paly of six; second and third a saltire: impaling, barry of four, in chief an escutcheon ermine.

Underneath are deposited the Remains of Henry Long, Esq. of Melksham, in the County of Wilts. who departed this life 23d of October, 1727, Aged 40 years.

And also of Henry Long, jun. his youngest Son, who departed this life 30th of August, 1739, Aged 26 years.

As likewise of Mrs. Ellin Long, Relict of the first, and Mother to the last of those Gentlemen. She was the youngest Daughter of William Trenchard, Esq. of Cutteridge, in this Parish, and Sister to the celebrated Author of the Independent Whig, and other valuable works. She inherited the Virtues of that ancient and worthy Family, in every stage of life pious and prudent, charitable to the Poor, and a most sincere Friend. Thus, much beloved whilst living, She died lamented July the 9th, 1752, at the Age of 65 years, and to her Memory particularly this Monument was erected by the appointment of her grateful Daughter, Mrs. Ellin Thresher, in May, 1756.

I know that my Redeemer liveth, and that he shall stand at the latter day upon the Earth.
Job the 19th, verse the 25th.

On Flat Stones in S. Aisle.

Here Lyeth the Body of Henry Long, Esq. late of Melksham, who departed this Life the 23 Oct. 1727, Aged 40 years.

Here Lyeth ye Body of William Trenchard, Esq. Jun. Son of William Trenchard, Esq. of Cutteridge, who dyed July 12th, Anno Dom. 1704, Aged 26 years.

Also here lieth Grace, Daughter of William Trenchard, Esq. who died June ye 11th, 1707, Aged 23 years.

Also here lieth the Body of Henry Long, Gent. Second Son of Henry Long, Esq. who lyeth interred under the next Stone by Ellen, his Wife, another Daughter of William Trenchard, Esq. and which said Henry Long, his Son, dyed August 30th, 1739, Aged 26 years.

Part of an Inscription in North Aisle.

Johannes Stafford, Obijt quinto die mensis Septembris, Anno Dom. Millesimo c c c c quadra.....

Hatchment.

Azure, a fess dancette, ermine, between six crosslets fitchy argent, in chief an annulet of the last: impaling or, dancette, two bars, azure, charged with two dancette, argent, a chief, azure.

Mrs. Rachel Long gave three Pounds annually to Six poor Families of this Parish.

The Church consists of a Chancel, Nave, North and South Aisles. The Nave is supported on each side by three pointed arches. In the windows of the chancel and the aisles is a little painted glass.

Archdeacon Daubeny Vicar.

WESTBURY.

On a Monument against the north wall of Chancel.

In Memory of Edward Bailey, Gent. who died July 12th, 1728.

And of Sarah, his Wife, who died May 20, 1707.

Also of Edmund Baily, their Son, who died Decem. 20th, 1728.

And of Ann, his Wife, who died Dec. 27th, 1728.

William, the Son of Edmund Baily, sen. Died July, 1711.

And Elizabeth, Daughter of Edmund Bailey, Jun. Died June 2d, 1742, Aged 19 years.

With five of her Brothers and Sisters, who died Infants.

This Monument was Erected by Mrs. Sarah Baily, the only surviving Branch of the Family in this Place.

Also Sarah Baily, who died Nov. 11th, 1761. Æt. 71.

Arms—Or, on a fess ingrailed azure, three fleur-de-lis of the first, between three horses heads erased of the second; impaling per fess azure, a bend indented argent, within a border ingrailed of the same, in base, argent, three bars, sable.

On the left side of the above.

This Monument was erected by the leave of Thomas Bennet, Esq. who is proprietor of the Chancel.

Flat Stones in Chancel.

This lyeth in Memory of Thomas and Elizabeth, Children of John Bennett, Esq.

Elizabeth, } dyed March ye 23d, 1675,
Thomas, } 3 1676.

Here Lyeth ye Body of Robert Wadham, of Imber, in ye County of Wilts. Esq. who Departed this life the 4th day of October, 1691. He married Hannah, ye Daughter of Samuel Trotman, of Bucknelll, in ye County of Oxon, Esq.

Here Lyeth the Body of Frances, second Wife of John Wadman, of Brook, in ye County of Wilts. Esq. who dyed the 28th day of August, 1681, and left to survive her, Robert, William, and Frances W . . . . was daughter of Robert Drew, of South Broome, In the same County, Esq. In Memory of . . ome this Stone was laid by her Sonn Robert Wadman, Esq. his Father, John Wadman dyed ye 3 of October, 1688, in ye 86th year of his Age, and lyeth interred at Imber, in ye aforesaid County.

Here Lyeth the Bodys of Michall, Stephen, and Hannah, ye Sons and Daughter of Stephen and Hester Whatly. Also Mary Rennell, their Grandmother, died ye 14th Day of November, 1690.

Also here lyeth the Body of Thomas Whatley, the Son of Stephen and Hester Whatley, who Departed this Life the 22d Day of September, 1714, in the 26 year of his Age.

In Memory of Thomas Huntley. Died Jan. 13th, 1766, Aged 63.

Also Mary his Wife. Died July 1st, 1762, Aged 66, with Eight of their Grand Children.

In Memory of Elizabeth, Daughter of Thomas and Hannah Paviour, who died August 12th, 1783, Aged 11 months.

Also here lieth the Remains of Thomas Paviour, who departed this life July ye 5th, 1785, Aged 30 years.

Underneath this Stone are deposited the Remains of Hannah, Wife of Arthur Paviour, who departed this life the 7th Day of December, 1790, Aged 30 years. Also James, (Son of the above) who died Sept. the 7th, 1790, Aged 2 years.

In a Vault underneath this Stone is Deposited the Mortal remains of Joseph Paviour, who departed this life the 27th Day of March, . . 03, Aged 71 years.

Reader, observe—beyond the Age of Man
Life extended—yet was but a span:
. . . . ider, then, how weak, at best thy trust,
. . . e of Clay, that's founded in the dust.

Also Hannah, the Daughter of Robert and Jane Paviour, who Departed this Life January the 8th, 1809, Aged 8 months.

And Mary Paviour, the Wife of Joseph Paviour, who Departed this Life March the 25th, 1810, Aged 77 years.

She was a virtuous Woman, She liv'd a sober life,
She was a tender Mother, and a loving Wife.

Underneath this Stone lieth the Remains of Eleanor Andrews, Widow, who departed this life March 22d, 1769, Aged 61 years.

Underneath this Stone lies ye Body of Sarah, Wife of John Gowen, Esq. eldest Sister and Coheiress of ye late Rev. William Sainsbury, Rector of Beckington, Somerset, who died ye 24th of December, 1780, Aged 64. Also the Remains of John Gowen, Esq. who died 19 July, 1801, Aged 89.

Arms—Ermine, on a saltire, azure, 5 fleur-de-lis . . impaling azure, three lozenges in bend within a border ingrailed, or.

Crest—A demi goat erect.

Here Lyeth the Body of Sarah, the Wife of Edmund Bayly, who departed this life the 20th of May, A. D. 1707, Aged 49 years.

Here Lyeth ye Body of Larance Hayward, who Departed this life Jan. the 26th, 1780, Aged 79 years.

Also here lieth the Body of Sarah, Wife of Larance Hayward, who Departed this life December the 27th, 1789, Aged 72 years.

Here Lyeth the Body of Abigail Bayly, of this Parish, who Departed this life April ye 16, 1706, Aged 51.

Also underneath this Stone lie deposited the remains of Elizabeth Earle, Widow of Joseph Earle, Esq. who died 8th October, 1762, Aged 62 years.

Also of Edmund Bayly, who died 15th Jan. 1781, Aged 77.

Son and Daughter of Edmund Bayly, late of this Parish, Gentleman.

Underneath this Stone Lieth the Mortal Remains of William Gaisford, jun. Esq. Died the 6th of July, 1762, Aged 22 years.

Also of Thomas Gaisford, Esq. Died the 14th of November, 1774, Aged 73 years.

Sarah Gaisford, Wife of Thomas Gaisford, Esq. Died the 11th of September, 1788, Aged 81.

John Gaisford, of Iford, Esq. Son of Thomas and Sarah Gaisford, Esq. died the 29th of July, 1810, Aged 63.

Arms—A chevron between three greyhounds courant.

Underneath are Deposited the Remains of Thomas Philly, late of this Place, Gent. who Died March 20th, 1782, Aged 66 years.

On a Monument against the north wall of the Vestry Room.

This Monument is erected, as a token of filial affection, by the only Daughter of Eleanor Andrews, Widow, who Departed this life March the 22d, 1769, Aged Sixty One years, and whose Remains are interred near this Place.

Arms—Argent, on a bend sable three mullets of the first; impaling gules, on a fess, argent, three mullets, sable, between two tigers passant, or.

On Flat Stones.

Here Lyeth ye Body of Samuel Gibbs, Gent. who Departed this life ye 5th of May, 1715, Aged 64 years.

Also here lyeth the Body of Edith Gibbs, Wife of Samuel Gibbs, Gent, who Departed this life ye 15th Feb. 1729, Aged 81 years.

Also here Lyeth the Bodies of John and Hannah, Son and Daughter of ye said Samuel Gibbs, who both died Decem. ye 12th, 1698, John Aged 23 years, Hannah Aged 13 years.

Samuel Gibbs, Son of the above Samuel Gibbs, Died 11th Jan. 1742, Aged 61 years.

And Mary Gibbs, his Wife died 21 November, 1755, Aged 69 years.

Here Lyeth the Body of Hannah, Daughter of Samuel Gibbs, who Departed this life the fifteenth day of Sept. 1728, Aged eleven years and six months.

Also Here Lyeth the Body of James, Son of the said Samuel and Mary Gibbs, who Departed this life the 11th Day of Dec. 1730, Aged Eleven Years and ten Months.

Here Innocence and Filiall duty Lye, whose Breath
Was snatch'd by Early, not untimely Death;
Hence did they go, Just as they did begin
Sorrow to know, before they knew to sin:
Death, that doth sin and sorrow thus prevent,
Is the next blessing to a life well spent.

Here lyeth the Body of Bridget, Daughter of Samuel Gibbs, who Departed this life ye 5th of February, 1717, Aged 4 years and 2 months.

Dear to the Memory of George Franklin . . . . . Died March the 25th 1817, Aged 72 years.

Betty Franklin, Wife of the above, who Died November the 30th, 1820, Aged 70 years.

Underneath this Stone Resteth the Body of George, Son of Richard and Mary Cockle, who departed this life ye 17th day of March, 1756, Aged 27 years.

Underneath lieth the Body of Ann, Wife of James Humphries, who departed this life July 28, 1802, Aged 81 years.

Also to the Memory of James Humphries, Wool-stapler, who departed this life June 9th, 1806, Aged 75 years.

To the respected Memory of Ebenezer Humphries, who died July 22, 1809, Aged 69 years.

In Memory of James Tree, Gent. who died May ye 20th, 1770, Aged 60 years.

Also Ann, Wife of James Tree, who Died July ye 20th, 1768, Aged 59 years.

Also James, Son of the above, who died Nov. ye 3d, 1766, Aged 22 years.

Also Ann, Daughter of Richard and Ann Kebby, who died Feb. 14th, 1770, Aged 11 months.

Also Ann, their Daughter, who died in her infancy.

Also to the Memory of the aforesaid Richard Kebby, who Departed this life December the 3d, 1805, Aged 66 years.

Also to the Memory of Ann, Wife of Richard Kebby, who Departed this life February the 16th, 1806, Aged 59 years.

On a small Mon. against south-west pillar of the Tower.

Underneath lyeth the Body of Roger Fricker, who Departed this life July the 16th, 1724, Aged 41 years.

On Flat Stones in Nave.

In Memory of Mary Harry, Wife of George Harry, of Westbury, Gent. She departed this life the 27th July, 1794, Aged 30 years.

Also of two Infant Children, namely, John and Sarah Harry.

Underneath this Stone lieth the Body of Elizabeth Axford, who died August the 31st, 1780, Aged 19 years.

Also underneath this Stone are deposited the Remains of James Killing, who departed this life the 11th day of April, 1788, in the 22 year of his Age.

Underneath this Stone are deposited the Remains of Jane, Wife of James Goringe Troke, who departed this Life the 4th day of Feb. 1791, Aged 58 years.

Also Benjm Peach Nupier died Feb. 18th, 1808, Aged 11 months.

Also James Goringe Troke died Feb. 28th, 1808, Aged 63 years.

In Memory of Richard Hillier, who died in 1749.

Also Hester Pickford died in 1766.

Mary Hillier died in 1768.

Bertie Hillier died in 1770.

Bridget Hillier died in 1780, Aged 63 years.

Beneath this Stone are deposited, with those of his Ancestors, the Remains of the late Jeffery Gawen, Esq. many years one of his Majesty's Justices of the Peace, and Sen. Alderman of the City of Salisbury, who departed this life the 12th of February, 1805, Aged 82.

Underneath are Deposited the Remains of Samuel Edwards, Gent. Obiit March, 23d, 1761, Æt. 43.

Also Elizabeth, his Wife. Obiit March 23, 1787, Æt. 69.

Also John Edwards, Son of the above Samuel and Elizabeth. Obiit June 2d, 1793, Æt. 46.

Sacred to the Memory of William Smith, sen. Yeoman, of Westbury, who departed this life May the 20th, 1800, Aged 76 years.

Underneath is laid Hannah, the Wife of Samuel Hales. Dyed July, 1731.

John Hales, jun. Dy'd July 22, 1762.

Mary, Wife of William Emblen, of Buckland, Dy'd Nov. 1771.

John Hales, sen. Dyed Feb. 12th, 1773.

Hannah Hales, ye Daughter of John Hales, sen. Died April 7th, 1788.

Also in Memory of Mary, Wife of the late John Hales, sen. who Departed this life Jan. the 16, 1795.

Underneath this Stone resteth the Body of William Bourne, who Departed this life October ye 15th, 1755, Aged 40 years.

Also Hannah, his Daughter, who December, 1770.

And of Hannah, his Wife, who died Jan. 1776, Aged 58 years.

On Monuments in N. Aisle.

Sacred to the Memory of Elizabeth Hooper, Wife of William Hooper, of Brook Mill, who departed this life Oct. 29, 1808, Aged 79 years.

Sacred to the Memory of Ann, Wife of Matthew Taylor, of Semington, who died March 13th, 1772, Aged 36 years.

Also of Ann and Mary, Daughters of Matthew and Ann Tayler. Ann died Oct. 25th, 1779, Aged 13 years, Mary died Oct. 17, 1784, Aged 15 years.

Also of Ann, second Wife of the above Matthew Tayler, who died Dec. 12th, 1800, Aged 64 years.

Also of Mathew Tayler, who died January 2d, 1814, Aged 77 years.

D. O. M.

Resurrectionem Justorum,
Hic juxta expectat, quod mortale fuit
Viri si quis alius, inculpabilis,
Georgii Turner, Arm. A.M.
Pietate sincera candore illibato
Ingenio suavi,
Moribusque integritate ornatis
Virtutis et Pietatis,
Exemplar illuxit,
Veritatis cultor, Pacis Amicus
Diu cum Morbo sævo luctatus est, et Dolores,
Tantum non omni patientia superiores,
Summo, suæ cum divina Voluntate consensu,
Quam mitissime tulit
Quievit
Die viii° Novembris, Anno Salutis
1768.
In illius Memoriam
Amoris et observantie, Ergo,
Martha, conjux altera,
Antonii Trew, de Wareham, in agro
Dorsetensi, Generosi, filia unica, poni curavit.

On Flat Stones in North Aisle.

Underneath this Stone lie the Remains of James Vine. Died 6th August, 1788, Aged 5 months and 8 days.

Lucy Vine died 22d Jan. 1791, Aged 11 Weeks.
Hannah Vine died 9th March, 1791, Aged 17 Weeks. } Twins.

Lucy Hewlett Vine died 18 Sept. 1795, Aged 2 years and 20 days.

Also Daniel Vine, gent. Died Oct. 7th, 1803, Aged 56 years.

Also William Vine, Gent. Eldest Son of the above, who died Oct. 10th, 1813, Aged 43 years.

In Memory of Richard Bidwood, who died July the 10th, 1756, Aged 51 years.

Also Hannah, his Wife, who died August the 15th, 1788, Aged 83 years.

In Memory of James Taylor, and Mary his Wife, and three of their Sons, William, James, and John.

Also in Memory of Ann Taylor, Wife of Matthew Tayler, who died March the 13th, 1772, Aged 36 years.

Also in Memory of Ann and Mary, Daughters of the above Matthew and Ann Taylor. Ann died Oct. the 25th, 1779, Aged 13 years. Mary died Oct. the 17th, 1784, Aged 15 years.

South Wall of South Aisle.

In Perpetuam Memoriam.

Paul Phipps, Esq. of Leigh, in this Parish, died Decem. first, 1722, Aged 62.

John Phipps, Esq. of Leigh, in this Parish, Son of the above Paul, died Nov. 5th, 1739, Aged 65.

James Phipps, Esq. Son of Thomas Phipps, Esq. of Leigh, in this Parish, died Dec. 5th, 1734, Aged 22.

Wilton Phipps, Esq. of Leigh, in this Parish, Son of the above-named John, died July 11th, 1741.

Thomas Phipps, Esq. of Leigh, in this Parish, Son of the above Paul, died Feb. 23d, 1747, Aged 66 years, High Sheriff of the County in 1734.

William Phipps, Esq. of Leighton House, in this Parish, Son of the above John, died Jan. 8th, 1778, Aged 71,
High Sheriff of the County in 1754.

Paul Phipps, Esq. of Leigh, in this Parish, Son of the above-named Thomas, died Nov. 5th, 1785, Aged 61.

Thomas Phipps, Esq. of Leigh, in this Parish, Son of the above Thomas, died August 25th, 1792, Aged 77, High Sheriff of the County in 1748, and Receiver-General for 57 years.

Thomas Hele Phipps, Esq. Son of the second-named Thomas, died Sept. 10th, 1790, and to whose Memory a Monument has been erected close by.

Arms—A trefoil between eight mullets.

Sacred to the Memory of Thomas Hele Phipps, Esq. of Leigh, in this Parish, who died September 11th, 1790, Aged 41.

He was a Man of strict Integrity, and one of his Majesty's Justices of the Peace for this County.

Also of three of his Children, who died in their Infancy.

His Widow has, through affectionate regard to his valued Memory, erected this Monument.

Arms—A trefoil between eight mullets; impaling, a lion rampant, in chief three roundels.

In the Vault beneath
Are the mortal Remains of Jacintha,
Youngest daughter of
the late Thomas Hele Phipps, Esq.
of Leighton House, in this Parish,
who departed this life of a typhus fever,
Feb. 17th, 1819, Aged 33 years.
In the short career of her Earthly Pilgrimage,
She exemplified the exercise
of every Female Virtue,
And left to her afflicted Relatives
A bright example for Christian imitation,
by whom it may be truly said, she
"did not live in vain,
But lived to die, and died to live again."
Mors janua Vitæ.

On Flat Stones in S. Aisle.

Underneath lieth the Body of the Rev. Thomas Hewett, Vicar of Westbury Forty-two years. He Departed this life the 1st day of August, 1792, Aged 76 years.

Also two of his Sons.

Underneath are Deposited the Remains of Henry Barker, who died April the 11th, 1766, Aged 53 years.

Also Martha, his Wife, who died November the 14th, 1766, Aged 46 years.

Also George Randall, Surgeon, who married Ann, Daughter of the said Henry and Martha Barker. He Departed this life August the 22d, 1788, Aged 50 years.

Also Ellen, Daughter of the said Henry and Martha Barker, who Departed this life April the 28th, 1793, Aged 45 years.

Also Ann, Relict of the above George Randell, who died the 2d of June, 1818, Aged 73 years.

In Memory of Sarah, Wife of Edward Salisbury, sen. who died Feb. 17th, 1766, Aged 62 years.

Also Edward Salisbury, sen. who died Decem. 23d, 1772, Aged 72 years.

Also Sarah, Wife of John Salisbury, sen. who died Sept. 6th, 1794, Aged 62 years.

On a Brass Plate.

Here lyes Henrietta Seymour, Wife of Edward Seymour, Esq. of Woodlands, Dorset, and Daughter of the Honourable James Phipps, late Governor of Cape Coast, Africa.

Hatchment—Quarterly, first and fourth gules, a lion rampant or; second and third argent, a fess reguly, azure, between three pellets: impaling argent, two chevrons between three cinque-foils, gules.

On Monuments in South Transept.

Near this Place lyeth interred the Body of William Phipps, Esq. of Heywood, near Westbury, in the County of Wilts. He was formerly Governour of Bombay, in the East Indies, which trust he executed with credit and reputation to himsslf, as well as to the advantage and satisfaction to the Company trading to those Parts. He departed this life the 21st day of August, 1748, Aged 67 years, leaving issue, by Hannah, his Wife, two Sons, Thomas and Edward Phipps, which Hannah, in affectionate regard to the Memory of her deceased Husband, has erected this Monument.

Here also lies interred the Body of Hannah, late the Wife of the above-said William Phipps, Esq. who Departed this life September 24, 1756, Aged 73.

Arms—Sable, a trefoil between eight mullets, argent: impaling per bend, sinister argent and sable, a lion rampant of the first.

D. O. M. S.

Hic in pace requiescunt ossa et cineres de Jacobi Ley, equestris ordinis viri et baronetti, filii Henrici Ley, de Teffont, cujus A. natu sexti, qui juvenis jurisprudentiæ studiis, mancipatus virtute meruit ut per omne, gradus ad summum, togatæ laudis fastigium ascenderet, regii in Hibernia banci justitiarius sufficiter capitalis, et in Angliam revocatus fit, pupillorum procurator regius, deinde Primarius in tribunall regio Justitiarius, quæ munia postquam magna, cum integritatis laude administraset illum Jacobus Rex Baronis Ley, de Ley, (suæ familiæ in Agro Devon antiqua sede) titulo ornavit in sanctius ads . . ut consilium summumq. Angliæ thesaurarium constituit, et rex Carolus, Marlbrigi comitis auctaris honoravit, regiiq. concilii instituit Presidens.

Uxorem duxit Mariam, filiam Johannis Pettey, de Stocktalmage, Oxon Com. Arm. (cujus corpus juxta ponitur) ex qua numerosam prolem procreavit: Henricum, nunc Marlbrigi comitem, Jacobum, Gulielmum, Elizabetham, Annam, Mariam, Dionysiam, Margaretam, Hesteram, Martham, Phœbem: qua conjuge fato functa Mariam despondit Gul. Bourer, Equitis, aurati viduam, post cujus obitum Janæ, Dom. Botteler filiæ, enupsit, ex quibus nullam prolem suscepit. Ita vir iste quem ad gravem prudentiam finxit natura, et doctrina excoluit, (publicis usq. ad declivem ætatem Magistratibus benefunctis) senio confectus animam de patria optime meritam placida morte Deo reddidit Londini in Hospitio Lincoln, sibi ante omnia delectissimo, Martii xiiii°, R. S. MDCXXVIII.

Henricus, Marlbrigi comes, optimis Parentibus hoc promunere extremo Monumentum uberibus lacrimis consecravit.

[*Under this Monument is a Tomb, with two Statues of a male and female lying upon it, the female placed on the right side of the male.*]

Arms—1. Argent, a chevron between three bears' heads, couped, sable.
2. Or, a chevron engrailed ermine, between three leopards' heads, caboshed sable.
3. Or, a chevron, argent, between three roses, gules.
4. Argent, a chevron between three birds, sable, beaks and legs, gules.
5. Argent, three trees, vert.
6. Ermine, a chevron, paly of six, between three leop rds' heads caboshed, vert.
7. Argent, on a chevron three . . . heads, or.
8. Argent, two chevrons gules, in chief a label, vert.
9. Gules, ten bezants, 4 3 2 1.
10. Or, a lion rampant between eight crosslets fitchy, vert.
11. Argent, a cross flory, or.
12. As the first.

Impaling quarterly, first and fourth or; second and third argent, over all, on a bend, vert, 3 martlets, or.

On Flat Stones in Transept.

Catherine Swinden Ob. Nov. 26th, 1720, Æt. 61.

Here lies interred the Body of Mrs. Elizabeth Smith, who departed this Life the 28th of February 1756, Aged 70 years.

Hatchments in Transept.

Sable, a trefoil, ermine, between eight mullets, or.

Sable, a trefoil, argent, between eight mullets of the same, over all an escutcheon, ermine: a chief, quarterly, first and fourth or, second and third gules.

Monuments in the South Wall of South Aisle.

In the Vault beneath are deposited the Remains of John Whittaker, the only Son of John and Anna Maria Whittaker, of Fairwood, in this Parish. It pleased the Almighty to remove this blessing from his afflicted Parents on the 29th day of August, 1819, in the 21 year of his Age.

The Lord gave, and the Lord hath taken away, Blessed be the name of the Lord.

Arms—Azure, three lozenges, argent.

In the adjoining Vault are deposited the remains of Lucy Mortimer, who left this world on the 11th day of April, 1820, in the 46th year of her Age. During the sufferings which arose from an infirm constitution, she endeavoured to render herself useful to her fellow creatures, and acceptable to her Creator, by deeds of charity and benevolence. In Memory of her Virtues and affectionate friendship, this Monument by her afflicted sister Anna-Maria Whittaker.

Benefactions.

In the South Aisle.

Henry Earle, of Marlburgh, conveyed by Indenture of Feoffment, in the year 1635, certain Lands, consisting of 5 A. 1 R. 24 P. situate near Britwell Springs, and also two Tenements and half an acre of Orchard, situate at Townsend, all in this Parish, to the Churchwardens of Westbury, as Trustees, for the use and benefit of the Church, or in keeping the Bells and Clock thereof in good repair. The said Lands have been valued at and now yield the yearly rent of £.8 : 2 : 0; and the said Tenements and Orchard the yearly Rent of £. 14 : 0 : 0, all free of Rates and Taxes.

N. B. Another half acre of arable Land, lying under Goosland Hedge, is included in the same Donation, but has not yet been recovered.

John Gibbs, Gent. left, by Will, dated the 14th of June, 1772, the whole Interest and Dividends (amounting to £. 17 : 1 : 10) of the sum of £. 569 : 16 : 0, vested in the 3 per cent. Consols, to be yearly laid out on the Feast of St. John the Evangelist in the purchase of Six strong Coats and Waistcoats, of an olive colour, to six poor Men, inhabitants of Westbury, receiving no alms from the Parish. The nomination of fit objects devolved, in the year 1814, to the Minister and Churchwardens.

This tablet was set up on the 1st Day of March, 1821, by James Tayler Singer, William Wilkins Hooper, } Churchwardens.

In the North Aisle.

BENEFACTION

To certain Poor in the Parish of Westbury.

Henry Smith, Esq. by Deed, enrolled in Chancery, dated the 26th of January, 1626, and in the 2d year of the Reign of King Charles the First, did order and appoint that there should be paid out of his Estates at Stoughton, in Leicestershire, for ever, a certain Sum of Money annually into the hands of the Churchwardens and Overseers of the Poor of the above Parish for the time being, to be applied by them, with the approbation of the Vicar, to the benefit of various descriptions of poor people of good character and reputation, being Parishioners, or having resided more than 5 years in the Parish.

The Sum divided to the said Parish Officers the present year for the use and purpose above mentioned, amounted to £. 13 : 8 : 10, exclusive of about £. 3 allowed towards necessary improvements.

This tablet was set up on the 1st day of March, 1804.

William Vince, Thomas White, } Churchwardens.

On a Brass Plate in Vestry Room.

Here Lyeth ye Bodie of Thomas Bennet, of Westbury, Gentleman, who took to Wife Margaret Buriton, the eldest Daughter and one of the Coheiresses of Thomas Buriton, of Streatley, in the County of Barkes, Esquire, which Margaret survivinge her saide Husband, hath, in token of their mutuall love whilst they lived together, and in testimonie of her continued affection after his decease, caused this Stone to be here placed in his Memorie, with whom as she lived, so after her death intendeth she, by gods permission, to rest in the same grave, as this Monument doth import. The said Thomas Bennett died . . . . th Day of June, Anno Dom. 1605. And the said Margaret died the . . . . Day of . . . . . . Anno Dom. . . . . .

Arms—Three demi lions rampant, mullet for difference.
Three grayhounds courant, crescent for difference.

Register commenced 1556.

The Rev. Thomas Cooke, Vicar.

Sir Manasseh Lopez Lord of the Manor.

BRATTON.

Against the South Wall of Chancel.

In Memory of Robert Long, late of this Parish, Gent. who departed this life Jan. 14th, 1745, Aged 55.

Arms—Long.

This Monument was erected by leave of Thos. Bennet, Esq. the Impropriator.

On a Flat Stone in Chancel.

Here lyeth the Body of Mary, late Wife of James Long, of this Parish, Gent. and Daughter of George Turner, heretofore of Penley, in this Parish. She departed this Life the 30th day of August, Anno Dom. 1755.

Arms—Long: impaling Turner.

On a Brass Plate.

Here lyeth buried Sefton Broomewhich, Gent. Deceased, who Purchased the Gravnge and Farme of Bratton, and Married Ann, the Daughter of W. Bower, of Lavington Epi. Gent. & left Issue W. Broomewhich, his Sonne & heire apparant, & Elizabeth, his Daughter, and Departed this Transitoric lyfe the 11 Day of July, Anno Dom. 1607.

On Flat Stone in Nave.

Here lyeth the Body of John Whittaker, sen. who departed this life the Sixth day of March, Anno Dom. 16. .

South Transept.

In Memory of William Whitaker, Gent. who died Feb. ye 12th, 1771, Aged 60 years.

And saying, Lord Jesus receive my spirit. Acts ye 7, & 59.

Also Elizabeth, his Wife, who died March ye 9th, 1775, Aged 61 years.

Sacred to the Memory of Mary Elizabeth Whitaker, wife of John Whitaker, Esq. who departed this life the 14th of October, 1806, in the 37 year of her Age.

Arms—Sable, three mascl. or; impaling per pale, sable and argent, a saltire engrailed and counter-charged.

Crest—A horse statant.

South Aisle.

Underneath lieth the Body of Humphry Whitaker, Gent. who Departed this life the 20th day of July, in ye year of our Lord God 1725, Ætat. suæ 45, he was buried in a Sepulchre.

Also underneath lyeth ye Body of William Emme, who Depd Oct. ye XIV. 1725, Ætat. suæ 43.

Underneath lyeth the Body of John Mansell, who Departed this life Dec. ye . . 1734, Ag . . . .

On Flat Stones in North Transept.

Underneath lyeth the Body of Jane, Wife of Thomas Dew, who Departed this life April the 3d, 1802, in the 70th year of her age.

O cruel Death, by whose right hand,
Ten thousand daily fall;
But Christ above, upon the cross,
Has purchased life for all.

Also of Sarah-Ann Dew, Daughter of Thomas and Jane Dew, who Departed this life August the 8th, 1802, in the 29th year of her Age.

Just in the bloom of my years,
I left my friends in floods of tears;
I soon sprung up, and soon was gone,
So frail is the life of every one.

Also of Thomas Dew, who departed this life June the 20th, 1814, Aged 78 years.

Underneath lyeth the Remains of Thomas Pepler, who died Nov. the 20th, 1775, Aged 55 years.

Also Jane, his Wife, died July the 15, 1779, Aged 48 years.

Likewise, at the outside, near this Place, lyeth James, Lea, and Rachel, Son and Daughters of the above, who all died young.

Now here together we do rest,
In hopes to rise again,

Hoping that we shall happy [illegible]
With Christ for to remain.

The Church consists of a Chancel, Nave, North and South Aisles, and North and South Transepts. The Nave is supported by two pointed arches on each side; in the windows of which and those of the north transept is some painted glass.

The Rev. Thomas Cooke Vicar.

~~Earl~~ of Bath Lord of the Manor.

DILTON.

Against south wall of Chancel.

Near this Place lyeth ye Body of Edward Line, who died April ye 20th, A. D. 1744, Aged 70 years.

In my full age here I doth ly:
If thou art old, prepare to die;
If thou art young prepare also,
When death doth call, we all must go.

Also in Memory of Margery, Wife of John Fripp, who died October ye 20, A. D. 1763, Aged 80 years.

To weep, alas, it is in vain,
For Christ, we hope, hath eas'd her pain,
Her soul with Angels for to joyne
In the Celestial Heavenly train.

Flat Stones in Chancel.

Here lyeth the Body of John Hayter, who Departed this life the 7th Day of Feb. 1738, Aged . . . .

Also in Memory of Thomas Hayter, who died July ye 29th, 1739, Aged 93 years.

Here lyeth the Body of Thomas Hanson, who Departed this life May the 28th, Anno Dom. 170 . Aged 79 years.

Here Lyeth the Body of John Wilkins, who Departed this life May the 28, A. D. 1730, Aged 81 years.

Against the South Wall of Nave.

Underneath lieth the Body of William Budd, who Departed this life the 5th day of August, 1766, Aged 45 years.

Also here lieth the Body of Mary, Daughter of William and Elizabeth Budd, who Departed this life the 28th day of Feb. 1776, Aged 18 years.

And also here lieth the Body of Thomas, Son of William and Elizabeth Budd, who departed this life the 28th day of May, 1775, Aged 9 years and 11 months.

And here also lieth the Body of James, Son of William and Elizabeth Budd, who departed this life the 9th day of August, 1779, Aged 26 years.

And also in Memory of William, their Son, who died abroad in June, 1782, Aged 32 years.

On a Monument in N. Aisle.

Underneath the large Pew at the west end of this aisle, are deposited the Remains of William Grant, of Broker's Gate, in this Chapelry, who departed this life Dec. 2d, 1769, Aged 46 years.

Also the Remains of Hannah, Relict of the above William Grant, who died Sept. 3d, 1802, Aged 82 years.

Likewise of William, Son of the above-named William and Hannah Grant, who died March 15, 1819, Aged 61.

And Fanny, his Wife, who died Jan. 3d, 1817, Aged 58.

On Flat Stones in North Aisle.

In Memory of Ralph Burgis, who departed this life August the 26, 1737, Aged 63 years.

Also in Memory of Mary, Wife of Thomas Burgis, who died Sept. the 3d, 1768, Aged 50 years.

Also of Thomas Burgis, who died April 5th, 1781, Aged 72 years.

Also of Edward, their Son, who died in his Infancy.

Also of Sarah, Daughter of Thomas and Mary Burgis, who died June the 17, 1797, Aged 55 years.

Under this Stone lyeth the Remains of Anna, Wife of Richard Iwnton, who Departed this life August the 3d, 1670.

Near this Place lyeth the Remains of Ann Gerrish, who departed this Life Decem. ye 24, 1777.

Also under this Stone lyeth the Remains of Elizabeth, Daughter of Philip and Margreat Blatch, who Departed this life May the 17, 1782, Aged 25 years.

And also under this Stone lyeth the Remains of Philip Blatch, sen. who Departed this life March . . . . 1788, Aged 56 years.

And also under this Stone are Deposited the Remains of Margreat, wife of the above Philip Blatch, who Departed this life April the 18, 1793, Aged 66 years.

Against North Wall of Nave.

ANTHONY SELF gave to the Poor of Dilton forty Pounds, to be as a Stock for them, and desired that the Churchwardens should yearly, at Easter, choose two honest men of Dilton, and that they, with them, should put forth ye forty pounds for ye best advantage, and that every Christmas ye Overseers, and ye two persons should, out of such advantage, buy apparel for such of the Poor as they thought fit.

WILLIAM GILBERT gave Twenty pounds, to be as a Stock, and the Interest thereof to be distributed yearly in Bread amongst the Poor.

CHRISTOPHER PIERCE gave ten pounds, to be as a Stock for poor labourers of Dilton, not having parish relief. The Interest thereof to be distributed yearly, on ye second day of January, amonst them.

JOHN CABLE gave five pounds to the poor of Dilton; the one-half of the Interest thereof to be bestowed on them yearly at Easter, and ye other half to be added to the principall.

WILLIAM TURNER gave Forty-five shillings; ye one-half of ye interest thereof to be distributed amongst ye poor of Dilton yearly, at Easter, and ye other half to be added to ye principall.

In March, 1679, JOHN WHATLEY, Constable of Westbury Hundred, by ye consent of ye Inhabitants of Dilton, did, with ye said Moneys & ye increase thereof, purchase, in ye names of Mr. Ivie, Minister, and Stephen Whatly and William Withy, Chaplewardens, of Dilton, three closes, called Croft and Corsley, containing by estimation twelve Acres, and a parrock, called Church Parrock, containing two Acres, in Beckington parish, Somersett, as appeareth by the Deed thereof remaining in this Chapple. THE VICCAR and Chapplewardens of Dilton, and ye ten Trustees, viz. Thomas Phipps, May Hill, William Wilkins, Roger Carter, Thomas Whatly, John Whatly, George Withy, Giles Adlam, William Rendell, and Thomas Hill, and the survivors of them, concerning the Rents and Profits of ye said Lands to observe these rules and directions following, as appeareth more at large by another Deed remaining in this Chapple, viz. They are yearly, for ever, to raise (if they can) out of the same rents and profits so much money as the yearly Interest of ye said severall sums given by the Donors above-named, would amount unto, and ye same Money to employ according to ye above expressed intention of ye said Donors. If any overplus of moneys shall be after such imploying, such overplus is to be imployed for ye poors benefitt in such manner as ye Vicar and Chapplewardens and ye Trustees, or ye major part of them, shall think fitt. If the same rents and profits shall not in any year amount to so much as ye yearly interest of the same severall sums given by the said Donors would amount to, then out of the same rents and profitts, the said directions of ye said severall Donors are to be pursued and performed as near as can be, regard being had to ye quantity of ye moneys raised by ye same rents and profitts. The Vicar and Chapelwardens are not at any time to lett or manure ye said lands, or any part thereof, or do any thing concerning the same without ye consent of ye trustees or ye survivors, or major of ym first had.

The Vicar, Chapplewardens and Trustees, are to meet in the Easter week yearly at this Chapple, giving notice thereof on Easter Sunday in Westbury Church and this Chapple, and consult concerning ye letting and managing of ye said lands for the poors benefitt, and to examine how ye rents and profits have been imployed for ye preceding year, and to imploy (as afore directed) ye moneys raised by ye rents and profitts yn unimployed; and if any of ym be absent at such meeting, yn such of ym as shall be present may consult and act as fully as if all were present. When the greater number of ye said Trustees are dead, ye survivors are, from time to time for ever, to get some of ye substantiallest Inhabitants in or about Dilton in ye room of ye deceased, so that ye said Directions of ye Donors may be ye more faithfully performed.

Dilton register commenced in 1600.
The Reverend Thomas Cooke, Vicar.
Sir Manasseh Lopez Lord of the Manor.

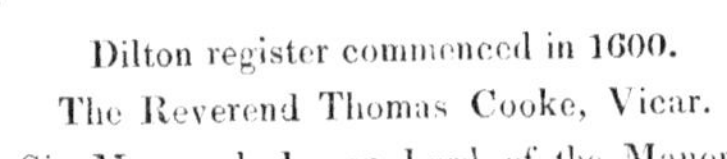

UPTON SCUDAMORE.

On Monuments against North Wall of Chancel.

In Memory of Lionel Seaman, D.D. Archdeacon of Wells, and Vicar of Frome. He married Jane, eldest Daughter of Dr. Edward Willes, Lord Bishop of Bath and Wells, by whom he had one Son, and three Daughters. He died the 21st day of February, 1760, Aged 53: And Margaret, his youngest daughter, dyed soon after him, and is buried in the same grave.

Arms—Argent, three bars azure, in fess point a crescent, or, impaling, argent, a chevron, azure, between three mullets, gules.

In this Chancel, near this Place, lyeth the Body of William Seaman, Rector of this Parish, who injoyed the sayd Rectory 52 years, and Departed this life Nov. the 7th, 1680.

Here also lyeth the Body of Mary Seaman, Wife of the said William Seaman, who Departed this life the 13th of June, 1671.

Here lieth the Body of Lionel Seaman, son of William Seaman, who died the 17th of January, 1685, Ætatis suæ 33.

Here also lieth the Body of Jane, the Wife of Lionel Seaman, who died July 1st, 1714, Aged 71.

On a Brass Plate.

Here lyeth the Body of Elizabeth Hungerford, ye Wife of Giles Hungerford, Gent. who departed this life 14th July, Anno Dom. 1632.

South Wall.

Near this Place lies interred the Body of Lionel Seaman, Esq. only Son of the late Rev. Dr. Lionel Seaman, and Jane, his Wife; who, after a short Pilgrimage of twenty four years (great part of which time it pleased God to afflict him with a declining state of health), was called out of this Life to the hope of a blessed eternity, but not before his many amiable Virtues had deeply engraven his Memory on the Hearts of his surviving Friends. His Mother erects this Monument as a final Tribute to the worth of an Affectionate and dutiful Son. He died July 20, 1783.

On Flat Stones.

Here lieth the Body of Mr. John Mountague, Rector of Upton Skidmore, Son of ye Honble James Mountague, of Lackham, in the County of Wilts. who departed this life the 19th of May, Anno Dom. 1691.

Here lieth the Body of Nicholas Barry, M.A. Son of Richard Barry, Rector of Upton Scudamore, who Departed this life August 3, Anno Dom. 1734.

Here also Lyeth the Body of William, (an infant) the Son of Richard Barry aforesaid, who died June 26, Anno Dom. 1694.

Here lieth the Body of ye Rev. Richard Barry, M.A. 58 years Rector of this Parish, died Nov. 21, 1749, Aged 84 years.

Underneath, in a Vault, lies the Body of the Rev. Richard Barry, Rector of this Parish, and Vicar of Bitton, in the County of Gloucester. He departed this life 21st Feb. 1766, Aged 73 years.

Also the Body of Catharine, his Wife. She died 14 October, 1774, Aged 71.

Here lieth the Body of Mary, the Wife of Richard Barry, Rector of Upton Scudamore, who departed this life May the 8, A. D. 1729.

Beneath lie interred the Reverend Richard Barry, Rector of this Parish, who died the 22d of Sept. 1779, Aged 51 years.

Also Elizabeth, his Wife, who died March 9th, in 1774, Aged 42 years.

Likewise Jane, their Daughter, who died December 6, 1769, Aged 6 years.

In Memory of Elizabeth, Daughter of the Rev. Richard Barry, Rector of this Parish. She died 25 March, 1770, Aged 78 years.

Here lieth the Body of Susanna Johnson, who was buried Dec. 27, 1701.

Here also lieth the Body of Jane Johnson, Daughter of the aforesaid Susanna Johnson. Buried Oct. 27, 1749, Aged 84 years.

On a Brass Plate.

Underneath lies interred the Remains of Mrs. Jane Seaman, who died 30th Nov. 1706, Aged 77 years.

North Aisle.

In Memory of Christopher Pearce, Son of Andrew and Mary Pearce, under-named, who Departed this life June the 9th, 1791, Aged 62 years.

Also in Memory of John Pearce, Son of Andrew and Mary Pearce, under-named, who departed this life May the 2d, 1798, Aged 67 years.

In Memory of Elizabeth, Daughter of Andrew and Mary Pearce, who departed this life July ye 22d, 1759, in the 33 year of her Age.

Also, of George, Son of Andrew and Mary Pearce, who departed this life June ye 13th, 1773, in the 33 year of his Age.

In Memory of Andrew Pearce, who departed this life Jan. ye 1st, 1778, in the 81 year of his Age.

Also in Memory of Mary Pearce, Wife of the above Andrew Pearce, who Departed this life Dec. ye 13th, 1785, in the 80 year of her Age.

Afflictions sore long time we bore,
Physicians was in vain;
But God was pleas'd that Death should cease,
And ease us of our pain.

With Christian Patience bear Affliction's Rod:
Reader, prepare to meet thy God.

Erected in Memory of Elizabeth, Wife of Andrew Pearce, who Departed this life on the 11th of Feb. 1807, in the 59th year of her Age.

Also in Memory of Andrew Pearce above named, who departed this life on the 11th of August, 1810, in the 74th year of his Age.

With soft compassion each kind heart was mov'd,
No Pomp, no Pride, no Affectation lov'd;
To all the World as to each other kind,
To social virtues faithful Friendship join'd.
Their grateful Children hold their mem'ry dear,
A Father's care, a Mother's love revere.

As time, like lightening, flies away,
So think of dying every Day.

In Memory of Christopher Pearce, who died May ye 20th, 1764, Aged 60 years.

Also Sarah, Wife of the above Christopher Pearce, Died Jan. 31, 1778, Aged 73 years.

Likewise Edward, Son of the above Christopher and Sarah Pearce, who Died Jan. ye 27, 1770, Aged 38 years.

Sacred to the Memory of William Pearce, and Ann his Wife. She died August 22, 1786, Aged 38 years, He died Feb. 19, 1809, Aged 69 years.

Keep conscience clear, avoid all broils and strife,
Forgive offences, lead a virtuous life,
Delight in doing good, and be content
With what allotment Providence hath sent.

Also of Edward, Son of William and Ann Pearce, who died June 4th, 1811, Aged 37 years.

Farewell, vain world, I've seen enough of thee,
And now am careless what thou say of me,
Thy smiles I court not, nor thy frowns I fear,
My cares are past, my body resteth here;
What fault thou see in me take care to shun,
And look at home, enough there's to be done.

In this Church are two stone statues, but much mutilated: one of them appears to be a knight templar.

Rev. Mr. Barry Rector.

WARMINSTER.

On Monuments against North Wall of Chancel.

In Memory of Roger Townsent, of this Town, Professor of Music. Died June 20th, 1730, Aged 39 years.

Our Maker's Praise his soft melodious Tongue,
By nature led, by Heaven directed, sung:
Harmonious Soul, thou always didst aspire
To imitate (now join) the heavenly Choir,
By hearing Angels sing, their notes improve,
And raise devotion to seraphic Love;
God's goodness view, enjoy, adore, proclaim,
And everlastingly extol his name.

Elizabeth, his Wife, Ob. Dec. 24th, 1769, Æt. 79.

James, their Son, Ob. Aug. 23, 1778, Æt. 60.

Ann	Wives of James, ob.	Feb. 23, 1747, Æt. 25.
Rachell		Sept. 28, 1750, Æt. 32.
Phillis		July 7, 1769, Æt. 66.

Elizabeth, his Daughter (by Ann) Ob. Dec. 9th, 1790, Æt. 46.

Lydia, Wife of Roger, Ob. Dec. 22, 1781, Æt. 31.

James their Son, in his Infancy. James, Son of Roger, by Elizabeth, Ob. July 12th, 1794, Æt. 7.

This Monument was erected by Roger, Son of James, who has given the sum of three Pounds a year for ever to the Clerk, Organist, and Choir of this Parish, to Sing the Anthem from the CL Psalm, as composed by him to whose Memory this is erected, during divine Service, on Sunday immediately preceding Midsummer day.

In Memory of Elizabeth, the Wife of Noah Chivers, of the City of Bath, and Daughter of the late William Bleeck, of this Town. Died 26th April, 1794, Aged 54 years.

Sacred to the Memory of James Grant Filkes, who Departed this Life on the 28th of January, 1813, Aged 64 years.

Near this Place are deposited the Remains of the Rev. Dacre Youngson, M. A. Formerly of St. John's College, Cambridge, Late Curate of this Parish, who died Jan. 31, 1783, Aged 37 years.

Tho' dead he yet speaketh, and still present in remembrance. Forcibly, tho' silently, admonished his once beloved Flock. To be cut off in the midst of a valuable and useful life, is one of the Mysteries of Divine Providence, which will be cleared up at the resurrection of the just.

George Wansey, after a few days Illness, Died March 19, 1807, Aged 50 years.

The love and esteem of all who knew him is the best Testimony to his real Character. The blessing of him that was ready to perish came upon him, and he caused the Widow's heart to sing for joy.

Brass Plate.

Here lieth the Body of Simon Sloper, Gentleman, desesed June 26, 1636.

Here Lyeth the Body of William Sloper, Son of Simon Sloper, Desesed Mar. 5, 1651.

Simon Sloper, William Sloper,
Robart Sloper, Ann Sloper.

Hic Jacet Gualterus Atwood, in Artibus Magister, hujus Parochiæ Vicarius, Collegii Reginalis in Academia Cantabrigiæ quondam alumnus, filius tertius Johannis Atwood, Armigeri, de Littleburie, in Parochia de Stanford Riveres, in Comitatu Essex. Obiit Sexto die Novembris, A° Dñi 1635, Ætatis suæ 33.

Arms—A lion rampant, argent, between five or.

Maria, Conjux pientissima dilectissima Pauli Lathom, A. M. hujus parochiæ Ministri, puerperio, necnon insequenti febre vexata, patientie, fidei, modestie, specimen exhibuit perillustrie, filioloque Joanne, superstite intravit gaudium Domini, prid. Cal. Oct. A. D. 1660, Æt. suæ 23.

Elizabetha, Pauli et Elizabethæ Lathom unica proles et delicia, variolis correpta, immaculatarum in Cœlis virginium adjungitur, chro. 7 Cal. Jul. A. D. 1668, Ætat. suæ 5.

Quod Mortale superfuit ultimæ clangorem tubæ præstolans, hoc obdormit pulvere vive memor læti fugit hora, hoc quod loquor vide est.

Brass Plate, south side.

To the living Memory of Hester Potticary, the only Daughter of Thomas Potticary of this Parish, who deceased August 31 . 1673.

God oft transplants his lovely flowers
From the Church garden heare below,
Them to secure from heat and showers,
In heavenly paradise to grow.
Here rests a virgin's earthly part,
Whom winter overtook in spring,
Whose soule, now freed from Satan's dart,
We hope doth Hallelujah sing.
Let persons in their younger years,
With her their Great Creator mind,
As they would be disarmed of fears
When death their outward man shall find.

CHRONAG.

Pure Vessels of Mercy enjoy happiness with God. 1673. Her age was 24 years.

CHRONAG.

Vertue in her is not Withering.

On Flat Stones within the Rails.

Here lieth the Body of Elizabeth, Wife of Edward Coward, who is left to lament ye loss of ye best of Wives, & prepare to follow her, who departed this life August 26, 1742, Aged 57 years.

Here Lieth the Body of James Ligertwood, M. A. Prebendary of Sarum, Rector of Brixton Deverell, and Vicar of Warminster, who Died 24 October, 1742, Aged 68 years.

Sacred to the Memory of the Rev. Millington Massey Jackson, A. M. formerly of Dunham Massey, in the County of Chester, and Fellow of St. John's College, Cambridge, 33 years Vicar of this Parish, and Rector of Kingston Deverell. He departed this life the 26 December, 1807, Aged seventy years.

Mariæ, uxor charissima Pauli Lathom, hujus Ecclesiæ Vicarii. Obijt 30 Die Sept. A. D. 1660, Æt. suæ 23.

On a Brass against S. E. Pillar of the Tower.

Prope hanc columnam, sub his tribus superioribus sedibus, corpus Mariæ, uxoris Francisci Bennett, de Smalebrooke, generosi, jacet sepulchrum. Obiit vicesimo sexto die Julii, Anno Domini millesimo sexcentissimo quinquagesimo-septimo, annoque Ætatis suæ quinquagesimo.

Underneath lieth the Body of William Wilton, Gent. who died on the 5 of August, 1752, in the 50th year of his Age.

He was descended from a Reputable family sittuated for many Generations in this Town. In the Middle part of his life he betook himself to the sea-service, in which he made so great a proficiency, that he was taken notice of by the two noble Brothers, the Lords Vere and Aubrey Beauclerk, and by the latter in Particular, who, for his advancement, Recommended him to the Command of a South Sea Sloop, in the West Indies. At his return home, the Right Honble Lord Viscount Weymouth was pleased to appoint him his House Steward, in which office he continued with great credit, and with the approbation of his Lord, for many years, who, during his Life, and at the time of his decease, most Generously and Nobly rewarded him for his faithfull Services.

Also Mary, Wife of Edward Wilton, who died May, 1759, Aged 36 years.

Also Jerrard, Son of Edward Wilton, who died February, 1785, Aged 10 years.

Also Edward Wilton, who died April, 1788, Aged 81 years.

Against N. E. Pillar of Tower.

Near this Place are deposited the Remains of Deborah Armstrong, who died November 6th, 1813, Aged 69.

N. W. Pillar.

Near this Place are deposited
the Remains
of Jane, Daughter of Joseph Bland,
Merchant of London,
who died May 17th, 1799,
Aged 23 years.

Arms—Argent, on a bend, sable, three pheons of the first.

S. W. Pillar.

Heus, Viator!
Siste gradum,
Pretium erit moræ,
Non nescire te quis infra jacet.
Hic jacet (..si Deus voluisset superstitem)
Willielmus, Willmi et Franciscæ Butler
Filius,
Juvenis integerrimus et consummatissimus,
Mira in dictis fides,
In Moribus suavitas,
In consuetudine facilitas fuit,
Hinc Parentum, fratres, atq. sorores,
Marito delictæ Scholæ Wellensis,
Absq. invidia
Flos et gloria
Cantabrigiæ futurus
idem et ornamentum,
sed proh dolor! variolis
nunquam magis invidendis
correptus candidissimam
efflavit animam
Jan: 21 . 1708, Ætat. suæ 18.
Abi jam & si possis, Lector, imitare.

Arms—Sable, on a fess, or, three estoils, gules, between three dragons heads, erased, or, crescent, gules, for difference.
Ermine, on a bend, gules, three escallops, or.

In Memory of Michael Webb, gent. who died July 10, 1788, Aged 74 years,
And lies interred on the other side of the Middle Isle.

Elizabeth Massey, his Daughter, died 11th November 1794, Aged 45 years.

Charles Webb, his Son, died 15 January, 1808, Aged 49 years.

West End of Nave.

In Memory of John Langley, Esq. who died on the 14th day of September, 1799, Aged 92 years.
He was a liberal Benefactor to the Poor of this Parish.

Arms—Paly of six, argent and vert.

To the Memory of John Maskelyn, Gent. who Departed this life the 24 of January, 1790, Aged 72 years.

On Flat Stones in Nave.

Here lyeth ye Body of William Langley, who died December 14, 1709, Aged 33 years.

And also William, Son of Wm. Langley, who died Jan. 1st, 1709, Aged 4 years.

Here also lieth the Body of Ann, the beloved Wife of Wm. Langley, who died Jan. 17, 1749, Aged 71 years.

Here lieth the Bodies of William, William, and Mary Sons and Daughter of William and Mary Bayly, of this Town. William died in October, 175. Aged 3 years; William died in January, 1755, in his infancy; Mary died in August, 1755, Aged 5 years.

Here lieth the Body of Mr. William Bayly, who departed this life November the 29th, 1772, Aged 63 years.

Here lieth the Body of Samuel Pikeman, who Departed this life May 19th, 1730, Aged 44.

Who in the several relations, a Husband, a Father, and a Friend, was affectionate, tender, and sincere; universally beloved, and equally lamented, by all that knew him.

Here also lyeth the Body of Hester, the Wife of Samuel Pikeman, who departed this life April 18, 1753, Aged 70 years.

Here also lyeth five of his Children, viz. John, Mary, Stephen, William, Aged 9 years, & Thomas, Aged 11 years.

Here also lyeth the Body of Sarah, his daughter, who died Feb: 14th, 1731, Aged Seven Years.

Here also lyeth the Body of Samuel, his Son, who died March 8, 1739, in the 25 year of his Age.

On a Brass Plate.

Underneath are deposited the Remains of John Butler, Mary his Wife, and John their Son, Marg. & Mary Iles, their Nieces, Ann, first Wife of Edward Butler, Ann Daughter of Ed. & Mar. Butler. Benj. Butler, Ob. 23 June, 1766, Æt. 42. Martha Butler, Ob. 17 Feb. 1773, Aged 57. Catherine, Daughter of Edward & Sarah Butler, Ob. Dec. 1785, Æt. 3 years. Edw. Butler, sen. Ob. 21 April, 1788, Æt. 70.

H. S. E.

Thomas Webb, Thomæ et Elizabethæ Webb, nuper de Warmininster, Filius natu maximus; spei optima juvenis, quidam literis egregie operam dedit in Schola Westmonasicrensi, variolis correptus, animam efflavit die Novembris VIIIto, Anno Ætatis suæ 27, Salutis Humanæ 1728.

Also here lieth the Body of the above-named Elizth Webb, who died Jan. 4th, 1732, Aged 45 years.

Here also lieth the Body of the above-named Thomas Webb, who died Nov. 10, 177· Aged 88 years.

Eliz. Hancock, died 29 August, 1794, Aged 47 years.
Eliz. Davis died 6 August, 1795, Aged 76 years.
Died 6th Novem. 1813, Aged 69 years, Deborah, Wife of Cuthbert Armstrong, Daughter of ye above Davis, and Sister of Eliz. Hancock.

George Lye died 10 April, 1797, Aged 17 years.

North Aisle.

Sacred to the Memory of Richard Samuel Wyche, who died Jan. 14, 1790, Aged 67.

Also of Mary, his Wife, who died July 3, 1801, Aged 76.

Also of Ann Webb, Sister of the above Mary Wyche, who died Decem. 6, 1813, Aged 87.

Sacred to the Memory of Charlotte Shoare, Daughter of John and Mary Shoare, who departed this life Oct. 2d, 1766, Aged 6 years.

Also of the above-named John Shoare, who departed this life Jan. 8th, 1777, Aged 68 years.

Also of the above-named Mary Shoare, who departed this life Nov. 5, 1787, Aged 66 years,

Also of William Shoare, Son of the above-named John and Mary Shoare, who departed this life March 21, 1789, Aged 32 years.

By whose direction this Tablet was Erected.

Underneath lie the Remains of Jane Shoare, first wife of John Shoare. Buried March the 9th, 1749.

And the Remains of John Shoare, Son of the above-named John and Jane Shoare, who died December the 3d, 1771, Aged 27 years.

This Tablet is erected by the surviving Daughter of the first named John and Jane Shoare, as a tribute of Respect to the Memory of an affectionate Mother and beloved Brother.

On a Brass Plate in S. Aisle.

Prope ab hoc pariete in medio ambula
Sepultus jacet Thomas Buckler, Gen.
Vir singulari erga Deum pietate,
Insigni in vicinos fide,
Edolore calculi multum diuq laboravit,
Quo peracuto morbo tandem plane confectus,
Mirâ cum patientia animam expiravit,
Dum vixit, amicos habuit homines,
Moriens conscientiam
Mortuus Deum.
Obijt Augusti 22 : 1704,
Circiter Ætat. 67.

Near this Place are deposited the Remains of Mr. Edward Slade, late Attorney-at-Law.

Also of Mary, his beloved Wife, and of Mr. William Slade, Gent. his Elder Brother.

Also of Mr. Edward Davis, late of Trowbridge, in this County.

Mr. John Slade, Gentleman, Ob. Feb. 13, 1773, Ætatis suæ 85.

Mrs. Ann Slade, his beloved Wife, Ob. Jan. 27, 1779, Ætatis 81.

Catharine Slade, their Daughter, ob. Nov. 25, 1761, Ætatis 25.

Edward Slade, their Son, who died in his Infancy.

Likewise the Rev. William Slade, A. M. Rector of Corsley. Ob. Nov. 27, 1782, Ætatis 53.

Also Martha, his Daughter, who died in her Infancy.

George Massey Slade. Ob. June 11, 1783, Aged 15 weeks.

Near this Place, under a Tomb in the Churchyard, Lye the Mortal Remains of Mr. Thos. Squire, lately of this Parish, Apothecary, who, to a singular skill and honesty in his Profession, a most active tenderness for the sick, an admirable sagacity in discerning the nature of Diseases, and an uncommon success in removing them, happily united the Christian and social Virtues of a tender Husband, an affectionate Parent, a chearful Companion, and a faithful Friend.

Mr. Squire

Was the 4th Son of the Rev. Samuel Squire, Formerly Vicar of Great Durnford, in this County. He married Susan, Daughter of the Rev. John Scott, Rector of Bishopstrow, with whom he lived 50 years. She was Interred under the same Tomb, August 9th, 1758, Aged 72, and near them eight of their Children. Their surviving Children are Samuel, now Lord Bishop of St. David's, Mary, and Eleanor, wife of the Rev. Mr. Twyford, Vicar of South Petherton, in Somersetshire. He dyed Nov. 30, 1761, Aged 74.

On Flat Stones.

Here lyeth ye Body of Anne, ye Beloved Daughter of William & Ann Adlam, who Departed this life ye 13th of January, Anno Dom. 1708, Aged 9 years 11 months.

As tender flowers are cut down,
And Dies away e're they are Growne;
So God was pleas'd to take my Breath,
And lay my Body in the Earth;
Whereas my Soul to Heaven did fly,
To rest with Christ Eternally.

In Memory of William Churchill, who Departed this life April the 12, 1769, Aged 80 years.

Also Elizabeth Holder, the Wife of William Holder, who departed this life April the 23, 1779, Aged 43 years.

Also the said William Holder, who departed this life Oct. the 16th, 1796, Aged 60 years.

East End of South Aisle.

In Memory of John Bodman, who departed this life in Nov. 1737, in the 42 Year of his Age.

An affectionate Husband, a tender Father, and sincere Friend.

Also 3 Children. Thos. Ob. 15th Feb. 1748, Aged 4 months; Mary, Ob. 31 March, 1748, Aged 8 years; John, Ob. 24th Jan. 1757, Aged 12 years.

Also of Mary, the Wife of the above John Bodman, who departed this life the 30th of August, 1759, in the 48 year of her age.

East End of South Aisle.

Benefactors to this Parish.

1799. John Langley, Esq. left by Will £.1000 stock 3 per cent. Consols, now standing in the names of the Vicar, Churchwardens, and Overseers. The Interest, £.30 to be given annually to 120 Poor Parishioners, who do not receive constant alms.

Henry Smith, Esq. gave £.10 per annum, to be distributed in Coats and Changes at Christmas for ever.

Mr. Stephen Pilchard gave £.120 for ever, and the use to be given to 20 poor native Inhabitants on St. Stephen's day, with a Sermon.

Mr. George Richardson, Vicar, gave £.10 at no interest.

Mr. Walter Atwood, another Vicar, gave £.5 at no interest.

Wm. Boys gave 7lb at no interest.

John Whithead gave 2lb at no interest.

Mr. Christopher Page gave 5lb at half interest.

Mr. John Wadman gave twenty half crowns, per annum to 20 poor inhabitants for ever.

Deans Stibbs gave 10lb at full Intrest.

Mr. Edward Scutt gave 5lb at full intrest.

Wm. Ridley gave 1lb at no Intrest.

Mr. Nicholas Butcher gave 5lb at no intrest.

Eliz. Gardner gave 20lb at full intrest.

Mr. Wm. Slade gave 20 half Crowns to 20 poor Houskeepers on 15 of January for ever.

Also, Mr. William King gave Forty Shillings a Year to be equally divided between Four poor Families, to continue for ever.

1807. Mr. George Wansey left by Will to the Minister, Churchwardens, and Overseers, One Thousand Pounds (since vested in the 4 per cent. Ann.) the Interest to be given away in Fifty Sums of One Pound each at Christmas for Ever, aged widows to have the preference, whether they have Pay from the Parish or not.

On the outside of the Church, west end.

Prox. ab hoc pariete sepultus jacet Georgius Carey, hujus oppidi Medicus, qui obivit Sept. ye 25, 1729, Ann. Ætatis 81.

The Church consists of a Chancel, Nave, North and South Aisles. The Nave is supported on each side by 4 semi arches. In the south wall of the south aisle is a small piscina.

The Rev. Mr. Rawlinson D. D. Vicar.

~~Earl~~ of Bath Lord of the Manor.

CORSLEY.

On Monument against South Wall of Chancel.

Near this Place Lyeth the Body of Mr. Thomas Aylesbury, who, after he had been Rector of this Parish 56 years, Dy'd March 22, Anno { Domini 1724, Ætatis 77.

Here also lyeth the Body of Sarah, his Wife. She dy'd Feb. 26, A. D. 1723, Aged 71 years.

Flat Stones in Chancel.

Here lyeth ye Body of John Mintey, who deceased this life ye 4th of November, Anno Dom. 1790.

Here lyeth the Body of Bridget Mintey, who Departed this life June 17th, 1714.

In Memoriæ Peerce Mintey, qui Obiit May 10, Anno Dom. 1723, Ætatis suæ 32.

Depositum Mortale Georgii Cary, de Corsly, generosi, qui vigesimo tertio die Novembris, Anno Ma . . . . Christiana MDCC Animam p . . . Deo reddidit postquam in corpore . . . peregrinata est ann. LXII.

Arms—On a bend three roses: a chevron lozengy, three cross crosslets.

Crest—A swan.

East End of Nave.

Sacred to the Memory of John Carpenter, an eminent Dyer in this Parish, who departed this life the 25th January 1812, Aged 58 years.

To enumerate the several amiable qualities that adorned the Character of this excellent and worthy Man, would far exceed the limits of this Tablet; suffice it to say, that his heart was expanded by every generous sympathy, and his life distinguished by the most sincere beneficence and disinterested friendship. He was an industrious and conscientious Tradesman, ever regulating his conduct by the divine precept, "Whatsoever ye would that men should do to you, do ye even so to them."

This Monument is erected and dedicated to his Memory by his affectionate Son-in-Law, H. A. Fussell, as a small token of gratitude and respect to his kind Father, and best Friend.

Against the South Wall of Nave.

In Memory of Robert Meares, Esquire, who died June 2d, 1779, Aged 51 years.

Also of Harrison Meares, (son of the above) who died May 5th, 1783, Aged 19 years.

Also of Mary, Wife of the above Robert Meares, Died March 23d, 1811, Aged 81 years.

Also of Robert Meares, late of Hackney, Middlesex, Gent. (Eldest Son of the aforesaid Robert and Mary) who died April 17th, 1816, Aged 64 years.

Also of John Meares, of Frome, gent. (second Son of the above Robert and Mary.) Died Jan. 31, 1818, Aged 61 years.

On a Flat Stone in Nave.

In the Vault underneath Lye deposited the Remains of Mr. William Jesser, late Citizen of London, who ended his life on earth the 6th day of August, 1762, in the 57 Year of his Age.

Also the Remains of Mrs. Elizabeth Jesser, Wife of the said Mr. William Jesser, who departed this life the 27 day of November, 1763.

And of Mrs. Mary Jesser, late of Frome, who left this Vain and transitory World for a blessed Eternity above, on the 29th of August, 1767.

Tablet against north wall of north aisle.

The Names of the Severall Benefactors of Corsley, and the particular Sums of Moneye Given by them to the use of the Poore of the said Parish for ever, to Continue; Viz.

William Hoore, Yeoman, Gave four Pounds.
Mr. John Cutlett, Minister, Gave five Pounds.
Mr. Moises Lye, vintner, Gave five Pounds.
Hugh Rogers, Yeoman, Gave fouer Pounds.
John Hill, Yeoman, Gave five Pounds.
Richard Holwey, Yeoman, Gave five Pounds.
Mr. John Lambe, Upholster, Gave Ten Pounds.
Mr. Richard Jenkins, Minister, Gave Five Pounds.
Mr. Moises Mayor, Vintner, Gave Five Pounds, Anno Dom. 1676.
Katherine Titford, Widowe, Gave this Tablet, 1634.

H. Hugh Rogers, once of worthy fame, is dead, and and layd in Chest, Aprill the xith.

U. Upon Hughs grave there is Hughs name, whereas Hugh's corps doth rest, A° Di 1611.

G. God gave Hugh great gifts with good successe, to advise to heal, to cure;

H. He blest Hughs works with perfectness, that divers Hugh did pleasure,
Hughs skill, Hughs counsaile, and Hughs ayde, was unto many a treasure:

R. Regarding poore folkes ease and healthe, for Gods glory, not for gains,

O. of charity freely Hugh gave his wealth, his salves, his plaisters, and his paynes.

G. given hath Hugh fower pounds likewise to this parrish by his last Will,

E. even so that a Crowne of the yearly encrease be added to the stock still,

R. remembring the day of his death, and not els the residewe be yearly paid

S. same to the parson, clark, poore, and bells, as in his will it is said.

H. Hugh was a Christian good, a Subject trewe, a comonwealths man rare,
Hughs Judgment so great, as many knew, Hughs knowledge none can declare.

R. Rogers is gone, whose deathe many moane, both rich and poore doe Rogers Misse,
Rogers, we trust, through Christ Jesus, we shall meet thee in blisse.

who list to know where Hughs body lyes, ^faxit Deus^
Neere to the Font let him cast his eyes.

The names of the Benefactors of Corsly, and the particular Sums of Money given by them to the use of the Poore of the said Parish for ever.

Mr. Jeremiah Hollway, Merchant, gave Fifty Pounds.
Mrs. Jane Hollway gave Five Pounds.
John Carr, Yeoman, gave five Pounds.

The Benefactors of Corsley, & the Sums of Money given by them to the use of the Poor for ever.

Mr. Jeremiah Hollway, Merchant, gave 50 Pounds.
Mr. John Carr, Yeoman, Gave 5 pounds.
Mrs. Jane Hollway Gave 5 Pounds.
Mr. Michael Parot Gave 5 pounds.
Robert Hopkins, Victualler, Gave this Tablet, 1688.

In North Aisle is some painted glass.

The Rev. Mr. Griffiths Vicar.

~~Earl~~ of Bath Lord of the Manor.

BISHOPSTROW.

Outside of Chancel.

Here lyeth the Body of Walter Bisse, who lived Rector of Bishopsthrowe 47 years. Hee died the 24, and was Buryed the 30 Day of Jan. Anno Domini 1664, Ætat. suæ 77.

Underneath lieth the Body of
John Forman, A. M.
in Expectation of the . . . . .
when it will . . . .
What manner of . . . .
He was 28 Rector of this . .
And Died March 11th, 1756, Aged . . . .
Also Eight of his Children.
John died August 4, 1755, Aged 22 years . . .
with four Sons, and two Daughters,
who died in their Infancy,
Are interred near this Place,
waiting for the Redemption of their Bo . .
And to hear those gratious words,
Come ye blessed Children of my Father,
. . . the kingdom prepared for you
. . . . the foundation of the world.

Brass Plate.

Here Lyeth interred the Body of Elener Seaman, the Wife of Thomas Seaman, who Departed this life the three and Twentieth day of September, in the one & Twentieth yeare of her Age, Anno Dñi 1633.

Brass Plate within the Chancel, north side.

Here Lieth interred the Body of John Temple, Gent. whoe Decease this Life the 20th Day of July, Anno Domini 1637.

South Wall of Nave.

Underneath lyeth the Body of Ann Fisher, waiting for a glorious Re-union to a Soul endued with heavenly Virtues. It pleased the Lord to call her from these abodes of Vanity and Sorrow on the 9th Day of October, 1783, Æt. 64.

In Testimony of the highest Regard to her Memory, as a most tender Wife and sincere Friend, this Monument was erected by her much-afflicted Husband Thomas Fisher, M. A.

Also in the same Grave with his Dear Wife, Lyeth the Body of the Rev. Thomas Fisher, who died the 13th Day of August, 1794, Aged 64 years.

He was Rector of this Parish 27 years.

Flat Stone.

Underneath are deposited the remains of Elizabeth Galpine, who died Dec. 9th, 1796, Aged 22 years.

In the same Grave with her Daughter Lieth the Body of Elizabeth Galpine, who died April ye 4, 1801,* [*it should be 1810] Aged 71 years.

Register began in 1685.—The Rev. F. Ashley present Rector.—Wm. Temple, Esq. Lord of the Manor.

NORTON BAVANT.

On Flat Stones in Chancel.

Here Lyeth the Body of John Twogood, of Norton, who Departed this Life the 23d of January, in the Year of Our Lord God 1665.

. . . . h the Bo . . . . am Olever. Departed this life in the y . . . of our Lord God 1670.

The Rev. Mr. Abm Clavey, Vicar of this Place, died ye 14th of August, 1765, Aged 53 years.

On a Monument in S. Aisle.

In Memory of Mr. Thomas Bennet, of this Place, who Departed this life the 18th of August, 1653.

In Memory of Elizabeth, the Wife of Thomas Bennet, who Dep. this life the 4 Day of November, 1681.

Arms—Gules, a bezant between three demi lions rampant, or: impaling argent, three greyhounds in pale statant, sable.

M. S.

Frances Bennet, 7th Dau. of Thomas Bennet, Esq. and of Eth his Wife, died August 12, 1750, Aged 11 years 8 months and 7 days.

Flat Stones.

This Lyeth in Memory of Thomas Bennet, ye 3d Son of Thomas & Etheldred Bennet, of this Place, Esq. who Dyed Nov. ye 11, Anno Dom. 1720, Aged . . . . months & 3 weeks.

This Lyeth in Memory of Thomas Bennet, ye 4 Son of Thomas & Etheldred Bennet, of this Place, Esq. who dyed August ye 11th, Anno Dom. 1722, Aged 6 months and . . weeks.

This Lyeth in Memory of Elizabeth, 4th Daughter of Thomas & Etheldred Bennet, of this Place, Esq. who died March 17th, 1724, Aged 8 months & 17 days.

This also Lyeth in Memory of Wake Bennet, ye seventh Son of Thomas Bennet, Esq. of this Place, and Etheldred, his Wife, who departed this life the 6 of January, 1731, Aged 8 months and 8 days.

This Lyeth in Memory of John Bennet, of this place, Esq. who departed this life ye 11th day of January, Anno Dom. 1706.

Arms—A roundel between three demi lions rampant.

This Lyeth in Memory of William Benett, of this place, Barrister at Law, Recorder of Shaftsbury and Bridport, in ye County of Dorsett, Son of Thomas & Elizabeth Benett, and Brother to John Benett, who Departed this life ye 29th day of November, Annoq. Dom. 1707.

Arms—The same as the preceding.

Thos. Bennet, Esq. of Norton Bavant, Principal Register, of the Prerogative Court of Canterbury, died Jan. 2d, 1754, Aged Sixty two.

Arms—Quarterly, first and fourth gules, a bezant between three demi-lions rampant, argent; second argent, an eagle with two heads displayed, gules; third argent, a chevron sable, between three catherine wheels, azure: impaling quarterly, first and fourth or, a trefoil, argent, between two bars, gules, in chief three torteaux; second a crescent argent; third, gules, three roses slipped within a border, argent; over all, an escutcheon of the first and fourth impalement.

Mrs. Etheld Bennet, Widow, Relict of Thos. Bennet, of Norton Bavant, in the County of Wilts. Esq. and one of the Daughters and Coheiresses of Archbp Wake, died 2nd April, 1766, Aged Sixty Eight.

Arms—Quarterly, first and fourth, gules, a bezant between 3 demi-lions, rampant, argent; second per pale or & az., an eagle displayed, gules; third arg. a chevron, ermine, between three catherine wheels, argent: impaling, quarterly, first and fourth or, a tre oil argent, between two bars gules, in chief three torteaux; second sable, a crescent, argent; third, gules, three roses slipped within a border argent; over all, an escutcheon of the impalement.

This lieth in Memory of William Bennet, Esq. Eldest Son of Thomas Bennet, Esq. of this Place, And Etheldred, his Wife, who departed this life the 28th of April, 1749, Aged 33 years 6 months 11 days.

And also of Mary, Wife of the said William Benet, Esq. who departed this life the 27th of October, 1768, Aged 51 years.

Arms—Quarterly, first and fourth, a roundel between three demi lions rampant; second, an eagle with two heads displayed; third, a chevron between three catherine wheels: impaling quarterly, first and fourth a trefoil between two bars, in chief three roundels; second and third a crescent.

This Lyeth in Memory of Francis Bennet, the Second Son of Thomas Bennet, Esq. of this Place, and Etheldred his Wife, who Departed this life the 24th of September, 1734, Aged 15 years 4 months and 16 days.

Also Etheldred, their Second Daughter, who died 11th May, 1778.

Arms—A roundel between three demi lions rampant, crescent for difference; impaling quarterly, first and fourth a trefoil between two bars, in chief three roundels; second and third a crescent.

Here Lyeth in Memory of Anne, the Daughter of Thomas Benet, who Departed November ye 3d, 1673.

Hatchments.

Gules, a plate between three demi lions rampant argent; impaling gules, a fess between three swans or.

Gules, a bezant between three demi lions rampant argent: impaling, a chevron checky, or and azure, between three crosslets fitchy, sable, over all, on an escutcheon azure, a lion rampant argent, crowned or. Crescent for difference, azure.

Quarterly, first and fourth gules, a bezant between three demi lions rampant argent; second argent, an eagle displayed gules; third argent, a chevron, sable, between three catherine wheels, azure; over all, an escutcheon quarterly, first and fourth argent, a fleur-de-lis, gules, between two bars of the same, in chief three torteaux; second and third sable, a crescent argent.

In this aisle is a large piscina, in the chancel also is a smaller one, by the south wall.

M E R E.

On Monument against South Wall of Chancel.

To the Memory of Katharine Moore, a darling Child of Richard and Charlotte Moore, sometime of Deans Orchard, in this Parish, where she was accidentally Burnt, and soon afterwards expired, Decem. 27, 1799, Aged 3 Years four Months and Fourteen Days.

N. B. This accident happened from the Child being left in a room by herself with a lighted candle and a fire, and in this instance the Child was supposed to have set herself on fire by the Candle.

Flat Stones in Chancel.

H. S. E.

Edoardus Garrard, Edoardi Garrard,
De Novo Sarum, in Com. Wilts, Armigeri,
Filius natu Maximus,
In Academia Oxon. A. M.
Ecclesiæ filius, verus (sub Xto,) pastor,
Cujus vocem errabundæ hic loci[illegible]es
ſignoscentes illico redierunt,
Adversæ diu valetudinis ponderibus
Oppressus,
[illegible]s surrexit altiusq. usq. in Cœlum
Terris vale dixit
Martii die 3to Anno natu ætatis { Dom. 1695, suæ 3$\frac{4}{5}$

Hic jacet Jacobus Harding, Arm.
Qui obiit 21 Feb.
Anno { Dom. 1775. Ætat. 87.

Underneath this Stone lieth the Body of James Harding, who died June ye 25th, 1724, Aged 70 years.

Also Catherine, his Wife, who died March ye 1st, 1725, Aged 70 years.

Likewise Catherine their Daughter, who died Oct. ye 31st, 1723, Aged 4 years.

And Mary, their Daughter, who died Decem. ye 22, 1700, Aged 15 years.

Against the South Wall of Nave.

1712. This south side wall and Roof was repaired, Mr. John Hardcastle M.A. being Vicar, Wm. Harding & Wm. Forward, Churchwardens,
1711, At the Cost and Charge of the Parishioners of Mere, And Performed by Mr. Charles Stoakes, of London, Surveyor of Buildings.

On a Flat Stone in Nave.

Here Lyeth the Body of William Ball, who was the beloved Husband of Elizabeth Ball. He Departed this life June the 12, 1708, in the 27th year of his Age.

Also here lies ye Body of William, Son of ye abovementioned William Ball, who Departed this life March ye 12, 1739-40, Aged 31 years.

On Monuments in the North Aisle.

Near this Place lies Dr. Thomas Tatum, a Christian Physician, Sincere in his Religion, Virtuous in his life, Benevolent in his Practice. He died March 25th, 1767, Aged 55.

Arms—Azure, a fess between three greyhounds' heads erased, argent.

On Flat Stones in North Aisle.

In Memory of Captain Green, of Dunnidge Lodge, And Mary, his Wife.

And also of the two sons of Harry Jennings, Gent.

. . . lieth the Body of Mary Tatum, ... Mr. Thos. Tatum, and Daughter of Abi. Gapp. Esq. She died the 17th day of . . . 1749, Aged 63.

Also here lieth the Body of Thos. Tatum, M.D. of Salisbury, Son of the above Thomas and Mary Tatum.

In Memory of Henry Pitts Gapper, who died Jan. ye 17, 1780, in the 11th year of his Age.

Also of John Gapper, Surgeon, who died Jan. 26, 1790, Aged 67.

Here lyes ye Body of Richard Dove, of Pithouse, Esq. who dy'd August ye 25, 1727, Aged 53.

Arms—A fess indented, ermine, between three doves; impaling a fess of five fusils, in chief a canton . . .

In Memory of Virgin, the Wife of Wm. Willoughby, Gent. who died April the 19th, 1737, Aged 26 years.

And also Charles, Son of the said William and Virgin, who died March the 31, 1737, Aged 15 weeks.

Here lies the Body of William Willoughby, Gent. of Zeals, who died March the 2d, 1752, Aged 49.

Here lieth the Body of John ye Son of Randolph Baron, Gent. Cittyzen of London, who dyed in ye 25th year of his Age, 1718.

Arms—A chevron between three estoiles, within a border engrailed: impaling quarterly, first and fourth a cross ingrailed; second and third a cross moline within a border . . .

Here lieth the Body of Randolph Baron, Esq. of Laverstock, who died the 4th of Oct. 1755, Aged 62.

This belongs to John, Son of Randolph.

Also here lies ye Body of Jane, the Wife of John Baron, Gent. Daughter of Wm. Willoughby, of West Knoyle, Esq. Obiit 8 August, 1725, Ann. Ætatis 30.

And also the Body of Lieut. Will. Baron, who died the 24 Sep. 1757, Aged 39.

H. S. E.

Henry Thos. Still died the 22d Oct. 1778, Aged 4 months.

Here lies ye Body of Hannah, the Wife of James Pitman, who dy'd Feb. ye 11, 1724, Aged 33.

Also here lyes ye Body of James Pitman, Sen. who Dy'd July the 22, 1727, Aged 62.

Here Lieth the Body of Alexander Henshaw, Gent. who departed this life March the 26, 1778, Aged 26 years.

South Aisle.

Here lies ye Body of Michael Down, who dy'd Sep. 12, 1727, Aged . . .

And also ye Body of Mary, his Wife, who dy'd May . . . 1715, Age . . . .

Here lies the Body of Francis, the Son of Michael Down, who died Feb. . . . 1730, Aged 49 years.

Hic jacet Thomas Grove, hujusce Ecclesiæ nuper Vicarius. In expectatione Diei supremi . . .
Qualis erat dies iste indicabit. Obijt secdo die Aprilis, A. D. 1809, Ætatis suæ 64.

Near this place, in a full and perfect hope of a blessed Resurrection, lyeth the Body of William Chafin, of Zeals, in this Parish, Esq. Whilst he lived, he continued possess'd, as Heir, of the Antient Seat of his Family, and was chosen and served as High Sheriff for this County in the year 1685 : and when he dyed he left a double memoriall behind him, a sincerity that willingly lost his Interest rather than his Conscience, and a good Husbandry, in Plantations and Improvements of Land scarç to be paralell'd. He had Issue alive at his death, by Mary his only Wife, and Daughter of Thomas Freke, late of Hinton, Esq. who was one of the Younger Sons of Sir Thos. Freke, late of Shrowton, Kt, both in the County of Dorsett, 2 Sons, Thomas and Harry, and One Daughter, Mary, the Wife of John Grove, of the Parish of Chisenburey, in this County, Esq. He dyed the 13th day of May, in the Year of our Lord 1695, and in the year of his Age 56, happily seeing his Children at age, plentifully providing for them, and blessed with the beginning of a numerous offspring of Grand Children by his Daughter. And in Memory of whom, the said Mary, his Mournfull Widow, desiring to lye by him, as a testimony of her love, hath set up this Inscription.

By ye said William Chafin, Esq. lyeth Buried ye Body of ye said Mary, his Wife, who dyed Oct. ye 27, 1712, Aged 79 years.

Arms—Gules, a talbot passant or, a chief ermine; impaling, sable, two bars or, in chief three mullets of the last.

Flat Stones.

Heere Lieth the Bodie of Eliz. Chafin, Daughter to Rich. Chafin, of Zeales, Esq. & Lucie, his wife, which said Eliz : was heere buried the 21 of November, 1641, and of her Age the Fourth, and it is the earnest desire of the said Lucie, her sorrofull Mother, out of the most deare and tender Affectiō to her said daughter Eliz. to bee laid by her on the south side, whence they bothe expect a glorious Resurrection.

Also, here lieth the Body of Mary Grove, Daughter of John Grove, of Chisenborow, Esq. & of Mary, his Wife, who was born July ye 11, & buried Oct. ye 4th following, 1687.

Also here lieth ye Body of Jane Grove, Daughter of John Grove, late of Chisenborow, Esq. and of Mary, his Wife, who was buried June ye 14, 1704, Aged 14 years & a half.

Brass Plate.

Chafin Grove, Esq. died Jan. 31, 1761,
Aged 63 years.
Son of John, and Grandson of Hugh Grove, Esq. of Chisenbury, in this County,
the latter beheaded at Exeter,
16 May, 1655,
Pro Rege et Lege.

Wm. Grove, S.T.B. of Zeals, Died 12 Feb. 1768,
Aged 75 years.
Elder Brother of Chafin Grove, Esq.

Wm. Chafin Grove, Esq. Son of Chafin Grove, Esq.
Obijt Jan 27, 1793, Ætat. 62.

Ann Grove, Widow of Chafin Grove, Esq. died 27 Feb. 1794, Aged 83.

Caroline Grove died April 11, 1796, Aged 1 year.
Thomas Henry Grove, died Jan. 28, 1800,
Aged 2 years.
Ann Elizabeth Grove, died Dec. 19th, 1807,
Aged 8 years.
Children of Charles and Elizabeth Grove.

Charles Grove, Esq. Son of Chafin and Ann Grove, died Oct. 27, 1806, Aged 59 years.

Harry Grove, Clerk, Rector of Staplehurst, in the County of Kent, died 6 July, 1808, Aged 62 years.

Hatchments.

Ermine, on a chevron ingrailed gules, three escallops, or.

Ermine, on a chevron ingrailed or, three eecallops argent; impaling checky, argent and sable, a fess, gules.

Gules, a talbot passant, or, chief ermine; impaling sable, two bars or, three mullets of the last.—[in a lozenge.]

Quarterly, first and fourth gules, a talbot passant or, a chief ermine; second azure, a chevron between three escallop shells, or; third, argent, on a bend gules, three lozenges argent, in chief a trefoil gules; impaling sable, two bars or, in chief three mullets of the last.

Ermine, on a chevron, gules, three escallops or: impaling the same.

Ermine, on a chevron ingrailed gules, an escallop or, between two argent.

Gules, a talbot passant or, in chief ermine.

Argent, a cinquefoil, gules, on a chief of the same a demi lion rampant argent; impaling, sable, three bars or, on the chief bar three mullets, or.

104

This Gallery and ye Ringing loft were built at ye Cost of Mrs. Mary Chafin, and Mrs. Jane Weldon, Her Sister, and freely Given by them to the use of the Singers in Mere for ever. 1705.

Argent, a cinquefoil gules, on a chief of the last a demi lion rampant, argent; impaling sable, two bars, or, in chief three mullets of the same.

Gules, a talbot passant, or, crescent for difference of the same, a chief erminois; impaling argent, a chevron between three lozenges, or.

Sable, gutty de argent, three roses of the same; impaling azure, two towers and as many lions' rampant argent. tow. li. li. tow.

Churchyard.

South Side. On an Altar Tomb.

The Rev. Charles Wager Allfix, 20 years Vicar of this Place, died the 30 of Nov. 1795, Aged 47.

Head Stones.

In Memory of William Ford, who died Jan. 17, 1807, Aged 82 years.

Ah! what avails the flowing Tear,
Nothing but Earth and Dust lie here;
Lament for what thou'st done amiss,
For thou must shortly come to this.

Here Lyeth the Body of Reubin Burnit, who died April 12th, 1768, Aged 77.

In Memory of Deborah, Wife of Thomas Chislett, who departed this life the 20 of May, 1773, Aged 36.

Also in Memory of the said Thomas Chislett, who Departed this life the 7th July, 1788, Aged 51.

Sacred to the Memory of Robert Cross, who died June 12th, 1808, Aged 75 years.

Also of Mary, his Wife, who died April ye 4th, 1808, Aged 75 years.

Near this place lieth the Body of William Hull, who died Oct. 17th. 1765, Aged 63.

Also the Body of Rachel, his Wife, who died March 25th, 1764, Aged 68.

Here lies the Body of Abraham Fleet, who died March the 13, 1759, Aged 80.

Also Here lies the Body of Ann, Wife of Abraham Fleet, who died April, 1770, Aged 89.

In Memory of Wm. Gray, who Departed this life August ye 2d, 1788, Aged 84 years.

In Memory of Mary, Wife of Thomas Maidment, who departed this life Jan. ye 21, 1787, Aged 44 years.

Also of Peggy, Daughter of Thos. and Mary Maidment, who died April ye 3d, 1780, Aged 15 years.

Likewise Six of their Children, who died in their Infancy.

In Memory of William Maidment, who died July 10, 1798, Aged 64 years.

Also Mary, his Daughter, who was accidentally shot, Jan. 28, 1794, Aged 22 years.

Thos. Seagram died Oct. 6, 1742, Aged 58 years.
Joan, Wife of Thomas Seagram, died Feb. 21, 1762, Aged 84 years.

Robert Butt died May 1st, 1784, Aged 78 years.
Francis, Wife of Robt. Butt, & Daughter of Thos. & Joane Seagram, died April 9th, 1799, Aged 93 years.

Mary Becketts, Daughter of Robert & Frances Butt, died April 16, 1816, Aged 69 years.

In Memory of John Moors, who Dep. this life Sep. 4, 1785, Aged 66.

Also Elizth his Wife, who Departed this life Sept. 26, 1776, Aged 54.

Likewise John, Eliz. Samuel, George, and Mary, their Children; Viz. Mary departed this life Feb. 22, 1777, Aged 27, the rest Infants.

East End of the Church.

In Memory of Sarah, Wife of John Lander, who died Jan. 1st, 1786, Aged 51 years.

Also Martha, Daughter of John and Sarah Lander, who died July 25, 1791, Aged 32 years.

Also of John Lander, who died July 30, 1805, Aged 72 years.

Stop, Reader, just one moment stay,
My admonition's brief:
Sin is the Soul's disease, take care
In Christ to find Relief.

In Memory of Elizabeth, Wife of Michael Lander who died Jan. ye 6, 1761, Aged 56 years.

Also of Wm. their Son, who died in the 8 year of his Age.

In Memory of Michael Lander, who died April ye 14 1780, Aged 78 years.

Near this Place Lyeth ye Body of Jane, ye Dau. of Osmond and Melior Hill, who departed this Life ye 27 Day of June, 1693, and in ye 13 year of her Age.

Head Stones.

Here lieth the Body of Betty, Wife of Samuel Lander, who died Feb. 6, 1755, Aged 41.

Also Samuel, Son of the before mentioned Samuel and Betty Lander, who died Dec. 28, 1762, Aged 22.

Here lieth the Body of Edward Fleet, who died Sept. ye 21, 1739, Aged 79.

Also ye Body of Mary, Wife of Edward Fleet, who dy'd August ye 1st, 1726, Aged 57.

In Memory of James Coward, who Depd this life May 30, 1791, Aged 61 years.

Also Mary, Wife of James Coward, who Depd this life April ye 21, 1793, Aged 63 years.

Here Resteth ye Body of Mr. Wm. Hix. Dy'd Jan. ye 6, 1711.

In Memory of Edward Dalling, who dy'd of ye Small Pox (which he designedly took), Sept. 6, 1737, Aged 21 years.

In Memory of Elizabeth, Wife of John Andrews, who died Jan. 23d, 1780, Aged 46.

Also in Memory of John Andrews, who Depd this life Nov. 6, 1806, Aged 78.

Likewise Mary, Daughter of John & Eliz. Andrews, & Wife of Edwd Butt, who died April 19th, 1786, Aged 30.

Also Ann, Daughter of John and Eliz. Andrews, who died May 30, 1781, Aged 20.

In Memory of Elizth, Wife of John Coleman, who Depd this life Feb. ye 27, 1781, Aged 71 years.

In Memory of John Coleman, who Depd this life Jan. ye 31, 1784, Aged 74 years.

In Memory of Harry Frith, who Depd this life March 21, 1769, Aged 67 years.

Also in Memory of Martha, ye Wife of ye said Harry Frith, who Depd this life Dec. ye 2d, 1776, Aged 63 years.

North Side. On an Altar Tomb.

James Butt died Nov. 15th, 1802, Aged 58 years.

Also Betty, the Wife of James Butt, who Depd this life Feb. ye 2, 1818, Aged 73 years.

In Memory of Eliz. wife of John Beckett, who died March 10, 1778, Aged 57.

Also in Memory of Elizabeth, 2d Wife of the said John Beckett, who died June 20, 1790, Aged 70.

Also Sarah, their Daughter, who died March ye 18, 1776, Aged 27.

Elizth, Wife of Nicholas Larkham, and Daughter of John and Eliz. Beckett, died in May, 1792, Aged 39 years.

John Beckett died Feb. 12, 1803, Aged 77 years.

John, Son of Nich. and Elizabeth Larkham, died in Feb. 1795, Aged 15 years.

In Memory of Richard Coleman, who Departed this life April 5, 1810, Aged 67 years.

In Memory of Martin Beckett, who died Jan. 10th, 1771, Aged 25.

Also Mary, Wife of Joseph Beckett, and Mother of the said Martin Beckett. She died July 28, 1794, Aged 87.

In Memory of Joseph Beckett, who died June 28, 1791, Aged 73.

In Memory of John Suter, who died Sept. 3, 1729, Aged 45.

Also Hannah, his Wife, who died May 27, 1777, Aged 82.

Also Abraham, their Son, who died Nov. 7th, 1788, Aged 69.

Also Elizabeth, their Daughter, who died Nov. 30th, 1799, Aged 72.

Also Charles, their Son, who died August 5, 1804, Aged 82.

Also Hannah, their Daughter, who died Jan. 25, 1805, Aged 82.

Here lieth the Body of John Harding Saxton, who dy'd April ye 14, 1719.

Altar Tomb.

In Cœlo quies

John Ford, Charles Ford, Sarah Jesse, Mary Ford, and Alicia Faugoin, Children of the said John and Mary Ford. John died Dec. 3, 1768, Aged 29, buried at Wincanton. Charles June 27, 1782, Aged 28. Sarah, Nov. 5, 1785, Aged 43, & buried at Charlton Musgrove. Mary Feb. 20th, 1792, Aged 54. Alicia, Sept. 10th, 1797, Aged 50.

Sacred to the Memory of Richard Ford, who died Feb. 18, 1752, Aged 82 years.

Also of Mary, his Wife, who died Sept. 21, 1752, Aged 79 years.

And of Richard, their Son, who died March 16, 1772, Aged 70 years.

James Ford, Son of John & Mary Ford, who died Nov. 6, 1802, Aged 58 years.

And by his Will gave £100 for an Organ for the adjoining Church, £40 to the Salisbury Infirmary, & £10 to the second poor of the Hamlet of Zeals.

Also of John, the Son of Richard and Mary Ford, who died March 12, 1770, Aged 59 years.

And of Mary, the Wife of the said John Ford, who died May 31, 1780, Aged 67 years.

In Memory of Martin Butt, who Departed this life Jan. 22, 1801, Aged 49 years.

In Memory of Ann, the Wife of Martin Butt, who Departed this life Nov. 14, 1792, Aged 30 years.

To the Memory of Joel Perman, who died 28th Nov. 1814, Aged 86 years.

Also of Ann, his Wife, who died 10 April, 1813, Aged 85 years.

To the Memory of Margaret Butt, who died 17 August, 1817, Aged 87 years.

Also of Benjamin Rayment, who died 2d March, 1809, Aged 48 years.

Here lies ye Body of Walter Alford, who died March ye 31, 1731, Aged 53 years.

Here also lieth the Body of Rose, Wife of Walter Alford, who died April ye 16, 1744, Aged 61 years.

In Memory of Thomas Toogood, who was accidentally Shot March ye 1st, and died ye 6th, 1786, Aged 22 years.

Also in Memory of Edith, Wife of John Toogood, who Departed this life Dec. 4, 1801, Aged 72 years.

In Memory of Thomas Toogood, who Departed this life April 12, 1763, Aged 61.

In Memory of Jane Cook, who Departed this life March 12, 1800, Aged 77.

Also of Rebecca Clement, Sister of the above, who Departed this life Oct. 11, 1798, Aged 88.

Sacred to the Memory of Elizth Moore, Daughter of Thos. and Grace Moore, who Departed this life June 6, 1802, Aged 52 years.

In Memory of Mary, Daughter of Stephen and Elizabeth Butt, who died August 24th, 1756, in the 21 year of her age.

Also two Sons, who died in their Infancy.

In Memory of Eliz. Wife of the before-mentioned Stephen Butt, who died March 29, 1730, in the 66 year of her Age.

In Memory of John Perman, who died April the 28, 1773, in the 59 year of his Age.

Here lieth ye Body of Margaret, Wife of John Perman, who died Oct. 21, 1756, Aged 34.

Here Resteth the Body of John Down, who died June 28, 1782, Aged 62.

Also William, his Son, died March 14, 1768, Aged 2 years.

Here also resteth the Body of Sarah, Wife of John Down, who Died July 20, 1785, Aged 59 years.

Here lieth ye Body of Ann, ye Wife of George Parrett, who died Oct. ye 8, 1741, Aged 28 years.

In Memory of James Jukes, who died March 31, 1791, Aged 57 years.

Also in Memory of Rachel, wife of James Jukes, who died June the 11, 1795, Aged 62 years.

In Memory of Edward Jukes, who died April 19, 1772 . . . . 48.

Altar Tomb.

In Memory of Thos. Bliss, who died Feb. 19, 1767, Aged 84.

In Memory of Wm. Harding, who Died Dec. 21, 1775, Aged 64.

Also of Lydia, his Wife, who died August 27, 1770, Aged 74.

In Memory of Betty and Michal, Daughters of Wm. and Lydia Harding, Viz. Betty died April 14, 1763, Aged 27 years, Michal died April the 10, 1783, Aged 44 years. Also in Memory of Virtue, Wife of Wm. Harding, Jun. who died Nov. 27, 1784, Aged 50. Likewise of Wm. Son of Wm. and Lydia Harding, who died April 22, 1803, Aged 70 years.

Here lieth the Body of Michal Harding, who died August 28, 1742, Aged 56 years.

In Memory of John Evered, who died June 4, 1815, Aged 81 years.

In Memory of Elizth, the Wife of John Evered, who died March 7th, 1805, Aged 62 years.

Here lieth the Body of Richard Coward, who died Oct. ye 24, 1726, Aged 42.

Here also lieth the Body of Jane, Wife of Richard Coward, who died June ye 5, 1750, Aged 66 years.

In Memory of Richard Hanham, who was Buried April 21, 1802, Aged 78.

Also in Memory of Ann, his Wife, who was buried Jan. 16, 1808, Aged 70.

Also of Rose, the Wife of Benjn Welsh, and Daugh of the aforesaid Rich. and Ann Hanham, who was buried March 25, 1796, Aged 38.

In Memory of Sarah, Wife of Andrew Glover, who died August 16, 1759, Aged 51.

Also in Memory of Semer Glover, who died Nov. 21, 1812, Aged 67 years.

Also of the said Andrew Glover, who died Dec. 15, 1786, Aged 79.

In Memory of Richd Sly, who dyed Dec. 9, 1778, Aged 89.

Also of Jane, his Wife, who dy'd Sept. 4, 1761, Aged 73.

Also in Memory of James Sly, their Son, who dy'd April 8, 1775, Aged 48.

Also in Memory of Phillip, Son of Richard and Jane Sly, who died Feb. 3, 1819, Aged 87 years.

In Memory of Nath. Goldsborough, who departed this life Aug. ye 4, 1796, Aged 48.

Also, in Memory of Nath. Goldsborough, who Departed this life April ye 2d, 1788, Aged 55.

In Memory of Joseph Sparrow, who died Nov. 17, 1793, Aged 68 years.

Also of Hannah Sparrow, his Wife, who died Nov. 16, 1806, Aged 81 years.

William, their Son, died July 31, 1793, Aged 34 years.

Sarah, their Daugh. died Nov. 31, 1804, Aged 53 years.

Charles, their Son, died August 22, 1806, Aged 44 years.

Altar Tomb.

Here Lieth the Body of Henry Clarke, who departed this life November, 1700.

Head Stones.

Memoriæ Sacrum Johannis Walker, qui obiit vicesimo secundo die Decembri, Anno Domini Millecimo Septingentecimo Octogecimo Octavo, Ætatis suæ Octogecimo Anno. & Item Marthæ, uxoris Johannis Walker, qui Obijt decimo tertio die Novembri, Anno Domini Millecimo Septingentecimo et Sexagecimo, Ætatis suæ quadragecimo Secundo Anno.

Item

Mariæ, Filiæ Johannis Walker, et Martha Uxor, qui Obijt decimo secundo Januari, Anno Domini Millecimo Septugentecimo et Sexagecimo Octavo, Ætatis suæ decimo nono anno.

Here lieth the Body of Wm. Rhore, who died April ye 20, 1742, Aged 37 years.

This Stone is Erected to the Memory of Mrs. Mary Rogers Phillips, (of Bayton) who departed this life April 26, 1814, Aged 70 years.

Here lieth the Body of John Rogers, who Departed this life Jan. ye 3d, 1753, Aged 43 years.

Here also lieth the Body of Mary, ye Wife of John Rogers, who departed this life June ye 4, 1785, Aged 74 years.

In Memory of Wm. Jones, who departed this life August, 22d, 1789, Aged 46.

In Memory of John Taylor, who departed this life Feb. 3, 1789, Aged 63.

Mary, his Daughter, died an Infant.

Also in Memory of Mary, Wife of the said John Taylor, who died Jan. 14, 1816, Aged 90 years.

Also in Memory of Charles, the Son of John and Mary Taylor, who Depd this life Oct. 14, 1789, in the 16 year of his age.

Here lies ye Body of Thomas Tailler, who died ye 3d of June, 1760, Aged 56 years.

Here lies the Body of Fanny, the Wife of Thos. Tailler, who died August the 28, 1778, Aged 80 years.

In Memory of John Taylor, who died Nov. 22, 1813, Aged 54.

In Memory of Thomas Taylor, who died Jan. 7, 1793, Aged 43 years.

Also of Mary, his Wife, who died Feb. 13th, 1820, Aged 70 years.

Flat Tomb.

Here lieth ye Body of Elizabeth, Daughter of Andrew Dewdney, who died May . . . 1741.

And also Mary, her Daug. who died in her Infancy.

Also here lieth the Body of John Dewdney, who died March ye 22, 1789, Aged 39 years.

Here also lieth ye Body of Andrew Dewdney, who died Nov. ye 3, 1712, Aged 51.

Here also lieth ye Body of Mary, Wife of the abovesaid Andrew Dewdney, who died Sep. ye 12, 1711 . . .

Here also lieth the Body of Aaron, son of the above Andrew and Mary Dewdney, who died July ye 20, 1783, Aged 47 years.

Also Eliz. Wife of the said Aaron Dewdney, who died Sept. 12, 1783, Aged 43 years.

Here lies ye Body of William Forward, who dy'd July ye 7, 1720, Aged 59.

Also his . . . . Jonathan, who dyed May 18, 1722.

In Memory of Charles Burfitt, of Zeals, in this Parish, who died July 28, 1804, Aged 73 years.

In Memory of Susanna, the Wife of John Gover, who died Oct. 28, 1802, Aged 55.

Also Elizh and Charles died in their Infancy.

Also Charles, their Son, died August 25, 1806, Aged 25.

In Memory of Thomas Mansfield, who died Dec. 25, 1775, Aged 75.

Also of his first Wife Eliz. who died Oct. 8, 1743, Aged 46.

And of Rebecca, his second Wife, who died Dec. 20, 1773, Aged 57.

North Wall of the Church.

Here lieth ye Body of Thomas Spinks, who Departed this life November ye 21, 1750, Aged 61 years.

Here also lies the Body of Robert, Son of Thomas and Dorothy Spinks, who dy'd ye 19 July, 1770, Aged 52 years.

Here lieth the Body of Dorothy, Wife of Thomas Spinks, who Died Sept. the 29, 1746, Aged 61.

Also Edward, their Son.

INDEX OF PERSONS

An asterisk (*) denotes more than one entry on a page. English forms of first names have been abbreviated in this index, as follows:

Abr	Abraham Abram Ebraham
Alex	Alexander
Alice	Alicia Allice Alys
And	Andr Andrew Andw
Ann	An Anna Anne
Ant	Anthony Anthonye Antony
Arthur	Arthure
Barb	Barbara Barbarah Barbary Barbon
Bart	Barth Barthol Bartholomew
Benj	Ben Benjamin
Brid	Bridged Bridget Brudgett
Cath	Catharine Catherine Cathorn Cathrine Kath Katharine Katherine Kathrin
Chas	Car Carle Charles
Chr	Christ Christopher
Cicely	Cecilia Ciscilica Coecilia Cyscely
Constance	Constant Constantia
Dan	Daniel Daniell
Deb	Deborah
Dor	Dorothe Dorothea Dorothie Dorothy
Edith	Edeth Edetha Edithiate
Edm	Edmond Edmund
Edw	Ed Edward Edwd
Eleanor	Eleaner Elenor Eliner Elinor Eleaner Eliner
Eliz	Elizab Elizabeth Elizth
Ellen	Allen Ellin Elline
Frances	Fra Francisca Fraunces Frauncys
Francis	Franc Francisco Frauncis
Frederick	Fredrick
Fulk	Foulke Fulke
Gabriel	Gabriell
Geo	Geor George
Gertrude	Gartrude Gertrud
Gifford	Giff
Gilbert	Gilbart
Giles	Gyles
Grace	Grachus
Han	Hanna Hannah
Harriet	Harriett Harriot
Hen	Harry Henrie Henry Henrye
Hum	Humfray Humfrey Humfry Humphrey Humphry
Isaac	Isac
Jane	Jayne
Janet	Jannet
Jas	James
Jean	Jeane
Jn	Jhn Joh Johan John
Joan	Joane Joon
Joanna	Joannae Johanna
Judith	Judeth
Laur	Laurence Lawrence
Lucy	Lucia Luci
Marg	Margaret Margarita Margit Margreat Margret Margt
Mary	Maria
Mat	Mathew Matthew
Mic	Michael Michal Michall
Millicent	Milicent Milisent Millesaint
Moses	Moyses
Nat	Nath Nathanael Nathaniel
Nevill	Nevel Nevell Nevil
Nic	Nichol Nicholai Nicholas
Olive	Oliffe Oliv
Phil	Philip Phillip
Phyllis	Phillis
Rach	Rachel Rachell
Reb	Rebecca Rebekah
Ric	Rich Richard
Rob	Robert Robt Robtus
Sam	Saml Samuel
Sar	Sara Sarae Sarah
Sus	Sewsan Susan Susana Susanna Susannah
Thos	Tho Thom Thomas
Wal	Walter
Wm	Will William Willm Willyam

INDEX OF PLACES

An asterisk (*) denotes multiple entries on a page; bold type indicates pages relating to a church where monuments have been transcribed.

WILTSHIRE RECORD SOCIETY
(As at March 2000)

President: PROF. C.R. ELRINGTON, F.S.A.
General Editor: DR JOHN CHANDLER
Acting Honorary Treasurer: IVOR SLOCOMBE
Honorary Secretary: JOHN N. D'ARCY

Committee:
D CHALMERS
MRS J. COLE
DR D.A. CROWLEY
S.D. HOBBS
M.J. MARSHMAN
MRS I.L. WILLIAMS
K.H. ROGERS, F.S.A., representing the Wiltshire Archaeological and Natural History Society

---

Honorary Auditor: J.D. FOY
Correspondent for the U.S.A.: CHARLES P. GOULD

PRIVATE MEMBERS

ADAMS, MS S, 23 Rockcliffe Avenue, Bathwick, Bath BA2 6QP
ANDERSON, MR D M, 20 Shakespeare Road, Stratford sub Castle, Salisbury SP1 3LA
APPLEGATE, MISS J M, 55 Holbrook Lane, Trowbridge BA14 0PS
ASAJI, PROF K 1-2-401 gakuen-higahi, Nishi, Kobe 651-21 Japan
AVERY, MRS S, c/o 46 The Close, Salisbury SP1 2EL
BADENI, COUNTESS JUNE, Norton Manor, Norton, Malmesbury SN16 0JN
BAINES, MRS B M, 32 Tybenham Road, Merton Park, London SW19 3LA
BAINES, MR R T, The Woodhouse, 52 St Mary Street, Chippenham SN15 3JW
BALL, MR S T, 19 The Mall, Swindon SN1 4JA
BARNETT, MR B A, 17 Alexandra Road, Coalpit Heath, Bristol BS17 2PY
BATHE, MR G, Byeley in Densome, Woodgreen, Fordingbridge, Hants SP6 2QU
BAYLIFFE, MR B G, 3 Green Street, Brockworth, Glos GL3 4LT
BEARD, MRS P S, The Anchorage, Port-e-Vullen, Maughold, Isle of Man
BERRETT, MR A M, 10 Primrose Hill Road, London NW3 3AD
BERRY, MR C, 9 Haven Road, Crackington Haven, Bude, Cornwall EX23 0PD
BLAKE, MR P A, 18 Rosevine Road, London SW20 8RB
BLAKE, MR T N, Glebe Farm, Tilshead, Salisbury SP3 4RZ
BLEASE, MRS S, 9 Royal Field Close, Hullavington, Chippenham SN14 6DY
BOX, MR S D, 73 Silverdale Road, Earley, Reading RG6 2NF
BRAND, DR P A, 155 Kennington Road, London SE11 6SF
BROOKE-LITTLE, MR J P, Heyford House, Lower Heyford, Bicester, Oxon OX6 3NZ
BROWN, MR D A, 36 Empire Road, Salisbury SP2 9DF
BRYANT, MRS D, 1 St John's Court, Devizes SN10 1BJ
BUCKERIDGE, MR J M, 147 Herrick Road, Loughborough, Leics LE11 2BS
BURGESS, MR I D, 29 Brackley Avenue, Fair Oak, Eastleigh, Hants SO5 7FL
BURGESS, MR J M, Tolcarne, Wartha Mill, Porkellis, Helston, Cornwall TR13 0HX
BURNETT-BROWN, MISS J M, Lacock Abbey, Lacock, Chippenham SN15 2LG
CARDIGAN, RT HON EARL OF, Savernake Estate Office, Marlborough SN8 1PA

CAREW HUNT, MISS P H, Cowleaze, Edington, Westbury BA13 4PJ

CARR, PROF D R, Dept. of History, 140 7th Ave South, St Petersburg, Florida 33701 USA

CARTER, DR B J, JP, PHD, BSC, FSG, 28 Okus Road, Swindon SN1 4JQ

CAWTHORNE, MRS N, Dawn, 47 London Road, Camberley, Surrey GU15 3UG

CHALMERS, MR D, 8 Isles Court, Ramsbury, Marlborough SN8 2QW

CHANDLER, DR J H, 53, The Tynings, Westbury BA13 3PZ

CHAVE, MR R A, 39 Church Street, Westbury BA13 3BZ

CHURCH, MR T S, Mannering House, Bethersden, Ashford, Kent TN26 3DJ

CHURN, MR R H, 5 Veritys, Hatfield, Herts AL10 8HH

CLARK, MR A G, Highlands, 51a Brook Drive, Corsham SN13 9AX

CLARK, MRS V, 29 The Green, Marlborough SN8 1AW

COLCOMB, MR D M, 38 Roundway Lane, Devizes SN10 2EO

COLE, MRS J A, 113 Groundwell Road, Swindon SN1 2NA

COLEMAN, MISS J, 16 Den Road, Bromley BR2 0NH

COLLINS, MR A T, 11 Lemon Grove, Whitehill, Bordon, Hants GU35 9BD

COLMAN, MRS P, 28 Abbey Mill, Church St, Bradford on Avon BA15 1HB

CONGLETON, LORD, West End Farm, Ebbesbourne Wake, Salisbury SP5 5JW

COOMBES, MR J, 85 Green Pastures, Heaton Mersey, Stockport SK4 3RB

COOMBES-LEWIS, MR R J, 45 Oakwood Park Road, Southgate, London N14 6QP

COOPER, MR S, 12 Victory Row, Wootton Bassett, Swindon SN4 7BE

CORAM, MRS J E, London House, 51 The Street, Hullavington, Chippenham SN14 6DP

COULSTOCK, MISS P H, 15 Pennington Crescent, West Moors, Wimborne, Dorset BH22 0JH

COVEY, MR R V, Lower Hunts Mill, Wootton Bassett, Swindon SN4 7QL

COWAN, COL M, 24 Lower Street, Harnham, Salisbury SP3 8EY

CRITTALL, MISS E, 3 Freshwell Gardens, Saffron Walden, Essex CB10 1BZ

CROUCH, MR J W, Kensington House, Pensford Hill, Pensford, Som BS39 4AA

CROWLEY, DR D A, 16 Greater Lane, Edington, Westbury BA13 4QP

D'ARCY, MR J N, The Old Vicarage, Edington, Westbury

DIBBEN, MR A A, 18 Clare Road, Lewes, East Sussex BN7 1PN

EDE, DR M E, 12 Springfield Place, Lansdown, Bath BA1 5RA

EDWARDS, MR P C, 33 Longcroft Road, Devizes SN10 3AT

ELRINGTON, PROF C R, 34 Lloyd Baker Street, London WC1X 9AB

FAY, MRS M, 40 North Way, Porton Down, Salisbury SP4 0JN

FLOWER-ELLIS, DR J G, Swedish Univ of Agric Sciences, PO Box 7072 S-750 07, Uppsala, Sweden 1972

FORBES, MISS K G, Bury House, Codford, Warminster

FOSTER, MR R E, The New House, St Giles Close, Gt Maplestead, Halstead, Essex CO9 2RW

FOY, MR J D, 28 Penn Lea Road, Bath BA1 3RA

FREEMAN, DR J, Queens Birmingham, Somerset Road, Edgbaston, Birmingham B15 2QH

FROST, MR B C, Red Tiles, Cadley, Collingbourne Ducis, Marlborough SN8 3EA

FULLER, MRS B, 65 New Park Street, Devizes SN10 1DR

GARNISH, MRS E A, 9 Rue de Hoek, 1630 Luikebeek, Brussels, B-1630, Belgium

GHEY, MR J G, 18 Bassett Row, Bassett, Southampton SO1 7FS

GIBBS, MRS E, Sheldon Manor, Chippenham SN14 0RG

GODDARD, MR R E H, Sinton Meadow, Stokes Lane, Leigh Sinton, Malvern, Worcs WR13 5DY

GOODBODY, MR E A, Stockmans, Rectory Hill, Amersham, Bucks HP6

GOODFELLOW, MR P S, Teffont Selby, 47 High Street, Mow Cop, Cheshire ST7 3NZ

GOSLING, REV DR J, 1 Wiley Terrace, Wilton, Salisbury SP2 0HN

GOUGH, MISS P M, 39 Whitford Road, Bromsgrove, Worcs B61 7ED

GOULD, MR C P, 1200 Old Mill Road, San Marino, California 91108 USA

GOULD, MR L K, 263 Rosemount, Pasadena, California 91103 USA

GRIFFITHS, MR T J, 29 Saxon Street, Chippenham SN15

GRUBER VON ARNI, COL E E, 11 Park Lane, Swindon SN1 5HG

GUNSTONE, MR L, 47 St Michaels Road, Bath BA2 1PZ

HAMILTON, CAPTAIN R, West Dean, Salisbury SP5 1JL

HARE, DR J N, 7 Owens Road, Winchester, Hants SO22 6RU

HARTCHER, REV DR G N, 3-5 Vincentia Street, Marsfield, NSW 2122, Australia

HATCHWELL, MR R C, Cleeve House, Rodbourne Bottom, Malmesbury SN16 0EZ

HAWKINS, MR M J, 121 High Street, Lewes, East Sussex BN7 1XJ

HAYWARD, MISS J E, Pleasant Cottage, Crockerton, Warminster BA12 8AJ

HELMHOLZ, PROF R W, Law School, 1111 East 60th Street, Chicago, Illinois 60637 USA

Henly, Mr H R, 99 Moredon Road, Swindon SN2 2JG
Herron, Mrs Pamela M, 25 Anvil Crescent, Broadstone, Dorset BH18 9DY
Hickman, Mr M R, 184 Surrenden Road, Brighton BN1 6NN
Hicks, Mr I, 20 Virginia Drive, Warminster BA12 8RW
Hilliker, Mr S, Box 184, Sutherland, NSW 2232, Australia
Hillman, Mr R B, 18 Carnarvon Close, Chippenham SN14 0PN
Hinton, Mr A E, Glenside Cottage, Glendene Avenue, East Horsley, Surrey KT24 5AY
Hobbs, Mr S, 63 West End, Westbury BA13 3JQ
Holley, Mr R J, 120 London Road, Calne SN11 0AH
Hornby, Miss E, 70 Archers Court, Castle Street, Salisbury SP1 3WE
Horton, Mr P.R.G, OBE, Hedge End, West Grimstead, Salisbury SP5 3RF
Howells, Ms Jane, 7 St Mark's Rd, Salisbury SP1 3AY
Hughes, Prof C J, Old House, Tisbury, Salisbury SP3 6PS
Hughes, Mr R G, 60 Hurst Park Road, Twyford, Reading RG10 0EY
Hull, Mr J L F, Sandown Apartments, 1 Southerwood Drive, Sandy Bay, Tasmania 7005, Australia
Humphries, Mr A G, Rustics, Blacksmith's Lane, Harmston, Lincoln LN5 9SW
Ingram, Dr M J, Brasenose College, Oxford OX1 4AJ
Jackson, Mr D, 2 Byways Close, Salisbury SP1 2QS
James, Mr J F, 3 Sylvan Close, Hordle, Lymington, Hants SO41 0HJ
Jeacock, Mr D, 16 Church Street, Wootton Bassett, Swindon
Jellicoe, Rt Hon Earl, Tidcombe Manor, Tidcombe, Marlborough SN8 3SL
Johnston, Mrs J M, Greystone House, 3 Trowbridge Road, Bradford on Avon BA15 1EE
Kent, Mr T A, Rose Cottage, Isington, Alton, Hants GU34 4PN
King, Mr S F, Church Mead House, Woolverton, Bath BA3 6QT
Kirby, Mr J L, 209 Covington Way, Streatham, London SW16 3BY
Kneebone, Mr W J R, 20 Blind Lane, Southwick, Trowbridge BA14 9PG
Komatsu, Prof Y, c/o Yushodo Co, 29 San-ei-cho, Shinjuku-Ku, Tokyo 160 Japan
Kunikata, Mr K, Dept of Economics, 1-4-12, Kojirakawa-machi, Yamagata-shi 990, Japan
Laurence, Miss A, c/o Arts Faculty, Open University, Milton Keynes MK7 6AA
Laurence, Mr G F, St Cuthberts, 20 Church Street, Bathford, Bath BA1 7TU
Leggate, Mr A, 48 High Street, Worton, Devizes SN10 5RG
Light, Mr L, 12 Canford Cliffe Avenue, Poole BH14 9QN
Lodge, Mr O R W, Southridge House, Hindon, Salisbury SP3 6ER
London, Miss V C M, 55 Churchill Road, Church Stretton, Salop SY6 6EP
Long, Mr S H, 12 Goulton Close, Yarm, Stockton on Tees, Cleveland TS15 9RY
Lush, Dr G J, 5 Braeside Court, West Moors, Ferndown, Dorset BH22 0JS
Marsh, Rev R, Maybridge Vicarage, 56 The Boulevard, Worthing BN13 1LA
Marshman, Mr M J, 13 Regents Place, Bradford on Avon BA15 1ED
Martin, Ms Jean, 21 Ashfield Road, Chippenham SN15 1QQ
Maslen, Mr A, 8 Alder Walk, Frome, Som BA11 2SN
Mathews, Mr R, P O Box R72, Royal Exchange, NSW 2000, Australia
Matthews, Canon W A, Holy Trinity Vicarage, 18a Woolley St, Bradford on Avon BA15 1AF
Mattingly, Mr N, Freshford Manor, Freshford, Bath BA3 6EF
Merryweather, Mr A, 60 Trafalgar Road, Cirencester, Glos GL7 2EL
Millington, Mrs P, Hawkstone, Church Hill, Lover, Salisbury SP5 2PL
Moles, Mrs M I, 40 Wyke Road, Trowbridge BA14 7NP
Montague, Mr M D, 115 Stuarts Road, Katoomba, NSW 2780, Australia
Moody, Mr R F, Harptree House, East Harptree, Bristol BS18 6AA
Morioka, Prof K 3-12, 4-chome, Sanno, Ota-ku, Tokyo, Japan
Morland, Mr T E, 47 Shaftesbury Road, Wilton, Salisbury SP2 0DU
Morrison, Mrs J, Priory Cottage, Bratton, Westbury BA13
Moulton, Dr A E, The Hall, Bradford on Avon BA15
Newbury, Mr C Coles, 6 Leighton Green, Westbury BA13 3PN
Newman, Mrs R, Tanglewood, Laverstock Park, Salisbury SP1 1QJ
Nokes, Mr P A, Wards Farm, Ditcheat, Shepton Mallet, Somerset BA4 6PR
O'Donnell, Miss S J, 42 Wessington Park, Calne SN11 0AU
Ogbourne, Mr J M V, 14 Earnshaw Way, Beaumont Park, Whitley Bay, Tyne and Wear NE25 9UN
Ogburn, Chief Judge Robert W, 317 First Avenue, Monte Vista, CO 81144, USA
Osborne, Col R, Unwins House, 15 Waterbeach Road, Landbeach, Cambridge CB4 4EA
Parker, Dr P F, 45 Chitterne Road, Codford St

Mary, Warminster BA12 0PG

Parrott, Mrs M G, 81 Church Road, Christian Malford, Chippenham SN15 4BW

Patience, Mr D C, 29 Priory Gardens, Stamford, Lincs PE9 2EG

Patrick, Dr S, The Thatchings, Charlton All Saints, Salisbury SP5 4HQ

Paveley, Mr A W, 135 Lower Camden, Chislehurst, Kent BR7 5JD

Perry, Mr S H, Priory Cottage, Broad Street, Bampton, Oxon

Platt, Mr A J, Daubeneys, Colerne, Chippenham SN14 8DB

Powell, Mrs N, 4 Verwood Drive, Bitton, Bristol BS15 6JP

Radnor, Earl of, Longford Castle, Salisbury SP5 4EF

Ramsay, Mrs R, 15 Chalbury Road, Oxford OX2 6UT

Rathbone, Mr M G, Craigleith, 368 Snarlton Lane, Melksham SN12 7QW

Raybould, Miss F, 20 Radnor Road, Salisbury SP1 3PL

Reeves, Dr M E, 38 Norham Road, Oxford OX2 6SQ

Rogers, Mr K H, Silverthorne House, East Town, West Ashton, Trowbridge BA14 6BE

Rooke, Miss S F, The Old Rectory, Little Langford, Salisbury SP3 4NU

Sheddan, Miss J A, 8 Sefton Avenue, Auckland 2, New Zealand

Shelburne, Earl of, Bowood House, Calne SN11 0LZ

Sheldrake, Mr B, 28 Belgrave Street, Swindon SN1 3HR

Shewring, Mr P, 73 Woodland Road, Beddau, Pontypridd, Mid-Glamorgan CF38 2SE

Sims-Neighbour, Mr A K, 2 Hesketh Crescent, Swindon SN3 1RY

Slocombe, Mr I, 11 Belcombe Place, Bradford on Avon BA15 1NA

Smith, Mr P J, 6 Nuthatch, Longfield, Kent DA3 7NS

Sneyd, Mr R H, Court Farm House, 22 Court Lane, Bratton, Westbury BA13 4RR

Sopp, Mr G A, 23952 Nomar Street, Woodland Hills, California 91367, USA

Spaeth, Dr D A, School of History and Archaeology, 1 University Gardens, University of Glasgow G12 8QQ

Steele, Mrs N D, 46 The Close, Salisbury SP1 2EL

Sterry, Ms K, 8 Watercrook Mews, Westlea, Swindon SN5 7AS

Stevenage, Mr M R, 49 Centre Drive, Epping, Essex CM16 4JF

Stevens, Miss M L E, 11 Kingshill Close, Malvern, Worcs WR14 2BP

Steward, Dr H J, Graduate School of Geography, 950 Main Street, Worcester, Mass 01610-1477, USA

Stewart, Miss K P, 6 Beatrice Road, Salisbury SP1 3PN

Stratton, Mr M J, Manor Farm, Stockton, Warminster BA12 0SQ

Sykes, Mrs M, Conock Manor, Conock, Devizes SN10 3QQ

Sylvester, Mr D G H, Almondsbury Field, Tockington Lane, Almondsbury, Bristol BS12 4EB

Taylor, Dr A J, Rose Cottage, Lincolns Hill, Chiddingfold, Surrey GU8 4UN

Taylor, Mr C C, 13 West End, Whittlesford, Cambridge CB2 4LR

Taylor, Mrs J B, 3915 Ivy Terrace Court NW, Washington DC, DC20007, USA

Thompson, Mrs A M, 18 Burnaston Road, Hall Green, Birmingham B28 8DJ

Thompson, Mr & Mrs J B, 1 Bedwyn Common, Great Bedwyn, Marlborough SN8 3HZ

Thomson, Mrs Sally M, Shirley House, High St, Codford, Warminster BA12 0NB

Tighe, Mr M F, Strath Colin, Pettridge Lane, Mere, Warminster BA12 6DG

Tsushima, Mrs J, Malmaison, Church Street, Great Bedwyn, Marlborough SN8 3PE

Turner, Mr I D, Warrendene, 222 Nottingham Road, Mansfield, Notts NG18 4AB

Vincent, Ms M A, 28 Rochester Road, Lodge Moor, Sheffield S10 4JQ

Waite, Mr R E, 18a Lower Road, Chinnor, Oxford OX9 4DT

Walker, Mr J K, 82 Wainsford Road, Everton, Lymington, Hants SO41 0UD

Warneford, Mr F E, New Inn Farm, West End Lane, Henfield, West Sussex BN5 9RF

Warren, Mr P, 6 The Meadows, Milford Hill Road, Salisbury SP1 2RT

Weinstock, Baron, Bowden Park, Lacock, Chippenham

Weller, Mr R B, 9a Bower Gardens, Salisbury SP1 2RL

Wenden, Mrs P, 21 Eastern Parade, Fareham, Hants PO16 0RL

Whorley, Mr E E, 190 Stockbridge Road, Winchester, Hants SO22 6RW

Williams, Mrs I L, 7 Chandler Close, Devizes SN10 3DS

Wordsworth, Mrs G, Quince Cottage, Longbridge Deverill, Warminster BA12 7DS

Wright, Mr D P, Haileybury, Hertford SG13 7NU

Young, Mrs D L, 25 Staveley Road, Chiswick, London W4 3HU

Younger, Mr C, 8 Ailesbury Way, Burbage, Marlborough SN8 3TD

UNITED KINGDOM INSTITUTIONS

Aberystwyth
- National Library of Wales
- University College of Wales

Bath. Reference Library
Birmingham
- Central Library
- University Library

Brighton. University of Sussex Library
Bristol
- Central Library
- University Library

Cambridge. University Library
Chippenham. Technical College
Coventry. University of Warwick Library
Devizes. Wiltshire Archaeological and Natural History Society
Dorchester. Dorset County Library
Durham. University Library
Edinburgh
- National Library of Scotland
- University Library

Exeter. University Library
Glasgow. University Library
Gloucester. Bristol and Gloucestershire Archaeological Society
Leeds. University Library
Leicester. University Library
Liverpool. University Library
London
- British Library
- College of Arms
- Guildhall Library
- Inner Temple Library
- Institute of Historical Research
- London Library
- Public Record Office
- Royal Historical Society
- Society of Antiquaries
- Society of Genealogists
- University of London Library

Manchester. John Rylands Library
Marlborough
- Memorial Library, Marlborough College
- Merchant's House Trust

Norwich. University of East Anglia Library
Nottingham. University Library
Oxford
- Bodleian Library
- Exeter College Library
- New College Library

Poole. Bournemouth University
Reading
- Central Library
- University Library

St Andrews. University Library
Salisbury
- Bourne Valley Historical Society
- Cathedral Library
- Salisbury and South Wilts Museum

Sheffield. University Library
Southampton. University Library
Swansea. University College Library
Swindon
- Royal Commission on the Historical Monuments of England
- Swindon Borough Council
- Wiltshire Family History Society

Taunton. Somerset Archaeological and Natural History Society
Trowbridge
- Wiltshire County Council, Library and Museum Service
- Wiltshire and Swindon Record Office

Wetherby. British Library Document Supply Centre
York. University Library

INSTITUTIONS OVERSEAS

AUSTRALIA

Adelaide. Barr Smith Library, Adelaide University
Canberra. National Library of Australia
Kensington. Law Library, University of New South Wales
Melbourne
- Baillieu Library, University of Melbourne
- Victoria State Library

Nedlands. Reid Library, University of Western Australia
Sydney. Fisher Library, University of Sydney

CANADA

Halifax, Nova Scotia. Dalhousie University Library
London, Ont. D.B.Weldon Library, University of Western Ontario
Montreal, Que. Sir George Williams University
Ottawa, Ont. Carleton University Library
St John's, Newf. Memorial University of Newfoundland Library
Toronto, Ont
- Pontifical Inst of Medieval Studies
- University of Toronto Library

Victoria, B.C. McPherson Library, University of Victoria

DENMARK

Copenhagen. Royal Library

EIRE

Dublin. Trinity College Library

GERMANY

Gottingen. University Library

JAPAN

Osaka. Institute of Economic History, Kansai University

Sendai. Institute of Economic History, Tohoku University

NEW ZEALAND

Wellington. National Library of New Zealand

SWEDEN

Uppsala. Royal University Library

UNITED STATES OF AMERICA

Ann Arbor, Mich. Hatcher Library, University of Michigan

Athens, Ga. University of Georgia Libraries

Atlanta, Ga. The Robert W Woodruff Library, Emory University

Baltimore, Md. George Peabody Library, Johns Hopkins University

Binghamton, NY. State University of New York

Bloomington, Ind. Indiana University Library

Boston, Mass.
- Boston Public Library
- New England Historic and Genealogical Society

Boulder, Colo. University of Colorado Library

Cambridge, Mass.
- Harvard College Library
- Harvard Law School Library

Charlottesville, Va. Alderman Library, University of Virginia

Chicago.
- Newberry Library
- University of Chicago Library

Dallas, Texas. Public Library

Davis, Calif. University Library

East Lansing, Mich. Michigan State University Library

Eugene, Ore. University of Oregon Library

Evanston, Ill. United Libraries, Garrett/Evangelical, Seabury

Fort Wayne, Ind. Allen County Public Library

Haverford, Pa. Magill Library, Haverford College

Houston, Texas. M.D. Anderson Library, University of Houston

Iowa City, Iowa. University of Iowa Libraries

Ithaca, NY. Cornell University Library

Las Cruces, N.M. New Mexico State University Library

Los Angeles.
- Public Library
- University Research Library, University of California

Minneapolis, Minn. Wilson Library, University of Minnesota

New Haven, Conn. Yale University Library

New York.
- Columbia University of the City of New York
- Public Library

Notre Dame, Ind. Memorial Library, University of Notre Dame

Piscataway, N.J. Rutgers University Libraries

Princeton, N.J. Princeton University Libraries

Salt Lake City, Utah. Family History Library

San Marino, Calif. Henry E. Huntington Library

Santa Barbara, Calif. University of California Library

South Hadley, Mass. Williston Memorial Library, Mount Holyoke College

Stanford, Calif. Green Library, Stanford University

Tucson, Ariz. University of Arizona Library

Urbana, Ill. University of Illinois Library

Washington. The Folger Shakespeare Library

Winston-Salem, N.C. Z.Smith Reynolds Library, Wake Forest University

LIST OF PUBLICATIONS

The Wiltshire Record Society was founded in 1937, as the Records Branch of the Wiltshire Archaeological and Natural History Society, to promote the publication of the documentary sources for the history of Wiltshire. The annual subscription is £15 for private and institutional members. In return, a member receives a volume each year. Prospective members should apply to the Hon. Secretary, c/o Wiltshire and Swindon Record Office, Bythesea Road, Trowbridge, Wilts BA14 8BS. Many more members are needed.

The following volumes have been published. Price to members £15, and to non-members £20, postage extra. Available from the Hon. Treasurer, c/o Wiltshire and Swindon Record Office, Bythesea Road, Trowbridge, Wilts BA14 8BS

1. *Abstracts of feet of fines relating to Wiltshire for the reigns of Edward I and Edward II*, edited by R.B. Pugh, 1939
2. *Accounts of the parliamentary garrisons of Great Chalfield and Malmesbury, 1645-1646*, edited by J.H.P. Pafford, 1940
3. *Calendar of Antrobus deeds before 1625*, edited by R.B. Pugh, 1947
4. *Wiltshire county records: minutes of proceedings in sessions, 1563 and 1574 to 1592*, edited by H.C. Johnson, 1949
5. *List of Wiltshire boroughs records earlier in date than 1836*, edited by M.G. Rathbone, 1951
6. *The Trowbridge woollen industry as illustrated by the stock books of John and Thomas Clark, 1804-1824*, edited by R.P. Beckinsale, 1951
7. *Guild stewards' book of the borough of Calne, 1561-1688*, edited by A.W. Mabbs, 1953
8. *Andrews' and Dury's map of Wiltshire, 1773: a reduced facsimile*, edited by Elizabeth Crittall, 1952
9. *Surveys of the manors of Philip, earl of Pembroke and Montgomery, 1631-2*, edited by E. Kerridge, 1953
10. *Two sixteenth century taxations lists, 1545 and 1576*, edited by G.D. Ramsay, 1954
11. *Wiltshire quarter sessions and assizes, 1736*, edited by J.P.M. Fowle, 1955
12. *Collectanea*, edited by N.J. Williams, 1956
13. *Progress notes of Warden Woodward for the Wiltshire estates of New College, Oxford, 1659-1675*, edited by R.L. Rickard, 1957
14. *Accounts and surveys of the Wiltshire lands of Adam de Stratton*, edited by M.W. Farr, 1959
15. *Tradesmen in early-Stuart Wiltshire: a miscellany*, edited by N.J. Williams, 1960
16. *Crown pleas of the Wiltshire eyre, 1249*, edited by C.A.F. Meekings, 1961
17. *Wiltshire apprentices and their masters, 1710-1760*, edited by Christabel Dale, 1961
18. *Hemingby's register*, edited by Helena M. Chew, 1963
19. *Documents illustrating the Wiltshire textile trades in the eighteenth century*, edited by Julia de L. Mann, 1964
20. *The diary of Thomas Naish*, edited by Doreen Slatter, 1965

21-2. *The rolls of Highworth hundred, 1275-1287*, 2 parts, edited by Brenda Farr, 1966, 1968

23. *The earl of Hertford's lieutenancy papers, 1603-1612*, edited by W.P.D. Murphy, 1969
24. *Court rolls of the Wiltshire manors of Adam de Stratton*, edited by R.B. Pugh, 1970
25. *Abstracts of Wiltshire inclosure awards and agreements*, edited by R.E. Sandell, 1971
26. *Civil pleas of the Wiltshire eyre, 1249*, edited by M.T. Clanchy, 1971
27. *Wiltshire returns to the bishop's visitation queries, 1783*, edited by Mary Ransome, 1972

28. *Wiltshire extents for debts, Edward I - Elizabeth I*, edited by Angela Conyers, 1973
29. *Abstracts of feet of fines relating to Wiltshire for the reign of Edward III*, edited by C.R. Elrington, 1974
30. *Abstracts of Wiltshire tithe apportionments*, edited by R.E. Sandell, 1975
31. *Poverty in early-Stuart Salisbury*, edited by Paul Slack, 1975
32. *The subscription book of Bishops Tounson and Davenant, 1620-40*, edited by B. Williams, 1977
33. *Wiltshire gaol delivery and trailbaston trials, 1275-1306*, edited by R.B. Pugh, 1978
34. *Lacock abbey charters*, edited by K.H. Rogers, 1979
35. *The cartulary of Bradenstoke priory*, edited by Vera C.M. London, 1979
36. *Wiltshire coroners' bills, 1752-1796*, edited by R.F. Hunnisett, 1981
37. *The justicing notebook of William Hunt, 1744-1749*, edited by Elizabeth Crittall, 1982
38. *Two Elizabethan women: correspondence of Joan and Maria Thynne, 1575-1611*, edited by Alison D. Wall, 1983
39. *The register of John Chandler, dean of Salisbury, 1404-17*, edited by T.C.B. Timmins, 1984
40. *Wiltshire dissenters' meeting house certificates and registrations, 1689-1852*, edited by J.H. Chandler, 1985
41. *Abstracts of feet of fines relating to Wiltshire, 1377-1509*, edited by J.L. Kirby, 1986
42. *The Edington cartulary*, edited by Janet H. Stevenson, 1987
43. *The commonplace book of Sir Edward Bayntun of Bromham*, edited by Jane Freeman, 1988
44. *The diaries of Jeffery Whitaker, schoolmaster of Bratton, 1739-1741*, edited by Marjorie Reeves and Jean Morrison, 1989
45. *The Wiltshire tax list of 1332*, edited by D.A. Crowley, 1989
46. *Calendar of Bradford-on-Avon settlement examinations and removal orders, 1725-98*, edited by Phyllis Hembry, 1990
47. *Early trade directories of Wiltshire*, edited by K.H. Rogers and indexed by J.H. Chandler, 1992
48. *Star chamber suits of John and Thomas Warneford*, edited by F.E. Warneford, 1993
49. *The Hungerford cartulary: a calendar of the earl of Radnor's cartulary of the Hungerford family*, edited by J.L. Kirby, 1994
50. *The Letters of John Peniston, Salisbury architect, Catholic, and Yeomanry Officer, 1823-1830*, edited by M. Cowan, 1996
51. *The Apprentice Registers of the Wiltshire Society, 1817- 1922,* edited by H R Henly, 1997
52. *Printed Maps of Wiltshire 1787-1844: a selection of topographical, road and canal maps in facsimile*, edited by John Chandler, 1998

VOLUMES IN PREPARATION

The First General Entry Book of the City of Salisbury, edited by D.R. Carr; *Wiltshire papist returns and estate enrolments, 1705-87*, edited by J.A. Williams; *Wiltshire glebe terriers*, edited by S.D. Hobbs and Susan Avery; *Marlborough probate inventories*, edited by Lorelei Williams; *Crown pleas of the Wiltshire eyre, 1268*, edited by Brenda Farr; *The Hungerford cartulary, vol.2: the Hobhouse cartulary*, edited by J.L. Kirby; *The Parish registers of Thomas Crockford, 1613-29*, edited by C.C. Newbury; *Devizes area income tax assessments, 1842-60*, edited by Robert Colley; *The Diary of William Henry Tucker*, edited by Helen Rogers. The volumes will not necessarily appear in this order.

A leaflet giving full details may be obtained from the Hon. Secretary, c/o Wiltshire and Swindon Record Office, Bythesea Road, Trowbridge, Wilts. BA14 8BS.